The Women's Rights Movement in the United States 1848-1970

A Bibliography and Sourcebook

by

ALBERT KRICHMAR

assisted by

Barbara Case
Barbara Silver
Ann E. Wiederrecht

The Scarecrow Press, Inc.
Metuchen, N.J.   1972

Library of Congress Cataloging in Publication Data

Krichmar, Albert.
  The women's rights movement in the United States,
1848-1970.

  1. Woman--History and condition of women--United
States--Bibliography. 2. Woman--Rights of women--
Bibliography. I. Title.
Z7964.U49K75   016.30141'2'0973   72-4702
ISBN 0-8108-0528-6

Copyright 1972 by Albert Krichmar

FOR MY PARENTS

CONTENTS

INTRODUCTION

This partially annotated bibliography of the women's rights movement in the United States brings together much of the important literature published between 1848 and 1970. Topics covered concern the legal, political, economic, religious, educational, and professional status of women since 1848. It is hoped that users of this compilation will be able to select works pertaining not only to women's status in these particular topics, but also to opinions and attitudes about and by women as well as state and federal legislation brought about for their protection and, in a number of instances, for their suppression.

The date, 1848, was chosen as a starting point because the first women's rights convention in this country was held in Seneca Falls, New York, on July 19th and 20th of that year. The time limits of 1848 to 1970 are not strictly adhered to since much important literature has been published in 1971. Some material has also been included previous to 1848. Because several American women were denied representation there, a number of items have been included for the World Anti-Slavery Convention held in London in 1840. This incident contributed to the convention in America eight years later.

The types of materials included consist of books, periodical articles, doctoral dissertations, pamphlets, and a number of state and federal government publications, primarily from the United States Women's Bureau. Where possible, reprints of books have been indicated.

To provide the researcher with further sources, a selected listing of manuscript collections has been included. The main publication used to put this section together was the National Union Catalog of Manuscript Collections. Another large source of information consisted of the several hundred letters received from state historical societies, and from public, state, and academic libraries, each giving information about their holdings. The collections are arranged first by state, and then by the name of the library in which they are found.

Another section offering further research possibilities is the list of women's rights and liberation serial publications. These are very important since they offer articles written by women who are actively participating in the current movement. The largest collection of literature on the current women's movement and women's liberation is located in the Women's History Research Center, Inc., 2325 Oak St., Berkeley, California 94708. For a small donation and a self-addressed, stamped envelope, the Center will provide price lists of its available publications, including bibliographies of its holdings.

Soon to be available on microfilm from Bell and Howell will be the collection of women's serial publications at the Center. The collection will be international in scope and will include civic, religious, professional, and women's liberation journals, newsletters, and newspapers.

Another section consists of biographical sources for a few of the many men and women who took part or are taking part in the women's movement. The entries are arranged by the individual's last name, with cross-references being used to lead the user to related entries within the main portion of the book.

A number of reference sources have also been listed. These represent a few of the more important sources for further information on various aspects of the movement.

The literature of the movement since 1848 is immense, but unfortunately is scattered throughout many indexes and many collections around the country. A number of special libraries have collections which help document the movement, such as the National Woman's Party Library in Washington, D. C., as well as the special collections of Smith College and Radcliffe College. The names of other special collections can be obtained from two publications: Subject Collections, by Lee Ash, published by R. R. Bowker, New York, 1967, and the Directory of Special Libraries and Information

Centers, edited by Anthony Kruzas, and published by Gale Research, Detroit, 1968.

I would like to thank the several hundred librarians, students, and faculty throughout the country who provided this work with many valuable bibliographic citations, especially for the manuscript section. Also to be thanked is the Women's History Research Center in Berkeley which contributed to a great extent to the list of women's liberation serial publications. Finally, this work could not have been put together by this time without the funds provided by both the Library of the University of California at Santa Barbara and the UCSB Academic Senate, as well as the many hours of work put in by Barbara Case, Barbara Silver, Ann Wiederrecht, and Jon Houghton in helping to compile, type, and proofread the material.

Albert Krichmar

Santa Barbara, California

GENERAL; LEGAL AND POLITICAL STATUS

1. ABBOTT, L. Marriage and divorce. Outlook, v. 53 (14 March 1896), 477-9.
2. ADAMS, Elsie and Mary Louise Briscoe., comps. Up against the wall, mother...On women's liberation. Beverly Hills, Cal., Glencoe, 1971. 393p.
3. ADDAMS, Jane. Larger aspects of the woman's movement. American Academy of Political and Social Science, annals, v. 56 (November 1914), 1-8.
4. _____. New impulse to an old gospel. Forum, v. 14 (November 1892), 345-58.
5. ALEXANDER, S. Feminine eye; McCall's editor's views of women's liberation. McCall's, v. 97 (July 1970), 8+.
6. ALLEN, A. T. Economic relation of the college woman to society. Education, v. 22 (February 1902), 351-62.
7. ALLEN, Lucy Ann. Mrs. L. A. Allen's appeal to the legislature of the state of Connecticut for the protection of women. n.p., 1878. 115p.
8. ALLEN, Pamela. Free space; a perspective on the small group in women's liberation. New York, Times Change Press, 1970. 63p.
9. ALMY, Charles and H. W. Fuller. Law of married women in Massachusetts. Boston, G. B. Reed, 1876.
10. AMERICAN Academy of Political and Social Science, Philadelphia. Woman's work and organizations. Philadelphia, The Academy, 1906. 159p. The influence of women's clubs.
11. _____. Women in the modern world. Philadelphia, The Academy, 1929. 396p. The woman's movement; her work outside the home as well as in business.
12. _____. Women's opportunities and responsibilities. Edited by Louise M. Young. Philadelphia, The Academy, 1947. 224p.
13. AMERICAN female; symposium. Harper's magazine, v. 225 (October 1962), 117-80. Discussion, v. 225 (December 1962), 6+.
14. AMERICAN Personnel and Guidance Association. On the position of women in society. By Joanne B. Lantz. Washington, The Association, 1971. 8p.
15. The AMERICAN woman. Trans-action, v. 8, no. 1 & 2 (November/December 1970), special double issue. Articles on women in industry, black women, double standards, Equal Rights Amendment, and general articles on women's liberation.
16. AMERICAN woman: history and HERstory. Senior scholastic, v. 97 (9 November 1970), 7-12.

17. The AMERICAN woman: today and tomorrow; jobs, education, income, security, role in the home. Changing times, v. 18 (February 1964), 42-6.

18. AMERICAN woman; why can't she be politically effective? Life, v. 21 (21 October 1946), 36.

19. AMERICAN women: status and future. Pioneer woman monthly, v. 39 (January 1964), 16.

20. AMERICAN women: what price liberation? New generation, v. 51 (Fall 1969), special issue. Partial contents: Economics of women's liberation; The professions; The black woman.

21. AMSLER, M. H. New married woman's statutes: meaning and effect. Baylor law review, v. 15 (Spring 1963), 145.

22. AMUNDSEN, Kirsten. The silenced majority; women and American democracy. Englewood Cliffs, N. J., Prentice-Hall, 1971. 184p.

23. ANDERSON, Amber Wallin. Jury service for women [1870-1948]. Georgia Bar journal, v. 11 (November 1948), 196-99.

24. ANDERSON, Sherwood. Perhaps women. New York, Liveright, 1931. 144p.

25. ANSWERING opponents of equal rights. Independent woman, v. 26 (October 1947), 302.

26. ANTHONY, C. W. Is there a prejudice against women in the United States? American Medical Women's Association, journal, v. 24 (October 1969), 787-8.

27. ANTHONY, Susan Brownell. Men and women; their province in the household. Independent, v. 54 (8 May 1902), 1126-8. The wife as an unequal owner of the combined earnings as the main reason for discontent in the household.

28. APTHEKER, Herbert. The Negro woman. Masses and mainstream, v. 2 (February 1949), 10-17. On her "militant history" since 1862.

29. ARCHARD, E. Woman question. Radical, v. 2 (1867), 715.

30. ARE American women making the most of the rights and privileges for which they fought: the loss of the adventurous spirit, by Agnes Rogers; People in skirts, by W. T. Hedden. American scholar, v. 19 (Winter 1949-50), 89-97.

31. ARE married women people? Independent woman, v. 17 (December 1938), 376-8+.

32. ARE Negro women smarter than their men? Sepia, v. 7 (December 1959), 70-4.

33. ARE women morally superior to men? Current literature, v. 39 (September 1905), 288-9.

34. ARKANSAS. Governor's Commission on the Status of Women. Report. Little Rock, 1970. 61p.

35. ARMSTRONG, A. O. Stop telling women they're unhappy. Information, v. 75 (August 1961), 3-9.

36. ARMSTRONG, M. F. Mission of educated women. Popular science monthly, v. 36 (1890), 601.

37. ARNOLD, Marguerite. Are women intelligent? Century magazine, v. 100 (December 1920), 264-72. A sketch of the woman's rights movement prior to the centennial celebration of 1876.
38. ARROW, Jeanne. Dangers in the pro-women line and consciousness-raising. New York, The Feminists, [1970?] 13p.
39. ASIMOV, Isaac. You've come a long way, baby--but look where you're going tomorrow! Trends, a journal of resources, v. 3 (October 1970), 25-6. The status of the young woman in 1991.
40. ASSOCIATIONS for the advancement of women. Open court, v. 1 (1887), 561.
41. ATHERTON, Gertrude Franklin. Can women be gentlemen? Boston, Houghton Mifflin, 1938. 207p.
42. ATKINSON, Ti-Grace. Radical feminism. New York, The Feminists, 1969. 8p.
43. _____. Vaginal orgasm as a mass hysterical survival response. New York, The Feminists, 1968. 3p.
44. AUSTIN, M. Sex emancipation through war. Forum, v. 59 (May 1918), 609-20.
45. AUSTIN, Mary Hunter. The young woman citizen. New York, Woman's Press, 1918. 186p.
46. BAKER, M. L. Legal emancipation of married women. Florida law journal, v. 11 (June 1937), 211-15.
47. BAKER, T. and M. Bird. Urbanization and the position of women. Sociological review, v. 7 (July 1959), 99-122.
48. BANKS, Elizabeth. The educated American drudge. North American review, v. 179 (September 1904), 433-8. The life of a college educated woman as a wife with no outside activities.
49. BANNING, M. C. Women come to judgment. Harper's magazine, v. 149 (October 1924), 562-75.
50. BARACH, Alvan L. Modern woman's defenses against living. North American review, v. 237 (February 1934), 151-9. Women's unhappiness despite many beneficial changes.
51. BARBER, Bernard and Lyle S. Lobel. Fashion in women's clothes and the American social system, 1930-1950. Social forces, v. 31 (December 1952), 124-31.
52. BARKER-BENFIELD, Graham John. The horrors of the half known life: aspects of the exploitation of women by men. 859p. PhD thesis, University of California, Los Angeles, 1968. A discussion of the male psychology which subordinated women in the 19th century.
53. BARNETT, Avrom. Foundations of feminism, a critique. New York, R. M. McBride, 1921. 245p. The sexes considered from biological, psychological, physiological, and sociological viewpoints.
54. BARRS, B. Married women; a summary of the laws of Florida relating to disabilities of coverture. Florida law journal, v. 9 (May 1935), 428-32.
55. BARRY, Herbert. Cross cultural perspectives on how to minimize the adverse effect of sex differentiation. Pre-

sented at a Symposium on Behavior Sciences of the American Psychological Association, Washington, D.C., 3
September 1969. Pittsburgh, Know, Inc., [1969?] 10p.
56. BART, Pauline. Mother Portnoy's complaints. Trans-action,
v. 8 (November 1970), 69-74.
57. BASCOM, J. Relations of women and men. Putnam's monthly
magazine, v. 14 (1859), 713.
58. BATTLE of the sexes is over, who won? We did. Ladies
home journal, v. 84 (February 1967), 66+.
59. BATTLE of the sexes; reversal of male-female roles. Newsweek, v. 70 (7 August 1967), 52.
60. BAUMGOLD, Julie. You've come a long way, baby. New
York, v. 2 (9 June 1969), 26-32.
61. BAYLES, George James. Woman and New York law. New
York, Law Press, 1912. 197p.
62. _____. Woman and the law. New York, Century, 1901.
267p. Reprinted by Greenwood Press, Westport, Conn.,
1971.
63. BEAL, Frances. Double jeopardy: to be black and female.
Washington, D.C., D.C. Women's Liberation, [1970?]. 9p.
64. BEARD, Mary Ritter, ed. America through women's eyes. New
York, Macmillan, 1933. 558p. Reprinted by Greenwood
Press, Westport, Conn., 1972. The contributions of wom-
en to American society from the 17th century to the present
using excerpts of well known publications.
65. _____. A changing political economy as it affects women.
Washington, American Association of University Women,
1934. 57p.
66. _____. On understanding women. New York, Longmans
Green, 1931. 541p. Reprinted by Greenwood Press,
Westport, Conn., 1972.
67. _____. The status of woman and the modern state. Woman's press, v. 30 (September 1936), 376-7.
68. _____. A test for the modern woman. Current history,
v. 37 (November 1932), 179-83. Effects of the depression on the feminist movement.
69. _____. Woman as force in history; a study in traditions
and realities. New York, Macmillan, 1946. 369p.
70. _____. Woman's role in society. American Academy of
Political and Social Science, annals, v. 251 (May 1947),
1-9.
71. BEAUMAN, S. Who's so liberated? Why? Vogue, v. 156
(1 September 1970), 382-3+.
72. BEECHER, Catharine Esther. The evils suffered by American
women and American children: the causes and the remedy. New York, Harper, 1846. 36p.
73. _____. The true remedy for the wrongs of woman; with a
history of an enterprise having that for its object. Boston, Phillips, Sampson, 1851. 263p. Main emphasis is
on the necessity for the organization of women.
74. BEEMAN, Alice L. and Shirley McCune. Changing styles:
Women's groups in the seventies. AAUW journal, v. 64
(November 1970), 24-6.

75. BELL, Inge P. The double standard. Trans-action, v. 8
    (November 1970), 75-80.
76. BELL, Ralcy H. Woman from bondage to freedom. New
    York, Critic and Guide, 1921. 230p.
77. BELLANGEE, J. Sexual purity and the double standard: de-
    pendence upon social conditions. Arena, v. 11 (February
    1895), 370-7.
78. BEM, Sandra L. and Daryl J. Bem. Training the woman to
    know her place: The power of a nonconscious ideology.
    Women; a journal of liberation, v. 1 (Fall 1969), 8-14.
79. BENNETT, Arnold. Our women; chapters on the sex-discord.
    New York, Doran, 1920. 264p.
80. BENNETT, L., Jr. Negro woman: crumbling matriarchate
    poses new problems. Ebony, v. 17 (September 1963),
    86-90+.
81. BENNETT, Margaret. Alice in womanland; or, The feminine
    mistake. Englewood Cliffs, N.J., Prentice-Hall, 1967.
    189p.
82. BENSON, E. Woman question. Galaxy, v. 2 (1866), 751.
83. BERNARD, Jessie. Changing life styles for women: their
    significance to families. Journal of home economics,
    v. 62 (October 1970), 575-83.
84. _____. The status of women in modern patterns of culture.
    American Academy of Political and Social Science, annals,
    v. 375 (January 1968), 3-14. Sexual equality not likely
    to be achieved because of domestic obligations of women
    and women's lack of interest in equal responsibilities.
85. BETTELHEIM, Bruno. Growing up female. Harper's maga-
    zine, v. 225 (October 1962), 120-8. The contradictions
    between how a girl in America is raised and the goals
    that are set for her.
86. _____. Women: emancipation is still to come. New re-
    public, v. 151 (7 November 1964), 48-58. Discussion;
    v. 151 (28 November 1964), 37; (12 December 1964),
    28-9.
87. BINSWANGER, Augustus Caesar. Married women: property
    and contractual rights [in Maryland]. Baltimore, Cur-
    lander, 1903.
88. BIRD, Caroline. The new woman; out to finish what the suf-
    fragette started. AAUW journal, v. 64 (November 1970),
    3-5.
89. _____. On being born female. Vital speeches, v. 35 (15
    November 1968), 88-91.
90. BISCH, L. E. Are women inferior, or are they trying to
    side-track nature? Century magazine, v. 113 (April
    1927), 674-81.
91. BISHOP, J. Prentiss. Commentaries on law of married wom-
    en, under statutes of the several states and at common
    law and in equity. Boston, Little, Brown, 1873-5. 2v.
92. BLACK women; double discrimination. Sepia, v. 18 (Septem-
    ber 1969), 18-19.
93. BLACKMAN, Lucy Worthington. The Florida Federation of
    Women's Clubs, 1895-1939. Jacksonville, Southern His-

torical Publishing Associates, 1939. 59p.
94. BLACKWELL, Alice Stone. Woman's 75 year fight. Nation,
     v. 117 (18 July 1923), 53-4. The story of the first
     woman's rights convention, held in Seneca Falls, N.Y.,
     July 1848.
95. BLACKWELL, Antoinette Louisa Brown. The sexes through-
     out nature. New York, G. P. Putnam, 1875. 240p.
     On the equality of the sexes based on evolutionary pro-
     cesses.
96. BLAIR, Emily Newell. The job of being a feminist, small
     town style. Outlook and independent, v. 151 (24 April
     1929), 643-6. The greater problems of a woman living
     in a small community.
97. _____. Married feminist's predicament. Outlook and in-
     dependent, v. 153 (4 September 1929), 7-9+. The prob-
     lem of whether a married couple should move due to
     the wife's better income rather than the husband's.
98. BLAKE, Lillie Devereux. Woman's place today. New York,
     J. W. Lovell, 1883. 173p.
99. BLAKELY, P. L. Are we men better than women? Ameri-
     ca, v. 68 (6 March 1943), 601.
100. BLANC, Marie Therese. The condition of woman in the
     United States. A traveller's notes. Translated by
     Abby Langdon Alger. Boston, Roberts, 1895. 285p.
     Reprinted by Greenwood Press, Westport, Conn., 1971.
101. BLATCH, Harriot Stanton. Do women want protection? Na-
     tion, v. 116 (31 January 1923), 115-16.
102. _____. Women and their work. Current literature, v. 29
     (September 1900), 307-8.
103. BLAUVELT, Mary Taylor. Race problem. American journal
     of Sociology, v. 6 (March 1901), 662-72. On the Mich-
     igan State Federation of Colored Women's Clubs.
104. BLEDSOE, Albert Taylor. The mission of woman. Washing-
     ton, GPO, 1913. 16p. Originally printed in the South-
     ern review for October 1871.
105. BLISS, B. His and hers. U.S. Catholic and jubilee, v. 35
     (June 1970), 31-5.
106. BOATWRIGHT, Eleanor M. The political and civil status of
     women in Georgia, 1783-1860. Georgia historical quar-
     terly, v. 25 (December 1941), 301-24.
107. BOEMLER, Charles. Woman. A treatise. St. Louis, W.
     Raine, printer, 1877. 61p.
108. BOHRER, Florence F. Legal status of women in Illinois.
     Illinois Bar journal (1931), 261-7.
109. BOOTHE, Viva B., ed. Women in the modern world. Amer-
     ican Academy of Political and Social Science, annals,
     v. 143 (May 1929), 1-373. Concerning the significance
     of the movement, woman's contribution to the modern
     home, women in industry, business and the professions,
     social attitudes.
110. BORGESE, Elisabeth Mann. Ascent of woman. New York,
     Braziller, 1963. 247p.
111. BOSTON. Woman's Rights Meeting, 1859. Report of the

Woman's Rights Meeting, at Mercantile Hall, May 27, 1859. Boston, S. Urbino, 1859. 32p.

112. BOUTELLE, Martin J. Community and separate in California. Pasadena, Cal., Boutelle, 1914. 36p. "An exposition of the laws, governing the acquisition, possession and distribution of property, a compendium of the rights of married persons."

113. BOWDITCH, William Ingersoll. Taxation of women in Massachusetts. Cambridge, J. Wilson, 1875. 71p.

114. BOYD, Mary Sumner. Are you your husband's ward? Ladies' home journal, v. 37 (April 1920), 87-8.

115. _____. Wanted: equality. Good housekeeping, v. 72 (March 1921), 18-19.

116. BOYER, E. Equal opportunity for women--in our time. Women lawyers journal, v. 56 (Winter 1970), 5.

117. BOYNE, Mrs. E. M. Verdict on women jurors. New York Times magazine (21 May 1950), 4+.

118. BRAGDON, Elizabeth. Women today: Their conflicts, their frustrations, and their fulfillments. Indianapolis, Bobbs-Merrill, 1953. 335 p. On career vs. home, emotional problems, and roles a woman must play.

119. BRECKINRIDGE, Sophonisba Preston. Family and the law. National Conference of Social Work, proceedings (1925), 290-7.

120. _____. The family and the state. Chicago, University of Chicago Press, 1934. 565p.

121. _____. Marriage and the civic rights of women; separate domicile and independent citizenship. Chicago, University of Chicago Press, 1931. 158p.

122. _____. Political equality for women and women's wages. American Academy of Political and Social Science, annals, v. 56 (November 1914), 122-33.

123. _____. Women in the twentieth century; a study of their political, social, and economic activities. New York, McGraw-Hill, 1933. 364p.

124. BRES, Rose Falls. The law and the woman. Brooklyn, American Printing Office, 1917. 170p.

125. BREUER, Elizabeth. Feminism's awkward age. Harper's magazine, v. 150 (April 1925), 545-51.

126. BRILL, E. H. Is marriage dying, too? Christian century, v. 84 (1 March 1967), 268-70.

127. BRISTED, C. A. Rights of women. Galaxy, v. 16 (1873), 196.

128. _____. Woman question. Galaxy, v. 9 (1870), 841.

129. BRITTEN, Emma Hardinge. The place and mission of woman. An inspirational discourse, delivered ... at the Melodeon, Boston, Sunday afternoon, February 13, 1859. Boston, H. W. Swett, 1859. 12p.

130. BROMLEY, Dorothy Dunbar. Feminist--new style. Harper's magazine, v. 155 (October 1927), 552-60. The new feminist as a person who can combine a family life with activities outside the home.

131. BROPHY, Brigid. Speaking out; women are prisoners of

their sex. Saturday evening post, v. 236 (2 November 1963), 10+. Freedom for women is only psychological, not actual.

132. BRORUP, Rasmus Peterson. Modesty, courtship and woman's right. Chicago, International Book Co., 1899. 203p.

133. BROWER, B. Long day's monotony of TV. Saturday evening post, v. 237 (26 September 1964), 76-8.

134. BROWN, H. E. Unequal justice under law: women and the Constitution. Washington, National Woman's Party, 1943. 15p.

135. _____. Worth of the Constitution to American women. Women lawyers journal, v. 36 (Winter 1950), 13-18.

136. BROWN, Ira V. The woman's rights movement in Pennsylvania, 1848-1873. Pennsylvania history, v. 32, no. 2 (1965), 153-65.

137. BROWN, Judith and Beverly Jones. Toward a female liberation movement. Boston, New England Free Press, [1970?].

138. BROWN, W. Kennedy. Gunethics; or, The ethical status of women. New York, Funk and Wagnalls, 1887. Arguments based on the Bible that women should be and are the equal of men.

139. BROWNMILLER, Susan. ...woman is often her own worst enemy--the enemy within. Mademoiselle, v. 70 (February 1970), 184+.

140. BROWNSON, Orestes A. Woman question. Catholic world, v. 9 (1869), 145.

141. BRUCE, Henry Addington Bayley. Woman in the making of America. Boston, Little, Brown, 1912. 257p. From the earliest settlements.

142. BRUCE, Margaret K. An account of United Nations action to advance the status of women. American Academy of Political and Social Science, annals, v. 375 (January 1968), 163-75.

143. BRUEMMER, L. Condition of women in society today. National Association of Women Deans and Counselors, journal, v. 33 (Fall 1969), 18-22; v. 33 (Winter 1970), 89-95.

144. BRUMMOND, K. Are wives people? Independent woman, v. 25 (November 1946), 329-30.

145. BRUORTON, J. A. Lining up women for democracy. New England magazine, v. 52 (October 1914), 74-7.

146. BRUTON, Margaret Perry. Present-day thinking on the woman question. American Academy of Political and Social Science, annals, v. 251 (May 1947), 10-16.

147. BRYANT, Florence V. A liberation woman looks at women's liberation. Trends, a journal of resources, v. 3 (October 1970), 11-14.

148. BUCK, Pearl S. America's gunpowder women; privileged and discontented. Harper's magazine, v. 179 (July 1939), 126-35. On the lack of initiative on the part of women.

149. _____. Of men and women. New York, John Day, 1941. 203p. Reasons for the discontent of women.

150. BUCKLEY, W. F., Jr. Women's lib watching. National review, v. 22 (8 September 1970), 964-5.
151. BUCKMAN, G. Life of a wife. Mademoiselle, v. 58 (January 1964), 96-7+.
152. BULLOCK, Alexander H. The centennial situation of woman, address ... at the commencement anniversary of Mount Holyoke Seminary, Massachusetts, June 22, 1876. Worcester, C. Hamilton, 1876. 45p.
153. BUNCH-WEEKS, Charlotte. A broom of one's own. Washington, D.C., D.C. Women's Liberation [1970?], 19p. On raising consciousness in areas of employment, civil rights, education, abortion and health.
154. BURKS, Martin Parks. Notes on the property rights of married women in Virginia.... Lynchburg, Va., J. P. Bell, 1893. 87p.
155. BURNHAM, S. Women's lib; the idea you can't ignore. Redbook, v. 135 (September 1970), 78-9+.
156. BUTTER, Stephen H. Legal rights of women in Florida. Miami, Hurricane House, 1968. 86p.
157. BYRNE, K. Who wants an intellectual wife? Today, v. 15 (June 1960), 10-12.
158. CABELL, I. C. Man's inhumanity to woman. Everybody's magazine, v. 11 (1904), 373.
159. CADE, Toni. The black woman; an anthology. New York, New American Library, 1970. 256p.
160. CADWALLADER, M. Marriage as a wretched institution. Atlantic monthly, v. 218 (November 1966), 62-6.
161. CALDWELL, Taylor. Speaking out; women get a dirty deal. Saturday evening post, v. 236 (25 May 1963), 8+.
162. CALIFORNIA. Advisory Commission on the Status of Women. California women. Sacramento, State of California, Documents Section, 1967. 51p. Public and private employment, education, civil and political rights.
163. _____. Laws, statutes, etc. California laws relating to women and children. Sacramento, California State Printing Office, 1926. 282p.
164. CALISHER, Hortense. "...no important woman writer, I think, has really wanted to write 'like a man.' They had too much taste." Mademoiselle, v. 70 (February 1970), 188-9+.
165. CALLAHAN, Parnell Joseph. Legal status of women. Dobbs Ferry, N.Y., Oceana, 1963. 95p.
166. CALLAHAN, Sidney C. The illusion of Eve; modern woman's quest for identity. New York, Sheed and Ward, 1965. 214p.
167. CAMPBELL, Dorcas. Equal rights. Wilson library bulletin, v. 20 (September 1945), 16-17.
168. CANNON, M. M. Status of women in the United States, 1952. Mysore labour gazette (November 1952), 5-12.
169. CANTAROW, Ellen. I am furious (female). Detroit, Radical Education Project [1970?]. 20p. The history and nature of women's oppression, devices that reinforce it and its relation to other liberation struggles.

170. CANTWELL, M., ed. I can't call you my sister yet. Mada-
     moiselle, v. 73 (May 1971), 182-3+.
171. CAPPER, A. Family; marriage and divorce laws need feder-
     al control and regulation. American mercury, v. 125
     (June 1938), 172.
172. CAREY, F. K. Rights of married women. Appleton's jour-
     nal, v. 24 (1880), 385.
173. CARLSON, A. D. When marriage handicaps; promotion for
     husband or wife often means moving. Woman's journal,
     v. 14 (May 1929), 10-11.
174. CARPENTER, C. E. Political evangelism, or Equal rights
     for women and men. Napa, Cal., Smith and Wilson,
     1884. 11p.
175. CARSON, Gerald. The woman movement: after one hundred
     years. Scribner's magazine, v. 88 (September 1930),
     263-9. On the slowing down of the feminist movement
     and on the previous work of Margaret Fuller.
176. CARSON, Josephine. Silent voices; the southern Negro wom-
     an today. New York, Delacorte, 1969. 273p.
177. CARSTENS, C. C. Marriage laws and their administration
     in Massachusetts. National Conference of Social Work,
     proceedings (1919), 381-2.
178. CARTER, M. E. Wives, widows, and wills. Arena, v. 27
     (May 1902), 518-24.
179. CASSARA, Beverly Benner, ed. American women: The
     changing image. Boston, Beacon, 1962. 141p.
180. CASSIDY, Jessie J., comp. Legal status of women. New
     York, National American Woman Suffrage Association,
     1897.
181. CATT, Carrie Chapman. Sixty years of stepping forward.
     Woman's journal, v. 14 (December 1929), 7-8.
182. CAWOOD, Rose. Tennessee Federation of Women's Clubs.
     Midland monthly, v. 7 (1897), 132.
183. CENTENNIAL of women's rights initiation. Monthly labor
     review, v. 66 (April 1948), 408-9.
184. CENTER for Information on America. Full partnership for
     women--what still needs to be done? Vital issues,
     v. 3 (November 1963). 4p.
185. CHAFE, William H. Separate but equal: The American wom-
     an's search for identity, 1920-1950. PhD thesis, Co-
     lumbia University, in progress.
186. CHAMBERLAIN, J. P. Changes in the law of the family,
     persons and property. American Academy of Political
     and Social Science, annals, v. 136 (March 1928), 15-25.
187. _____. Further statutory changes in the legal status of
     women. American Bar Association, journal, v. 11
     (May 1925), 317-19.
188. CHANDLER, L. B. Woman movement. Arena, v. 4 (Novem-
     ber 1891), 704-11.
189. CHARLOTTE Perkins Gilman's dynamic social philosophy.
     Current literature, v. 51 (July 1911), 67-70.
190. CHATON, J. H. UNESCO long-range program for the ad-
     vancement of women. American Academy of Political

and Social Science, annals, v. 375 (January 1968), 145-53.

191. CHESSER, Elizabeth Sloan. Woman, marriage, and mother-hood. New York, Funk and Wagnall's, 1913. 287p.

192. CHICAGO Regional Conference on the Changing Status of Women, Roosevelt University, 1962. The changing status of women; report. Washington, GPO [1962?], 48p.

193. CHRISTENSEN, J. Status of women in Oregon. Women lawyers journal, v. 49 (Spring 1963), 11.

194. CHRISTIAN, Stella L. The history of the Texas Federation of Women's Clubs. Houston, Dealy-Adey-Elgin, 1919. 398p.

195. CHRISTIAN feminism. Messenger of the sacred heart, v. 90 (September 1955), 10-12.

196. CLAGETT, S. H. Woman question. Nation, v. 10 (1870), 61.

197. CLARENBACH, Kathryn. Women are people. Symposium on the Behavioral Sciences, American Psychological Association, 1969. Pittsburgh, Know, Inc., [1969?] 22p.

198. _____. Women: second class citizens. Marriage, v. 49 (December 1967), 28-35.

199. CLARK, Robert Emmet. Community of property and the family in New Mexico. Albuquerque, Department of Government, University of New Mexico, 1956. 51p.

200. CLARK, T. C. Equal rights for women in America. Washington, U.S. Department of Justice, Tom Clark, 1949. 7p.

201. CLARK, Walter, 1846-1924. Can a prior registered mortgage acknowledged before a duly appointed and acting deputy clerk, be set aside merely because the deputy happens to be a woman? Raleigh, Edwards and Broughton Printing Co., 1916. 10p.

202. _____. The legal status of women in North Carolina; address before the Federation of Women's Clubs, New Bern, N.C., 8 May 1913. n.p., n.d. 23p.

203. _____. Some of the discriminations against women in North Carolina. n.p., n.d. 6p.

204. CLARK, Walter, 1885-1933. Paper presented to the State Federation of Women's Clubs by Walter Clark, Jr. and J. Melville Broughton, Jr. Raleigh, N.C., Federation of Women's Clubs, 1914. 26p.

205. CLASSIFICATION on the basis of sex and the 1964 Civil Rights Act. Iowa law review (Spring 1965), 778-98.

206. CLAWSON, A. H. Home problems of employed women. Practical home economics, v. 23 (April 1945), 199-200.

207. CLEARY, Josephine. Notes from the lower classes II. New York, The Feminists, 1969. 1p.

208. CLUB women who get results. Good housekeeping, v. 154 (January 1962), 126. Concerning the General Federation of Women's Clubs.

209. COBBE, Frances Power. The duties of women. New York, National American Woman Suffrage Association, 1882. 161p.

210. COHANE, R. F.   Group action among women.   Women law-
        yers journal, v. 33 (Spring 1947), 72-6.
211. COLBURN, W. G.   Property of married women.   North
        American review, v. 99 (1864), 34.
212. COLLIER, Robert Laird.   Follies of the woman movement,
        an address.   New York, Rand, McNally & Co., print-
        ers, 1871.   8p.
213. COLON, Clara.   Enter fighting: today's woman.   A Marxist-
        Leninist view.   New York, New Outlook, 1970.   95p.
214. _____. An outline on the fight for women's freedom.   New
        York, Communist Party, National Education Department,
        1969.   19p.
215. COLQUHOUN, E.   Modern feminism and sex antagonism.
        Living age, v. 278 (6 September 1913), 579-94.
216. COLUM, M. M.   Life and literature; are women outsiders?
        Forum, v. 100 (November 1938), 222-6.
217. COMER, Nancy.   Women are discriminated against; but they
        deserve it.   Mademoiselle, v. 70 (February 1970),
        248-9+.   "Women want the privileges, but not the re-
        sponsibilities. "
218. COMMANDER, Lydia K.   How does the access of women to
        industrial occupations react on the family?--The self-
        supporting woman and the family.   American journal
        of Sociology, v. 14 (May 1909), 752-57.   On the neces-
        sity of women to take part in the industrial world.
219. COMMISSION on status of women (established by the United
        Nations Economic and Social Council): promoting
        equality with men.   United Nations weekly bulletin,
        v. 2 (11 February 1947), 113-15.
220. COMMISSION on status of women: first session completed
        and plan of work evolved (Lake Success, N.Y., Febru-
        ary 10-24, 1947).   United Nations weekly bulletin, v. 2
        (4 March 1947), 200-3.
221. COMMISSION on the status of women.   United Nations bulle-
        tin, v. 14 (15 April 1953), 273-5.
222. CONANT, Mrs. C. E.   North Dakota Federation of Women's
        Clubs.   Midland monthly, v. 8 (1897), 362.
223. CONFERENCE on the role of the State Commissions on the
        Status of Women in Ten Western States, Portland, Ore.,
        1968.   Expanding women's effectiveness in the commun-
        ity; a report.   n.p., 1968.   31p.
224. CONFERENCE on Women's Work and Their Stake in Public
        Affairs, March 28-30, 1935, New York.   Proceedings.
        New London, Conn., Institute of Women's Professional
        Relations, 1935.   329p.
225. CONFESSIONS of an ex-feminist.   New republic, v. 46 (14
        April 1926), 218-20.   Unhappiness in marriage due to
        a wife's inability to extend herself beyond the home
        and to her husband's apathy.
226. CONGRESS to get bills on equal treatment for women.   Con-
        gressional quarterly weekly report, v. 20 (28 Decem-
        ber 1962), 2298-2300.
227. CONNECTICUT.   Governor's Committee on the Status of Wom-

en. Report of the Governor's Committee on the Status of Women. Connecticut women. Hartford, 1967. 55p.

228. CONROY, S. B. Set stage for new equal rights battle. McCall's, v. 98 (May 1971), 37.

229. CONSORTIUM, domestic services, and the emancipation of women. U.S. law review, v. 70 (September 1936), 487-90.

230. CONSTITUTIONAL law: exclusion of women from jury does not deny equal protection. Minnesota law review, v. 51 (January 1967), 552+.

231. CONVENTION debate and action on legislation. American Association of University Women, journal, v. 47 (October 1953), 31-5.

232. CONVENTION on political rights of women; text. U.S. Department of State, bulletin, v. 49 (26 August 1963), 327-8.

233. CONWELL, Russell H. Woman and the law. [Boston, Russell?] 1876.

234. COOKE, Joanne and Robin Morgan, comps. The new women: a Motive anthology on women's liberation. Indianapolis, Bobbs-Merrill, 1970. 196p.

235. COOKE, Rose Terry. The real rights of women. North American review, v. 149 (September 1889), 347-54.

236. COOPER, Anna Julia. A voice from the South. By a woman of the South. Xenia, Ohio, Aldine Printing House, 1892. 304p. Afro-American Press, Chicago, 1970. The status of woman at the close of the 19th century and especially the status of the black woman in the South.

237. COOPER, S. W. Legal rights of women. American magazine, v. 20 (1890), 448.

238. COPE, E. D. Oppression of women. Open Court, v. 8 (1894), 4103.

239. CORBETT-ASHBY, Margery. Women's place in democracy. Woman's press, v. 31 (July/August 1937), 305-6.

240. CORBIN, Caroline Elizabeth. Socialism and Christianity in reference to the woman question. Chicago, C. F. Corbin, 1905.

241. _____. Woman's rights in America, a retrospect of sixty years, 1848-1908. n.p., Illinois Association Opposed to the Extension of Suffrage to Women, 1908. 12p.

242. CORD, William Harland. Treatise on legal and equitable rights of married women. 2d ed. Philadelphia, Bisel, 1885. 2v.

243. CORELLI, M. Man's war against woman. Harper's bazaar, v. 41 (May-June 1907), 425-8, 550-3.

244. CORNELL Conference on Women, January 22-25, 1969. Proceedings. Edited by Sheila Tobias and others. Pittsburgh, Know, Inc., [1970?] 100p. Partial contents: Abortion and contraception; Psychological differences between men and women; The black woman in America; Equality and the education of women.

245. COWELL, Margaret. Women and equality. New York,
         Workers' Library, 1942.
246. _____. Women's place in the fight for a better world.
         New York, New Century, 1947.
247. COWLEY, Joyce. Pioneers of women's liberation. New
         York, Merit, 1969. 15p. General, historical discus-
         sion of the movement from the 16th century to the pres-
         ent.
248. COX, O. C. Marital status and employment of women: with
         special reference to Negro women. Sociology and so-
         cial research, v. 25 (November 1940), 157-65.
249. CRABITES, P. Woman and her purse; history of the property
         rights of the married woman. Catholic world, v. 131
         (June 1930), 319-26.
250. CRANSTON, M. W. Modern woman's place in the home.
         Atlantic monthly, v. 178 (July 1946), 106-8.
251. CRAVEN, M. B. Criticism on the Apostle Paul, in defense
         of women's rights. Intemperance, war, and Biblical
         theology, the three great obstructions to Christianity.
         Philadelphia, Barclay, 1872. 61p.
252. CRAZY-QUILT divorce-law pattern. Literary digest, v. 122
         (15 August 1936), 31-2.
253. CROCE, A. Sexism in the head. Commentary, v. 51
         (March 1971), 63-8.
254. CROLY, Jane Cunningham. The history of the woman's club
         movement in America. New York, H. G. Allen, 1898.
         1184p.
255. CRONAN, Sheila. Marriage. New York, The Feminists,
         [1970?] 7p.
256. CRONAU, Rudolph. Woman triumphant; the story of her
         struggles for freedom, education and political rights....
         New York, R. Cronau, 1919. 300p.
257. CROSBY, J. F. Advisability of inserting the word sex before
         the word race in the Fifteenth Amendment of the Con-
         stitution of the United States. Washington, Georgetown
         University, 1910. 16p.
258. CROSS, K. Patricia. College women: A research descrip-
         tion. Washington, National Association of Women Deans
         and Counselors, 1968. 19p. A paper discussing the
         difference in backgrounds of men and women, expecta-
         tions of families on each, and a recommendation to en-
         courage academic programs suitable for women's wants
         and needs.
259. CROZIER, Blanche. Constitutionality of discrimination based
         on sex. Boston University law review, v. 15 (Novem-
         ber 1935), 723-55.
260. CRUMMELL, Alexander. The black woman of the South; her
         neglects and her needs. Washington, Byron S. Adams,
         1883. 16p.
261. CUNNINGHAM, Robert M. Women who made it offer insights
         (some unintended) into their problems. College and
         university business, v. 48 (Feburary 1970), 56-61.
262. CURTIS, George William. Equal rights for all.... Speech

by George W. Curtis in the New York State Constitutional Convention, 1867. Rochester, N.Y., New York
State Constitutional Convention Campaign Committee,
1867. 24p.

263. CUTLER, John Henry. What about women? An examination
of the present characteristics, nature, status, and position of women as they have evolved during this century.
New York, I. Washburn, 1961. 241p.

264. DAHLINGER, Charles W. The dawn of the woman's movement: An account of the origin and history of the
Pennsylvania married woman's property law of 1848.
Western Pennsylvania historical magazine, v. 1 (1918),
68-84.

265. DALE, Laura H. The law and today's woman. Part I.
American Association of University Women, journal,
v. 53 (October 1959), 23-6. Concerning women jurors
and the property rights of women.

266. _____. The law and today's woman. Part II. American
Association of University Women, journal, v. 53 (January 1960), 90-2. Concerning women's legal status within the family.

267. DALL, Caroline Wells Healey. Woman's rights under the
law: in three lectures, delivered in Boston, January,
1861. Boston, Walker, Wise, 1861. 164p.

268. DAS, Sonya Ruth. The American woman in modern marriage.
New York, Philosophical Library, 1948. 185p.

269. DAVIDICA, Maureen. Women and the radical movement. No
more fun and games, no. 1 (December 1969). 2p. [re-
print issue]. On the advocacy of radical feminism; i.e.,
a complete breaking away from the male sector in order
to achieve complete equality on the part of women.

270. DAVIES, Emily. Thoughts on some questions relating to wom-
en, 1860-1908. New York, Macmillan, 1910. Reprinted
by Kraus Reprint, N.Y., 1972.

271. DAVIS, Elizabeth L. The story of the Illinois Federation of
Colored Women's Clubs, 1900-1922. [Chicago?], n.p.,
1922. 137p.

272. DAVIS, H. E. To raise the status of women in all fields. Independent woman, v. 25 (September 1946), 258-60. On the
United Nations Commission on the Status of Women.

273. DAVIS, Paulina Wright. A history of the national woman's
rights movement, for twenty years, with the proceedings
of the Decade Meeting held at Apollo Hall, New York
City, October 20, 1870, from 1850 to 1870. New York,
Journeymen Printers' Cooperative Association, 1871.
Kraus Reprint, N.Y., 1972. 152p.

274. DEBATING women's status. Independent woman, v. 19 (February 1940), 62.

275. DEBENEDICTIS, Daniel J. Legal rights of married women.
New York, Cornerstone, 1969. 127p.

276. DEBS, Eugene Victor. Woman--comrade and equal. n.p.,
n.d. 4p.

277. DECKER, Sarah S. Meaning of the woman's club movement.

American Academy of Political and Social Science, annals, v. 28 (September 1906), 199-204.

278. DECLARATION on the elimination of discrimination against
women adopted by the United Nations General Assembly.
International labour review, v. 97 (June 1968), 587-8.

279. DECOST, Dorothy K. Local government's role in program to
advance the status of women. Municipal South, v. 11
(April 1964), 20-1.

280. DECTER, Midge. Liberated woman. Commentary, v. 50
(October 1970), 33-44.

281. _____. The liberated woman and other Americans. New
York, Coward, McCann, 1971. 256p.

282. DE FORD, Miriam A. The feminist future. New republic,
v. 56 (19 September 1928), 121-3. Concerning the
growing equality of men and women.

283. DEGLER, Carl N. Charlotte Perkins Gilman on the theory
and practice of feminism, 1898-1923. American quarterly, v. 8 (Spring 1956), 21-39.

284. The DEMAND for citizenship for women. Americana, v. 7
(December 1912), 1114-16. A brief list of important
events in the history of the woman's movement.

285. DEMOTT, Benjamin. In and out of women's lib. Atlantic
monthly, v. 225 (March 1970), 110-17.

286. DENGEL, A. Woman question. Poise, v. 4 (November 1942),
7+.

287. DENSMORE, Dana. Chivalry--The iron hand in the velvet
glove. No more fun and games, no. 3 (November 1969),
60-7. On the polite behavior of modern men towards
women as a sign of men's status.

288. _____. On the temptation to be a beautiful object. No
more fun and games, no. 2 (February 1969), 43.

289. _____. Our place in the universe. No more fun and
games, no. 1 (December 1969). 5p. [reprint issue].
On the degrading role women are now enduring and the
necessity of their revolting.

290. _____. Sex and the single girl. No more fun and games,
no. 2 (February 1969), 74.

291. _____. Sex roles and female oppression; a collection of
articles. Boston, New England Free Press [1969?].
29p.

292. _____. The slave's stake in the home. No more fun and
games, no. 2 (February 1969), 14-20. The problem of
the woman in marriage and the problem of making her
understand her situation.

293. _____. Women's magazines and womanhood, 1969. No
more fun and games, no. 3 (November 1969), 30-9.
Thoughts on various magazines and their influence on
women.

294. DENSMORE, Emmet. Sex equality; solution of the woman
problem. New York, Funk, 1907.

295. DE RHAM, Edith. The love fraud; why the structure of the
American family is changing and what women must do
to make it work. New York, Potter, 1965. 319p.

296. DEUTCH, V. L. Equal rights. Saturday review of litera-
     ture, v. 31 (7 August 1948), 23.
297. DEVEREUX, Mrs. Roy. Ascent of woman. Boston, Roberts,
     1896.
298. DEVLIN, Polly. Many seem to think that being unhappy has
     more merit to it than being happy.... Mademoiselle,
     v. 70 (February 1970), 190-1+. The difficulties of
     simply becoming a woman.
299. DIALOGUE on women. By Esther Milner and others. In-
     dianapolis, Bobbs-Merill, 1967. 98p. Partial con-
     tents: Women in history; The mother's role; Sex
     equality.
300. DICKINSON, M. L. Woman; a half century of progress.
     Arena, v. 15 (1896), 361.
301. DIKE, S. W. Uniform marriage and divorce laws. Arena,
     v. 2 (September 1890), 399-408.
302. DINER, Helen. The story of the Amazons. New York, The
     Feminists [1970?] 2p.
303. DINGWALL, Eric John. The American woman: A historical
     study since 1620. New York, Rinehart, 1957. 309p.
     On the problem of why American women are so domi-
     nant in American society and yet so restless and dis-
     satisfied.
304. DISCRIMINATION against women. America, v. 78 (24 January
     1948), 451.
305. DISENCHANTMENT of motherhood. Science digest, v. 53
     (June 1963), 42.
306. DIX, Dorothy. Handicap of sex. Good housekeeping, v. 57
     (August 1913), 215-18.
307. _____. Woman's inhumanity to woman. Everybody's
     magazine, v. 10 (May 1904), 633-5. On the theory
     that the dependence of women on men for happiness
     and pleasures resulted in women regarding each other
     with suspicion for fear of losing their "ideal" conditions.
308. DIXON, Marlene. Why women's liberation? San Francisco,
     Bay Area Radical Education Project, 1970. 15p. Also
     in: Ramparts, v. 8 (December 1969), 57-63.
309. DO women need to be liberated; symposium. Sign, v. 50
     (August 1970), 32-3.
310. DODGE, Mary Abigail. Woman's worth and worthlessness.
     The compliment to "A new atmosphere." New York,
     Harper, 1871. 291p.
311. _____. Woman's wrongs: a counter-irritant. Boston,
     Ticknor and Fields, 1868. 212p. Reprinted by Green-
     wood Press, Westport, Conn., 1971.
312. DOES my liberation mean not your liberation? Detroit, Radi-
     cal Education Project, 1970. 6p.
313. DOLAN, Julia B. Another version of the legal status of
     women in Wisconsin. Marquette law review, v. 15
     (April 1931), 139-57.
314. DOLE, E. P. Legal rights of married women in New Hamp-
     shire. Granite monthly, v. 3 (1880), 264.
315. DONLON, Mary H. Status or stature? American Association

of University Women, journal, v. 51 (January 1958),
82-4. On the gaining of greater status, but little
stature.

316. DORR, Rheta Child. Breaking into the human race. Hampton's magazine, v. 27 (September 1911), 317-29. The
fact that women are made to conform to a certain type
whereas men are expected to differ from each other.

317. _____. Free and equal citizens. Good housekeeping, v.
87 (July 1928), 38-9.

318. _____. Problems of divorce. Forum, v. 45 (January
1911), 68-79.

319. DOYLE, Patricia Martin. The women's rights movement--
past. Trends, a journal of resources, v. 3 (October
1970), 5-9.

320. DRAFT declaration on the elimination of discrimination against
women; discussion in United Nations third committee.
UN monthly chronicle, v. 4 (November 1967), 37-9.

321. DRAKE, Durant. The ethics of the women's cause. North
American review, v. 200 (November 1914), 771-80.
On the necessity to consider women's duties rather
than their rights.

322. DREW, Althea Jompen. "...femininity is about as ambiguous
a matter as patriotism...." Mademoiselle, v. 70 (February 1970), 185+. The fear of not being a "feminine
woman" when among men.

323. DUDAR, H. Women's lib: the war on sexism; with views of
social scientists. Newsweek, v. 75 (23 March 1970),
71-6+.

324. DUNBAR, Roxanne. Female liberation as the basis for social
revolution. New Orleans, Southern Female Rights Union,
1971.

325. _____. Poor white woman. Women; a journal of liberation, v. 1 (Fall 1969), 15-17.

326. _____. What is to be done? No more fun and games,
no. 1 (December 1969), 3p. [reprint issue]. On the
necessity of attaining equality without male help and to
rid society of the small number of ruling males.

327. DURRANCE, R. B. Equality in Florida. Florida law journal, v. 21 (July 1947), 207-13.

328. _____. Married Woman's Act of 1943--is it an emancipation act? Florida law journal, v. 19 (October 1945),
237-43.

329. DYER, E. O. Marital happiness and the two-income family.
Southwestern social science quarterly, supp. v. 40
(1959), 95-102.

330. EATON, Amasa Mason. Woman's legal condition in Rhode
Island. n.p., n.d. 65p.

331. ECONOMIC and legal status of women. American Association
of University Women, journal, v. 40 (April 1947), 140-
6. Efforts of the AAUW between 1940 and 1947 to
achieve economic equality for women.

332. ELLICKSON, Katherine P. Progress of the [President's]
Commission on the Status of Women. Monthly labor

review, v. 86 (February 1963), 141-44.
333. ELLIS, H. Equal rights; a paradox. Pictorial review, v. 26 (November 1924), 5.
334. ELLIS, Julie E. Revolt of the second sex. New York, Lancer, 1970.
335. ENDLICH, Gustav Adolf and Louis Richards. Rights and liabilities of married women under common and statute law of Pennsylvania. Philadelphia, T. & J. W. Johnson, 1889.
336. EPSTEIN, Cynthia and William J. Goode, eds. The other half; roads to women's equality. Englewood Cliffs, N.J., Prentice-Hall, 1971. 207p. Articles by Lionel Tiger, Kate Millett, Jessie Bernard, Alice S. Rossi, and others.
337. EQUAL political rights for women; resolution adopted by United Nations General Assembly. UN bulletin, v. 1 (24 December 1946), 63.
338. EQUAL rights. Commonweal, v. 27 (18 February 1938), 465.
339. EQUAL rights for women. University of Florida law review, v. 15 (Summer 1962), 134.
340. EQUALITY, not protection. Science news, v. 94 (23 November 1968), 516-17. Concerning the Civil Rights Act and Title VII.
341. EQUALITY of the sexes. Family digest, v. 9 (March 1954), 53-4.
342. EQUALITY of the sexes. Month, v. 156 (December 1930), 542-4.
343. ERNEST, E. Women's present status. Kansas Medical Society, journal, v. 31 (December 1930), 427-32.
344. ERNST, George Alexander. Legal status of married women in Massachusetts. Boston, Massachusetts Woman Suffrage Association, 1895. 81p.
345. EVANS, Alvin Eleazer. The legal interests of married women in the state of Kentucky. Lexington, University of Kentucky Press, 1928. 54p.
346. EVANS, E. P. Woman question. Nation, v. 9 (1869), 112.
347. FAIRCHILD, J. E., ed. Women, society, and sex. New York, Sheridan House, 1952. 255p. The changing role of women in contemporary society.
348. FARBER, Seymour M., ed. The challenge to women. New York, Basic Books, 1966. 176p.
349. _____. Man and civilization: The potential of woman; a symposium. New York, McGraw-Hill, 1963. 328p.
350. FARLEY, G. M. Women on Washington [State] juries. Independent, v. 75 (3 July 1913), 50-2.
351. FARLEY, Jennie Tiffany. Women on the march again: the rebirth of feminism in an academic community. 282p. PhD thesis, Cornell University, 1970.
352. FARNHAM, Marynia F. Battles won and lost. American Academy of Political and Social Science, annals, v. 251 (May 1947), 113-19. On whether women's equal rights efforts have succeeded.

353. FAUST, Jean. Words that oppress. Pittsburgh, Know, Inc.,
        1970. 2p. On the feminizing of titles to differentiate
        and emphasize differences between the sexes.
354. FELTON, C. C. Rights and wrongs of women. Christian
        examiner, v. 52 (1852), 194.
355. FEMALE sexuality and the family. Wildflowers, v. 11
        (1969?), 26.
356. FEMININE vs. feminist. Living age, v. 272 (9 March 1912),
        587-92.
357. FEMINISM as a social phenomenon, by Mary R. Beard;
        Toward a new role for women, by Margaret Mead.
        Woman's press, v. 34 (November 1940), 464-7.
358. FEMINISM in the federal Constitution. World's work, v. 45
        (November 1922), 20-1.
359. FEMINISM moves on. Science news, v. 98 (5 September
        1970), 199.
360. FENBERG, Matilda. Jury service for women? Women law-
        yers journal, v. 33 (Spring 1947), 45-8.
361. FENNER, Mildred Sandison. One hundred years ago history
        was made at Seneca Falls. National Education Associa-
        tion, journal, v. 37 (November 1948), 534-5.
362. FERRISS, Abbott L. Indicators of trends in the status of
        American women. New York, Russell Sage Foundation,
        1971. 451p. A collection of data from federal govern-
        ment sources indicating women's educational status, in-
        come, employment, and other characteristics from
        around 1940 to the present.
363. FIELD, A. E. Woman's place in a changing world. National
        Education Association of the United States, proceedings
        (1939), 555-7.
364. FIGUEROA, Ana. Three stages of the convention on political
        rights of women [as passed in the UN Economic and
        Social Council sessions]. UN bulletin, v. 13 (1 July
        1952), 36-7.
365. FIRESTONE, Shulamith. The dialectic of sex; the case for
        feminist revolution. New York, Morrow, 1970. 274p.
366. FIRKEL, E. Women in the modern world. Notre Dame,
        Ind., Fides, 1963.
367. FISHER, B. E. Woman's place is--where? interview with
        Ida Tarbell. Christian science monitor weekly maga-
        zine (23 December 1936), 5.
368. FISHER, Marguerite J. Jury service--women as jurors; the
        present status of women as to jury service. American
        Bar Association, journal, v. 33 (February 1947), 113-
        15.
369. _____. Status of juror service for women. Independent
        woman, v. 26 (November 1947), 315+.
370. FISHMAN, Nathaniel. Married woman's bill of rights. New
        York, Liveright, 1943. 282p.
371. FITCH, George L. Humanity's wrongs alias woman's rights.
        San Francisco, n.p., 1895. 33p.
372. FIVE passionate feminists; symposium. McCalls, v. 97
        (July 1970), 52-5+. Interviews with Mrs. Malcolm

Peabody, civil rights worker; Judy Stein, founder of a
high school woman's liberation group; Anne Koedt,
founder of the New York Radical Feminists; James
Clapp, mathematician and women's rights advocate;
and Ellen Willis, rock-music critic.

373. FLEISCHMAN, Doris E. Notes of a retiring feminist. American mercury, v. 68 (February 1949), 161-8. The
problems of a married woman using her own name.

374. FLEMING, E. D. When a wife is second best. Cosmopolitan, v. 144 (January 1958), 62-5.

375. FLEXNER, Eleanor. Century of struggle; the woman's rights
movement in the United States. Cambridge, Harvard
University Press, 1959. 384p. Suffrage and the
rights movement through 1920.

376. FLORIDA. Governor's Commission on the Status of Women.
Women in Florida. Tallahassee, 1966. 53p.

377. FLORIDA wins legislative victory; married women may control their own property. Independent woman, v. 22
(July 1943), 215.

378. FLOWER, B. O. Era of woman. Arena, v. 4 (August 1891),
382-4.

379. FLYNN, Elizabeth Gurley. The feminine ferment: a discussion of the fight for women's rights. New masses,
(13 May 1947), 6-9.

380. FOLEY, Paul. Whatever happened to women's rights? Atlantic
monthly, v. 213 (March 1964), 63-5. Discussion: v. 214
(July 1964), 24+. The fact that most women, since 1920,
are not active voters, and do not seek professional careers
beyond college, but would rather get married.

381. FORSYTH, Z. D. and F. H. Forsyth. Trend toward sex equality in homemaking. Journal of Home Economics, v. 31
(April 1939), 249-57.

382. FORTUNE survey: Women in America. Fortune, v. 34 (August 1946),   5-6+ ; v. 34 (September 1946), 5-6. Questionnaire results pertaining to the status of women in
the home and their employment.

383. FORTUNE survey: Women in jobs. Fortune, v. 14 (October
1936), 222+. Results of questionnaires concerning
whether women should work outside the home.

384. FOSTER, G. B. Philosophy of feminism. Forum, v. 52
(July 1914), 10-22.

385. FOSTER, Mrs. J. E. Woman's political evolution. North
American review, v. 165 (November 1897), 600-9.

386. FOSTER, Lemuel Hill. The legal rights of women ... a brief
synopsis of the laws relating to property rights, dower,
divorce, the rights of a widow in the estate of her husband, etc. Detroit, Woman's Publishing Co., 1913.
295p. Consists of a summary of laws for each state.

387. FOWLER, William W. Women on the American frontier. Hart-
ford, Conn., S. S. Scranton, 1877. 527p. Reprinted by
Plutarch Press, Detroit, 1972 and Source Book Press,
N.Y., 1972.

388. FOX, Louis Hewitt. Pioneer women's rights magazine. New

York Historical Society, quarterly, v. 42 (January
1958), 71-4. A short history of "The Lilly," a feminist magazine, lasting from 1849 to around 1856.

389. FRANCIS, Philip. Legal status of women. Dobbs Ferry,
N.Y., Oceana, 1963. 95p.

390. FRANKLIN, Fabian. The intellectual powers of woman.
North American review, v. 166 (January 1898), 40-53.
Refutation of the theory that women are intellectually
inferior to men.

391. FRASER, Clara. Which road toward women's liberation?
Women; a journal of liberation, v. 2 (Fall 1970), 54-5.
The question of whether the movement is a matter for
liberals or radicals, and whether it is separated from
or concerned with race, class, and caste.

392. FRAZIER, George. Masculine mystique. Mademoiselle, v.
71 (July 1970), 63-4+. Many of men's problems might be
solved if women gained their equality.

393. FREEMAN, Diana. The feminist's husband. New republic,
v. 52 (24 August 1927), 15-16. An unhappy marriage
caused by the wife's taking on much of the economic
burden.

394. FREEMAN, Jo. The Bitch Manifesto. Pittsburgh, Know,
Inc., 1970. 7p. The female as a Bitch; i.e., aggres-
sive, assertive, free, and seeking their identity through
themselves.

395. _____. The building of the gilded cage. Pittsburgh,
Know, Inc., 1970. 16p. Concerning the social control of women.

396. _____. Growing up girlish. Trans-action, v. 8 (November 1970), 36-43. Concerning sex roles.

397. _____. The new feminists. Nation, v. 208 (24 February
1969), 241-4. Inequities in employment and a discussion of several modern-day women's liberation and
rights groups such as WITCH, WRAP, and NOW.

398. FREEMAN, Mary. The marginal sex; modern woman. Commonweal, v. 75 (2 February 1962), 483-6. The contra-
dictory nature of women's greater freedom and equality.

399. FRIEDAN, Betty. Emptiness is a housewife's complaint.
Practical forecast, v. 9 (October 1963), 44+.

400. _____. Feminine fulfillment; is this all? excerpt from
The Feminine Mystique. Mademoiselle, v. 55 (May
1962), 146-7+.

401. _____. The feminine mystique. New York, Dell, 1970.
410p. Refutation of the stereotyped image of women.

402. _____. Fraud of femininity; excerpts from The Feminine
Mystique. McCalls, v. 90 (March 1963), 81+; Discussion: v. 90 (August 1963), 38+.

403. _____. Have American housewives traded brains for
brooms? Ladies home journal, v. 80 (January 1963),
24+.

404. _____. Opinion; on the conventions. Mademoiselle, v.
67 (October 1968), 22+. The ignoring of women's interests during political conventions.

405. FROTHINGHAM, O. B. Woman question. Nation, v. 8
      (1869), 87.
406. FULTON, David Bryant. A plea for social justice for the
      Negro woman. Issued by the Negro Society for His-
      torical Research, Yonkers, N.Y., New York, Lincoln,
      1912. 11p.
407. FULTON, Justin Dewey. Woman as God made her; the true
      woman. Boston, Lee and Shepard, 1869. 262p.
408. FURER, Howard B. The American city: a catalyst for the
      women's rights movement. Wisconsin magazine of his-
      tory, v. 52 (Summer 1969), 285-305. Covers the peri-
      od from around 1840 to 1920.
409. FURNAS, J. C. Woman power. Ladies home journal, v.
      59 (November 1942), 20-1+.
410. The FUTURE of free womanhood. Living age, v. 277 (12
      April 1913), 119-21. The necessity of disregarding
      sex differences as a basis for equality.
411. GAGE, Matilda Joslyn. Speech of Mrs. M. E. J. Gage, at
      the Women's rights convention, held at Syracuse, Sep-
      tember, 1852. Syracuse, N.Y., Masters' Print.,
      [1852?] 8p. [Woman's Rights Tracts, no. 7.] Com-
      ments on the inequality in marriage and the necessity
      of women for self-reliance.
412. _____. Woman, church and state: a historical account
      of the status of woman through the Christian ages:
      with reminiscences of the matriarchate. Chicago, C.
      H. Kerr, 1893. 554p.
413. GALLAHER, Ruth Augusta. Legal and political status of
      women in Iowa; an historical account of the rights of
      women in Iowa from 1838 to 1918. Iowa City, State
      Historical Society of Iowa, 1918. 300p.
414. GALLUP, George. American woman. Saturday evening post,
      v. 235 (22 December 1962), 15-32.
415. GAMBLE, Eliza Burt. The evolution of woman; an inquiry
      into the dogma of her inferiority to man. New York,
      G. P. Putnam, 1894. 356p.
416. GARSKOF, Michele H. Roles women play: readings toward
      women's liberation. Belmont, Cal., Brooks/Cole,
      1971. 210p.
417. GASS, Gertrude Dorothy. The attitudes of eighty-five women
      in their middle years toward their narrowing role and
      the relationship of these attitudes to their contentment.
      220p. PhD thesis, University of Michigan, 1957. A
      study showing that women's discontent could be re-
      moved through more outside activities.
418. GEORGE, Walter Lionel. The intelligence of woman. Boston,
      Little, Brown, 1916. 244p.
419. GEORGIA. Governor's Commission on the Status of Women.
      Report. Atlanta, 1965. 35p.
420. GIBBES, Emily Oliver. Gleanings; a gift to the women of
      the world. New York, Caxton, 1892. 545p.
421. _____. A woman's idea for woman's good. Newport,
      R.I., C. E. Hammett, Jr., 1889. 76p.

422. GILLILAND, Mary S. Women in the community and in the
         family. International journal of ethics, v. 5 (October
         1894), 28-43. The necessity for women to widen their
         activities beyond the home.
423. GILMAN, Charlotte Perkins. Divorce and birth control.
         Outlook, v. 148 (25 January 1928), 130-1.
424. _____. The duty of surplus women. Independent, v. 58
         (19 January 1905), 126-30.
425. _____. The growing power of woman. Booklover's maga-
         zine, v. 4 (September 1904), 385-90.
426. _____. The home. Its work and influence. New York,
         Charlton, 1910. 347p. Reprinted by Source Book
         Press, New York, 1970.
427. _____. Home: its work and influence. Critic, v. 43
         (December 1903), 568-70.
428. _____. The man-made world, or, Our androcentric cul-
         ture. New York, Charlton, 1911. 260p. Reprinted
         by Source Book Press, New York, 1970. Pertains to
         the results of the unlimited dominance of men.
429. _____. Modesty: feminine and other. Independent, v.
         58 (29 June 1905), 1447-50. Modesty as inferiority
         and pride, and as a differentiation of the sexes.
430. _____. Reaction of home conditions upon the family.
         American journal of Sociology, v. 14 (March 1909),
         592-605. On the evils of economic dependence of
         women.
431. _____. Wash-tubs and woman's duty. Century, v. 110
         (June 1925), 152-9.
432. _____. What are women anyway? Collier's, v. 43 (5
         June 1909), 19.
433. _____. The Woman's Congress of 1899. Arena, v. 22
         (September 1899), 342-50.
434. _____. Women and social service. Warren, Ohio, Na-
         tional American Woman Suffrage Association [1907?].
         12p. On the necessity for women to take a greater
         part in social service rather than solely in family
         service.
435. GIRVIN, Ernest A. Domestic duels; or, Evening talks on
         the woman question.... San Francisco, E. D. Bron-
         son, 1898. 277p.
436. GITTELSON, N. Love, sex, and the silken curtain. Har-
         per's bazaar, v. 101 (February 1968), 33+.
437. GLADSTONE, Rose. Planned obsolescence: the middle-
         aged woman. Up from under, v. 1 (May/June 1970),
         29-31.
438. GLASGOW, Maude. The subjection of woman and traditions
         of men. New York, M. I. Glasgow, 1940. 341p.
439. GLYNN, Edward. How to unnerve male chauvinists. Ameri-
         ca, v. 123 (12 September 1970), 144-6; Discussion:
         v. 123 (10 October 1970), 247. On a number of
         groups such as NOW, WITCH, etc., and on the Equal
         Rights Amendment.
440. GODKIN, E. L. Agitation on rights of women. Nation,

v. 11 (1870), 346.

441. _____. Another delicate subject. Nation, v. 11 (14 July 1870), 21-3. Comments on the movement in general.

442. _____. Female influence. Nation, v. 5 (25 July 1867), 73-4.

443. _____. The feud in the woman's rights camp. Nation, v. 11 (24 November 1870), 346-7. Comments on articles in several journals: Woman's Advocate, Revolution, and the Woman's Journal.

444. _____. The neglected side of woman. Nation, v. 7 (1868), 434-5.

445. _____. The other side of the question. Nation, v. 5 (17 October 1867), 316-17.

446. _____. Woman question. Nation, v. 8 (1869), 409-10.

447. GOLDBERG, Cecile Sylvia. Law of married women in Pennsylvania. Philadelphia, Bisel, 1940. 321p.

448. GOLDIN, D. R. Present status of married women in Georgia. Georgia bar journal, v. 7 (May 1945), 436-44.

449. GOLDMAN, Emma. The traffic in women and other essays on feminism. New York, Times Change Press, 1970. 63p.

450. _____. Tragedy of woman's emancipation. New York, Mother Earth Publishing Assn., 1909.

451. GOLDSTEIN, Valerie Saiving. The human situation: A feminine viewpoint. Journal of religion, v. 40 (April 1960), 100-12. The irrelevance of masculine experience on a feminine society.

452. GOLDWATER, Ethel. Women's place: The new alliance of "science" and anti-feminism. Commentary, v. 4 (December 1947), 578-85. The problem of the dependent housewife.

453. GORDON, L. M. Marriage by proxy: The need for certainty and equality in the laws of the American states. Social service review, v. 20 (March 1946), 29-48.

454. GORDON, Linda. Families. Boston, New England Free Press, 1970. 24p. Families and the oppression of women.

455. GORNICK, Vivian and Barbara K. Moran. Woman in sexist society; studies in power and powerlessness. New York, Basic Books, 1971. 515p.

456. _____. Women's liberation: The next great moment in history is theirs. Pittsburgh, Know, Inc., [1970?]. 5p.

457. GOUGER, Helen M. Constitutional rights of the women of Indiana: An argument in the superior court of Tippecanoe County, Indiana. Judge F. B. Everett, presiding. January 10, 1895. n.p., [1895?] 57p.

458. GRAHAM, Abbie. Ladies in revolt. New York, Woman's Press, 1934. 222p. On the freedoms attained by women from around 1790 to 1890.

459. GRAHAM, Lee. Who's in charge here? not women! New York Times magazine, (2 September 1962), 8+. Inequities in wages and in politics.

460. GRAND, Sarah. The new aspect of the woman question.
     North American review, v. 158 (March 1894), 270-6.
461. GRANT, Jane. Confession of a feminist. American mercury,
     v. 57 (December 1943), 684-91.
462. GRANT, R. Marriage and divorce. Yale review, n.s., v.
     14 (January 1925), 223-38.
463. GRANT, Robert. Women and property. Scribner's maga-
     zine, v. 62 (November 1917), 585-91.
464. GREENE, Mary Anne. Legal status of women under the laws
     of Rhode Island, 1892. Providence, n.p., 1893. 7p.
465. GRIMKE, Angelina Emily. Letter from Angeline Grimke
     Weld, to the Woman's Rights Convention, held at Syra-
     cuse, September, 1852. Syracuse, N.Y., Masters' Print.,
     [1852?]. 8p. [Woman's Rights Tracts, no. 8.] On the
     difference between human, artificial, and natural organi-
     zations and their power in relation to women's rights.
466. GRIMKE, Sarah Moore. Letters on the equality of the sexes,
     and the condition of woman. Boston, I. Knapp, 1838.
     128p. Reprinted by B. Franklin, New York, 1970 and
     Source Book Press, N.Y., 1972.
467. GROSS, Amy. Women's lib loves you. Mademoiselle, v. 70
     (February 1970), 232-3+.
468. GROSSMAN, E. M. and G. A. McNulty. Right of women to
     serve on juries in Missouri. St. Louis law review,
     v. 12 (February 1927), 138-44.
469. GROVER, Alonzo J. The Bible argument against woman
     stated and answered from a Bible standpoint. Earl-
     ville, Ill., Cook County Woman's Suffrage Association,
     1870. 23p.
470. GROVES, Ernest Rutherford. The American woman: the
     feminine side of a masculine civilization. New York,
     Greenberg, 1937. 438p. The changing status of wom-
     en from colonial times.
471. GRUENBERG, Sidonie Matsner. Changing conceptions of the
     family. American Academy of Political and Social Sci-
     ence, annals, v. 251 (May 1947), 128-36.
472. _____. Woman's place today. Child study, v. 16 (May
     1939), 185-8.
473. HACKER, Helen Mayer. Women as a minority group. Social
     forces, v. 30 (October 1951), 60-9. [Also: Bobbs-
     Merrill reprint, Indianapolis. number S-108.]
474. HAHN, L. B. Discussions on status of women. U.S. De-
     partment of State bulletin, v. 30 (26 April 1954), 646-
     51.
475. _____. Promoting the progress and equality of women.
     U.S. Department of State bulletin, v. 41 (13 July 1959),
     62-4.
476. _____. United Nations and equality for women. U.S. De-
     partment of State bulletin, v. 33 (1 August 1955), 206-
     8.
477. _____. United Nations promotion of equality for women.
     U.S. Department of State bulletin, v. 38 (2 June 1958),
     930-3.

478. HALE, E. E. Independence of women. Lend a hand, v. 1
      (1886), 660.
479. HALL, Gus. Working class approach to women's liberation.
      New York, New Outlook, 1970. 12p. A speech at the
      Women's Commission of the U.S. Communist Party,
      January 5, 1970, pertaining to women in the work
      force and their efforts for political independence.
480. HALLS, John H. Woman and her emancipation. New York,
      New York Labor News Co., 1908. 46p.
481. HALONEN, Kae. Man's world and welcome to it. Detroit,
      Radical Education Project [1970?]. 8p. The problem
      of channelling women into female roles as well as their
      problems in society.
482. HAMILTON, Cicely. Marriage as a trade. New York, Mof-
      fat Yard, 1909. 257p. Reprinted by Singing Tree
      Press, Detroit, 1971.
483. HARD, W. Protected wives of Louisiana. Delineator, v. 80
      (July 1912), 12-14.
484. HARDWICK, Elizabeth. Women "...are demanding equal
      rights in something that is itself losing ground as a
      fulfillment." Mademoiselle, v. 70 (February 1970),
      186-7+.
485. HARE, Nathan and Julia Hare. Black women, 1970. Trans-
      action, v. 8 (November 1970), 65-8+.
486. HARPER, Ida Husted. Changing conditions of marriage. In-
      dependent, v. 61 (6 December 1906), 1329-32.
487. _____. Man versus women: an indictment. Independent,
      v. 64 (2 April 1908), 741-4. Concerns the fact that
      lawmaking power is in the hands of men, and the in-
      equality in jobs and education.
488. _____. Women as jurors. National magazine, v. 20
      (1904), 40.
489. HARPER, L. Woman's place is not where you think it is.
      Catholic layman, v. 79 (June 1965), 40-4.
490. HARRIS, George E. Law of contracts by married women.
      New York, Banks and Co., 1887.
491. HART, W. O. Rights of women in Louisiana. Louisiana
      historical quarterly, v. 4 (October 1921), 437-58. A
      study, in part historical, of the civil code of Louisiana
      and acts of the legislature as regards the rights of
      women.
492. HATHAWAY, C. C. Woman's demand for man's full civil
      rights. Current history magazine of the New York
      Times, v. 17 (January 1923), 642-5.
493. HAUGHTON, R. The weaker sex. Clergy, v. 51 (November
      1966), 849-62.
494. HAWAIIAN women want jury service. Woman's journal, v.
      16 (March 1931), 27.
495. HAWKES, A. L. Changing patterns in women's lives in 1960.
      Teachers College record, v. 61 (April 1960), 404-14.
496. HAYDEN, C. and M. King. Sex and caste. Liberation, v.
      11 (April 1966), 35-6.
497. HAYDEN, M. P. The Bible and woman; a critical and com-

prehensive examination of the teaching of the Scriptures concerning the position and sphere of woman. Cincinnati, Ohio, Standard Publishing Co., 1902. 74p.

498. HAYS, Hoffman Reynolds. The dangerous sex; the myth of feminine evil. New York, Putnam, 1964. 316p. Reasons in the psychology of women's low status.

499. HEBARD, Grace Raymond. The first woman jury. Journal of American history, v. 7, no. 4 (1913), 1293+.

500. HEDGEMAN, Anna A. The role of the Negro woman. Journal of educational Sociology, v. 17 (April 1944), 463-72.

501. HEINRICH, Louise Dudley. Sex distinction in the Virginia law. Richmond, Legislative Reference Bureau, 1925. 12p.

502. HEINZEN, K. Rights of women and the sexual relations. Boston, B. R. Tucker, 1891.

503. HENROTIN, Ellen M. Evolution of women. World to-day, v. 5 (1903), 1308.

504. _____. General Federation of Women's Clubs. Outlook, v. 55 (1897), 442.

505. _____. State federations of women's clubs. Review of reviews, v. 16 (October 1897), 437-40.

506. HENSHAW, S. E. Are they inferior? Galaxy, v. 7 (1869), 125.

507. HENTOFF, Margot. Women's liberation, the time is now. Parents' magazine, v. 45 (December 1970), 44+.

508. HENTOFF, Nat. Women's liberation, but how soon will it happen? Parents' magazine, v. 45 (December 1970), 45+.

509. HERTELL, T. Right of married women to hold property. new ed. Boston, Mendum, 1867.

510. HERZFELD, Norma Krause. The status of women. Commonweal, v. 71 (5 February 1960), 515-18. Primarily on the status of American women, with comments on a number of women's organizations.

511. HEYWOOD, Ezra Harvey. Uncivil liberty: an essay to show the injustice and impolicy of ruling woman without her consent. Princeton, Mass., Cooperative Publishing Co., 1873. 23p.

512. HICKEY, Margaret A. Never underestimate the brainpower of a woman, Mr. President. Ladies' home journal, v. 79 (November 1962), 44.

513. HICKOX, George A. Legal disabilities of married woman in Connecticut. Hartford, 1871. 40p. [Tracts of the Connecticut Woman Suffrage Association, no. 1.]

514. HICKS, William Watkin. The banner with the new device; woman's place in nature, in civilization, and in government. Boston, Sanctuary Publishing Co., 1913. 280p.

515. HIGGINS, Edwin, comp. A compilation of Maryland laws of interest to women. Baltimore, Press of Baltimore Methodist, 1897. 83p.

516. HIGGINSON, Thomas Wentworth. Common sense about women. Boston, Lee and Shepard, 1882. 403p. Reprinted by

Greenwood Press, Westport, Conn., 1971.
517.   _____. Concerning all of us. New York, Harper, 1892.
         210p.
518.   _____. Ought women to learn the alphabet? Boston, For
         sale at the office of "The Woman's Journal," 1871.
         23p. Reprinted from the Atlantic monthly of February
         1859.
519.   _____. Woman and her wishes. New York, Fowler and
         Wells, 1853. 23p. The necessity of women to have
         influence.
520. HIGH school girls deny that women's place is in the home.
         Senior scholastic, v. 46 (5 March 1945), 26.
521. HINCKLE, Warren and Marianne Hinckle. History of the rise
         of the unusual movement for women power in the United
         States, 1961-1968. Ramparts magazine, v. 6 (February
         1968), 22-31. Discussion: v. 6 (May 1968), 4.
522. HINKLE, Beatrice M. Woman's subjective dependence upon
         man. Harper's magazine, v. 164 (January 1932), 193-
         205. Psychological dependence on men despite the re-
         moval of many restrictive laws.
523. HINSON, M. R. Outlook for college women in our democracy.
         Southern Association quarterly, v. 4 (August 1940),
         462-5.
524. HOAR, George Frisbie. Woman's rights and the public wel-
         fare. Remarks before a Joint Special Committee of
         the Massachusetts Legislature, April 14, 1869. Boston,
         C. K. Whipple, 1869. 16p.
525. HOBBS, Lisa. Love and liberation; up front with the femi-
         nists. New York, McGraw-Hill, 1970. 161p.
526. HOLLINGWORTH, Leta S. Science and feminism. Scientific
         monthly, (September 1916), 277-84.
527. HOLMES, L. M. Woman's future position in the world.
         Arena, v. 20 (September 1898), 333-43.
528. HOOKER, John. Woman question. Nation, v. 9 (1869), 386.
529. HORACK, Frank Edward. Legislation pertaining to women
         and children in Iowa. Iowa City, University of Iowa
         Press, 1934. 67p.
530. HORNE, L. Three-horned dilemma facing Negro women.
         Ebony, v. 21 (August 1966), 118-22+.
531. HORNER, Matina. A bright woman is caught in a double
         bind. In achievement-oriented situations she worries
         not only about failure but also about success. Psy-
         chology today, v. 3 (November 1969), 36+.
532. HOW bosses feel about women's lib; job policies unaffected.
         Business week, (5 September 1970), 18-19. Varied
         opinions of employers indicating primarily that women
         are, in fact, getting their rights.
533. HOW can we raise women's status? Symposium. Independent
         woman, v. 17 (September 1938), 280-1+.
534. HOW do women rate? Nations schools, v. 37 (March 1946),
         45.
535. HOWARD, J. Political status of women. Chautauquan, v.
         18 (1894), 477.

536.   HOWELLS, W. D. Civic equality for woman. Harper's
        monthly magazine, v. 118 (May 1909), 965-8.
537.   HOWES, Ethel Puffer. The meaning of progress in the wom-
        an movement. American Academy of Political and So-
        cial Science, annals, v. 143 (May 1929), 14-20.
538.   HOWORTH, L. S. Wheels spin faster; developments in the
        women's movement. American Association of University
        Women, journal, v. 38 (April 1945), 150-1.
539.   HOYT, R. Toward a revalorization of bitchery. National
        Catholic reporter, v. 7 (27 November 1970), 1+.
540.   HUBBELL, Thelma Lee and Gloria R. Lothrop. The Friday
        Morning Club, a Los Angeles legacy. Southern Cali-
        fornia quarterly, v. 50, no. 1 (1968), 59-90. On the
        Friday Morning Club, founded by Caroline M. Severance
        in 1891, and which was a means for working for wom-
        en's rights and educational activities.
541.   HUBERT, L. D., Jr. Effect of recent acts on the incapaci-
        ties and disabilities of married women in Louisiana.
        Tulane law review, v. 8 (December 1933), 107-20.
542.   HUGHES, S. T. The half-citizen. Texas Bar journal, v. 2
        (April 1939), 99-100, 108. Concerning jury service for
        women.
543.   HUMPHREY, Mattie L. The black woman's survival kit.
        Trends, a journal of resources, v. 3 (October 1970),
        21-4.
544.   HUNDRED years' war. Time, v. 36 (9 December 1940), 16-
        17. The Woman Centennial Congress in New York to
        celebrate 100 years of the women's rights struggle.
545.   HUNSUCKER, Suzanne. Who wants equality? Women in
        Wyoming. Nation, v. 211 (9 November 1970), 465-8.
546.   HUNT, Harry E., comp. Michigan laws relating to women
        and girls. Detroit, Michigan Equal Suffrage Associa-
        tion, 1911.
547.   HUNT, Morton. Her infinite variety; the American woman
        as lover, mate and rival. New York, Harper & Row,
        1962. 333p.
548.   _____. Up against the wall, male chauvinist pig! Play-
        boy, v. 15 (May 1970), 95+.
549.   HUNT, R. L. Legal status of women. Wisconsin journal of
        education, v. 73 (March 1941), 350-1.
550.   HUNTINGTON, F. D. Position of women. Monthly religious
        magazine, v. 14 (1855), 241.
551.   HURST, Fannie. Crisis in the history of women: let us have
        action instead of lip-service. Vital speeches, v. 9
        (15 May 1943), 479-80. Criticism of government and
        industry for the low number of women in these areas.
552.   HURST, Helen Harrison. Woman's changing role. Journal
        of home economics, v. 40 (May 1948), 263.
553.   HUSBANDS, Clement M. Law of married women in Pennsyl-
        vania, with a view of law of trusts in that state. Phila-
        delphia, T. & J. W. Johnson, 1878.
554.   HYER, M. Long road to freedom. National Catholic re-
        porter, v. 7 (13 November 1970), 1+.

555. _____. Tougher issues surfacing in women's lib debates.
National Catholic reporter, v. 7 (26 March 1971), 3+ .
556. HYMER, E. W. [United Nations] Commission on the Status
of Women. Independent woman, v. 34 (May 1955), 190.
557. _____. It behooves the other half to listen. Independent
woman, v. 30 (April 1951), 90-2. Concerning the U.N.
Commission on the Status of Women.
558. ILLINOIS. Commission on the Status of Women. Report of
the status of women. Springfield, 1965. 64p.
559. _____. _____. Women--agents of change; Second report on the status of women, 1967. Springfield, 1967.
52p. A third report was issued in 1969, also 52p.
560. IN the same boat; battle of the sexes. Ebony, v. 17 (October 1962), 72-3.
561. INFLUENCES and capabilities of women. National quarterly
review, v. 7 (1863), 111.
562. INMAN, Mary. In woman's defense. Los Angeles, Committee to Organize the Advancement of Women, 1940. 174p.
563. _____. Woman-power. Los Angeles, Committee to Organize the Advancement of Women, 1942. 88p.
564. INTER-AMERICAN Commission of Women. A comparison of
the political and civil rights of men and women in the
United States. Washington, GPO, 1936. 249p. Indicates equal and unequal treatment of women in all
states, regarding minimum wage, right to contract,
sue and be sued, etc.
565. _____. Historical review on the recognition of the political rights of American women. Washington, Pan American Union, 1965. 29p.
566. IS a uniform divorce law necessary or desirable? Review of
reviews, v. 45 (March 1912), 372-3.
567. IS a women's revolution really possible? Yes, by Leslie
Aldridge Westoff; No, by John Gagnon and William
Simon. McCall's, v. 97 (October 1969), 76+ .
568. IS Wisconsin's equal rights law proving beneficial to women?
Pro and con. Congressional digest, v. 3 (March 1924),
205-6.
569. IS woman inferior to man? Sign, v. 27 (March 1948), 56.
570. JACKSON, James Caleb. American womanhood: its peculi-
arities and necessities. 3d ed. New York, Baker,
Pratt, 1870. 159p.
571. JAHODA, Marie and Joan Havel. Psychological problems of
women in different social roles. Educational record,
v. 36 (October 1955), 325-35.
572. JAM session; is a woman's place in the home? Senior scholastic, v. 56 (5 April 1950), 21-2.
573. JAMES, H. Woman question. Putnam's monthly magazine,
v. 1 (1853), 279.
574. JANEWAY, Elizabeth. Happiness and the right to choose.
Atlantic monthly, v. 225 (March 1970), 118-26.
575. _____. Man's world, woman's place; a study in social
mythology. New York, Morrow, 1971. 319p.
576. JENSEN, Oliver Ormerod. The revolt of American women;

a pictorial history of the century of change from
bloomers to bikinis--from feminism to Freud. New
York, Harcourt, Brace, 1952. 224p.

577. JESSUP, Henry Wynans. Law for wives and daughters; their
rights and their obligations. New York, Macmillan,
1927. 208p.

578. JIAGGE, A. R. Introduction to the Declaration on elimination of discrimination against women. UN monthly
chronicle, v. 5 (March 1968), 55-61.

579. JOHNSEN, Julia Emily, comp. Special legislation for wom-
en. New York, H. W. Wilson, 1926. 142p.

580. JOHNSON, Nora. Captivity of marriage. Atlantic monthly,
v. 207 (June 1961), 38-42. Discussion: v. 208
(August 1961), 24-5.

581. JONES, Beverly and Judith Brown. Toward a female liberation movement. Boston, New England Free Press
[1969?]. 32p. Criticism of the Manifesto of the female caucus of the national SDS convention in 1967 and
suggestions for a stronger movement.

582. JONES, Irma T. History of the Michigan State Federation
of Women's Clubs. Michigan history magazine, v. 10
(January 1926), 60-75; (April 1926), 221-32; (October
1926), 534-49.

583. JURY discrimination against women, mandamus. Illinois law
review, v. 22 (March 1928), 777-9.

584. JURY service for women. State government, v. 10 (April
1937), 81.

585. JURY service for women. University of Florida law review,
v. 12 (Summer 1959), 224.

586. JURY service for women extended. National municipal review, v. 26 (June 1937), 312.

587. JURY service for women voted in Oklahoma. Independent
woman, v. 30 (July 1951), 209.

588. KANE, John Joseph. Are men equal to women? Ave maria,
v. 82 (27 August 1955), 17-20.

589. _____. The changing roles of father and mother in contemporary American society. American Catholic sociological review, v. 11 (October 1950), 140-51.

590. KANOWITZ, Leo. Constitutional aspects of sex-based discrimination in American law. Nebraska law review,
v. 48 (November 1968), 131.

591. _____. Law and the married woman. St. Louis University law journal, v. 12 (Fall 1967), 3.

592. _____. Legal status of American women. Family law
quarterly, v. 2 (June 1968), 121.

593. _____. Sex-based discrimination in American law: law
and the single girl. St. Louis University law journal,
v. 11 (Spring 1967), 293-330.

594. _____. Women and the law; the unfinished revolution.
Albuquerque, University of New Mexico Press, 1969.
312p. Concerns the Equal Pay Act of 1963; Title VII
of the 1964 Civil Rights Act; and the legal status of
married women.

595. KANSAS. Governor's Commission on the Status of Women.
     Report. Topeka, 1968. 44p.
596. _____. University. Bureau of General Information. Laws
     affecting women in Kansas. By M. B. Virtue. Topeka,
     1939. 45p.
597. KARP, Walter. Feminine utopia. Horizon, v. 13 (Spring
     1971), 4-13. The ascendancy of the male due to his
     dominance in the family.
598. KATZ, Maude W. The Negro woman and the law. Freedom-
     ways, v. 2 (Summer 1962), 278-86.
599. KEARON, Pamela. Man-hating. New York, The Feminists,
     1969. 2p.
600. _____. Power as a function of the group--some notes.
     New York, The Feminists, 1969. 4p.
601. _____. Rules and responsibility in a leaderless feminist
     revolutionary group. New York, The Feminists, 1969.
     3p.
602. KELLEY, Florence. Family and the woman's wage. Con-
     ference on charities and corrections (1909), 118-21.
603. _____. The new woman's party. Survey, v. 45 (5 March
     1921), 827-9.
604. _____. Should women be treated identically with men by
     law? American review, v. 1 (May 1923), 276-84.
605. KELLY, D. The status of women; report of the President's
     Commission. Catholic nurse, v. 12 (December 1963),
     16-17.
606. KELLY, John Francis. Contracts of married women.
     Newark, N.J., Soney & Sage, 1882.
607. KELTNER, E. H. Texas married women. Suggested legis-
     lative action to liberalize the contractual and property
     rights of Texas married women. Texas law review,
     v. 25 (June 1947), 657-67.
608. KEMPTON, Sally. Cutting loose; a private view of the wom-
     en's uprising. Esquire, v. 74 (July 1970), 53-7.
609. KENDRICK, Ruby M. They also serve; the National Associa-
     tion of Colored Women, Inc. [1896-1954]. Negro his-
     tory bulletin, v. 17 (May 1954), 171-5.
610. KENTUCKY. Governor's Commission on the Status of Wom-
     en. Kentucky women. Frankfort [1966?]. 68p.
611. KENYON, Dorothy. The awakening of women. American As-
     sociation of University Women, journal, v. 42 (Fall
     1948), 9-15. Comments on the Seneca Falls convention
     of 1848.
612. _____. Equality and freedom. Independent woman, v. 28
     (March 1949), 66-8. Partly on the United Nations
     Commission on the Status of Women.
613. _____. How women have achieved as citizens. American
     Association of University Women, journal, v. 33 (Janu-
     ary 1940), 67-73. On the Seneca Falls Convention in
     1848.
614. _____. Women in our changing political economy. Ameri-
     can Association of University Women, journal, v. 29
     (January 1936), 78-83.

615. KEY, Ellen Karolina. The woman movement. New York,
      G. P. Putnam, 1912. 224p.
616. KIELL, Norman and Bernice Friedman. Culture lag and
      housewifemanship: the role of the married female col-
      lege graduate. Journal of educational Sociology, v. 31
      (October 1957), 87-95.
617. KING, H. H. Black woman and women's lib. Ebony, v. 26
      (March 1971), 68-70+.
618. KINGSLEY, C. Woman question. Every Saturday, v. 8
      (1870), 556.
619. KLEIN, D. How much of a man's world is it? Seventeen,
      v. 26 (November 1967), 210+.
620. KNOPF, Olga. The art of being a woman. New York, Blue
      Ribbon, 1932. 307p. Primarily the status of married
      women.
621. _____. Women on their own. Boston, Little, Brown,
      1935. 306p.
622. KNOX, D. Divorce conflict. Forum, v. 62 (July 1919), 48-
      59.
623. KNOX, Reuben, comp. Law of married women in New Jer-
      sey. Plainfield, N.J., New Jersey Law Journal Pub-
      lishing Co., 1912. 561p.
624. KNUDSON, Dean. The declining status of women: Popular
      myths and the failure of functionalist thought. Social
      forces, v. 48 (December 1969), 183-93.
625. KOEDT, Anne. The myth of the vaginal orgasm. Boston,
      New England Free Press [1970?]. 5p.
626. KOMAROVSKY, Mirra. Blue-collar marriage. New York,
      Random House, 1967. 395p.
627. _____. Functional analysis of sex roles. American soci-
      ological review, v. 15 (August 1950), 508-16. The
      status of women in the family structure.
628. KOMISAR, Lucy. New feminism. New York, Watts, 1971.
629. _____. New feminism. Saturday review, v. 53 (21 Febru-
      ary 1970), 27-30+. Concerning refutations of men's
      superiority and the fact that motherhood should not be
      the main part of a woman's life.
630. KRADITOR, Aileen S., ed. Up from the pedestal; selected
      writings in the history of American feminism. Chicago,
      Quadrangle, 1968. 372p.
631. KRAMER, Jane. Profiles; founding cadre; personalities of
      and dialogues among some members of a woman's lib-
      eration group. New Yorker, v. 46 (28 November 1970),
      52-6+.
632. KREPS, Juanita M. The status of women; the economic
      change. Vital speeches, v. 28 (1 September 1962),
      698-701. Pertains to employment and marriage trends.
633. KRESGE, Pat. The human dimensions of sex discrimination.
      AAUW journal, v. 64 (November 1970), 6-9.
634. KUGLER, Israel. The women's rights movement and the
      National Labor Union, 1866-1872; what was the nature
      of the relationship between the National Labor Union
      and the woman's rights movement and what may serve

to explain periods of cooperation and subsequent diver-
gence? 570p. PhD thesis, New York University, 1954.
635. LA BARR, M. E. Women jurors in North Carolina. Independent woman, v. 16 (February 1937), 53.
636. LADNER, Joyce A. Tomorrow's tomorrow: The black woman. Garden City, N.Y., Doubleday, 1971. 304p.
637. LADY'S law; marriage. Atlantic monthly, v. 90 (October
1902), 570-2.
638. LA FOLLETTE, Suzanne. Concerning women. New York,
A. & C. Boni, 1926. 306p. Partial contents: Beginnings of emancipation; women's status, past and present;
institutional marriage and its economic aspects.
639. LANDY, Avrom. Two questions on the status of women under
capitalism. Communist, v. 20 (September 1941), 818-
33.
640. LAPHAM, E. C. Woman's duty to her own sex. Forum,
v. 1 (1886), 455.
641. LA RUE, Linda J. Black liberation and women's lib. Trans-
action, v. 8 (November 1970), 59-64.
642. LAW and the wife. Harper's bazaar, v. 34 (5 January 1901),
60.
643. LAW of married women. American law review, v. 6 (1872),
57.
644. LAWRENCE, D. H. The real thing. Scribner's magazine,
v. 87 (June 1930), 587-92. The unhappiness of women
despite their greater freedoms.
645. _____. What will woman do with her freedom? Virginia
quarterly review, v. 6 (July 1930), 372-81.
646. LAWRENCE, Emmeline Pethick and Charlotte Perkins Gilman.
Does a man support his wife? New York, National
American Woman Suffrage Association, 1911. 20p.
647. LAWS, Judith L. The social psychology of women: shibboleths and lacunae. Pittsburgh, Know, Inc., [1969?].
12p.
648. LEAGUE of Nations. Status of women. Communications from
governments and women's international organizations
[since September 27, 1935] ... Geneva, 1936- .
649. _____. Assembly. First Committee. Status of women.
Geneva, 1935. 2p.
650. LEAGUE of Women Voters of the United States. Committee
on the Legal Status of Women. A survey of the legal
status of women in the 48 states. rev. ed. Washington, The League, 1930. 228p.
651. _____. _____. Toward equal rights for men and wom-
en. Washington, 1929. 139p.
652. LEAR, W. M. Second feminist wave. New York Times
magazine (10 March 1968), 24-5+; Discussion: (31
March 1968), 14+.
653. LEARY, John P. Woman in American society today. Thought,
v. 42 (Spring 1967), 112-20.
654. LEGAL conditions of women. Western law journal, v. 6
(1849), 145.
655. LEGAL rights of married women in Texas. Southwestern law

journal, v. 13 (Winter 1959), 84.
656. LEGAL rights of women. American, v. 21 (1891), 27.
657. LEGAL rights of women. New Englander, v. 22 (1863), 22.
658. LEMONS, James Stanley. The new woman in the new era:
     The woman movement from the great war to the great
     depression. 399p. PhD thesis, University of Mis-
     souri, 1967.
659. LEON, S. de. What is a liberated woman? Sign, v. 50
     (August 1970), 5-10.
660. LEONARD, E. A. St. Paul on the status of women. Catholic
     biblical quarterly, v. 12 (July 1950), 311-20.
661. LEONARD, P. Ideal of equality for men and women. Har-
     per's bazaar, v. 43 (May 1909), 525-6.
662. LERNER, Gerda. The feminists: a second look. Columbia
     forum, v. 13 (Fall 1970), 24-30.
663. LEVITT, Morris. The political role of American women.
     Journal of human relations, v. 15 (First quarter 1967),
     23-35.
664. LEVY, N. Law and the lady. Pictorial review, v. 37
     (March 1936), 16-17.
665. LEWIS, Edwin C. Developing woman's potential. Ames,
     Iowa State University Press, 1968. 389p.
666. LEWIS, Helen Matthews. The woman movement and the
     Negro movement, parallel struggles for equal rights.
     Charlottesville, University of Virginia, 1949. 89p.
667. LIBERATING magazines. Newsweek, v. 77 (8 February
     1971), 101-2.
668. LIBERATING the Journal. Newsweek, v. 76 (3 August 1970),
     44. Occupying the offices of the Ladies' Home Journal
     by militant feminists.
669. LIBERATING women. Time, v. 95 (15 June 1970), 93. Re-
     belling against the distorted view of women in advertise-
     ments.
670. LICHTENBERGER, James P. Divorce legislation. American
     Academy of Political and Social Science, annals, v. 160
     (March 1932), 116-23.
671. LICHTMAN, Ronnie. Getting together; the small group in
     women's liberation. Up from under, v. 1 (May/June
     1970), 23-4.
672. LIFTON, Robert Jay, ed. The woman in America. Boston,
     Houghton Mifflin, 1965. 293p. Psychological aspects
     of women's place in society and the fact that public
     opinion forces women with family responsibilities to
     refrain from professional work.
673. LILLEY, Celinda A. Centenary tract. The coming centen-
     nial, A.D. 1876. East Calais, Vt., The Author,
     1873. 16p.
674. LIMPUS, Laurel. Liberation of women; sexual repression
     and the family. Boston, New England Free Press,
     [1969?] 15p.
675. LINCOLN, A. Who will revere the black woman? Negro
     digest, v. 15 (September 1966), 16-20.
676. LITTLE, R. F. Shall women serve on juries in Illinois?

Illinois State Bar Association (1930), 278-84.
677. A LITTLE dearer than his horse: Legal stereotypes and the
feminine personality. Harvard civil rights-civil liberties law review, v. 6 (March 1971), 260-87.
678. LIVERMORE, Mary Ashton Rice. Advance of woman during
the last fifty years. Bostonian, v. 1 (1893), 81.
679. _____. What shall we do with our daughters? Superfluous
women and other lectures. Boston, Lee & Shepard,
1883. 208p.
680. _____. Women's views of divorce. North American review, v. 150 (January 1890), 110-35.
681. LOCKWOOD, Belva A. Present phase of woman. Cosmopolitan, v. 5 (1888), 467.
682. LOEB, Isidor. The legal property relations of married parties;
a study in comparative legislation. New York, Columbia
Univ. Press, 1900. 197p. Rep., AMS Press, N.Y., 1972.
683. LONGWELL, Marjorie. The American woman then and now.
Delta Kappa Gamma bulletin, v. 36 (Fall 1969), 28-32.
684. LOUISIANA. Governor's Commission on the Status of Women.
Report. Baton Rouge, 1967. 39p.
685. LUKENS, E. C. Shall women throw away their privileges?
American Bar Association, journal, v. 11 (October
1925), 645-6.
686. LUNDBERG, Ferdinand. Modern woman: the lost sex. New
York, Grosset and Dunlap, 1958. 497p.
687. LUTZ, Alma. Case for women jurors. Independent woman,
v. 15 (January 1936), 19-20+ .
688. _____. Crusade for freedom; women in the anti-slavery
movement. Boston, Beacon, 1968. Concerns the first
fifty years of the abolition movement and the drive for
women's voice in national affairs.
689. _____. The first woman's rights convention, Seneca Falls,
New York, July 19-20, 1848. More books, v. 23
(September 1948), 243-50.
690. LYELLS, Ruby E. Stutts. Woman-power for a better world;
civilizing influence in a man's world. Vital speeches,
v. 14 (15 January 1948), 217-20.
691. MS America; ending Miss and Mrs. as form of address.
Newsweek, v. 77 (26 April 1971), 61-2.
692. MABEE, Carleton. Women and Negroes march. Midwest
quarterly, v. 6, no. 2 (1966), 163-74. A comparison
of early women's rights movements between 1850 and
1920 and the Negro civil rights movement in the 1960's.
693. MCAFEE, Kathy and Myrna Wood. What is the revolutionary
potential of women's liberation? Boston, New England
Free Press [1969?]. 16p.
694. MCBEE, S. Report on the status of women. McCall's, v. 97
(September 1970), 128. A discussion of the Report of
the President's Task Force on Women's Rights and Responsibilities.
695. MCCASKILL, J. M. What about rights of married women?
Are they really wronged and oppressed? Florida law
journal, v. 11 (July 1937), 274-7.

696. MACCOBY, Eleanor. Is there any special way of thinking,
      feeling, or acting that is characteristically female...?
      Mademoiselle, v. 70 (February 1970), 180-1+.
697. MACCORRIE, J. P. Woman question. Catholic world, v.
      63 (1896), 605.
698. MCCRACKEN, Elizabeth. The women of America. New
      York, Macmillan, 1904. 397p. Partial contents: The
      pioneer woman of the West; Woman suffrage in Colo-
      rado; Social ideals of American women; The woman
      from the college.
699. MCCRIMMON, Abraham Lincoln. The woman movement.
      Philadelphia, Griffith and Rowland, 1915. 254p.
700. MCCULLOCH, Catharine Waugh. Chronology of woman's
      rights movement in Illinois. Chicago, Illinois Equal
      Suffrage Association [1903?]. 4p.
701. MCDOUGALD, E. J. Double task; the struggle of Negro
      women for sex and race emancipation. Survey, v. 53
      (1 March 1925), 688-91.
702. MCGALLIARD, H. W. A wife's personal property. Popular
      government (January 1937), 10.
703. MCKELWAY, A. J. Standards of legislation for women and
      children in the southern states. Conference on charities
      and corrections (1911), 186-90.
704. MCLEAN, H. H. Effect of the Nineteenth Amendment on
      qualifications of jurors. Illinois law review, v. 21
      (November 1926), 292-4.
705. MCMAHON, Theresa Schmid. Women and economic evolu-
      tion; or, The effects of industrial changes upon the
      status of women. 131p. PhD thesis, University of
      Wisconsin, 1909.
706. MCSWEENY, E. Advancement of women. Catholic world,
      v. 49 (1889), 326.
707. MCWILLIAMS, Nancy R. Feminism and femininity; an as-
      sertion of positive difference. Commonweal, v. 92
      (15 May 1970), 219-21. A criticism of feminists who
      want to do away with distinctions between men and wom-
      en.
708. MAILER, Norman. The prisoner of sex. Boston, Little,
      Brown, 1971. 240p.
709. MAINARDI, Pat. The politics of housework. Boston, New
      England Free Press [1968?]. 3p.
710. MAINE. Governor's Advisory Council on the Status of Wom-
      en. Maine women, 1971. Report to His Excellency
      Kenneth M. Curtis, Governor of the State of Maine.
      [Augusta?], 1971. 24p.
711. MALE and female; war between the sexes in the media.
      Newsweek, v. 75 (18 May 1970), 74. Sex discrimina-
      tion charges against the Washington, D.C., newspapers
      and against Time, Inc.
712. MANDATE of Title VII of the Civil Rights Act of 1964: to
      treat women as individuals. Georgia law review, v.
      59 (October 1970), 221+.
713. MANN, Horace. A few thoughts on the powers and duties of

woman. Syracuse, N.Y., Hall, Mills, 1853. 141p.
714. MANNING, Agnes M. Because it was woman's. A paper
read before the Woman's Press Association, March,
1891. San Francisco, P. J. Thomas, Printer, 1891.
24p.
715. MARDEN, Orison Swett. Woman and home. New York,
Crowell, 1915. 350p.
716. MARLOW, Holt Carleton. The ideology of the woman's
movement, 1750-1860. 374p. PhD thesis, University
of Oklahoma, 1966.
717. The MARRIED women's property acts. John Marshall law
journal, v. 80 (21-28 December 1935), 414+.
718. MARSH, Harold. Marital property in conflict of laws.
Seattle, University of Washington Press, 1952. 263p.
719. MARSHALL, J. E. Divorce law reform. Quarterly review,
v. 251 (October 1928), 256-69.
720. MARTIN, Anne. Feminists and future political action. Nation, v. 120 (18 February 1925), 185-6. On the lack
of an organized feminist movement.
721. _____. Political methods of American and British feminists. Current history magazine of the New York
Times, v. 20 (June 1924), 396-401.
722. _____. Woman's inferiority complex. New republic,
v. 27 (20 July 1921), 210-12. The need for more
women to demand their rights.
723. MARTIN, Edward Sandford. The unrest of women. New
York, Appleton, 1915. 146p.
724. MARTIN, George Madden. American women and paternalism.
Atlantic monthly, v. 133 (June 1924), 744-53.
725. MARTIN, John. Feminism, its fallacies and follies. New
York, Dodd, Mead, 1916. 359p.
726. MARTIN, Kate Byam. The social status of European and
American women. Chicago, C. H. Kerr, 1887. 47p.
727. MATTHEWS, B. S. Legal discriminations against women
existing in the United States today. Congressional digest, v. 3 (March 1924), 16-17.
728. _____. Women should have equal rights with men: a
reply. American Bar Association, journal, v. 12
(February 1926), 117-20.
729. MAY, Samuel Joseph. The rights and condition of women:
a sermon, preached in Syracuse, November, 1845.
Syracuse, N.Y., Lathrop's print., [1853?] 16p. A
rebuttal to reasons why women should not have equal
rights with men. [Woman's Rights Tracts, no. 1.]
730. MAYNARD, Douglas H. The world's anti-slavery convention
of 1840. Mississippi Valley historical review, v. 47
(December 1960), 452-71.
731. MAYO, Amory Dwight. Woman's movement in the South.
New England magazine, v. 5 (October 1891), 249-60.
732. MEAD, Margaret, ed. American women, the report of the
President's Commission on the Status of Women, and
other publications of the Commission. New York,
Scribner, 1965. 274p. Contains the final report of

the Commission, including the final reports of each of
the seven committees.

733. _____. De we undervalue full-time wives? Appraisal of
report by the President's Commission on the Status of
Women. Redbook, v. 122 (November 1963), 22+.

734. _____. What shall we tell our children? Redbook, v. 135
(June 1970), 35+. The fact that most women still live
in the traditional pattern, i.e., men's and women's
separate roles, despite greater numbers of militant
feminists.

735. _____. What women want: a candid appraisal of U.S.
women today. Fortune, v. 34 (December 1946), 172-
5+. Women's discontent in the home.

736. _____. Women: a time for change. Redbook, v. 134
(March 1970), 60+.

737. _____. Women's social position. Journal of educational
Sociology, v. 17 (April 1944), 453-62.

738. MEARKLE, Annie L. Woman not man's equal. Midland
monthly, v. 9 (1898), 173.

739. MEHLINGER, K. Sexual revolution. Ebony, v. 21 (August
1966), 57-60+.

740. MEHRHOF, Barbara. Class structure in the women's movement. New York, The Feminists, 1969. 5p.

741. _____ and Sheila Cronan. The rise of man; the origins
of woman's oppression: One view. New York, The
Feminists, 1969. 6p.

742. MEIKLE, Wilma. Towards a sane feminism. New York,
McBride, 1917. 168p.

743. MELDER, Keith Eugene. The beginnings of the women's
rights movement in the United States, 1800-1840. 500p.
PhD thesis, Yale University, 1964.

744. MEN and women: equality or equity? America, v. 123 (19
September 1970), 167-8. Women's liberation people
should demand equity, not equality. Also, disadvantages
of the Equal Rights Amendment as expressed by the National Council of Catholic Women.

745. MEN, women: Declaration on the elimination of discrimination against women. UNESCO courier, v. 21 (November 1968), 30-1.

746. MENCKEN, Henry Louis. In defense of women. New York,
Knopf, 1926. 210p.

747. MERCKX, Fernand J. The bolshevism of sex; femininity and
feminism. New York, Higher Thought Publishing Co.,
1921. 207p.

748. MERRIAM, Eve. After Nora slammed the door; American
women in the 1960's: The unfinished revolution.
Cleveland, World, 1964. 236p.

749. MERRILL, D. P. Women on the march; growth of women's
organizations in the past three-quarters of a century.
Independent woman, v. 19 (October 1940), 330-2.

750. MERSAND, Joseph E. The inferiority of women, and other
fairy tales. New York, n.p., 1937. 20p.

751. MEYER, Annie N., ed. Woman's work in America. New

York, Holt, 1891. 457p.
752. MICHAELS, Sheila. The archetypal woman. New York, The
Feminists, 1970. 4p.
753. MICHIGAN. Governor's Commission on the Status of Women.
Report. Lansing, 1965. 47p.
754. MICOSSI, Anita L. Conversion to women's lib. Trans-action,
v. 8 (November 1970), 82-90.
755. MILLER, Alice Duer. Who is Silvia? An aspect of feminism.
Scribner's magazine, v. 56 (July 1914), 53-60. Wom-
en's status in the home, in education, and politics, as
well as men's fear of women as one factor in feminine
equality.
756. MILLER, D. I lack the courage of my convictions though
deep within me beats a Lucy Stone heart. Century illustrated monthly magazine, v. 115 (January 1928),
326-8.
757. MILLER, E. G. Equal rights: a debate. New York Times
magazine (7 May 1944), 14+.
758. MILLER, Leo. Woman and the divine republic. Buffalo,
Haas & Nauert, 1874. 213p.
759. MILLER, N. DuBois. Legal status of married women in
Pennsylvania. Philadelphia, American Academy of Political and Social Science, 1876.
760. MILLER, Robert Stevens. Sex discrimination and Title VII
of the Civil Rights Act of 1964. Minnesota law review,
v. 51 (April 1967), 877-97.
761. MILLER, Ruthann. In defense of the women's movement.
New York, Merit, 1970. 15p.
762. MILLETT, Kate. Sexual politics. Garden City, N.Y.,
Doubleday, 1970. 393p.
763. MINOR, F. Political status of woman. Forum, v. 9 (1890),
150.
764. MISSISSIPPI. Governor's Commission on the Status of Wom-
en. Status of women in Mississippi. Jackson, 1970.
31p.
765. MISTER, J. F. Law of married women. American law review, v. 20 (1886), 359.
766. MITCHELL, Bonnie. League of Women Voters marks 50
years. Wisconsin then and now, v. 16, no. 2 (1969),
1-3. A short historical sketch of the League, founded
by two Wisconsin women, Carrie Chapman Catt and
Jessie Jack Hooper.
767. MITCHELL, Juliet. Women; the longest revolution. Boston,
New England Free Press [1967?]. 29p. Reprinted
from the New Left Review, (November/December 1966),
11-37. Pertains to women's situation as related to
needed changes in production, reproduction, socializa-
tion, and sexuality.
768. MODIFY divorce rules. Outlook, v. 149 (13 June 1928), 246-
7.
769. MONCURE, D. A. Women are not 'persons' and have no
civil rights other than the right to vote. Women lawyers journal, v. 44 (Winter 1958), 15.

770. MONTAGU, Ashley. Are women as creative as men? Satur-
      day review, v. 36 (30 May 1953), 18-19+. Discussion:
      v. 36 (27 June 1953), 25.
771. _____. The natural superiority of women. Rev. ed. New
      York, Macmillan, 1968. 235p.
772. _____. The triumph and tragedy of the American woman.
      Saturday review, v. 41 (27 September 1958), 13-15+.
      The problem of women, in their attempts at equality,
      striving to be like men.
773. _____. Women are not second-rate men. Ladies' home
      journal, v. 73 (December 1956), 108.
774. MONTANA. Montana Governor's Commission on the Status
      of Women. Annual report of the Montana Governor's
      Commission on the Status of Women. [Helena?], 1970.
      6p.
775. MOODY, Helen Watterson. The unquiet sex. New York, C.
      Scribner, 1898. 159p.
776. _____. The unquiet sex: women's clubs. Scribner's
      magazine, v. 22 (October 1897), 486-91. Activities
      of women's clubs with mention of the General Federa-
      tion of Women's Clubs.
777. MOORE, Dorothea. Work of women in California. American
      Academy of Political and Social Science, annals, v. 28
      (1906), 257.
778. MORGAN, Robin. Goodbye to all that. Pittsburgh, Know,
      Inc., [1970?]. 7p.
779. _____. Sisterhood is powerful; an anthology of writings
      from the women's liberation movement. New York,
      Random House, 1970. 602p.
780. MORRIS, N. Limitations of sex. North American review,
      v. 132 (1881), 79.
781. MOTT, Lucretia. Slavery and "the woman question":
      Lucretia Mott's diary of her visit to Great Britain to
      attend the World's Anti-Slavery Convention of 1840.
      Edited by Frederick B. Tolles. Haverford, Pa.,
      Friends' Historical Association, 1952. 86p.
782. MOYER, M. H. Property of married women in Florida.
      Florida State Bar Association law journal, v. 4
      (August 1930), 154-67.
783. MUIR, Edwin. Women--free for what? Nation, v. 119 (6
      August 1924), 140-2. The unhappiness of women de-
      spite their greater freedom.
784. MURPHY, B. How the church understands rights of women.
      Catholic world, v. 15 (1872), 78.
785. MURRAY, Pauli. Jane Crow and the law: sex discrimina-
      tion and Title VII. George Washington law review,
      v. 34 (December 1965), 232-56.
786. _____. Women's liberation--pattern for the 70's? Church
      woman (January 1970), 11-14.
787. MURRELL, Ethel Ernest. Equality--the leading question.
      Women lawyers journal, v. 31 (Winter 1945), 9.
788. _____. Florida's new Married Women's Act; a discussion
      of its constitutionality. Florida law journal, v. 17

(November 1943), 266-9.
789. MUZZEY, A. L.   Hour and the woman.   Arena, v. 22
      (August 1899), 263-72.
790. MYTH of the movement.   Wildflowers, v. 1 (November 1970),
      4-5+.   On the myth of what a woman should be and
      what she actually is.
791. NATIONAL Conference of Governor's Commissions on the
      Status of Women.   Progress and prospects; the report
      of the Second National Conference of Governors' Com-
      missions on the Status of Women.   Cosponsored by the
      Interdepartmental Committee on the Status of Women
      and the Citizens' Advisory Council on the Status of Wom-
      en, Washington, D.C., July 28-30, 1965.   Washington,
      GPO, 1966.   80p.
792. NATIONAL Council of Women of the United States.   History
      and minutes of the National Council of Women of the
      United States, organized in Washington, D.C., March
      31, 1888.   Edited by Louise Barnum Robbins.   Boston,
      E. B. Stillings, 1898.   343p.
793. NATIONAL Woman's Party.   How Virginia law discriminates
      against women.   n.d.   12p.
794. _____.   Legal position of women in Virginia.   n.d.   44p.
795. _____.   The present campaign for equality of rights for
      women.   Washington, 1945.   24p.
796. _____.   [The National Woman's Party], what it is, what it
      has done, and what it is doing.   Washington, 1922.   8p.
797. [NATIONAL] Woman's Rights Conventions.   Proceedings of the
      Woman's Rights Conventions held at Seneca Falls and
      Rochester, N.Y., July and August, 1848.   New York,
      R. J. Johnston, 1870.   2v in 1.   44p.   Reprinted by
      Arno Press, New York, 1969.
798. NATIONAL Woman's Rights Convention.   Proceedings of the
      Woman's Rights Convention, held at Worcester, October
      23 and 24, 1850.   Boston, Prentiss & Sawyer, 1851.
      84p.
799. NATIONAL Woman's Rights Convention, Second, Worcester,
      October 15 & 16, 1851.   Proceedings.   New York,
      Fowler & Wells, 1852.   112p.
800. [NATIONAL] Woman's Rights Convention, Syracuse, N.Y.,
      September 8, 9, and 10, 1852.   Proceedings.   Syra-
      cuse, N.Y., J. E. Masters, 1852.   98p.
801. NATIONAL Women's Rights Convention.   Proceedings of the
      National Women's Rights Convention, held at Cleveland,
      Ohio, on Wednesday, Thursday, and Friday, October 5,
      6, and 7, 1853.   Cleveland, Gray, Beardsley, Spear,
      1854.   188p.
802. NATIONAL Woman's Rights Convention held in New York City,
      at the Broadway Tabernacle, on Tuesday and Wednesday,
      November 25 and 26, 1856.   Proceedings.   New York,
      Edward O. Jenkins, printer, 1856.
803. NATIONAL Woman's Rights Convention.   Proceedings of the
      National Woman's Rights Convention, held in New York
      City, Thursday, May 12, 1859, with a phonographic re-

port of the speech of Wendell Phillips. Rochester,
N.Y., Steam Press of A. Strong, 1859. 20p.
804. NATIONAL Woman's Rights Convention held at the Cooper
Institute, New York City, May 10 and 11, 1860. Proceedings. Boston, Printed by Yerrinton & Garrison,
1860.
805. NATIONAL Women's Trade Union League of America. Equal
rights, yes, but how? Chicago, The League, [1920?].
806. NEBRASKA. Governor's Commission on the Status of Women.
April 1971 report of the Governor's Commission on the
Status of Women. [Lincoln?], 1971.
807. _____. _____. Women power; women in service.
Second state women's conference. [Lincoln, 1969?]
44p.
808. NECARSULMER, E. U. The market-place or the home?
Standard, v. 15 (May 1929), 269-73.
809. NEED of legislative protection for women. Social economist,
v. 7 (1894), 88.
810. NEFF, Lawrence W. The legal status of women in Texas.
Dallas, n.p., 1905. 98p.
811. NEGRIN, Su. A graphic notebook on feminism. New York,
Times Change Press, 1970. 64p. Photographs and
drawings of well-known feminists, posters and exploitation of women.
812. The NEGRO woman in retrospect: blueprint for the future.
Negro history bulletin, v. 29 (December 1965), 55-6+.
813. The NEGRO woman; special issue of Ebony. Ebony, v. 21
(August 1966), 25+.
814. NEIDER, Charles, ed. Man against woman; a vade mecum
for the weaker sex and a caution to women. New
York, Harper, 1957. 210p.
815. NEILL, E. W. Do women want equal rights? Poise, v. 5
(May 1943), 42.
816. NELSON, J. F. So it's a man's world? Woman's press,
v. 34 (July 1940), 317-19+.
817. NEVADA. Governor's Commission on the Status of Women.
Biennial report. 1st--1964/66--[Carson City?].
818. _____. _____. Training women to meet the challenge
of today's new dimensions. Proceedings. Carson City,
1970. 90p.
819. NEVADA League of Women Voters. Annual bulletin of the
Nevada League of Women Voters, containing review of
Nevada laws concerning women and children. Compiled
by Mrs. Sadie D. Hurst. Reno, The League, 1923.
38p.
820. NEVIN, J. W. Rights of women. American Whig review,
v. 8 (1851), 367.
821. NEW feminism. Ladies' home journal, v. 87 (August 1970),
64-71. Discussion: v. 87 (November 1970), 69+.
822. NEW Jersey. Governor's Commission on the Status of Wom-
en. New Jersey women. [Trenton, 1967?] 19p.
823. NEW measures to advance women's status proposed. United
Nations bulletin, v. 4 (1 February 1948), 97-8.

824. NEW Pennsylvania laws for women and children. Survey, v. 22 (15 May 1909), 243-4.
825. NEW state laws affecting women's work. Survey, v. 30 (3 May 1913), 161-2.
826. The NEW woman. Current history, v. 27 (October 1927), 1-48.
827. NEW York (State). Library Legislative Reference Section. Married women's rights in New York State. Albany, 1923. 4p.
828. _____. _____. The status of women under the equal rights law in Wisconsin. By Zona Gale. Albany, 1925. 38p.
829. NICHOL, Charles Ready. God's woman; the place of women in the social and religious life as revealed in the Bible. Clifton, Texas, Mrs. C. R. Nichol, 1938. 183p.
830. NICHOLS, Mrs. C. I. H. The responsibilities of woman. A speech by Mrs. C. I. H. Nichols, at the woman's rights convention, Worcester, October 15, 1851. [Rochester, N.Y., Steam press of Curtis Butts, 185-?] 18p. [Woman's rights tracts, no. 5.]
831. NICHOLS, J. P. Nurture of feminism in the United States. Harvard educational review, v. 11 (May 1941), 347-58.
832. NICHOLS, W. H. and I. Vern. Three million woman power. Collier's, v. 121 (14 February 1948), 12-13+. Concerning the General Federation of Women's Clubs.
833. NIZER, L. Verdict on women as jurors. New York Times magazine (11 March 1962), 20+.
834. NOBLE, Lulu Gray. Agitation by a looker-on. Nation, v. 10 (20 January 1870), 38-9.
835. _____. An explanation from the "looker-on." Nation, v. 10 (10 March 1870), 155-6. Comments on the movement.
836. NORTH, Sandie. Reporting the movement. Atlantic monthly, v. 225 (March 1970), 105-6. The movement as being opposed to the mass media.
837. NORTH Carolina. Commission on the Education and Employment of Women. Report to the Governor and the General Assembly of North Carolina. Raleigh, 1967. 18p.
838. _____. Governor's Commission on the Status of Women. The many lives of North Carolina women; report. [Raleigh?], 1964. 95p.
839. _____. University Extension Division. Special legal relations of married women in North Carolina as to property, contracts, and guardianship. By M. P. Smith. Chapel Hill, University of North Carolina Press, 1928. 76p.
840. NORTH Dakota. Governor's Commission on the Status of Women. New horizons for North Dakota women. Report of the Governor's Commission on the Status of Women. Bismark, 1964. 27p. The last report since 1964.
841. NOTES from the first year. New York, New York Radical Women, 1968.

842. NOTES from the second year: Women's liberation; major
      writings of the radical feminists. New York, Notes,
      1970. 126p. A number of articles (as in no. 841)
      concerning the radical feminist movement; abortion,
      housework, feminist theater, class structure, love, etc.
843. NOTES on women's liberation; we speak in many voices.
      Detroit, News & Letters, 1970. 86p. Thirty articles
      on a number of feminist topics.
844. NOVACK, George. Revolutionary dynamics of women's libera-
      tion. New York, Merit, 1969. 22p.
845. NUGENT, Elinor Roth. The relationship of fashion in wom-
      en's dress to selected aspects of social change from
      1850 to 1950. 249p. PhD thesis, Louisiana State
      University, 1962. Shows that women's fashions changed
      according to the degree of their freedom and status.
846. O'BRIEN, Charles. The growth in Pennsylvania of the prop-
      erty rights of married women. American law register,
      v. 49 (1901), 524-30.
847. O'CONNOR, Lynn. Male supremacy. San Francisco, Wom-
      en's Page [1970?]. 8p.
848. O'CROWLEY, I. R. Laws affecting women. Practical home
      economics, v. 19 (January 1941), 5-7.
849. OHIO Women's Convention, Salem, 1850. Proceedings of the
      Ohio Women's Convention, held at Salem, April 19 and
      20, 1850.... Cleveland, Smead & Cowles' Press,
      1850. 48p. Includes text of letters from Elizabeth
      Cady Stanton, Lucy Stone, Lucretia Mott, and others.
850. OLDHAM, James C. Sex discrimination and state protective
      laws. Denver law review, v. 44 (Summer 1967), 344.
851. OLNEY, Warren. Some phases of the woman question. Oak-
      land, Cal., Enquirer Publishing Co., 1896. 13p.
852. ON the liberation of women: a special double issue. Motive,
      v. 29 (March/April 1969), 4-89.
853. ONATIVIA, Elizabeth. Give us our privileges. Scribner's
      magazine, v. 87 (June 1930), 593-8.
854. ONEAL, Marion Sherrard. New Orleans scenes. Louisiana
      history, v. 6, no. 2 (1965), 189-209. Reminiscences
      of a women's rights meeting in 1903 including comments
      of Carrie Chapman Catt, Charlotte Perkins Gilman, and
      Anna Howard Shaw.
855. O'NEILL, William L. Everyone was brave--the rise and fall
      of feminism in America. Chicago, Quadrangle, 1969.
      369p.
856. _____. The woman movement; feminism in the United
      States and England. New York, Barnes & Noble, 1969.
      208p.
857. OREGON. Governor's Committee on the Status of Women in
      Oregon. Expanding women's effectiveness in the com-
      munity. A report of the Conference on the Role of the
      State Commissions on the Status of Women in Ten
      Western States, January 26-28, 1968, Portland, Ore-
      gon. Salem, 1968. 31p.
858. _____. _____. The world of women in Oregon; the

second major report. Salem, 1968. 73p.
859. _____ . _____ . Year-end report. Salem, 1965. 28p.
860. ORGANIZATIONAL principles and structure. New York, The
Feminists [1970?]. 10p. Structure of The Feminists,
a New York group.
861. OSSOLI, Sarah Margaret Fuller. Woman in the nineteenth
century and kindred papers related to the sphere, condition and duties of women. Boston, Jewett, 1855.
420p. Reprinted by Greenwood Press, Westport, Conn.,
1968, and by Library Reprints, Ltd., N.Y., 1972.
862. OUR chaotic divorce laws. Unpopular review, v. 3 (January
1915), 61-75.
863. PAINTER, E. G. Women: the last of the discriminated.
National Association of Women Deans and Counselors,
journal, v. 34 (Winter 1971), 59-62.
864. PALFREY, John G. The eligibility of women for public office under the constitution of Massachusetts. Massachusetts law quarterly, v. 11 (February 1922), 147-63.
865. PALMER, Gretta. The feminist surrenders. Today, (5 December 1936), 16-17+.
866. PALMER, Paul E. Christian breakthrough in women's lib.
America, v. 124 (19 June 1971), 634-7.
867. PARKER, Theodore. A sermon of the public function of
woman, preached at the Music-hall, Boston, March
27, 1853. [Rochester, N.Y., Steam press of Curtis,
Butts, 185?.] 24p. [Woman's rights tracts, no. 2.]
868. PARKHURST, Genevieve. Great necessity; national uniform
marriage and divorce laws. Pictorial review, v. 31
(February 1930), 1.
869. _____ . Is feminism dead? Harper's magazine, v. 170
(May 1935), 735-45. Problems in the organization of
women, apathy, lack of great leaders, and their in-
ability to stand together. Covers the period from 1920
to 1935.
870. PARKMAN, Francis. Woman question. North American review, v. 129 (1879), 303-21.
871. PARSONS, Alice B. Woman's dilemma. New York, T.
Crowell, 1926. 311p. On whether men and women
should have different social functions and whether the
home will be in danger if the wife works outside the
home.
872. PARSONS, E. C. Feminism and the family. International
journal of ethics, v. 28 (October 1917), 52-8.
873. PARSONS, F. Shall our mothers, wives, and sisters be our
equals or our subjects? Arena, v. 40 (July 1908),
92-4.
874. PATRICK, C. Relation between government and the status
of women. Journal of social Psychology, v. 23 (May
1946), 163-74.
875. PAUL, Alice. Outline of the legal position of women in
Pennsylvania. Philadelphia, Pennsylvania State Wom-
en's Suffrage Association, 1911. 42p.
876. PECK, Ellen. The baby trap. New York, Geis, 1971. 245p.

877. PEDERSEN, Inger Margrete. Status of women in private law.
      American Academy of Political and Social Science, an-
      nals, v. 375 (January 1968), 44-51. Marriage law,
      property rights, and family support.
878. PEDERSEN, Victor Cox. The woman a man marries; an
      analysis of her double standard. New York, G. H.
      Doran, 1927. 276p.
879. PEEBLES, Isaac Lockhart. Are men and women equal? The
      question answered. Nashville, Tenn., M. E. Church,
      South, 1918. 23p. Contents: The make of each class;
      The Scriptures teach that men and women are not equal.
880. PENNSYLVANIA. Governor's Commission on the Status of
      Women. Pennsylvania women; law and politics, educa-
      tion, employment, volunteering. Report of the Gover-
      nor's Commission on the Status of Women. Harrisburg,
      1965. 46p.
881. PETERSON, Esther. The status of women in the United
      States; brief account of the findings of the President's
      Commission on the Status of Women. International la-
      bour review, v. 89 (May 1964), 447-60.
882. PETERSON, Frederick. Normal women not neurotic. New
      York, National American Woman Suffrage Association,
      1914. 7p. Criticism of the low status given to women
      on the basis of strictly biological comparisons.
883. PHILLIPS, F. L. Changed status of women. Education,
      v. 87 (December 1966), 246-7.
884. PHILLIPS, R. LeClerc. The real rights of women. Har-
      per's magazine, v. 153 (October 1926), 609-14.
885. PIDGEON, Mary Elizabeth. The laws of Virginia as they af-
      fect women and children. Charlottesville, Va., The
      University, 1926. 29p.
886. PIEPHO, I. Proposed study of status of women. Catholic
      action, v. 29 (March 1947), 12-13.
887. PIER, Florida. The masculine and the feminine mind. Har-
      per's weekly, v. 54 (24 September 1910), 21.
888. PIERCY, Marge. The Grand Coolie Damn. Boston, New
      England Free Press, 1969. 14p. Concerns some of
      the problems of the women's movement and criticism
      of men.
889. PIERSON, W. W. Property rights of married women in
      Pennsylvania. University of Pennsylvania bulletin,
      series 17, no. 1 (1916), 339-58.
890. PIMENOFF, Lydia L. Science and the woman's question.
      North American review, v. 156 (February 1893), 248-
      51.
891. PINCHOT, G. M. Surprises in an investigation of birth con-
      trol. Survey, v. 53 (15 March 1925), 751-3. Reply
      by Margaret Sanger: v. 54 (15 April 1925), 116.
892. PITKIN, Walter B. Can intellectual women live happily?
      North American review, v. 227 (June 1929), 699-705.
893. PLACE of woman. American, v. 6 (1883), 6.
894. PLATT, Horace Garvin. The law as to the property rights
      of married women, as contained in the statutes and

decisions of California, Texas and Nevada. San Francisco, Sumner Whitney, 1885. 366p.
895. POGREBIN, Letty Cottin. It's still a man's world; with reports by seven women who speak out. Good housekeeping, v. 171 (November 1970), 73-5.
896. POLITICAL position of women. American literary magazine, v. 2 (1848), 246.
897. POLITICAL rights of women; 56 years of progress. New York, Columbia University Press, 1949.
898. POLITICAL rights of women; resolution unanimously approved by General Assembly of the United Nations. UN bulletin, v. 1 (25 November 1946), 22-3.
899. POOR black woman. Boston, New England Free Press [1968?] 4p.
900. POPENOE, Paul. Can the family have two heads? Sociology and social research, v. 18 (September 1933), 12-17.
901. PORTER, John William. Feminism. Louisville, Ky., Baptist Book Concern, 1923. 165p.
902. POSITION of woman and the home. Popular science monthly, v. 23 (1883), 412.
903. PRATT, A. New feminist criticism; with reply by L. S. Robinson. College English, v. 32 (May 1971), 872-89.
904. PRESIDENT'S Commission on the Status of Women. American women: their status and education. Practical forecast for home economics, v. 9 (November 1963), 26-7+.
905. PRESSMAN, Sonia. Quiet revolution. Family law quarterly, v. 4 (March 1970), 31.
906. PRIESTLY, John Boynton. Speaking out; women don't run the country. Saturday evening post, v. 237 (12 December 1967), 8+. Concerning the need for women to take a greater part in American society.
907. PRINGLE, H. F. What do the women of America think about the double standard? Ladies' home journal, v. 55 (November 1938), 22-3+.
908. PROFFATT, John. Woman before the law. New York, Putnam, 1874. 137p. The status of married women.
909. PROPERTY of married women. Godey's lady's book, v. 45 (1852), 542.
910. QUESTION of a uniform marriage and divorce law; history, statistics, synopsis of laws; pro and con discussion. Congressional digest, v. 6 (June 1927), 183-208.
911. A QUESTION of woman's status. Confrontation (April 1971), 1-20.
912. RAINEY, Luretta. History of Oklahoma State Federation of Women's Clubs. Guthrie, Oklahoma, Co-operative Publishing Co., 1939. 341p.
913. RAPACZ, M. P. Progress of the property law relating to married women. University of Kansas City law review, v. 11 (June 1943), 173-86.
914. RAPPAPORT, Philip. Looking forward; a treatise on the status of woman and the origin and growth of the family and the state. Chicago, C. H. Kerr, 1913. 234p.
915. RAUSCHENBUSCH, W. Moral aspects of the woman move-

ment. Bible World, v. 42 (October 1913), 195-99.
916. REAL nature of woman's inferiority to man. Current literature, v. 42 (April 1907), 445-7.
917. REED, Evelyn. The myth of women's inferiority. Boston,
New England Free Press [1969?] 9p. Concerns
"certain false claims regarding the social superiority
of the male sex" in the home, industry, etc.
918. _____. Problems of women's liberation; a Marxist approach. New York, Merit, 1969. 63p.
919. REEVES, Nancy. Womankind; beyond the stereotypes. Chicago, Aldine-Atherton, 1971. 434p.
920. REMBAUGH, Bertha. The political status of women in the
United States: a digest of the laws concerning women
in the various states and territories. New York, G.
P. Putnam, 1911. 164p.
921. REPORT of the President's Commission on the Status of
Women. Monthly labor review, v. 86 (October 1963),
1166-9. Excerpts from the Report.
922. RESOLUTIONS on status of women. School and society, v.
70 (24 December 1949), 427.
923. REVOLUTION II: thinking female. College and university
business, v. 48 (February 1970), 51-86. Seven articles on the role and status of women.
924. RHODE Island. Commission on the Status of Women. Women
in Rhode Island; their state and their status. A report
to the governor on the status of women in Rhode Island
with recommendations for a program of constructive
action. Providence, Oxford Press [1965?] 68p.
925. RICE, C. D. Are women the weaker sex? Family digest,
v. 9 (July 1954), 53.
926. RICHARDSON, Eudora Ramsay. A woman leader challenges
discriminations. New York, National Federation of
Business and Professional Women's Clubs, Inc., 1935.
24p.
927. RIDLEY, Jeanne Clare. Demographic change and the roles
and status of women. American Academy of Political
and Social Science, annals, v. 375 (January 1968), 15-
25.
928. RIEGEL, Robert E. American women; a story of social
change. Rutherford, N.J., Fairleigh Dickinson University Press, 1970. 376p.
929. _____. Split of the feminist movement in 1869. Mississippi valley historical review, v. 49 (December 1962),
485-96. The split of the American Equal Rights Association into the National Woman Suffrage Association
and the American Woman Suffrage Association.
930. _____. Woman's rights and other 'reforms' in Seneca
Falls. A contemporary view. New York history, v.
46 (January 1965), 41-59. Pages 42-57 consist of an
article by Mary S. Bull on the events from 1840 to
and including the first day of the Seneca Falls Convention, 19 July 1848.
931. _____. Women's clothes and women's rights. American

quarterly, v. 15 (Fall 1963), 390-401. The effects on clothing styles of the rights movement between 1848 and 1927.

932. RIGHTS and responsibilities. Ladies' home journal, v. 65 (July 1948), 11.
933. RIGHTS of women. Democratic review, v. 30 (1852), 180.
934. RIGHTS of women. Democratic review, v. 34 (1854), 434.
935. RIGHTS of women. Democratic review, v. 43 (1859), 175.
936. RIGHTS of women. National quarterly review, v. 20 (1870), 79.
937. RIGHTS of women as affected by Catholicism and Protestantism. Catholic world, v. 14 (1872), 467.
938. RIGHTS of women in Massachusetts. Historical magazine [Dawson's], v. 12 (1867), 121.
939. RIGHTS of women--progress and problems. United Nations review, v. 2 (June 1956), 18-21. Report on the 10th session of the United Nations Commission on the Status of Women.
940. ROBINS, Joan. Handbook of women's liberation. North Hollywood, Cal., National Organization for Women Library Press, 1970. 279p.
941. ROBINSON, M. V. A balance sheet for feminism. Woman's press, v. 29 (November 1935), 490-1+.
942. ROLLIN, B. What's women's lib doing to the family? Plenty! Look, v. 35 (26 January 1971), 40.
943. ROOSEVELT, Eleanor. It's up to the women. New York, F. Stokes, 1933. 263p.
944. ROOSEVELT, Theodore. Women's rights; and the duties of both men and women. Outlook, v. 100 (3 February 1912), 262-6. A belief in equality between men and women, but with a "complete dissimilarity of function between them."
945. ROOT, Melvin A. Legal conditions of girls and women [in Michigan]. Lansing, Mich., Reprogle, 1894.
946. ROSE, Ernestine Louise. Speech of Mrs. E. L. Rose, at the Women's Rights Convention, held at Syracuse, September, 1852. Syracuse, N.Y., Masters' print., 1852. 8p. [Woman's rights tracts, no. 9.] The rights of women in general. Also includes the Declaration of Sentiments of the Seneca Falls convention of 1848.
947. _____. An address on women's rights, delivered before the people's Sunday meeting, in Cochituate Hall, on Sunday afternoon, October 19, 1851. Boston, J. P. Mendum, 1851. 21p.
948. ROSSI, Alice S. Equality between the sexes: An immodest proposal. Daedalus, v. 93 (Spring 1964), 607-52. The reasons for the decline of the early feminist movement, reasons for achieving equality, and the means by which equality can be reached.
949. _____. Position paper--models of sex equality. New York Academy of Sciences, annals, v. 175 (30 October 1970), 950-2.

950. _____. The roots of ambivalence in American women.
     Chicago, University of Chicago, National Opinion Re-
     search Center, Committee on Human Development,
     1969. 34p.
951. _____. Sex equality: the beginning of ideology. Humanist,
     v. 29 (September/October 1969), 3-6.
952. ROSTOW, Edna G. Best of both worlds: Feminism and
     femininity. Yale review, v. 51 (March 1962), 384-99.
953. ROSZAK, Betty and Theodore Roszak, eds. Masculine/femi-
     nine: readings in sexual mythology and the liberation
     of women. New York, Harper & Row, 1969. 316p.
954. ROYDEN, Agnes Maude. What is marriage? Atlantic month-
     ly, v. 132 (September 1923), 297-307.
955. RUTLEDGE, W. Women's rights. Vital speeches, v. 14 (1
     June 1948), 508-11.
956. SADE, Janine. History of the equality issue in the contem-
     porary women's movement. New York, The Feminists,
     1969. 3p. Concerning the National Organization for
     Women.
957. SAGE, Mrs. Russell. Opportunities and responsibilities of
     leisured women. North American review, v. 181
     (1905), 712-21.
958. SALPER, Roberta. Female liberation: history and current
     politics. New York, Random House, 1971.
959. SALTER, William M. What is the real emancipation of woman?
     Atlantic monthly, v. 89 (January 1902), 28-35.
960. SAMUELS, G. Verdict on women jurors. New York Times
     magazine (7 May 1950), 22+.
961. SANGER, Margaret. Birth control raid on the birth control
     clinical research bureau in New York City. New re-
     public, v. 58 (1 May 1929), 305-6.
962. _____. The case for birth control. New York, Modern
     Art Printing Co., 1917. 251p.
963. _____. Case for birth control. Woman citizen, v. 8 (23
     February 1924), 17.
964. _____. Every child a wanted child. Time, v. 88 (16
     September 1966), 96+.
965. _____. Family limitation. Revised. 6th ed. [New
     York?], 1917. 16p.
966. _____. Is race suicide probable? Collier's, v. 76 (15
     August 1925), 25.
967. _____. Motherhood in bondage. New York, Brentano's, 1928.
     446p. Rep., Maxwell Reprint, Elmsford, N.Y., 1972.
968. _____. My fight for America's first birth control clinic.
     Reader's digest, v. 76 (February 1960), 49-54.
969. _____. My fight for birth control. New York, Farrar & Rine-
     hart, 1931. 360p. Rep., Maxwell Reprint, Elmsford,
     N.Y., 1972.
970. _____. National security and birth control. Forum, v. 93
     (March 1935), 139-41.
971. _____. The new motherhood. London, J. Cape, 1922. 243p.
     Rep., Maxwell Reprint, Elmsford, N.Y., 1972.
972. _____. The pivot of civilization. New York, Brentano's, 1922.

284p. Rep., Maxwell Reprint, Elmsford, N.Y., 1972.

973. _____. Should legal barriers against birth control be re-
moved? Congressional digest, v. 10 (April 1931), 104-
8.

974. _____. Status of birth control: 1938. New republic, v.
94 (20 April 1938), 324-6.

975. _____. War against birth control. American mercury,
v. 2 (June 1924), 231-6.

976. _____. Woman and the new race. New York, Brentano's, 1920.
234p. Rep., Maxwell Reprint, Elmsford, N.Y., 1972.

977. _____. Woman, morality, and birth control. New York,
New York Women's Publishing Co., 1922. 55p.

978. _____. Women and birth control. North American review,
v. 227 (May 1929), 529-34.

979. SAUNDERS, Jessie Jane. The legal status of women. New
York, National American Woman Suffrage Association,
1897. 116p. Property rights, divorce laws, suffrage,
and guardianship of children in each state.

980. SAWYER, F. W. Legal rights of women. North American
review, v. 90 (1860), 538.

981. SAYERS, Dorothy L. Are women human? Grand Rapids,
Mich., Eerdmans, 1971. 47p.

982. SCHEINFELD, Amram. How equal are women? Collier's,
v. 112 (18 September 1943), 15+.

983. SCHMID, Margaret. Sex roles and survival. Women; a
journal of liberation, v. 1 (Fall 1969), 7.

984. SCHMIEDELER, E. Near equality with men; so what!
Homiletic and pastoral review, v. 45 (October 1944),
11-22.

985. SCHREIBER, F. R. and M. Herman. Battle of the sexes.
Science digest, v. 61 (April 1967), 22-4.

986. SCHREINER, Olive. Woman movement of our day. Harper's
bazaar, v. 36 (January-March 1902), 3-8, 103-7, 222-7.

987. _____. The woman question. Cosmopolitan, v. 28 (November 1899), 182-92.

988. SCHULDER, Diane. Women and the law. Atlantic monthly,
v. 225 (March 1970), 103-4.

989. SCHUMAN, Pat and Gay Detlefsen. Sisterhood is serious:
An annotated bibliography. Library journal, v. 96
(1 September 1971), 2587-94. General discussion of
the movement followed by a short bibliography.

990. SCOTT, Anne Firor. After suffrage: Southern women in the
twenties. Journal of southern history, v. 30, no. 3
(1963), 298-318. The lack of much of an increase of
women in public life since 1925 and the lack of any
real voice by women in political party decisions.

991. _____, ed. The American woman. Who was she? Englewood Cliffs, N.J., Prentice-Hall, 1971. 182p. The
relationship between the changing role of women in
American society and the changes in women's education,
work, views of family life, and her participation in
social movements. Excerpts of articles from mid-
nineteenth century to the present.

992. _____. The "new woman" in the new South. South At-
      lantic quarterly, v. 61 (Autumn 1962), 473-83. The
      struggle for women's rights in the South from around
      1830 to 1920.
993. _____. The southern lady: from pedestal to politics,
      1830-1930. Chicago, University of Chicago Press,
      1970. 247p.
994. SEDGWICK, A. G. Rights of married women. Nation,
      v. 37 (1883), 266.
995. SEGERS, Mary C. New civil rights: fem lib! Catholic
      world, v. 211 (August 1970), 203-7. The necessity
      to destroy the traditional feminine and masculine
      stereotypes, and on the "genuinely laudable aims of
      the women's liberation movement."
996. SEIDENBERG, Faith A. The submissive majority: Modern
      trends in the law concerning women's rights. Cornell
      law review, v. 55 (January 1970), 262-72.
997. SEX discrimination and the Constitution. Stanford law re-
      view, v. 2 (July 1950), 691-730. Comments on exist-
      ing discriminatory laws and the constitutionality of
      such laws.
998. SEX discrimination joker in Civil Rights Act. Automation,
      v. 14 (June 1967), 23.
999. SEX equality and protective laws. Editorial research re-
      ports (13-19 July 1926), 525-64.
1000. SHEED, Wilfrid. The second sex, etc., etc. Commonweal,
      v. 80 (27 March 1964), 15-16. Criticism of Betty
      Friedan and others.
1001. SHELL, Louise. The lonely girl in the big city. Boston,
      New England Free Press, 1971. 13p.
1002. SHOULD women serve as jurors in divorce cases? Current
      opinion, v. 70 (April 1921), 511-12.
1003. SHOWALTER, Elaine, comp. Women's liberation and litera-
      ture. New York, Harcourt, Brace, 1971. 338p.
      Anthology of fiction and non-fiction by Ibsen, Woll-
      stonecraft, Mill, Woolf, Friedan, Millett, and others.
1004. SIEGEL, R. Right of a married woman to sue her husband
      on a contract. Dickinson law review, v. 38 (June
      1934), 270-6.
1005. SINCLAIR, Andrew. The better half; the emancipation of
      the American woman. New York, Harper and Row,
      1965. 401p.
1006. SLADE, Mrs. F. L. Women as jurors. Woman citizen,
      v. 9 (20 September 1924), 19.
1007. SMITH, Cyril J. Tradition of Eve. San Antonio, Texas,
      Naylor, 1961. 308p.
1008. SMITH, Elizabeth Oakes. Sanctity of marriage. Syracuse,
      N.Y., Lathrop's print., 185? 8p. Criticism of mar-
      riage as a "commercial co-partnership" instead of as
      a "sacrament," and on the necessity of legal equality.
1009. _____. Woman and her needs. New York, Fowler &
      Wells, 1851. 120p.
1010. SMITH, Ethel M. Toward equal rights for men and women.

Washington, National League of Women Voters, 1929.
139p.

1011. _____. What is sex equality. Century, v. 118 (May
1929), 96-106.

1012. SMITH, Francis Ormond. The sphere and influence of woman, over the well-being of society. Boston, Printed
by Bazin & Chandler, 1853. 24p.

1013. SMITH, G. Place of woman in the state. Forum, v. 8
(1890), 515.

1014. SMITH, Harrison. Feminism in reverse. Saturday review,
v. 37 (25 December 1954), 20. The growing number
of gifted women who prefer marriage to a profession.

1015. _____. The war of the sexes: An interim report. Saturday review, v. 33 (22 April 1950), 22. Discussion:
v. 33 (20 May 1950), 26-7.

1016. _____. Women are coming! Saturday review, v. 31 (17
July 1948), 18.

1017. SMITH, J. N. To end discrimination against women. Independent woman, v. 16 (May 1937), 132+.

1018. SMITH, M. P. Special legal relations of married women
in North Carolina as to property, contracts, and
guardianship. Chapel Hill, University of North Carolina Press, 1928. 76p.

1019. SMITH, Paul Jordan. The soul of woman; an interpretation
of the philosophy of feminism. San Francisco, P.
Eider, 1916. 66p.

1020. SMITH, Thelma M. Feminism in Philadelphia, 1790-1850.
Pennsylvania magazine of history and biography, v.
68 (July 1944), 243-68.

1021. SMITH, Thomas Robert, comp. The woman question. New
York, Boni & Liveright, 1919. 229p.

1022. SOCHEN, June. Now let us begin: Feminism in Greenwich
Village, 1910-1920. 213p. PhD thesis, Northwestern
University, 1967.

1023. SOCIAL condition of women. Knickerbocker magazine, v. 61
(1863), 381.

1024. SONTHEIMER, M. Do women have equal rights? Good
housekeeping, v. 127 (December 1948), 38-9+.

1025. SORENSEN, M. Quest for equality. International concilia-
tion, v. 507 (March 1956), 311-13.

1026. SOTHESON, A. H. Work of women's clubs. Forum, v. 12
(December 1891), 519-28.

1027. SPAHR, Margaret. Are you a "person?" Journal of home
economics, v. 46 (May 1954), 303-6. Concerning the
legal status of married women in New York State.

1028. SPEAKE, P. Woman's super rights. Alabama law journal,
v. 3 (December 1927), 26-31.

1029. SPEER, Ocie. A treatise on the law of marital rights in
Texas, including marriage, divorce, children, community property, homestead, administration and statutory actions. Rochester, N.Y., Lawyer's Co-operative Publishing Co., 1929. 1051p.

1030. SPENCER, Anna Garlin. The drama of the woman of genius.

Forum, v. 47 (January 1912), 34-54. The need for
women to work much harder than men in order to at-
tain a position equal to them.

1031. _____. Legal position of married women. Popular science monthly, v. 18 (1881), 643.

1032. _____. Woman and the state. Forum, v. 48 (October
1912), 394-408.

1033. SPENCER, H. Status of women and children. Popular science monthly, v. 11 (1877), 433.

1034. SPENT crusade. Time, v. 51 (1 March 1948), 15-16. Com-
memoration of the first equal rights convention; but
with little enthusiasm.

1035. SPRAGUE, Henry Harrison. Women under the law of Massachusetts. 2d ed. Boston, Little, Brown, 1903.

1036. STAMBLER, Sookie. Women's liberation; blueprint for the
future. New York, Ace Books, 1970. 283p.

1037. STANTON, Elizabeth Cady. Address to the Legislature of
New York, adopted by the State Woman's Rights Convention, held at Albany, Tuesday and Wednesday, February 14 and 15, 1854. Albany, Weed, Parsons,
1854. 19p.

1038. _____. Are homogeneous divorce laws in all states desirable? North American review, v. 170 (March
1900), 405-9.

1039. _____. Divorce versus domestic warfare. Arena, v. 1
(April 1890), 560-9.

1040. _____. Has Christianity benefited? North American review, v. 140 (1885), 389.

1041. _____. Progress of the American woman. North American review, v. 171 (December 1900), 904-7.

1042. _____. Solitude of self; an address delivered by Elizabeth Cady Stanton, before the United States Congressional Committee on the Judiciary, Monday, January
18, 1892. Edited by Harriot Stanton Blatch. [New
York, 1910?] 20p.

1043. _____. Woman question. Radical, v. 3 (1868), 18.

1044. _____. The woman's Bible.... New York, European
Publishing Co., 1898. 2v. Commentaries on woman's status in the Old and New Testaments.

1045. STANTON, Theodore. Seneca Falls and women's rights.
Independent, v. 111 (4 August 1923), 42-3. News-
paper reactions to the Seneca Falls convention and
Susan B. Anthony's part in the movement.

1046. STARRETT, H. E. Future of American women. Forum,
v. 10 (1891), 185.

1047. STATUS of Wisconsin women under the equal rights law, by
Zona Gale; Status of women under the equal rights
law: discussion of chapter 529 of the Wisconsin laws
of 1921, by A. E. Matheson. Wisconsin State Bar
Association, proceedings (1922), 168-97.

1048. STATUS of women. American magazine, v. 13 (1887), 376.

1049. STATUS of women; great scope of Commission's work. UN
bulletin, v. 1 (16 September 1946), 11-13.

1050. STAWELL, F. Melian. Women and democracy. International
        journal of ethics, v. 17 (April 1907), 329-36.
1051. STEARNS, Bertha-Monica. Reform periodicals and female
        reformers, 1830-1860. American historical review,
        v. 37 (1932), 678-99.
1052. STEINBERG, E. and J. Starke. Woman's liberation: a
        woman's view; a man's view. Senior scholastic, v.
        97 (9 November 1970), 16-17.
1053. STEINEM, Gloria. After black power, women's liberation.
        New York, v. 2 (7 April 1969), 8-10.
1054. _____. What it would be like if women win. Time, v.
        96 (31 August 1970), 22+.
1055. STERN, Edith M. Women are household slaves. American
        mercury, v. 68 (January 1949), 71-6.
1056. STERN, Paula. The womanly image; character assassination
        through the ages. Atlantic monthly, v. 225 (March
        1970), 87-90.
1057. STEVENS, D. New freedom in divorce; can it be secured
        by uniformity in marriage laws? Forum, v. 76 (Sep-
        tember 1926), 321-38. Reply: v. 76 (November 1926),
        788-9.
1058. STEWARD, Gustavus. The black girl passes. Social forces,
        v. 6 (September 1927), 99-103.
1059. STINSON, Alvah La Forrest. Woman under the law. Bos-
        ton, Hudson Printing Co., 1914. 406p.
1060. STOKES, Rose H. Phelps. Condition of women from their
        own point of view. American Academy of Political
        and Social Science, annals, v. 27 (1906), 627.
1061. STONE, M. Liberation struggle generates tension on race,
        sex issues. Christian century, v. 87 (10 June 1970),
        736-9.
1062. STOUT, Claude D. Legal status of women in Wisconsin.
        Marquette law review, v. 14 (February-June 1930),
        66-89, 121-69, 198-211. Historical viewpoint.
1063. STOW, Marietta Lois Beers. Unjust laws which govern
        woman. 2d ed. Boston, Rand, Avery, printer, 1877.
        370p. Concerning the property rights of women.
1064. STUART, Mrs. R. J. New political power of women.
        Ladies' home journal, v. 81 (September 1964), 68+.
1065. SUELZLE, Marijean. What every woman should know about
        the women's liberation movement. Berkeley, Cal.,
        Women's Research Associates [1971?].
1066. SWANWICK, Helena M. Future of the women's movement.
        New York, Macmillan, 1914. 208p. Primarily on
        the status of women around 1914.
1067. SYCKLE, R. Van. Contractual capacity and property rights
        of married women in Michigan. Detroit law review,
        v. 5 (April-June 1935), 69-83, 124-35.
1068. SYMES, Lillian. Still a man's game; reflections of a
        slightly tired feminist. Harper's magazine, v. 158
        (May 1929), 678-86.
1069. SYMPOSIUM--Women and the law. Valparaiso University
        law review, v. 5, no. 2 (1971), 203-488.

1070. TAEUBER, Irene B. and Hope T. Eldridge. Some demo-
       graphic aspects of the changing role of women. Amer-
       ican Academy of Political and Social Science, annals,
       v. 251 (May 1947), 24-34.
1071. TAFT, Julia Jessie. Woman movement from the point of
       view of social consciousness. Chicago, University of
       Chicago Press, 1916. 62p.
1072. TALBOT, G. F. Political rights and duties of women.
       Popular science monthly, v. 49 (1896), 80.
1073. TALMAGE, T. Dewitt. Woman: her power and her priv-
       ileges. A series of sermons on the duties of the
       maiden, wife, and mother, and of their influence in
       the home and society. New York, Ogilvie, 1888.
       200p.
1074. TANNER, Leslie B., ed. Voices from women's liberation.
       New York, Signet, 1970.
1075. TARBELL, Ida Minerva. The American woman. American
       magazine, v. 69 (January-April 1910), 363-77, 468-
       81, 656-69, 801-14; v. 70 (May 1910), 60-73. A
       series of articles dealing with the emancipated Ameri-
       can woman.
1076. _____. Business of being a woman. American magazine,
       v. 73 (March 1912), 563-8.
1077. _____. Making a man of herself. American magazine,
       v. 73 (February 1912), 427-30.
1078. _____. Uneasy woman. American magazine, v. 73
       (January 1912), 259-62.
1079. TAX, Meredith. Woman and her mind: the story of daily
       life. Cambridge, Mass., Bread and Roses, 1970.
       20p.
1080. TAYLOR, A. W. Property first! Christian century, v. 40
       (26 April 1923), 530-1.
1081. _____. Woman's rights and duties. Christian century,
       v. 40 (4 October 1923), 1265-6.
1082. TAYLOR, Isaac N. The woman question. According to
       Moses and Paul. Boston, Arena, 1894. 72p.
1083. TEMPLE, M. L. Our greatest privilege, to be tried by
       our peers. Independent woman, v. 32 (June 1953),
       197+.
1084. TENNESSEE State Federation of Women's Clubs. Fifteen
       reasons why the law of Tennessee governing the prop-
       erty rights of married women should be changed.
       [Nashville, Brandon Printing Co., 1912?] 31p.
1085. TEXAS. Governor's Commission on the Status of Women.
       Report. Austin, State of Texas, Executive Depart-
       ment, 1968. 67p.
1086. TEXAS. Legislative Council. Legal status of married wom-
       en in Texas. Austin, 1956. 104p. [Its Staff Re-
       search Report no. 54-3.]
1087. THAXTER, S. W. Women's rights under Maine law. Maine
       State Bar Association, journal, v. 43 (1954), 39-46.
1088. THOMAS, J. E. Role of the Negro woman in the battle for
       equality. Negro digest, v. 13 (February 1964), 68-73.

1089. THOMAS, W. I. The older and newer ideals of marriage.
       American magazine, v. 67 (April 1909), 548-552.
       The need for the extension of women's activities be-
       yond the home.
1090. THOMPSON, E. B. What weaker sex? Ebony, v. 21
       (August 1966), 84-6+.
1091. THOMPSON, Flora McDonald. Retrogression of the Ameri-
       can woman. North American review, v. 171 (Novem-
       ber 1900), 748-53. On women's status at the time
       along with views of De Tocqueville on women's status
       in the United States.
1092. THOMPSON, Jessie. History of jury service for women,
       compiled under the auspices of the Wyoming B & PW
       Clubs. Thermopolis, Wyoming, March 1953. Mimeo-
       graphed. 31p.
1093. THOMPSON, Mary Lou, ed. Voices of the new feminism.
       New York, Beacon, 1970. 160p.
1094. TIGER, Lionel. Male dominance? Yes, alas. A sexist
       plot? No. New York Times magazine (25 October
       1970), 35-7+ ; Discussion: (15 November 1970), 26+ ;
       (22 November 1970), 22+.
1095. TILLETT, Gladys A. Elimination of discrimination against
       women; report on 19th session. U.S. Department of
       State, bulletin, v. 55 (22 August 1966), 284-88. Con-
       cerning the United Nations Commission on the Status
       of Women.
1096. _____. Existing law and measures to improve the status
       of women in the western hemisphere. U.S. Depart-
       ment of State, bulletin, v. 51 (27 July 1964), 128-32.
1097. _____. Progress report on the status of women. U.S.
       Department of State, bulletin, v. 47 (30 July 1962),
       197-99. Concerning the United Nations Commission
       on the Status of Women.
1098. TO chart the next century of women's progress; celebrating
       one hundredth anniversary of first declaration of wom-
       en's rights. Independent woman, v. 27 (April 1948),
       118.
1099. TOOMY, A. J. The woman question among Catholics.
       Catholic world, v. 57 (1893), 669-84.
1100. TORNABENE, L. Bored housewife. Ladies home journal,
       v. 83 (November 1966), 97-9+ ; Discussion: v. 84
       (February 1967), 8.
1101. TOWARD equality for women in Jewish law. Reconstruction-
       ist, v. 32 (27 May 1966), 3-4.
1102. TOWARD improving the status of women. UN bulletin, v.
       10 (1 May 1951), 451+.
1103. TOWNER, Harriet C. Federation of women's clubs of Iowa.
       Midland monthly, v. 7 (1897), 548.
1104. _____. Missouri Federation of Women's Clubs. Mid-
       land monthly, v. 7 (1897), 372.
1105. TREATISE on marriage, divorce, and legal rights of married
       women. Indianapolis, Coons, 1887.
1106. TRENT, W. P. Position of women. Chautauquan, v. 9

(1889), 505.
1107.   TRIED and approved; the woman juror. Literary digest,
        v. 70 (17 September 1921), 46-9.
1108.   TRILLING, Diana. Female biology in a male culture.
        Saturday review, v. 53 (10 October 1970), 16-18+.
1109.   TROTH, A. How we won jury service in Georgia. In-
        dependent woman, v. 33 (February 1954), 64.
1110.   TRUEX, D. Focus on feminine ferment. Journal of college
        student personnel, v. 11 (September 1970), 323-31.
1111.   TRUTH, Sojourner. Speech at the Women's Rights Conven-
        tion, Akron, Ohio, May 29, 1851. (In: Mark, Irving,
        ed. The faith of our fathers; an anthology expressing
        the aspirations of the American common man, 1790-
        1860. New York, Knopf, 1952. pp. 33-4.)
1112.   TUCKER, George Fox. Advising a woman as to her legal
        rights. Chicago, Blackstone Institute, 1920. 24p.
1113.   TURLAY, W. W. Plea for liberality in divorce legislation.
        Arena, v. 23 (January 1900), 98-102.
1114.   TUTTLE, Florence Guertin. The awakening of woman: sug-
        gestions from the psychic side of feminism. New
        York, Abingdon, 1915. 164p.
1115.   UHLRICH, E. Woman man's equal. Midland monthly, v. 10
        (1898), 60.
1116.   UNDERPRIVILEGED majority. Economist, v. 210 (4 Janu-
        ary 1964), 24. Commenting on the report of the
        President's Commission on the Status of Women.
1117.   UNDERWOOD, O. Women's jury service law in Tennessee.
        Independent woman, v. 30 (June 1951), 173.
1118.   UNIFORM divorce laws. Independent, v. 55 (29 October
        1903), 2591-2.
1119.   UNIFORM divorce legislation. Independent, v. 54 (4 Sep-
        tember 1902), 2150-2.
1120.   UNITED Nations. Commission on the Status of Women. The
        legal status of married women; a report to the Secre-
        tary General. New York, 1958.
1121.   _____. Department of Economic and Social Affairs.
        Civic and political education of women. New York,
        1964. 92p. Discusses certain factors influencing the
        status of women in various societies as well as con-
        taining a list of women's rights organizations.
1122.   _____. _____. The convention on the political rights
        of women; history and commentary. New York, 1956.
        46p.
1123.   _____. _____. Political education of women; pamphlet
        produced at the request of the Commission on the
        Status of Women. New York, 1951. 43p.
1124.   _____. Office of Public Information. The United Nations
        and the status of women; a survey of United Nations
        work in this field. New York, 1964. 30p.
1125.   _____. Secretary-General, 1946- (Lie). Preliminary
        report on the political rights of women. Lake Suc-
        cess, 1947. 81p.
1126.   _____. Secretary-General, 1946-1953 (Lie). Property

rights of women; report. New York, 1953. 136p.

1127. _____. Secretary-General, 1953- (Hammarskjöld). Legal status of married women; report submitted by the Secretary-General. New York, Commission on the Status of Women, United Nations, 1958. 103p.

1128. _____. Secretary-General, 1961- (Thant). United Nations assistance for the advancement of women; report of the Secretary-General. New York, 1967. 75p.

1129. _____. Seminar on the Status of Women in Family Law. Seminar on the Status of Women in Family Law. New York, 1961- annual.

1130. The UNITED Nations and the status of women. United Nations review, v. 8 (March 1961), 22-7; (April 1961), 26-32. "A survey of the work of the United Nations to promote the civil and political rights of women."

1131. UNITED States. Citizens Advisory Council on the Status of Women. Reports of the Task Force on Social Insurance and Taxes. Washington, GPO, 1968. 139p. The extent of social protection and taxation of women workers.

1132. _____. Department of State. Human rights; some next steps; address. Texts of conventions on slavery, forced labor, and political rights of women and President Kennedy's letter transmitting the conventions to the Senate. By Richard N. Gardner. Washington, GPO, 1963. 21p.

1133. _____. Interdepartmental Committee on the Status of Women. American women; 1963-1968. Report. Washington, GPO, 1968. 31p. Articles concerning women in employment, legal rights, home and community, education, and a report on other commissions on the status of women.

1134. _____. _____. Annual report. Washington, GPO, 1964- . Various articles dealing with equal pay and employment, education, home and community, Title VII of the Civil Rights Act, activities of state commissions on the status of women, etc.

1135. _____. _____. Progress report on the status of women October 11, 1963, through October 10, 1964. Washington, GPO, 1964. 27p. Advances in states concerning legislation; list of governors' commissions; federal advances.

1136. _____. President's Commission on the Status of Women. American women. Report of the President's Commission on the Status of Women. Washington, GPO, 1963. 86p. Results of a two-year study on the achievements and inequities of American women, with recommendations.

1137. _____. _____. Report of the Committee on Civil and Political Rights. Washington, GPO, 1963. 83p. A study of inequities and recommendations in the areas of jury service, personal and property rights of married women, means for achieving greater legal recognition (e.g., Equal Rights Amendment), etc.

1138. _____. _____. Report of the Committee on Home
and Community. Washington, GPO, 1963. 51p. A
discussion of needed services such as child care,
health services, family services, services related to
employment, along with deployment of responsibility.

1139. _____. _____. Report of the Committee on Social
Insurance and Taxes. Washington, GPO, 1963. 81p.
A discussion of inequities and recommendations for
women in areas of social insurance and federal taxes.

1140. _____. President's Task Force on Women's Rights and
Responsibilities. A matter of simple justice. Washington, GPO, 1970. 33p. A study proposing legislation in order to remedy inequities against women.

1141. _____. Women's Bureau. The changing status of women.
Chicago Regional Conference, May 18-19, 1962. Washington, GPO, 1964.

1142. _____. _____. Conference on the American Woman,
Her Changing Role as Worker, Homemaker, and Citizen, Washington, 1948. Report. Washington, GPO,
1948. 210p. [Bulletin no. 224.]

1143. _____. _____. Conference on Woman's Destiny--
Choice or Chance? Seattle, University of Washington,
1963. Report. Washington, GPO, 1965. 86p.

1144. _____. _____. The effective use of womanpower, report of the conference, March 10 and 11, 1955.
Washington, GPO, 1955. 113p. [Bulletin no. 257.]

1145. _____. _____. International documents on the status
of women. By Mary Elizabeth Pidgeon. Washington,
GPO, 1947. 116p. [Bulletin no. 217.]

1146. _____. _____. The legal status of women in the
United States of America, January 1, 1938. By Sara
L. Buchanan. Washington, GPO, 1938-1940. [Bulletin
no. 157.]

1147. _____. _____. The legal status of women in the
United States of America, January 1, 1938: report for
Alabama. Washington, GPO, 1938. 10p. [Bulletin
no. 157-1.]

1148. _____. _____. The legal status of women in the
United States of America: report for Alabama, as of
January 1, 1959. Washington, GPO, 1959. 13p.
[Bulletin 157-1, rev.]

1149. _____. _____. The legal status of women in the
United States of America, January 1, 1938: report for
California. Washington, GPO, 1939. 20p. [Bulletin
no. 157-4.]

1150. _____. _____. The legal status of women in the
United States of America, January 1, 1948: report for
California. Washington, GPO, 1950. 21p. [Bulletin
no. 157-4, rev.]

1151. _____. _____. The legal status of women in the
United States of America: report for California as of
July 1, 1963. Washington, GPO, 1963. 38p. [Bul-

letin no. 157-4, rev.]

1152. ____. ____. The legal status of women in the United States of America, January 1, 1948: report for Colorado. Washington, GPO, 1949. 15p. [Bulletin no. 157-5.]

1153. ____. ____. The legal status of women in the United States of America, January 1, 1948: report for the District of Columbia. Washington, GPO, 1950. 10p. [Bulletin no. 157-8.]

1154. ____. ____. The legal status of women in the United States of America, January 1, 1948: report for Georgia. Washington, GPO, 1948. 15p. [Bulletin no. 157-10, rev.]

1155. ____. ____. The legal status of women in the United States of America, January 1, 1948: report for Louisiana. Washington, GPO, 1950. 16p. [Bulletin no. 157-17.]

1156. ____. ____. The legal status of women in the United States of America, January 1, 1948: report for Nevada. By S. L. Buchanan. Washington, GPO, 1949. 16p. [Bulletin no. 157-27, rev.]

1157. ____. ____. The legal status of women in the United States of America, January 1, 1938: report for New York state. Washington, GPO, 1938. 14p. [Bulletin no. 157-31.]

1158. ____. ____. The legal status of women in the United States of America, January 1, 1948: report for Pennsylvania. Washington, GPO, 1949. 14p. [Bulletin no. 157-37.]

1159. ____. ____. The legal status of women in the United States of America, January 1, 1948: report for Tennessee. Washington, GPO, 1949. 13p. [Bulletin no. 157-41, rev.]

1160. ____. ____. The legal status of women in the United States of America, January 1, 1948: report for Texas. Washington, GPO, 1949. 12p. [Bulletin no. 157-42, rev.]

1161. ____. ____. The legal status of women in the United States of America as of January 1, 1948: summary for all states combined. By Sara L. Buchanan. Washington, GPO, 1951. 105p. [Bulletin no. 157.]

1162. ____. ____. The legal status of women in the United States of America; United States summary as of January 1, 1953. Washington, GPO, 1956. 103p. [Bulletin no. 157.]

1163. ____. ____. The political and civil status of women in the United States of America: summary, including principal sex distinctions, as of January 1, 1948. Washington, GPO, 1948. 6p.

1164. ____. ____. The President's Commission on the Status of Women; why a commission? Function, operational procedures, ongoing results. Washington, GPO, 1966. 9p.

1165. _____. _____. State laws of special value to women. Washington, GPO, 1951. 50p.

1166. _____. _____. The status of women in the United States, 1953. By Lucile N. Furman. Washington, GPO, 1953. 26p. [Bulletin no. 249.]

1167. _____. _____. Today's woman in tomorrow's world; report of a conference commemorating the 40th anniversary of the Women's Bureau, June 2-3, 1960. Washington, GPO, 1960. 138p. [Bulletin no. 276.]

1168. URCH, Erwin J. Other half of history. Social education, v. 25 (April 1961), 189-92. The lack of women in written history.

1169. USEEM, R. H. Changing cultural concepts in women's lives. National Association of Women Deans and Counselors, journal, v. 24 (October 1960), 29-34.

1170. UTAH. Governor's Committee on the Status of Women in Utah. Utah women; opportunities, responsibilities; Report of the Governor's Committee on the Status of Women in Utah, June 15, 1966. Salt Lake City, 1966. 66p.

1171. VAIL, R. W. The Lily. New York Historical Society quarterly, v. 36 (October 1952), 375. A short history of the feminist periodical, with its locations in certain libraries.

1172. VEBLEN, Thorstein. Barbarian status of women. American journal of Sociology, v. 4 (January 1899), 503-14.

1173. _____. The economic theory of woman's dress. Popular science monthly, v. 46 (December 1894), 198-205. On the theory that "woman's dress...involves the implication that the woman is a chattel," and that the "...function of civilized womankind is the conspicuous consumption of goods."

1174. VERMILYE, J. On women's legal rights. Florida law review, v. 12 (February 1938), 63-6.

1175. VERNON, Dorothy. [Describes a collection of letters written to Paulina Wright Davis of Providence, R.I., by leading feminists, ca. 1850-ca. 1888.] Month at Goodspeeds, v. 19 (1948), 160-62.

1176. VERY volcanic. Newsweek, v. 76 (31 August 1970), 47. On the Women's Strike for Equality, 26 August 1970.

1177. VIGMAN, Fred. Beauty's triumph; or, The superiority of the fair sex invincibly proved; a social history of the rise of sex equalitarianism, gentility, feminism, and hedonist ideals of modern women and the consequences thereof, from the Renaissance to modern times. Boston, Christopher, 1966. 202p.

1178. VIRGINIA. Commission on the Status of Women. Status of women. Report of the Commission on the Status of Women to the Governor and the General Assembly of Virginia. Richmond, 1966. 69p.

1179. VIRTUE, Maxine Boord. 111 laws affecting women in Kansas. Topeka, S. C. Austin, state printer, 1939.

1180. VON ZAHN-HARNACK, A. University women and the woman's movement. American Association of University Women, journal, v. 23 (October 1929), 1-3.

1181. WARBASSE, Elizabeth B. The changing legal rights of married women, 1800-1861. PhD thesis, Radcliffe College, 1960.

1182. WARD, Dearing. The decline of women. Forum, v. 82 (November 1929), 300-3.

1183. WARE, Cellestine. Woman power; the movement for women's liberation. New York, Tower, 1970. 176p.

1184. WARREN, Joseph. Husband's right to wife's services. Harvard law review, v. 38 (February-March 1925), 421-46, 622-50.

1185. WARRINGTON, Carina C. What has been done to remove legal discriminations against women? Washington, National League of Women Voters, 1922. 30p.

1186. WARRIOR, Betsy. Sex roles and their consequences. No more fun and games, no. 2 (February 1969), 21-31.

1187. WATERS, Gola E. Sex, state protective laws and the Civil Rights Act of 1964. Labor law journal, v. 18 (June 1967), 344-52.

1188. WATERS, Mary-Alice. The politics of women's liberation today. New York, Pathfinder, 1970. 23p. A discussion of the radical aspects of the movement.

1189. WATKINS, Mel and Jay David. To be a black woman: Portraits in fact and fiction. New York, Morrow, 1970. 285p. An anthology of articles from the ante-bellum period to the present.

1190. WEATHERS, Mary Ann. An argument for black women's liberation as a revolutionary force. No more fun and games, no. 2 (February 1969), 66-70.

1191. WEBB, Marilyn Saltzman. Women as secretary, sexpot, spender, sow, civic actor and sickie. Motive, v. 6 (March-April 1969), 48-59.

1192. WEBSTER, Thomas. Woman man's equal. Cincinnati, Hitchcock and Walden, 1873. 297p.

1193. WEILLER, H. E. No justice for the ladies. Independent woman, v. 30 (March 1951), 61-2.

1194. WEISS, John. Woman question. Christian examiner, v. 56 (1854), 1-34.

1195. WEISSTEIN, Naomi. Kinder, küche, kirche. Radical therapist, v. 1 (August-September 1970), 12-13. Also: Boston, New England Free Press, 1970. 7p. Criticism of psychologists' and psychiatrists' view of women.

1196. WELLS, J. C. Treatise on the separate property of married women under the recent enabling acts. Cincinnati, Clarke, 1878.

1197. WELLS, Lyn. American women; their use and abuse. Boston, New England Free Press, 1969. 17p.

1198. WELLS, Mildred White. Unity in diversity; the history of the General Federation of Women's Clubs since 1889. Washington, General Federation of Women's Clubs, 1953. 525p.

1199. WELTER, Barbara. Anti-intellectualism and the American
      woman: 1800-1860. Mid-America, v. 48, no. 4
      (1966), 258-70. The dilemma of the American woman
      striving for opportunities against the theory that wom-
      anhood and intellect do not go together.
1200. _____. The cult of true womenhood: 1820-1860. Ameri-
      can quarterly, v. 18 (Summer 1966), 151-74. Con-
      cerns the reasons for women's confinement in the
      home and the eventual banding together of women to
      eradicate their problems.
1201. WENTWORTH, Franklin Harcourt. Woman's portion: An
      address delivered in Carnegie Hall, New York City,
      Sunday afternoon, February 27, 1910, under the
      auspices of the women of the Socialist Party. New
      York, Socialist Literature Co., 1910. 24p.
1202. WEST, A. Who takes advantage of American women? Men.
      Vogue, v. 151 (May 1968), 198-9+.
1203. WEST, Rebecca. This is the suspicion I have about the
      scene. I suspect it is unfair to women. Mademoi-
      selle, v. 70 (February 1970), 182-3+. The depend-
      ence of women on men, making women feel inferior
      and therefore unhappy.
1204. WESTERVELT, Esther M. Are we ready for equality?
      AAUW journal, v. 64 (November 1970), 20-3.
1205. _____. Woman as a compleat human being. National
      Association of Women Deans and Counselors, journal,
      v. 29 (Summer 1966), 150-5.
1206. _____. Womanpower--wanton waste or wishful thinking?
      Vocational guidance quarterly, v. 10 (Winter 1962),
      78-84.
1207. WHAT is liberation? Women; a journal of liberation, v. 1
      (Winter 1970), special issue.
1208. WHAT the feminists are reading. McCall's, v. 98 (April
      1971), 44.
1209. WHAT to do about discrimination. Panel suggests 12 ways
      to make rights a reality. AAUW journal, v. 64
      (November 1970), 10-13.
1210. WHITE, Frederick Augustus, comp. Laws on marriage,
      divorce and property rights of married women of all
      states and Alaska, Hawaii, Arizona, New Mexico, and
      District of Columbia. San Francisco, Bender-Moss,
      1910. 423p.
1211. WHITE, Martha E. Work in New England. New England
      magazine, v. 28 (June 1903), 447-63. Pertaining to
      women's clubs.
1212. _____. The work of the woman's clubs. Atlantic month-
      ly, v. 93 (May 1904), 614-23. The General Federa-
      tion of Women's Clubs and its work.
1213. WHO'S come a long way, baby? Time, v. 96 (31 August
      1970), 16-21. The current women's rights movement
      with views of Lionel Tiger and Kate Millett.
1214. WHY not one national divorce law? Woman's home com-
      panion, v. 71 (January 1944), 12.

1215. WILBUR, Emma G. St. Paul's view of woman. Presby-
       terian quarterly, v. 13 (1899), 589-607.
1216. WILCOX, Susanne. Unrest of modern woman. Independent,
       v. 67 (8 July 1909), 62-6.
1217. WILENSKY, R. W. In my opinion: women's liberation is
       long overdue. Seventeen, v. 29 (June 1970), 198.
1218. WILLARD, Frances E. Cause of woman is man's cause.
       Arena, v. 5 (1892), 712-25.
1219. _____. The dawn of woman's day. Our day, v. 2
       (November 1888), 345-60.
1220. WILLIAMS, Catharine Plasterer. The true rights of woman.
       Huntington, Ind., n.p., 1868.
1221. WILLIAMS, Essie W. Legal status of women and children
       in Minnesota. St. Paul, Review Publishing Co., 1911.
       32p.
1222. WILLIAMS, Fannie B. Present status and intellectual prog-
       ress of colored women. Address delivered...before
       the Congress of Representative Women, World's Co-
       lumbian Exposition. Chicago, May, 1898. [i.e.,
       1893?] n.p., 1893? 15p.
1223. WILLIS, Ellen. Whatever happed to women? Nothing.
       That's the trouble; a report on the new feminism.
       Mademoiselle, v. 69 (September 1969), 206+.
1224. WILSON, Elizabeth. A scriptural view of woman's rights
       and duties, in all the important relations of life.
       Philadelphia, W. S. Young, printer, 1849. 376p.
1225. WILSON, Jennie Lansley. The legal and political status of
       women in the United States. Cedar Rapids, Iowa,
       Torch Press, 1912. 336p. Supplement: 1922. 105p.
1226. _____, comp. The legal status of women in Iowa. Des
       Moines, Iowa, J. L. Wilson, 1894.
1227. WINCHESTER, B. The new woman. Arena, v. 27 (1902),
       367.
1228. WINSLOW, Helen M. Influence of women. Critic, v. 44
       (1904), 237.
1229. _____. The story of the woman's club movement. New
       England magazine, v. 37 (July 1908), 543-57.
1230. WOLD, E. The changing legal scene. Independent woman,
       v. 16 (April 1937), 105+.
1231. WOLFSON, Alice. Women vs. health industry; health care
       may be hazardous to your health. Detroit, Radical
       Education Project, 1970. 4p. Victimization of women
       by the health profession.
1232. WOMACK, Marcella. Women in society, or, Woman's place
       is in the home. Kansas City, Mo., n.p., [1969?] 5p.
1233. WOMAN, a "must" on the impartial jury. Boston University
       law review, v. 28 (January 1948), 55-60. On jury
       service for women, 1904-1947.
1234. WOMAN and the law. American Bar Association, journal,
       v. 26 (February 1940), 157.
1235. The WOMAN in America. Daedalus, v. 93 (Spring 1964),
       special issue. Articles on working women, equality
       between the sexes, professional women, as well as

several articles on Jane Addams and Eleanor Roosevelt. [Also published as a paperback: Robert J.
Lifton, editor. Boston, Beacon Press, 1965.]

1236. The WOMAN market. Up from under, v. 1 (May/June
       1970), 15-18. Effects of advertisement on women.
1237. WOMAN power. Newsweek, v. 75 (30 March 1970), 61.
       Feminists' demands on the Ladies' Home Journal.
1238. WOMAN question. Brownson's quarterly review, v. 22
       (1873), 508.
1239. WOMAN question. Monthly religious magazine, v. 18 (1857),
       234, 399.
1240. WOMAN question. Monthly religious magazine, v. 19 (1858),
       65.
1241. WOMAN question. Monthly religious magazine, v. 20 (1858),
       225.
1242. WOMAN question. Monthly religious magazine, v. 21 (1859),
       179.
1243. WOMAN question. Nation, v. 8 (1869), 311.
1244. WOMAN question. Nation, v. 9 (1869), 434.
1245. WOMAN question. North American review, v. 130 (1880),
       16.
1246. WOMAN question among Catholics. Catholic world, v. 57
       (August 1893), 668-84.
1247. WOMAN question among Catholics. Catholic world, v. 59
       (June 1894), 229+.
1248. WOMAN'S declaration of sentiments drawn up at Seneca Falls,
       July 1848. Independent woman, v. 27 (July 1948), 216.
1249. WOMAN'S dual role causes domestic strife. Science news
       letter, v. 67 (14 May 1955), 316.
1250. WOMAN'S fight for equal rights. Congressional digest, v.
       25 (December 1946), special issue. Partial contents:
       Questions before the United Nations, the movement in
       the United States, legal obstacles, pro and con dis-
       cussions.
1251. WOMAN'S Party--right or wrong? The woman's party is
       wrong, by Elizabeth Glendower Evans. The woman's
       party is right, by Carol A. Rehfisch. New republic,
       v. 36 (26 September 1923), 123-4.
1252. WOMAN'S place. Atlantic monthly, v. 225 (March 1970),
       81-112+. Ten articles concerning job discrimination
       and other aspects of the movement.
1253. A WOMAN'S protest. Monthly religious magazine, v. 32
       (1864), 213.
1254. WOMAN'S Rights Convention, New York City, September 6
       and 7, 1853. New York, Fowler & Wells, 1853. 96p.
1255. WOMAN'S Rights Convention, Rochester, N.Y., 1848. Re-
       port of the Woman's Rights Convention, Rochester,
       1848. University of Rochester Library bulletin, v. 4
       (Autumn 1948), 13-17.
1256. WOMEN fight for liberation. The Red Papers 3. San Fran-
       cisco, Bay Area Revolutionary Union, 1970. 62p.
       Partial contents: Women and the home; Women on the
       job; Battles of Working-class women; Black Panther

sisters on women's liberation.
1257. WOMEN jurors. United States law review, v. 71 (February 1937), 75-8.
1258. WOMEN of America, now is the time to arise: Yes! No! Maybe (?) By Richard H. Rovere, Robert Alan Aurthur, and Eleanor Perenyi. Esquire, v. 58 (July 1962), 31-5+.
1259. WOMEN take stock of themselves.... New York, Woman's Press [1941?] 28p. Articles by Mary R. Beard, Margaret Mead, Pearl S. Buck and others.
1260. WOMEN under the law. Old and new, v. 3 (1871), 119.
1261. WOMEN'S clubs and social reform. Gunton's magazine, v. 17 (1899), 179.
1262. WOMEN'S legal rights in 50 states. McCall's, v. 98 (February 1971), 90-5.
1263. WOMEN'S lib; a second look. Time, v. 96 (14 December 1970), 50.
1264. WOMEN'S lib: Mailer vs. Millett. Time, v. 97 (22 February 1971), 70-1.
1265. WOMEN'S lib: The war on "sexism"; special report. Newsweek, v. 75 (23 March 1970), 71-6+.
1266. WOMEN'S liberation and the movement in Seattle. Socialist revolution, v. 1 (September/October 1970), 115-36.
1267. WOMEN'S liberation in a Christian perspective--Symposium. Saint Anthony messenger, v. 78 (March 1971), 4-48.
1268. WOMEN'S liberation meeting at the ALA conference. AB bookman's weekly, v. 46 (20-27 July 1970), 90.
1269. WOMEN'S liberation: who, what, when, where, why, and some how; an introductory pamphlet. Los Angeles, Everywomen Publishing Co., 1970. 9p.
1270. WOMEN'S lit; the feminist press. Newsweek, v. 77 (26 April 1971), 65.
1271. WOMEN'S rights: How GH readers feel about liberation and equality. Good housekeeping, v. 172 (March 1971), 34+.
1272. WOOD, Clement. Modern sex morality. New republic, v. 36 (12 September 1923), 68-70. A discussion of a William Jennings Bryan speech, part of which concerns doing away with the double standard.
1273. WOOD, Mary I. The history of the General Federation of Women's Clubs for the first twenty-two years of its organization. New York, History Department, General Federation of Women's Clubs, 1912. 445p.
1274. _____. The woman's club movement. Chautauquan, v. 59 (June 1910), 13-64.
1275. WOODHULL, Victoria Claflin and Tennessee C. Claflin. The human body the temple of God; or, The philosophy of Sociology...together with other essays.... Also press notices of extemporaneous lectures delivered throughout America and England from 1869 to 1882.... London, n.p., 1890.
1276. WOOLLEN, C. J. Failure of feminism. Homiletic and pastoral review, v. 48 (October 1947), 30-9.

1277. WOOLSEY, Kate T.   Women's inferior position in a republic.
       North American review, v. 177 (August 1903), 242-6.
       Rejoinder: v. 177 (September 1903), 544-51.
1278. WOOTEN, Mattie Lloyd.   The status of women in Texas.
       PhD thesis, University of Texas, 1941.
1279. WRIGHT, Marcus Joseph.   The social evolution of women.
       Philadelphia, Martin & Allardyce, 1912.   48p.
1280. WYDEN, Peter.   The revolt of Texas women.   Saturday
       evening post, v. 234 (14 January 1961), 25+.   At-
       tempts on the part of Texas women to get rid of ob-
       solete laws now considered unfair.
1281. WYOMING.   Governor's Commission on the Status of Women.
       Wyoming women.   Report of the Governor's Commis-
       sion on the Status of Women.   [Cheyenne?], 1966.
       53p.
1282. YOUNG, Louise M., ed.   Women's opportunities and respon-
       sibilities.   American Academy of Political and Social
       Science, annals, v. 251 (May 1947), 1-185.   Articles
       on women's education, the family, women's role in
       society, women in industry, etc.
1283. YOUNG mothers answer back: you don't have to feel trapped!
       letters; with editorial comment.   Redbook, v. 129
       (July 1967), 61+.

EQUAL RIGHTS AMENDMENT

1284. ANTHONY, Susan B., II. The "equal rights" amendment; an attack on labor. Lawyer's guild review (January 1943), 12-17.
1285. BOSONE, R. B. and K. St. George. Equal Rights Amendment. American Association of University Women, journal, v. 45 (May 1952), 210-13.
1286. BRESSETTE, L. E. Perils of equal rights measures cited. Catholic action, v. 26 (August 1944), 8+.
1287. BREWER, F. M. Equal Rights Amendment. Editorial research reports (4 April 1946), 219-36.
1288. BROPHY, M. L. An Equal Rights Amendment: would it benefit women; takes the position that such an amendment is unnecessary and might seriously endanger modern social legislation intended to protect women from exploitation. American Bar Association journal, v. 38 (May 1952), 393-5.
1289. BROWN, H. E. Woman lawyer defends proposed Equal Rights Amendment. American Bar Association journal, v. 26 (April 1940), 356-8.
1290. BROWN, M. A. Equal Rights Amendment. American Association of University Women, journal, v. 47 (October 1953), 20-7.
1291. CAMPAIGN headquarters opened: to work for the Equal Rights Amendment. Independent woman, v. 26 (April 1947), 112.
1292. CATHOLIC leaders register opposition to Equal Rights Amendment. Catholic action, v. 20 (March 1938), 4-5.
1293. CONGRESS and the Equal Rights Amendment. Congressional digest, v. 50 (January 1971), 1-32.
1294. CONNELLY, M. M. Equal Rights Amendment. Women lawyers journal, v. 41 (Fall 1955), 18.
1295. CRABLE, E. C. Pros and cons of the Equal Rights Amendment. Women lawyers journal, v. 35 (Summer 1949), 7-9.
1296. CRAMER, J. S. Should women support the Equal Rights Amendment? Independent woman, v. 14 (May 1935), 148-9.
1297. DICKINSON, Mrs. L. Position on Equal Rights Amendment. Congressional digest, v. 25 (December 1946), 304+.
1298. DOCK, L. L. Lucretia Mott Amendment. Public health nurse, v. 16 (March 1924), 135-6. Reply by Florence Kelley: v. 16 (April 1924), 191-2.
1299. DORSEN, Norman and Susan Deller Ross. The necessity of a constitutional amendment. Harvard civil rights-

civil liberties law review, v. 6 (March 1971), 216-24.
1300. EMERSON, Thomas I. In support of the Equal Rights Amend-
       ment. Harvard civil rights-civil liberties law review,
       v. 6 (March 1971), 225-33.
1301. EQUAL Rights Amendment. Ave maria, v. 65 (1 February
       1947), 133.
1302. EQUAL Rights Amendment. National Education Association,
       journal, v. 33 (October 1944), 168.
1303. EQUAL Rights Amendment. Sign, v. 23 (February 1944),
       388.
1304. EQUAL Rights Amendment. Social justice review, v. 37
       (March 1945), 383-4.
1305. EQUAL Rights Amendment and the woman worker. Catholic
       action, v. 25 (February 1943), 18.
1306. The EQUAL Rights Amendment: equal rights movement in
       American history; progress of equal rights in foreign
       countries; legal discriminations against women exist-
       ing today in the United States; a summary of special
       labor laws for women in the United States; pending
       Equal Rights Amendment to the U.S. Constitution;
       Equal Rights Amendment discussed pro and con. Con-
       gressional digest, v. 3 (March 1924), 192-207.
1307. The EQUAL Rights Amendment: is it the next step to wom-
       en's freedom? American Association of University
       Women, journal, v. 47 (October 1953), 20-7. Argu-
       ments for and against.
1308. EQUAL Rights Amendment; opposition by labor and women's
       groups. Social service review, v. 19 (March 1945),
       111-13.
1309. EQUAL Rights Amendment: pro: a step toward freedom, by
       Katharine St. George; con: action by states, a better
       solution, by R. B. Bosone. American Association of
       University Women, journal, v. 45 (May 1952), 210-13.
1310. EQUAL Rights Amendment, pro and con. Congressional di-
       gest, v. 22 (April 1943), 99-128.
1311. The EQUAL Rights Amendment revised: have recent develop-
       ments removed the grounds for opposition? American
       Association of University Women, journal, v. 37 (Octo-
       ber 1943), 10-14.
1312. EQUAL rights and democracy: proposed Equal Rights Amend-
       ment. Independent woman, v. 23 (December 1944),
       387+.
1313. EQUAL rights bill wins House group approval. Commercial
       and financial chronicle, v. 162 (2 August 1945), 551.
1314. EQUAL rights for women. America, v. 70 (29 January
       1944), 463. Editorial opposed to the Equal Rights
       Amendment.
1315. EQUAL rights for women. America, v. 79 (15 May 1948),
       128. Editorial advocating H.R. 2007 (rather than the
       Equal Rights Amendment) which would take into ac-
       count physical, biological, and social differences.
1316. EQUAL rights for women? New republic, v. 94 (16 Febru-
       ary 1938), 34. Criticism of the Equal Rights Amend-
       ment.

1317. EQUAL rights for women. Senior scholastic, v. 56 (15
      February 1950), 10-11.
1318. EQUAL rights for women: A symposium on the proposed
      constitutional amendment. Harvard civil rights-civil
      liberties law review, v. 6 (March 1971), 215-87.
1319. EQUAL rights for women? pro and con discussion. Senior
      scholastic, v. 62 (6 May 1953), 7-8.
1320. EQUAL rights for women? Things may never be the same.
      U.S. news and world report, v. 69 (24 August 1970),
      29-30. Attempts by Representative Martha Griffiths
      to get the Equal Rights Amendment passed; and pos-
      sible effects of the proposed Amendment.
1321. EQUAL rights for women workers; a new push. U.S. news
      and world report, v. 69 (3 August 1970), 51-2. Legal
      action taken against various industries for alleged sex
      discriminations, by the Equal Employment Opportunity
      Commission.
1322. EQUAL rights NOW. Newsweek, v. 75 (2 March 1970), 75.
      On the National Organization for Women.
1323. EQUALITY of women. America, v. 109 (26 October 1963),
      473. View of the National Council of Catholic Women
      on the Equal Rights Amendment.
1324. FREUND, Paul A. The Equal Rights Amendment is not the
      way. Harvard civil rights-civil liberties law review,
      v. 6 (March 1971), 234-42.
1325. GREATHOUSE, Rebekah S. The effect of constitutional equal-
      ity on working women. American economic review,
      supplement (March 1944), 227-36. The Equal Rights
      Amendment and minimum wage.
1326. HARRISON, Gladys Amelia. Against "equal rights" by con-
      stitutional amendment. Washington, National League
      of Women Voters, 1928. 15p.
1327. HEARING on the Equal Rights Amendment. Independent wom-
      an, v. 17 (March 1938), 88-9.
1328. HELMES, Winifred. Equal rights, where do we stand?
      American Association of University Women, journal,
      v. 46 (March 1953), 165. The AAUW position on the
      Equal Rights Amendment.
1329. HORNADAY, M. Showdown on equal rights: amending the
      Constitution. Christian Science Monitor magazine, (9
      October 1943), 5.
1330. IRWIN, Inez Haynes. Equal Rights Amendment. Good house-
      keeping, v. 78 (March 1924), 18-19.
1331. JORDAN, Joan. Comment: working women and the Equal
      Rights Amendment. Trans-action, v. 8 (November
      1970), 16+ .
1332. KELLEY, Florence, comp. Twenty questions about the feder-
      al amendment proposed by the National Woman's Party.
      New York, National Consumers' League, 1922. 7p.
1333. KENTON, E. Ladies' next step; case for the Equal Rights
      Amendment. Harper's magazine, v. 152 (February
      1926), 366-74.
1334. KEYES, F. P. Equal rights bill. Good housekeeping. v. 76

(February 1923), 28-9.
1335. KITCHELT, Florence L. Equal Rights Amendment. Independent woman, v. 25 (April 1946), 122.
1336. _____. Equal Rights Amendment: with reply. New republic, v. 113 (17 December 1945), 840-1.
1337. KOONTZ, Elizabeth D. The Women's Bureau looks to the future. Monthly labor review, v. 93 (June 1970), 3-9. Concerns the Equal Rights Amendment, equal employment, and the Equal Employment Opportunity Commission.
1338. KUHNE, C. Equal Rights Amendment before new Congress. Independent woman, v. 34 (March 1955), 91+.
1339. KURLAND, Philip B. The Equal Rights Amendment: some problems of construction. Harvard civil rights-civil liberties law review, v. 6 (March 1971), 243-52.
1340. LADIES' day. Newsweek, v. 76 (24 August 1970), 15-16. On the passing of the Equal Rights Amendment by the House of Representatives, 350-15.
1341. LUTZ, Alma. Only one choice: Taft-Wadsworth legal status bill vs. Equal Rights Amendment. Independent woman, v. 26 (July 1947), 199+.
1342. _____. Why bar equality? Equal Rights Amendment. Christian Science Monitor magazine (22 July 1944), 3.
1343. MANNING, A. L. Congress upholds women's rights; subcommittees in Senate and House report favorably on Equal Rights Amendment. Independent woman, v. 20 (September 1941), 276.
1344. _____. We buckle on our armour and return to the fray; unfavorable vote by the House judiciary committee on the Equal Rights Amendment. Independent woman, v. 22 (November 1943), 338+.
1345. MORRISSY, Elizabeth. Face Equal Rights Amendment realistically. Catholic action, v. 27 (November 1945), 18.
1346. _____. The status of women; to be equal does not mean to be identical. Vital speeches, v. 15 (1 November 1948), 55-60.
1347. MURRAY, Pauli. The Negro woman's stake in the Equal Rights Amendment. Harvard civil rights-civil liberties law review, v. 6 (March 1971), 253-9.
1348. MURRELL, Ethel Ernest. Full citizenship for women: an Equal Rights Amendment. American Bar Association, journal, v. 38 (January 1952), 47-9.
1349. NATIONAL business woman, v. 36 (July 1957), 1-21+. Special issue on equal rights for women.
1350. NATIONAL Consumers' League. Blanket equality bill proposed by the National Woman's Party for state legislatures; why it should not pass. New York, The League, 1922. 8p.
1351. NATIONAL Council of Catholic Women protests passage of Equal Rights Amendment. Catholic action, v. 15 (July 1933), 30.
1352. NATIONAL Woman's Party. Equal Rights Amendment: questions and answers. By H. H. Weed. Washing-

ton, GPO, 1946. 20p.

1353. _____. Equal Rights Amendment. Questions and answers on the Equal Rights Amendment prepared by
the Research Department of the National Woman's
Party. Edited by Ethel E. Murrell. Washington,
GPO, 1951. 8p.

1354. _____. Equal Rights Amendment; questions and answers.
Edited by Margery C. Leonard. 4th ed. Washington, GPO, 1963. 30p.

1355. NATIONAL Woman's Party explains its proposal for an Equal
Rights Amendment. Congressional digest, v. 22
(April 1943), 102-4.

1356. NATIONAL Women's Trade Union League of America. Opposing the so-called Equal Rights Amendment. By
Blanch Freedman. Washington, The League, 1943.
12p.

1357. NEW victory in an old crusade. Time, v. 96 (24 August
1970), 10-12.

1358. NEWMAN, P. M. Equal Rights Amendment. American
federationist, v. 45 (August 1938), 815-17.

1359. NEXT step in the emancipation of women--an Equal Rights
Amendment? American Association of University
Women, journal, v. 31 (April 1938), 160-4.

1360. OPPOSITION to the proposed Equal Rights Amendment.
Congressional digest, v. 22 (April 1943), 125-6.

1361. PALMER, H. Here we stand, we can do no other; Equal
Rights Amendment. Independent woman, v. 32 (December 1953), 433-4+.

1362. PORTNOW, Billie. What's wrong with the Equal Rights
Amendment? Jewish currents, v. 25 (July/August
1971), 4-9.

1363. POWER of a woman; the Equal Rights Amendment. Ladies'
home journal, v. 87 (August 1970), 50.

1364. PROPOSED constitutional amendment to grant women equal
rights is favorably reported by subcommittees of
Senate and House judiciary committees. Commercial
and financial chronicle, v. 144 (26 June 1937), 4263.

1365. PROPOSED Equal Rights Amendment to the U.S. Constitution: fact material, and pro and con discussion.
Congressional digest, v. 22 (April 1943), 99-128.

1366. PULLER, Edwin S. When equal rights are unequal. Virginia law review, v. 13 (June 1927), 619-30. The
National Woman's Party's efforts to promote the
Equal Rights Amendment and problems it has encountered.

1367. REASONS for opposing the proposed Equal Rights Amendment. American Association of University Women,
journal, v. 32 (April 1939), 153-7. Excerpts from
hearings in Congress (February 7-10, 1938) from
persons opposed to the Amendment, a position then
adopted by the AAUW.

1368. REED, G. E. Equal Rights Amendment. Catholic mind,
v. 44 (January 1946), 6-8.

1369. RIGHTS for women. Newsweek, v. 28 (29 July 1946), 17.
1370. SACHAR, Libby E. and Joyce Capps. A brief in favor of
       an Equal Rights Amendment. Prepared for the Civil
       and Political Rights Committee of the President's
       Commission on the Status of Women, presented by the
       National Federation of Business and Professional Wom-
       en's Clubs, Inc., April, 1963. n.p., n.d. 103p.
1371. SANDLER, Bernice. The equal rights for women amend-
       ment. Statement of Dr. Bernice Sandler before the
       Senate Judiciary Committee, Subcommittee on Con-
       stitutional Amendments, May 6, 1970. Pittsburgh,
       Know, Inc., 1970. 17p.
1372. SENATE scuttles full partnership; Equal Rights Amendment.
       Independent woman, v. 32 (August 1953), 300.
1373. SEX discrimination and equal protection: Do we need a con-
       stitutional amendment? Harvard law review, v. 84
       (April 1971), 1499-1524.
1374. SHALL women be equal before the law? Yes! by Elsie
       Hill. No! by Florence Kelley. Nation, v. 114 (12
       April 1922), 419-21.
1375. SHERRILL, R. That Equal Rights Amendment; what, exactly,
       does it mean? New York Times magazine (20 Septem-
       ber 1970), 25-7+.
1376. SISTERS of Abigail Adams. Time, v. 55 (6 February 1950),
       12-13. Discussion of those in favor of the Amend-
       ment (Alice Paul, The General Federation of Women's
       Clubs, The American Medical Women's Association,
       etc.) and those opposed (The National League of Wom-
       en Voters, The American Association of University
       Women, etc.).
1377. SMITH, Ethel M. Equal rights and equal rights; what is
       wrong with the Woman's Party amendment? Chicago,
       National Women's Trade Union League of America
       [1925?]. 8p.
1378. _____. Toward equal rights for men and women. Wash-
       ington, National League of Women Voters, 1929. 139p.
1379. SNIPING at the Equal Rights Amendment: introduction of
       H.R. 1972, calling for establishment of a commission
       on legal status of women. Independent woman, v. 26
       (March 1947), 88.
1380. STATEMENT of The Feminists on the Equal Rights Amend-
       ment: for the hearings on the Equal Rights Amend-
       ment before the Senate Judiciary Committee, Septem-
       ber 9, 10, 11, 15, 1970. New York, The Feminists,
       1970. 3p.
1381. STEVENS, Doris and Alice Hamilton. Blanket amendment;
       debate. Forum, v. 72 (August 1924), 145-60.
1382. TEMPLE, M. L. Is your representative among those
       present? Equal Rights Amendment. Independent
       woman, v. 33 (June 1954), 223-4+.
1383. _____. Pyrrhic victory; Equal Rights Amendment. In-
       dependent woman, v. 32 (September 1953), 327-8.
1384. _____. What do our congressmen think about the Equal

Rights Amendment? Independent woman, v. 32
(April 1953), 127-8+.

1385. U.S. Congress. Senate. Committee on the Judiciary.
Equal rights for men and women. Hearing before a
subcommittee of the Committee on the Judiciary, U.S.
Senate, 73d Congress, 1st session, on S.J. Res. 1,
a joint resolution proposing an amendment to the Constitution of the United States relative to equal rights
for men and women. May 27, 1933. Washington,
GPO, 1933. 32p.

1386. _____. _____. _____. _____. Equal rights
for men and women. Hearings before a subcommittee
of the Committee on the Judiciary, U.S. Senate, 75th
Congress, 3d session, on S.J. Res. 65, a joint resolution proposing an amendment to the Constitution of
the United States relative to equal rights for men and
women. Washington, GPO, 1938. 2v.

1387. _____. _____. _____. _____. Equal rights.
Hearings before a subcommittee of the Committee on
the Judiciary, U.S. Senate, 84th Congress, 2d session, on S.J. Res. 39, proposing an amendment to
the Constitution of the United States relative to equal
rights for men and women. April 11 and 13, 1956.
Washington, GPO, 1956. 79p.

1388. _____. _____. _____. _____. The "equal
rights" amendment. Hearings, 91st Congress, 2d
session, on S.J. Res. 61, proposing an amendment
to the Constitution of the United States relative to
equal rights for men and women. May 5, 6, and 7,
1970. Washington, GPO, 1970. 793p.

1389. VAN DEN HAAG, Ernest. Women; how equal? National review, v. 22 (8 September 1970), 945+.

1390. WOMEN lawyers journal, v. 57 (Winter 1971), special issue
on the Amendment.

1391. WOMEN'S rights; Senate approves Equal Rights Amendment.
Senior scholastic, v. 56 (8 February 1950), 12.

1392. ABBOTT, Edith. Woman voter and the spoils system in
       Chicago. National municipal review, v. 5 (July 1916),
       460-5.
1393. ABBOTT, Frances M. Comparative view of the woman suf-
       frage movement. North American review, v. 166
       (February 1898), 142-51.
1394. ABBOTT, Lyman. Advance of women. World's work, v. 8
       (1904), 5033.
1395. _____. Answer to the arguments in support of woman
       suffrage. American Academy of Political and Social
       Science, v. 35 (May 1910), 28-32.
1396. _____. Assault on womanhood. Outlook, v. 91 (3 April
       1909), 784-8.
1397. _____. Why the vote would be injurious to women. La-
       dies' home journal, v. 27 (February 1910), 21-2.
1398. _____. Why women do not wish the suffrage. Atlantic
       monthly, v. 92 (September 1903), 289-96. Primarily
       because women feared a change in the structure of
       society (home, church, etc.), a change they were op-
       posed to.
1399. _____. Women's rights. Outlook, v. 100 (10 February
       1912), 302-4.
1400. ABBOTT, Virginia C. The history of woman suffrage and
       The League of Women Voters in Cuyahoga County,
       1911-1945. Cleveland, League of Women Voters of
       Cuyahoga County, 1949. 178p.
1401. ACKERMANN, Jessie. What women have done with the vote.
       New York, W. B. Feakins, 1913. 86p.
1402. ADAMS, Mildred. The right to be people. Philadelphia,
       Lippincott, 1966. 248p.
1403. ADDAMS, Jane. Aspects of the woman's movement. Sur-
       vey, v. 64 (1 August 1930), 384-7+.
1404. _____. The modern city and the municipal franchise for
       women. New York, National American Woman Suf-
       frage Association, n. d. 15p.
1405. _____. Votes for women and other votes. Survey, v. 28
       (1 June 1912), 367-8. Concerning the fact that wom-
       en without the vote are much worse off than any dis-
       franchised men could be since so many of life's im-
       portant activities take place beyond the immediate
       family to which women are confined.
1406. _____. Why women should vote. New York, National
       American Woman Suffrage Association, 1912. 20p.
       The necessity of women to extend their interests out-

side the home if the preservation of the home is to be continued.

1407. _____. Women, war and suffrage. Survey, v. 35 (6 November 1915), 148+. A plea for women to organize after the war.

1408. ADVANTAGES of equal suffrage, by Andreas Ueland and Josephine Schain; Disadvantages of equal suffrage, by L. C. Gilfillan and Mrs. E. L. Carpenter. Minnesota Academy of Social Sciences, papers and proceedings (1915), 142-98.

1409. ADVISORY Committee Opposed to Woman Suffrage. The Virginia General Assembly and Womans' suffrage. Respectfully submitted by the Advisory Committee Opposed to Woman Suffrage.... [Richmond, Va., 1919?] 12p.

1410. AIRING the argument for woman's suffrage. Current literature, v. 46 (April 1909), 367-74.

1411. ALDERSON, Mary L. Women suffrage in Montana, 1904. A half century of progress for Montana women. n.p., 1935.

1412. ALGEO, Sara M. MacCormack. The story of a sub-pioneer. Providence, R.I., Snow & Farnham, 1925. 318p. Primarily the suffrage movement in Rhode Island.

1413. ALLEN, Florence E. and Mary Welles. The Ohio woman suffrage movement. "A certain unalienable right." What Ohio women did to secure it. n.p., Committee for the Preservation of Ohio Woman Suffrage Records, 1952. 55p.

1414. ALLEN, J. C. The South and suffrage. New republic, v. 13 (5 January 1918), 282-3.

1415. ALLEN, William Harvey. Woman's part in government, whether she votes or not. New York, Dodd, Mead, 1911. 377p.

1416. ALMA-TADEMA, L. Suffrage danger. Living age, v. 274 (10 August 1912), 330-5.

1417. AMERICAN Academy of Political and Social Science, Philadelphia. Significance of the woman suffrage movement. Philadelphia, The Academy, 1910. 37p.

1418. _____. Women in public life. Edited by James P. Lichtenberger. Philadelphia, The Academy, 1914. 194p. Partial contents: Economic basis of feminism; Social legislation; Education of women; Suffrage in Pennsylvania and other areas.

1419. AMERICAN Equal Rights Association. Proceedings of the first anniversary of the American Equal Rights Association, held at the Church of the Puritans, New York, May 9 and 10, 1867. New York, R. J. Johnston, printer, 1867. 80p.

1420. AMERICAN Woman Suffrage Association. Constitution of the American Woman Suffrage Association and the history of its formation with the times and places in which the Association has held meetings up to 1880. Boston, Press of George H. Ellis, 1881. 8p.

1421. _____. Woman suffrage in Wyoming. (Boston, 188?) 2p.
1422. AMERICAN woman voter arrives. Literary digest, v. 66
        (28 August 1920), 9-11.
1423. AMERICAN women in the long fight for the vote. Literary
        digest, v. 66 (4 September 1920), 52-4.
1424. AMES, K. Woman suffrage in California. Overland, v. 51
        (June 1908), 513-14.
1425. ANALYSIS of the House vote: House vote state by state.
        Woman citizen, v. 3 (31 May 1919), 1152, 1156-7.
1426. ANNUAL invasion of Congress by the woman suffragists.
        Current opinion, v. 56 (January 1914), 9-11.
1427. ANOTHER example of the unfavorable press encountered by
        the early exponents of suffrage for women. Kansas
        historical quarterly, v. 18 (May 1950), 208-9. Re-
        port from the Topeka Weekly Leader, 12 September
        1862, on speeches by Elizabeth Cady Stanton and
        Susan B. Anthony.
1428. ANTHONY, Susan B. Fifty years of work for women. In-
        dependent, v. 52 (15 February 1900), 414-17.
1429. _____. Status of women, past, present, and future.
        Arena, v. 17 (May 1897), 901-8.
1430. _____. Woman's half-century of evolution. North Ameri-
        can review, v. 175 (December 1902), 800-10. The
        improvement of women's status from 1848 to 1902.
1431. ANTI-SUFFRAGE essays by Massachusetts women. Boston,
        J. A. Haien, 1916. 152p. Partial contents: Woman
        suffrage a menace to social reform; True function of
        the normal woman; Woman suffrage versus woman-
        liness; also includes a brief chapter (the introduction)
        on the anti-suffrage victory in Massachusetts in 1915.
1432. An APPEAL against anarchy of sex to the constitutional con-
        vention and the people of the state of New York, by a
        member of the press.... New York, J. A. Gray &
        Green, printers, 1867. 21p.
1433. ARGUMENT against woman suffrage. Independent, v. 75
        (7 August 1913), 301-2.
1434. ARTHUR, J. Suffrage for women in Washington territory.
        American magazine, v. 16 (1888), 347.
1435. AULT, Nelson Allen. The earnest ladies: The Walla Walla
        Woman's Club and the Equal Suffrage League of 1886-
        1889. Pacific Northwest quarterly, v. 42 (1951), 123-
        37.
1436. AUSTIN, Mary Hunter and Anne Martin. Suffrage and gov-
        ernment; the modern idea of government by consent
        and woman's place in it, with special reference to
        Nevada and other western states. New York, Na-
        tional American Woman Suffrage Association, 1914.
        14p.
1437. BABCOCK, E. S. Melancholia and the silent woman. Out-
        look, v. 93 (18 December 1909), 868-74.
1438. BAILEY, C. H. How Washington women regained the ballot.
        Pacific monthly, v. 26 (July 1911), 1-11.
1439. BAILY, Muriel. Women's suffrage in the Americas. Pan

American Union bulletin, v. 52 (January 1921), 35-47.
A brief history of the movement in the United States.

1440. BAKER, Abby Scott. The Woman's Party. Outlook, v. 113
(23 August 1916), 1002-4.

1441. BARNES, E. Suffrage in Idaho. Twentieth century magazine, v. 6 (September 1912), 441-8.

1442. BASSETT, T. D. The 1870 campaign for woman suffrage in
Vermont. Vermont quarterly, v. 14 (April 1946), 47-
61.

1443. BEARD, Charles A. Woman suffrage and strategy. New republic, v. 1 (12 December 1914), 22-3.

1444. _____. The Woman's Party. New republic, v. 7 (29
July 1916), 329-31.

1445. BEARD, Mary Ritter. Amending state constitutions: a study
of state constitutions which lack suffrage amendments.
Chicago, National Office of the Socialist Party, 1916.
3p.

1446. _____. Legislative influence of unenfranchised women.
American Academy of Political and Social Science, annals, v. 56 (November 1914), 54-61.

1447. BEECHER, Catharine Esther. Woman suffrage and woman's
professions. Hartford, Conn., Brown & Gross, 1871.
210p. In opposition to woman suffrage because of the
division of labor between man and wife; but an advocate of education for women.

1448. _____. Woman's profession as mother and educator, with
views in opposition to woman suffrage. Philadelphia,
G. Maclean, 1872. 223p.

1449. BEECHER, Henry Ward. Woman's duty to vote. Speech by
Henry Ward Beecher, at the eleventh National Woman's
Rights Convention, held in New York, May 10, 1866.
New York, American Equal Rights Association, 1867.
31p.

1450. _____. Woman's influence in politics: an address delivered by Henry Ward Beecher, at the Cooper Institute, New York, February 2, 1860. Boston, R. F.
Wallcut, 1860. 18p.

1451. BELL, Alden. Shall the ballot be given to women? Gunton's
magazine, v. 17 (December 1899), 474-84. Suffrage
in Virginia.

1452. BELMONT, Mrs. Oliver Hazard Perry. American suffragist
on the defensive. Review of reviews, v. 41 (January
1910), 100-1.

1453. _____. How can women get the suffrage? Independent,
v. 68 (31 March 1910), 686-9.

1454. _____. Liberation of a sex. Hearst's magazine, v. 23
(April 1913), 614-16.

1455. _____. Why I am a suffragist. World to-day, v. 21
(October 1911), 1171-8.

1456. _____. Woman suffrage as it looks today. Forum, v.
43 (March 1910), 264-8.

1457. _____. Woman's right to govern herself. North American review, v. 190 (November 1909), 664-74. On

suffrage and anti-suffrage.
1458. BENNETT, E. L. Federal amendment chimera. New re-
       public, v. 8 (26 August 1916), 94-5.
1459. BENSON, A. L. Mrs. Oliver Hazard Perry Belmont's
       views on suffrage. Pearson's magazine, v. 22 (Octo-
       ber 1909), 530-7.
1460. BERNBAUM, Ernst. Anti-suffrage essays by Massachusetts
       women. n.p., 1916.
1461. BJORKMAN, Frances Maule. The blue book: woman suf-
       frage, history, arguments and results. Rev. ed.
       New York, National Woman Suffrage Publishing Co.,
       1917. 244p.
1462. _____. Where women vote. New York, National Ameri-
       can Woman Suffrage Association, 1912. 39p. Facts
       about woman suffrage in each suffrage country or state.
1463. _____. Why women want to vote. New York, National
       American Woman Suffrage Association, 1912. 12p.
       The absence of suffrage hampers women's efficiency
       as a housekeeper.
1464. _____. Woman suffrage and the liquor interests. New
       York, National Woman Suffrage Pub. Co., [19--?].
1465. BLACKWELL, Alice Stone. Do interests conflict? Woman
       citizen, v. 3 (19 October 1918), 416.
1466. _____. Equal suffrage: why? Arbitrator, v. 1 (Decem-
       ber 1918), 3-6.
1467. _____. Federal route. Woman citizen, v. 3 (12 October
       1918), 396.
1468. _____. An object lesson. Independent, v. 61 (26 July
       1906), 198-9. Anti-suffrage activities in Oregon on
       the part of wealthy women, railroads, and the liquor
       interests.
1469. _____. Objections answered. New York, National Ameri-
       can Woman Suffrage Association, n.d.
1470. _____. Women and the school vote. New York, National
       American Woman Suffrage Association, 1908. 7p.
       Statements from various school superintendents as to
       the value of women's vote in school elections.
1471. BLACKWELL, F. H. Electorate of men and women. North
       American review, v. 195 (June 1912), 803-19.
1472. BLACKWELL, Henry Brown. Objections to woman suffrage
       answered. Boston, American Woman Suffrage Associa-
       tion, 1888. 2p.
1473. _____. Woman suffrage problems considered. Forum,
       v. 3 (April 1887), 131-41.
1474. BLAIR, Emily Newell. What women may do with the ballot.
       An address by Mrs. Emily Newell Blair...before the
       Democratic Women's Luncheon Club of Philadelphia,
       August 28, 1922. [Philadelphia, 1922?] 21p.
1475. BOCK, Annie. Woman suffrage. Address opposing an
       amendment to the Constitution of the United States
       extending the right of suffrage to woman, written for
       presentation to the Committee on woman suffrage,
       United States Senate. Washington, GPO, 1913. 10p.

1476. BORAH, W. E. Why I am for suffrage for women. Delineator, v. 76 (August 1910), 85.
1477. BOWDITCH, William Ingersoll. Taxation of women in Massachusetts. Cambridge, J. Wilson, 1875. 62p. The
idea that if women are to be taxed, they should have
the right to vote.
1478. _____. Woman suffrage a right, not a privilege. Cambridge, Mass., University Press, 1879. 52p. Restriction of suffrage to men is contrary to the theory
of the American Constitution.
1479. BOWNE, Borden Parker. A man's view of woman suffrage.
Boston, n.p., [189?] 8p.
1480. _____. Woman and democracy. North American review,
v. 191 (April 1910), 527-36.
1481. BOYD, Mary Sumner. State constitutional obstructions. New
York, National Woman Suffrage Pub. Co., 1917. 12p.
1482. _____. The woman citizen; a general handbook of civics,
with special consideration of women's citizenship.
New York, Stokes, 1918. 260p.
1483. BOYER, R. P. Oklahoma's victory; Michigan's sweeping
triumph. Woman citizen, v. 3 (30 November 1918),
545, 547.
1484. BRADFORD, M. C. Equal suffrage victory in Colorado.
Outlook, v. 48 (23 December 1893), 1205-6.
1485. BRASHERE, Ora M. Science and suffrage; an inquiry into
the causes of sex differences.... [Salt Lake City?]
n.p., 1909. 15p.
1486. BRAY, W. E. Do women want the vote? Atlantic monthly,
v. 117 (April 1916), 433-41. A survey.
1487. A BRIEF history of the Rhode Island Woman Suffrage Association, during the 24 years, from 1868 to 1893. Providence, E. L. Freeman, 1893. 20p.
1488. BRIEF on woman suffrage: political suffrage for women sub-
versive to American ideals. New York, Man Suffrage
Association, 1915. 17p. States reasons why suffrage
should not be given to New York women.
1489. BROCKETT, Linus Pierpont. Woman: her rights, wrongs,
privileges, and responsibilities. Containing a sketch
of her condition in all ages and countries, from her
creation and fall in Eden to the present time: her
present legal status in England, France, and the United
States...and woman suffrage; its folly. Hartford,
Conn., L. Stebbins, 1869. 447p. Reprinted by Books
for Libraries Press, Freeport, New York, 1970.
1490. BROWN, D. Where votes for women came from. Catholic
digest, v. 23 (March 1959), 56-60.
1491. BROWN, Dee Alexander. The gentle tamers; women of the
old wild west. Lincoln, University of Nebraska Press,
1968. 317p. Part of which concerns the suffrage
movement in the West.
1492. BROWN, G. Stewart. Is the nineteenth amendment legal?
Review of reviews, v. 4 (19 January 1921), 54-5.
1493. _____. The nineteenth amendment. Virginia law review,

v. 8 (February 1922), 237-45.

1494. BROWN, Joseph Granville. History of equal suffrage in Colorado, 1868-1898. Denver, News Job Printing Co., 1898. 59p.

1495. BROWN, L. A. Suffrage and prohibition. North American review, v. 203 (January 1916), 93-100.

1496. BRYAN, W. J. Strong appeal to Christian conscience in behalf of prohibition and woman suffrage. Union signal, v. 43 (13 December 1917), 5-7+.

1497. BUCKLEY, James Monroe. The wrong and peril of woman suffrage. New York, Revell, 1909. 128p.

1498. BURNHAM, Carrie S. Suffrage--the citizen's birthright. An address delivered before the Constitutional convention of Pennsylvania, January 16, 1873.... Philadelphia, Cooperative Printing Co., 1873. 11p.

1499. _____. Woman suffrage. The argument of Carrie S. Burnham before Chief Justice Reed, and Associate Justices Agnew, Sharswood and Mercur, of the Supreme Court of Pennsylvania, in banc, on the 3d and 4th of April, 1873. With an appendix containing the opinion of Hon. George Sharswood and a complete history of the case. Philadelphia, Citizen's Suffrage Association, 1873. 112p.

1500. BUSHNELL, Horace. Women's suffrage; the reform against nature. New York, C. Scribner, 1869. 184p. Reprinted by Greenwood Press, Westport, Conn., 1971.

1501. BUTLER, Sarah Schuyler. Women as citizens. Review of reviews, v. 69 (June 1924), 642-5. The question of whether woman suffrage will be a success.

1502. CAIRNES, J. E. Woman suffrage:--a reply. Macmillan's magazine, v. 30 (September 1874), 377-88.

1503. CALDWELL, Martha B. The woman suffrage campaign of 1912. Kansas historical quarterly, v. 12 (August 1943), 300-18.

1504. CALIFORNIA. University. University Extension Division. Woman Suffrage. Berkeley, University of California, 1915. 15p.

1505. CARTER, Marion Hamilton. The woman with empty hands; the evolution of a suffragette.... New York, Dodd, Mead, 1913. 76p.

1506. CATHOLIC view of woman suffrage. Literary digest, v. 44 (8 June 1912), 1211-12.

1507. CATT, Carrie Chapman. Address to the Congress of the United States. New York, National Woman Suffrage Pub. Co., 1917. 26p.

1508. _____, comp. Ballot and the bullet. New York, National American Woman Suffrage Association, 1897. 73p.

1509. _____. A bit of history. New York, Interurban Woman Suffrage Council, 1908. 3p. Criticism of the New York State Legislature for not submitting the woman suffrage amendment to the voters.

1510. _____. Cave man complex vs. woman suffrage. Woman citizen, v. 8 (5 April 1924), 16-17.

1511. _____. How to work for suffrage in an election district
or voting precinct. New York, National Woman Suffrage Pub. Co., 1917. 12p.

1512. _____. Perhaps. Warren, Ohio, National American
Woman Suffrage Association [1910?]. 16p.

1513. _____. Ready for citizenship. Public, v. 20 (24 August
1917), 818+.

1514. _____. What women have done with the vote. Independent,
v. 115 (17 October 1925), 447-8.

1515. _____. Why the federal amendment? New York, National
Woman Suffrage Pub. Co., 1917. 12p.

1516. _____. Will of the people. Forum, v. 43 (June 1910),
595-602.

1517. _____. Woman suffrage and its basic argument. New
York, Interurban Woman Suffrage Council, 1907. 8p.
The basic argument being that "taxation without representation is tyranny" and "Governments derive their
just powers from the consent of the governed."

1518. _____. Woman suffrage and the home. New York, Interurban Woman Suffrage Council, 1907. 8p.

1519. _____. Woman suffrage by federal constitutional amendment. New York, National Woman Suffrage Pub. Co.,
1917. 100p. Reasons why an amendment to the Constitution is the best method for obtaining the vote.

1520. _____. Woman suffrage movement. Public, v. 17 (12
June 1914), 568-70.

1521. _____. Woman suffrage only an episode in age-old movement. Current history, v. 27 (October 1927), 1-6.

1522. _____, ed. Woman's century calender. New York, National American Woman Suffrage Association, 1899.
81p.

1523. _____. Women voters at the crossroads. Public, v. 22
(31 May 1919), 569-70.

1524. _____. World politics and women voters. Woman's
home companion, v. 47 (November 1920), 4.

1525. _____ and Nettie R. Shuler. Woman suffrage and politics:
the inner story of the woman suffrage movement.
Seattle, University of Washington Press, c.1926, 1969.
504p.

1526. CHACE, Elizabeth Buffum and Lucy Buffum Lovell. Two
Quaker sisters. New York, Liverite, 1937. From
their diaries; concerning the woman suffrage movement in Rhode Island and of education in the early
19th century.

1527. CHAPMAN, C. H. Right of woman to the ballot. Arena,
v. 16 (September 1896), 570-80.

1528. CHITTENDEN, Alice Hill. The counter influence to woman
suffrage. Independent, v. 67 (29 July 1909), 246-9.
Problems of the suffrage movement, especially in
Oregon, due to open anti-suffrage activities.

1529. CHURCH of Jesus Christ of Latter Day Saints. "Mormon"
women's protest. An appeal for freedom, justice and
equal rights. The ladies of the Church of Jesus Christ

of Latter Day Saints protest against the tyranny and indecency of federal officials in Utah, and against their own disfranchisement without cause. Full account of proceedings at the great mass meeting, held in the theatre, Salt Lake City, Utah, Saturday, March 6, 1886. Salt Lake City, Deseret News Co., Printers, 1886. 91p.

1530. CLARK, C. W. Suffrage for women; pro and con. Atlantic monthly, v. 65 (1890), 310.

1531. CLARK, James I. Wisconsin women fight for suffrage. Madison, State Historical Society of Wisconsin, 1956. 20p.

1532. CLARK, Walter, 1846-1924. Ballots for both; an address at Greenville, North Carolina, 8 December 1916. Raleigh, Commercial Printing Co., n.d. 16p.

1533. _____. Equal suffrage; address before the Equal Suffrage League, Greensboro, North Carolina, 22 February 1915. n.p., n.d. 8p.

1534. _____. Legal status of women in North Carolina...address before the Federation of Women's Clubs, New Bern, North Carolina, 8 May 1913. n.p., n.d. 24p.

1535. CLARKE, Ida Clyde. Suffrage in the southern states; a brief history of the progress of the movement in fourteen states...Nashville, Tenn., Williams Printing Co., 1914.

1536. CLARKE, James F. Woman suffrage; reasons for and against. Boston, National American Woman Suffrage Association [1888?]. 4p.

1537. CLEMENS, Lois Gunden. Woman liberated. Scottsdale, Pa., Herald Press, 1971. 158p. Religious aspects of women's equality.

1538. CLEMENT, Cora. A woman's reasons why women should not vote. Boston, J. E. Farwell, printers, 1868. 16p.

1539. CLEVELAND, G. Would woman suffrage be unwise? Ladies' home journal, v. 22 (October 1905), 7-8.

1540. CLUBWOMEN for suffrage. Literary digest, v. 49 (4 July 1914), 4-5.

1541. COCKERELL, T. D. Votes for women. Dial, v. 51 (16 July 1911), 45-8.

1542. COLLEGE Equal Suffrage League of Northern California. Winning equal suffrage in California; reports of committees of the College Equal Suffrage League of Northern California in the campaign of 1911. San Francisco, The League, 1913. 139p.

1543. COMMITTEE of Women of Southern California. Woman suffrage. Washington, GPO, 1914. 22p.

1544. CONANT, W. C. Suffrage for women. Scribner's monthly, v. 3 (1872), 73, 209.

1545. CONNECTICUT. General Assembly. Joint Special Committee on Woman's Suffrage. Report of the Joint Special Committee of the Legislature of Connecticut on Woman Suffrage, May session, 1870. Hartford, Conn., Case,

Lockwood and Brainard, 1870. 19p. (Connecticut
Woman Suffrage Association. Tracts, no. 4.)

1546. CONSISTENT democracy. The elective franchise for women.
Twenty-five testimonies of prominent men, viz: ex-
Gov. Anthony of Rhode Island, Rev. Henry Ward
Beecher, Rev. William H. Channing, etc. Worcester,
T. W. Higginson, 1858. 4p.

1547. CONSTITUTIONAL provisions for the suffrage in Iowa. Iowa
journal of history and politics, v. 22 (April 1924),
163-216. pp. 212-16 are specific to the extension of
suffrage to women in Iowa.

1548. COOK, Tennessee Celeste Claflin. Constitutional equality a
right of woman; or, A consideration of the various
relations which she sustains as a necessary part of
the body of society and humanity; with her duties to
herself--together with a review of the Constitution
of the United States, showing that the right to vote is
guaranteed to all citizens. New York, Woodhull,
Claflin, 1871. 148p.

1549. COOKE, G. W. Social idealism and suffrage for woman.
Chautauquan, v. 58 (April 1910), 166-83.

1550. COOLEY, W. H. Future of women. Arena, v. 27 (1902),
373.

1551. _____. Suffragists and suffragettes; a record of actual
achievement. World to-day, v. 15 (October 1908),
1066-71.

1552. _____. Younger suffragists. Harper's weekly, v. 58
(27 September 1913), 7-8.

1553. COOLIDGE, M. R. Try-out of women voters. Harper's
weekly, v. 59 (10 October 1914), 355-6.

1554. COOLIDGE, Olivia E. Women's rights: the suffrage movement in America, 1848-1920. New York, Dutton,
1966. 189p.

1555. COOPER, S. F. Suffrage for women. Harper's magazine,
v. 41 (1870), 438.

1556. COPE, Edward Drinker. The relation of the sexes to government. New York, New York State Association
Opposed to Woman Suffrage [1888?]. 9p.

1557. CORBIN, Caroline Elizabeth F. Woman's rights in America,
a retrospect of sixty years, 1848-1908. n.p., Illinois Association Opposed to the Extension of Suffrage to Women, 1909. 12p.

1558. COREY, G. Utah. American Academy of Political and
Social Science, annals, v. 19 (January 1902), 145-7.

1559. COULTER, Thomas Chalmer. A history of woman suffrage
in Nebraska, 1856-1920. 212p. PhD thesis, Ohio
State University, 1967.

1560. CREEL, George. Measuring up equal suffrage. New York,
National American Woman Suffrage Association [1911?].
32p. Suffrage in Colorado.

1561. _____. What have women done with the vote? Century,
v. 87 (March 1914), 663-71.

1562. CREPAZ, Adele. Emancipation of women and its probable

consequences. New York, Scribner's Sons, 1893.
1563. CROLY, H. Obligation of the vote. New republic, v. 4
       (9 October 1915), 5-10.
1564. CRONYN, D. Suffrage for women. Radical, v. 3 (1868),
       382.
1565. CROTHERS, Samuel McChord. Meditations on votes for
       women, together with animadversions on the closely
       related subject of votes for men. Boston, Houghton
       Mifflin, 1914. 81p.
1566. CRUMBS for women. Independent, v. 71 (16 November 1911),
       1104-5.
1567. CURTIS, George William. Equal rights for women. Boston,
       American Woman Suffrage Association, 1867. 4p. A
       plea for woman suffrage in New York State.
1568. CUTLER, H. G. Why do women want the ballot? Forum,
       v. 43 (June 1915), 711-27.
1569. DAGGETT, M. P. New chapter in woman's program. Good
       housekeeping, v. 56 (February 1913), 148-55.
1570. _____. Suffrage enters the drawing-room. Delineator,
       v. 75 (January 1910), 37-8.
1571. _____. Wanted: women voters to vote. Good house-
       keeping, v. 79 (July 1924), 40-1.
1572. DAHLGREN, Madeline Vinton. Thoughts on female suffrage,
       and in vindication of woman's true rights. Washing-
       ton, Blanchard & Mohun, 1871. 22p. Anti-suffrage.
1573. DALLYING with suffrage. Public, v. 21 (12 October 1918),
       1281-2.
1574. DANENBAUM, R. College Equal Suffrage League. World
       to-day, v. 17 (October 1909), 1107-8.
1575. DAVIS, Paulina Wright. A history of the national woman's
       rights movement, for twenty years, with the proceedings
       of the decade meeting held at Apollo Hall, October 20,
       1870, from 1850 to 1870, with an appendix containing the
       history of the movement during the winter of 1871, in the
       national capitol. New York, Journeyman printers, 1871.
       Reprinted by Source Book Press, N. Y., 1970.
1576. DAVIS, Reda. California women; a guide to their politics,
       1885-1911. San Francisco, California Scene, 1967.
       201p. Includes biographical sketches of a number of
       California suffragists as well as a discussion of the
       suffrage movement in California.
1577. _____. Woman's republic. San Francisco, California
       Scene, 1969. The California suffrage movement.
1578. DAWSON, J. W. Woman suffrage. Catholic world, v. 112
       (November 1920), 145-56.
1579. DECKER, E. W. The legal status of woman: an address
       before the Woman Suffrage Convention at St. Louis,
       May 1869. St. Louis, Industrial Age Printing Co.,
       1872. 14p.
1580. DEERING, M. C. Women's demonstration; how they won
       and used the vote in California. Collier's, v. 48
       (6 January 1912), 17-18.
1581. DEFEAT of the federal amendment for woman suffrage in

the United States. Pan American magazine, v. 28
(December 1918), 112-14.
1582.   DEFEAT of woman suffrage in New Jersey. Independent,
v. 84 (1 November 1915), 168-9.
1583.   DELAND, Margaret. Change in the feminine ideal. Atlantic
monthly, v. 105 (March 1910), 297-301.
1584.   _____. Third way in woman suffrage. Ladies' home
journal, v. 30 (January 1913), 11-12.
1585.   DE LEON, Daniel. The ballot and the class struggle. New
York, New York Labor News Co., 1947. 48p. First
published in 1909 under the title "Woman suffrage."
1586.   DEMOCRACY advancing. Public, v. 21 (18 January 1918), 74-5.
1587.   DE VOU, Mary R. Woman suffrage movement in Delaware.
(In: Reed, Henry Clay, ed. Delaware; a history of
the first state. New York, Lewis Historical Pub. Co.,
1947. 3v. v. 1, pp. 349-70.)
1588.   DEXTER, Henry Martyn. Common sense as to woman suffrage. Boston, W. L. Greene, 1885. 33p.
1589.   DICEY, A. V. Arguments against woman suffrage. Living
age, v. 261 (10 April 1909), 67-84.
1590.   DO women wish to vote? Outlook, v. 94 (19 February 1910),
375-7.
1591.   DOANE, William Croswell. Some later aspects of woman
suffrage. North American review, v. 163 (November
1896), 537-48.
1592.   _____. Why women do not want the ballot. North American review, v. 161 (September 1895), 257-67. Reply:
Arena, v. 15 (March 1896), 642-53.
1593.   DODGE, Mrs. Arthur M. Woman suffrage opposed to woman's rights. American Academy of Political and
Social Science, annals, v. 56 (November 1914), 99-
104. An article by the president of the National Association Opposed to Woman Suffrage, New York.
1594.   DORR, Rheta Childe. The battle for woman suffrage.
Broadway magazine, v. 21 (July 1908), 1-11.
1595.   _____. Eternal question. Collier's, v. 66 (30 October
1920), 5-6.
1596.   _____. What eight million women want. Boston, Small,
Maynard, 1910. 330p. An argument for suffrage
based on a study of women's organizations. Reprinted
by Kraus Reprint, N. Y., 1972.
1597.   _____. What women have already achieved. Hampton's
magazine, v. 23 (October 1909), 545-54.
1598.   _____. Women did it in Colorado. Hampton's magazine,
v. 26 (April 1911), 426-38.
1599.   DOUGLASS, Frederick. [Two letters, edited by Joseph
Borome], Journal of Negro history, v. 33 (October
1948), 469-71. Two letters, dated, Rochester, September 27, 1868, and District of Columbia, January
17, 1893, concerning woman suffrage and Negro rights.
1600.   DUBOIS, W. E. Burghardt. Disfranchisement. New York,
National American Woman Suffrage Association, [191?]
10p. Refutation of arguments against suffrage.

1601. EASIER to amend one than forty-eight; Senator Shafroth ex-
       plains "a very serious obstacle." Woman citizen,
       v. 3 (31 August 1918), 267+.
1602. EASTERN suffrage campaigns. Review of reviews, v. 52
       (November 1915), 518-20.
1603. EASTMAN, Max. Is woman suffrage important? North
       American review, v. 193 (January 1911), 60-71.
1604. _____. Values of the vote. New York, Men's League
       for Woman Suffrage, 1912. 12p.
1605. _____. Woman's suffrage and sentiment. New York,
       Equal Franchise Society, 1909. 11p. An attack on
       anti-suffrage advocates.
1606. EASTWARD the tide of woman suffrage takes its way. Cur-
       rent opinion, v. 59 (November 1915), 297-9.
1607. ECKERT, F. W. Effects of woman's suffrage on the political
       situation in the city of Chicago. Political Science
       quarterly, v. 31 (March 1916), 105-21.
1608. EFFECT of the Nineteenth Amendment. Illinois law review,
       v. 23 (December 1928), 398-9.
1609. ELLARD, V. G. Effect of equal suffrage in Colorado. Lip-
       pincott's magazine, v. 64 (1899), 411.
1610. ELLIOTT, E. C. Let us therewith be content: indifference
       of women to suffrage. Popular science, v. 51 (July
       1897), 341-8.
1611. ELLIOTT, Sarah Barnwell. A study of the woman suffrage
       movement in America. New York, Equal Franchise
       Society, 1910. 44p.
1612. ELLIS, Mrs. H. Political militancy. Forum, v. 49 (April
       1913), 385-400.
1613. EMERSON, Ralph Waldo. A reasonable reform. New York,
       National American Woman Suffrage Association [1881?].
       4p. A refutation of the objections that if women are
       able to vote, they will become politically contaminated
       and unsexed.
1614. EMINENT opinions on woman suffrage. New York, National
       American Woman Suffrage Association [19--?]. 55p.
       Short opinions by 141 suffrage advocates.
1615. EQUAL Suffrage League of Virginia. Virginia state laws
       concerning women. Richmond, Whittet & Shepperson
       [1910?]. 16p.
1616. EQUAL suffrage tide. Chautauquan, v. 67 (June 1912), 13-
       14.
1617. ERBE, Carl H. Constitutional provisions for the suffrage in
       Iowa. Iowa journal, v. 22 (April 1924), 163-216.
1618. EXPANSION of equality. Independent, v. 73 (14 November
       1912), 1143-5.
1619. EXPERIENCES of woman's suffrage. Independent, v. 66
       (20 May 1909), 1091-2.
1620. EXTENSION of woman suffrage. Outlook, v. 116 (2 May
       1917), 10-11.
1621. FAIRCHILD, James Harris. Woman's right to the ballot.
       Oberlin, G. H. Fairchild, 1870. 67p.
1622. FAMED biologist's warning of the peril in votes for women.

Current literature, v. 53 (July 1912), 59-62.
1623. FERRIN, Mary Upton. Woman's defense: a reply to Horace
       Greeley's lecture, recently delivered in Providence,
       R.I. Peabody, Mass., Printed by C. D. Howard,
       1869. 16p.
1624. FIELD, Sara Bard. Nevada's fight for woman suffrage.
       Out West, n.s., v. 8 (August 1914), 51-76.
1625. FIELDING, W. J. President will endorse the federal suf-
       frage amendment: when? Call magazine, (2 Decem-
       ber 1917), 3.
1626. FINCH, Jessica Garretson. How the ballot would help the
       working woman. New York, Equal Franchise Society,
       1909. 3p. The need of the vote to keep legislators
       honest.
1627. FINCK, Henry T. Woman's glorious opportunities. Inde-
       pendent, v. 53 (30 May 1901), 1238-42. Activities
       women could take up rather than seeking the vote.
1628. FIRST and last suffrage maps of United States: 1869 and
       1917. Woman citizen, v. 1 (22 September 1917), 317.
1629. FISHER, M. J. Mid-nineteenth century attitudes against
       women suffrage. Social studies [Philadelphia], v. 44
       (May 1953), 184-7. Covers the period 1848 to 1854.
1630. FITCH, Charles Howard. The light under the bushel: wom-
       anhood suffrage.... Denver, Col., Coleman & Haigh
       print., 1888. 12p.
1631. FLEXNER, Simon. The biological argument against women
       suffrage. New York, National American Woman Suf-
       frage Association, 1914. 14p. Refutation of argu-
       ments against women based on biological differences
       with men.
1632. FOR the federal suffrage amendment. Woman citizen, v. 2
       (2 February 1918), 193, 196.
1633. FORSYTH, A. Campaigning for the vote: touring Connecticut
       for suffrage. Collier's, v. 50 (28 September 1912),
       20-1; (5 October 1912), 16-17.
1634. FOWLER, Nathaniel Clark. The principle of suffrage. New
       York, Sully and Kleinteich, 1916. 59p.
1635. FOX, Karolena M. History of the equal suffrage movement
       in Michigan. Michigan history magazine, v. 2 (Janu-
       ary 1918), 90-109.
1636. FOXCROFT, F. Check to woman suffrage in the United
       States. Nineteenth century, v. 56 (November 1904),
       833-41.
1637. FRANKLIN, Christine Ladd. Intuition and reason. Monist,
       v. 3 (January 1893), 211-19. Case for suffrage based
       on the refutation of the thought that men's and women's
       minds are made differently, but rather that society has
       created two separate fields of interest for men and
       women.
1638. FRAUENGLASS, William. A study of attitudes toward woman
       suffrage found in popular humor magazines, 1911-1920.
       232p. PhD thesis, New York University, 1967.
1639. FRIGGENS, P. What Wyoming did for women. Reader's

digest, v. 77 (September 1960), 197-201+.
1640. FROTHINGHAM, D. B.   Real case of the "Remonstrances"
       against woman suffrage.   Arena, v. 2 (July 1890),
       175-81.   Reply: v. 2 (November 1890), 752-5.
1641. FROTHINGHAM, Eugenia Brooks.   Fears of the anti-suffra-
       gist.   New York, National Woman Suffrage Pub. Co.,
       1914.   Arguments against anti-suffrage.
1642. FRY, Amelia.   Along the suffrage trail: from west to east
       for freedom now!   American West, v. 6, no. 1 (1969),
       16-25.   On the efforts of Sara Bard Field to deliver
       a petition to President Woodrow Wilson for passage
       of the 19th Amendment, in 1915.
1643. FULTON, Justin Dewey.   The true woman and woman vs.
       ballot.   Boston, Lee and Shepard, 1869.
1644. GAGE, Matilda Joslyn.   Arguments before the Committee on
       the District of Columbia of the U.S. Senate and House
       of Representatives upon the Centennial woman suffrage
       memorial of the women citizens of this nation, intro-
       duced in the U.S. Senate by Hon. A. A. Sargent...
       January 25, 1876, and in the House of Representatives,
       by Hon. S. S. Cox... March 31, 1876, asking for equal
       suffrage for men and women in the District of Colum-
       bia.   Washington, Gibson Brothers, printers, 1876.
       12p.
1645. _____.   Woman's rights catechism.   n.p., 1871.   3p.
1646. GALE, Zona.   What women won in Wisconsin.   Nation,
       v. 115 (23 August 1922), 184-5.
1647. _____.   What women won in Wisconsin.   Washington, Na-
       tional Woman's Party, 1922.   17p.
1648. GAMBLE, Harry Pollard.   An open letter to U.S. Senator
       Ransdell opposing the federal amendment for woman
       suffrage.   New Orleans, n.p., 1918.   31p.
1649. GARRISON, William Lloyd.   A plea for universal suffrage.
       Boston, National American Woman Suffrage Associa-
       tion [1881?].   2p.
1650. GIBBON, J. C.   Why women should have the ballot.   North
       American review, v. 163 (July 1896), 91-7.
1651. GIGLIOTTI, Cairoli.   Woman suffrage; its causes and pos-
       sible consequences.   Chicago, Press of Barnard and
       Miller, 1914.   92p.
1652. GILFILLAN, Harriet Woodbridge.   The disadvantages of
       equal suffrage.   n.p., 1915.
1653. GILMAN, Charlotte Perkins.   Are women human beings?   A
       consideration of the major error in the discussion of
       woman suffrage.   Harper's weekly, v. 56 (25 May
       1912), 11.
1654. _____.   Women and social service.   [Warren, Ohio, Na-
       tional American Woman Suffrage Association, 1907?]
       12p.
1655. GLEASON, Ida Riner.   Wyoming started something.   Nation-
       al historical magazine, v. 72, no. 7 (1938), 36-9.
       Story of the start of woman suffrage in Wyoming in
       1870.

1656. GODKIN, E. L. Report on women suffrage for 1879. Nation, v. 29 (1879), 286.
1657. _____. Suffrage for women. Nation, v. 36 (1883), 204.
1658. _____. Suffrage for women in Michigan. Nation, v. 18 (1874), 311.
1659. GOODMAN, Nathan G. The extension of the franchise to women. Historical outlook, v. 18 (April 1927), 157-60.
1660. GOODWIN, Grace Duffield. Anti-suffrage: ten good reasons. New York, Duffield, 1912. 141p.
1661. GOODWIN, H. M. Suffrage for women. New Englander, v. 43 (1884), 193.
1662. GRAEME, Betty. Woman suffrage in a new entente. Woman citizen, v. 1 (28 July 1917), 152-3.
1663. GRAHAM, Abbie. Ladies in revolt. New York, Woman's Press, 1934.
1664. GRAVES, Lawrence L. The Wisconsin woman suffrage movement, 1846-1920. PhD thesis, University of Wisconsin, 1954.
1665. GREENE, M. A. Results of the woman suffrage movement. Forum, v. 17 (June 1894), 413-24.
1666. GRIMES, Alan Pendleton. The puritan ethic and woman suffrage. New York, Oxford University Press, 1967. 159p. On the conservativeness of the woman suffrage movement in the western U.S.
1667. GRINNELL, Katherine Van Allen. Woman's place in government; from the scientific and Biblical viewpoint. New York, H. W. Merton, 1914. 184p.
1668. GULE, Janet. Social change in the feminine role: A comparison of woman's suffrage and woman's temperance, 1870-1920. PhD thesis, Radcliffe College, 1961.
1669. GUTHRIE DARUSMONT, Frances Sylva. Memorial on suffrage. Washington, n.p., 1874. 4p.
1670. HADLEY, H. D. The Woman's Party and the presidential campaign. National magazine, v. 44 (July 1916), 562-8.
1671. HAINES, Helen. Catholic womanhood and the suffrage. Catholic world, v. 102 (October 1915), 55-67.
1672. HALE, Annie Riley. The Eden sphinx. New York, n.p., 1916. 4p.
1673. _____. Woman suffrage. Article on the biological and sociological aspects of the woman question. Washington, GPO, 1917. 8p.
1674. HALE, Beatrice Forbes-Robertson. What women want; an interpretation of the feminist movement. New York, Stokes, 1914. 307p. A history of feminism from Mary Wollstonecraft to 1914 and a discussion of problems and hopes for the future.
1675. HALE, M. Useless risk of the ballot for women. Forum, v. 17 (June 1894), 406-12.
1676. HANSER, Elizabeth J. Woman suffrage movement in Ohio. Ohio magazine, v. 4 (February 1908), 83-92.
1677. HARPER, Ida Husted. American woman gets the vote. Re-

view of reviews, v. 62 (October 1920), 380-4.

1678.   . Brief history of the movement for woman suffrage
in the United States. New York, National Woman Suffrage Pub. Co., 1919. 40p.

1679.   . Evolution of the woman suffrage movement.
World to-day, v. 19 (September 1910), 1017-21.

1680.   . Getting the vote for women. Harper's bazaar,
v. 44 (February 1910), 90-1.

1681.   . History of the movement for woman suffrage in
the United States. New York, Interurban Woman Suffrage Council, 1907. 15p. Covers the period 1647-
1907.

1682.   . National amendment for woman suffrage. Washington, Congressional Union for Woman Suffrage, 1915.
16p.

1683.   . National Constitution will enfranchise woman.
North American review, v. 199 (May 1914), 709-21.

1684.   . New state for woman suffrage; Washington. Harper's bazaar, v. 45 (January 1911), 38.

1685.   . President and the suffragists. Independent,
v. 68 (28 April 1910), 902-4. On President William
Howard Taft's remarks to woman suffragists.

1686.   . Recent elections and woman suffrage. North
American review, v. 200 (December 1914), 893-9.

1687.   . Status of woman suffrage in the United States.
North American review, v. 189 (April 1909), 502-12.
Information showing how woman suffrage had to con-
tend against the liquor interests.

1688.   . Suffrage--a right. North American review,
v. 183 (21 September 1906), 484-98.

1689.   . Suffrage and a woman's centenary. North American review, v. 202 (November 1915), 730-5.

1690.   . Suffrage snapshots. Washington, n.p., 1915.
96p.

1691.   . Votes for three million women. Review of reviews, v. 46 (December 1912), 700-4.

1692.   . Votes for women. Harper's bazaar, v. 43 (December 1909), 1215.

1693.   . Votes for women. Harper's bazaar, v. 44 (Sep-
tember-October 1910), 558, 616.

1694.   . War and woman suffrage. Harper's weekly, v. 61
(4 December 1915), 548-9.

1695.   . What the suffragists are doing. Harper's bazaar,
v. 43 (February-November 1909), 201-3, 303-5, 421-3,
523-4, 625-7, 727-9, 829-30, 931-2, 1049-50, 1167-8.

1696.   . Why women cannot vote in the United States.
North American review, v. 179 (July 1904), 30-41.

1697.   . Winning of the vote. Woman citizen, v. 10 (8
August 1925), 7-8.

1698.   . Woman suffrage in six states. Independent,
v. 71 (2 November 1911), 967-70. Sketches of Washington, California, Wyoming, Colorado, Utah, and
Idaho in their giving suffrage to women.

1699. _____. Woman suffrage news. Harper's bazaar, v. 44
(June-August 1910), 412, 472, 500.
1700. _____. The world movement for woman suffrage. Review of reviews, v. 44 (December 1911), 725-9.
1701. _____. Would woman suffrage benefit the state and woman herself? North American review, v. 178 (March
1904), 362-74.
1702. HARRIS, Mrs. L. H. The women and the future. Independent, v. 64 (14 May 1908), 1090-2.
1703. HARRISON, Frederic. Realities and ideals. New York,
Macmillan, 1908. Anti-suffrage.
1704. HARVEY, G. Inherent right. North American review,
v. 191 (May 1910), 701-20.
1705. _____. Working of equal suffrage. North American review, v. 199 (March 1914), 338-43.
1706. HARWOOD, W. S. Constitutional suffrage for women. North
American review, v. 162 (May 1896), 632-4.
1707. HASKELL, Oreola Williams. Banner bearers; tales of the
suffrage campaigns. Geneva, N.Y., W. F. Humphrey,
1920. 350p.
1708. HAUSER, Elizabeth J. Woman suffrage movement in Ohio.
Ohio magazine, v. 4 (February 1908), 83-92.
1709. HAVEMEYER, L. W. Memories of a militant. Scribner's
magazine, v. 71 (May 1922), 528-39; (June 1922),
661-76.
1710. HAWAII--suffrage. Woman citizen, v. 2 (4 May 1918), 448.
1711. HAWAII--suffrage. Woman citizen, v. 3 (22 June 1918), 67.
1712. HAZELTON, John Hampden. Just a few thoughts upon the
woman suffrage question. New York, E. W. Whit-
field, 1918. 69p.
1713. HECKER, Eugene Arthur. A short history of women's rights
from the days of Augustus to the present time. With
special reference to England and the United States.
2d ed. rev. New York, Putnam, 1914. 313p. Reprinted by Greenwood Press, Westport, Conn., 1970.
1714. HEINEMAN, Charlotte C. Suffrage in California. Public,
v. 14 (3 November 1911), 1117.
1715. HENRY, J. K. New woman of the new South. Arena, v. 11
(February 1895), 353-62.
1716. HERTWIG, John George. Woman suffrage. New York,
Eckler, printer, 1883. 16p.
1717. HIGGINSON, Thomas Wentworth. Unsolved problems of suffrage for women. Forum, v. 2 (1887), 439.
1718. Hill, C. M. Woman's battle for the ballot in Chicago.
Collier's, v. 43 (3 April 1909), 26-7.
1719. HILLYER, Curtis Justin. The winning of Nevada for woman's suffrage, delivered before a joint session of the
Nevada Legislature in 1869. Carson City, Nevada
Printing Co., 1916. 29p.
1720. HISTORY of woman suffrage in Missouri. Missouri historical
review, v. 14 (April-June 1920), 281-384.
1721. HOAR, George Frisbie. The right and expediency of woman
suffrage. Century magazine, n.s., v. 26 (August

1894), 605-13.
1722. _____. Woman suffrage essential to the true republic.
Boston, American Woman Suffrage Association [187?].
4p.
1723. _____. Woman's right and the public welfare. Remarks
of Hon. George F. Hoar, before a joint special committee of the Massachusetts Legislature, April 14,
1869. Boston, New England Woman's Suffrage Association, 1869. 16p. [Woman's suffrage tracts,
no. 6.]
1724. HOLLISTER, Horace Adelbert. The woman citizen, a problem in education. New York, D. Appleton, 1919.
307p.
1725. HOLMES, James H. A report on the condition of the cause
of woman suffrage, made to the Universal Franchise
Association.... Washington, Universal Franchise Association, 1868. 12p.
1726. HOLZAPFEL, Gottlieb. Woman suffrage facts cartooned.
Cleona, Pa., Printed by Holzapfel Pub. Co., 1915.
32p.
1727. HOOKER, John. Bible and woman suffrage.... Hartford,
Conn., Printed by Case, Lockwood and Brainard,
1870. 17p. [Tracts of the Connecticut Woman Suffrage Association, no. 1.]
1728. HORACK, Frank Edward. Equal suffrage in Iowa. Iowa
City, Iowa, State Historical Society, 1914. 48p.
Also in: Applied history, v. 2 (1914), 275-314.
1729. HOW California women voters "made good." Review of
reviews, v. 47 (May 1913), 608-10. Women voters
in San Francisco.
1730. HOW it feels to be the husband of a suffragette, by him.
New York, Doran, 1915. 63p.
1731. HOW suffrage is organized. Woman citizen, v. 1 (2 June
1917), 16-17.
1732. HOWE, Julia Ward. Case for woman suffrage. Outlook,
v. 91 (3 April 1909), 780-4.
1733. _____. Suffrage for women. Galaxy, v. 7 (1869), 364.
1734. _____. Suffrage for women as a weapon in vital reforms.
Our day, v. 9 (1892), 23.
1735. HOWES, Harvey. A last resort. Fair Haven, Vt., D.
Lyman Crandall, pr., 1870. 9p.
1736. HUBBARD, Benjamin Vestal. Socialism, feminism, and suf-
fragism, the terrible triplets, connected by the same
umbilical cord and fed from the same nursing bottle.
Chicago, American, 1915. 301p.
1737. HUGHES, J. L. Last protest against woman's enfranchisement. Arena, v. 10 (July 1894), 201-13.
1738. HURD, Ethel Edgerton. Woman suffrage in Minnesota; a
record of the activities in its behalf since 1847....
Minneapolis, Published for the Minnesota Suffrage Association by the Inland Press, 1918. 52p.
1739. HUTCHINSON, Emilie J. Socializing influence of the ballot upon
women. American Academy of Political and Social

Science, annals, v. 56 (November 1914), 105-10.
1740. ILLINOIS. Attorney General's Office. Woman's suffrage in
Illinois. P. J. Lucey, attorney general. Springfield,
Schnepp & Barnes, state printers, 1916. 13p.
1741. _____. Supreme Court. William J. Scown vs. Anthony
Czarnechi, et al. Woman's suffrage decision with
dissenting opinions of Justice Farmer and Justice
Cooke. (Springfield, Ill.?) Attorney General [1913?].
53p.
1742. ILLINOIS Association Opposed to the Extension of Suffrage to
Women. Annual report. Chicago. The Association,
1911.
1743. ILLINOIS Equal Suffrage Association. Mayors of Illinois on
Chicago woman's suffrage. n.p., n.d. 23p.
1744. IMPROVED prospects. Harper's weekly, v. 51 (6 July 1907),
975-6.
1745. INDIANA decision and the federal suffrage amendment. Woman citizen, v. 1 (3 November 1917), 429.
1746. IRWIN, Inez Haynes. Angels and amazons, a hundred years
of American women. Garden City, N.Y., Doubleday,
Doran, 1933. 531p. Primarily education and suffrage,
as well as trade unions, the professions, etc. between
1833 and 1933.
1747. _____. The story of the Woman's Party. New York,
Harcourt, Brace, 1921. 486p. The struggle for suffrage from around 1912 to 1920.
1748. _____. Up hill with banners flying. Penobscot, Me.,
Traversity, 1964. 501p. The suffrage movement
from 1913 to 1920.
1749. IS suffrage her right? Outlook, v. 49 (20 May 1894), 908-9.
1750. IS the suffrage a duty? Outlook, v. 49 (19 May 1894), 860-1.
1751. IS woman suffrage failing? Symposium. Woman citizen,
v. 8 (22 March 1924), 7-9; (5 April 1924), 8-10; (19
April 1924), 14-16; (3 May 1924), 17.
1752. IVINSON, E. How woman suffrage came to Wyoming.
Wyoming State Historical Department, collections and
proceedings, v. 1 (1919-1920), 135-52.
1753. JACKSON, W. Turrentine. Governor Francis E. Warren,
a champion of woman suffrage. Letters in the National
Archives. Annals of Wyoming, v. 5 [1943?], 143-9.
History of woman suffrage in the territory of Wyoming
from 1869 to 1889. Reprint of six letters from other
states showing interest in the Wyoming suffrage experiment.
1754. JACOBI, Mary Putnam. "Common sense" applied to woman
suffrage; a statement of the reasons which justify the
demand to extend the suffrage to women, with consideration of the arguments against such enfranchisement, and with special reference to the issue presented to the New York State convention of 1894. New
York, G. P. Putnam, 1894. 236p.
1755. _____. The status and future of the woman suffrage movement. Forum, v. 18 (December 1894), 406-14. On

the lack of positive action by women against their condition in New York.
1756. JEPSON, Nels Peter. The woman's suffrage from a religious
and judicial point of view; address delivered at Eau
Claire, Wisconsin. Menomonie, Wis., Boothby Printing Shop, 1912. 23p.
1757. JOHNSON, E. S. Discovering Pennsylvania. Survey, v. 35
(9 October 1915), 38-42.
1758. JOHNSON, Helen Kendrick. Woman and the republic; a survey of the woman-suffrage movement in the United
States and a discussion of the claims and arguments
of its foremost advocates. New York, National League
for the Civic Education of Women, 1909. 359p. Reprinted by Greenwood Press, Westport, Conn., 1971.
Woman suffrage as related to education, the professions, the church, and the home.
1759. _____. Woman suffrage and education. Popular science
monthly, v. 51 (June 1897), 222-31.
1760. JOHNSON, Kenneth Ray. The woman suffrage movement in
Florida. 332p. PhD thesis, Florida State University,
1966. Covers the period 1890 to 1920.
1761. JOHNSTON, Mary and Thomas Nelson Page. Two Virginia
novelists on woman's suffrage. Virginia magazine of
history and biography, v. 64 (July 1956), 286-90.
Concerns an exchange of letters, 1910.
1762. JONES, Mrs. Gilbert E. Facts about suffrage and anti-suffrage. Forum, v. 43 (May 1910), 495-504.
1763. _____. Impediments to woman suffrage. North American
review, v. 190 (August 1909), 158-69. The individual
state constitutions as a major impediment to suffrage.
1764. _____. Position of the anti-suffragists. American Academy of Political and Social Science, annals, supp.
v. 35 (May 1910), 16-22.
1765. KATZENSTEIN, Caroline. Lifting the curtain: the state and
national woman suffrage campaigns in Pennsylvania as
I saw them. Philadelphia, Dorrance, 1955. 376p.
Covers the period 1910 to 1920.
1766. KEITH, L. E. Female filosofy, fished out and fried. [Cal-
lowell?] Ohio, 1894. 293p.
1767. KELLEY, Florence. Campaign for the enfranchisement of
women in Oregon. Outlook, v. 83 (21 July 1906),
675-6.
1768. _____. Some ethical gains through legislation. New York,
Macmillan, 1905. 341p.
1769. KENDRICK, Lowell Clapp and Harold Preston Salisbury.
General constitutional and statutory provisions relative
to suffrage. Providence, Rhode Island State Library,
Legislative Reference Bureau, 1912. 99p.
1770. KENNEALLY, James J. Catholicism and woman suffrage in
Massachusetts. Catholic historical review, v. 53,
no. 1 (1967), 43-57. The changing of the attitudes of
the Catholic community from anti-suffrage to an attitude of neutrality.

1771. _____. Woman suffrage and the Massachusetts referendum
of 1895. Historian, v. 30 (August 1968), 617-33.
1772. KENT, William. Concerning woman suffrage--from a man's
viewpoint. Washington, n.p., 1913. 6p. Address of
William Kent of California, delivered at the Columbia
Theater, Washington, D.C., Sunday, August 31, 1913.
1773. KIDDER, M. G. Woman suffrage. Overland, v. 53 (January 1909), 3-8.
1774. KING, Della Robinson. Thoughts of a thoughtful woman.
Scotland, S.D., Messenger Office, 1898. 50p.
1775. KINKAID, M. H. Feminine charms of the woman militant.
Good housekeeping, v. 54 (February 1912), 146-55.
1776. KNOBE, B. D. Recent strides of woman suffrage. World's
work, v. 22 (August 1911), 14733-45.
1777. _____. Spectacular woman suffrage in America. Independent, v. 71 (12 October 1911), 804-10.
1778. _____. Votes for women. Harper's weekly, v. 52 (25
April 1908), 20-1.
1779. KRADITOR, Aileen S. The ideas of the woman suffrage
movement, 1890-1920. New York, Columbia University Press, 1965. 313p.
1780. _____. Tactical problems of the woman suffrage movement in the South. Louisiana studies, v. 5, no. 4
(1966), 289-305.
1781. KRONE, Henrietta L. Dauntless women; the story of the
woman suffrage movement in Pennsylvania, 1910-1920.
PhD thesis, University of Pennsylvania, 1947.
1782. LABOR and woman suffrage. American federationist, v. 27
(October 1920), 937-9.
1783. LABOR'S position on woman suffrage. New republic, v. 6
(11 March 1916), 150-2.
1784. LA FOLLETTE, Fola. Will the women vote together? Independent, v. 86 (12 June 1916), 440-1.
1785. LAIDLAW, Harriet Burton. The woman's hour. Forum,
v. 56 (November 1916), 531-43.
1786. LARSON, Taft Alfred. Petticoats at the polls; woman suffrage in territorial Wyoming. Pacific Northwest quarterly, v. 44 (April 1953), 75-9. Covers the period
1869 to 1891.
1787. _____. Woman suffrage in western America. Utah historical quarterly, v. 38, no. 1 (1970), 7-19. Suggests that mere chance had more to do with women
acquiring the vote in the West rather than the frontier
spirit.
1788. _____. Woman suffrage in Wyoming. Pacific Northwest
quarterly, v. 56, no. 2 (1965), 57-66. Reasons why
woman suffrage was granted in Wyoming first.
1789. LASKI, H. J. The federal suffrage amendment. Dial, v. 66
(31 May 1919), 541-3.
1790. LAST ditch. New republic, v. 22 (10 March 1920), 45-6.
1791. LEAGUE of Women Voters of the United States. XL (forty)
years of a great idea. Washington, The League,
1960. 52p.

1792. LEATHERBEE, Ethel Brigham. Anti-suffrage campaign
       manual. Endorsed by Woman's Anti-Suffrage Associa-
       tion of Massachusetts.... Boston, Mrs. A. T. Leath-
       erbee, 1915. 28p.
1793. LEE, E. M. Suffrage for women in Wyoming. Galaxy,
       v. 13 (1872), 755.
1794. LEONARD, Priscilla. Woman suffrage in Colorado. Out-
       look, v. 55 (20 March 1897), 789-92.
1795. LEROY, V. B. Should women vote? World to-day, v. 15
       (October 1908), 1061-6.
1796. LEWIS, Laurence. How woman suffrage works in Colorado.
       Outlook, v. 72 (27 January 1906), 167-78.
1797. LINDSEY, Ben B. If I were a woman. New York, National
       American Woman Suffrage Association [1912?]. 8p.
       The necessity of getting involved in the suffrage move-
       ment in order to bring about legal equality.
1798. _____. Reply to anti-suffragists, at a meeting held under
       the auspices of the Equal Franchise Society in the As-
       sembly Chamber, Albany, N.Y., February 24, 1911.
       New York, Equal Franchise Society, 1911. 53p. Pri-
       marily concerns suffrage in Colorado.
1799. LINKUGEL, W. A. Woman suffrage argument of Anna
       Howard Shaw. Quarterly journal of speech, v. 49
       (April 1963), 165-74.
1800. LIPPMANN, Walter. Vote as a symbol. New republic,
       v. 4 (9 October 1915), 4-5.
1801. LIVERMORE, Daniel Parker. Woman suffrage defended by
       irrefutable arguments, and all objections to woman's
       enfranchisement carefully examined and completely
       answered. Boston, Lee & Shepard, 1885. 224p.
1802. LIVERMORE, Henrietta Jackson. How to raise money for
       suffrage. New York, National Woman Suffrage Pub-
       lishing Co., 1917. 16p.
1803. LIVERMORE, Mary Ashton Rice. Suffrage for women.
       North American review, v. 143 (1886), 371.
1804. LOCKWOOD, George Robinson. Why I oppose woman suf-
       frage. By George R. Lockwood of the St. Louis Bar.
       St. Louis, n.p., 1912. 23p.
1805. LONDON, J. Why I voted for equal suffrage. Independent,
       v. 75 (11 September 1913), 634-5.
1806. LOSE, R. J. Platform for women. Forum, v. 45 (January
       1911), 91-3.
1807. LOUISIANA Ratification Campaign Committee. Expert legal
       opinions on the ratification of the federal amendment
       to the Constitution for woman suffrage. New Orleans,
       Enterprise Printing Co., 1920. 19p.
1808. LOW, A. Maurice. Mission of woman. North American
       review, v. 196 (August 1912), 204-14.
1809. _____. Women in the election. Yale review, v. 10
       (January 1921), 311-22.
1810. LOWRY, William H. Woman suffrage denied, a catchy
       dialogue based on facts and practical life. Princeton,
       Mo., W. C. Price Printing Co., 1902. 11p.

1811. LYON, Peter. The day the women got the vote. Holiday,
       v. 24 (November 1958), 68-9+. The winning of suf-
       frage in Tennessee.
1812. MCCAULEY, Doris T. A brief history of woman suffrage in
       Arizona. n.p., 1964.
1813. MCCRACKEN, Elizabeth. Woman suffrage in the tenements.
       Atlantic monthly, v. 96 (December 1905), 750-9.
1814. _____. Woman's suffrage in Colorado. Outlook, v. 75
       (28 November 1903), 737-44.
1815. MCCULLOCH, Catharine Waugh, comp. The bench and bar
       of Illinois on equal suffrage. Chicago, n.p., 1903.
       53p.
1816. MCGOWAN, J. Decade of equal rights. Commonweal, v.
       13 (11 February 1931), 401-3.
1817. MACK, Mrs. O. H. History of the suffrage movement in
       Nevada, 1900-1920. New York, The Author, 1920.
       23p.
1818. MCKEE, J. V. Shall women vote? Catholic world, v. 102
       (October 1915), 45-54. Anti-suffrage article.
1819. MCKEE, O., Jr. Ten years of woman suffrage. Common-
       weal, v. 12 (16 July 1930), 298-300.
1820. MACKENZIE, W. D. Suffrage movement in the District of
       Columbia. Public, v. 17 (17 July 1914), 680-1.
1821. MCKIM, J. M. The vexed question. Nation, v. 10 (24
       March 1870), 189-90. Comments on a pro-suffrage
       speech by Henry Ward Beecher.
1822. _____. The vexed question. Nation, v. 10 (31 March
       1870), 205-6. Comments on John Stuart Mill's and
       Wendell Phillips' views of the women's movement.
1823. _____. The vexed question. Nation, v. 10 (14 April
       1870), 237-8. Comments on John Stuart Mill's views
       of the suffrage movement in the United States.
1824. MACLAY, Arthur Collins. Is Christianity hostile to the
       cause of woman suffrage? A monograph embodying a
       citizen's protest against female enfranchisement as
       being an undemocratic and unjust innovation. Plain-
       field, N.J., Courier-news Job Department, 1913. 31p.
1825. MACLEOD, A. Should women vote? Ladies home journal,
       v. 75 (February 1958), 6.
1826. MCNAUGHT, M. S. Enfranchised woman teacher: her op-
       portunity. School and society, v. 6 (11 August 1917),
       155-60.
1827. MCPHERSON, James M. Abolitionists, woman suffrage, and
       the Negro, 1865-1869. Mid-America, v. 47, no. 1
       (1965), 40-7. The problem after the Civil War of the
       abolitionists wanting to obtain suffrage for the Negro
       while postponing it for women.
1828. MAHONEY, Joseph F. Woman suffrage and the urban masses.
       New Jersey history, v. 87 (Autumn 1969), 151-72.
1829. MARBURY, William L. The Nineteenth Amendment and
       after. Virginia law review, v. 7 (October 1920), 1-29.
1830. MARCHING for equal suffrage. Hearst's magazine, v. 21
       (June 1912), 2497-2501.

1831. MARQUIS, N. Woman and the California primaries. Inde-
         pendent, v. 72 (13 June 1912), 1316-18.
1832. MARTIN, Edward Sandford. The unrest of women. New
         York, D. Appleton, 1913. 146p.
1833. MASON, Lucy Randolph. The divine discontent. Richmond,
         Va., Equal Suffrage League of Virginia, n.d. 16p.
1834. MASSIE, E. M. Woman's plea against woman suffrage.
         Living age, v. 257 (11 April 1908), 84-8.
1835. MEAD, L. A. Violence and votes. Independent, v. 72 (27
         June 1912), 1416-19.
1836. MELONEY, William Brown. What women have accomplished
         without the ballot. Munsey's magazine, v. 44 (Novem-
         ber 1910), 197-203.
1837. MEREDITH, E. Do women vote? National municipal re-
         view, v. 3 (October 1914), 663-71.
1838. _____. What it means to be an enfranchised woman in
         Colorado. Atlantic monthly, v. 102 (August 1908),
         196-202.
1839. MERK, Lois Bannister. Boston's historical public school
         crisis. New England quarterly, v. 31 (June 1958),
         172-99. On school suffrage for women.
1840. _____. Massachusetts and the woman suffrage movement.
         PhD thesis, Radcliffe College, 1956.
1841. METCALF, H. H. Why New Hampshire should give votes to
         women. Granite monthly, v. 42 (January 1910), 23-7.
1842. MEYER, Annie N. Woman's assumption of sex superiority.
         North American review, v. 178 (January 1904), 103-9.
1843. MICHELSON, M. Vice and the woman's vote. Sunset,
         v. 30 (April 1913), 344-8.
1844. MILL, Mrs. John Stuart. Enfranchisement of women. Re-
         printed from the Westminster and Foreign Quarterly
         Review, for July, 1851. Syracuse, N.Y., Lathrop's
         print., 1852. 24p. [Woman's Rights Tracts, no. 3.]
         Speaking about the American suffrage movement, in
         part.
1845. MILLER, Alice Duer. Women are people! New York, G.
         H. Doran, 1917. 98p.
1846. MILLER, Francis. Argument before the Judiciary Commit-
         tee of the House of Representatives upon the petition
         of 600 citizens asking for the enfranchisement of the
         women of the District of Columbia, January 21, 1874,
         ...in the case of Sara J. Spencer vs. the Board of
         Registration, and Mary Webster vs. the judges of
         election, now pending in the Supreme Court of the
         United States. Washington, Gibson Brothers, print-
         ers, 1874. 8p.
1847. MINOR, Francis. Citizenship and suffrage: the Yarbrough
         decision. Arena, v. 5 (December 1891), 68-75.
1848. _____. Woman's legal right to the ballot. Forum, v. 2
         (December 1886), 351-60.
1849. _____. Woman's political status. Forum, v. 9 (April
         1890), 150-8.
1850. MISGIVINGS of a male suffragette. Scribner's magazine,

v. 58 (October 1915), 494-502. A feminist's doubts about the movement.

1851. MITCHELL, A. F. Suggestions of A. F. Mitchell, to the Committee, on the merits of a bill granting suffrage to women on all educational and school matters.... Southbury, Conn., n.p., 1883. 12p.

1852. MOORE, E. W. Suffrage question in the far West. Arena, v. 41 (July 1909), 414-24.

1853. MORRIS, John R. The women and governor Waite. Colorado magazine, v. 44, no. 1 (1967), 11-19. With governor Waite's help women gained the right to vote in Colorado in 1893; but the governor turned against suffrage after his defeat in 1894, believing that the women had voted against him.

1854. MORRIS, Monia Cook. The history of woman suffrage in Missouri, 1867-1901. Missouri historical review, v. 25 (October 1930), 67-82.

1855. MORRISSON, M. F. Votes for women; story of the fight for equal suffrage. Woman's home companion, v. 67 (November 1940), 8+.

1856. MORSE, Howard Newcomb. A study in the problems presented by the integration into the Constitution of certain articles amendatory thereto. Alabama lawyer, v. 10 (January 1949), 98-104. Also in: New York State Bar Association, bulletin, v. 21 (February 1949), 18-23. Concerning rescissions of the ratification of the 13th, 14th, 15th, and 19th amendments, 1865-70, 1919-20.

1857. MORTON, Katharine A. A historical review of woman suffrage. Wyoming annals, v. 12 (1940), 21-34.

1858. MOTT, Lucretia. Discourse on woman, delivered at the assembly buildings, December 17, 1849, by Lucretia Mott. Philadelphia, T. B. Peterson, 1850. 20p. Concerns the necessity for the rights of women in various spheres: political, legal, etc.

1859. MUNGER, George G. Shall women vote? Argument in favor of woman suffrage. New York, Strouse, 1882.

1860. NATHAN, Mrs. F. Woman suffrage an aid to social reform. American Academy of Political and Social Science, annals, supp. v. 35 (May 1910), 33-5.

1861. NATIONAL American Woman Suffrage Association. Big drive for presidential suffrage. New York, The Association, [1917?]. 2p.

1862. _____. First and last steps in the suffrage movement. New York, The Association, 1919. 4p.

1863. _____. Twenty-five answers to antis; five minute speeches on votes for women by eminent suffragists. New York, The Association, [1912?]. 43p.

1864. _____. Victory, how women won it; a centennial symposium, 1840-1940. New York, Wilson, 1940. 174p.

1865. _____. Woman suffrage, arguments and results; a collection of eight popular booklets covering together practically the entire field of suffrage claims and evi-

dence. Designed especially for the convenience of suffrage speakers and writers and for the use of debaters
and libraries. New York, The Association, [1911?].
222p.

1866. NATIONAL Woman Suffrage and Educational Committee, Washington, D.C. An appeal to the women of the United
States. Hartford, Conn., Case, Lockwood and Brainard, Printers, 1871. 4p. A petition for signatures
of those in favor of suffrage.

1867. The NECESSITY of woman suffrage. North American review, v. 183 (5 October 1906), 688-9. The first
editorial by the North American review advocating
woman suffrage.

1868. NELSON, A. D. First ladies of the ballot box. American
mercury, v. 90 (March 1960), 57-8.

1869. NEVADA State Equal Suffrage Association. Proceedings of
the state convention held in Reno, Nevada, October
29 and 30, 1895. Reno, State Journal print., 1895.
36p.

1870. NEVER give up Nebraska. Woman citizen, v. 3 (8 February
1919), 749-51+.

1871. NEW status of suffrage. Nation, v. 103 (13 July 1916), 28-9.

1872. NEW York (state)--woman suffrage. Public, v. 20 (2 November 1917), 1049.

1873. NEW York State Woman's Rights Committee. Appeal to the
women of New York. n.p., 1860. 4p.

1874. NINE equal suffrage states. Chautauquan, v. 69 (January
1913), 127-8.

1875. NINE years' experience of woman suffrage in Wyoming.
Boston, W. K. Moody, printers, 1879. 12p.

1876. NINETEENTH Amendment. America, v. 95 (8 September
1956), 515.

1877. NO votes for New Jersey women. Literary digest, v. 51
(30 October 1915), 946-7.

1878. NORTON, C. E. Suffrage and education for women. Nation, v. 5 (1867), 152.

1879. NOUN, Louise R. Strong-minded women; the emergence of
the woman suffrage movement in Iowa. Ames, Iowa
State University Press, 1970. 322p.

1880. OBJECTIONS to the Federal Amendment. New York, National American Woman Suffrage Association, 1917.
24p. Arguments against seven objections to woman
suffrage, among them the objection that women do not
really want the ballot, and woman suffrage in the
South would interfere with white supremacy.

1881. OBJECTIONS to woman suffrage answered by college women.
New York, National American Woman Suffrage Association, 1900. 16p.

1882. O'CONNELL, D. M. Should Catholic women vote? America, v. 44 (14 March 1931), 553-4.

1883. O'HAGAN, Anne. Advance of woman suffrage in America.
Munsey's magazine, v. 56 (October 1915), 56-66.

1884. OHIO women win. Independent, v. 89 (26 February 1917), 345.

1885.   OHIO'S greater victory. National suffrage news, v. 3 (May
        1917), 20.
1886.   OHIO'S rebuilt constitution. Literary digest, v. 45 (14 Sep-
        tember 1912), 405-6.
1887.   OKLAHOMA. University. Woman's suffrage; arguments for
        and against. Norman, University of Oklahoma, 1914.
        79p.
1888.   O'NEAL, Emmet. The Susan B. Anthony Amendment. Ef-
        fect of its ratification on the rights of the states to
        regulate and control suffrage and elections. Virginia
        law review, v. 6 (February 1920), 338-60.
1889.   OREGON Equal Suffrage Association. Argument in favor of
        equal suffrage constitutional amendment.... [Portland,
        Ore., 1905?] 7p.
1890.   OUT West. The clash in Nevada. A history of woman's
        fight for enfranchisement. The Nevada suffrage fight.
        Articles by Jane Addams, Charlotte Perkins Gilman,
        Carrie Chapman Catt, Mary Roberts Coolidge, Mary
        Austin, Anne Martin, Sara Bard Field, Inez Haynes
        Gillmore, Gail Laughlin, Dr. Anna Howard Shaw. Re-
        printed from Out West (August 1914), 51-76.
1891.   OVERTON, Gwendolen. Past, present and future. North
        American review, v. 194 (August 1911), 271-81.
1892.   OWEN, E. Von R. Woman's vote in Utah. Harper's week-
        ly, v. 58 (2 May 1914), 18.
1893.   OWEN, R. L. Discussion of equal suffrage for women.
        American Academy of Political and Social Science,
        annals, v. 35 (May 1910), 6-9.
1894.   PARADING in New York for woman suffrage. Current litera-
        ture, v. 52 (June 1912), 627-8.
1895.   PARK, Maud Wood. Front door lobby. Boston, Beacon,
        1960. 278p. Account of the suffrage campaign in
        Washington, D.C.
1896.   PARKER, William. The fundamental error of woman suf-
        frage. New York, F. H. Revell, 1915. 125p.
1897.   PARKHURST, Charles H. Inadvisability of woman suffrage.
        American Academy of Political and Social Science,
        annals, supp. v. 35 (May 1910), 36-7.
1898.   PARKMAN, Francis. Some of the reasons against woman
        suffrage. Boston, Massachusetts Association Opposed
        to the Further Extension of Suffrage to Women [1884?]
        16p.
1899.   PARSONS, Elsie Clews. Anti-suffragists and the war. Sci-
        entific monthly, v. 1 (October 1915), 44-6.
1900.   PATTON, E. E. The first suffrage convention. Daughters
        of the American Revolution magazine, v. 82 (August
        1948), 591-2. Concerning the convention in Seneca
        Fall, New York, in 1848.
1901.   PATTON, George Smith. Why women should not be given the
        vote. [Los Angeles?] 1911. 16p.
1902.   PEARCE, Stella E. Suffrage in the Pacific Northwest; old
        Oregon and Washington. Pacific Northwest quarterly,
        v. 3 (April 1912), 106-14. Covers the period from

1840 to 1912.

1903. PEEBLES, Isaac Lockhart. Is woman suffrage right? The question answered. Meridian, Miss., T. Farmer, printer, 1918. 25p.

1904. PELLEW, George. Woman and the commonwealth; or a question of expediency. Boston, Houghton Mifflin, 1888. 38p. Pro-suffrage argument, with refutations of the arguments against suffrage.

1905. PHELPS, Edith May, comp. Selected articles on woman suffrage. 3d ed. Minneapolis, H. W. Wilson, 1916. 274p.

1906. PHILLIPS, Wendell. Speech of Wendell Phillips, Esq., at the Convention, held at Worcester, October 15 and 16, 1851. Syracuse? 1851. 24p. [Woman's Rights Tracts, no. 2.] The necessity of women to be equal to men in all spheres. Pages 21-24 includes a speech by Abby Kelly Foster.

1907. _____. Speeches on rights of women. Philadelphia, Press of A. J. Ferris, 1898. 65p.

1908. PICKENS, William. Woman voter hits the color line. Nation, v. 111 (6 October 1920), 372-3. The possibility of Negro women in the South being denied the right to vote despite passage of the 19th Amendment.

1909. PILLSBURY, H. History of woman suffrage in New Hampshire. Granite monthly, v. 58 (August 1926), 260-8.

1910. PILLSBURY, Parker. The mortality of nations: an address delivered before the American Equal Rights Association, in New York, Thursday evening, May 9, 1867. New York, R. J. Johnston, printer, 1867. 13p.

1911. A PLEA for impartial suffrage, by a lawyer of Illinois. Chicago, Western News Co., 1868. 95p.

1912. PLIGHT of the suffrage amendment. World's work, v. 39 (January 1920), 225-6.

1913. PLUNKETT, H. Working of woman suffrage in Wyoming. Fortnightly review, v. 53 (May 1890), 656-69.

1914. POLING, Daniel Alfred. Mothers of men. Harrisburg, Pa., Publishing House of the United Evangelical Church, 1914. 44p.

1915. POLL of women on the suffrage. Outlook, v. 104 (7 June 1913), 268-70.

1916. POLLARD, Edward B. The subjection of women according to St. Paul. An address before the Equal Suffrage League of Richmond, Virginia. New York, National Woman Suffrage Pub. Co., 1917. An interpretation of the Bible in favor of woman suffrage.

1917. POLLARD, Vickie and Donna Keck. They almost seized the time! Detroit, Radical Education Project, 1970. 13p. The part women played in the suffrage and trade union movements in the 19th century.

1918. PORRITT, Annie Gertrude. Laws affecting women and children in the suffrage and non-suffrage states. 2d ed. New York, National Woman Suffrage Pub. Co., 1917. 168p. Arranged by state, giving information as to labor legislation, wages, property rights, guardianship of children, etc.

1919. PORTER, D. G. Suffrage for women. Christian quarterly, v. 6 (1874), 471.

1920. PORTER, Kirk Harold. A history of suffrage in the United States. Chicago, University of Chicago Press, 1918. 260p. Reprinted by Greenwood Press, Westport, Conn., 1969.

1921. POSITION of organized labor on woman suffrage. n.p., Illinois Legislative Reference Bureau, 1916. 4p.

1922. POTTER, Frances Boardman. Women, economics and the ballot. [Youngstown, Ohio, Vindicator, 1909?] 8p. A plea for suffrage to bring about economic independence of married women.

1923. POWELL, Thomas Reed. Woman suffrage. Academy of Political Science, proceedings, v. 5 (October 1914), 73-81.

1924. PRESCOTT, Grace Elizabeth. The woman suffrage movement in Memphis: its place in the state, sectional and national movements. Western Tennessee Historical Society, papers, v. 18 (1964), 87-106. The movement in Tennessee from 1872 to 1920, including Elizabeth Avery Meriwether, the first southerner to lecture for woman suffrage.

1925. PRESIDENT and the Senate. Woman citizen, v. 3 (19 October 1918), 410-11.

1926. PRESIDENT Wilson calls suffrage vital aid to victory. Woman citizen, v. 3 (5 October 1918), 366-7.

1927. PRIDDY, Bessie Leach. Woman mind on politics. National municipal review, v. 10 (March 1921), 171-6.

1928. PROCESSION of victories. Woman citizen, v. 1 (27 October 1917), 409-10.

1929. PROGRESS of woman's suffrage. Outlook, v. 102 (26 October 1912), 375-6.

1930. PROPOSED constitutional amendments in Iowa, 1857-1909. Iowa journal of history and politics, v. 8 (April 1910), 171-210. Pages 192-197 are specific to woman suffrage and proposed legislative action.

1931. PROS and cons of woman suffrage; review of a legislative report, by one of the sex. Boston, W. B. Clarke, 1882.

1932. PROSPECTS of federal amendment. Woman citizen, v. 3 (29 June 1918), 88.

1933. PUSHING suffrage at Washington. Woman citizen, v. 2 (2 February 1918), 188.

1934. PUTNAM, Mabel Raef. The winning of the first bill of rights for American women. Milwaukee, F. Putnam, 1924. 92p. Pertains primarily to Wisconsin.

1935. RAINE, W. M. Colorado legislation and results. Chautauquan, v. 34 (February 1902), 482-4.

1936. RAMSEY, A. R. Woman suffrage in America. Lippincott's magazine, v. 82 (July 1908), 101-4.

1937. RATIFICATION schedule. Woman citizen, v. 4 (28 June

1919), 86.
1938.   READ, Humphrey. The birth of equality, being a call to the
        ballot. Wilkes-Barre, Pa., Printed by E. B. Yordy
        Co., 1915. 14p.
1939.   REED, Dorinda Riessen. The woman suffrage movement in
        South Dakota. Vermillion, S.D., Governmental Re-
        search Bureau, University of South Dakota, 1958.
        126p.
1940.   REYNOLDS, M. J. Why suffrage failed in New Jersey.
        New republic, v. 5 (13 November 1915), 43-4.
1941.   RICHARDSON, A. S. Truth about equal suffrage. Woman's
        home companion, v. 37 (October 1910), 17-18; (No-
        vember 1910), 13-14.
1942.   The RIGHT of the silent woman. Outlook, v. 101 (18 May
        1912), 105-6. The apathy of nearly one million New
        York City women towards the suffrage movement.
1943.   ROBERTS, H. H. Woman suffrage and municipal politics in
        Wyoming. American Academy of Political and Social
        Science, annals, v. 18 (November 1901), 556-8.
1944.   ROBINSON, Harriet Jane. Massachusetts in the woman suf-
        frage movement. A general political, legal and legis-
        lative history from 1774 to 1881. 2d ed. Boston,
        Roberts, 1883. 279p.
1945.   ROBINSON, Helen Ring. Preparing women for citizenship.
        New York, Macmillan, 1918. 130p.
1946.   _____. What about the Woman's Party? Independent,
        v. 87 (11 September 1916), 381-3.
1947.   ROBINSON, M. C. Suffrage prophets. Unpopular review,
        v. 4 (July 1915), 127-39.
1948.   ROESSING, Jennice B. The equal suffrage campaign in Penn-
        sylvania. American Academy of Political and Social
        Science, annals, v. 56 (November 1914), 153-60.
1949.   ROGERS, Henry Wade. Federal action and state rights.
        New York, National Woman Suffrage Pub. Co., n.d.
        14p.
1950.   RORKE, Margaret Hayden, comp. Letters and address on
        woman suffrage, by Catholic ecclesiastics. New York,
        Devin-Adair, 1914. 32p.
1951.   ROSSIGNOL, J. E. Woman suffrage and municipal politics
        in Colorado. American Academy of Political and So-
        cial Science, annals, v. 18 (November 1901), 552-6.
1952.   RUDY, Belle L. Franchise. Lima, Ohio, Press of the
        Parmenter Printing Co., 1895. 32p.
1953.   RUSSELL, Charles Edward. Is woman suffrage a failure?
        Century, v. 107 (March 1924), 724-30.
1954.   _____. Obstructions in the way to justice. [Warren,
        Ohio, National American Woman Suffrage Association,
        1908?] 14p.
1955.   RYLANCE, Joseph H. Woman suffrage question, an argu-
        ment and an appeal. New York, Whittaker, 1894.
1956.   SAMS, Conway Whittle. Shall women vote? A book for men.
        New York, Neale, 1913. 345p. Anti-suffrage; a dis-
        cussion of the rights of men in relation to their wives

and children.
1957. SAYLER, D. M. Indiana's double somersault into both suffrage and prohibition columns. New republic, v. 10 (17 March 1917), 192-4.
1958. SCHAFFER, Ronald. The Montana woman suffrage campaign, 1911-1914. Pacific Northwest quarterly, v. 55, no. 1 (1964), 9-15. The efforts of Jeannette Rankin and others in gaining the vote for women in Montana.
1959. SCHAIN, Josephine. Women and the franchise. Chicago, McClurg, 1918. 127p. Review of arguments against woman suffrage and why suffrage should be granted.
1960. SCHMIDT, Nathaniel. Government by the people. Address at the Ontario County Woman Suffrage Convention at Phelps, New York, May 24, 1909. New York, National American Woman Suffrage Association, 1909.
1961. SCOTT, Mary Semple, ed. History of the woman suffrage movement in Missouri. Missouri historical review, v. 14 (April-July 1920), 281-384. Covers the period from 1842 to 1920.
1962. SCOTT, Mrs. W. F. Woman's relation to government. North American review, v. 191 (April 1910), 549-58.
1963. SEAWELL, Molly Elliot. The ladies battle. New York, Macmillan, 1911. 119p. Anti-suffrage; a criticism of suffragists on their lack of knowledge of politics.
1964. _____. Two suffrage mistakes: proposed suffrage amendment to the constitution and opposition to the payment of the income tax. North American review, v. 199 (March 1914), 366-82.
1965. SEDGWICK, M. K. Some scientific aspects of suffrage for women. Gunton's magazine, v. 20 (1901), 333.
1966. SELDEN, Henry R. Rights of women under the late constitutional amendments. Argument of Hon. Henry R. Selden in behalf of Susan B. Anthony, on Habeas Corpus, before the Hon. N. K. Hall, U.S. District Judge for the Northern District of New York, at Albany, January 21, 1873. The United States vs. Susan B. Anthony. Rochester, N.Y., Tracy & Rew, pr., 1873. 16p. On the defense of Susan B. Anthony by Mr. Selden after she had voted "without having a lawful right to vote."
1967. SEVERN, Bill. Free but not equal: how women won the right to vote. New York, Messner, 1967. 189p.
1968. SHALL women vote? Symposium. Outlook, v. 101 (3 August 1912), 754+.
1969. SHARP, Evelyn. Rebel women. New York, John Lane, 1910. 131p. Sketches of suffragist activities.
1970. SHAW, Anna Howard. Address delivered December 1915 upon retiring from the presidency of the National Association. New York, National Woman Suffrage Pub. Co., n.d.
1971. _____. Alabama speech. New York, National Woman Suffrage Pub. Co., 1915.
1972. _____. Equal suffrage--a problem of political justice. American Academy of Political and Social Science, an-

nals, v. 56 (November 1914), 93-8.
1973. _____. Men of America on trial for democracy. Public,
v. 20 (24 August 1917), 813-14.
1974. _____. Passages from speeches of Dr. Shaw's. New
York, National Woman Suffrage Pub. Co., n.d.
1975. _____, comp. The yellow ribbon speaker; readings and
recitations. Boston, Lee and Shepard, 1891. 243p.
1976. SHEARMAN, T. G. Suffrage for women. Nation, v. 3
(1866), 498.
1977. SHILLING, D. C. Woman's suffrage in the constitutional
convention of Ohio. Ohio archaeological and historical
quarterly, v. 25 (April 1916), 166-74.
1978. SHOULD women vote? Important affirmative testimony.
Grand Haven, Mich., Herald print., 1874.
1979. SHULER, Marjorie. For rent--one pedestal. New York,
National Woman Suffrage Pub. Co., 1917. 126p. The
kind of work suffrage workers experienced.
1980. _____. Where are the women voters? Review of reviews, v. 69 (April 1924), 419-22.
1981. The SILENT suffragists of America. Century, v. 85 (April
1913), 953-4. On the possibility of militant suffrage
tactics.
1982. SIMKINS, M. E. Suffrage and anti-suffrage. Living age,
v. 260 (6 February 1909), 323-9.
1983. SLATER, L. Woman's suffrage. McCall's, v. 88 (September 1961), 84-93.
1984. SMITH, G. Woman's place in the state. Forum, v. 8 (January 1890), 515-30.
1985. SMITH, Helena Huntington. Weighing the women's vote. Outlook, v. 151 (23 January 1929), 126-9. On the potential of the woman's vote.
1986. SMITH, Munroe. Consent of the governed. New York, Man-
suffrage Association, 1914. 8p. Also in: Academy
of Political Science, proceedings, v. 5 (October 1914),
82-8.
1987. SMITH, W. Woman suffrage on trial. Outlook, v. 99 (2
September 1911), 50-1.
1988. SOLOMONS, Selina. How we won the vote in California; a
true story of the campaign of 1911. San Francisco,
New Woman Pub. Co., 1912. 71p.
1989. SOMERSET, Isabel. Renaissance of women. North American review, v. 159 (October 1894), 490-7. Suffrage
and employment beyond the home.
1990. SPENCER, A. G. Logical basis of woman suffrage. American Academy of Political and Social Science, annals,
v. 35 (May 1910), 10-15.
1991. _____. Woman and the state. Forum, v. 48 (October
1912), 394-408.
1992. SPENCER, Sara Jane. Problems on the woman question,
social, political, and scriptural. Washington, Langran,
Ogilvie, 1871. 17p.
1993. SPRAGUE, William Forrest. Women and the West. Boston,
Christopher, 1940. 294p. Hardships of women in the

American West in the 19th century, including the
western suffrage movement.

1994.   SQUIRE, Belle. The woman movement in America; a short
account of the struggle for equal rights. Chicago,
McClurg, 1911. 285p. A brief study of the woman
suffrage movement from around 1790, especially in
Illinois.

1995.   STANTON, Elizabeth Cady. Address in favor of universal
suffrage, for the election of delegates to the constitutional convention. Before the Judiciary Committees of
the Legislature of New York, in the Assembly Chamber, January 23, 1867, in behalf of the American
Equal Rights Association. Albany, Weed, Parsons,
1867. 24p. A speech asking for the right of all people of that state to vote for delegates.

1996.   _____. History of woman suffrage. New York, Fowler &
Wells, 1881-1922. 6v. Reprinted by Source Book
Press, New York, 1970, and by Arno Press, New
York, 1969.

1997.   _____. Letter from Mrs. Elizabeth Cady Stanton to the
Woman's Rights Convention, held at Worcester, October, 1850. Syracuse, Masters' print., [1850?].
pp. 1-4. [Woman's Rights Tracts, no. 10.] Refutation of the theory that attainment of the suffrage by
women will cause a breakdown of the family.

1998.   _____. Letter from Mrs. Elizabeth Cady Stanton to the
Woman's Rights Convention, held at Syracuse, September, 1852. Syracuse, N.Y., Masters' print.,
[1852?]. pp. 5-8. [Woman's Rights Tracts, no. 10.]
Suggests that possibly all property-holding women
should refuse to pay taxes unless given the right to
vote. Also on equal education.

1999.   _____. Memorial of Elizabeth Cady Stanton, Isabella
Beecher Hooker, Elizabeth L. Bladen, Olympia Brown,
Susan B. Anthony, and Josephine L. Griffing, to the
Congress of the United States, and the arguments
thereon.... Washington, D.C., Chronicle Pub. Co.,
1872. 30p. Arguments by the above persons for a
law giving women the right to vote.

2000.   STATEMENT of the District of Columbia Association Opposed
to Woman Suffrage. Congressional record, v. 54
(19 February 1917), 3977-82.

2001.   STATE'S wrongs. New republic, v. 23 (28 July 1920), 242-3.

2002.   STEPHENS, C. C. Legal disabilities of women in California.
2d ed. San Jose, Mercury Steam Print., 1873. 8p.

2003.   STEUNENBERG, F. Woman suffrage in Idaho. Harper's
bazaar, v. 33 (26 May 1900), 220-1.

2004.   STEVENS, Doris. Jailed for freedom. New York, Boni &
Liveright, 1920. 388p.

2005.   STEWART, Ella S. Woman suffrage and the liquor traffic.
American Academy of Political and Social Science,
annals, v. 56 (November 1914), 143-52.

2006.   STONE, Lucy. Reasons why the women of New Jersey

should vote as shown from the Constitution and statutes of New Jersey. n.p., n.d. 4p.
2007. _____. Suffrage for women in Massachusetts. American
magazine, v. 3 (1882), 233.
2008. _____. A woman suffrage catechism. Boston, American
Woman Suffrage Association, 1888. 2p.
2009. _____ and Frances E. Willard. Suffrage for women; a
symposium. Chautauquan, v. 13 (1891), 72.
2010. STRAKER, David Augustus. Citizenship, its rights and
duties--woman suffrage; a lecture delivered by D.
Augustus Straker, esq., at the Israel A.M.E. Church,
and before the Pioneer Lyceum, at Hillsdale, Washington, D.C., April 13 and 14, 1874. Washington,
New National Era Print., 1874. 22p.
2011. STRAUBE, Melvin M. A scientific demonstration of the
dangers of woman suffrage. Huntsville, Mo., Times
Pub. Co., 1921. 116p.
2012. STRONG, Henry. Address before the California Woman's
Club, San Francisco, May 30, 1907. [San Francisco,
n.p., 1907?] 19p.
2013. SUCCESS of woman suffrage. Independent, v. 73 (8 August
1912), 334-5.
2014. SUFFRAGE and higher education for women. Nation, v. 29
(1879), 364.
2015. SUFFRAGE as a national issue. Literary digest, v. 48 (4
April 1914), 745-6.
2016. SUFFRAGE conquest of Illinois. Literary digest, v. 46 (28
June 1913), 1409-10.
2017. SUFFRAGE convention in Chicago. National magazine, v. 49
(April 1920), 92.
2018. SUFFRAGE for women. Every Saturday, v. 9 (1870), 690.
2019. SUFFRAGE for women. Every Saturday, v. 10 (1871), 490.
2020. SUFFRAGE for women. Historical magazine (Dawson's),
v. 1 (1857), 360.
2021. SUFFRAGE for women. Nation, v. 4 (1867), 136.
2022. SUFFRAGE for women. New eclectic, v. 6 (1870), 459.
2023. SUFFRAGE for women. Outlook, v. 64 (1900), 573.
2024. SUFFRAGE for women. Republic, v. 3 (1874), 36.
2025. SUFFRAGE for women. Southern quarterly review, v. 21
(1852), 322.
2026. SUFFRAGE for women; Apollo Hall meeting, 1871. Every
Saturday, v. 10 (1871), 554.
2027. SUFFRAGE for women in the West. Outlook, v. 65 (1900),
430.
2028. SUFFRAGE for women on school committees in Massachusetts. Nation, v. 29 (1879), 272.
2029. SUFFRAGETTES in America. Current literature, v. 44
(April 1908), 350-2.
2030. SUFFRAGETTES on the stump. Letter from the Political
Equality League of Wisconsin, 1912. Wisconsin magazine of history, v. 38 (Autumn 1954), 31-4. Letter
from Crystal Eastman Benedict, campaign manager
of the Political Equality League, to Mrs. C. W.

Steele on how to organize an auto tour for the suffrage campaign.
2031. SUFFRAGIST fight over industrial equality. Literary digest, v. 89 (12 June 1926), 10-11.
2032. SUFFRAGISTS take New York State. Literary digest, v. 55 (17 November 1917), 14-15.
2033. SUMNER, Helen Laura. Equal suffrage; results of an investigation in Colorado made for the Collegiate Equal Suffrage League of New York State. New York, Harper, 1909. 282p.
2034. SUTHERLAND, R. L. Appeal of politics to woman. North American review, v. 191 (January 1910), 25-86.
2035. SWETT, H. P. Ballot as a cultural instrument. Historical outlook, v. 19 (April 1928), 165-6.
2036. SWIDLER, Arlene. Brownson and the woman question. American benedictine review, v. 19 (June 1968), 211-19. Views of anti-suffragist Orestes A. Brownson.
2037. TACTICS of woman suffrage. Independent, v. 64 (23 April 1908), 930-2.
2038. TARBELL, Ida Minerva. Is woman's suffrage a failure? Good housekeeping, v. 79 (October 1924), 18-19.
2039. TAYLOR, Antoinette Elizabeth. The origin of the woman suffrage movement in Georgia. Georgia historical quarterly, v. 28 (June 1944), 63-79. Development of suffrage in Georgia after 1890.
2040. _____. A short history of the woman suffrage movement in Tennessee. Tennessee historical quarterly, v. 2 (September 1943), 195-215.
2041. _____. The woman suffrage movement in Arkansas. Arkansas historical quarterly, v. 15 (Spring 1956), 17-52.
2042. _____. The woman suffrage movement in Mississippi, 1890-1920. Journal of Mississippi history, v. 30, no. 1 (1968), 1-34. Shows the activities of the Mississippi Woman Suffrage Association in its efforts to obtain the vote for women.
2043. _____. The woman suffrage movement in North Carolina, Part 1. North Carolina historical review, v. 38 (January 1961), 45-62. Covers the period from 1863 to 1917.
2044. _____. The woman suffrage movement in North Carolina, Part 2. North Carolina historical review, v. 38 (April 1961), 173-89. Covers the period from 1917 to 1921.
2045. _____. The woman suffrage movement in Tennessee, 1870-1920. New York, Bookman, 1957. 150p.
2046. _____. The woman suffrage movement in Texas. Journal of southern history, v. 17 (May 1951), 194-215.
2047. TAYLOR, Edward Thomas. Equal suffrage in Colorado: speech. Washington, GPO, 1912. 55p.
2048. TAYLOR, G. Women socializing politics. Survey, v. 31 (7 February 1914), 595-6.
2049. _____. Women's voting significantly tested in Illinois.

Survey, v. 32 (18 April 1914), 69-70.
2050. TEN thousand women marching for votes. Literary digest,
       v. 44 (18 May 1912), 1024-6.
2051. TERRY, Edmund R. Votes for women, why? New York,
       Hamilton, 1917. 63p.
2052. THEODORE Roosevelt and Elihu Root on woman's suffrage.
       Outlook, v. 90 (19 December 1908), 848-9.
2053. THOMAS, C. S. Woman suffrage. Congressional record,
       v. 53 (19 February 1916), 3239-40. Tells where
       women vote, how much use they make of the vote,
       and gives testimony of governors of suffrage states.
2054. THOMAS, E. A. Suffrage for women in Wyoming. Potter's
       American monthly, v. 18 (1882), 492.
2055. THOMAS, M. Carey. A new-fashioned argument for woman
       suffrage. New York, National College Equal Suffrage
       League, 1911. 21p. The working woman's need of
       the ballot written by the president of Bryn Mawr Col-
       lege.
2056. THOMAS, Thaddeus P. Why equal suffrage has been a suc-
       cess. Hartford, Connecticut Woman Suffrage Associa-
       tion, [1910?]. 14p.
2057. THOMAS, W. I. Votes for women. American magazine,
       v. 68 (July 1909), 292-301.
2058. _____. Woman and the occupations. American maga-
       zine, v. 68 (September 1909), 463-70. The need of
       the vote for working women.
2059. THOMPSON, C. M. A decade of women's suffrage. Cur-
       rent history, v. 33 (October 1930), 13-17.
2060. TIBBLES, Charles Edwin. Nonpartisan political lecture,
       universal suffrage; the Republican National Conven-
       tion held in Chicago, June 1912, and Colonel Roose-
       velt's reversal of doctrine on woman suffrage. Chi-
       cago, C. E. Tibbles, 1912. 16p.
2061. TILTON, Theodore. The Constitution a title-deed to wom-
       an's franchise. A letter to Charles Sumner. New
       York, Published at the Office of the Golden Age, 1871.
       17p.
2062. _____. The rights of women. A letter to Horace Greeley.
       New York, Published at the Office of the Golden Age,
       1871. 11p.
2063. TIME to stop it. Independent, v. 73 (19 December 1912),
       1439-40.
2064. TODD, John. Woman's rights. Boston, Lee and Shepard,
       1867. 27p.
2065. TRIUMPH of woman suffrage. Current history magazine of
       the New York Times, v. 13 (October 1920), 138-42.
2066. TROUT, Grace Wilbur. Sidelights on Illinois suffrage his-
       tory. Illinois State Historical Society, journal, v. 13
       (April 1920), 145-79. Covers the period from 1869
       to 1920.
2067. TUBBS, Ella E. Judgment reversed. Binghamton, N.Y.,
       n.p., 1912.
2068. TUCKER, Henry St. George. Woman's suffrage by consti-

tutional amendment. New Haven, Conn., Yale University Press, 1916. 204p.

2069.   TYER, P. Idaho's twenty years of woman suffrage. Outlook, v. 114 (6 September 1916), 35-9.

2070.   UNDER which flag, ladies, order or anarchy? Century, v. 86 (June 1913), 309-10. Pennsylvania Association for Woman Suffrage disagrees with militant suffrage methods.

2071.   UNITED Nations. Department of Economic and Social Affairs. The convention on the political rights of women; history and commentary. New York, 1955 [i.e. 1956]. 46p.

2072.   _____. _____. The road to equality; political rights of women. New York, 1953. 21p.

2073.   _____. Secretary-General. Constitutions, electoral laws and other legal instruments relating to the political rights of women; memorandum. 1948- . New York. Annual.

2074.   UNIVERSAL suffrage. Female suffrage. By a Republican (not a "Radical"). Philadelphia, J. B. Lippincott, 1867. 116p.

2075.   VAN RENSSALAER, Mariana Griswold. Should we ask for the suffrage? New York, New York State Association Opposed to Woman Suffrage [191?] 15p.

2076.   VICTORY map of 1918. Woman citizen, v. 3 (7 December 1918), 570-1.

2077.   VOTES for women by federal amendment. New republic, v. 13 (17 November 1917), 64-5.

2078.   WAITE, Davis H. and Lorenzo Crounse. Woman suffrage in practice. North American review, v. 158 (June 1894), 737-44. Articles by the governors of Colorado and Nebraska concerning suffrage in the West.

2079.   WALL, Louise H. Moving to amend; campaign of the College Equal Suffrage League in California. Sunset, v. 27 (October 1911), 377-84.

2080.   WALSH, Correa Moylan. Feminism. New York, Sturgis & Walton, 1917. 393p.

2081.   WALSH, Robert C. Anti-woman suffrage and criticisms. St. Louis, Wilson Printing Co., 1916. 31p.

2082.   WARD, Lester F. Genius and woman's intuition. Forum, v. 9 (June 1890), 401-8. Refutes the theory that woman's intuition in dealing with public questions would be lost if she acquired the right to vote.

2083.   WARREN, M. Housekeepers' need of the ballot. World today, v. 12 (April 1907), 418-21.

2084.   WATSON, A. R. Attitude of southern women on the suffrage question. Arena, v. 11 (February 1895), 363-9.

2085.   WATSON, Ellen H. Pros and cons of woman suffrage; review of a legislative report. By one of the sex. Boston, W. B. Clarke and Carruth, 1882.

2086.   _____. Rights of men and women, natural, civil, political. With replies to popular speakers and writers. Boston, Cupples, Upham, 1883. 62p.

2087. WEBB, J. A.   Legal view of suffrage for women in America.
       American law review, v. 31 (1897), 404.
2088. WEISS, J.   Suffrage for women.   Radical, v. 5 (1869), 445.
2089. WELLS, M. M.   Some effects of woman suffrage.   American
       Academy of Political and Social Science, annals, v.
       143 (May 1929), 207-16.
2090. WEYL, W. E.   Working for the inevitable.   New republic,
       v. 4 (9 October 1915), 15-16.
2091. WHAT America thinks of votes for women.   Literary digest,
       v. 51 (9 October 1915), 753-6.
2092. WHAT the National American Woman Suffrage Association has
       done: half a century of work.   Woman citizen, v. 3
       (9 November 1918), 487.
2093. WHAT woman suffrage does.   World's work, v. 17 (April
       1909), 11419-20.
2094. WHEELER, E. P.   Federal woman suffrage amendment.   Re-
       joinder, by Alice Stone Blackwell; Reply to Miss Black-
       well, by E. P. Wheeler.   Arbitrator, v. 1 (December
       1918), 6-14.
2095. _____. Home rule.   New York, Man-suffrage Association,
       1916.   6p.   Brief on argument before the Judiciary
       Committee, House of Representatives, March 1914,
       against proposition for a constitutional amendment
       compelling the states to adopt woman suffrage.
2096. _____. What women have done without the ballot.   New
       York, Man-Suffrage Association, 1915.   8p.
2097. _____. Why women in rural communities do not need the
       vote.   Cornell countryman, v. 15 (November 1917),
       80-1.
2098. WHERE government is of the people.   Woman citizen, v. 3
       (6 July 1918), 110-11.   Consists of a suffrage map.
2099. WHERE women have municipal suffrage.   Woman citizen,
       v. 3 (24 May 1919), 1136.
2100. WHITE, Carlos.   Ecce femina: an attempt to solve the
       woman question.   Being an examination of arguments
       in favor of female suffrage by John Stuart Mill and
       others, and a presentation of arguments against the
       proposed change in the constitution of society.   Boston,
       Lee & Shepard, 1870.   258p.
2101. WHITE, Eliza A.   As it should be.   Philadelphia, J. B.
       Lippincott, 1874.   274p.   Anti-suffrage text.
2102. _____. As she would have it.   Philadelphia, J. B. Lip-
       pincott, 1873.   105p.
2103. WHITE, H. M.   Open letter on woman suffrage.   Outlook,
       v. 103 (26 April 1913), 893-4.
2104. WHITEHEAD, W. A.   A brief statement connected with the
       origin, practice and prohibition of female suffrage in
       New Jersey.   New Jersey Historical Society, pro-
       ceedings, ser. 1, v. 8 (1856-1859), 101-5.
2105. WHITEHOUSE, Mrs. N.   Woman suffrage in New York.   Na-
       tion, v. 106 (1 June 1918), 647-8.
2106. WHITEHOUSE, V. B.   Immigrant woman and the vote.   Im-
       migrants in America review, v. 1 (September 1915),

63-9.
2107. WHITNEY, Orson Ferguson. Speeches of Hon. D. F. Whit-
       ney in support of woman suffrage delivered in the Con-
       stitutional Convention of Utah, March 30, April 2, and
       April 5, 1895. n.p., Utah Woman Suffrage Associa-
       tion [1895?]. 23p.
2108. WHO wants the suffrage federal amendment? Woman citizen,
       v. 3 (22 June 1918), 70-1.
2109. WHY more women voters don't vote. Literary digest, v. 81
       (24 May 1924), 5-7.
2110. WHY votes should be given to women. Americana, v. 6
       (June 1911), 621-2. Concerns New Jersey.
2111. WILCOX, Hamilton. Freedom's conquests; the great spread
       of woman suffrage through the world. With a roll of
       honor, showing over one hundred regions where it now
       exists, in America, Africa, Europe, Asia, and Ocean-
       ica. 2d ed. New York, J. W. Lovell, 1889. 9p.
2112. WILD, Laura H. Woman suffrage in Ohio. Public, v. 15
       (20 September 1912), 895-6.
2113. WILHELM, Donald. Entering the promised land; four inter-
       views concerning suffrage. Independent, v. 103 (11
       September 1920), 299-300+. Comments by Calvin
       Coolidge, Franklin D. Roosevelt, and others.
2114. WILHITE, Ann L. Wiegman. Sixty-five years till victory:
       a history of woman suffrage in Nebraska. Nebraska
       history, v. 49, no. 2 (1968), 149-63. The movement
       in Nebraska from 1855, including comments on the
       Nebraska Woman Suffrage Association, as well as a
       speech in Omaha by Amelia Bloomer.
2115. WILL New York women vote now that they can? Woman
       citizen, v. 1 (17 November 1917), 478.
2116. WILL the states ratify suffrage? Literary digest, v. 61
       (7 June 1919), 22-3.
2117. WILL they use the ballot? Woman citizen, v. 1 (8 Septem-
       ber 1917), 269.
2118. WILLCOX, James K. Wyoming: the true cause and splendid
       fruits of woman suffrage there...correcting the errors
       of Horace Plunkett and Professor Bryce, and supplying
       omissions in the history of woman suffrage, by Mrs.
       Stanton, Mrs. Gage, and Miss Anthony. New York,
       n.p., 1890. 28p.
2119. WILLIAMS, Albert. Prohibition and woman suffrage. Speech
       of Hon. Albert Williams, of Ionia, Michigan, made at
       Charlotte, Mich., October 9, 1874. [Lansing?] 1874.
       30p.
2120. WILLIAMS, Mattie L. History of woman suffrage in Arizona
       and other states. Arizona historical review, v. 1
       (January 1929), 69-73.
2121. WILSON, W. S. Suffrage in North Carolina. North Carolina
       State Literary and Historical Association, proceedings,
       v. 17 (1917), 70-7.
2122. WILSON, Woodrow. Address at suffrage convention, Atlantic
       City, N.J., September 8, 1916. Washington, GPO,

1916. 5p.
2123. _____. Address by the President of the United States.
        Congressional record, v. 56 (30 September 1918),
        11849-50.
2124. WINNING of Nevada for woman suffrage: including oration of
        Hon. Curtis J. Hillyer, delivered before a joint ses-
        sion of the Nevada Legislature in 1869: an unanswer-
        able argument for the suffrage cause. Carson City,
        Nevada Printing Co., 1916. 29p.
2125. WINSOR, M. Suffrage amendment. Public, v. 21 (13 July
        1918), 896-7.
2126. WOLD, Clara. We don't want nothin' new. Independent,
        v. 102 (1920), 79+. A suffragist's interview with
        Delaware legislators.
2127. WOMAN and the suffrage. American Academy of Political
        and Social Science, annals, v. 56 (November 1914),
        93-160.
2128. WOMAN suffrage. Chicago, Civics Society, 1913. 265p.
        (Woman Citizen's Library, v. 7.)
2129. WOMAN suffrage. Outlook, v. 49 (31 March 1894), 577-8.
        Concerns suffrage in New York.
2130. WOMAN suffrage. Outlook, v. 126 (8 September 1920), 52-3.
2131. WOMAN suffrage and national prohibition. Searchlight on
        Congress, v. 2 (December 1917), 7-10.
2132. WOMAN suffrage and the church. Literary digest, v. 50
        (15 May 1915), 1156.
2133. WOMAN suffrage and the liquor interests; some exhibits.
        New York, National American Woman Suffrage As-
        sociation [1916?]. 16p. Reprints of articles of por-
        tions of the liquor and brewing industry journals show-
        ing their open opposition to woman suffrage, especially
        in Wisconsin, Illinois, and Michigan.
2134. WOMAN suffrage declared a failure. Literary digest, v. 81
        (12 April 1924), 12-13.
2135. WOMAN suffrage in Colorado. Current literature, v. 38
        (May 1905), 425-7.
2136. WOMAN suffrage in Colorado. Outlook, v. 56 (12 June 1897),
        405-8.
2137. WOMAN suffrage in operation; symposium. Independent,
        v. 66 (20 May 1909), 1056-70.
2138. WOMAN suffrage in practice. North American review,
        v. 158 (June 1894), 737-44.
2139. WOMAN suffrage in the Senate. Woman citizen, v. 2 (9
        March 1918), 288.
2140. WOMAN suffrage in the United States; correction of mis-
        statements. Educational review, v. 37 (April 1909),
        405-8.
2141. WOMAN suffrage marches on. Independent, v. 99 (9 August
        1919), 174-6.
2142. WOMAN suffrage marching on. Current literature, v. 51
        (December 1911), 596-600.
2143. The WOMAN suffrage movement. Chautauquan, v. 59 (June
        1910), 69-78.

2144. The WOMAN suffrage movement in the United States, a study;
          by a lawyer. Boston, Arena, 1895. 153p.
2145. WOMAN suffrage question. Outlook, v. 49 (12 May 1894),
          820-2.
2146. WOMAN suffrage stirring the states. Literary digest, v. 46
          (29 March 1913), 697-8.
2147. WOMAN suffrage triumphant. Pan American magazine, v.
          31 (October 1920), 221-5.
2148. WOMAN suffrage victory in sight. Literary digest, v. 64
          (27 March 1920), 25-6.
2149. WOMAN suffragists chortle with joy. Current literature,
          v. 53 (December 1912), 612-14.
2150. WOMAN'S arguments against woman suffrage. North Ameri-
          can review, v. 184 (1 March 1907), 558-60.
2151. WOMAN'S hand in Maine. Literary digest, v. 66 (25 Sep-
          tember 1920), 13-14.
2152. WOMAN'S inherent right to vote. North American review,
          v. 183 (19 October 1906), 830-1.
2153. WOMAN'S National Republic Committee. Woman suffrage
          and political parties. New York, 1888. 8p.
2154. The WOMAN'S rights almanac for 1858. Containing facts,
          statistics, arguments, records of progress, and
          proofs of the need of it. Worcester, Mass., Z.
          Baker [1857?]. 35p.
2155. WOMAN'S victory in Washington. Collier's, v. 46 (7 Janu-
          ary 1911), 25.
2156. WOMEN suffragists and party politics. New republic, v. 9
          (9 December 1916), 138-40.
2157. WOMEN vote in Illinois. Outlook, v. 106 (7 March 1914),
          509-11.
2158. WOMEN voters have made our politics very, very different.
          Saturday evening post, v. 233 (27 August 1960), 10.
2159. WOMEN voters in Colorado. Public, v. 14 (22 September
          1911), 981-2.
2160. WOMEN voters' view on woman's suffrage. Outlook, v. 97
          (28 January 1911), 143-4.
2161. WOMEN'S suffrage; arguments for and against. Oklahoma
          University bulletin, n.s., no. 80, University Extension
          ser. no. 17, 1914. 80p.
2162. WOMEN'S votes in Illinois. Survey, v. 32 (25 July 1914),
          442.
2163. WOODBURY, Helen Laura. Equal suffrage; the results of
          an investigation in Colorado made for the Collegiate
          Equal Suffrage League of New York State. New York,
          Harper, 1909. 281p.
2164. WOODHULL, Victoria Claflin. The argument for woman's
          electoral rights under amendment XIV and XV of the
          Constitution of the United States. n.p., n.d. 202p.
2165. YALE University Debating Association. A discussion of
          woman suffrage, by the Yale University debating teams,
          in the 1914 triangular debates with Harvard and Prince-
          ton. New Haven, Conn., Yale Co-operative Corpora-
          tion, 1914. 38p.

2166.   YEAR of equal suffrage.   World's work, v. 27 (November
            1913), 14-15.
2167.   YOUMANS, Theodora W.   How Wisconsin women won the
            ballot.   Wisconsin magazine of history, v. 5 (1921-
            22), 3-32.   Covers the period from 1849 to 1920.
2168.   YOUNG, Rose.   Keeping up with the suffrage procession.
            Life and labor, v. 7 (May 1917), 78-9.
2169.   _____. Women who get together.   Good housekeeping,
            v. 57 (December 1913), 742-50.
2170.   ZANGWILL, Israel.   Human suffrage.   Call magazine (7
            October 1917), 3.
2171.   ZEAL of the woman suffragists.   Current literature, v. 47
            (December 1909), 598-603.

2172. ABBOTT, Edith. Employment of women in industries.
Journal of political economy, v. 14 (January 1906),
14-40.

2173. _____. Employment of women in industries: cigar-
making--its history and present tendencies. Journal
of political economy, v. 15 (January 1907), 1-25.

2174. _____. History of industrial employment of women in
the United States: An introductory study. Journal
of political economy, v. 14 (October 1906), 461-501.

2175. _____. History of the employment of women in the American cotton mills. Journal of political economy, v. 16
(November/December 1908), 602-21, 680-92.

2176. _____. The history of trade-unionism among women in
Boston. A report to the Executive Committee of the
Women's Trade Union League of Massachusetts....
Boston, The League, 1906. 33p.

2177. _____. The wage-earning woman and the state. Boston,
Boston Equal Suffrage Association for Good Government, 1912. 22p.

2178. _____. Women in industry. Survey, v. 23 (15 January
1910), 513-14.

2179. _____. Women in industry; a study in American economic
history. New York, Appleton, 1913. 408p. Reprinted
by Arno Press, New York, 1969, and by Source Book
Press, New York, 1970.

2180. _____. Women in industry: the Chicago stockyards.
Journal of political economy, v. 19 (October 1911),
632-54.

2181. _____. Women in industry: The manufacture of boots
and shoes. American journal of Sociology, v. 15
(November 1909), 335-60. Development of the industry
and economic problems of women such as decreases in
wages and strikes in Lynn, Massachusetts.

2182. _____. Women's wages in Chicago. Journal of political
economy, v. 21 (February 1913), 143-58.

2183. ACADEMY of Political Science, New York. The economic
position of women. New York, 1910. 193p.

2184. ADDAMS, Jane. Reaction of simple women to trade union
propaganda. Survey, v. 36 (1 July 1916), 364-6.

2185. ADMISSION of women to union membership. Monthly labor
review, v. 55 (November 1942), 1006-7.

2186. ADVENTURES in economic independence. Harper's weekly,
v. 61 (25 December 1915), 608-9.

2187. ALEXANDER, S. T. M. Negro women in our economic life.

Opportunity, v. 8 (July 1930), 201-3.

2188. ALEXANDER Hamilton Institute, New York. Women in industry. New York, The Institute, 1918. 44p.

2189. AMERICAN federationist (August 1929), special issue. Devoted to women workers, trade unionists, wages, the U.S. Women's Bureau, compensation, etc.

2190. AMERICAN scholar forum; are American women making the most of the rights and privileges for which they fought? Symposium. American scholar, v. 19 (January 1950), 89-97. Discussion: v. 19 (April 1950), 231-4.

2191. AMERICAN woman's dilemma. Life, v. 22 (16 June 1947), 101-11.

2192. AMERICAN women and the labor problem. Public opinion, v. 22 (1897), 748.

2193. AMES, Azel. Sex in industry; a plea for the working girl. Boston, J. R. Osgood, 1875. 158p.

2194. AMIDON, Beulah. Arms and the women: From now on, for the duration, the women of America will be replacing millions of men at jobs in war production and civilian services. Survey graphic, v. 31 (May 1942), 244-8+.

2195. _____. Woman's place in the defense program. Educational record, v. 22 (July 1941), 403-13.

2196. _____. Women breadwinners; they don't work for pin money. Survey graphic, v. 27 (March 1938), 151-2. On the necessity of women to work, with differences in salaries between men and women.

2197. ANDERSON, H. W. Employing married women. Educational law and administration, v. 6 (October 1938), 43-4.

2198. ANDERSON, Mary. Behind the counters in the "five-and-tens." American federationist, v. 39 (March 1932), 283-6.

2199. _____. Economic status of wage-earning homemakers. Journal of home economics, v. 24 (October 1932), 864-8.

2200. _____. Hours of work. American federationist, v. 32 (September 1925), 769-72.

2201. _____. Importance of women in industry. Personnel journal, v. 6 (February 1928), 329-30.

2202. _____. Industrial standards for women. American federationist, v. 32 (July 1925), 769-72.

2203. _____. King cotton and the woman worker. American federationist, v. 39 (April 1932), 429-35.

2204. _____. The Negro woman worker. American federationist, v. 39 (October 1932), 1114-20.

2205. _____. The postwar role of American women. American economic review, supp. v. 34 (March 1944), 237-44.

2206. _____. Report of committee on women in industry. U.S. Bureau of Labor bulletin, v. 653 (1938), 74-85.

2207. _____. Status of women in industry, 1935-1936; report of committee with discussion. U.S. Bureau of Labor bulletin, v. 629 (1937), 102-24.

2208. _____. Uphill way of women workers. Woman's journal, v. 14 (December 1929), 15.

2209. _____. What use is the Women's Bureau to the woman
worker? American federationist, v. 36 (August 1929),
939-42.

2210. _____. Will women retire from industry with return of
peace? Academy of Political Science, proceedings,
v. 8 (February 1919), 139-40.

2211. _____. With women workers in the stockyards. American federationist, v. 39 (May 1932), 556-60.

2212. _____. The woman office worker: her outlook today.
American federationist, v. 42 (March 1935), 267-71.

2213. _____. Woman's place. Safety engineering (March 1943),
20-3.

2214. _____. Women at work: "woman power" can be used ef-
fectively in the defense program when health and safety
measures are adequate. National safety news (July
1941), 10-11+.

2215. _____. Women in industry, September 1, 1938, to September 1, 1939; report of the committee, with summary of laws and major events. U.S. Bureau of Labor
bulletin, v. 678 (1940), 178-87.

2216. _____. Women in laundries. American federationist, v.
39 (February 1932), 182-7.

2217. _____. Women in war industry. American federationist,
v. 49 (March 1942), 18-19+.

2218. _____. Women who enamel stoves. American federationist, v. 40 (January 1933), 49-53.

2219. _____. Women work long hours in southern mills. American labor legislation review, v. 18 (March 1928), 35-6.

2220. _____. Women workers in textiles. American federationist, v. 36 (June 1929), 696-9.

2221. _____. Women's role in war production. Labor information bulletin (April 1942), 1-4.

2222. _____. Working conditions. American federationist,
v. 32 (October 1925), 946-9.

2223. ANDREWS, N. Organizing women. American federationist,
v. 36 (August 1929), 976-7.

2224. ANGELL, Frances. Compete! Philadelphia, Dorrance, 1935.
104p.

2225. ANTHONY, Katharine Susan. Mothers who must earn; a
study in New York's west side. Survey, v. 32 (4
April 1914), 17-22.

2226. ANTHONY, Susan B., II. Out of the kitchen, into the war;
woman's winning role in the nation's drama. New
York, S. Daye, 1943. 246p.

2227. APPLEBAUM, Stella B. Working wives and mothers. New
York, Public Affairs Committee, 1952. 32p. The
status of married women in industry.

2228. ARE many women replacing soldiers in industrial work?
Current opinion, v. 64 (January 1918), 60-1.

2229. ARE women advancing? Public, v. 21 (20 April 1918),
491-2.

2230. ATTACK Illinois ten-hour law. Survey, v. 27 (16 December 1911), 1351-2.

2231. BAER, Amelia. Some problems of working mothers. Family, v. 23 (January 1943), 386-91.

2232. BAERS, M. Women workers and home responsibilities. International labour review, v. 69 (April 1954), 338-55.

2233. BAKER, Elizabeth F. At the crossroads in the legal protection of women in industry. American Academy of Political and Social Science, annals, v. 143 (May 1929), 265-79.

2234. _____. Protective labor legislation, with special reference to women in the state of New York. New York, Columbia University Press, 1925. 467p.

2235. BAKER, Melba. Women who work: discrimination against women in the United States; extent of this problem and prospect for its solution. International socialist review, v. 23 (Summer 1962), 80-3+.

2236. BANNING, M. C. Will they go back home? Rotarian, v. 63 (September 1943), 28-30.

2237. BARBASH, J. Industrialism and woman's status. Vocational guidance quarterly, v. 13 (Autumn 1964), 21-7.

2238. BARNARD, E. F. Home, job, or both? The woman's problem. Nation, v. 122 (2 June 1926), 601-2.

2239. BARNES, Earl. Economic independence of women. Atlantic monthly, v. 110 (August 1912), 260-5. Property rights and especially unequal income and job rights of women.

2240. _____. Women in industry. Atlantic monthly, v. 110 (July 1912), 116-24.

2241. BARNES, F. The young girl worker. American federationist, v. 36 (August 1929), 984.

2242. BARRY, V. J. Statutes prohibiting employment of married women in public service. Boston University law review, v. 19 (November 1939), 661-5.

2243. BATTEN, Samuel Zane. The industrial menace to the home. Philadelphia, American Baptist Publication Society, 1914. 32p.

2244. BEINHAUER, Myrtle T. State labor laws applicable to women and their effect on women's employment opportunities. 336p. PhD thesis, University of Minnesota, 1955. Analysis of maximum hours, minimum wages, safety and health, and equal pay and their impact on women's employment opportunities.

2245. BEM, Sandra L. and Daryl J. Bem. Sex-segregated want ads: do they discourage female job applicants? Pittsburgh, Carnegie-Mellon University, Department of Psychology. Reprinted by Know, Inc., Pittsburgh, 1969.

2246. BENN, W. J. Women have a place in business and industry but they must not surrender their place in the home. America, v. 61 (27 May 1939), 154-5.

2247. BENSLEY, M. S. Labor organization among women. Charities and the commons, v. 15 (16 December 1905), 384-5.

2248. BENSTON, Margaret. The political economy of women's liberation. Monthly review, v. 21 (September 1969), 13-27. Also: Boston, New England Free Press, 1969. The women's movement in relation to the class structure of society, primarily concerning industry and production.

2249. BERRY, G. H. Mothers in industry. American Academy of Political and Social Science, annals, v. 143 (May 1929), 315-24.

2250. BEST, Harry. Extent of organization in the women's garment making industries of New York. American economic review, v. 9 (December 1919), 776-92.

2251. BIRD, Caroline. Born female; the high cost of keeping women down. New York, McKay, 1968. 288p.

2252. BLACKWELL, E. Industrial position of women. Popular science monthly, v. 23 (1883), 388.

2253. BLAIR, Emily Newell. Women in war industries. Current history magazine of the New York Times, v. 9 (January 1919), 95-100.

2254. BLANKENHORN, M. D. Do working women want it? Consumers' League report on the 48-hour law. Survey, v. 57 (15 February 1927), 630-1.

2255. BLISS, H. L. Eccentric official statistics. American journal of Sociology, v. 3 (November 1897), 355-77. Employment of women and children and the possible economic effects on the head of the family.

2256. BLOOD, R. O., Jr. Long-range causes and consequences of the employment of married women. Journal of marriage and the family, v. 27 (February 1965), 43-7.

2257. B'NAI B'rith. Vocational Service Bureau. Five thousand women college graduates report: findings of a national survey of the social and economic status of women graduates of liberal arts colleges of 1946-1949. By Robert Shosteck. Washington, 1953. 66p.

2258. BODICHON, Barbara Leigh. Women and work. New York, C. S. Francis, 1859. 35p.

2259. BONDFIELD, M. G. Women within the trade union. American federationist, v. 34 (November 1927), 1360-2.

2260. BOONE, Gladys. The Women's Trade Union Leagues in Great Britain and the United States of America. New York, Columbia University Press, 1942. 283p. Reprinted by AMS Press, New York, 1968. Concerns women in industries leading up to the American Women's Trade Union League and its progress to around 1940. Emphasizes the American movement.

2261. BOOTHE, Viva B. Gainfully employed women in the family. American Academy of Political and Social Science, annals, v. 160 (March 1932), 75-85.

2262. BOYNTON, N. Working girls. Arena, v. 2 (August 1890), 370-2.

2263. BRANCH, Mary S. Women and wealth; a study of the economic status of American women. Chicago, University of Chicago Press, 1934. 153p.

2264. BRANDEIS, Louis Dembitz. Anna Hawley, plaintiff in error,
       vs. Joseph H. Walker, constable for the township of
       Montgomery, Franklin County, Ohio, defendant in er-
       ror. Brief and argument for defendant in error. By
       Louis D. Brandeis, counsel for the defendant in error,
       assisted by Josephine Goldmark.... n.p., 1914. 622p.
       Concerns the restricting of hours for women.

2265. _____. The people of the state of New York, respondent,
       against Charles Schweinler Press, a corporation, de-
       fendant-appellant. A summary of "facts of knowledge"
       submitted on behalf of the people. Prepared April
       1914, by Louis D. Brandeis and Josephine Goldmark.
       New York, National Consumers' League, 1918. 452p.
       Concerns night work restriction for women.

2266. _____ and Josephine C. Goldmark. Women in industry;
       decision of the United States Supreme Court in Curt
       Miller vs. State of Oregon, upholding the constitution-
       ality of the Oregon ten-hour law for women and brief
       for the State of Oregon. Reprinted for the National
       Consumers' League. New York, 1908. 113p. Re-
       printed by Arno Press, New York, 1969.

2267. BRECKINRIDGE, Sophonisba Preston. Illinois ten-hour law.
       Journal of political economy, v. 18 (June 1910), 465-
       70.

2268. _____. Legislative control of women's work. Journal of
       political economy, v. 14 (February 1906), 107-9.

2269. BREWER, F. M. Women workers after the war. Editorial
       research reports (22 April 1944), 285-300.

2270. BRIEF for the eight-hour day for women. Monthly labor re-
       view, v. 8 (May 1919), 1430-5.

2271. BRINK, V. E. Paychecks or homes for women: A knotty
       problem for postwar solution. Commerce (September
       1944), 16-18+.

2272. BRITTON, V. Gainfully employed homemakers. Journal of
       Home Economics, v. 30 (March 1938), 72-4+.

2273. BROOKS, T. R. Working women. Dun's review and modern
       industry, v. 82 (August 1963), 62-3.

2274. BROPHY, Loire. If women must work. New York, Appleton-
       Century, 1936. 153p.

2275. BROWN, C. What's going to happen to our women workers?
       Good housekeeping, v. 117 (December 1943), 42+.

2276. BROWN, E. S. Working women in New York. American
       journal of social science, v. 25 (1888), 78.

2277. BROWN, Jean Collier. The economic status of Negro women.
       Southern workman, v. 60 (October 1931), 428-37.

2278. BROWNE, H. F. Employment of women after marriage.
       Conference board management record, v. 1 (October
       1939), 149-56.

2279. BRYN MAWR College. Summer School for Women Workers
       in Industry. Women workers and family support; a
       study made by students in the economics course at the
       Bryn Mawr summer school. Washington, GPO, 1925.
       10p. [Bulletin of the U.S. Women's Bureau, no. 49.]

2280. BRYNER, E. Taking stock of American women as wage
      earners. Industrial arts magazine, v. 7 (June 1918),
      207-9.
2281. BUCKLEY, L. College women and the labor market. Cath-
      olic counselor, v. 7 (Spring 1963), 98-101.
2282. _____. More change. Community, v. 24 (July/August
      1965), 15.
2283. BULLARD, Washington Irving. Women's work in war time.
      Boston, Merchants National Bank, 1917. 85p.
2284. BULLOCK, Edna Dean, comp. Selected articles on the em-
      ployment of women. Minneapolis, H. W. Wilson, 1911.
      147p.
2285. BUNTING, Mary I. Huge waste: educated womanpower.
      New York Times magazine (7 May 1961), 23+.
2286. BUTLER, Elizabeth Beardsley. Industrial environment of
      Pittsburgh's working women. Charities and the com-
      mons, v. 21 (6 March 1909), 1117-42.
2287. _____. Women and the trades, Pittsburgh, 1907-1908.
      New York, Charities Publication Committee, 1909.
      440p.
2288. _____. Work of women in the mercantile houses of Pitts-
      burgh. American Academy of Political and Social Sci-
      ence, annals, v. 33 (March 1909), 326-37.
2289. _____. Working women of Pittsburgh. Charities and the
      commons, v. 21 (2 January 1909), 570-80.
2290. CADBURY, Edward. Women's work and wages. Chicago,
      University of Chicago Press, 1906.
2291. CAIN, Glen George. Married women in the labor force--an
      economic analysis. Chicago, University of Chicago
      Press, 1966. 159p. Historical study of the deter-
      minants of participation of married women in the labor
      force.
2292. CALIFORNIA Industrial Welfare Committee. What California
      has done to protect the women workers. Sacramento,
      1927. 27p.
2293. CALIFORNIA--Minimum wages for women in mercantile es-
      tablishments. Monthly review, v. 5 (September 1917),
      116-17.
2294. CALLING the dishonor roll of states seeking to legislate
      against the married woman worker. Independent wom-
      an, v. 18 (May 1939), 149.
2295. CAMMON, H. M. Work and wages of women. Harper's
      magazine, v. 38 (1869), 665.
2296. CAMPBELL, Helen Stuart. Prisoners of poverty. Women
      wage-earners, their trades and their lives. Boston,
      Little, Brown, 1900. 257p. Reprinted by Greenwood
      Press, Westport, Conn., 1970.
2297. _____. Women wage-earners: their past, their present,
      and their future. Boston, Roberts, 1893. 213p. Re-
      printed by Greenwood Press, Westport, Conn., 1971.
      In part, on the inequalities of wages between men and
      women.
2298. _____. Working women of today. Arena, v. 4 (August

1891), 329-39.
2299. CAMPBELL, M. E. Employment bureaus for women.
Academy of Political Science, proceedings, v. 1 (October 1910), 151-61.
2300. CAN a woman run a home and a job, too? Literary digest,
v. 75 (11 November 1922), 40-63.
2301. CANNON, P. Pin-money slaves. Forum, v. 84 (August 1930), 98-103.
2302. CAREY, H. Career or maternity? North American review,
v. 228 (December 1929), 737-44.
2303. CARNER, L. Shorter hours for women workers. American
federationist, v. 35 (October 1928), 1246-9.
2304. CARPENTER, Elizabeth. More truth about woman in industry. North American review, v. 179 (August 1904),
215-25. A refutation of an argument showing how
poorly women stand in industry, especially in regard
to salary and physical conditions.
2305. CARROLL, M. S. Working wife and her family's economic
position. Monthly labor review, v. 85 (April 1962),
366-74. Reply: v. 85 (August 1962), 898-9.
2306. CARSEL, Wilfred. A history of the Chicago Ladies' Garment
Workers' Union. Chicago, Normandie House, 1940.
323p.
2307. CASSELL, Kay Ann. The legal status of women. Library
journal, v. 96 (1 September 1971), 2600-3. Problems
of Title VII and the Equal Employment Opportunity
Commission as well as salary differences, and other
matters.
2308. CHAMBERLAIN, Mary. Women after the war. Survey,
v. 34 (14 August 1915), 450-2.
2309. The CHANGING status of Negro women workers. Monthly
labor review, v. 87 (June 1964), 671-3.
2310. CHASS, B. P. American women who are earning wages.
Current history magazine of the New York Times,
v. 22 (May 1925), 253-6.
2311. CHENERY, W. L. The new position of women. Survey,
v. 45 (8 January 1921), 539-40. The economic status
of women before, during, and after World War I and
the need to give men the same safeguards as women
rather than to tear down the laws set up for women.
Also concerns the work of the U.S. Women's Bureau.
2312. CHERVENIK, E. Employment status of University of Wisconsin women graduates of 1945, 1946, and 1947. National Association of Deans of Women, journal, v. 11
(March 1948), 150-2.
2313. CHEYNEY, A. S. Negro woman in industry. Survey, v. 46
(23 April 1921), 119.
2314. CHICAGO Trade and Labor Assembly. New slavery: investigation into the sweating system as applied to the
manufacturing of wearing apparel. Chicago, Rights of
Labor Office, 1891.
2315. CHISHOLM, Shirley. The 51% minority. An address by
Representative Shirley Chisholm delivered at the Con-

ference on Women's Employment, sponsored by the
Chicago Area Chapter of the National Organization for
Women, Chicago, 24 January 1970. Pittsburgh, Know,
Inc., 1970. 7p.

2316. CHOLLET, L. E. A working-woman's statement. Nation,
v. 4 (1867), 155.

2317. CHURCH, E. R. Employment for women. Harper's monthly magazine, v. 65 (1882), 112.

2318. CHUTE, C. L. Women and children in the glass industry.
Survey, v. 26 (17 June 1911), 437-8.

2319. CLARK, I. C. Negro woman worker, what now? Opportunity, v. 22 (April 1944), 84-5+.

2320. CLARK, Sue Ainslie. Making both ends meet; the income
and outlay of New York working girls. New York,
Macmillan, 1911. 270p.

2321. CLEVELAND. Chamber of Commerce. A report on the
problem of the substitution of woman for manpower in
industry; approved by the Board of Directors, July 17,
1918...Cleveland, 1918. 49p.

2322. CLINCH, Mary. The phenomenon of the working wife. Social order, v. 6 (October 1956), 362-6.

2323. COHN, F. M. Women and the labor movement. American
federationist, v. 32 (December 1925), 1186-8.

2324. COIT, E. G. and M. H. Esgar. Married women in industry.
Woman's press, v. 23 (February 1929), 126-9.

2325. _____ and E. D. Harper. Why do married women work?
Survey, v. 64 (15 April 1930), 79-80.

2326. COLON, Clara. Equality for working women. Political affairs, v. 47 (November 1968), 20-33.

2327. COLORED women in industry in Philadelphia. Monthly labor
review, v. 12 (May 1921), 1046-8.

2328. COMMANDER, Lydia Kingsmill. Self-supporting woman and
the family. American journal of Sociology, v. 14
(May 1909), 752-7.

2329. COMMENTS on womanpower 4F. Independent woman, v. 22
(November 1943), 234+ ; (December 1943), 367+ .

2330. CONFERENCE on Employment problems of Working Women.
Report. Held at Kellogg Center, Michigan State Uni-
versity, East Lansing, Michigan, September 30, 1961.
Washington, GPO, 1962. 23p.

2331. CONFERENCE on Expanding Employment Opportunities for
Career Women, Los Angeles, 1966. Exploding the
myths; a report. Washington, GPO, 1967. 67p.

2332. CONFERENCE on Work in the Lives of Married Women,
Columbia University, 1957. Work in the lives of married women. New York, Columbia University Press,
1959. 220p.

2333. CONNECTICUT. Bureau of Labor. Report on the conditions
of wage-earning women and girls. By C. M. Hollo-
way. n.p., Connecticut State Library, 1914. 139p.

2334. CONSTITUTIONALITY of a bill to prohibit the employment of
married women. Michigan State Bar journal, v. 12
(April 1933), 231-2.

2335. CONSUMERS' League of Cincinnati. Bulletin on conditions
       of saleswomen in Cincinnati mercantile establishments.
       Cincinnati, The League, 1915. 16p.
2336. _____. What girls live on--and how. A study of the ex-
       penditures of a sample group of girls employed in
       Cincinnati in 1929. By Frances R. Whitney. Cincin-
       nati, The League, 1930. 42p.
2337. _____. Women workers in factories: A study of working
       conditions in 275 industrial establishments in Cincin-
       nati and adjoining towns. By Annette Mann. Cincin-
       nati, The League, 1918. 45p.
2338. CONSUMERS' League of Eastern Pennsylvania, Philadelphia.
       Colored women as industrial workers in Philadelphia;
       a study made by the Consumers' League of Eastern
       Pennsylvania. [Philadelphia, 1920?] 47p.
2339. CONSUMERS' League of New York. Behind the scenes in
       a hotel. New York, The League, 1922. 47p.
2340. _____. Behind the scenes in a restaurant; a study of
       1017 women restaurant employees. New York, The
       League, 1916. 48p.
2341. _____. Behind the scenes in candy factories. By Lillian
       Symes. New York, The League, 1928. 65p.
2342. _____. The forty-eight hour law; do working women want
       it? By Lillian Symes. New York, The League, 1927.
       36p.
2343. _____. Less than a living wage. New York, The League,
       1921. 9p.
2344. _____. New day for the colored woman worker. New
       York, The League, 1919. 39p.
2345. CONSUMERS' League of Oregon. Report of the Social Survey
       Committee on the wages, hours, and conditions of
       work and cost and standard of living of women wage
       earners in Oregon with special reference to Portland.
       Portland, The League, 1913. 12p.
2346. COOK, Alice H. Women and American trade unions. Amer-
       ican Academy of Political and Social Science, annals,
       v. 375 (January 1968), 124-32. A study of unions'
       attitudes toward women and the effect of "equality"
       legislation on women's opportunities.
2347. CORSON, John J. Wasting of manpower. Atlantic monthly,
       v. 170 (August 1942), 75-8. The necessity of married
       women to work to replace men in the Armed Forces.
2348. COTTON, D. W. The case for the working mother. New
       York, Stein and Day, 1965. 212p.
2349. COUSINS, Norman. Will women lose their jobs? Current
       history, v. 51 (September 1939), 14-18. Against
       defeminization of jobs in order to alleviate job short-
       age for men.
2350. CROOK, D. P. Not guilty! Married woman who follows
       woman's work outside the home. Independent woman,
       v. 19 (June 1940), 179-80.
2351. DAGGETT, M. P. New chapter in woman's progress. Good
       housekeeping, v. 56 (February 1913), 148-55.

2352. DALL, Caroline Wells. Woman's right to labor; or, low
       wages and hard work. Boston, Walker, Wise, 1860.
       184p. Social obstacles for women as well as women
       creating their own problems.
2353. DAVENEL, G. F. When Johnny comes marching home. In-
       dependent woman, v. 24 (July 1945), 182-3+ .
2354. DAVIES, R. J. Are women taking men's jobs? Political
       quarterly, v. 2 (January 1931), 126-30.
2355. DAVIS, Allen F. The Woman's Trade Union League; origins
       and organization. Labor history, v. 5, no. 1 (1964),
       3-17.
2356. DAVIS, B. H. New look at working wives. America,
       v. 107 (18 August 1962), 616+ ; Discussion: v. 107
       (22 September 1962), 782-5.
2357. DAY, Lincoln H. Status implications of the employment of
       married women in the United States. American jour-
       nal of Economics and Sociology, v. 20 (July 1961),
       391-7.
2358. DECTER, Midge. Women at work. Commentary, v. 31
       (March 1961), 243-250.
2359. DEGLER, Carl N. Revolution without ideology: The chang-
       ing place of women in America. Daedalus, v. 93
       (Spring 1964), 653-70. The role of the industrial
       revolution as a force in changing women's place.
2360. DEVINE, Edward Thomas. Economic function of woman.
       New York, Teachers College Press, 1910. 16p.
2361. DICKASON, Gladys. Women in labor unions. American
       Academy of Political and Social Science, annals,
       v. 251 (May 1947), 70-8.
2362. DISNEY, D. C. She sought refuge from domestic chaos in
       a job. Ladies' home journal, v. 80 (October 1963),
       10+ .
2363. DO women want protection? Wrapping women in cotton-
       wool, by Harriot Stanton Blatch; What is equality? by
       Clara Mortenson Beyer. Nation, v. 116 (31 January
       1923), 115-16. Concerning special legislation for
       working women.
2364. DO working women get a fair break: one of them says no;
       an employer says yes. Changing times, (October
       1949), 8-11.
2365. DORR, Rheta Childe. Bullying the woman-worker. Harper's
       weekly, v. 51 (30 March 1907), 458-9+ ; On long work-
       ing hours and low pay for women in industry.
2366. _____. Should there be labor laws for women? Good
       housekeeping, v. 81 (September 1925), 52-3.
2367. _____. Woman wage-earners. Nation, v. 82 (1906),
       152-3. On working conditions in industry and the
       lack of sophisticated studies.
2368. DREIER, M. E. Women in industry. Academy of Political
       Science, proceedings, v. 8 (February 1919), 139-40.
2369. DUNLOP, F. Social result of legislation affecting women
       workers. National Conference of Social Work (1927),
       309-12.

2370. DURAND, J. D. The post-war employment of women in the
      United States: a statistical forecast. International
      labour review, v. 48 (December 1943), 695-713.
2371. EARNINGS and hours in woman-employing industries of
      Hawaii. Monthly labor review, v. 52 (February
      1941), 363-8.
2372. EARNINGS and hours of women in Kentucky, 1937. Monthly
      labor review, v. 47 (August 1938), 309-12.
2373. EARNINGS and hours of working women in Utah. Monthly
      labor review, v. 50 (March 1940), 630-4.
2374. EATON, Charles Henry. The industrial position of woman.
      A lecture by Charles H. Eaton...delivered before the
      School of Social Economics, New York. New York,
      Press of W. R. Jenkins [189?]. 23p.
2375. ECONOMIC progress of women. Social economist, v. 2
      (1892), 337.
2376. EDELMAN, Judy. Unions on the line; myth. Reality. Up
      from under, v. 1 (May/June 1970), 34-7. Criticism
      of unions' discrimination against women.
2377. EDUCATED woman's struggle to support herself. American
      magazine, v. 62 (1906), 281.
2378. EFFECT of modern industry on women. Outlook, v. 92 (22
      May 1909), 137-8.
2379. EFFECT of plant shut-down on woman workers. Monthly
      labor review, v. 37 (December 1933), 1355-8.
2380. EFFECT of technological changes on employment of women.
      Monthly labor review, v. 42 (January 1936), 81-4.
2381. EFFECTS of labor legislation on employment opportunities
      for women. Monthly labor review, v. 27 (November
      1928), 911-22.
2382. ELKUS, Abram I. Social investigation and social legislation.
      American Academy of Political and Social Science, an-
      nals, v. 48 (July 1913), 54-65. Attempts to improve
      the conditions under which women in industry worked.
2383. ELLIOTT, C. W. Work and wages of women. North Ameri-
      can review, v. 135 (1882), 146.
2384. EMPLOYMENT and wages of women in Pennsylvania. Monthly
      labor review, v. 47 (December 1938), 1276-82.
2385. EMPLOYMENT for women in San Francisco. Overland month-
      ly, n.s., v. 4 (1884), 387.
2386. EMPLOYMENT of married women. Social service review,
      v. 13 (June 1939), 280-1.
2387. EMPLOYMENT of married women in the United States. In-
      dustrial and labor information, v. 54 (13 May 1935),
      223-6.
2388. EMPLOYMENT of older women. International labour review,
      v. 72 (July 1955), 61-77.
2389. EMPLOYMENT of women after marriage. Monthly labor re-
      view, v. 50 (January 1940), 78-82.
2390. EMPLOYMENT of women and children in Indiana. Monthly
      labor review, v. 16 (May 1923), 1051-4.
2391. EMPLOYMENT of women in California, March, 1943. Month-
      ly labor review, v. 57 (July 1943), 105-6.

2392. EMPLOYMENT of women in clerical work. Monthly labor
       review, v. 40 (May 1935), 1225-32.
2393. EMPLOYMENT of women in industrial occupations in Oregon.
       Monthly labor review, v. 11 (December 1920), 1242-5.
2394. EMPLOYMENT of women in New York State factories, 1942.
       Monthly labor review, v. 56 (February 1943), 282-3.
2395. EMPLOYMENT of women in peacetime and war jobs in New
       York State. Industrial bulletin, v. 21 (October 1942),
       346-8.
2396. EMPLOYMENT of women in the United States. Industrial and
       labour information, v. 49 (15 January 1934), 84-9.
2397. EMPLOYMENT of women in war production. Social security
       bulletin (July 1942), 4-15.
2398. EMPLOYMENT of women in wartime. Monthly labor review,
       v. 55 (September 1942), 441-5.
2399. ERSKINE, Lillian. Women in productive industry. American
       Academy of Political and Social Science, annals, v. 91
       (September 1920), 93-7.
2400. EXPLOITATION of women workers. Social justics review,
       v. 35 (September 1942), 158-9.
2401. FAIVRE, B. M. Strangers in our midst: the plight of the
       young girl industrial worker. Catholic charities re-
       view, v. 26 (April 1942), 87-9.
2402. FARMER, H. S. Helping women to resolve the home-career
       conflict. Personnel and guidance journal, v. 49 (June
       1971), 795-801.
2403. FAWCETT, E. Woes of the New York working girl. Arena,
       v. 5 (December 1891), 26-35.
2404. FEDERAL policy in the employment of women. Monthly labor
       review, v. 7 (November 1918), 1332-40. The work of
       the National War Labor Board.
2405. FEMALE labor arouses hostility and apprehension in union
       ranks. Current opinion, v. 64 (April 1918), 292-4.
       The problem of replacing men during the war by wom-
       en working for lower wages.
2406. FIFTY year goal near for women workers.... Business
       week (21 January 1956), 46+. Women's growth in the
       American labor force and the part played by the U.S.
       Women's Bureau.
2407. FIGHT against married women on payrolls. American busi-
       ness, v. 9 (August 1939), 37.
2408. FILENE, E. A. Betterment of the conditions of working
       women. American Academy of Political and Social
       Science, annals, v. 27 (May 1906), 613-23.
2409. FISCH, Edith L. and M. D. Schwartz. State laws on the em-
       ployment of women. Metuchen, N.J., Scarecrow,
       1953. 377p.
2410. FISHER, Katharine. Women workers and the A. F. of L.
       New republic, v. 27 (3 August 1921), 265-7. Prob-
       lems of women in being recognized by unions.
2411. FISHER, Lettice. Economic position of the married woman.
       New York, Oxford University Press, 1924.
2412. FLOERKE, Jill. Conference on women's rights sponsored

by the National Organization for Women. Christian
century, v. 87 (11 March 1970), 304-6. Conference
in Chicago, 24 January 1970, primarily concerning
rights in employment.

2413. FREUND, E. Constitutional aspect of the protection of wom-
en in industry. Academy of Political Science, proceedings, v. 1 (October 1910), 162-84.

2414. FRIEDAN, Betty. Woman: the fourth dimension. Ladies'
home journal, v. 81 (June 1964), 48-55; Discussion:
v. 81 (June 1964), 47; (September 1964), 34+.

2415. FRIES, F. W. Should women work? Catholic digest, v. 2
(May 1938), 29-31.

2416. FROM the women: "What about our job rights?" U.S. news
and world report, v. 61 (4 July 1966), 61-2. Criticism of the Equal Employment Opportunity Commission
by Representative Martha Griffiths.

2417. FULL employment means women, too. American Association
of University Women, journal, v. 39 (October 1945),
37.

2418. FURTHER information asked on economic opportunities for
women. United Nations review, v. 5 (May 1959),
35-8.

2419. FUTURE of woman as Olive Schriner sees it. Current literature, v. 50 (May 1911), 515-17.

2420. GAMET, D. M. The problem of married women in public
employment. Bar Association of Kansas, journal,
v. 9 (February 1941), 271-6.

2421. GILES, N. What about the women? Do they want to keep
their factory jobs when the war is over? Ladies' home
journal, v. 61 (June 1944), 22-3+.

2422. GILMAN, Charlotte Perkins. Woman's economic place. Cosmopolitan, v. 27 (July 1899), 309-13.

2423. _____. Women and economics: a study of the economic
relation between men and women as a factor in social
evolution. Boston, Small, Maynard, 1898. 340p.
Reprinted by Source Book Press, New York, 1970.

2424. GINZBERG, Eli. Life styles of educated women. New York,
Columbia University Press, 1966. 224p. Analysis of
choice concerning employment opportunities and family
duties made by college educated women.

2425. _____. Paycheck and apron--Revolution in womanpower.
Industrial relations; a journal of economy and society,
v. 7 (May 1968), 193-203. Concerns part-time work,
types of jobs held by women, statistics for 1947 and
1966, and the amount of education as related to whether
a woman works regularly.

2426. GLEASON, Caroline J. For working women in Oregon; revised code of rulings on wage, hour and sanitary conditions issued by the Industrial Welfare Commission.
Survey, v. 36 (9 September 1916), 585-6.

2427. _____. Legislation for women in Oregon. 153p. PhD
thesis, Catholic University of America, 1924.

2428. GLEASON, G. Job market for women: a department chair-

man's view; with reply by M. A. Ferguson. College
English, v. 32 (May 1971), 927-33.
2429.   GLOVER, Katherine. Women at work in wartime. New
York, Public Affairs Committee, 1943. 31p.
2430.   GOLDBERG, Marilyn. New light on the exploitation of wom-
en. Liberation, v. 14 (October 1969), 22-7.
2431.   GOLDMAN, R. S. Should mothers work? Social service review, v. 23 (March 1949), 74-87.
2432.   GOLDMARK, Josephine. Fatigue and efficiency; a study in
industry. Containing also the substance of four briefs
in defense of women's labor laws. New York, Charities Publication Committee, 1912. 302p.
2433.   _____. Labor laws for women. Survey, v. 29 (January
1925), 552-5.
2434.   _____. Legislative gains for women in 1912. Survey,
v. 28 (13 April 1912), 95-7.
2435.   _____. Some considerations affecting the replacement of
men by women workers. American journal of public
health, v. 8 (April 1918), 270-6.
2436.   _____. Working women and the laws. American Academy
of Political and Social Science, annals, v. 28 (September 1906), 261-76.
2437.   GOLDMARK, P. Facts as to women in war industries.
New republic, v. 13 (29 December 1917), 251-2.
2438.   GOVE, G. F. Holding your own is not enough; steps necessary to advancement and security. Independent woman,
v. 25 (July 1946), 207-8.
2439.   GRAFFENREID, Clare de. The condition of wage-earning
women. Forum, v. 15 (March 1893), 68-82.
2440.   _____. Trade-unions for women. Lend a hand, v. 10
(1893), 103.
2441.   GRAHAM, I. J. Working hours of women in Chicago. Journal of political economy, v. 23 (October 1915), 822-31.
2442.   GRAVES, Elsa. Will women stay in industry? Womans
press, v. 38 (December 1944), 543-4.
2443.   GRAY, Albert. America's womanpower: will wartime wom-
en workers in industry become permanent? Advertising and selling (May 1943), 68+.
2444.   GREEN, Constance. The role of women as production workers in war plants in the Connecticut Valley. Northampton, Mass., Smith College, 1946. 84p.
2445.   GREEN, W. Women who work, and trade unions. American
federationist, v. 55 (March 1948), 19.
2446.   GREENBAUM, L. Wall Street: man's world. New York
Times magazine (13 May 1945), 21.
2447.   GREENBIE, M. B. New skills and how to acquire them;
women in defense industry. Independent woman,
v. 20 (June 1941), 175+.
2448.   GREENWALD, Shirley E. and William I. Greenwald. His-
toric bases for female labor force participation.
Journal of Home Economics, v. 55 (May 1963), 348-
52. Primarily concerns the 19th century.
2449.   GROAT, G. G. Judicial views of the restriction of women's

hours of labor. Political Science quarterly, v. 25
(September 1910), 420-34.

2450. GROSS, Edward. Plus ça change...the sexual structure of
occupations over time. Social problems, v. 16 (Fall
1968), 198-208. Study of the sociological aspects and
trends in the employment of women and the effect on
the division of the sexes in the occupational structure
between 1900 and 1960.

2451. GROVE, K. Escape from baby talk. Mademoiselle, v. 48
(March 1959), 94-5. Concerning the employment of
married women.

2452. GROVE and union agree to arbitration, election. Publisher's
weekly, v. 197 (27 April 1970), 55-7.

2453. GROVE fires union activists; women's lib seizes offices.
Publisher's weekly, v. 197 (20 April 1970), 38. Wom-
en liberationists, led by Robin Morgan, take over
Grove Press offices due to firing of a number of wom-
en, allegedly, because of union activities.

2454. GROVE loses arbitration; four must be rehired. Publisher's
weekly, v. 198 (31 August 1970), 248.

2455. HRW's job discrimination handbook. Washington, Human
Rights for Women, National Press Building, 1971.

2456. HAGER, A. R. Occupations and earnings of women in industry. American Academy of Political and Social
Science, annals, v. 143 (May 1929), 65-73.

2457. HAHN, L. B. Economic opportunities for women. U.S.
Department of State, bulletin, v. 34 (18 June 1956),
1033-5. Concerning the United Nations Commission
on the Status of Women.

2458. HALL, H. O. Can the home town girls make good? Journal
of business education, v. 14 (February 1939), 9-10.

2459. HAMILTON, Alice. The eight-hour day for women in industry. Mid-Pacific magazine, v. 36 (October 1928),
333-7.

2460. _____. Protection for women workers. Forum, v. 72
(August 1924), 152-60.

2461. HANSL, Eva. The utilization of womanpower: An unnecessary waste of human resources. Vital speeches,
v. 18 (1 September 1952), 689-93.

2462. HARBESON, Gladys Evans. Choice and challenge for the
American woman. Cambridge, Mass., Schenkman,
1967. 185p.

2463. HARPER, Ida Husted. Women ought to work. Independent,
v. 53 (16 May 1901), 1123-7. The relationship of a
working woman to her family.

2464. HARRISON, Ethel B. "The woman who toils" in America.
Nineteenth century, v. 54 (December 1903), 1020-5.
Differences between men's and women's work in
factories.

2465. HARRISON, Evelyn. The working woman: barriers in employment. Public administration review, v. 24 (June
1964), 78-85.

2466. HAWES, E. Do women workers get an even break? New

York Times magazine (19 November 1944), 13+.
2467. _____. The woman problem. Antioch review, v. 5
(March 1945), 46-55.
2468. HAWKS, M. G. Return of the working mother to the home.
Catholic action, v. 15 (August 1933), 12-14.
2469. HAYNES, E. R. Two million Negro women at work. Southern workman, v. 51 (February 1922), 64-72.
2470. HEBERT, Robert S. Laws affecting the employment of wom-
en. Columbus, Ohio, Legislative Service Commission,
1967. 42p.
2471. HEDGES, Janice N. Women workers and manpower demands
in the 1970's. Monthly labor review, v. 93 (June
1970), 19-29.
2472. HENLE, F. Does it pay for a wife to work? American
home, v. 70 (September 1967), 44-5+.
2473. HENRY, Alice. The trade union woman. New York, Appleton, 1915. 314p.
2474. _____. Women and the labor movement. New York,
Doran, 1923.
2475. HERRICK, E. M. What about women after the war? New
York Times magazine (5 September 1943), 7+.
2476. HERRON, Belva M. The progress of labor organization
among women; together with some considerations concerning their place in industry. Urbana, Ill., University Press, 1905. 79p.
2477. HESS, Edith. State regulation of woman and child labor in
Kansas. Kansas State Historical Society, collections,
v. 15 (1923), 279-333.
2478. HICKEY, Margaret A. Bound for the future; women's responsibility in new age. Vital speeches, v. 10 (1
November 1943), 49-51.
2479. HICKS, J. M. Special legislation for women in industry.
Washington, National League of Women Voters, 1927.
8p.
2480. HILL, Helen. Freedwomen. Virginia quarterly review,
v. 8 (January 1932), 33-40. On economic inequality
of women and the fact that society expects them to do
no work.
2481. HILTON, M. N. Earnings and employment of women factory
workers, April 1954. Monthly labor review, v. 78
(October 1955), 1126-32.
2482. HINES, F. T. The ladies want postwar jobs too: figures
show war increase of women workers to be overrated.
Commerce (June 1944), 18-19+.
2483. _____. Post-war employment of women. Women's work
and education (Winter 1944), 1-4.
2484. HOBBS, M. A. War-time employment of women. American
labor legislative journal, v. 8 (December 1918), 332-8.
2485. HOFFMAN, Lois Norma. Some effects of the employment
of mothers on family structure. 227p. PhD thesis,
University of Michigan, 1958.
2486. HOLLOBON, J. Are women people? Continuous learning,
v. 4 (November/December 1965), 245-50. Discrim-

ination in employment opportunities despite equal educational level with men in many instances.

2487. HOLLOWELL, O. L. Women and equal employment: from
romantic paternalism to 1964 Civil Rights Act. Wom-
en lawyers journal, v. 56 (Winter 1970), 28.

2488. HOURS and earnings in Connecticut laundries, 1933 and 1934.
Monthly labor review, v. 41 (November 1935), 1334-41.

2489. HOURS and earnings in Connecticut laundries, 1934 and 1935.
Monthly labor review, v. 43 (September 1936), 609-10.

2490. HOURS and earnings of men and women in Michigan factories.
Monthly labor review, v. 60 (January 1945), 159-61.

2491. HOURS and earnings of women in five New York industries.
Monthly labor review, v. 18 (May 1924), 1049-50.

2492. HOURS and earnings of women in New Jersey laundries.
Monthly labor review, v. 45 (October 1937), 885-9.

2493. HOURS and night work of women in New York war plants.
Monthly labor review, v. 61 (September 1945), 507-9.

2494. HOURS and working conditions of women in industry in Iowa.
Monthly labor review, v. 14 (March 1922), 543-6.

2495. HOURS and working conditions of women in Maryland industries. Monthly labor review, v. 16 (March 1923),
573-4.

2496. HOURS, earnings, and conditions of labor of women in Indiana mercantile establishments and garment factories.
U.S. Bureau of Labor Statistics, bulletin, v. 160
(1914), 1-198.

2497. HOURS, earnings, and duration of employment of wage-earning
women in selected industries in the District of Columbia. U.S. Bureau of Labor bulletin, v. 116 (1913),
1-68.

2498. HOURS laws for women in New York State compared with
those of other states. Industrial bulletin, (November
1931), 39+.

2499. HOURS, wages, and working conditions for women in Kentucky. Monthly labor review, v. 17 (October 1923),
846-9.

2500. HOURS, wages, and working conditions of Rhode Island wom-
en in nontextile industries. Monthly labor review,
v. 14 (June 1922), 1209-13.

2501. HOW women's role in U.S. is changing. U.S. news and
world report, v. 60 (30 May 1966), 58-60. More
women wanting to get out of the home; their problems
in industry and the professions.

2502. HOW working women fare in Connecticut. Survey, v. 33
(27 March 1915), 684-5.

2503. HOW would you solve it? The modern woman's greatest
problem: economic independence. Delineator, v. 90
(January 1917), 2.

2504. HOWE, Julia Ward. Industrial value of woman. North
American review, v. 135 (1882), 433.

2505. HUBER, Charlotte. Working wives are "on the spot": move
to bar married women from government jobs now
spreading to private industry...first step in the cam-

paign to drive all women back to the kitchen;....
Retail executive (12 July 1939), 6+.

2506. HUTCHINS, Grace. Women who work. New York, International, 1934. 285p.

2507. HUTCHINSON, Emilie J. The economic problems of women. American Academy of Political and Social Science, annals, v. 143 (May 1929), 132-6. Problems of employing the married woman; wages and the economic status of women.

2508. IF jobs get scarce, will women be squeezed out? Business week (14 November 1953), 178-9.

2509. IF layoffs come, women go first. U.S. news and world report, v. 35 (31 July 1953), 56-7.

2510. ILLINOIS ten-hour law held valid. Outlook, v. 95 (14 May 1910), 50-1.

2511. INMAN, Mary. Woman power. Los Angeles, Committee to Organize the Advancement of Women, 1942.

2512. INSTITUTE of Women's Professional Relations. Proceedings of the Conference on Women's Work and Their Stake in Public Affairs, March 28-29-30-1935. New London, Conn., The Institute, 1935. 329p.

2513. INTERNATIONAL Association for Labor Legislation. Ten-hour maximum working-day for women and young persons. Washington, GPO, 1913. 71p.

2514. INTERNATIONAL Labor Office. The law and women's work; a contribution to the study of the status of women. Geneva, 1939. 590p.

2515. _____. Women workers in a changing world. Geneva, 1963-64. 2v.

2516. IRVIN, H. B. Conditions in industry as they affect Negro women. National Conference of Social Work, proceedings (1919), 521-4.

2517. JACOBSON, Betty. "Women's work...." A job description. Library journal, v. 96 (1 September 1971), 2596.

2518. JAFFE, A. J. Trends in the participation of women in the working force. Monthly labor review, v. 79 (May 1956), 559-67.

2519. JAMIE, Wallace. Women: our other great resource; present status of working women. Journal of college placement, v. 18 (December 1957), 14-16.

2520. JOHNSON, Alvin. Job discrimination and the law. Woman's press (January 1946), 14+.

2521. JOHNSON, E. M. Forty-eight hour law in Massachusetts. Survey, v. 45 (23 October 1920), 125-6.

2522. _____. Why protection? Woman citizen, v. 9 (9 August 1924), 16-17.

2523. JOHNSON, G. G. Feminism and the economic independence of women. Journal of social forces, v. 3 (May 1925), 612-16.

2524. JOHNSTONE, Elizabeth. Women in economic life: rights and opportunities. American Academy of Political and Social Science, annals, v. 375 (January 1968), 102-14. The work of the International Labour Organization to

promote equal rights in all areas of life.
2525.   JOINT Committee to Study the Employment of Colored Women
        in New York City and Brooklyn.   A new day for the
        colored woman worker; a study of colored women in
        industry in New York City.   By Nelle Swartz and oth-
        ers.   New York, C. P. Young Co., printers, 1919.
        39p.
2526.   JONES, Katherine A.   Working girls of Chicago: their
        wages, their homes, and their summer outings.   Re-
        view of reviews, v. 4 (September 1891), 167-72.
2527.   JONSBERG, A. A.   Women invade men's industrial meetings;
        then organize their own section.   National safety news,
        v. 20 (October 1929), 89-90+.
2528.   JORDAN, Joan.   The place of American women; economic
        exploitation of women.   Boston, New England Free
        Press, 1969.   22p.
2529.   _____.   Protective laws.   Detroit, Radical Education
        Project, 1970.   22p.   The exploitation of women in
        industry, especially in California; and criticism of the
        National Organization for Women.
2530.   JOSEPHSON, Hannah G.   The golden threads; New England's
        mill girls and magnates.   New York, Duell, Sloan and
        Pearce, 1949.   325p.   Reprinted by Russell and Rus-
        sell, New York, 1967.
2531.   JOSSELYN, I. M.   Should mothers work?   Social service re-
        view, v. 23 (March 1949), 74-87.
2532.   KANSAS.   Commission of Labor and Industry.   Women work-
        ers in Kansas: industrial welfare orders of the Com-
        mission of Labor and Industry, 1930.   Topeka, 1930.
        10p.
2533.   _____.   Department of Labor and Industry.   Report of
        wages and hours of women and minors in industry,
        November 1, 1937 to January 1, 1938.   Topeka, 1938.
        39p.
2534.   KELLEY, Florence.   Invasion of family life by industry.
        American Academy of Political and Social Science, an-
        nals, v. 34 (July 1909), 90-6.
2535.   _____.   Labor legislation for women and its effects on
        earnings and conditions of labor.   American Academy
        of Political and Social Science, annals, v. 143 (May
        1929), 286-300.
2536.   _____.   Leisure by statute for women.   New York, Na-
        tional Consumers' League, 1924.   1p.   Also in:
        Woman citizen, v. 8 (17 May 1924), 16-17.
2537.   _____.   Limiting women's working hours.   Survey, v. 25
        (21 January 1911), 651-2.
2538.   _____.   Married women in industry.   Academy of Political
        Science, proceedings, v. 1 (October 1910), 90-6.
2539.   _____.   Progress of labor legislation for women.   Na-
        tional Conference of Social Work, proceedings (1923),
        112-16.
2540.   _____.   The war and women workers.   Survey, v. 39
        (9 March 1918), 628-31.

2541. _____. Women in industry: the eight hours day and rest
       at night upheld by the U.S. Supreme Court. New
       York, National Consumers' League, 1916. 4p.
2542. _____. Women in trade unions. Outlook, v. 84 (15 De-
       cember 1906), 926-31.
2543. KELLEY, M. E. Women and the labor movement. North
       American review, v. 166 (April 1898), 408-17.
2544. _____. Women factory workers. Outlook, v. 58 (29
       January 1898), 269-70.
2545. KENISTON, Ellen and Kenneth Keniston. An American
       anachronism: the image of women and work. Ameri-
       can scholar, v. 33 (Summer 1964), 355-75. Concerns
       the need to emphasize woman's work outside the home
       and to get away from the era when womanliness was
       associated with family duties.
2546. KEYSERLING, Mary Dublin. Exploding the myths, a report
       of a conference on expanding employment opportunities
       for career women. Washington, GPO, 1967. Discus-
       sion of means of training and employing women as well
       as the social prejudices against them.
2547. KIEVIT, M. B. Women in gainful and useful employment.
       Journal of Home Economics, v. 60 (November 1968),
       697-702. The dual role of the female worker and the
       need to develop programs to make both sexes aware
       of male-female expectations in the family.
2548. KINGSBURY, Susan M. Relation of women to industry.
       American Sociological Society, proceedings and publi-
       cations, v. 15 (1920), 141-62.
2549. KIRKWOOD, M. M. Women's right to work. Woman's
       press, v. 31 (November 1937), 481-2.
2550. KOONTZ, Elizabeth D. Women and jobs in a changing world.
       American vocational journal, v. 45 (December 1970),
       13-15.
2551. KRAMER, Gerson B. and Abraham Bluestone. Factory em-
       ployment of women, 1950 to 1954. Monthly labor re-
       view, v. 77 (November 1954), 1210-13. The number
       of women employed in certain types of industries and
       the percent change.
2552. KREPS, Juanita. Sex in the marketplace: American women
       at work. Baltimore, Johns Hopkins University Press,
       1971. 117p.
2553. KYRK, Hazel. Who works and why. American Academy of
       Political and Social Science, annals, v. 251 (May
       1947), 44-52.
2554. LABARRE, H. Working wives. Cosmopolitan, v. 142
       (March 1957), 48-53.
2555. LABOR laws for women in industry in Indiana. Monthly
       labor review, v. 8 (April 1919), 1134-6.
2556. LABOR legislation and the rights of women. Journal of
       Home Economics, v. 21 (September 1929), 664-6.
2557. LA FOLLETTE, Cecile Tipton. A study of the problems of
       652 gainfully employed married women homemakers.
       New York, Teachers College, Columbia University

Press, 1934. 208p.
2558. LA FOLLETTE, R. M. Message to labor. American
          federationist, v. 29 (September 1922), 636.
2559. LAPE, E. E. Women in industry. New republic, v. 25
          (26 January 1921), 251-3.
2560. LARONGE, M. N. Where working women stand today. Iron
          age, v. 201 (20 June 1968), 68-9.
2561. LASELLE, Mary A. The young woman worker. Boston,
          Pilgrim Press, 1914. 189p.
2562. LATEST rules on jobs for women. U.S. news and world
          report, v. 68 (22 June 1970), 87. Guidelines set up
          by the U.S. Department of Labor.
2563. LATTIMORE, Eleanor Larrabee. Legal recognition of in-
          dustrial women. New York, Young Women's Christian
          Association, 1919. 91p.
2564. LAUGHLIN, Clara E. The work-a-day girl: a study of
          some present-day conditions. New York, F. H. Revell,
          1913. 320p.
2565. LAW, H. S. Man for the job--and the woman. Technical
          world magazine, v. 21 (April 1914), 187-92.
2566. The LAW and women's welfare. Outlook, v. 93 (18 Decem-
          ber 1909), 837-9. On the ten hour working day for
          women in Oregon and Illinois.
2567. LAW and women's work; a contribution to the study of the
          status of women. Washington, International Labor Of-
          fice, 1939. 590p.
2568. LAWS in the United States concerning labor of women.
          American labor legislation review, v. 2 (October 1912),
          495-501.
2569. LAWS relating to the employment of women and children.
          U.S. Bureau of Labor, bulletin, v. 15 (November
          1907), 655-816.
2570. LAWS relating to women industrially employed. Monthly
          labor review, v. 30 (February 1930), 264-85. Sum-
          mary of laws for each state governing night work for
          women, rest provisions, and prohibitory provisions
          relating to employment of women.
2571. LEE, Kendrick. Women in war work. Washington, Editorial
          research reports, 1942. 17p.
2572. LEE, Vernon. The economic dependence of women. North
          American review, v. 175 (July 1902), 71-90.
2573. LEGISLATION for women in industry. American labor legis-
          lation review, v. 6 (December 1916), 356-418.
2574. LEGISLATION on hours of labor of women and minors up to
          January 1, 1929. Monthly labor review, v. 28 (Febru-
          ary 1929), 256-69. Summary for each state concern-
          ing working hours.
2575. LEVINE, Louis. The Women's Garment Workers Union: a
          history of the International Ladies Garment Workers
          Union. New York, n.p., 1924.
2576. LITTELL, Jane. Meditations of a wage-earning wife. At-
          lantic monthly, v. 134 (December 1924), 728-34.
          Thoughts of a wife who supports the family.

2577. LOCKE, Harvey and Muriel Mackeprang. Marital adjust-
       ment and the employed wife. American journal of
       Sociology, v. 54 (May 1949), 536-8.
2578. LONG thrust toward economic equality. Ebony, v. 21
       (August 1966), 38-40+. The employment of Negro
       women.
2579. LOUGHLIN, Ann. Women trade unionists. American feder-
       ationist, v. 42 (November 1935), 1178-9.
2580. LUCAS, Bertha June. The woman who spends, a study of
       her economic function. Boston, Whitcomb and Bar-
       rows, 1916. 161p.
2581. LUTZ, Alma. Shall woman's work be regulated by law?
       Atlantic monthly, v. 146 (September 1930), 321-7.
       The fact that many protective laws actually hinder wom-
       en and that any new laws should apply equally to both
       sexes.
2582. _____. Which road, women workers? Equal pay and
       special protective laws. Christian Science Monitor
       magazine (2 February 1946), 2.
2583. MCADOO, L. S. Woman's economic status in the South.
       Arena, v. 21 (June 1899), 741-56.
2584. MACARTHUR, Kathleen. Shibboleths or security. Womans
       press, v. 39 (April 1945), 11-13. Women and post-
       war employment.
2585. MACDONALD, Norval. Women in industry--what can't they
       do? Journal of occupational medicine, v. 12 (March
       1970), 85-6. Primarily on weight-lifting restrictions.
2586. MCDOWELL, M. E. Need for a national investigation into
       women's work. Charities and the commons, v. 17
       (5 January 1907), 634-6.
2587. MACE, D. R. Does a wife have a right to work? McCall's,
       v. 89 (October 1961), 70+.
2588. MCILROY, A. L. Problems of the working mother: mar-
       riage and motherhood should not be cause for dismis-
       sal of women from work. Nation's health, v. 4
       (March 1922), 132-5.
2589. MACINTOSH, E. Women in industry discussed by club.
       Trans-Pacific, v. 20 (15 December 1932), 12.
2590. MCKNIGHT, E. C. Jobs, for men only? Shall we send
       women workers home? Outlook, v. 159 (2 September
       1931), 12-13.
2591. MACLEAN, Annie Marion. Factory legislation for women in
       the United States. American journal of Sociology,
       v. 3 (September 1897), 183-205. A listing of hours
       of labor and other laws for each state.
2592. _____. Wage-earning women. New York, Macmillan,
       1910. 202p.
2593. _____. Women workers and society. Chicago, A. C.
       McClurg, 1916. 135p.
2594. MCNALLY, Gertrude Bancroft. Patterns of female labor
       force activity. Industrial relations; a journal of
       economy and society, v. 7 (May 1968), 204-18. Labor
       force participation by sex between 1947 and 1967 and

problems in discrimination; in particular the problems
of enforcing Title VII of the Civil Rights Act of 1964.

2595.   MAFFETT, M. L.   Under-use of womanpower slows war ef-
fort.   Independent woman, v. 22 (August 1943), 230-1+.

2596.   MAHER, Amy G.   The employment of women.   Social service
review, v. 5 (March 1931), 28-36.

2597.   _____.   Ohio's women workers.   American Academy of
Political and Social Science, annals, v. 143 (May
1929), 94-103.

2598.   _____.   Women trade unionists in the United States.   International labour review, v. 11 (March 1925), 366-80.

2599.   MAILLY, William.   Working girls' strike; the shirtwaist
makers of New York.   Independent, v. 67 (23 December 1909), 1416-20.   Activities of the Women's Trade
Union League during the strike.

2600.   MARCUS, M. R.   Women in the labor force.   Social case-
work, v. 41 (June 1960), 298-302.

2601.   MARGOLIN, B.   Equal pay and equal employment opportunities for women.   New York University Conference on
Labor, v. 19 (1966), 297.

2602.   MARRIED women who work.   Woman worker (September
1939), 3-5.

2603.   MARSDEN, Dora.   Bondwoman.   New York, National American Woman Suffrage Association, 1912.   14p.   The
necessity for working women and changes in the professions, industry, etc.

2604.   MARTIN, Anne.   Equality laws vs. women in government.
Nation, v. 115 (16 August 1922), 165-6.

2605.   MASON, Lucy Randolph.   The shorter day and women workers.   Richmond, Va., Virginia League of Women
Voters, 1922.   26p.

2606.   MASSACHUSETTS.   Bureau of Statistics of Labor.   Women
in industry.   Boston, Wright & Potter Printing Co.,
1890.

2607.   _____.   Supreme Judicial Court.   Opinions of the honor-
able justices of the Supreme Judicial Court as to the
constitutionality of certain measures designed to limit
the employment of married women in the public service.   Boston, 1939.   35p.

2608.   MATTHEWS, Lillian Ruth.   Women in trade unions in San
Francisco, Berkeley, University of California Press,
1913.   100p.

2609.   MEREDITH, E.   Woman and the industrial problem.   Arena,
v. 23 (1900), 438.

2610.   MEYER, Annie Nathan, ed.   Woman's work in America.
New York, Holt, 1891.   457p.   Reprinted by Greenwood Press, Westport, Conn., 1971.

2611.   MILLER, Frieda S.   They need the money; that's the reason
why women work.   American federationist, v. 57 (January 1950), 28-31.

2612.   _____.   Woman's place: what will determine it?   American federationist, v. 39 (March 1932), 287-90.

2613.   _____.   Women at work, then and now.   American federationist, v. 58 (July 1951), 10-11+. On women working outside their homes since 1639.

2614. _____. Women in the labor force. American Academy of Political and Social Science, annals, v. 251 (May 1947), 35-43.

2615. _____. Women's hours of work: a survey. Personnel, v. 23 (March 1947), 332-8.

2616. MISSOURI. Commission on Human Rights. Sex discrimination in Missouri; an analysis of the Missouri law regulating hours of work for women--its relationship to the Missouri Fair Employment Practices Act and to the Federal Civil Rights Act of 1964. Prepared by Sandra A. Neese and Peter C. Robertson. Jefferson City, The Commission, 1967. 65p.

2617. _____. _____. A survey of Missouri and federal laws relating to discrimination in employment because of sex. A staff study for the Missouri Commission on the Status of Women. Prepared by Sandra A. Neese and Peter C. Robertson. Jefferson City, The Commission, 1966. 30p.

2618. MUNTZ, Earl E. Women's changing role in the United States employment market. International labour review, v. 74 (November 1956), 415-36.

2619. MURPHY, B. Work of woman as a breadwinner. Catholic world, v. 17 (1873), 223.

2620. MUSSEY, Henry Raymond. The law and a living for women. Survey, v. 61 (1 November 1928), 156-8. The question of whether protective laws for women actually prevent them from getting jobs.

2621. MY wife works: many economists have insisted that wives of employed men should give up their jobs. Nations business (September 1940), 23-4+.

2622. NATHAN, Maud. The story of an epoch-making movement. Garden City, N.Y., Doubleday, Page, 1926. 245p.

2623. _____. Working women and women who spend. American Academy of Political and Social Science, annals, v. 27 (1906), 642.

2624. NATIONAL Association of Manufacturers of the United States of America. A tale of 22 cities; report on Title VII of the Civil Rights Act of 1964. Edited by Charles A. Kotke. New York, 1965. 168p.

2625. NATIONAL Consumers' League. Campaign against sweating. By Walter Lippmann. New York, The League, 1915. 29p.

2626. _____. Eight hours day for wage-earning women; United States Supreme Court upholds the California law; list of eight hours laws. New York, The League, 1916. 12p.

2627. _____. Equal opportunity for women wage earners: facts vs. fiction. New York, The League, 1920. 10p.

2628. NATIONAL Education Association. Committee on Equal Opportunity. Protecting the employment status of women. Washington, The Association, 1939.

2629. NATIONAL Federation of Business and Professional Women's
       Clubs. Occupational discriminations against women:
       an inquiry into the economic security of American busi-
       ness and professional women. By I. L. Peters. New
       York, The Federation, 1935. 16p.
2630. _____. Position of married women in the economic world.
       New York, The Federation, 1940. 69p.
2631. _____. Recent legislative and executive action restricting
       the right of married women to work. rev. ed. New
       York, The Federation, 1940. 15p.
2632. NATIONAL Industrial Conference Board. Women in factory
       work. New York, The Board, 1942. 52p.
2633. NATIONAL Manpower Council. Womanpower; a statement,
       with chapters by the Council staff. New York, Colum-
       bia University Press, 1957. 371p. On women in the
       labor force between 1890 and 1956.
2634. NATIONAL Women's Trade Union League of America. Action
       needed: post-war jobs for women. Washington, The
       League, 1944. 24p.
2635. _____. Some facts regarding unorganized working women
       in the sweated industries. Chicago, The League, 1914.
2636. _____. Women in trade unions in the United States.
       Chicago, The League, 1919. 15p.
2637. NEAL, A. B. Employment of women. Godey's lady's book,
       v. 45 (1852), 125+.
2638. NEARING, Scott. Woman and social progress; a discussion
       of the biologic, domestic, industrial, and social pos-
       sibilities of American women. New York, Macmillan,
       1912. 285p.
2639. _____. Women in American industry. Philadelphia,
       American Baptist Publication Society, 1915. 18p.
2640. NEGRO women in industry. Monthly labor review, v. 15
       (July 1922), 116-18.
2641. NEGRO women in industry. Monthly labor review, v. 29
       (September 1929), 554-6.
2642. NELSON, Nell. The white slave girls of Chicago. Chicago,
       Burkley, 1888. 139p.
2643. NESTOR, Agnes. Working women after victory. American
       federationist, v. 52 (February 1945), 17-18.
2644. NET contribution of working wives in Texas to family income.
       Monthly labor review, v. 85 (December 1962), 1383-4.
2645. NEW hazards in new jobs for women. Survey, v. 39 (19
       January 1918), 452-3. Protection of women in industry
       as asked for by the Women's Trade Union League of
       New York.
2646. NEW Jersey. Department of Labor. Bureau for Women and
       Children. Compiled labor laws governing the employ-
       ment of women and children, 1929. Trenton, 1929.
       100p.
2647. NEW legislation to eliminate discrimination against women in
       the civil service. National business woman, v. 36
       (March 1957), 8.
2648. NEW paper work for employers; women's job rights: advice

from Equal Employment Opportunity Commission. U.S. news and world report, v. 59 (6 December 1965), 93.

2649. The NEW position of women in American industry. Monthly labor review, v. 12 (January 1921), 153-7.

2650. NEW York (state). Department of Labor. Employers' postwar plans for women workers. New York, 1945. 6p.

2651. _____. _____. Employment of women in the first post-reconversion year in New York State, 1946-47. New York, 1947. 41p.

2652. _____. _____. Long hours and night work: experience and views of women workers in New York State. New York, 1946. 16p.

2653. _____. _____. Post-war changes in the employment of women in New York State, 1944-46. New York, 1946. 41p.

2654. _____. _____. Women who work at night. New York, 1948. 47p.

2655. _____. _____. Women who work in New York. By E. S. Marconnier. New York, 1941. 58p.

2656. _____. Governor Rockefeller's Conference on Women. Governor Rockefeller's Conference on Women, New York Hilton Hotel, New York, New York, May 26-27, 1966. [New York, 1966?] 67p. Problems and laws affecting women, consumer and other problems facing women.

2657. _____. Governor's Committee on the Education and Employment of Women. New York women and their changing world. Albany, 1964. 96p.

2658. NEW York Tribune. Occupations of women and their compensation: a compilation of essays by prominent authorities on all the leading trades and professions in America in which women have asserted their ability, with data as to the compensation afforded in each one. New York, The Tribune, 1898. 133p.

2659. NIENBURG, B. M. Women in the nation's economy. American Association of University Women, journal, v. 32 (April 1939), 131-5.

2660. NIGHT-WORK law for women upheld in Connecticut. Monthly labor review, v. 51 (October 1940), 951.

2661. NIGHT work; women and the New York courts. Charities and the commons, v. 17 (3 November 1906), 183-4.

2662. NORRIS, L. W. The role of women in American economic life. Association of American Colleges, bulletin, v. 42 (March 1956), 51-60.

2663. NORTH Carolina. University. Studies in the social and industrial condition of women as affected by the war. By Mrs. T. W. Lingle. Chapel Hill, 1919. 19p.

2664. NORTON, E. Women in war industries. New republic, v. 13 (15 December 1917), 179-81.

2665. NOTTINGHAM, Elizabeth K. Toward an analysis of the effects of two world wars on the role and status of middle-class women in the English speaking world. American sociological review, v. 12 (December 1947), 666-75.

2666.   NYE, Francis I. and Lois N. Hoffman, eds. The employed
        mother in America. Chicago, Rand McNally, 1963.
        406p.
2667.   OBENAUER, M. L. Working hours, earnings, and duration
        of employment of women workers in Maryland and
        California. U.S. Bureau of Labor, bulletin, v. 23
        (September 1911), 347-465.
2668.   OCCUPATION: housewife; employment is rising in the largest
        of all the occupations, but jobs are becoming less se-
        cure. Vocational trends, (October 1939), 18-19.
2669.   ODENCRANTZ, Louise C. Employment of women and chil-
        dren in selected industries. Survey, v. 31 (24 Janu-
        ary 1914), 498-9. Comments on a Federal Govern-
        ment report indicating lower wages for women than for
        men and the need for individual community effort rath-
        er than the Government in alleviating women's economic
        problems.
2670.   The OFFICIAL word on job rights for women; official guid-
        ance by Equal Employment Opportunity Commission.
        U.S. news and world report, v. 59 (22 November
        1965), 90-1.
2671.   OHIO Industrial Commission. Wages and hours of labor of
        women and girls employed in mercantile establish-
        ments in Ohio in 1913. n.p., 1914. 33p.
2672.   OLIPHANT, Rosamond D. Woman's work. Cincinnati, C.
        T. Woodrow & Co., printers, 1881. 35p.
2673.   ON-THE-JOB oppression of working women; a collection of
        articles. Boston, New England Free Press, 1968.
2674.   ON the job, women act much like men...but mostly they are
        lower on the ladder. Business week (12 October 1963),
        114-15. Comparison of male and female federal em-
        ployees in salaries, promotions, and reasons for quit-
        ing.
2675.   OPPENHEIMER, Valerie Kincade. The female labor force
        in the United States; demographic and economic factors
        governing its growth and changing composition. Berke-
        ley, University of California, Institute of International
        Studies, 1970. 197p. Concerns the changing patterns
        of female labor force participation, segregation of
        male and female labor markets, different female labor
        markets, etc.
2676.   _____. The sex-labeling of jobs. Industrial relations;
        a journal of economy and society, v. 7 (May 1968),
        219-34.
2677.   OPPOSITION tactics against women's 48-hour bill in New
        York. American labor legislative review, v. 16
        (March 1926), 20-1.
2678.   ORDEN, Susan R. and Norman M. Bradburn. Working
        wives and marriage happiness. American journal of
        Sociology, v. 74 (January 1969), 392-407. Reply:
        v. 75 (November 1969), 412-15. A study showing
        that greater marriage happiness results where greater
        freedom to choose is present for the wife.

2679. OSBORNE, M. H. Should mothers have outside jobs? Better homes and gardens, v. 30 (January 1952), 16-17+.
2680. OTEY, Elizabeth L. Women and children in southern industry. American Academy of Political and Social Science, annals, v. 153 (January 1931), 163-9. A comparison with men's wages; legislation, health, etc.
2681. OUR double-standard prosperity. Literary digest, v. 101 (18 May 1929), 83-5. Concerning the greater number of married women in industry.
2682. PALMER, Gladys L. Women's place in industry. Current history, v. 6 (January 1944), 19-24. Economic status of women during and after the war.
2683. PALMER, H. Womanpower survey progress report. National business woman, v. 37 (May 1958), 10.
2684. PARMELEE, M. Economic basis of feminism. American Academy of Political and Social Science, annals, v. 56 (November 1914), 18-26.
2685. PARRISH, John B. Revolution in employment for women. Education digest, v. 30 (October 1964), 50-2.
2686. PARSONS, Elsie Clews. How does the access of women to industrial occupations react on the family?--Higher education of women and the family. American journal of Sociology, v. 14 (May 1909), 758-63.
2687. PATTEN, Simon N. Some new adjustments for women. Independent, v. 61 (20 September 1906), 674-81. The value of married women in industry.
2688. _____. Young wives in industry. Independent, v. 57 (1 December 1904), 1244-9.
2689. PENN, E. S. Labor's kinship: the problem of the colored woman as a "newcomer" in the field of industry. Woman's press, v. 21 (January 1927), 12-14+.
2690. PENNSYLVANIA. Department of Labor and Industry. Bureau of Women and Children. Hours and earnings of men and women in the silk industry. By Jessie Beatrice McConnell. Harrisburg, 1929. 74p.
2691. PENNY, Virginia. Think and act. A series of articles pertaining to men and women, work and wages. Philadelphia, Claxton, Remsen & Haffelfinger, 1869. 372p.
2692. PEPPER, Mary. Women in industry. Welfare magazine, v. 19 (September 1928), 978-84.
2693. PERKINS, Frances. Do women in industry need special protection? Survey, v. 55 (15 February 1926), 529-32.
2694. _____. The future of the woman who works for wages. Better times (5 June 1933), 6-7.
2695. _____. Should women take men's jobs? Woman's journal, v. 15 (April 1930), 7-9+.
2696. PERRELLA, Vera C. Women and the labor force. Monthly labor review, v. 91 (February 1968), 1-12. Trends in the participation of Negro and white women in the labor force, as well as equal pay, educational level, etc.
2697. PERRY, Lorinda. The millinery trade in Boston and Philadelphia, a study of women in industry. Binghamton,

N.Y., Vail-Ballou, 1916. 122p.
2698. PERSONS, C. E. Women's work and wages in the United
States. Quarterly journal of Economics, v. 29 (February 1915), 201-34.
2699. PETERSON, Esther. Are women taking men's jobs? Personnel journal, v. 41 (February 1962), 83-4.
2700. _____. Outlook for women. American Association of
School Administrators, official report (1965), 62-74.
2701. _____. Working women. Daedalus, v. 93 (Spring 1964),
671-99. Women in industry from around 1940 and
comparisons with men in various types of jobs as to
number of workers, wages, and ways to eliminate the
problem.
2702. PICKEL, M. B. How come no jobs for women? New York
Times magazine (27 January 1946), 20+.
2703. PIDGEON, Mary Elizabeth. Changes in women's employment
during the war. Monthly labor review, v. 59 (November 1944), 1029-30.
2704. _____. Changes in women's occupations, 1940 to 1950.
Monthly labor review, v. 77 (November 1954), 1205-9.
2705. _____ and Margaret T. Mettert. Women workers and
family support. Monthly labor review, v. 50 (January 1940), 1-5.
2706. PLACING a want ad? There are federal rules to follow now;
Equal Employment Opportunity Commission. U.S. news
and world report, v. 59 (4 October 1965), 100-1.
2707. POLAKOFF, S. Memorable day: achievements of the union.
American federationist, v. 37 (December 1930), 1483-9.
2708. POLICY of War Manpower Commission on woman workers.
Monthly labor review, v. 56 (April 1943), 669-71.
2709. POPE, E. Is a working mother a threat to the home?
McCall's, v. 82 (July 1955), 29+.
2710. POSSIBILITIES and limitations of the employment of women
in industry, by Alice Hamilton; Problem of the married
woman in industry, by Florence Kelley; Discussion, by
the members. Pennsylvania Department of Labor and
Industry, bulletin, v. 5, no. 1 (1918), 36-42. 55-62.
2711. POTTER, F. S. Women's trade unions. Survey, v. 29 (22
March 1913), 886-7.
2712. PRESSMAN, Sonia. Discrimination in employment because of
sex. Washington, Equal Employment Opportunity Commission, 1969.
2713. _____. Legal revolution in women's employment rights.
Florida bar journal, v. 44 (June 1970), 332.
2714. _____. Sex discrimination in employment and what you
can do about it. Women lawyers journal, v. 54 (Fall 1968), 6.
2715. PRICE, Hazel M. Women's contribution to industrial development in America. Hays, Fort Hays Kansas State College, 1962. 71p.
2716. PRINCETON University. Industrial Relations Section. Sex
discrimination in employment. Princeton, N.J., 1969.
4p.

2717. _____. _____. Women in war industries. Princeton,
          N.J., 1942. 82p.
2718. PROBLEMS in fair employment and equal pay for women.
          Stores, v. 50 (March 1968), 14-18.
2719. PROBLEMS on job rights of women. U.S. news and world
          report, v. 59 (30 August 1965), 77. Problems of the
          Equal Employment Opportunity Commission in deter-
          mining exactly what constitutes discrimination and in-
          equality.
2720. PROGRESS of Economic and Social Council: action on eco-
          nomic rights of women. United Nations bulletin, v. 6
          (15 March 1949), 260-3.
2721. PROHIBITION of employment of married women in public
          service held void by Supreme Judicial Court of Mas-
          sachusetts. Monthly labor review, v. 49 (August
          1939), 382-3.
2722. PROPORTION of women in selected industries. Newsweek,
          v. 22 (23 August 1943), 54. Chart showing percent
          of women in selected industries in May 1942 and May
          1943 and percent increase.
2723. PROTECTION of women; some laws and lawsuits: a review.
          Outlook, v. 106 (28 March 1914), 670-3. Concerning
          hours and minimum wages for women.
2724. PRUETTE, Lorine. Equal rights or easier work? Woman's
          journal, v. 14 (January 1929), 14-15.
2725. _____. Women and leisure, a study of social waste.
          New York, E. P. Dutton, 1924. 225p.
2726. PUNKE, Harold H. Democracy and the employment of wom-
          en. South Atlantic quarterly, v. 41 (October 1942),
          425-36. Equal wages and reasons for discrimination
          in industry.
2727. _____. What they think about such matters as the home
          and gainful employment of married women. Journal
          of Home Economics, v. 35 (December 1943), 642-3.
2728. QUINN, Francis X. Women at work--the facts. Social
          order, v. 12 (February 1962), 65-71. Statistical sum-
          mary of women in the labor force in 1960.
2729. RAMSEY, Glenn V. Some attitudes and opinions of employed
          women. National Association of Women Deans and
          Counselors, journal, v. 26 (April 1963), 30-6.
2730. RAY, Mary. Come out of the kitchen. Survey, v. 37 (16
          December 1916), 300-1.
2731. The RECONVERSION of women: the industrial future of wom-
          en seems assured. Current history, n.s., v. 8
          (March 1945), 200-6.
2732. REGULATION of women's working hours in the United States.
          American labor legislation review, v. 8 (December
          1918), 339-54.
2733. REICHERT, Anita. The homemaker as employed mother.
          Journal of Home Economics, v. 53 (January 1961),
          18-22.
2734. REID, I. DeA. The Negro woman worker: how is the eco-
          nomic situation affecting two million Negro workers?

Womans press, v. 26 (April 1932), 204-6.
2735. REID, Margaret G. The economic contribution of home-
        makers. American Academy of Political and Social
        Science, annals, v. 251 (May 1947), 61-9.
2736. REILY, A. E. Have women any choice? Independent woman,
        v. 34 (April 1955), 129-30.
2737. RELATIVE importance of male and female workers in Cleve-
        land and Cuyahoga County, Ohio, 1923 and 1928.
        Monthly labor review, v. 33 (September 1931), 529-30.
2738. RELATIVE position of men and women in government employ-
        ment. Monthly labor review, v. 23 (October 1926),
        717-18.
2739. RENNE, R. R. Womanpower and the American economy.
        Journal of Home Economics, v. 49 (February 1957),
        83-6.
2740. REPORT on woman workers in New York State. Monthly
        labor review, v. 15 (July 1922), 120-3.
2741. RHODES, A. Employment of women. Galaxy, v. 21 (1876),
        45.
2742. RIGHT to a job; discussion based on articles in Good house-
        keeping. Catholic charities review, v. 16 (November
        1932), 289.
2743. ROBBINS, Jhan and June Robbins. Why young mothers feel
        trapped. Reader's digest, v. 78 (January 1961), 99-
        102.
2744. ROBERTS, Peter. Employment of girls in textile industries
        of Pennsylvania. American Academy of Political and
        Social Science, annals, v. 23 (May 1904), 434-44.
2745. ROBINSON, Harriet Jane. Loom and spindle: or, Life among
        the early mill girls. With a sketch of "The Lowell
        Offering" and some of its contributors. New York,
        Crowell, 1898. 216p.
2746. ROE, C. Can the girls hold their jobs in peacetime? Satur-
        day evening post, v. 216 (4 March 1944), 28-9+.
2747. ROGERS, Agnes. Women are here to stay; the durable sex
        in its infinite variety through half a century of Ameri-
        can life. New York, Harper, 1949. 220p. Shows
        feminine occupations and attitudes between 1866 and
        1948.
2748. ROOSEVELT, A. E. Place of women in the community.
        National Education Association of America, proceed-
        ings (1935), 313-16.
2749. ROSENBERG, A. How our unions were built. American
        federationist, v. 36 (December 1929), 1453-61.
2750. ROSENFELD, Carl and Vera C. Perrella. Why women start
        and stop working: a study in mobility. Monthly labor
        review, v. 88 (September 1965), 1077-82.
2751. ROSHCO, B. Jobs that women don't get. New York Times
        magazine (17 March 1957), 26+.
2752. ROSS, Mary. Shall we join the gentlemen? Survey, v. 57
        (1 December 1926), 263-7.
2753. ROSSI, Alice S. The case against full-time motherhood.
        Redbook, v. 124 (March 1965), 51+.

2754. _____. A good woman is hard to find. Transaction,
v. 2 (November/December 1964), 20-3. Married
women's "re-entry" into employment.

2755. _____. Job discrimination and what you can do about it.
Atlantic monthly, v. 225 (March 1970), 99-102. On
Title VII of the Civil Rights Act of 1964.

2756. ROWE, Edna. How high can a woman climb? Nation's
business (April 1929), 41-3+.

2757. RUSSELL, Thomas H. The girl's fight for a living; how to
protect working women from dangers due to low wages.
An impartial survey of present conditions, results of
recent investigations, and remedies proposed. Chicago,
M. A. Donahue, 1913. 200p.

2758. SACHAR, Libby E. It's no longer a man's world. National
business woman, v. 37 (April 1958), 10-11.

2759. SAINT, A. M. Women in the public service: the city of
Berkeley, California. Public personnel studies, v. 8
(July 1930), 104-7.

2760. SALLEY, R. E. and R. G. Weintraub. Women college
graduates report on employment. Journal of educational research, v. 42 (January 1949), 376-80.

2761. SCHAUFFLER, M. C. Women for defense industries.
American Association of University Women, journal,
v. 44 (January 1951), 69-71.

2762. SCHNEIDER, Florence Hemley. Defense and the woman
worker. Journal of educational Sociology, v. 15 (January 1942), 260-71.

2763. _____. Economic challenge to American women. New
York, National Federation of Business and Professional
Women's Clubs, 1941. 26p.

2764. SCHNITZLER, William F. A new world for working women.
American federationist, v. 70 (August 1963), 18-22.

2765. SCHONBERGER, Richard J. Ten million U.S. housewives
want to work. Labor law journal, v. 21 (June 1970),
374-9. Responsibilities employers should take on to
allow women to work.

2766. SCHREINER, Olive. Woman and labor. 8th ed. New York,
F. A. Stokes, 1911. 299p. The need for women to
work outside the home.

2767. _____. The woman question. Cosmopolitan, v. 28 (November 1899), 45-54; (December 1899), 182-92. The
economic status of women.

2768. SCHWARTZ, Jane. Part-time employment; employer attitudes on opportunities for the college-trained women:
report of a pilot project. New York, Alumnae Advisory Center, 1964. 62p.

2769. SCHWARTZ, Rosalind. Notes from the working class: A
Jewish woman speaks her mind. New York, The
Feminists, 1970. 3p.

2770. SCOBEY, J. Best of both worlds. Mademoiselle, v. 57
(May 1963), 171-3+.

2771. SEIPPEL, Clara P. Medical aspect of women's ills in industry. Monthly labor review, v. 13 (November 1921),

945-50.
2772. SEX and equal employment rights.   Monthly labor review,
      v. 90 (August 1967), III-IV.   The work of the Equal
      Employment Opportunity Commission.
2773. SEX and nonsense.   New republic, v. 153 (4 September
      1965), 10.   Reply: v. 153 (18 September 1965), 26+.
      Criticism of Title VII of the Civil Rights Act and of
      the Equal Employment Opportunity Commission.
2774. SEX and VII; Equal employment opportunity section.   Time,
      v. 86 (9 July 1965), 62.
2775. SEX and the job.   Newsweek, v. 66 (12 July 1965), 72.
2776. SEXTON, Patricia Cayo.   Speaking for the working-class
      wife.   Harper's magazine, v. 225 (October 1962), 129-
      33.
2777. SHAFFER, Helen B.   Woman's place in the economy.   Edi-
      torial research reports (13 February 1957), 105-21.
      Women vs. men in the labor market; legislation on
      employment of women; factors for and against women
      workers.
2778. SHALL women lose their new jobs?   Literary digest, v. 60
      (11 January 1919), 14-15.
2779. SHALLCROSS, Ruth E.   Should married women work?   New
      York, Public Affairs Committee, 1940.   31p.
2780. SHARE of wage-earning women in family support.   Monthly
      labor review, v. 17 (July 1923), 140-2.
2781. SHEPHERD, Jack.   Is someone kidding the college girl?
      Look, v. 30 (11 January 1966), 37-8.   The shunting
      of college girls into typically feminine jobs by em-
      ployers.
2782. SHOULD married women work?   Business women's federa-
      tion girds for battle.   Business week (27 July 1940),
      34.
2783. SHOULD married women work?   Symposium.   Current his-
      tory, v. 51 (September 1939), 16+.
2784. SHOULD mother take a job or stay home with the kids?
      Changing times, v. 7 (September 1953), 22-4.
2785. SHOULD mothers of young children work?   Ladies' home
      journal, v. 75 (November 1958), 58-9+.
2786. SHOULD wives be wage earners?   Gunton's magazine, v. 27
      (July 1904), 25-33.
2787. SIMPSON, S. E.   Womanpower: a time for action.   Voca-
      tional guidance quarterly, v. 16 (December 1967),
      134-6.
2788. SKINNER, J.   Postwar employment of women.   Independent
      woman, v. 23 (September 1944), 278.
2789. SMITH, Alfred E.   Labor laws and women workers.   Survey,
      v. 64 (15 May 1930), 182-3.
2790. SMITH, Ethel M.   Equal opportunity for women wage earners.
      Current history, v. 29 (February 1929), 793-7.
2791. SMITH, Georgina M.   The changing woman worker; a study
      of the female labor force in New Jersey and in the
      nation from 1940 to 1958.   New Brunswick, N.J.,
      Rutgers, The State University, 1960.   23p.

2792. SMITH, M. P. Legal and administrative restrictions af-
       fecting the rights of married women to work. Ameri-
       can Academy of Political and Social Science, annals,
       v. 143 (May 1929), 255-64.
2793. SMITH girls; job market opens wide for college graduates as
       war reduces manpower. Life, v. 13 (28 September
       1942), 53-4.
2794. SMUTS, Robert W. Women and work in America. New
       York, Columbia University Press, 1960. 180p. The
       conditions under which women worked from the turn
       of the century as well as comments from 19th century
       feminists.
2795. SOMERVILLE, A. Missouri's nine-hour women's bill. Sur-
       vey, v. 22 (24 July 1909), 576-7.
2796. SONTHEIMER, M. Is one man worth two women? Cosmo-
       politan, v. 135 (September 1953), 129-31.
2797. SOUTHARD, H. F. Mother's dilemma: to work or not?
       New York Times magazine (17 July 1960), 39.
2798. SPECIAL legislation for women workers. New republic,
       v. 21 (28 January 1920), 252-3.
2799. SPEEK, F. V. Economic and legal status of women.
       American Association of University Women, journal,
       v. 38 (June 1945), 222-6.
2800. SPENCER, Anna Garlin. Should married women work out-
       side the home? Eugenics, v. 4 (January 1931), 21-5.
2801. The SPIRIT of women wage-earners. Survey, v. 34 (19
       June 1915), 262-3. Concerning the National Women's
       Trade Union League.
2802. SPOOR, Lillie M. Women and the problem of earning a liv-
       ing. Denver, Col., Ward & Saunders, printers, 1912.
       62p.
2803. STANDARDS for employment of women in defense program.
       Monthly labor review, v. 51 (September 1940), 564-7.
2804. STATEWIDE Conference on the Changing Status of Women,
       Ohio State University, Columbus, 1963. Proceedings:
       Focus on employment. [Columbus, Ohio State Univer-
       sity, 1965?] 61p.
2805. STERN, Edith M. Brains in the kitchen. Nation, v. 158
       (22 January 1944), 95-6. The need for women in in-
       dustry.
2806. STEVENS, Eleanour Virginia. Some development in national
       equal wage and employment policy for women with em-
       phasis on the years, 1962-1966. 270p. PhD thesis,
       University of Illinois, 1967. A study of the Equal Pay
       Act of 1963 and Title VII of the Civil Rights Act of
       1964 and their positive effects.
2807. STEVENS, R. D. Those perverse women who want to work.
       American Association of University Women, journal,
       v. 39 (January 1946), 97-8.
2808. STEWART, J. A. National Women's Trade Union League.
       Chautauquan, v. 59 (June 1910), 116-20.
2809. STEWART, M. W. Our sacred heritage: legal status of
       women and of those who work with their hands. Amer-

ican law review, v. 54 (September 1920), 641-61.
2810. STITT, Louise. Women's wartime employment: expanding
needs; increasing problems. American Association of
University Women, journal, v. 35 (April 1942), 136-40.
2811. STOKES, R. H. Condition of working women from the working-woman's viewpoint. American Academy of Political
and Social Science, annals, v. 27 (May 1906), 627-37.
2812. STOLZ, Lois Meek. Woman's search for a new self. National Association of Women Deans and Counselors,
journal, v. 22 (April 1959), 125-30. The employment
of married women with some comparisons between
1890 and 1957.
2813. STRATTON, D. C. Our great unused resource, womanpower. New York Times magazine (1 October 1950),
17+.
2814. _____. Women after the war. Independent woman, v. 24
(October 1945), 279+.
2815. STUDY of Negro women in industry. Southern workman, v.
58 (September 1929), 420-2. Covers the period from
1910 to 1922.
2816. SUBPOENAING the toxim of fatigue; the injunction against the
enforcement of the Illinois ten-hour law for women.
Survey, v. 23 (11 December 1909), 344-6.
2817. SUELZLE, Marijean. Women in labor. Transaction, v. 8
(November 1970), 50-8.
2818. SWARTZ, Nelle. Women who work. Survey, v. 48 (13 May
1922), 243-4. A survey of the number of women in
various jobs in New York State.
2819. _____ and Edith Hilles. Women workers in the five and
ten. Survey, v. 47 (12 November 1921), 244-5.
Wages and hours of women compared with men.
2820. SWEET, James A. Family composition and the labor force
activity of married women in the United States. 259p.
PhD thesis, University of Michigan, 1968.
2821. SWETT, Maud. Woman's work. Madison, Wis., Parson's
Printery, 1909.
2822. A SYMPOSIUM: women in the labor force. Industrial relations, v. 7 (May 1968), 187-248.
2823. TAYLOR, G. Illinois ten-hour law. Survey, v. 23 (6 November 1909), 205-6.
2824. _____. Ten-hour day for women upheld. Survey, v. 24
(30 April 1910), 170-1.
2825. TECHNIQUES for the task ahead; economic and legal status
of women. American Association of University Women,
journal, v. 37 (June 1944), 228-33.
2826. TENNESSEE. State Board for Vocational Education. More
efficient use of women in industry; a composite report
of five training conferences for management and women
representatives of industry. Nashville, 1944. 91p.
2827. TERLIN, Rose and J. F. Nelson. Married women are working! Womans press, v. 35 (January 1941), 14-15+.
2828. TEXAS. Bureau of Labor Statistics. Laws of Texas relating
to employment of women and children. Austin, 1936.

14p.

2829. _____. University. Bureau of Research in the Social
Sciences. The labor of women in the production of
cotton. By Ruth Allen. Austin, 1931. 285p.

2830. THOMPSON, Flora McDonald. The truth about women in industry. North American review, v. 178 (May 1904),
751-60.

2831. THOMPSON, W. Gilman. Women and heavy war work.
Scribner's magazine, v. 65 (January 1919), 113-16.
The extent to which women can replace men in heavy
industries and suggestions for accomplishing this.

2832. THWING, Charles F. What becomes of college women?
North American review, v. 161 (November 1895),
546-53.

2833. TRENDS in employment of women. Industrial bulletin, v. 20
(November 1941), 340-1.

2834. TURNER, Marjorie B. Women and work. Los Angeles,
Institute of Industrial Relations, University of California, 1964. 73p.

2835. TURNER, Ralph H. The nonwhite female in the labor force.
American journal of Sociology, v. 56 (March 1951),
438-47.

2836. UNEMPLOYMENT among women in the early years of the
depression. Monthly labor review, v. 38 (April
1934), 790-5.

2837. UNITED Electrical, Radio and Machine Workers of America
(UE). UE fights for women workers: end rate discrimination; end job discrimination. New York, UE,
1952. 39p.

2838. U.S. Bureau of Labor. Employment and economic status of
older men and women. Washington, GPO, 1952. 58p.
[Bulletin no. 1902.]

2839. _____. _____. Report on condition of woman and
child wage-earners in the United States. Washington,
GPO, 1910-1913. 19v.

2840. _____. _____. Summary of the Report on condition
of woman and child wage earners in the United States.
Washington, GPO, 1915. 445p. [Bulletin no. 175.]

2841. _____. Bureau of the Census. Statistics of women at
work, based on unpublished information derived from
the schedules of the twelfth census: 1900. Washington, GPO, 1907. 399p.

2842. _____. _____. Women in gainful occupations, 1870-
1920: A study of the trend of recent changes in the
numbers, occupational distribution, and family relationship of women reported in the census as following
a gainful occupation. By Joseph A. Hill. Washington, GPO, 1929. 416p. [Census monographs no. 9.]

2843. _____. Citizens Advisory Council on the Status of Women.
Equal employment opportunities for women under Title
VII of the Civil Rights Act of 1964; a memorandum on
policy.... Washington, GPO, 1965. 12p.

2844. _____. _____. Report of the Task Force on Labor

Standards. Washington, GPO, 1968. 58p. Labor
legislation, standards, wages, benefits, etc.

2845. _____. Civil Service Commission. The first year: A
study of women's participation in federal defense activities. By L. F. McMillin. Washington, GPO,
1941. 39p.

2846. _____. _____. Investigating complaints of discrimination in federal employment, on grounds of race, color,
religion, sex, and national origin. Washington, GPO,
1967. 28p.

2847. _____. _____. Occupations and salaries of women in
the federal service. Washington, GPO, 1962.

2848. _____. _____. Study of employment of women in the
federal government, 1966- . Washington, GPO, 1968- .
Annual reports of statistics concerning federal employment of women and areas where greater efforts for
equal opportunity for women should be made.

2849. _____. Congress. Senate. History of women in industry in
the United States. By Helen Laura Sumner. Washington, GPO, 1910. 277p. [Senate Document no. 645.
61st Congress, 2d session.]

2850. _____. _____. _____. History of women in trade
unions, 1825-1890, through the Knights of Labor. By
John B. Andrews. Washington, GPO, 1911. [Senate
Document no. 645, part 10, pp. 9-132. 61st Congress, 2d session.]

2851. _____. Equal Employment Opportunity Commission.
Equal employment opportunity report--job patterns for
minorities and women in private industry. Washington, GPO, 1968- . Annual report on statistics concerning discrimination in private industry.

2852. _____. _____. Help wanted...or is it? A look at
white collar job inequalities for minorities and women.
Washington, GPO, 1968. 15p.

2853. _____. Interdepartmental Committee on the Status of
Women. Federal employment of women. Washington,
GPO, 1966. 22p.

2854. _____. Manpower Administration. Womanpower policies
for the 1970's. By Wilbur J. Cohen. Washington,
GPO, 1967. 40p.

2855. _____. President, 1921-1923 (Harding). Address of the
President of the United States on social justice, wom-
en, and labor, at Helena, Mont., June 29, 1923.
Washington, GPO, 1923. 10p.

2856. _____. President's Commission on the Status of Women.
Four consultations: private employment opportunities,
new patterns in volunteer work, portrayal of women by
the mass media, problems of Negro women. Washington, GPO, 1963. 38p.

2857. _____. _____. Report of the Committee on Federal
Employment. Washington, GPO, 1963. 195p. The
status of women in the Federal Government, concerning promotions, health and insurance, military ser-

vices, as well as a short history of women in the
civil service.

2858. ____. ____. Report of the Committee on Private
Employment. Washington, GPO, 1963. 55p.
A study
of barriers to women and recommendations in equal
employment opportunities, equal pay, employment service policy, and several recommendations.

2859. ____. ____. Report of the Committee on Protective
Labor Legislation. Washington, GPO, 1963. 38p.
Study of findings and recommendations for women in
areas of equal pay, collective bargaining, hours of
work, minimum wages, etc.

2860. ____. War Manpower Commission. Women's Advisory
Committee. Recommendations on separation of women
from wartime jobs. Monthly labor review, v. 61
(September 1945), 506.

2861. ____. Women's Bureau. Background facts on women
workers in the United States, 1962- . Washington,
GPO, 1962- . Annual report of statistics concerning
age groups, marital status, educational level, and occupational structure of the female labor force.

2862. ____. ____. Baltimore women war workers in the
post-war. Washington, GPO, 1948. 61p.

2863. ____. ____. Changes in women's occupations,
1940-1950. By Mary Elizabeth Pidgeon. Washington,
GPO, 1954. 104p. [Bulletin no. 253.]

2864. ____. ____. Chronological development of labor
legislation for women in the United States. By
Florence Patteson Smith. Washington, GPO, 1932.
176p. [Bulletin no. 66-2.]

2865. ____. ____. Conference on unions and the changing
status of women workers, Rutgers University, 1964.
Report. Washington, GPO, 1965. 29p.

2866. ____. ____. Earnings and hours in Hawaii woman-
employing industries. By Ethel Erickson. Washington, GPO, 1940. 53p. [Bulletin no. 177.]

2867. ____. ____. Earnings in the women's and children's
apparel industry in the spring of 1939. By Arthur
Theodore Sutherland. Washington, GPO, 1940. 91p.
[Bulletin no. 175.]

2868. ____. ____. The economic responsibilities of wom-
en workers as shown by a Women's Bureau study of
women war workers and their postwar plans. Washington, GPO, 1946. 4p.

2869. ____. ____. Economic status of university women
in the United States of America. By Susan M. Kingsbury. Washington, GPO, 1939. [Bulletin no. 170.]

2870. ____. ____. The effects of labor legislation on the
employment opportunities of women. Washington,
GPO, 1928. [Bulletin no. 65.]

2871. ____. ____. The effects on women of changing
conditions in the cigar and cigarette industries. By
Caroline Manning and H. A. Byrne. Washington, GPO,

1932. 187p. [Bulletin no. 100.]

2872. _____. _____. The employed woman homemaker in
the United States; her responsibility for family support. By Mary Elizabeth Pidgeon. Washington, GPO,
1936. 22p. [Bulletin no. 148.]

2873. _____. _____. Employed women and family support.
By Mary Elizabeth Pidgeon. Washington, GPO, 1939.
57p. [Bulletin no. 168.]

2874. _____. _____. Employed women under N.R.A. codes.
By Mary Elizabeth Pidgeon. Washington, GPO, 1935.
144p. [Bulletin no. 130.] Concerning the National
Recovery Administration.

2875. _____. _____. Employment in service and trade industries in Maine. By Arthur Theodore Sutherland.
Washington, GPO, 1940. 30p. [Bulletin no. 180.]

2876. _____. _____. The employment of women in offices.
By Ethel Erickson. Washington, GPO, 1934. 126p.
[Bulletin no. 120.]

2877. _____. _____. Employment of women in Tennessee
industries. By Ethel Erickson. Washington, GPO,
1937. 63p. [Bulletin no. 149.]

2878. _____. _____. Employment of women in the early
postwar period with background of prewar and war
data. By Mary Elizabeth Pidgeon. Washington, GPO,
1946. 14p. [Bulletin no. 211.]

2879. _____. _____. Employment of women in the federal
government, 1923-1939. By R. F. Nyswander and
J. M. Hooks. Washington, GPO, 1941. 60p. [Bul-
letin no. 182.]

2880. _____. _____. Facts about working women; a graphic
presentation based on census statistics and studies of
the Women's Bureau. Washington, GPO, 1925. 64p.
[Bulletin no. 46.]

2881. _____. _____. Handbook on women workers. Washington, GPO. Published periodically, and containing
information pertaining to the participation of women in
the labor force, income, occupations, federal and
state laws affecting their employment, and the civil
and political status of women.

2882. _____. _____. History of labor legislation for women
in three states; Massachusetts, New York, and California. By Clara E. M. Beyer. Washington, GPO,
1929. 288p. [Bulletin no. 66.]

2883. _____. _____. Hours and conditions of work for wom-
en in industry in Virginia. Washington, GPO, 1920.
32p.

2884. _____. _____. Hours, earnings, and employment in
cotton mills. By Ethel Lombard Best. Washington,
GPO, 1933. 78p. [Bulletin no. 111.]

2885. _____. _____. Iowa women in industry. Washington,
GPO, 1922. 73p. [Bulletin no. 19.]

2886. _____. _____. Know your rights: what a working
wife should know about her legal rights. By Harriet

F. Pilpel and Minna P. Peyser. Washington, GPO, 1965. 14p. [Leaflet no. 39.]

2887. _____. _____. Labor laws affecting women, a capsule summary. Washington, GPO, 1944- .

2888. _____. _____. Labor laws for women in industry in Indiana. Washington, GPO, 1919. 29p. [Bulletin no. 2.]

2889. _____. _____. Labor laws for women in the states and territories. By Florence Patteson Smith. Washington, GPO, 1934. 71p. [Bulletin no. 98.]

2890. _____. _____. Laws on sex discrimination in employment; Federal Civil Rights Act, Title VII, state fair employment practices laws, July 1965-1970. Washington, GPO, 1965-1970. 5v.

2891. _____. _____. The Negro woman worker. By Jean Collier Brown. Washington, GPO, 1938. 17p. [Bulletin no. 165.]

2892. _____. _____. Negro women and their jobs. By Miriam Keeler. Washington, GPO, 1954. 10p.

2893. _____. _____. Negro women in industry. Washington, GPO, 1922. 65p. [Bulletin no. 20.]

2894. _____. _____. Negro women in industry in 15 states. By Mary Elizabeth Pidgeon. Washington, GPO, 1929. 74p. [Bulletin no. 70.]

2895. _____. _____. Negro women in the population and in the labor force. Washington, GPO, 1968. 41p.

2896. _____. _____. Negro women war workers. Washington, GPO, 1945. 23p. [Bulletin no. 205.]

2897. _____. _____. Negro women workers in 1960. By Helen O. Nicol. Washington, GPO, 1964. 55p. [Bulletin no. 287.]

2898. _____. _____. The new position of women in American industry. Washington, GPO, 1920. 158p. [Bulletin no. 12.]

2899. _____. _____. The occupational progress of women, 1910-1930. Washington, GPO, 1933. 90p. [Bulletin no. 104.]

2900. _____. _____. Oregon legislation for women in industry. By Sister Miriam Theresa (Caroline J. Gleason). Washington, GPO, 1931. 40p. [Bulletin no. 90.]

2901. _____. _____. Preliminary report: hours, wages, and working conditions for women in industry in Kentucky. Washington, GPO, 1922. 13p.

2902. _____. _____. Preliminary report on the working conditions and hours of labor for women in industry in Maryland. Washington, GPO, 1922. 16p.

2903. _____. _____. A preview as to women workers in transition from war to peace. By Mary Elizabeth Pidgeon. Washington, GPO, 1944. 26p. [Special bulletin no. 18.]

2904. _____. _____. The share of wage-earning women in family support. Washington, GPO, 1923. 170p. [Bulletin no. 30.]

2905. _____. _____. Some effects of legislation limiting
hours of work for women. Washington, GPO, 1921.
26p. [Bulletin no. 15.] Emphasis is on Massachusetts and New Jersey.

2906. _____. _____. Standards for employment of women
in industry. Washington, GPO, 1939. 8p. [Bulletin
no. 173.]

2907. _____. _____. State hour laws for women. Washington, GPO, 1953. 114p. [Bulletin no. 250.]

2908. _____. _____. State labor laws for women, December 31, 1937: Part 1, Summary; Part 2, Analysis of
hour laws for women workers. By Florence P. Smith.
Washington, GPO, 1938. [Bulletin no. 156.]

2909. _____. _____. State labor laws for women, December
31, 1940: Part 1, Summary. By Florence P. Smith.
Washington, GPO, 1940. 18p. [Bulletin no. 156-1.]

2910. _____. _____. State labor laws for women: hours,
home work, prohibited or regulated occupations, seats,
minimum wage. By Florence P. Smith. Washington,
GPO, 1937. 93p. [Bulletin no. 144.]

2911. _____. _____. State labor laws for women with wartime modifications, December 15, 1944. Washington,
GPO, 1945. 5 parts. [Bulletin no. 202.]

2912. _____. _____. State laws affecting working women.
Washington, GPO, 1921. 49p. [Bulletin no. 16.]

2913. _____. _____. State laws affecting working women:
hours, minimum wage, home work. Washington, GPO,
1927. 51p. [Bulletin no. 63.]

2914. _____. _____. The status of women in the government service in 1925. By Bertha Marie von der Nienburg. Washington, GPO, 1926. 103p. [Bulletin no.
53.]

2915. _____. _____. Summaries of studies on the economic
status of women. Washington, GPO, 1935. [Bulletin
no. 134.]

2916. _____. _____. Summary of state labor laws for
women, February, 1967. Washington, GPO, 1967.
18p.

2917. _____. _____. Technological changes in relation to
women's employment. By Ethel L. Best. Washington, GPO, 1935. [Bulletin no. 107.]

2918. _____. _____. Toward better working conditions for
women; methods and policies of the National Women's
Trade Union League of America. By Mary Elizabeth
Pidgeon. Washington, GPO, 1953. 71p. [Bulletin
no. 252.]

2919. _____. _____. Trends in the employment of women,
1928-1936. By Mary Elizabeth Pidgeon. Washington,
GPO, 1938. 48p. [Bulletin no. 159.]

2920. _____. _____. Underutilization of women workers?
Washington, GPO, 1967. 23p. Statistics showing
employment policy discrimination. Summaries of
findings concerning wage discrimination and under-

utilization of both Negro and white women.
2921. _____. _____. Utilization of women workers--a reprint from the 1967 Manpower report. Washington,
GPO, 1967. 12p.
2922. _____. _____. What industry means to women workers. By Mary Van Kleeck. Washington, GPO, 1923.
10p. [Bulletin no. 31.]
2923. _____. _____. What the wage-earning woman con-
tributes to family support. By Agnes Lydia Peterson.
Washington, GPO, 1929. 21p. [Bulletin no. 75.]
2924. _____. _____. The woman wage earner, her situation today. By Elizabeth D. Benham. Washington,
GPO, 1939. 56p. [Bulletin no. 172.]
2925. _____. _____. Women at work; a century of industrial change. Washington, GPO, 1939. 80p. [Bul-
letin no. 161.]
2926. _____. _____. Women in Alabama industries; a study
of hours, wages, and working conditions. Washington,
GPO, 1924. 86p. [Bulletin no. 34.]
2927. _____. _____. Women in Arkansas industries: a
study of hours, wages, and working conditions. Washington, GPO, 1923. 86p. [Bulletin no. 26.]
2928. _____. _____. Women in Delaware industries: a
study of hours, wages, and working conditions. Washington, GPO, 1927. 156p. [Bulletin no. 58.]
2929. _____. _____. Women in Florida industries. Washington, GPO, 1930. 115p. [Bulletin no. 80.]
2930. _____. _____. Women in Georgia industries: a study
of hours, wages, and working conditions. Washington,
GPO, 1922. 89p. [Bulletin no. 22.]
2931. _____. _____. Women in Illinois industries: a study
of hours and working conditions. Washington, GPO,
1926. 108p. [Bulletin no. 51.]
2932. _____. _____. Women in Kentucky industries: a
study of hours, wages, and working conditions. Washington, GPO, 1923. 114p. [Bulletin no. 29.]
2933. _____. _____. Women in Maryland industries: a
study of hours and working conditions. Washington,
GPO, 1922. 96p. [Bulletin no. 24.]
2934. _____. _____. Women in Mississippi industries: a
study of hours, wages, and working conditions. Washington, GPO, 1926. 89p. [Bulletin no. 55.]
2935. _____. _____. Women in Missouri industries: a
study of hours and wages. Washington, GPO, 1924.
127p. [Bulletin no. 35.]
2936. _____. _____. Women in New Jersey industries: a
study of wages and hours. Washington, GPO, 1924.
99p. [Bulletin no. 37.]
2937. _____. _____. Women in Ohio industries: a study
of hours and wages. Washington, GPO, 1925. 137p.
[Bulletin no. 44.]
2938. _____. _____. Women in Oklahoma industries: a
study of hours, wages, and working conditions. Wash-

ington, GPO, 1926. 118p. [Bulletin no. 48.]

2939. _____. _____. Women in Rhode Island industries: a study of hours, wages, and working conditions. Washington, GPO, 1922. 73p. [Bulletin no. 21.]

2940. _____. _____. Women in South Carolina industries: a study of hours, wages, and working conditions. Washington, GPO, 1923. 128p. [Bulletin no. 32.]

2941. _____. _____. Women in Tennessee industries: a study of hours, wages, and working conditions. Washington, GPO, 1927. 120p. [Bulletin no. 56.]

2942. _____. _____. Women in Texas industries: hours, wages, working conditions, and home work. By Mary Loretta Sullivan. Washington, GPO, 1936. 81p. [Bulletin no. 126.]

2943. _____. _____. Women in the economy of the United States of America: a summary report. By Mary Elizabeth Pidgeon. Washington, GPO, 1937. 137p. [Bulletin no. 155.]

2944. _____. _____. Women in the federal service, 1923-1947. By Mary Elizabeth Pidgeon. Washington, GPO, 1949-1950. 2v. [Bulletin no. 230.]

2945. _____. _____. Women office workers in Philadelphia. By H. A. Byrne. Washington, GPO, 1932. 17p. [Bulletin no. 96.]

2946. _____. _____. Women who work in offices: study of employed women; study of women seeking employment. By H. A. Byrne. Washington, GPO, 1935. 27p. [Bulletin no. 132.]

2947. _____. _____. Women workers and their dependents. By Mary Elizabeth Pidgeon. Washington, GPO, 1952. 117p. [Bulletin no. 239.]

2948. _____. _____. Women workers in ten war production areas and their postwar employment plans. Washington, GPO, 1946. 56p. [Bulletin no. 209.]

2949. _____. _____. Women workers in the third year of the depression: a study. Washington, GPO, 1933. 16p. [Bulletin no. 103.]

2950. _____. _____. Women workers in their family environment. Washington, GPO, 1941. 82p. [Bulletin no. 183.]

2951. _____. _____. Women's employment in West Virginia. By H. A. Byrne. Washington, GPO, 1937. 27p. [Bulletin no. 150.]

2952. _____. _____. Women's hours and wages in the District of Columbia in 1937. By Ethel Lombard Best. Washington, GPO, 1937. 44p. [Bulletin no. 153.]

2953. _____. _____. Women's occupations through seven decades. Washington, GPO, 1947. 257p. [Bulletin no. 218.]

2954. _____. _____. Women's wages and hours in Nebraska. By Arthur Theodore Sutherland. Washington, GPO, 1940. 51p. [Bulletin no. 178.]

2955. VALENTIN, A. Employment of women since the war. In-

ternational labour review, v. 25 (April 1932), 480-92.
2956. VAN ETTEN, Ida M. The condition of women workers under
the present industrial system. New York, Concord
Cooperative Print., 1891. 16p.
2957. VAN KLEECK, Mary. The effect of labor laws upon women
in industry. U.S. Bureau of Labor bulletin, v. 429
(1927), 19-27.
2958. _____. Federal policies for women in industry. American Academy of Political and Social Science, annals,
v. 81 (January 1919), 87-94. The position of women
in industry following World War I.
2959. _____. For women in industry. Survey, v. 37 (23 December 1916), 327-9. The beginnings of the U.S.
Women's Bureau.
2960. _____. How women wage earners fare. World's work,
v. 15 (December 1907), 9683-90.
2961. _____. Places for American women in industry after the
war. Official bulletin [District of Columbia]. v. 3
(8 January 1919), 27.
2962. _____. What shall be done with women who have replaced
men in industry during the war? U.S. Employment
Service, bulletin, v. 1 (26 November 1918), 7.
2963. _____. Women and machines. Atlantic monthly, v. 127
(February 1921), 250-60. Feminism versus modern
industry following World War I.
2964. _____. Working hours of women in factories. Charities
and the commons, v. 17 (6 October 1906), 13-21.
2965. VAN RENSSELAER, M. G. Waste of women's intellectual
force. Forum, v. 13 (July 1892), 616-28.
2966. VAN VORST, Bessie. The woman who toils. New York,
Doubleday, 1903.
2967. VARIATIONS in employment trends of male and female workers. Monthly labor review, v. 31 (July 1930), 19-28.
2968. VOGEL, Lise. Women workers; some basic statistics.
Boston, New England Free Press, 1970. 19p. Statistics on age of working women, kinds of jobs held
by women, salaries, nonwhite women, and women in
labor unions.
2969. VON ELTZ, Eleonore. Hearing from the people; fight for
the 48 hour week for women workers in New York
State. Survey, v. 56 (15 May 1926), 235+.
2970. WAGES and family responsibilities of employed women on relief in New York City. Monthly labor review, v. 42
(June 1936), 1525-7.
2971. WAGES and hours of women in clothing industries in Rhode
Island. Monthly labor review, v. 45 (October 1937),
889-91.
2972. WAGES and hours of women in Kansas, 1937. Monthly labor
review, v. 47 (November 1938), 1021-3.
2973. WAGES and hours of women in retail trade in New York,
1944. Monthly labor review, v. 61 (August 1945),
299-300.
2974. WAGGAMAN, Mary T. The National Women's Trade Union

League of America. Monthly labor review, v. 8
(April 1919), 237-45.

2975. WALD, L. D. Organization among the working women.
American Academy of Political and Social Science,
annals, v. 27 (May 1906), 638-45.

2976. WALDMAN, Elizabeth. Changes in the labor force activity
of women. Monthly labor review, v. 93 (June 1970),
10-18. Concerns women's earnings, the Negro woman,
and types of occupations.

2977. _____. Marital and family status of workers. Monthly
labor review, v. 91 (April 1968), 14-22.

2978. WALDO, R. J. Should industry employ women? Boston,
business (June 1950), 184-6.

2979. WALLERSTEIN, Bertha. The working-woman's idea. Nation, v. 116 (30 May 1923), 627-8.

2980. WALTERS, J. E. Women in industry. American Academy
of Political and Social Science, annals, v. 229 (September 1943), 56-62. Company policies concerning
the employment of women during World War II.

2981. WARTIME relaxation of California's woman and child labor
laws in 1943. Monthly labor review, v. 59 (July
1944), 121-2.

2982. WEATHERLY, U. G. Employment of women in industry and
its effect on the family. American Sociological Society,
proceedings and publications, v. 3 (1908), 124-49.

2983. _____. How does the access of women to industrial occupations react on the family? American journal of
Sociology, v. 14 (May 1909), 740-52.

2984. WEBER, Gustavus A. The Women's Bureau; its history,
activities and organization. Baltimore, Johns Hopkins
Press, 1923. 31p.

2985. WELLS, Emilie Louise. Woman and child wage-earners in
the United States. American economic review, v. 2
(June 1912), 436-42. A summary of the 19 volume
study of the conditions of women and child workers in
the United States issued by the U.S. Bureau of Labor.

2986. WELLS, Jean A. Employment of June 1956 women college
graduates. Monthly labor review, v. 81 (July 1958),
752-6.

2987. _____. Employment of June 1957 women college graduates.
Monthly labor review, v. 82 (June 1959), 663-6.

2988. _____. Women college graduates seven years later.
Monthly labor review, v. 90 (July 1967), 28-32. Pertains to employment status, salaries, and continuing
education.

2989. WELLS, Lyn. American women; their use and abuse. Boston, New England Free Press, 1969. 17p. Concerning employment and home life.

2990. WHAT shall be done with women who have replaced men in
industry? Current opinion, v. 66 (February 1919),
124-5. The danger of male employees trying to force
women out of jobs; also concerns lower wages for
women.

2991. WHAT Uncle Sam does not do for women in industry. New
       republic, v. 7 (29 July 1916), 324-6.
2992. WHEN is the difference unequal? question of sex bias.
       Time, v. 86 (10 December 1965), 36. The Equal
       Employment Opportunity Commission and its enforce-
       ment of the Civil Rights Act of 1964.
2993. WHEN mother works: pro and con discussion. Practical
       Home Economics, v. 6 (February 1961), 26-7+.
2994. WHITE, E. Should wives work? Rotarian, v. 55 (October
       1939), 19-22. Discussion: v. 55 (December 1939), 2.
2995. WHITELOCK, F. Married women in today's labor force.
       Journal of Home Economics, v. 41 (December 1949),
       549-51.
2996. WHY mothers work. America, v. 114 (29 January 1966),
       166. Reply: v. 114 (5 March 1966), 312.
2997. WHY women are wage earners. Current literature, v. 29
       (October 1900), 385-6.
2998. WIFE'S place? More say "in a job." U.S. news and world
       report, v. 28 (2 June 1950), 34+. More women work-
       ing outside the home, but with a number of inequities
       still present.
2999. WILENSKY, Harold L. Women's work: Economic growth,
       ideology, structure. Industrial relations, v. 7 (May
       1968), 235-48.
3000. WILLETT, Mabel H. The employment of women in the cloth-
       ing trade. New York, Macmillan, 1902. 206p. Re-
       printed by AMS Press, New York, 1968. The em-
       phasis is on New York: working conditions, wages,
       work at home, trade unions, labor legislation, etc.
3001. WILLIS, Margaret. Working women. Journal of educational
       Sociology, v. 14 (April 1944), 473-8. Women in the
       postwar world.
3002. WINGO, Walter. Here come the girls. Nation's business,
       v. 57 (December 1969), 38-41. Concerns the advances
       of women in industry; but also some problems of Title
       VII and the Equal Employment Opportunity Commission,
       women in trade unions, along with views of Lionel
       Tiger, Margaret Chase Smith, and others.
3003. WINKLER, Ilene. Woman workers: the forgotten third of
       the working class. New York, International Socialists,
       1968. 13p.
3004. WINSLOW, Mary Nelson. The effects of labor legislation on
       women's work. American Academy of Political and
       Social Science, annals, v. 143 (May 1929), 280-5.
3005. _____. Married women in industry. Journal of social
       hygiene, v. 9 (October 1923), 385-95.
3006. WISCONSIN. Legislative Reference Library. Special labor
       legislation for women: summary of the statutes...in
       all states which place restrictions upon the employ-
       ment of adult women; do not apply to men. Madison,
       1926. 11p.
3007. WITTE, Edwin E. The effects of special labor legislation
       for women. Quarterly journal of Economics, v. 42

(November 1927), 153-64.
3008. WOLFE, A. B. and H. Olson. War-time industrial employment of women in the United States. Journal of political economy, v. 27 (October 1919), 639-69.
3009. WOLFE, F. E. Admission to American Trade unions.
Johns Hopkins University Studies in Historical and
Political Science, v. 30 (1912), 528-49.
3010. WOLFE, Helen B. Women in the world of work. Albany,
University of the State of New York, State Education
Department, Division of Research, 1969. 65p.
3011. WOLFSON, Theresa. Equal rights in the union. Survey,
v. 57 (15 February 1927), 629-30.
3012. _____. Trade union activities of women. American
Academy of Political and Social Science, annals,
v. 143 (May 1929), 120-31.
3013. _____. Where are the organized women workers? American federationist, v. 32 (June 1925), 455-7.
3014. _____. The woman worker and the trade unions. New
York, International, 1926. 224p.
3015. WOLMON, Leo. Are women hard to organize? Survey,
v. 53 (15 March 1925), 741-2.
3016. WOMAN--her "place" and her problems. Economic outlook,
(July 1945), special issue.
3017. WOMAN wage earners in Minnesota. Monthly labor review,
v. 11 (September 1920), 543-7.
3018. WOMAN workers in the District of Columbia, 1937. Monthly
labor review, v. 45 (September 1937), 626-31.
3019. WOMAN workers in the third year of the depression.
Monthly labor review, v. 37 (August 1933), 303-5.
3020. WOMAN-POWER. Time, v. 95 (30 March 1970), 59.
Charges of discrimination against "Newsweek" and the
"Ladies' Home Journal."
3021. WOMAN'S changing role in America. U.S. news and world
report, v. 67 (8 September 1969), 44-6. Pressure
on the Federal Government, private business, and industrial firms to do away with discriminatory practices against women. Charts show pay differences in
selected types of jobs and the growing number of
women in the professions.
3022. A WOMAN'S place: diminishing justification for sex discrimination in employment. Southern California law
review, v. 42 (Fall 1968), 183-211. Problems of
enforcement of the Civil Rights Act.
3023. WOMAN'S place in work force. Business week (16 March
1957), 160-1. Findings of the National Manpower
Council concerning trends in the female labor force.
3024. WOMAN'S place: surveys show they not only can do the job
but that they often do it better; obstacles to employment are giving way; nation appraises its womanpower. Business week (16 May 1942), 20+.
3025. WOMAN'S work after the war. New republic, v. 17 (25
January 1919), 358-9.
3026. WOMAN'S work: legislation of 1911. American labor legis-

lation review, v. 1 (October 1911), 144-7.
3027. WOMAN'S work: legislation of 1912. American labor legislation review, v. 2 (October 1912), 495-501.
3028. WOMAN'S work: legislation of 1913. American labor legislation review, v. 3 (October 1913), 433-47.
3029. WOMAN'S work: legislation of 1914. American labor legislation review, v. 4 (October 1914), 492-4.
3030. WOMAN'S work: legislation of 1915. American labor legislation review, v. 5 (December 1915), 792-805.
3031. WOMEN and children in industry in Maryland. Monthly labor review, v. 16 (June 1923), 1326-8.
3032. WOMEN as wage-earners. Current literature, v. 37 (September 1904), 240-2.
3033. WOMEN at work; anything he can do.... Senior scholastic, v. 97 (9 November 1970), 15.
3034. WOMEN at work; revolt against the kitchen. Time, v. 95 (11 May 1970), 100. More women are getting jobs, but old prejudices are still present, such as lower pay for women and few memberships in unions.
3035. WOMEN in Alabama industries. Monthly labor review, v. 19 (August 1924), 400-2.
3036. WOMEN in Arkansas industries. Monthly labor review, v. 16 (June 1923), 1323-6.
3037. WOMEN in labor unions. Monthly labor review, v. 60 (June 1945), 1269-70.
3038. WOMEN in New York retail and service jobs. 1945. Monthly labor review, v. 62 (June 1946), 931-2.
3039. WOMEN in post-war industries. Touchstone, v. 5 (May 1919), 160-1.
3040. WOMEN in South Carolina industries. Monthly labor review, v. 18 (March 1924), 571-3.
3041. WOMEN in the government service. Monthly labor review, v. 10 (January 1920), 208-17.
3042. WOMEN in trade unions. Monthly labor review, v. 19 (August 1924), 398-400.
3043. WOMEN in unions. Woman worker (January 1940), 10-11.
3044. WOMEN unite to protect women. Survey, v. 41 (28 December 1918), 405-6. Attempts in New York State at minimum wages, 8-hour day, and other changes for women.
3045. WOMEN wage-earners. Nation, v. 82 (22 February 1906), 152-3. On the unequal proportion of women to men in industry.
3046. WOMEN will stay: they're enjoying their first taste of industrial equality, and surveys indicate many will hang on to jobs after the war. Business week (March 1944), 46+.
3047. WOMEN workers after the war. Woman citizen, v. 3 (21 December 1918), 612-13.
3048. WOMEN workers: conditions in the United States. Industrial and labour information, v. 54 (1 April 1935), 12-18.
3049. WOMEN workers: employment trends, 1900 to 1950. Month-

ly labor review, v. 72 (January 1951), 52.

3050. WOMEN workers: fact vs. fantasy. Management review,
v. 46 (January 1957), 47-8.

3051. WOMEN workers' platform. Survey, v. 41 (15 March 1919),
868-9. A number of bills pending in the New York
State Legislature.

3052. WOMEN'S equality in industry. New republic, v. 57 (28
November 1928), 31-2. Discussion: v. 57 (2 January
1929), 193-4.

3053. WOMEN'S industry after the war. Journal of Home Economics, v. 8 (May 1916), 263-4.

3054. WOMEN'S right to work; symposium. Woman's journal,
v. 15 (May 1930), 28-9.

3055. WOMEN'S strike; the ladies' waist-makers of New York.
Outlook, v. 93 (11 December 1909), 799-89.

3056. WOMEN'S Trade Union League of Massachusetts. The history of trade unionism among women in Boston. Boston, The League, 1915. 33p.

3057. WOMEN'S wages and hours in Nebraska, 1938. Monthly labor
review, v. 52 (April 1941), 859-63.

3058. WOMEN'S working hours. American labor legislation review,
v. 1 (January 1911), 90-3.

3059. WOODHOUSE, Chase Going. Conference on women's work
and their stake in public affairs. Association of
American Colleges, bulletin, v. 21 (May 1935), 384-8.

3060. _____. Some trends in women's work. Social forces,
v. 16 (May 1938), 543-52.

3061. _____. The status of women. American journal of Sociology, v. 35 (May 1930), 1091-6; v. 36 (May 1931),
1011-16.

3062. _____. Women. American journal of Sociology, v. 37
(May 1932), 956-62. The increasing unemployment
problems of women.

3063. _____. Women. American journal of Sociology, v. 38
(May 1933), 889-95. Comparisons of the male and
female labor force between 1900 and 1930.

3064. WOODS, E. H. Inter-state convention of women workers.
Charities and the commons, v. 21 (14 November 1901),
276-8.

3065. WOODS, Katharine Pearson. Queens of the shop, the work-
room and the tenement. Cosmopolitan, v. 10 (November 1890), 99-105. Concerns the working women in
New York.

3066. WOODWARD, N. Married woman in industry. Suburban
life, v. 18 (April 1914), 238.

3067. WORK and women. Outlook, v. 88 (8 February 1908), 286-
7. On the right of the state to "regulate the working
hours of adult women."

3068. WORK for women. Independent, v. 73 (25 July 1912), 182-6.
The need for women to work outside the home.

3069. WORTMAN, M. S. and F. Luthans. The incidence of anti-
discrimination clauses in union contracts. Labor law
journal, v. 16 (September 1965), 523-32. Anti-dis-

crimination clauses would be necessary in trade union
labor contracts to ensure equal employment.

3070. YELLOWITZ, I. Labor and the progressive movement in
New York State. Ithaca, Cornell University Press,
1965. 288p. Historical development of the labor
movement and legislation for protection of workers,
including women.

3071. YOUNG Women's Christian Association. War Work Council.
Colored Work Committee. The work of colored women.
Compiled by Jane Olcott. New York, 1919. 136p.

3072. _____. _____. Industrial Committee. Legal recognition of industrial women. By E. L. Lattimore and R.
S. Trent. New York, 1919. 91p.

3073. YOUNGER, Maud. The NRA and protective laws for women.
Literary digest, v. 117 (2 June 1934), 27. Concerning the National Recovery Administration.

3074. YUDELSON, Sophie. Woman's place in industry and labor
organizations. American Academy of Political and
Social Science, annals, v. 24 (September 1904), 343-53.

3075. ZAPOLEON, Marguerite Wykoff. Women in defense occupations. Occupations, v. 19 (April 1941), 509-11.

3076. _____. Women's work: Facts, findings, and apparent
trends. National Association of Women Deans and
Counselors, journal, v. 24 (October 1960), 40-7.

3077. ZUEBLIN, Charles. Effect on woman of economic dependence. American journal of Sociology, v. 14 (March
1909), 606-21.

3078. ADAMS, Elizabeth K. Women professional workers, a study made for the Women's Educational and Industrial Union. Chautauqua, N. Y., Chautauqua Press, 1921. 302p.

3079. ALVAREZ, Robert S. Women's place in librarianship. Wilson bulletin for libraries, v. 13 (November 1938), 175-8. Reply: v. 13 (January 1939), 336.

3080. ARMSTRONG, A. W. Are business women getting a square deal? Atlantic monthly, v. 140 (July 1927), 28-36.

3081. ASTIN, Helen S. The woman doctorate in America; origins, career, and family. New York, Russell Sage Foundation, 1969. 196p.

3082. BAILYN, Lotte. Notes on the role of choice in the psychology of professional women. Daedalus, v. 93 (Spring 1964), 200-10. The obstacles to free choice in the lives of married professional women.

3083. BAY, C. U. Executive leadership shortage and barriers against women. Commercial and financial chronicle, v. 185 (28 February 1957), 998.

3084. BAYNG, G. Girl in the business world. World review, v. 3 (8 November 1926), 126-7.

3085. BECK, E. L. Prospect for advancement in business of the married woman college graduate. National Association of Women Deans and Counselors, journal, v. 27 (Spring 1964), 114-19.

3086. BENNETT, Walter Wilson. Institutional barriers to the utilization of women in top management. 162p. PhD thesis, University of Flordia, 1964.

3087. BIRD, Caroline. Women in business: the invisible bar. Personnel, v. 45 (May/June 1968), 29-35.

3088. BLAIR, Emily Newell. Discouraged feminists. Outlook and independent, v. 158 (8 July 1931), 302-3+. The problem of the division of "men's" and "women's" professions.

3089. BLANKENSHIP, W. C. Head librarians: How many men: How many women? College and research libraries, v. 28 (January 1967), 41-8.

3090. BOCK, E. Wilbur. Farmer's daughter effect: the case of the Negro female professionals. Phylon, v. 30 (Spring 1969), 17-26.

3091. BOOTH, A. N. Future of women in business and professions. Vital speeches, v. 26 (1 October 1960), 761-3.

3092. BORING, Edwin G. The woman problem. American psychologist, v. 6 (December 1961), 679-82. The status

of women in the American Psychological Association.
3093. BOWEN, Catherine Drinker. We've never asked a woman before. Atlantic monthly, v. 225 (March 1970), 82-6.
3094. BOWKER, R. R. Women in the library profession. Library journal, v. 45 (June 1920), 545-9.
3095. _____. Women in the library profession. Library journal, v. 45 (July 1920), 587-92.
3096. _____. Women in the library profession. Library journal, v. 45 (August 1920), 635-40.
3097. BUREAU of Vocational Information, New York. Marriage and careers; a study of one hundred women who are wives, mothers, homemakers and professional workers. By Virginia MacMakin Collier. New York, Channel Bookshop, 1926. 121p.
3098. BOWMAN, Garda W. Are women executives people? Harvard business review, v. 43 (July/August 1965), 14-16+. Report of a survey of 2000 executives, half of them men, half of them women.
3099. BRUCE, N. Problem of women in business. Forbes, v. 23 (1 May 1929), 56-7.
3100. BRYAN, Alice I. Women in American psychology: factors affecting their professional careers. American psychologist, v. 2 (January 1947), 3-20.
3101. BUCHANAN, E. H. Women in management. Personnel administration, v. 32 (September 1969), 21-6.
3102. CAPEK, K. Woman and the professions. Atlantic monthly, v. 157 (May 1936), 579-80.
3103. COMSTOCK, S. Marriage or career? Good housekeeping, v. 94 (June 1932), 32-3.
3104. CUMMINGS, Edith Mae. Pots, pans and millions; a study of woman's right to be in business; her proclivities and capacity for success. Washington, National School of Business Science for Women, 1929. 376p.
3105. CUSSLER, M. The woman executive. New York, Harcourt, Brace and World, 1958.
3106. DAINTON, P. M. Women executives; is there room at the top? Personnel management, v. 49 (March 1967), 15-19.
3107. DAVIS, Ann E. Women as a minority group in higher academics. American sociologist, v. 4 (May 1969), 95-8.
3108. DAWKINS, Lola B. Women executives in business, industry, and the professions. 218p. PhD thesis, University of Texas, 1962.
3109. DETLEFSEN, Ellen G. Overdue; the women's liberation movement. Wilson library bulletin, v. 44 (May 1970), 962-5+. Primarily women's status as librarians.
3110. DIGMAN, Dorothy. More women in advertising now than in World War I. A look backward and ahead through feminine eyes. Printers ink, v. 199 (29 May 1942), 16-17+.
3111. DOES business play fair with women? American business, v. 6 (October 1936), 33-5.
3112. DOLSON, M. T. Where women stand in administration.

Modern hospital, v. 108 (May 1967), 100-5.
3113. DUBLIN, L. I. Home-making and careers. Atlantic monthly, v. 138 (September 1926), 335-43.
3114. EBERLY, Marion. The executive woman. American Association of University Women, journal, v. 54 (May 1961),
215-18.
3115. ECONOMIC position of married business and professional
women. Monthly labor review, v. 51 (December 1940),
1371-4.
3116. ELLIOTT, Margaret. Earnings of women in business and the
professions. Ann Arbor, University of Michigan,
School of Business Administration, 1930. 215p.
3117. ELLIOTT, Margaret and Grace E. Manson. Some factors
affecting earnings of business and professional women.
American Academy of Political and Social Science,
annals, v. 143 (May 1929), 137-45.
3118. ELLIS, E. D. What chance for women? Women's professional status. Forum, v. 105 (March 1946), 590-4.
3119. EPSTEIN, Cynthia Fuchs. Encountering the male establish-
ment: sex-status limits on women's careers in the
professions. New York, Bureau of Applied Social Research, Columbia University, 1970. 18p. [Reprinted
from American journal of Sociology, v. 75, no. 6
(May 1970), 965-82.]
3120. _____. Woman's place; options and limits in professional
careers. Berkeley, University of California Press,
1970. 221p.
3121. EYDE, L. D. Eliminating barriers to career development
of women. Personnel and guidance journal, v. 49
(September 1970), 24-8.
3122. FAIRCHILD, S. C. Women as librarians in American public
libraries. Library journal, v. 29 (1904), 157.
3123. FAMULARD, Joseph J. Women at the top--the record, the
obstacles, the outlook. Management review, v. 56
(August 1967), 55-8. The gradual lowering of barriers
for women in business.
3124. FARMER'S daughter effect: The case of the Negro female
professional. Phylon, v. 30 (Spring 1969), 17-26.
3125. FAVA, Sylvia Fleis. The status of women in professional
Sociology. American sociological review, v. 25 (April
1960), 271-6.
3126. FICHTER, Joseph H. Career expectations of Negro women
graduates. Monthly labor review, v. 90 (November
1967), 36-42.
3127. FIDELL, L. S. Empirical verification of sex discrimination
in hiring practices in Psychology. American psychologist, v. 25 (December 1970), 1094-8.
3128. FISHER, Dorothy Canfield. Women, education, and democracy. American Association of University Women,
journal, v. 33 (April 1940), 131-6. The necessity for
women to move into new areas of work after their
formal education rather than taking up typically "female" professions.

3129. FOR women, a difficult climb to the top: few get through
sex barriers.... Business week, (2 August 1969),
42-4+.
3130. FRANCIS, Clarence. Do women belong in business? Forecast for home economics, v. 57 (November 1941), 23+.
3131. FREEDMAN, J. Liberated librarian: a look at the second
sex in the library profession. Library journal, v. 95
(1 May 1970), 1709-11.
3132. GERARD, G. B. Financial independence for professional
women. Journal of home economics, v. 52 (February
1960), 91-4.
3133. GINDER, Charles E. Factor of sex in office employment.
Office executive, v. 36 (February 1961), 10-13.
3134. GOETZ, Arthemise. Shackles for business women. Outlook
and independent, v. 159 (16 December 1931), 494-5.
Single working women are not, in fact, more independent than married women.
3135. GRACEY, G. So, you'd like to be a woman boss? Personnel journal, v. 40 (July/August 1961), 119-20+.
3136. GREENE, Katharine B. The social and professional status
of women. Teachers College record, v. 42 (December 1940), 206-11.
3137. GRIEDER, Frieda Anne. Women in professions and higher
education [1870-1940]. Faculty studies [Western Carolina Teachers College], v. 29 (July 1952), 13-22.
3138. HAHN, M. C. Equal rights for women in career development. Personnel, v. 47 (July 1970), 55-9.
3139. HALL, E. Can it be done? Problems of the two-career
woman. Independent woman, v. 23 (October 1944),
308-9+.
3140. HAMILL, K. Women as bosses. Fortune, v. 53 (June
1956), 104-8+.
3141. HARRIS, William T. The relation of woman to the trades
and professions. Educational review, v. 20 (October
1900), 217-29.
3142. HILTON, M. E. Professional women and the war. School
and society, v. 63 (12 January 1946), 35-7.
3143. HOLDEN, Miriam Y. The status of women librarians.
Antiquarian bookman, v. 36 (23 August 1965), 647-8.
3144. HOLSEY, A. L. Negro women and business. Southern
workman, v. 56 (August 1927), 343-9.
3145. HOWE, F. Report on women and the professions. College
English, v. 32 (May 1971), 847-54.
3146. HOWE, Julia Ward. Women in the professions. Chautauquan,
v. 7 (1888), 460.
3147. HUMAN Engineering Laboratory. Characteristics common to
professional women in law and other non-structural
fields. Hoboken, Human Engineering Laboratory,
1938. 83p.
3148. IS there room at the top? Woman citizen, v. 3 (22 February, 26 April, 10 May 1919), 796-7, 818-19, 840-1,
843, 860-1, 965+; 990-1, 1016-17, 1068-9.
3149. JACQUET, Constant H., Jr. The professional woman in the

United States: A bibliographical essay. Information
service [National Council of Churches, New York],
v. 48 (31 May 1969), 1-7.

3150. JAMES, M. S. Future of women as librarians. Public libraries, v. 7 (1902), 1.

3151. _____. Women as librarians. Library journal, v. 18
(1893), 146.

3152. JEROME, Lucy B. Business women of California. Overland
monthly, n.s., v. 45 (1905), 58.

3153. KANDEL, I. L. Homemaking and the career woman. School
and society, v. 70 (31 December 1949), 444.

3154. KASS, Babette. The economic strength of business and professional women. New York, National Federation of
Business and Professional Women's Clubs, 1954.
140p.

3155. KAY, R. R. Women desert kitchen for managerial suite.
Iron age, v. 192 (26 December 1963), 40.

3156. KEIFFER, Miriam G. and Dallas M. Cullen. Discrimination
experienced by academic female psychologists. Pittsburgh, Know, Inc., [1970?]. 19p. Results of a questionnaire sent to female and male psychologists and
discussed at the 7th annual meeting of the APA, Washington, D.C., 1 September 1969.

3157. KELLY, M. E. Women in business. Lippincott's magazine,
v. 57 (1896), 850.

3158. KOMAROVSKY, Mirra. Cultural contradictions and sex roles.
American journal of Sociology, v. 52 (November 1946),
184-9. Contradictions of college girls as to their professional careers and homemaker.

3159. LANHAM, Elizabeth and Lola B. Dawkins. Women in business; equal pay for equal work? Austin, Bureau of
Business Research, University of Texas, 1959. 14p.

3160. LEWIS, R. H. Women in business. Commonweal, v. 13
(18 February 1931), 437-8.

3161. LOWENTHAL, Helen. A healthy anger. Library journal,
v. 96 (1 September 1971), 2597-9. Primarily on discrimination against female librarians.

3162. MCCRACKEN, Elizabeth. Women in the professions. Outlook, v. 77 (1904), 699.

3163. MACY, John W., Jr. Unless we begin now; womanpower.
Vital speeches, v. 32 (1 September 1966), 678-82.
Trends since 1961 to bring about equal opportunities
for women in employment.

3164. MANDIGO, P. Wife-with-career. Woman's journal, v. 15
(October 1930), 14-15+.

3165. MARKETING'S lady MBA: Can an ornament become a fix-
ture? Sales management, v. 102 (1 May 1969), 38-
40+.

3166. MATTHEWS, R. E. Married women librarians. Library
journal, v. 66 (August 1941), 650-1.

3167. MEITNER, Lise. The status of women in the professions.
Physics today, v. 13 (August 1960), 16-21.

3168. MERCER, Marilyn. Women at work: Is there room at the

top? Saturday evening post, v. 241 (27 July 1968),
17-21+. The difficulty of women in moving up in the
business world.

3169. MERRITT, Doris H. Discrimination and the woman executive: Convention blocks use of a resource. Business
horizons, v. 12 (December 1969), 15-22.

3170. MILLER, J. S. Women and top-level jobs. American Association of University Women, journal, v. 44 (October 1950), 7-10.

3171. MITCHELL, Mildred B. Status of women in the American
Psychological Association. American psychologist,
v. 6 (June 1951), 193-201.

3172. MITCHELL, Susan Barber. Women and the doctorate; a
study of the enabling or impeding factors operative
among Oklahoma's women doctoral recipients in the
attainment and use of the degree. Final report.
Stillwater, Oklahoma State University, Research
Foundation, 1968. 154p.

3173. MOON, Eric. Tokenism at the top? Library journal, v. 90
(1 October 1965), 4019.

3174. MOORE, L. W. Using the power of womanpower, the need
for enlightenment. Vital speeches, v. 35 (1 December
1968), 105-8.

3175. MORRISON, Anne H. Women and their careers; a study of
306 women in business and the professions. New
York, National Federation of Business and Professional Women's Clubs, 1934. 187p.

3176. MURPHY, E. O. Women and blacks; sexual discrimination
in the library profession. Library journal, v. 95 (15
March 1970), 959.

3177. NATIONAL Education Association. Research Division. Wom-
en in the professions: a wartime survey. Berkeley,
University of California Press, 1945. 142p. Contents: Personal status; Professional status; Economic
status; War and postwar status.

3178. NATIONAL Federation of Business and Professional Women's
Clubs. A study of employability of women in selected
sections of the United States. By Iva Lowther Peters.
New York, The Federation, 1936. 34p. Results of an
interview with 212 business and professional women.

3179. NORRIS, Marion Lela. The ways of a business woman; a
discussion of the problems confronting business women.
Battle Creek, Mich., Gage Printing Co., 1924. 186p.

3180. PARRISH, John B. Professional woman-power as a national
resource. Quarterly review of education and business,
(February 1961), 54-63. The decline of the number
of women in the professions and reasons for this decline.

3181. PAYNE, C. H. Problems of the woman scholar. American
Association of University Women, journal, v. 33 (January 1940), 80-4.

3182. PETTICOATS rustle on executive ladder: University of
Michigan's all-female conference on management in-

dicates that the ladies are overcoming male prejudice
to women in high spots. Business week, (29 September 1962), 50-2+.

3183.   The PLACE of women in the modern business world as affecting home-life, the marital relation, health, mortality and the future of the race. American Academy
of Medicine, v. 9, no. 5 (1908), 335-84.

3184.   PRINCE, E. G. Laws to protect professional women. Independent woman, v. 17 (June 1938), 170+.

3185.   RAYNE, Martha Louise. What can a woman do; or, Her
position in the business and literary world. Peters-
burgh, N. Y., Eagle, 1893. 528p.

3186.   REBELLING women, the reason. U.S. news and world report, v. 68 (13 April 1970), 35-7. Comparisons of
pay scales for men and women between 1957 and 1968
as well as problems in entering the professions, politics, and business.

3187.   ROSSI, Alice S. Ambivalence in women: should we plan for
the real or the ideal? Adult leadership, v. 16 (September 1967), 100-2+. Ambivalence of women toward
their roles concerning the family and career.

3188.   RUSSIN, J. M., ed. What educated women want; marriage,
yes--but the career drive is strong. Newsweek, v.
67 (13 June 1966), 68-72+.

3189.   RYAN, L. C. Women in the professions. Women lawyers
journal, v. 31 (Summer 1945), 5+.

3190.   SCHILLER, Anita R. The disadvantaged majority. American libraries, v. 1 (April 1970), 345-9.

3191.   _____. Widening the sex gap. Library journal, v. 94
(15 March 1969), 1098-1100.

3192.   SCHUMAN, B. Women in business. Lippincott's magazine,
v. 57 (1896), 850.

3193.   SCHUMAN, Pat. Status of women in libraries: task force
meets in Detroit. Library journal, v. 95 (August
1970), 2635.

3194.   SHOULD the preponderance of women in the American library
profession be considered an evil? Wilson bulletin for
libraries, v. 8 (March 1934), 403-7.

3195.   SCHWARTZ, Eleanor B. An evaluation of the application and
implementation of Title VII as it applies to women in
management. 251p. PhD thesis, Georgia State College, 1969. On the ineffectiveness of Title VII since
its enactment in 1964, the continuing discrimination
against women, and recommendations.

3196.   SEAGOE, May V., ed. Professional women in modern society. Journal of social issues, v. 6, no. 3 (1950),
entire issue. Partial contents: The stereotype of
femininity; Women in the professions; Women in education; The woman physician's dilemma.

3197.   SELLERS, M. Future of women in business. Independent
woman, v. 27 (July 1948), 197-8.

3198.   SHERWOOD, Catherine. Professional woman at home.
South Atlantic quarterly, v. 30 (April 1931), 134-40.

Southern professional women and home life.
3199. SIMPSON, Richard L.   Occupational choice among career-oriented college women.   Marriage and family living, v. 23 (November 1961), 377-83.
3200. SLOTE, C. T.   Women executives: fact and fancy.   Dun's review and modern industry, v. 72 (December 1958), 90-5.
3201. SMALL, V.   Having their say.   Mademoiselle, v. 41 (September 1955), 136-7.
3202. SPENCER, S. J.   World's need of business women.   National Education Association of the United States, proceedings, v. 32 (1893), 800-3.
3203. STOCKTON, Frank Tenney.   Salaried women in upper level positions in Kansas business firms.   Lawrence, Center for Research in Business, University of Kansas, 1959. 38p.
3204. SURETTE, R. F.   Career versus homemaking: perspectives and proposals.   Vocational guidance quarterly, v. 16 (December 1967), 82-6.
3205. TORNABENE, L.   How separate careers live happily together.   Cosmopolitan, v. 147 (July 1959), 50-7.
3206. TUTTLE, Helen W.   Women in academic libraries.   Library journal, v. 96 (1 September 1971), 2594-6.
3207. U.S. Department of Labor.   The age factor as it relates to women in business and the professions.   By H. A. Byrne.   Washington, GPO, 1934. 66p. [Bulletin no. 117.]
3208. VAN DE WARKER, E.   Relations of women to professions.   Popular science monthly, v. 6 (1875), 454.
3209. VERMONT, M. B.   Child vs. career.   Today's health, v. 32 (March 1954), 30-1+.
3210. VIVIAN, M. E.   Discrimination against women in the professions; a survey of recent literature.   Pacific Northwest Library Association, quarterly, v. 16 (January 1952), 83-9.
3211. VOLANTE, E. M.   What is the status of women executives in personnel administration?   Personnel administration, v. 26 (September 1963), 59-60.
3212. The WEAKER sex.   Library journal, v. 63 (15 March 1938), 232.
3213. WHITEHURST, S. A., ed.   Women in high level positions (national and state).   Washington, General Federation of Women's Clubs, 1954. 49p.
3214. WHITMAN, A.   Problem that plagues the thoughtful woman; marriage-versus-career.   Redbook, v. 122 (February 1964), 50-1+.
3215. WHY women cause problems in business.   Management review, v. 20 (June 1961), 85-6.
3216. WILE, Ira and M. D. Winn.   The wife in business.   Hygeia, v. 7 (February 1929), 129-32.
3217. WILKINS, Zora Putnam.   Letters of a business woman to her daughter, and letters of a business girl to her mother.   Boston, Marshall Jones, 1923. 151p.

180

180   The Women's Rights Movement

3218.   WOMEN in business.   Fortune, v. 12 (July 1935), 50-7;
        (August 1935), 50-5+; (September 1935), 81+.   His-
        torical 3-part survey showing how women attempted to
        gain equality in industry.
3219.   WOMEN in the learned professions.   Public opinion, v. 14
        (1893), 401.
3220.   WOMEN supervisors, pro and con.   Independent woman,
        v. 21 (October 1942), 306+.
3221.   WOMEN want more say in business and a new federation
        (Federation of Women Shareholders in American Busi-
        ness) is helping them to get more recognition in big
        corporations.   Changing times, v. 3 (May 1949), 31-2.
3222.   WOMEN'S chances slim for top industry posts.   Occupations,
        v. 29 (December 1950), 225.
3223.   WRIGHT, C. D.   Women in business.   Are they hurting the
        chances of the men?   Chautauquan, v. 26 (1898), 79.
3224.   ZAPOLEON, Marguerite Wykoff.   Expanding occupational op-
        portunities for women.   Monthly labor review, v. 76
        (April 1953), 381-3.

                              WOMEN IN LAW

3225.   ARMSTRONG, Barbara.   2997 women practice law in U.S.,
        still find going tough, survey shows.   Harvard Law
        School record, v. 13 (6 December 1951), 1+.
3226.   BAR women; New York City Bar Association decides to ad-
        mit women.   Time, v. 29 (24 May 1937), 44.
3227.   BLAUSTEIN, Albert P.   America's women lawyers: The
        1949 lawyer count.   Women lawyers journal, v. 37,
        no. 2 (1951), 18-20.
3228.   BURNSIDE, A.   The woman lawyer--why?   Arkansas Bar
        Association (1936), 141-6.
3229.   CONNABLE, R.   Case for girls in law.   Mademoiselle,
        v. 61 (May 1965), 188-90+.
3230.   DINERMAN, Beatrice.   Sex discrimination in the legal pro-
        fession.   American Bar Association, journal, v. 55
        (October 1969), 951.
3231.   DREW, E. H.   Women and the law.   Women lawyers jour-
        nal, v. 47 (Winter 1961), 20.
3232.   DULIN, I. L.   Progress of women in the law.   Journal of
        the Missouri Bar, v. 4 (August 1948), 163+.
3233.   EFFECT of war on employment of woman lawyers.   Monthly
        labor review, v. 57 (September 1943), 502-3.
3234.   EPSTEIN, Cynthia Fuchs.   Women and professional careers:
        The case of the woman lawyer.   PhD thesis, Colum-
        bia University, 1968.
3235.   FRANK, J. N.   Women lawyers.   Women lawyers journal,
        v. 31 (Winter 1945), 4-5+.
3236.   HARVARD University to admit women to its law school.
        School and society, v. 70 (22 October 1949), 267-8.
3237.   ILLINOIS.   Courts.   Supreme Court.   From the Chicago
        legal news, 5 February 1870.   A woman cannot prac-

tice law or hold any office in Illinois. Full report of
the proceedings in the Supreme Court of Illinois upon
the application of Myra Bradwell to be admitted to the
bar. Chicago, Church, Goodman & Donnelley, printers, 1870. 12p.

3238. KENYON, Dorothy. Case (by one of them) for women lawyers. New York Times magazine (19 February 1950),
144.

3239. KNIGHT, H. Women and the legal profession. Contemporary,
v. 103 (May 1913), 689-96.

3240. KOLIS, M. N. There is a place for women in law. Detroit
lawyer, v. 24 (August 1956), 100.

3241. LOCKED out? Women and the legal profession. Student
lawyer journal, v. 16 (November 1970), special issue.

3242. MACMILLAN, C. Women and the legal profession. Living
age, v. 293 (23 June 1917), 750-3.

3243. MARTIN, J. O. Women lawyers. To my sisters in law.
Tennessee law review, v. 19 (February 1946), 109-12.

3244. ROBINSON, L. J. Women as lawyers in the United States.
Green bag, v. 2 (1890), 10.

3245. SASSOWER, D. L. Women in the law: the second hundred
years. American Bar Association journal, v. 57
(April 1971), 329+.

3246. STRICKLAND, M. Women as lawyers. Green bag, v. 3
(1891), 240.

3247. WHITE, James J. Women in the law. Michigan law review,
v. 65 (April 1967), 1051-1122. The status of women
in the legal profession--based on replies to a questionnaire to 2219 women and 2151 men graduated from 108
accredited American law schools, 1955-1965.

3248. WILBANKS, Elizabeth Johnson. Women in law in Alabama
[1909-1950]. Alabama lawyer, v. 12 (January 1951),
43-6.

3249. WOMEN as lawyers. Lippincott's magazine, v. 23 (1879),
387.

3250. No entry.

WOMEN IN MEDICINE

3251. AITKIN, J. K. Status of women doctors in medicine today.
Medicine illustrated, v. 6 (March 1952), 131-33.

3252. AUSTIN, M. History of women in medicine; symposium.
Medical Library Association, bulletin, v. 44 (January
1956), 12-24.

3253. BLACKWELL, Elizabeth. Pioneer work in opening the med-
ical profession to women. New York, Longmans
Green, 1895. 264p. Reprinted by Source Book Press,
New York, 1970.

3254. BLAKE, John B. Women and medicine in ante-bellum America. Bulletin of the history of medicine, v. 39, no.
2 (1965), 99-123. Covers the period 1849 to 1861 and

Elizabeth Blackwell, her sister Emily, Dr. Harriot
K. Hunt, and Dr. Marie E. Zakrewska.
3255. BLUESTONE, N. Marriage... and medicine. American Medical Women's Association, journal, v. 20 (November
1965), 1048-53.
3256. BOWERS, J. Z. Special problems of women medical students. Journal of medical education, v. 43 (May
1968), 532-7.
3257. _____. Wife, mother, and physician. American Medical
Women's Association, journal, v. 22 (October 1967),
760-4.
3258. BROWN, Adelaide. The history of the development of women
in medicine in California. Medical woman's journal,
v. 33 (January 1925), 17-20.
3259. BROWN, S. W. Colored women physicians. Southern workman, v. 52 (December 1923), 580-93.
3260. CHADWICK, J. R. Women as physicians. International review, v. 7 (1879), 444.
3261. CRAIGHILL, M. D. Analysis of women in medicine today.
Women in medicine. American Medical Women's Association, journal, v. 71 (January 1941), 7-8.
3262. DENKO, J. D. Managing a practice and a home simultane-
ously: one woman physician's solution. American
Medical Women's Association, journal, v. 20 (August
1965), 762-5.
3263. DYKMAN, R. A. Survey of women physicians graduating
from medical school, 1925-1940. Journal of medical
education, v. 32, no. 13, part 2 (1957), 3-38.
3264. ECKMAN, F. M. Why can't more women be doctors? Redbook, v. 137 (May 1971), 77+.
3265. EQUALITY for women doctors. Time, v. 41 (26 April 1943),
46.
3266. FAY, M. Why don't more women apply to medical schools?
Journal of medical education, v. 37 (May 1962), 500-1.
3267. _____. Why so few women doctors? Today's health,
v. 41 (June 1963), 46-9+.
3268. FRANKLIN, C. L. Women and medicine. Nation, v. 52
(1891), 131.
3269. GREGORY, S. Women as physicians. Living age, v. 73
(1861), 243.
3270. HIGHER education of women at Johns Hopkins. Nation,
v. 52 (1891), 71.
3271. HOLTON, S. C. The woman physician: a study of role
conflict. American Medical Women's Association,
journal, v. 24 (August 1969), 638-45.
3272. HUNT, Harriot K. Glances and glimpses; or, Fifty years
social, including twenty years professional life. Boston, J. P. Jewett, 1856. 418p. Reprinted by Source
Book Press, New York, 1970.
3273. HURD-MEAD, Kate Campbell. A study of the medical education of women. American Medical Association,
journal, v. 116 (25 January 1941), 339-47. Pertains
primarily to the 19th century.

3274. JACOBI, Mary Putnam. Women as physicians. North
       American review, v. 134 (1882), 52.
3275. JEFFRYS, M. Comparison of men and women in medical
       training. Lancet, v. 1 (26 June 1965), 1381-3.
3276. KETTLE, M. H. Fate of the population of women medical
       students. Lancet, v. 1 (13 June 1936), 1370-4.
3277. KOSA, John. The female physician in public health: Con-
       flict and reconciliation of the professional and sex
       roles. Sociology and social research, v. 49 (April
       1965), 295-305.
3278. LAKE, A. Drop those prejudices against women doctors.
       American Medical Women's Association, journal,
       v. 22 (June 1967), 402-6.
3279. LET woman doctors serve too. Saturday evening post,
       v. 215 (20 February 1943), 100.
3280. LOPATE, Carol. Women in medicine. Baltimore, Johns
       Hopkins Press, 1968. 204p.
3281. LUTZKER, Edythe. Women gain a place in medicine. New
       York, McGraw-Hill, 1969.
3282. MCGREW, Elizabeth. Medical womenpower: Can it be used
       more effectively? American Medical Women's Associ-
       ation, journal, v. 17 (December 1962), 973-85.
3283. MANN, K. Medical women's handicap. Harper's weekly,
       v. 58 (28 February 1914), 32.
3284. MARMOR, Judd. Women in medicine: importance of the
       formative years. American Medical Women's Associ-
       ation, journal, v. 23 (July 1968), 7.
3285. MEAD, Kate Campbell. A history of women in medicine.
       Haddam, Conn., Haddam, 1938.
3286. _____. Women doctors today and yesterday. Independent
       woman, v. 18 (May 1939), 138-40+.
3287. MEDICAL education for women called worthwhile. Science
       digest, v. 44 (November 1958), 48.
3288. MORROW, L. E. Physicians can be female. American
       Medical Women's Association, journal, v. 24 (October
       1969), 826-7.
3289. MOTT, Lucretia. A sermon to the medical students, de-
       livered by Lucretia Mott at Cherry Street Meeting
       House, Philadelphia, on first-day evening, second
       month 11th, 1849. Philadelphia, W. B. Zeiber, 1849.
       21p.
3290. O'CONNOR, K. Women in medicine: opportunities and
       problems. American Medical Women's Association,
       journal, v. 18 (November 1963), 885-90.
3291. ONE way to meet the doctor shortage. Independent woman,
       v. 26 (February 1947), 44-6+.
3292. PARKER, E. Why not more women in medicine? Medical
       annals of the District of Columbia, v. 32 (November
       1963), 473-4.
3293. POPE, E. A. Women as physicians. American journal of
       social science, v. 14 (1881), 178.
3294. PUBLIC demands and the education of women as physicians.
       Nation, v. 50 (1890), 237.

3295. PULLUM, C. A. Women, medicine and misconceptions.
       American Medical Women's Association, journal,
       v. 18 (July 1963), 563-5.
3296. ROSENLUNG, M. L. Women in medicine. Annals of in-
       ternal medicine, v. 66 (May 1967), 1008-12.
3297. SEAVER, J. Women doctors, in spite of everything. New
       York Times magazine (26 March 1961), 27+.
3298. SHRYOCK, Richard Harrison. Women in American medicine
       (1850-1950). American Medical Women's Association,
       journal, v. 5 (September 1950), 371-9.
3299. THELANDER, Hulda E. Aesculapius beckoning: some
       thoughts on medical education for women. American
       Medical Women's Association, journal, v. 18 (Novem-
       ber 1963), 897-9.
3300. _____. Is medicine a career for girls? National Associ-
       ation of Deans of Women, journal, v. 15 (January
       1952), 74-7.
3301. U.S. Women's Bureau. Conference on Meeting Medical
       Manpower Needs--the Fuller Utilization of the Woman
       Physician, Washington, D.C., 1968. Report. Wash-
       ington, GPO, 1968. 104p.
3302. UPLAND, B. Women as physicians. American magazine,
       v. 3 (1882), 302.
3303. VICTORY long overdue; commissioning women physicians in
       the Medical Corps of Army and Navy. Independent
       woman, v. 22 (May 1943), 132.
3304. WAGER, M. A. Women as physicians. Galaxy, v. 6
       (1868), 774.
3305. WHITMAN, H. M.D. for men only? Woman's home com-
       panion, v. 73 (November 1946), 32-3+.
3306. WHY there aren't more woman doctors. Science digest,
       v. 53 (May 1963), 29.
3307. WILLARD, L. Campaigning for more opportunities in medi-
       cine; internships for women. Independent woman,
       v. 18 (June 1939), 174.
3308. WILLIAMS, Josephine J. Patients and prejudice: lay atti-
       tudes toward women physicians. American journal of
       Sociology, v. 51 (January 1946), 283-7.
3309. _____. The professional status of women in medicine.
       PhD thesis, University of Chicago, 1949.
3310. _____. The women physicians dilemma. Journal of social
       issues, v. 6, no. 3 (1950), 38-44.
3311. WILLIAMS, M. J. Underemployment of women physicians.
       Annals of internal medicine, v. 71 (October 1969),
       862-3.
3312. WOMEN as physicians. American magazine, v. 2 (1881),
       299.
3313. WOMEN as physicians. Every Saturday, v. 6 (1868), 407.
3314. WOMEN as physicians. Every Saturday, v. 11 (1871), 27.
3315. WOMEN in medical schools. Journal of medical education,
       v. 41 (February 1966), 184-5.
3316. WOMEN or doctors? Newsweek, v. 26 (12 November 1945),
       84. Refutations of reasons for limiting the number of

women in medical schools.
3317. WULSIN, J. H.   Admission of women to medical school.
      American Medical Women's Association, journal, v. 21
      (August 1966), 674-6.
3318. YARRELL, Zuleika.   Women in medicine.   Journal of educa-
      tional Sociology, v. 17 (April 1944), 492-7.

WOMEN IN POLITICS

3319. ALLEN, Florence E.   Participation of women in government.
      American Academy of Political and Social Science, an-
      nals, v. 251 (May 1947), 94-103.
3320. _____.   Women in public office.   Women lawyers journal,
      v. 44 (Summer 1958), 12.
3321. ANDERSON, G. E.   Women in Congress.   Commonweal,
      v. 9 (13 March 1929), 532-4.
3322. BEECHER, Henry Ward.   Woman's influence in politics.
      Boston, R. F. Wallcut, 1860.   18p.
3323. BLAIR, Emily Newell.   Are women a failure in politics?
      Harper's magazine, v. 151 (October 1925), 513-22.
3324. _____.   Putting women into politics.   Woman's journal,
      v. 16 (March 1931), 14-15.
3325. _____.   Women in the political parties.   American
      Academy of Political and Social Science, annals,
      v. 143 (May 1929), 217-29.
3326. BLUNT, Katharine.   How about the women?   Their part in
      public service.   American Association of University
      Women, journal, v. 32 (October 1938), 17-20.
3327. BOYD, R. R.   Women and politics in the United States and
      Canada.   American Academy of Political and Social
      Science, annals, v. 375 (January 1968), 52-7.
3328. CARAWAY, Hattie W.   Women in Congress.   State govern-
      ment, v. 10 (October 1937), 203-4.
3329. _____.   Women in state capitols.   State government,
      v. 10 (October 1937), 213-15.
3330. COLON, Frank T.   The elected woman.   Social studies,
      v. 58, no. 6 (1967), 256-61.   Factors working against
      women seeking public office, such as prejudice of men
      office holders, conflict of work and household duties.
3331. DAVIS, Clare Ogden.   Politicians, female.   North American
      review, v. 229 (June 1930), 749-56.
3332. DONALDSON, Alice.   Women emerge as political speakers.
      Speech monographs, v. 18 (March 1951), 54-61.   On
      women as delegates to the Democratic and Republican
      national conventions, 1920.
3333. EVANS, Ernestine.   Women in the Washington scene.   Cen-
      tury magazine, v. 106 (August 1923), 507-17.   Bio-
      graphical sketches of women in politics, such as Alice
      Paul, Grace Abbott, and Harriet Taylor Upton.
3334. FISHER, Marguerite J.   Women in the political parties.
      American Academy of Political and Social Science, an-
      nals, v. 251 (May 1947), 87-93.

3335. GODKIN, E. L.   Sex in politics.   Nation, v. 12 (1871), 270.
3336. GOLDMAN, O. R.   The inexperienced politician: some ad-
       vantages and handicaps of a woman candidate.   Ameri-
       can Association of University Women, journal, v. 41
       (October 1947), 17-19.
3337. KINNICUTT, Eleonora.   The American woman in politics.
       Century magazine, v. 49 (1895), 302-4.
3338. LEE, Percy Maxim.   Why not more women in public office?
       National municipal review, v. 43 (June 1954), 307-8.
3339. LENROOT, Katharine F.   Women in public office.   State
       government, v. 10 (October 1937), 205-6.
3340. LOCKWOOD, B. A.   Women in politics.   American journal
       of politics, v. 2 (1893), 385.
3341. MATHESON, F. P.   Natural debarments of women from po-
       litical service.   American magazine of civics, v. 7
       (1895), 591.
3342. NEGRO women in politics.   Ebony, v. 21 (August 1966), 96-
       100.
3343. NEW York (State).   Library Legislative Reference Section.
       Statements by state Democratic Party officials relative
       to representation of women on state and local party
       committees.   Compiled by June Lambert.   Albany,
       1936.   6p.
3344. _____ . _____ .   Statements by state Republican Party
       officials relative to representation of women on state
       and local party committees.   Compiled by June Lam-
       bert.   Albany, 1939.   6p.
3345. PARISH, A.   Political role of women in America.   Phi Delta
       Delta, v. 35 (June 1957), 12.
3346. PATRICK, C.   Attitudes about women executives in govern-
       ment positions.   Journal of social psychology, v. 19
       (February 1944), 3-34.
3347. PEAK, Mayme Ober.   Women in politics.   Outlook, v. 136
       (23 January 1924), 147-50.
3348. PHELPS, W. W.   Women in politics.   American journal of
       politics, v. 2 (1893), 578.
3349. POLITICS of women.   Lippincott's magazine, v. 8 (1871),
       168.
3350. REPUBLICAN Party.   National Committee, 1960-1964.   Wom-
       en's Division.   The history of women in Republican
       national conventions and women in the Republican Na-
       tional Committee.   Compiled by Josephine L. Good.
       Washington, 1963.   58p.
3351. RICHARDSON, Eudora Ramsay.   Ladies of the lobby.   North
       American review, v. 227 (June 1929), 648-55.   On the
       apathy of women toward political office.
3352. RISHEL, Virginia.   More women in government: at least,
       more women are candidates for Congressional office.
       American Association of University Women, journal,
       v. 42 (October 1948), 21-4.
3353. ROBINSON, Helen Ring.   On being a woman senator.   In-
       dependent, v. 78 (20 April 1914), 130-2.
3354. ROGERS, E. N.   Women's new place in politics.   Nation's

business, (August 1930), 39-41+.

3355. ROOSEVELT, Eleanor. Women in politics. Good housekeeping, v. 110 (January 1940), 18-19+; (March 1940),
45+; (April 1940), 45+.
3356. ROOSEVELT, Theodore. Women and the New York constitutional convention. Outlook, v. 107 (1 August 1914),
796-8.
3357. ROSS, John Gordon. Ladies in politics. Forum and century,
v. 96 (November 1936), 209-15.
3358. SCHOONMAKER, N. M. Where does she stand; woman's
progress and position in politics. Century magazine,
v. 113 (January 1927), 354-60.
3359. SCHUCK, Victoria. A hundred years of women and politics.
Mt. Holyoke alumnae quarterly, v. 32 (November
1948), 117-19.
3360. SHILVOCK, A. R. and G. J. Schnepp. Women in politics:
Catholic collegiate attitudes: many American college
students manifest resistance to the prospect of women
taking an active part in political activities, men, in-
evitably, to a greater extent than women. Social
order, v. 3 (October 1953), 361-6.
3361. SPRINGER, A. I. Woman's role in the machinery of government. Vital speeches, v. 23 (1 April 1957), 373-6.
3362. STATUS of women in government service. Monthly labor review, v. 23 (December 1926), 1254-6.
3363. STONE, Kathryn H. Women as citizens. American Academy
of Political and Social Science, annals, v. 251 (May
1947), 79-86. The need for more women to take part
in public affairs.
3364. STORY, D. Woman in politics. Munsey's magazine, v. 29
(1903), 256.
3365. VAN DER VRIES, B. T. Women in government. Women
lawyers journal, v. 35 (Winter 1949), 9-11.
3366. WELLS, Kate G. Woman in office. National magazine,
v. 22 (1905), 133.
3367. WOMAN'S dilemma--home or politics: getting elected is just
one problem for office-holding wife. U.S. news and
world report, v. 44 (23 May 1958), 68-70.

WOMEN IN THE SCIENCES

3368. BOLTON, H. I. Women in science. Popular science monthly, v. 53 (August 1898), 506-11.
3369. CLANCY, Edward P. Women and physics. American journal of physics, v. 30 (September 1962), 626-9.
3370. DAVIS, W. Need sex desegregation. Science news letter,
v. 86 (11 July 1964), 22.
3371. DE BELLEFONDS, Josette. Women and engineering. Impact of science on society, v. 14, no. 4 (1964), 249-
67.
3372. DEMENT, A. L. College woman as a science major. Journal of higher education, v. 33 (December 1962), 487-90.

3373. DIAMOND, M. C. Women in modern science. American
       Medical Women's Association, journal, v. 18 (Novem-
       ber 1963), 891-6.
3374. DREWS, K. Women engineers; the obstacles in their way.
       Scientific American, v. 65 (7 March 1908), 147-8.
3375. EDGERTON, H. A. Women in science careers. National
       Association of Women Deans and Counselors, journal,
       v. 25 (June 1962), 166-9.
3376. EMPLOYMENT and characteristics of women engineers.
       Monthly labor review, v. 79 (May 1956), 551-4.
3377. GOFF, A. C. Women can be engineers. American Associ-
       ation of University Women, journal, v. 41 (January
       1948), 75-6.
3378. GOLDSMITH, Naomi F. Women in science: Symposium and
       job mart. Science, v. 168 (29 May 1970), 1124-7.
3379. INGELS, Margaret. Petticoats and slide rules. Midwest
       engineer, v. 5 (August 1952), 2-4+. On women as
       engineers between 1886 and 1921.
3380. INTERNATIONAL Conference of Women Engineers and Sci-
       entists, 1st, New York, 1964. Focus for the future:
       developing engineering and scientific talent; proceed-
       ings. [New York, 1965?]
3381. KUNDSIN, Ruth B. Why nobody wants women in science;
       reprint. Science digest, v. 58 (October 1965), 60-5.
3382. LANDIS, W. S. Women chemists in industry. Journal of
       chemical education, v. 16 (December 1939), 577-9.
3383. LEWIS, N. D. Women and modern science. American As-
       sociation of University Women, journal, v. 51 (Octo-
       ber 1957), 18-20.
3384. M. I. T. Symposium on American Women in Science and
       Engineering, 1964. Women and the scientific profes-
       sions. Edited by Jacquelyn Mattfield and Carol G.
       Van Aken. Cambridge, M. I. T. Press, 1965. 250p.
3385. MANGRAS, M. N. Women and science. Public opinion,
       v. 14 (1893), 305.
3386. OSTROFSKY, M. Woman mathematicians in industry: the
       road to success is difficult. AAUW journal, v. 57
       (March 1964), 114+.
3387. PATTERSON, J. S. Women and science. Radical, v. 7
       (1870), 169.
3388. _____. Women and science. Radical, v. 7 (1870), 287.
3389. PINES, M. Should women be trained in the sciences?
       Barbard alumnae magazine, v. 47, no. 3 (1958), 2-7.
3390. RETALIATA, J. T. Education of women engineers at
       snail's pace. Chemical and engineering news, v. 33
       (14 February 1955), 623.
3391. ROSSI, Alice S. Women in science, why so few? Science,
       v. 148 (28 May 1965), 1196-1202.
3392. SCHWARZ, G. and B. L. Dilmore. Employment of women
       in physics. American journal of physics, v. 22
       (April 1954), 184-6.
3393. SCIENCE'S sex desegregation. Science news letter, v. 81
       (3 March 1962), 138-9.

3394. SCIENTIST, wife and mother. Look, v. 20 (16 October
       1956), 51.
3395. SENDERS, Virginia L. The music is made by men. AAUW
       journal, v. 57 (March 1964), 115-18. Concerning fe-
       male mathematicians.
3396. SEX and scientific recognition. Scientific American, v. 104
       (21 January 1911), 58.
3397. SHAPLEY, V. B. Science in petticoats; in wartime and in
       peace. American Association of University Women,
       journal, v. 39 (April 1946), 148-50.
3398. TORPEY, W. G. The role of women in professional en-
       gineering. Journal of engineering education, v. 52
       (June 1962), 656-8.
3399. UNDERWOOD, S. A. Women's work in science. New Eng-
       land magazine, v. 3 (February 1891), 695-700.
3400. WEEKS, Dorothy W. Women in physics today. Physics
       today, v. 13 (August 1960), 22-3.
3401. WHITE, Martha S. Psychological and social barriers to
       women in science. Science, v. 170 (23 October 1970),
       413-16.
3402. WILLIAMSON, M. B. Some American women in science.
       Chautauquan, v. 28 (1899), 361.
3403. WOLFLE, D. Women in science and engineering. Science,
       v. 145 (25 September 1964), 1389.
3404. ZAHM, John Augustine. Woman in science; with an intro-
       ductory chapter on woman's long struggle for things
       of the mind. New York, D. Appleton, 1913. 452p.

3405. ABBOTT, Frances M. The pay of college women. North American review, v. 163 (September 1896), 337-44. An inquiry into pay inequities in a number of occupations.

3406. ABBOTT, Grace and Sophonisba P. Breckinridge. State regulation of the wages of women violates the fourteenth amendment. Social service review, v. 10 (September 1936), 483-9.

3407. ADDAMS, Jane. Minimum wage boards for women. Ladies home journal, v. 30 (March 1913), 27.

3408. ANDERSON, Mary. Wages for women workers. American Academy of Political and Social Science, annals, v. 81 (January 1919), 123-9.

3409. _____. Women's work and wages: the Women's Bureau and standards of women's work. National Conference of Social Work, proceedings, (1921), 285-7.

3410. _____. Year of the minimum wage. American federationist, v. 45 (April 1938), 369-75.

3411. ANNUAL earnings of women and men in Pennsylvania industries, 1929-1936. Monthly labor review, v. 48 (June 1939), 1302-4.

3412. AVERAGE weekly earnings of men and women in New York State factories. Monthly labor review, v. 17 (November 1923), 1095-6.

3413. BARRY, R. Insufficient pay for working girls, and resulting evils. Pearson's magazine, v. 25 (February 1911), 175-81.

3414. _____. Women's wages less than men's, and the reasons for. Pearson's magazine, v. 25 (March 1911), 293-300.

3415. BLAKE, L. D. Pay of women; are they fairly paid? Forum, v. 2 (1886), 201.

3416. BONNEY, W. L. Women and the wage system. Arena, v. 26 (1901), 172.

3417. BOSWORTH, Louise Marion, ed. The living wage of women workers; a study of incomes and expenditures of 450 women in the city of Boston. New York, Longmans Green, 1911. 90p. Also: American Academy of Political and Social Science, annals, v. 37; supp. (May 1911), 1-90.

3418. CARROLL, M. R. Women workers and the minimum wage. American federationist, v. 32 (December 1925), 1155-8.

3419. CASELLI, E. M. Men's and women's wages, 1920-1948.

Conference Board Management record, v. 11 (May 1949), 196-8.

3420. CHAMBERLAIN, Mary. Paper-box factory girl and the Constitution. Survey, v. 33 (26 December 1914), 330-1. The U.S. Supreme Court considering the constitutionality of an Oregon law providing minimum wages for women.

3421. CHENEY, E. D. Women; shall they work for pay? Chautauquan, v. 13 (1891), 215.

3422. CODES of fair competition and women's wages in the United States. International labour review, v. 29 (June 1934), 812-22.

3423. COMPARATIVE earnings of men and women in Indiana factories, March 1939. Monthly labor review, v. 49 (October 1939), 846-7.

3424. COMPARATIVE earnings and hours of men and women, 1937-38. Monthly labor review, v. 46 (April 1938), 900-2.

3425. COMPARATIVE earnings and hours of men and women, 1937-38. Monthly labor review, v. 48 (May 1939), 1003-6.

3426. COMPARATIVE earnings and hours of men and women, 1937-38. Monthly labor review, v. 47 (December 1938), 1272-3.

3427. COMPARATIVE earnings and hours of women and men, October 1940. Monthly labor review, v. 53 (November 1941), 1177-9.

3428. COMPARATIVE earnings and hours of women and men, September 1939. Monthly labor review, v. 50 (March 1940), 628-30.

3429. COMPARATIVE earnings and hours of women and men. March 1940. Monthly labor review, v. 51 (September 1940), 640-2.

3430. CONSUMERS' League of New York. Women's wages today; one reason for a legal minimum in New York State. New York, The League, 1920. 12p.

3431. DICKINSON, Z. Clark. Men's and women's wages in the United States. International labour review, v. 47 (June 1943), 693-720.

3432. EARNINGS of women factory employees in New York. Monthly labor review, v. 57 (December 1943), 1178.

3433. EARNINGS of women in Tennessee industries. Monthly labor review, v. 43 (August 1936), 467-70.

3434. EARNINGS of women in Illinois industries, June 1945. Monthly labor review, v. 61 (November 1945), 953-4.

3435. EARNINGS of women in Illinois industries, January 1944. Monthly labor review, v. 58 (May 1944), 1030-2.

3436. ECONOMIC status of university women. Monthly labor review, v. 50 (February 1940), 345-9. Indicates salaries for various jobs between 1925 and 1935.

3437. EDGEWORTH, F. Y. Women's wages in relation to economic welfare. Economic journal, v. 33 (December 1923), 487-95.

3438. EFFECT of minimum wages on women's earnings in Rhode Island. Monthly labor review, v. 47 (September 1938),

551-5.
3439. EFFECT of minimum wage in New York industries. Monthly
           labor review, v. 52 (February 1941), 359-63.
3440. GAINS under minimum wage in two New York industries,
           1940. Monthly labor review, v. 53 (September 1941),
           622-4.
3441. GEE, Henrietta. The married woman's wages. Woman's
           journal, v. 14 (February 1929), 16-17+.
3442. GILSON, M. B. Wages of women in industry. Industrial
           management, v. 61 (1 June 1921), 427-31; v. 62
           (1 July 1921), 37-42.
3443. GOLDMARK, Josephine. New menace in industry. Scrib-
           ner's magazine, v. 93 (March 1933), 141-3. Concern-
           ing the fall in earnings for women.
3444. HAMMOND, M. B. Wages of women in manual work. Po-
           litical Science quarterly, v. 15 (September 1900),
           508-35.
3445. HASKEL, B. Minimum wages in New York State. Common-
           weal, v. 28 (10 June 1938), 174-7.
3446. HAYES, F. C. Minimum wage and the wages paid to women.
           Wisconsin library bulletin, v. 9 (1913), 106.
3447. HERSTEIN, L. Women discuss wages. American federa-
           tionist, v. 36 (August 1929), 949-59.
3448. HODGE, R. W. and P. Hodge. Occupational assimilation as
           a competitive process. American journal of Sociology,
           v. 71 (November 1965), 249-64. Possible economic
           basis (high wages) as an employment policy for dis-
           crimination against Negroes and women.
3449. HOFFMAN, B. H. How much should they earn? Ladies
           home journal, v. 63 (July 1946), 20-3.
3450. HOLCOMBE, A. N. Effects of the legal minimum wage for
           women. American Academy of Political and Social
           Science, annals, v. 69 (January 1917), 34-41.
3451. HUTCHINSON, Emilie J. Women's wages; a study of the
           wages of industrial women and measures suggested to
           increase them. New York, Columbia University Press,
           1919. 179p. Reprinted by AMS Press, New York,
           1968.
3452. IN the wake of wages. Opportunist, v. 1 (August-September
           1916), 7-13.
3453. INCOME a working wife actually nets. Good housekeeping,
           v. 158 (April 1964), 163.
3454. INFORMATION Bureau on Women's Work. Trend of women's
           wages, Ohio, 1924. Toledo, 1926. 15p.
3455. INTERNATIONAL Ladies Garment Workers Union. Forty
           cent minimum wage for the women's apparel industry.
           By Lazare Teper. New York, 1941. 64p.
3456. JOHNSON, E. M. Fifteen years of minimum wage in Mas-
           sachusetts. American federationist, v. 35 (December
           1938), 1469-77.
3457. KAUN, D. E. Economics of the minimum wage; the effects
           of the Fair Labor Standards Act, 1945-1960. 333p.
           PhD thesis, Stanford University, 1964.

3458. KELLEY, Florence. The inescapable dilemma. Survey,
        v. 41 (22 March 1919), 885. The need for minimum
        wage statutes rather than strikes on the part of women.

3459. _____. The minimum wage law in Oregon under fire.
        Survey, v. 31 (14 March 1914), 740-1. The Oregon
        Supreme Court in a case involving the constitutionality
        of the first American minimum wage law for women.

3460. KUCZYNSKI, L. and M. Steinfeld. Fluctuations of wages of
        women and unskilled male workers. American feder-
        ationist, v. 34 (August 1927), 963-5.

3461. LESLIE, M. Minimum wage for women. American feder-
        ationist, v. 40 (April 1933), 390-3.

3462. LIST of states with references to the statutes which protect
        earnings of married women. U.S. Bureau of Labor
        Statistics, bulletin, v. 148 (1914), 79-80.

3463. LUCAS, Arthur F. The legal minimum wage in Massachu-
        setts. American Academy of Political and Social Sci-
        ence, annals, supp. v. 130 (March 1927), 1-84.

3464. LUTZ, Alma. Women and wages. Nation, v. 139 (17 Octo-
        ber 1934), 440-1. Minimum wage for women and op-
        position to it.

3465. MABEE, C. E. Minimum wages for women in California.
        Journal of applied Sociology, v. 8 (September 1923),
        31-6.

3466. MACKENZIE, F. W. Minimum wage for women and children.
        American labor legislation review, v. 13 (December
        1923), 254-5.

3467. MCNULTY, Donald J. Differences in pay between men and
        women workers. Monthly labor review, v. 90 (Decem-
        ber 1967), 40-3.

3468. MINIMUM wage decrees in Massachusetts. Monthly labor re-
        view, v. 7 (September 1918), 677-8.

3469. MINIMUM wage for women. Nation, v. 102 (8 June 1916),
        610-11.

3470. MORTENSON, C. E. Wages of women employed as cleaners,
        maids and elevator operators in buildings and theaters
        in the District of Columbia. Monthly labor review,
        v. 11 (November 1920), 976-82.

3471. NATIONAL Consumers' League. Earnings of women in fac-
        tories and a legal living wage. By M. W. Dewson.
        New York, 1921. 27p.

3472. _____. Living wage for women in the capitol of the na-
        tion: an important measure, the Trammell-Keating
        minimum wage bill. New York, The League, 1918.
        3p.

3473. _____. Remember the shrunken dollar: A living wage for
        women wage earners: minimum wage legislation in
        force in the District of Columbia, Arizona, Arkansas,
        California, Colorado, Kansas, Massachusetts, Minne-
        sota, North Dakota, Oregon, Texas, Utah, Washington,
        Wisconsin, Canadian border provinces, except New
        Brunswick. New York, The League, [1921?]. 4p.

3474. NATIONAL Industrial Conference Board. Wartime pay of

women in industry. By Geneva Seybold. New York,
The Board, 1943. 31p. [Studies in personnel policy,
no. 58.]

3475. NEW minimum wage for District of Columbia mercantile industry. Monthly labor review, v. 9 (October 1919),
1151-2.

3476. NEW minimum wage awards in Massachusetts, Minnesota,
and Wisconsin. Monthly labor review, v. 9 (September 1919), 856-64.

3477. NEW York (state). Department of Labor. Wages and hours
of work of organized women in New York state. Albany, 1925, 11p. [Special bulletin no. 136.]

3478. _____. _____. Women's war wages. New York, 1943.
7p.

3479. _____. _____. Women's wages on men's jobs. New
York, 1944. 33p.

3480. O'HARA, E. V. Wage legislation for women. Catholic
world, v. 100 (January 1915), 443-50.

3481. PENNSYLVANIA. Department of Labor and Industry. Earnings of women workers in Pennsylvania manufacturing
with special reference to the clothing industry. Harrisburg, 1938.

3482. PERSONS, C. E. Estimates of a living wage for female
workers. American Statistical Association, journal,
v. 14 (June 1915), 567-77.

3483. PETERSON, John M. Employment effects of state minimum
wages for women: Three historical cases re-examined.
Industrial and labor relations review, v. 12 (April
1959), 406-22.

3484. PITY the poor working girl. New republic, v. 133 (29
August 1955), 3. Shows the greater pay increase of
men as contrasted with women.

3485. PRESENT wages of women in New York state industries.
Economic world, n.s., v. 17 (1 February 1919), 158-9.

3486. QUESTION of fixing a minimum wage for women alone. Congressional digest, v. 15 (November 1936), 282-7.

3487. RELATION of women's to men's wages. Commerce reports,
no. 148 (25 June 1919), 1573-6.

3488. ROBERT, J. Women and the wage question. Review of reviews, v. 45 (April 1912), 439-42.

3489. ROBINS, M. D. One aspect of the menace of low wages.
Social hygiene, v. 1 (June 1915), 358-63.

3490. SAMUELSON, P. A. Prejudice; women's wages. Newsweek,
v. 75 (23 March 1970), 90.

3491. SANBORN, Henry N. Income differences between men and
women in the United States. Chicago, University of
Chicago Library, 1960.

3492. _____. Pay differences between men and women. Industrial and labor relations review, v. 17 (July 1964),
534-50.

3493. SAWHILL, Isabel Van Devanter. The relative earnings of
women in the United States. 201p. PhD thesis, New
York University, 1968.

3494. SEYBOLD, Geneva. War Labor Board decisions on women's
       pay. Conference Board management record, v. 6
       (January 1944), 3-6.
3495. _____. Wartime pay of women in industry. Conference
       board management record, v. 5 (October 1943), 402-5.
3496. SHORT, J. M. and N. K. Harrington. Women's wages com-
       pared with living costs and general community stand-
       ards, 1914-1932. Portland, Ore., Reed College,
       1933. 15p.
3497. SMITH, Ethel M. Congress grants inadequate raise to wom-
       en workers. Woman citizen, v. 3 (10 August 1918),
       215.
3498. STATUTE bars discrimination in pay based solely on sex:
       employers uphold principle. Industrial bulletin [N.Y.
       State Dept. of Labor], v. 25 (July 1946), 40-1.
3499. STEPHENS, K. Wages of women. North American review,
       v. 162 (1894), 377.
3500. STITT, Louise. Guaranteed living wage provisions of state
       minimum wage orders for women. Monthly labor re-
       view, v. 53 (September 1941), 572-7.
3501. SURVEY of women's wages on men's jobs in (New York)
       state industries. Industrial bulletin [N.Y. State Dept.
       of Labor], v. 23 (April 1944), 118-21.
3502. SWARTZ, Nelle. The trend in women's wages. American
       Academy of Political and Social Science, annals, v.
       143 (May 1929), 104-8.
3503. TAUSSIG, J. W. Minimum wages for women. Quarterly
       journal of Economics, v. 30 (May 1916), 411-42.
3504. TREND of women's wages in New York City since 1929.
       Monthly labor review, v. 32 (June 1931), 1332-4.
3505. TYLER, M. D. Wife's control over her own earnings.
       Woman citizen, v. 4 (29 May 1920), 1328-9.
3506. UNDERPAID women. Independent, v. 74 (6 March 1913),
       543-4.
3507. U.S. Women's Bureau. Differences in the earnings of wom-
       en and men. By Mary Elizabeth Pidgeon. Washing-
       ton, GPO, 1938. 57p. [Bulletin no. 152.]
3508. _____. _____. Differentials in pay for women.
       Washington, GPO, 1945. 17p.
3509. _____. _____. Earnings of women in selected manu-
       facturing industries, 1946. By Mary Elizabeth Pid-
       geon. Washington, GPO, 1948. 14p. [Bulletin no.
       219.]
3510. _____. _____. Fact sheet on the earnings gap.
       Washington, GPO, 1971. 6p. [Bulletin no. 71-86.]
3511. _____. _____. Minimum wage and the woman worker.
       By Regina Marsden Neitzey. Washington, GPO, 1960.
       16p.
3512. _____. _____. Special study of wages paid to women
       and minors in Ohio industries prior and subsequent to
       the Ohio minimum wage law for women and minors.
       Washington, GPO, 1936. 83p. [Bulletin no. 145.]
3513. _____. _____. Suggested language for a state act to

abolish discriminatory wage rates based on sex.
Washington, GPO, 1964.

3514. _____. _____. Wages of women in 13 states. By
Mary Elizabeth Pidgeon. Washington, GPO, 1931.
213p. [Bulletin no. 85.]

3515. _____. _____. Women's wages in Kansas. Washington, GPO, 1921. 104p. [Bulletin no. 17.]

3516. _____. _____. Women's wages in wartime. By
Elizabeth D. Banham. Washington, GPO, 1944. 10p.

3517. WAGE cuts for women [in New York City]. Survey, v. 66
(15 July 1931), 397.

3518. WAGES for women. Outlook, v. 63 (1899), 533.

3519. WAR Labor Board's decisions on women's pay. Conference
board management record, v. 6 (January 1944), 3-6.

3520. WEEKLY earnings of women in Pennsylvania industries.
Monthly labor review, v. 48 (June 1939), 1304-11.

3521. WHITTEMORE, Margaret. The wage-earning homemaker
and the family income. Journal of home economics,
v. 23 (November 1931), 998-1001.

3522. WINSLOW, Mary Nelson. Medians of women's earnings in
four states. American Statistical Association, journal,
v. 18 (March 1922), 106-8. Survey of wages of wom-
en in Kansas, Georgia, Rhode Island, and Kentucky.

3523. WOLFSON, Theresa. Wages of organized women workers.
American federationist, v. 32 (September 1925), 811-
13.

3524. WOMAN'S right to a living wage. Independent, v. 81 (4
January 1915), 4-6.

3525. WOMEN and wages. Woman citizen, v. 4 (7 June 1919), 8-9.

3526. WOMEN'S earnings in New York factories, September 1944.
Monthly labor review, v. 60 (June 1945), 1270-2.

3527. WOMEN'S earnings in service and trade in Maine. Monthly
labor review, v. 52 (March 1941), 612-16.

3528. WOMEN'S right to fair play. Outlook, v. 133 (14 February
1923), 295-6. On the constitutionality of minimum
wages for women.

3529. WOMEN'S wages. Nation, v. 108 (22 February 1919), 270-1.

3530. WOMEN'S wages in boom times. Industrial bulletin [N.Y.
State Dept. of Labor], v. 20 (October 1941), 296-8.

3531. WOMEN'S wages in Kansas. Monthly labor review, v. 13
(November 1921), 1037-41.

3532. WOMEN'S wages in New York. Monthly labor review, v. 8
(March 1919), 828-30.

3533. WOMEN'S wages on men's jobs in New York state. Monthly
labor review, v. 58 (June 1944), 1245-7.

3534. WOMEN'S war wages in New York state, 1943. Monthly
labor review, v. 58 (April 1944), 767-8.

3535. WORKINGWOMEN and wages; a poll of the press. Outlook,
v. 103 (29 March 1913), 705-7.

3536. WRIGHT, Carroll D. Why women are paid less than men.
Forum, v. 13 (July 1892), 629-39. The close and
necessary connection between the political and the industrial emancipation of women.

EQUAL WAGES

3537. ACTION on equal pay: Syracuse University students make pioneering study of New York's equal pay law: Equal pay: What it means. Industrial bulletin, v. 26 (July 1947), 5-14.

3538. AIKEN, S. C. Here's how: New Jersey federation's fight for equal pay. Independent woman, v. 31 (June 1952), 184-5.

3539. ANDERSON, Mary. Equal pay for equal work. Journal of home economics, v. 37 (November 1945), 581.

3540. _____. The women's equal pay act of 1945. Woman's press, v. 39 (November 1945), 33-4.

3541. APPLICATION of WLB equal pay principle: women held entitled to equal pay where work is in fact equal. Wage and hour reporter, v. 5 (5 October 1942), 763-4.

3542. BENGE, E. J. Can we pay women same wage rates as men? American business, v. 12 (December 1942), 12-13.

3543. BILL to give equal pay. Occupations, v. 24 (January 1946), 240.

3544. BLOODWORTH, B. Case for equal pay legislation. Independent woman, v. 31 (June 1952), 169-70.

3545. BRADY, Dorothy S. Equal pay for women workers. American Academy of Political and Social Science, annals, v. 251 (May 1947), 53-60.

3546. BRECKINRIDGE, Sophonisba Preston. Home responsibilities of women and the "equal wage." Journal of political economy, v. 31 (August 1923), 521-43.

3547. BUCK, D. P. Colorado's women go after equal pay. Independent woman, v. 33 (September 1954), 330-2+.

3548. _____. How Colorado won equal pay. Independent woman, v. 34 (June 1955), 3-5+.

3549. BUREAU of National Affairs. Equal pay for equal work: Federal Equal Pay Law of 1963. Washington, BNA, 1963. 124p.

3550. CAVANAGH, M. Equal pay: Catholic teaching on women's rights. Tablet, v. 205 (12 February 1955), 153.

3551. COCHRANE, D. H. Equal pay for comparable work. Independent woman, v. 22 (July 1943), 197+.

3552. _____., comp. Shall women have equal pay? Symposium. Independent woman, v. 23 (April 1944), 108-9+.

3553. CRANE, P. Equal pay for women. Tablet, v. 205 (26 February 1955), 210-11.

3554. DALE, L. H. Problems and progress of equal pay. Kappa Beta Pi quarterly, v. 38 (October 1954), 107-11.

3555. DECISIONS of National War Labor Board, August and Septem-

ber 1942: equal pay for woman workers. Monthly
labor review, v. 56 (January 1943), 63-4.

3556. EDGEWORTH, F. Y. Equal pay to men and women for
equal work. Economic journal, v. 32 (March 1920),
431-57.

3557. EQUAL Pay Act of 1963: its implementation and enforcement. American Association of University Women,
journal, v. 61 (March 1968), 117-19.

3558. EQUAL Pay Act of 1963. Monthly labor review, v. 86 (July
1963), 947.

3559. EQUAL pay for equal work. Women lawyers journal, v. 31
(Spring 1945), 12-13.

3560. EQUAL pay for equal work in the United States. International labour review, v. 50 (July 1944), 106-8.

3561. EQUAL pay for equal work in the United States. International labour review, v. 58 (September 1948), 391-4.

3562. EQUAL pay for men and women discussed by Economic and
Social Council. U.N. bulletin, v. 4 (1 March 1948),
172.

3563. EQUAL pay for the woman worker. Conference board management record, v. 5 (January 1943), 1-6.

3564. EQUAL pay for women. America, v. 91 (5 June 1954), 262.

3565. EQUAL pay for women. American federationist, v. 71 (June
1964), 14-17.

3566. EQUAL pay for women. Commonweal, v. 78 (7 June 1963),
293-4.

3567. EQUAL pay for women. It's effect. U.S. news and world
report, v. 56 (14 June 1964), 91-2.

3568. EQUAL pay for women under order of War Labor Board.
Wage and hour reporter, v. 6 (7 June 1943), 526-7.

3569. EQUAL pay law: how it will work. U.S. news and world
report, v. 54 (24 June 1963), 10.

3570. EQUAL pay principle. United Nations review, v. 4 (March
1958), 4.

3571. EQUAL pay principle in New York war industries. Monthly
labor review, v. 57 (July 1943), 102-4.

3572. 'EQUAL pay' principle in the replacement of men by women
in New York war industries. Industrial bulletin [N.Y.
State Dept. of Labor], v. 22 (March 1943), 110-12.

3573. EQUAL wages for women? debate. Rotarian, v. 77 (December 1950), 14-16; v. 78 (February 1951), 2.

3574. FAIRER wages for the fair sex; Fair Labor Standards Act.
Business week, (6 June 1964), 74.

3575. FINIGAN, Frederick T. Problems in fair employment and
equal pay for women...; and selling is selling--The
Equal Pay Act, by George L. Plant. Stores, v. 50
(March 1968), 14-18.

3576. FIRST equal pay law. Woman citizen, v. 3 (3 May 1919),
1050.

3577. FISHER, Marguerite J. Equal pay for equal work legislation.
Industrial and labor relations review, v. 2 (October
1948), 50-7.

3578. _____. Equal pay for equal work legislation. Labor law

journal, v. 2 (August 1951), 578-86.
3579. FLEMMING, A. S. Why can't a woman be paid like a man?
Good housekeeping, v. 155 (November 1962), 50+.
3580. GRANTTHAM, C. R. Why equal pay now? Independent
woman, v. 24 (November 1945), 319.
3581. GUITAR, M. A. Funny thing happened on her way to the
bank. Mademoiselle, v. 59 (September 1964), 179+.
3582. HOLLIS, C. Problems of equal pay when women are called
back to industry. Tablet, v. 189 (7 June 1947), 282-3.
3583. HOUSE passes bill requiring equal pay for women. Congressional quarterly weekly report, v. 20 (27 July 1962),
1243-4.
3584. HUNTER, L. B. Equal pay at work: record of New York
State's equal pay law. Independent woman, v. 27
(February 1948), 37-8+.
3585. HYMER, E. W. Dollar for dollar, equal pay for equal
work. Independent woman, v. 29 (April 1950), 117-18.
3586. IN behalf of equal pay; conference of representatives of
women's national organizations. Independent woman,
v. 23 (November 1944), 331.
3587. INTERNATIONAL Federation of Christian Trade Unions.
Equal pay for equal work; a memorandum on the
principle of women's work and women's wages, submitted to the United Nations' Economic and Social
Council and the International Labour Organization.
Utrecht, [1951?]. 55p.
3588. INTERNATIONAL Labor Office. Equal remuneration for men
and women workers for work of equal value. Fifth
item on the agenda. Geneva, 1949-50. 2v.
3589. _____. Equal remuneration for men and women workers
for work of equal value. Seventh item on the agenda.
Geneva, 1950-51. 2v.
3590. LANGENBACH, A. E. Equal pay for the fair sex. Banking,
v. 57 (December 1964), 38+.
3591. LANHAM, Elizabeth and Lola B. Dawkins. Women in business: equal pay for equal work? Austin, Bureau of
Business Research, University of Texas, 1959. 14p.
3592. LAW requiring equal pay for women held constitutional by
Supreme Court of Michigan. Monthly labor review,
v. 51 (December 1940), 1437-8.
3593. LEOPOLD, Alice K. Federal equal pay legislation. Labor
law journal, v. 6 (January 1955), 7-32.
3594. LYNCH, B. A. Equal wages for women? Rotarian, v. 78
(January 1951), 2.
3595. MACGAUGHEY, James R. Equal pay for equal work?
American school board journal, v. 82 (February 1931),
60.
3596. MCQUATTERS, G. F. Washington, our stand on equal pay
presented. Independent woman, v. 27 (April 1948),
117-18.
3597. MILLER, Freida S. Equal pay; its importance to the nation.
Independent woman, v. 25 (November 1946), 325-6+.
3598. MORAN, Robert D. Reducing discrimination: role of the

Equal Pay Act. Monthly labor review, v. 93 (June 1970), 30-4.

3599. MURPHY, T. E. Female wage discrimination: a study of the Equal Pay Act, 1963-1970. University of Cincinnati law review, v. 39 (Fall 1970), 615+.

3600. NATIONAL Conference on Equal Pay for Equal Work. Monthly labor review, v. 74 (May 1952), 559-60.

3601. NEW equal pay laws. Social service review, v. 23 (December 1949), 509-10.

3602. NIX, J. C. Equal pay for equal work. Monthly labor review, v. 47 (January 1952), 41-5. An analysis of clauses in collective bargaining agreements concerning equal pay for women.

3603. NORTHRUP, H. R. Equal opportunity and equal pay. Management of personnel quarterly, v. 3 (Fall 1964), 17-26.

3604. ON equal pay for women. U.S. news and world report, v. 56 (23 March 1964), 115-17. On the Equal Pay Act of 1963.

3605. OWEN, W. B. Equal pay for women, one view; summary of statement. U.S. news and world report, v. 54 (8 April 1963), 100.

3606. PAY women equal wages? Rotarian, v. 63 (September 1943), 26-7. Discussion, v. 63 (October 1943), 2.

3607. PLUNKETT, M. L. Equal pay for women workers. Monthly labor review, v. 63 (September 1946), 380-9.

3608. SEIGLER, Vernon. Equal pay for women laws: are they desirable? However wrong discrimination against working women may be, legislation will not provide a practical solution or cure. Labor law journal, v. 5 (October 1954), 663-88+.

3609. SHAPLEY, D. Sex discrimination on campus: Michigan wrestles with equal pay. Science, v. 173 (16 July 1971), 214-16.

3610. SHOULD industry favor the "equal pay" law: Yes, by C. D. Pepper; No, by C. T. Murchison. Modern industry, v. 11 (May 1946), 128-9+.

3611. SIMCHAK, Morag M. Equal Pay Act of 1963: its implementation and enforcement. AAUW journal, v. 61 (March 1968), 117-19.

3612. SKINNER, J. Master file and the U.S. census on equal pay. Independent woman, v. 23 (April 1944), 111.

3613. SMITH, F. S. Fairness for the fair sex. Christianity and crisis, v. 22 (17 September 1962), 146-7.

3614. SPRINGEN, P. J. Dimensions for the oppression of women. Vital speeches, v. 37 (15 February 1971), 265-7.

3615. SULLIVAN, J. E. Equal salaries for equal service. National Education Association of America, journal, v. 12 (November 1923), 373.

3616. TUCKER, B. F. Equal pay for equal work. Women lawyers journal, v. 31 (Spring 1945), 12-13.

3617. UNITED Nations. Commission on the Status of Women. Equal pay for equal work. New York, 1958.

3618.   _____. _____. Equal remuneration for men and wom-
en workers for work of equal value. New York, 1958.
3619.   _____. _____. Practical methods for the implementation of equal pay for equal work. New York, 1957.
3620.   _____. Secretary-General, 1953- (Hammarskjöld). Equal
pay for equal work. New York, 1960. 65p.
3621. U.S. Department of Labor. Wage and Hour Division.
Equal pay. Washington, GPO, 1971. 16p. [Publica-
tion number 1320.]
3622.   _____. Solicitor of the Department of Labor. Legislative
history of the Equal Pay Act of 1963. Washington,
GPO, 1963. 114p.
3623.   _____. Women's Bureau. Action for equal pay. Washington, GPO, 1965. 7p.
3624.   _____. _____. Case studies in equal pay for women.
Washington, 1951. 27p.
3625.   _____. _____. Digest of state equal pay laws. Washington, GPO, 1951. 14p.
3626.   _____. _____. Digest of state equal pay laws, June
1, 1955. Washington, GPO, 1955. 20p.
3627.   _____. _____. Digest of state equal pay laws. Washington, GPO, 1965. 26p.
3628.   _____. _____. Economic indicators relating to equal
pay, 1962. By Jean Alice Wells. Washington, GPO,
1962. 19p. [Pamphlet no. 9.]
3629.   _____. _____. Equal pay for women in war industries.
By Mary Elizabeth Pidgeon. Washington, GPO, 1942.
26p. [Bulletin no. 196.]
3630.   _____. _____. Equal pay for women means a rate
based on the job; not on the sex of the worker. rev.
ed. Washington, GPO, 1948. 1p. [Leaflet no. 2.]
3631.   _____. _____. Movement for equal pay legislation in
the United States. Washington, GPO, 1950. 5p.
3632.   _____. _____. Progress toward equal pay in the
meat-packing industry. By Ethel Erickson. Washington, GPO, 1953. 16p. [Bulletin no. 251.]
3633.   _____. _____. Report of the National Conference on
Equal Pay, March 31, and April 1, 1952. By Helen
Josephy Robison. Washington, GPO, 1952. 25p.
[Bulletin no. 243.]
3634.   _____. _____. What the equal pay principle means
to women. rev. ed. Washington, GPO, 1964.
3635.   _____. _____. What you want in state equal pay bill.
Washington, GPO, 1969. 3p.
3636.   _____. _____. Why state equal pay laws? Washington, GPO, 1966. 4p.
3637. WHEN women get paid as much as men.... U.S. news and
world report, v. 54 (3 June 1963), 97-8. Pending
equal pay legislation in Congress and how it would
operate.
3638. WOMEN at work. Monthly labor review, v. 93 (June 1970),
3-44. Special issue pertaining to the Equal Pay Act;
labor force activity of women; the U.S. Women's

Bureau; manpower demands in the 1970's.
3639. WOMEN workers and the Equal Pay Act of 1945. American
           Association of University Women, journal, v. 39 (Fall
           1945), 38-9. Editorial in favor of the Act.
3640. WORLD Federation of Trade Unions. Principle of equal pay
           for equal work for men and women workers. Lake
           Success, 1948. 2p.
3641. WYOMING passes state equal pay law. National business
           woman, v. 38 (May 1959), 28.

EDUCATION

3642. ACKER, Joan. The status of women at the University of Oregon. Report of an Ad Hoc Committee. Eugene, Oregon, University of Oregon, 1970. 20p.
3643. ADAMS, H. Education of women. North American review, v. 118 (1874), 140.
3644. AIKEN, W. Education of women in Texas. San Antonio, Naylor, 1957.
3645. ALBJERG, M. H. Why do bright girls not take stiff courses? Educational forum, v. 25 (January 1961), 141-4.
3646. ALMY, E. A. Year's progress for college women. Education, v. 10 (April 1890), 476-84.
3647. ALPENFELS, E. J. World of ideas: do women count? Educational review, v. 44 (January 1963), 40-3. Concerns women as educators.
3648. AMERICAN Association of University Professors. Activities of interest to Committee W in chapters and conferences. Memorandum. Washington, The Association, 3 February 1971. 2p. Lists a number of universities which "are interested in undertaking or actively engaged in projects related to faculty women on their campuses."
3649. _____. Committee on the Status of Women. Indiana University Chapter. Study of the status of women faculty at Indiana University. Bloomington campus. Bloomington? January 1971. 53p.
3650. _____. _____. Kansas State Teachers College Chapter. Report one of the Committee on the Status of Women. Emporia, 1970. 16p. A study of full-time faculty women at Kansas State Teachers College.
3651. AMERICAN Association of University Women. Campus 1970. Where do women stand? Research report of a survey on women in academe. By Ruth M. Oltman. Washington, 1970.
3652. _____. Economic status of university women in the United States of America. By Susan M. Kingsbury. Washington, GPO, 1939. 70p.
3653. _____. The evolving role of the women's liberation movement in higher education. By Ruth M. Oltman. Washington, 1971. 9p.
3654. _____, Tampa, Florida. Status of Women Committee: Faculty report. By Maxine Mackay. Tampa, 1970. 31p. A study of sex discrimination in the State University System of Florida.
3655. AMERICAN Council on Education. How fare American women? By Althea Hottel. Washington, The Council,

1955. 70p.
3656. AMERICAN Historical Association. Committee on the Status
of Women. (A draft report on the status of women
faculty in history departments at selected colleges and
universities.) Washington, The Association, 1970.
29p.
3657. AMERICAN women: their status and education. U.S. President's Commission on the Status of Women. Practical
forecast for home economics, v. 9 (November 1963),
26-7+.
3658. ARNOLD, S. L. Reconciliation of cross-purposes in the education of women. Journal of education, v. 68 (16
July 1908), 112-13.
3659. ASSOCIATION of Departments of English. The lot of women:
A report on the National Survey of Undergraduate English Programs. By Thomas Wilcox. New York, 1970.
7p. Also in: Association of Departments of English,
bulletin, no. 25 (May 1970), 53-9. Concerns discrimination against potential women college teachers of
English.
3660. BABEY-BROOKE, Anna M. and R. B. Amber. Discrimination against women in higher education. A 15 year
survey. Promotional practices at Brooklyn College
CUNY: 1955-1970, all ranks-tenured and untenured.
[New York?], 1970. 27p.
3661. BACKUS, H. H. Should the college train for motherhood?
Outlook, v. 61 (25 February 1899), 461-3.
3662. BALCH, E. G. Education and efficiency of women. Academy
of Political Science, proceedings, v. 1 (October 1910),
61-71.
3663. BARCLAY, D. For bright girls: what place in society?
New York Times magazine, (13 September 1959), 126.
Concerning the education of women.
3664. BASS, A. T. Development of higher education for women in
this country. Contemporary education, v. 41 (May
1970), 285-8.
3665. BAYER, Alan E. and Helen S. Astin. Sex differences in
academic rank and salary among science doctorates
in teaching. Journal of human resources, v. 3 (Spring
1968), 191-200. The extent of discrimination against
women as university teachers with respect to equal
pay and promotion opportunities.
3666. BAZELL, R. J. Sex discrimination; campuses face contract
loss over HEW demands. Science, v. 170 (20 November 1970), 834-5.
3667. BEARD, Mary Ritter. University discipline for women--
asset or handicap? American Association of University
Women, journal, v. 25 (April 1932), 129-33. Whether
a college education is more of a handicap for women
than for men.
3668. BEASLEY, I. M. Education is the key for women. American Academy of Political and Social Science, annals,
v. 375 (January 1968), 154-62.

3669. BEATLEY, B. Education of women; plea for realism.
       Journal of education, v. 124 (December 1941), 291-3.
3670. BELOK, M. V. A forgotten minority. Journal of thought,
       v. 4 (November 1969), 273-7. Problems of the aca-
       demic woman.
3671. BENEZET, Louis T. Modern mythology in women's educa-
       tion. American Association of University Professors,
       bulletin, v. 36 (Autumn 1950), 487-96.
3672. BERNARD, Jessie. Academic women. University Park, Pa.,
       Pennsylvania State University Press, 1964. 331p. On
       the social status, behaviour and acceptance of women
       as university teachers.
3673. BERRY, Sara and Mark Erenburg. Earnings of professional
       women at Indiana University. Bloomington, 1969. 21p.
3674. BIBBY, K. Colleges for women. Good housekeeping, v. 48
       (May 1909), 552-6.
3675. BIXLER, Julius Seelye. Shall we let the ladies join us?
       American scholar, v. 4 (October 1935), 474-83.
3676. BLACKWELL, G. W. College and the continuing education
       of women. Educational record, v. 44 (January 1963),
       33-9.
3677. BLANDIN, Isabella Margaret. History of higher education of
       women in the South prior to 1860. Washington, Neale,
       1909. 328p.
3678. BOAS, Louise Schutz. Woman's education begins: The rise
       of women's colleges. Norton, Mass., Wheaton Col-
       lege Press, 1935. 295p.
3679. BOK, E. College and the stove. Ladies' home journal,
       v. 20 (April 1903), 16.
3680. BRACKETT, Anna C., ed. Women and the higher education.
       New York, Harper, 1893. 214p. Reprinted by Green-
       wood Press, Westport, Conn., 1971. The articles
       were written between 1819 and 1892 by Emma Willard,
       Lucy M. Salmon, Anna C. Brackett and others con-
       cerning the evolution of women's education in the 19th
       century.
3681. BRAGDON, H. D. Second century faces the first; is it time
       to choose new goals in higher education for women?
       American Association of University Women, journal,
       v. 31 (June 1938), 206-15.
3682. BROOKS, Rozanne M. Woman's place is in the wrong; the
       "loyal opposition." Vital speeches, v. 28 (15 Decem-
       ber 1961), 151-4. Criticism of colleges and univer-
       sities.
3683. BROWN, H. D. How shall we educate our girls? Outlook,
       v. 53 (7 March 1896), 431.
3684. BROWNING, Oscar. Education of women and the universities.
       Forum, v. 24 (1898), 225.
3685. BULL, Jennie. High school women: oppression and libera-
       tion. Women: a journal of liberation, v. 1 (Winter
       1970), 42-6.
3686. CALIFORNIA. University. Academic Senate. Berkeley
       Division. Report of the Committee on Senate policy.

Report of the Subcommittee on the status of academic
women on the Berkeley campus. Berkeley, 1970.
78p. Nepotism at Berkeley, percentage of women at
different academic levels, admission to the Graduate
Division, status of women in research units, etc.

3687.   _____. _____. _____. Santa Barbara Division.
The status of academic women at UCSB. In: Minutes
of the Santa Barbara Division of the Academic Senate,
University of California, 10 June 1971, p. 9-17.

3688. CAMPBELL, Doak Sheridan. Problems in the education of
college women: a study of women graduates of southern colleges. Nashville, Tenn., Peabody College
Book Store, 1933.

3689. CARMICHAEL, O. C. Change in higher education. Association of American Colleges, bulletin, v. 32 (October
1946), 355-61.

3690. CHAMBLISS, Rollin. Women too are persons. American
Association of University Professors, bulletin, v. 37
(September 1951), 547-52. On the education of women.

3691. CHANGE and choice for the college woman. AAUW journal,
(May 1962), special issue. American culture and female roles, ways of working, self and society.

3692. CHICAGO. University. Committee on University Women.
Women in the University of Chicago; a report. Chicago, University of Chicago, 1970. 122p. Report on
the status and opportunities open to academic women,
with special attention to equality regarding salaries,
promotion, and tenure for faculty women.

3693. CHINAS, B. L. Women on college faculties. Science,
v. 168 (22 May 1970), 917.

3694. CLAPP, Margaret. Realistic education for women. American Association of University Women, journal, v. 43
(Summer 1950), 199-202. The issue here is not equal
education for both sexes, but rather different education for men and women because of their differing future roles.

3695. CLARK, S. Higher education for women in America. New
England magazine, v. 2 (1890), 711.

3696. CLAWSON, A. H. Liberation from low pay and limited opportunity. American vocational journal, v. 45 (December 1970), 31-2+ .

3697. CLESS, E. L. Modest proposal for the educating of women.
American scholar, v. 38 (Autumn 1969), 618-27.

3698. COLE, Arthur C. A hundred years of Mount Holyoke College; the evolution of an educational ideal. New
Haven, Conn., Yale University Press, 1940. Reflects
changing concepts in education and widening opportunities for women.

3699. COLLET, C. R. Educated working women. American
Academy of Political and Social Science, annals,
v. 20 (September 1902), 436-8.

3700. CONFERENCE on the Present Status and Prospective Trends
of Research on the Education of Women, Rye, New

York, 1957. The education of women: Signs for the
future; report. Washington, American Council on
Education, 1959. 153p.
3701. CONFERENCE on the Undergraduate Education of Women,
Cedar Crest College, Allentown, Pennsylvania, July
8-10, 1969. Allentown, 1969. 90p. Whether wom-
en's education should be different from men's, obligations of colleges towards women and further areas for
research.
3702. CONTINUING education for women: symposium. Adult leadership, v. 18 (May 1969), 5-36.
3703. COOK, Richard V. An address on the education and influence
of women; delivered before the Sabbath School Union,
in the Lutheran Church, January 11, 1858. Columbus,
Texas, Colorado Citizen, 1858. 20p.
3704. CORRALLO, S. B. Economic relevance of women's higher
education. National Association of Women Deans and
Counselors, journal, v. 31 (Winter 1968), 74-9.
3705. COUNCIL on the Education and Position of Women in a Democracy. Education of women in a democracy. New
London, Conn., Institute of Women's Professional Relations, 1940. 28p.
3706. CROSS, Barbara M., ed. The educated woman in America;
selected writings of Catharine Beecher, Margaret
Fuller, and M. Carey Thomas. New York, Teachers
College Press, 1965. 175p.
3707. CUTHBERT, Marion Vera. Education and marginality; a
study of the Negro woman college graduate. 167p.
PhD thesis, Columbia University, 1942.
3708. D'ALFONSO, N. Problem of the education of women. Education, v. 6 (1886), 360, 420.
3709. DALL, Caroline Wells. The college, the market, and the
court; or, Woman's relation to education, labor, and
law. Concord, N.H., Rumford, 1914. 511p.
3710. DAVID, Opal D. The education of women: Signs for the
future. Washington, American Council on Education,
1959.
3711. DAVIS, H. Collegiate education of women. Overland, v. 16
(October 1890), 337-44.
3712. DAVIS, Hazel. Equal pay for men and women teachers.
American School Board journal, v. 111 (September
1945), 31-3.
3713. DAVIS, Helen Edna. Women's professional problems in the
field of education; a map of needed research. [New
York?], Pi Lambda Theta, 1936. 24p.
3714. DAVIS, Paulina Wright. On the education of females...read
at the Convention in Worcester, Mass., October 16,
1851. Syracuse, N.Y., Lathrop's Print., 1851. 16p.
[Woman's rights tracts, no. 3.] Concerning equal
education for women, especially in the medical, legal,
and theological schools.
3715. DE GARMO, C. Higher education of women. Educational
review, v. 25 (April 1903), 341-7.

3716. DEMENT, A. L. Higher education of the housewife. Journal of higher education, v. 31 (January 1960), 28-32.
3717. DEWEY, J. Higher education of women. Popular science monthly, v. 28 (1886), 606.
3718. DIKE, Samuel W. Sociology in the higher education of women. Atlantic monthly, v. 70 (November 1892), 668-76.
3719. DOES graduate work for women pay dividends on the investment? School and society, v. 50 (9 December 1939), 750-1. Consists of a summary of a report by the American Association of University Women and the U.S. Women's Bureau.
3720. DOLAN, Eleanor F. and Margaret P. Davis. Anti-nepotism rules in colleges and universities; their effect on the faculty employment of women. Educational record, v. 41 (October 1960), 285-95.
3721. _____. Educated women: a mid-century evaluation. Educational forum, v. 20 (January 1956), 219-28.
3722. _____. Educational goals for college women. Association of American Colleges, bulletin, v. 39 (October 1953), 441-51.
3723. _____. Higher education for women: time for reappraisal. Higher education, v. 20 (September 1963), 5-13.
3724. DONLON, Mary H. Women's education today. Educational record, v. 39 (July 1958), 246-52.
3725. DRINKER, S. L. and J. Schrier. Patriarchal values in women's education. Journal of higher education, v. 25 (March 1954), 115-21.
3726. DUNBAR, E. Mother returns to the campus; Minnesota plan for the continuing education of women. Look, v. 26 (23 October 1962), 46-50.
3727. DUPANLOUP, F. A. Education and employment of women. American journal of education, v. 17 (1868), 623.
3728. DWIGHT, T. Education for women at Yale. Forum, v. 13 (June 1892), 451-63.
3729. ECKERT, R. E. and J. E. Stecklein. Academic woman. Liberal education, v. 45 (October 1959), 390-7.
3730. EDDY, Edward D., Jr. What's the use of educating women? Saturday review, v. 46 (18 May 1963), 66-8.
3731. EDMISTON, Susan. How is women's liberation doing in the high schools? Seventeen, v. 30 (April 1971), 48+.
3732. EDUCATION and the role of women: symposium. National Education Association, journal, v. 49 (December 1960), 48-53.
3733. EDUCATION for the mature woman: excerpts from American Woman, the report of the President's Commission on the Status of Women. Saturday review, v. 46 (16 November 1963), 90.
3734. EDUCATION for women. Adult education, v. 10 (March 1938), 227-36.
3735. EDUCATION of women. American journal of education, v. 5 (1858), 593.
3736. EDUCATION of women. American journal of education, v. 27 (1877), 733.

3737. EDUCATION of women; adaptation of report. U.S. President's Commission on the Status of Women. School life, v. 46 (November 1963), 17-19.
3738. EDUCATION of women at Harvard College. Literary world, v. 13 (1882), 396.
3739. The EDUCATION of women for social and political leadership; a symposium at Southern Methodist University.... Dallas, Southern Methodist University Press, 1967. 84p.
3740. EGGLESTON, G. C. Education of women. Harper's monthly magazine, v. 67 (1883), 292.
3741. ELLIS, A. Caswell. Preliminary report of Committee W on the Status of Women in College and University Faculties. American Association of University Professors, bulletin, v. 7 (1921), 21-32. Summary of questionnaires sent to 176 colleges and universities showing the number of men and women at different ranks, salary differences, and promotion differences.
3742. _____. Second report of Committee W on the Status of Women in College and University Faculties. American Association of University Professors, bulletin, v. 10 (November 1924), 65-73. Results of a questionnaire showing opinions that colleagues had of the success of women in important phases of their work.
3743. ELLIS, S. R. Social status of the American teacher. School and society, v. 31 (11 January 1930), 47-50.
3744. ELLMANN, Mary. Academic women. Commentary, v. 39 (March 1956), 67-70. The problem of breaking out of the female role even after beginning to teach.
3745. ELY, R. T. Higher education of women. Christian union, v. 45 (1892), 1025.
3746. EMORY University. United Campus Ministry. Discrimination against women in the University. Atlanta, Ga., 1970. 4p.
3747. FAWCETT, M. G. Higher education of women. Critic, v. 10 (1887), 272.
3748. FERBER, Marianne and Jane Loeb. Rank, pay, and representation of women on the faculty at the Urbana-Champaign campus of the University of Illinois. Report of the Committee on the Status of Women, presented to the Urbana AAUP chapter. [Urbana?], 1970. 28p.
3749. FISHER, Dorothy C. Women, education, and democracy. National Education Association, journal, v. 28 (October 1939), 197-8.
3750. FISHER, M. J. Educating women for what? Independent woman, v. 29 (August 1950), 231-2+.
3751. FITZPATRICK, E. A. New trends in women's education. School and society, v. 66 (23 August 1947), 129-31.
3752. FLETCHER, Robert S. and Ernest H. Wilkins. The beginning of college education for women and of co-education on the college level. Oberlin, Ohio, 1937. 14p. Bulletin of Oberlin College, n.s., 343.

3753. FLEY, J. A. Campus regulations: are girls different?
       National Association of Women Deans and Counselors,
       journal, v. 31 (Spring 1968), 116-22.
3754. FRANCIS, Barbara. The status of women at Cornell. Ithaca,
       N.Y., Cornell University, 1970. 6p.
3755. FRED, E. B. Women and higher education: with special
       reference to the University of Wisconsin. Journal of
       experimental education, v. 31 (December 1962), 158-
       72.
3756. FREEMAN, Jo. The revolution is happening in our minds.
       College and university business, v. 48 (February
       1970), 63-9. Suggestions for changing hiring practices
       of women educators.
3757. _____. Women on the social science faculties since 1892.
       Washington, American Political Science Association,
       1969. 14p. A study of the position of women in the
       social science faculties at the University of Chicago.
3758. FRIDERICH, N. M. Access to education at all levels.
       American Academy of Political and Social Science,
       annals, v. 375 (January 1968), 133-44.
3759. GARBER, J. P. Should the sexes be educated together?
       Education, v. 23 (December 1902), 235-41.
3760. GARDNER, J. Sexist counseling must stop. Personnel and
       guidance journal, v. 49 (May 1971), 705-14.
3761. GILDERSLEEVE, Virginia C. Present dangers in the educa-
       tion of women. Teachers College record, v. 30 (No-
       vember 1928), 122-5.
3762. _____. Whither educated women? Association of Ameri-
       can Colleges, bulletin, v. 25 (May 1939), 258-67.
3763. GILL, L. D. Women in higher education. Religious educa-
       tion, v. 9 (June 1914), 272-8.
3764. GLASS, M. Are the secondary schools and colleges helping
       the young woman to find her place in the present so-
       cial order? Department of Secondary School Princi-
       ples, bulletin, v. 22 (May 1938), 15-21.
3765. GOALS of women in higher education. American Association
       of University Women, journal, v. 48 (March 1955),
       161-7.
3766. GODARD, J. M. War and the woman's college. Southern
       Association quarterly, v. 8 (February 1944), 154-6.
3767. GOODSELL, Willystine. Education of women: its social
       background and its problems. New York, Macmillan,
       1923. 378p.
3768. _____. Educational opportunities of American women--
       theoretical and actual. American Academy of Political
       and Social Science, annals, v. 143 (May 1929), 1-13.
3769. GORREN, Aline. Womanliness as a profession. Scribner's
       magazine, v. 15 (May 1894), 610-15. The possibility
       that higher education of women will do away with fem-
       inity.
3770. GRAHAM, Patricia Albjerg. Women in academe. Science,
       v. 169 (25 September 1970), 1284-90. Discussion:
       v. 170 (18 December 1970), 1258+. Past and present

academic employment of women in American colleges
and universities and suggestions for changes to improve
women's academic status.

3771. GREEN, E. Unequal woman. College management, v. 5
(August 1970), 2-3.

3772. GREENLEAF, W. J. Centennial of education for women.
School life, v. 18 (June 1933), 186-7.

3773. GRUCHOW, Nancy. Discrimination; women charge universities, colleges with bias. Science, v. 168 (1 May
1970), 559-61.

3774. GRUMBACH, Doris. Woman's place. Commonweal, v. 74
(28 April 1961), 119-21. Discussion: v. 74 (19 May
1961), 207-9.

3775. HABEIN, M. Problems in women's education. National Association of Deans of Women, journal, v. 13 (March
1950), 117-23.

3776. HACKETT, Alice Payne. Wellesley: Part of the American
story. New York, Dutton, 1949. 320p.

3777. HADLEY, Arthur T. The admission of women as graduate
students at Yale. Educational review, v. 3 (May 1892),
486-9.

3778. HAHN, L. B. United Nations Commission on the Status of
Women; statements. U.S. Department of State, bulletin, v. 36 (29 April 1957), 704-5.

3779. HARRIS, Ann Sutherland. Second sex in academe. AAUP
bulletin, v. 56 (September 1970), 283-95. Discussion:
v. 57 (March 1971), 137+. The distribution of women
in academic institutions suggests discriminatory attitudes and practices.

3780. HARVARD examinations for women. Old and new, v. 8
(1873), 371.

3781. HAWKINS, Ruth R. The odds against women. Change in
higher education, v. 1 (November/December 1969),
34-6. Discrimination against women in industry,
government and as educators in terms of salary,
prestige, and power.

3782. HEALY, Ann Kirtland. A lady--and one third scholar.
Educational forum, v. 27 (March 1963), 313-18.

3783. HELMES, Winifred. Woman power and higher education.
American Association of University Women, journal,
v. 51 (May 1958), 203-6. The large number of un-
employed women as a potential labor force in the future.

3784. HIGGINSON, Thomas Wentworth. Education of women. Atlantic monthly, v. 3 (1859), 137.

3785. _____. Higher education of women. Critic, v. 9 (1886),
273.

3786. _____. Women and the alphabet. New York, Houghton
Mifflin, 1900. 360p.

3787. HIGHER education for women in America. Leisure hour,
v. 39 (1890), 757.

3788. HIGHER education of women. Academy, v. 1 (1887), 297.

3789. HIGHER education of women. School and society, v. 86 (27

September 1958), 342-3. Statement by the Education Committee of the American Association of University Women.

3790. HIGHER education of woman in America. New England magazine, v. 2 (August 1890), 711-14.

3791. HOTTEL, Althea K. Changing status of women. National Association of Deans of Women, journal, v. 17 (January 1954), 62-7.

3792. _____. Social change and women's education. Association of American Colleges, bulletin, v. 39 (May 1953), 312-16.

3793. HOUGHTON, D. D. Women in higher education. Association of Governing Boards of State Universities and Allied Institutes, proceedings, (1949), 106-19.

3794. HOW Harvard rules women. Cambridge, Mass., New University Conference, 1970. 77p. On women's treatment in Harvard's professional schools, student wives, women employees, black women, etc.

3795. HOWE, Florence. The education of women. Liberation, v. 14 (August/September 1969), 49-55.

3796. HOYLE, J. Who shall be principal: a man or a woman? National elementary principal, v. 48 (January 1969), 23-4.

3797. HUTCHINSON, Emilie Josephine. Women and the PhD; facts from the experiences of 1025 women who have taken the degree of doctor of philosophy since 1877. Greensboro, N.C., North Carolina College for Women, 1930. 212p.

3798. IF your daughter wants to go to college. U.S. news and world report, v. 58 (24 May 1965), 54-5. On whether coeducational colleges discriminate against women.

3799. INTERNATIONAL Conference on Public Education, 1952. Access of women to education. New York, Columbia University Press, 1952. 207p.

3800. INTERNATIONAL Council of Women. Report of the International Council of Women, assembled by the National Woman Suffrage Association, Washington, D.C., United States of America, March 25 to April 1, 1888. Washington, R. H. Darby, printer, 1888. 471p.

3801. IS woman ruining the country? Influence of women teachers. Literary digest, v. 102 (September 1928), 24.

3802. ITASCA Conference on the Continuing Education of Women, Itasca State Park, Minnesota, 1962. Education and a woman's life; proceedings. Washington, American Council on Education, 1963. 153p.

3803. JACOBI, Mary Putnam. Higher education of women. Science, v. 18 (27 November 1891), 245-6.

3804. JONES, David D. War and the higher education of Negro women. Journal of Negro education, v. 11 (July 1942), 329-37.

3805. JORDAN, D. S. Higher education of women. Popular science, v. 62 (December 1902), 97-107.

3806. JORDAN, Mary A. The college for women. Atlantic month-

ly, v. 70 (October 1892), 540-6.
3807. KAHN, R. W. Education of women. Education, v. 12 (1892), 20.
3808. KANSAS. University. Associated Women Students. Commission on the Status of Women, 1969-70. Reports. Lawrence, 1970. 30p. A study of female students and faculty members in seven normally male-dominated schools in Kansas University.
3809. KAUFMAN, Helen M. The status of women in administration in selected institutions of higher education in the United States. 199p. PhD thesis, New York University, 1961. A study showing that gender is a major factor in the making of administrative appointments, that few women hold administrative positions, and other important factors.
3810. KEEZER, D. M. Where are the able woman teachers? American Association of University Women, journal, v. 31 (April 1938), 149-51.
3811. KELLEY, F. Higher education of women in the universities. International review, v. 14 (1883), 130.
3812. KERR, M. What should college do for women? Woman's journal, v. 15 (November 1930), 24+.
3813. KINGSBURY, Susan M. Study of the economic status of university women. American Association of University Women, journal, v. 32 (June 1939), 224-8. Results of a questionnaire of about 10,000 AAUW members, concerning their employment, discrimination, earnings, and their responsibility for dependents.
3814. KIRKPATRICK, Wynona Jeanneret. The emerging role of women in institutions of higher education in the United States. 214p. PhD thesis, University of Arkansas, 1965. Historical study of women's growing opportunities for education.
3815. KITTRELL, F. P. Current problems and programs in the higher education of Negro women. Quarterly review of higher education among Negroes, v. 12 (January 1944), 13-15.
3816. KLUCKHOHN, Florence Rockwood. What education for women? Women in America, by Florence Kluckhohn; Another look at women's education, by Bancroft Beatley. Urbana, n.p., 1950. 31p.
3817. KOMAROVSKY, Mirra. Measuring the yardsticks. American Association of University Women, journal, v. 41 (June 1948), 209-11.
3818. _____. What should colleges teach women? Harper's magazine, v. 199 (November 1949), 33-7.
3819. _____. Women and education. Independent woman, v. 27 (July 1948), 196-7.
3820. _____. Women in the modern world: their education and their dilemmas. Boston, Little, Brown, 1953. 319p.
3821. LAMPHERE, Louise. Report of the AAUP Committee on the Employment and Status of Women Faculty and Women Graduates at Brown. Providence, R.I., 1970. 22p.

3822. LANDER, E. T. University education of women. Education,
       v. 1 (1881), 48.
3823. LANGE, Alexis F. Problem of the professional training for
       women. School and society, v. 3 (1 April 1916),
       480-5. The need for educating women to work outside
       the home as well.
3824. LANSING, Marion Florence. Seventy-five years of higher
       education for women. Outlook, v. 102 (19 October
       1912), 360-5. Concerning the celebration of the 75th
       anniversary of the founding of Mount Holyoke College.
3825. LA SORTE, M. A. Academic women's salaries: equal pay
       for equal work? Journal of higher education, v. 42
       (April 1971), 265-78.
3826. LATHROP, Virginia Terrell. Educate a woman. Chapel
       Hill, University of North Carolina Press, 1942.
3827. LAUGHLIN, Clara E. Better schooling and higher wages.
       Pearson's magazine, v. 28 (July 1912), 58-66.
3828. LAYTON, Elizabeth Nelson. Significant dates in the early
       history of institutions for the higher education of wom-
       en in the United States. Washington, U.S. Office of
       Education, 1948. 12p.
3829. LEGGETT, G. Female in academe: a partial and non-
       statistical view. AAUP bulletin, v. 49 (September
       1963), 237-9. Women as educators.
3830. LEONARD, E. A. Aims of higher education for women in
       the United States. School and society, v. 58 (16 Oc-
       tober 1943), 295-8.
3831. LEOPOLD, Alice K. The challenge of tomorrow: woman-
       power. Vital speeches, v. 24 (15 May 1958), 478-80.
3832. LEVER, Janet and Pepper Schwartz. Women at Yale; liber-
       ating a college campus. Indianapolis, Bobbs-Merrill,
       1971. 274p.
3833. LEWIS, E. C. Choice and conflict for the college woman.
       National Association of Women Deans and Counselors,
       v. 32 (Summer 1969), 176-82.
3834. LEWIS, N. D. American women and higher education.
       Southern university conference proceedings, (1958),
       64-71.
3835. _____. College women and their proper spheres. Amer-
       ican Association of University Women, journal, v. 47
       (May 1954), 207-12.
3836. LIBERATING academe. Saturday review, v. 54 (20 March
       1971), 48.
3837. LIKERT, Jane G., ed. Conversations with returning women
       students. Ann Arbor, University of Michigan, Center
       for Continuing Education for Women, 1967. 55p.
       Conversations with women and their continuing educa-
       tion problems concerning attitudes of husbands, facul-
       ty, discrimination and ways of managing at home,
       school, and at work.
3838. LIPMAN, Aaron. Educational preparation for the female
       role. Journal of educational sociology, v. 33 (Sep-
       tember 1959), 40-3.

3839. LIPSCOMB, A. A. Education of women in America. Harper's magazine, v. 15 (1857), 776.
3840. LITTLE, C. C. Women and higher education. Scribner's magazine, v. 86 (August 1929), 146-50.
3841. LIVERMORE, Mary Ashton Rice. What shall we do with our daughters? Superfluous women, and other lectures. Boston, Lee and Shepard, 1883. 208p.
3842. LOUTTIT, C. M. and M. L. Marksberry. Attitudes of women on higher education. Educational administration and supervision, v. 37 (November 1951), 385-95.
3843. LUDEMAN, W. W. Declining female college attendance: causes and implications. Educational forum, v. 25 (May 1961), 505-7.
3844. LUTZ, Alma. Women need education, too. Christian Science Monitor weekly magazine, (20 July 1946), 3.
3845. LYON, Rhee. Married women and the academic tradition. Journal of higher education, v. 35 (May 1964), 251-5.
3846. MCAFEE, Mildred H. Segregation and the women's colleges. American journal of Sociology, v. 43 (July 1937), 16-22. Development of women's higher education from around 1837.
3847. _____. War and the higher education of women. Journal of Negro education, v. 11 (July 1942), 262-6.
3848. _____. Woman's place then and now. Association of American Colleges, bulletin, v. 23 (November 1937), 376-83. Higher education of women.
3849. MCBRIDE, Katharine E. What is women's education? American Academy of Political and Social Science, annals, v. 251 (May 1947), 143-52.
3850. MCBRYDE, John M., Jr. Womanly education for woman. Sewanee review, v. 15 (October 1907), 467-84. On whether courses for women should differ from men's courses.
3851. MCCAIN, J. R. Colleges for women in the Southeast, a hundred years of higher education for women, progress and problems. American Association of University Women, journal, v. 30 (October 1936), 7-10.
3852. MCCORD, D. Radcliffe and education for women. New York Times magazine, (5 December 1954), 26-7+ .
3853. MCDONALD, Ellen E. Educated women: the last minority? Columbia University forum, v. 10 (Summer 1967), 30-4.
3854. MCGAUGHEY, J. R. Equal pay for equal work? American school board journal, v. 82 (February 1931), 60.
3855. MCGINLEY, P. Why educate women? excerpts from Profession: housewife. Ladies home journal, v. 79 (October 1962), 36+ .
3856. MCGUIGAN, Dorothy Gies. A dangerous experiment; 100 years of women at the University of Michigan. Ann Arbor, Center for Continuing Education of Women, 1970. 136p.
3857. MCHALE, K. Education for women. Journal of higher education, v. 6 (December 1935), 459-68. On colleges

for women.
3858. _____. Higher education for women today; with discus-
            sion. Association of American Colleges, bulletin,
            v. 22 (March 1936), 113-19. On colleges for women.
3859. MACKINTOSH, May. Women as professional teachers. Ed-
            ucation, v. 7 (1887), 556.
3860. MACLAER, Martha. The history of the education of girls
            in New York and in New England, 1800-1870. Wash-
            ington, Howard University Press, 1926. 123p.
3861. MCLEOD, B. Don't call it women's work. Education, v. 87
            (January 1967), 301-2. Women as educators.
3862. MALKIEL, M. R. Lida de. Free opportunity for intellectual
            pursuits. American Association of University Women,
            journal, v. 52 (October 1958), 5-8.
3863. MARBURY, E. Education of women. Education, v. 8 (1888),
            235.
3864. MARKLE, A. L. Education of women. Arena, v. 24 (1900),
            206.
3865. MARKLEY, Mary E. Some chapters on the history of higher
            education for Lutheran women. Lutheran quarterly,
            v. 53 (January 1923), 1-54.
3866. MARKSBERRY, M. L. and C. M. Louttit. University wom-
            en's opinion on their education. Urbana, University
            of Illinois Press, 1951.
3867. MARSH, G. P. Education of women. Nation, v. 3 (1866),
            165.
3868. MARTIN, G. H. Early education of girls in Massachusetts.
            Education, v. 20 (1900), 323.
3869. MARTIN, Gertrude S. The education of women and sex
            equality. American Academy of Political and Social
            Science, annals, v. 56 (November 1914), 38-46.
3870. MAYO, Amory Dwight. Southern women in the recent edu-
            cational movement in the South. Washington, GPO,
            1892.
3871. MEAD, Margaret. Is college wasted on women? Redbook,
            v. 118 (January 1962), 6.
3872. MENDENHALL, Thomas C. Women's education and the edu-
            cated woman. School and society, v. 88 (19 November
            1960), 436-9.
3873. MEYER, Annie Nathan. Higher education for women in New
            York City. Nation, v. 46 (1888), 68-9.
3874. MILANOVICH, A. Gentlemen before ladies? Women teach-
            ers aspiring to elementary principalships are being
            discriminated against. New York State education,
            v. 54 (December 1966), 18-19.
3875. MILLER, M. M. Women in university teaching. American
            Association of University Women, journal, v. 54
            (March 1961), 152-4.
3876. MINTURN, Leigh. Inequities in salary payments to faculty
            women. Memorandum. Boulder, University of Colo-
            rado, 1970. 6p. Inequities at the University of
            Colorado.
3877. MITCHELL, M. Collegiate education of women. Education,

v. 1 (1881), 433.
3878. MONCURE, J. C. Vassar's seventy-fifth anniversary.
American Association of University Women, journal,
v. 34 (October 1940), 35.
3879. MOORE, Bernice Milburn. Mothers, homemakers, and wage
earners. National Education Association journal, v.
54 (May 1965), 22-3.
3880. MORGAN, A. F. New look for the old-fashioned liberal education of women. American Association of University
Professors, bulletin, v. 39 (June 1953), 259-63.
3881. MORRISS, M. S. What next in women's education? Association of American Colleges, bulletin, v. 30 (March
1944), 111-17.
3882. MUELLER, Kate Hevner. Educating women for a changing
world. Minneapolis, University of Minnesota Press,
1954. 302p.
3883. _____. Sex differences in campus regulations. Personnel and guidance journal, v. 32 (May 1954), 528-32.
3884. _____. Women's education, for what? American Association of University Women, journal, v. 48 (March
1955), 136-40.
3885. MULLANE, M. K. Changing patterns in education of women.
American Medical Women's Association, journal, v. 20
(October 1965), 962-4.
3886. MULLER, L. C. and O. G. Muller. New horizons for college women. Washington, Public Affairs Press, 1960.
3887. NAPIER, T. H. Function of the college for women. Southern Association quarterly, v. 5 (August 1941), 342-5.
3888. NATIONAL Organization for Women, Fullerton, California,
North Orange County Chapter. A report on the status
of women at the California State College at Fullerton.
By Virginia Bratfisch and others. Fullerton, 1970.
18p.
3889. NEILSON, W. A. Should women be educated like men?
Forum, v. 81 (February 1929), 102-5.
3890. NEUMAN, R. R. When will the educational needs of women
be met? Journal of counseling psychology, v. 10
(Winter 1963), 378-83.
3891. NEWCOMER, Mabel. A century of higher education for
American women. New York, Harper, 1959. 266p.
3892. _____. Women's education: facts, findings, and apparent
trends. National Association of Women Deans and
Counselors, journal, v. 24 (October 1960), 35-40.
3893. NICOLSON, Marjorie. Rights and privileges pertaining
thereto. American Association of University Women,
journal, v. 31 (April 1938), 135-42. On the education
of women and women as educators.
3894. NIMKOFF, Meyer F. and Arthur L. Wood. Women's place
academically; the share of administrative and academic
leadership assigned to women in women's colleges.
Journal of higher education, v. 20 (January 1949),
28-36.
3895. NOBLE, Jeanne L. The Negro woman's college education.

New York, Teacher's College, Columbia University,
1956. 163p. An analysis of a survey of a "group of
Negro women who are college graduates," with an interpretation of the results "in the light of a historical
and philosophical review of higher education for Negro
women" since 1857.
3896. _____. Negro women today and their education. Journal
of Negro education, v. 26, no. 1 (1957), 86-91.
3897. NON humilis mulier triumpho. Time, v. 95 (29 June 1970),
45. Commencement address given by female student
at Harvard University demanding equal rights for wom-
en, especially in education.
3898. OLTMAN, Ruth M. Campus 1970-where do women stand?
AAUW journal, v. 64 (November 1970), 14-15.
3899. ON campus; women's lib. Madamoiselle, v. 71 (August
1970), 104. Reports on the status of women's liberation on a number of college campuses.
3900. PALMER, A. E. Review of the higher education of women.
Forum, v. 12 (September 1891), 28-40.
3901. PARK, R. Women's higher education. School and society,
v. 94 (22 January 1966), 35-9.
3902. PARRISH, Celestia S. Shall the higher education of women
be the same as that of men? Educational review, v.
22 (November 1901), 383-96. Comments and opinions
on a speech by M. Carey Thomas, president of Bryn
Mawr College, in: Educational review, v. 21 (January
1901), 1-10.
3903. PARRISH, John B. Coming crisis in women's higher education and work. AAUW journal, v. 64 (November
1970), 17-19.
3904. _____. Top level training of women in the United States,
1900-1960. National Association of Women Deans and
Counselors, journal, v. 25 (January 1962), 67-73.
Survey of doctorate training for selected disciplines.
3905. _____. Women in top level teaching and research. AAUW
journal, v. 55 (January 1962), 99-103+. A study of
the distribution of women (by rank, type of school, and
by discipline) in 20 leading colleges and universities,
showing that women occupy lower ranks and salaries
in these institutions.
3906. PATTERSON, J. S. Education and enfranchisement of
women. Radical, v. 7 (1870), 169, 287.
3907. PENDLETON, E. F. Wider-open gates to colleges. Journal of education, v. 83 (25 May 1916), 564-5.
3908. PERRY, J. B. Education of women. Critic, v. 30 (1897),
137.
3909. PETERS, David W. The status of the married woman teacher. New York, Teachers College, Columbia University Press, 1934.
3910. PHELPS, S. J. What should a state do in the education of
its women? High school quarterly, v. 23 (January
1935), 97-100.
3911. PHILLIPS, F. L. Changed status of women. Education,

v. 87 (December 1966), 246-7.

3912. PITTSBURGH. University. Advisory Council on Women's
Opportunities. Progress report to the chancellor.
Pittsburgh, 1970. 14p. Recommendations concerning
doing away with sex discrimination at Pittsburgh University.

3913. _____. _____. University Committee for Women's
Rights. Discrimination against women at the University of Pittsburgh. Pittsburgh, 1970. 71p.

3914. POLICIES and practices should reflect college commitment
to equality. College and university business, v. 48
(February 1970), 79-83. Nine recommendations to
eliminate discrimination in higher education for women.

3915. POLLARD, Lucille Addison. Women on college and university faculties; a historical survey and a study of their
present academic status. 346p. PhD thesis, University of Georgia, 1965. Covers the period 1835 to the
present.

3916. POPE, Ruth Vesta. Factors affecting the elimination of
women students from selected coeducational colleges of
liberal arts. New York, Teachers College, Columbia
University, 1931. 110p.

3917. PORTER, D. G. Collegiate education of women. Christian
quarterly, v. 5 (1873), 433.

3918. POUND, L. Graduate work for women. School and society,
v. 15 (27 May 1922), 573-8.

3919. POWERS, M. F. End discrimination to hold onto federal
funding; University of Pittsburgh. College management,
v. 6 (May 1971), 24-6.

3920. PRELIMINARY report on the status of women at Harvard.
Cambridge, Mass., Harvard University, 1970. 16p.

3921. PROGRAMS, problems and needs in women's continuing education; Proceedings of a statewide conference for institutions of higher education, community and government representatives, Seattle, Washington, November
8, 1968. Seattle, University of Washington, Office of
Women's Continuing Education, 1968. 70p.

3922. PUNKE, Harold H. Sex and equal opportunity in higher education. National Association of Secondary School
Principals, bulletin, v. 45 (November 1961), 121-8.

3923. RADCLIFFE College. Committee on Graduate Education for
Women. Graduate education for women; the Radcliffe
PhD; a report. Cambridge, Mass., Harvard University Press, 1956. 135p.

3924. RAND, E. A. Education of women at Harvard College.
Education, v. 2 (1882), 415.

3925. RANDOLPH, A. Is the American girl being miseducated?
Ladies home journal, v. 27 (1 September 1910), 9.

3926. RAUSHENBUSCH, Esther. Unfinished business: continuing
education for women. Educational record, v. 42 (October 1961), 261-9.

3927. REED, H. L. Women students at Chicago University. Outlook, v. 50 (7 July 1894), 19-20.

3928. REID, Marion. Woman, her education and influence. New
       York, Fowler & Wells, 1852. 192p.
3929. REINHARDT, A. H. Education of the women of the United
       States. National Education Association, proceedings
       and addresses, (1921), 65-74.
3930. RELLER, T. L. Women as members of boards of education.
       American school board journal, v. 88 (April 1934),
       25-6+.
3931. RICHARDSON, Eudora Ramsay. The case of the women's
       colleges in the South. South Atlantic quarterly, v. 29
       (April 1930), 126-39. The difference in the size of
       endowments given to men's and women's colleges since
       1772.
3932. RICHMOND, Winifred. Present practices and tendencies in
       the secondary education of girls. Pedagogical semi-
       nary, v. 23 (June 1916), 184-98.
3933. RIDER, Linda. Emancipation of the woman teacher. Educa-
       tion, v. 39 (September 1918), 46-54. The question of
       equal salary and all-male boards of education.
3934. RIESMAN, David. Some dilemmas of women's education.
       Educational record, v. 46 (Fall 1965), 424-34.
3935. _____. Women: their orbits and their education. Amer-
       ican Association of University Women, journal, v. 51
       (January 1958), 77-81.
3936. ROBINSON, Frederick B. Women as prospective college
       presidents. School and society, v. 30 (24 August
       1929), 245-52.
3937. ROBINSON, Lora H. The status of academic women. Wash-
       ington, ERIC Clearinghouse on Higher Education, 1971.
       30p.
3938. ROSSI, Alice S. Discrimination and demography restrict op-
       portunities for academic women. College and univer-
       sity business, v. 48 (February 1970), 74-8. The sta-
       tus of women faculty in academic institutions from
       1940 to the present, with future trends.
3939. RUDMAN, H. C., ed. Woman principal: going the way of
       the buffalo? symposium. National elementary princi-
       pal, v. 45 (April 1966), 6-11.
3940. RUETHER, R. Are women's colleges obsolete? Critic,
       v. 27 (October/November 1968), 58-64. Discrimina-
       tion in Catholic women's colleges.
3941. RYDER, S. Room at the top; for whom? Changing educa-
       tion, v. 4 (Fall 1969), 25.
3942. SACK, Saul. The higher education of women in Pennsylvania.
       Pennsylvania magazine of history and biography, v. 83
       (January 1959), 29-73.
3943. SANDLER, Bernice. Sex discrimination at the University of
       Maryland. Washington, Women's Equity Action League,
       1969. 12p.
3944. SANFORD, Nevitt. Is college education wasted on women?
       Ladies home journal, v. 74 (May 1957), 78-9+.
3945. SAYERS, Joseph. Woman's rights: or, A treatise on the
       inalienable rights of woman, carefully investigated, and

inscribed to the female community of the United
States of America. Cincinnati, Applegate, 1856. 72p.
3946. SCHINDLER, S. Flaw in our public school system; preponderance of women teachers. Arena, v. 6 (June
1892), 59-63.
3947. SCOTT, Anne Firor. The half-eaten apple: A look at sex
discrimination in the University. Buffalo, New York
State University, 1970. 26p. Identifies problem
areas at SUNY-Buffalo.
3948. SEDGWICK, A. G. Education of women. Nation, v. 36
(1883), 118.
3949. SENDERS, Virginia L. Minnesota plan for women's continuing education: a progress report. Educational
record, v. 42 (October 1961), 270-8.
3950. SERGEANT, E. S. Educated for what? New republic,
v. 5 (1 January 1916), 219-20.
3951. SETON, W. Higher education of women and posterity.
Catholic world, v. 73 (1901), 147.
3952. SEX discrimination in higher education: constitutional
equality for women? Journal of family law, v. 10
(1971), 327+.
3953. SHEPHERD, J. Is someone kidding the college girl? Cre-
ating in college, then typing in a New York office.
Look, v. 30 (11 January 1966), 36-8.
3954. SHIEBLER, H. A. Do high schools neglect the girls?
Changing times, v. 8 (January 1954), 21-2.
3955. SHINN, M. W. Women as school-directors. Overland
monthly, n.s., v. 8 (1886), 628.
3956. _____. Women on school boards. Overland monthly,
n.s., v. 12 (1888), 547.
3957. SHORTCOMINGS in the education of women. Critic, v. 31
(21 August 1897), 97-8.
3958. SHORTRIDGE, Kathleen. Women as university nigger; How
the 'U' keeps females in their place; or, How a young
female student sought sexual justice at the 'U' and
couldn't find it anywhere. Pittsburgh, Know, Inc.,
1970. 5p. Discrimination at the University of Michigan.
3959. SIMON, Rita James. Of nepotism, marriage, and the pur-
suit of an academic career. Sociology of education,
v. 39 (Fall 1966), 344-58.
3960. _____. The woman PhD: a recent profile. Social
problems, v. 15 (Fall 1967), 221-36. Covers the
period 1958 to 1963.
3961. SIMPSON, Lawrence A. A myth is better than a miss:
Men get the edge in academic employment. College
and university business, v. 48 (February 1970), 72-3.
3962. _____. A study of employing agents' attitudes toward
academic women in higher education. 150p. PhD
thesis, Pennsylvania State University, 1968. Findings
of a study which show discrimination towards women on
the part of employing agents (i.e., deans, depart-
mental chairmen, and total faculty).

3963. SINCLAIR, M. E. Centennial in college education for wom-
          en. American Association of University Women,
          journal, v. 31 (October 1937), 36-8.
3964. SMITH, Charles Foster. The higher education of women in
          the South. Educational review, v. 8 (October 1894),
          287-90.
3965. SMITH, L. J. College education is for women, too! Jour-
          nal of home economics, v. 50 (June 1958), 436.
3966. SMITH, M. C. Education of women at Harvard College.
          Education, v. 6 (1886), 568.
3967. SMITH, M. Leonita. Catholic viewpoints about the psycholo-
          gy, social role, and higher education of women. 227p.
          PhD thesis, Ohio State University, 1961. A study
          showing that Catholic educators believe that women
          are different physically and psychologically from men
          and that their education should reflect these differences.
3968. SMITH, M. R. Recent tendencies in the education of wom-
          en. Popular science, v. 48 (November 1895), 27-33.
3969. SPICE and sympathy: women students and staff. Harvard
          Law School bulletin, v. 21 (June 1970), 14.
3970. SPIEGLER, C. G. Are our girls getting boys' education?
          New York Times magazine, (14 May 1950), 29+.
3971. STATUS of women in college and university faculties.
          School and society, v. 21 (3 January 1925), 16-17.
3972. STEINMETZ, K. E. Women administrators in higher edu-
          cation. NEA journal, v. 41 (September 1952), 342.
3973. STEPHENS, K. Higher education of women. Forum, v. 7
          (1889), 41.
3974. STODDARD, George Dinsmore. On the education of women.
          New York, Macmillan, 1950. 101p.
3975. STRACHAN, Grace C. Equal pay for equal work; the story
          of the struggle for justice being made by the women
          teachers of the city of New York. New York, B. F.
          Buck, 1910. 570p.
3976. STRAINCHAMPS, Ethel. Plight of the intellectual girl.
          Saturday review, v. 43 (19 November 1960), 63-4+.
          Criticism of stifling a girl's intellectual efforts in high
          school and molding her into the typically stereotyped
          female.
3977. SUGGESTIONS on the education of women. American journal
          of education, v. 13 (1863), 495.
3978. TALBOT, M. Looking backward--and forward--in AAUW.
          American Association of University Women, journal,
          v. 30 (June 1937), 207-11.
3979. _____. Women in the university world; the story of a
          century's progress. American Association of Univer-
          sity Women, journal, v. 32 (June 1939), 203-14.
3980. TALBOT, Marion. Present-day problems in the education
          of women. Educational review, v. 14 (October 1897),
          248-58. The problem of different courses and dif-
          ferent methods of teaching women as opposed to men's
          instruction, as well as a lack of intellectual freedom
          for women.

3981. TAYLOR, H. Are women's colleges obsolete? New York
       Times magazine, (7 September 1958), 24+.
3982. TAYLOR, James Monroe. Before Vassar opened; a con-
       tribution to the history of the higher education of
       women in America. Boston, Houghton Mifflin, 1914.
       287p.
3983. _____. College education for girls in America. Educa-
       tional review, v. 44 (October-November 1912), 217-33,
       325-47. A study of the movement for the higher edu-
       cation of women prior to the opening of Vassar College
       in 1865.
3984. _____. Education of women. World's work, v. 6 (August
       1903), 3751-3.
3985. TEAD, Ordway. Women's higher education: past, present,
       and future. Harvard educational review, v. 17 (Sum-
       mer 1947), 151-61.
3986. TEMPLIN, Lucinda. Some defects and merits in the higher
       education of women in Missouri. Columbia, University
       of Missouri Press, 1927. 32p.
3987. TETLOW, John. Colleges for the education of women in the
       eastern states. Education, v. 1 (1881), 465.
3988. _____. The education of women for the learned profes-
       sions. Educational review, v. 11 (February 1896),
       105-25. Preparation of women before higher educa-
       tion, for professions such as law, medicine, and the
       ministry.
3989. THOMAS, M. Carey. Present tendencies in women's college
       and university education. Educational review, v. 35
       (January 1908), 64-85.
3990. _____. Should the higher education of women differ from
       that of men? Educational review, v. 21 (January
       1901), 1-10. A speech by the president of Bryn
       Mawr College.
3991. THOMPSON, E. W. Education for ladies, 1830-1860. New
       York, King's Crown Press, 1947.
3992. THWING, C. F. College education of young women. Public
       opinion, v. 16 (1894), 9.
3993. _____. Recent movements in the education of women.
       Harper's magazine, v. 62 (1881), 101.
3994. _____. Should woman's education differ from man's?
       Forum, v. 30 (February 1901), 728-36.
3995. TOMPKINS, Pauline. Change and challenge for the educated
       woman. Saturday review, v. 46 (18 May 1963), 69-
       70+. The necessity for higher education to take into
       account the problems women will have: e.g., difficul-
       ties in being hired and the problem of role expecta-
       tions.
3996. TRENT, W. P. Reflections on the education of women--and
       men. Columbia University quarterly, v. 12 (March
       1910), 195-9.
3997. TRUAX, Anne. Research on the status of faculty women,
       University of Minnesota. Minneapolis, University of
       Minnesota, Office for Student Affairs, 1970. 15p. A

comparison of ratio of male/female faculty, mean and
median salary, and percentage differentials by rank,
college, and term.
3998. TWEEDY, A. B. Higher education of women. Is it opposed
to motherhood? Popular science, v. 36 (1890), 751.
3999. TYLER, Dorothy. Higher education of women. Washington,
American Association of University Women, 1942. 45p.
4000. UNITED Nations. Economic and Social Council. Access of
women to the teaching profession. New York, 1961.
4001. U.S. Department of the Interior. The legal status of married women teachers. By Ward W. Keesecker.
Washington, GPO, 1934. 22p.
4002. U.S. President's Commission on the Status of Women. Report of the Committee on Education. Washington, GPO,
1963. 71p. A discussion and recommendations for
women in elementary, secondary, and college education, research on the education of women.
4003. U.S. Women's Bureau. Trends in educational attainment
of women, 1965-1969. Washington, GPO, 1965-69.
5v.
4004. UNIVERSITY education for women. Review of reviews, v. 6
(August 1892), 48-50.
4005. USEEM, R. H. Who needs women? National Association of
Women Deans and Counselors, journal, v. 24 (June
1961), 171-8.
4006. VAN DE WARKER, E. Is the education of women with men
a failure? Harper's weekly, v. 48 (20 August 1904),
1288-9.
4007. VAN HISE, C. R. Educational tendencies in state universities. Educational review, v. 34 (December 1907),
504-20.
4008. VAN KLEECK, Mary. Social challenge to university women.
American Association of University Women, journal,
v. 29 (January 1936), 67-72.
4009. VAN RENSSELAER, M. G. Waste of women's intellectual
force. Forum, v. 13 (July 1892), 616-28.
4010. VASSAR: the kind of education girls get. Business week,
(26 May 1956), 92-4+.
4011. VON RAUMER, K. Education of women. American journal
of education, v. 10 (1861), 227.
4012. WARREN, C. For what are we educating women? National
Association of Deans of Women, journal, v. 7 (June
1944), 152-6.
4013. WASHINGTON. University. Associated Students. Women's
Commission. Report on the status of women at the
University of Washington; Part 1: Faculty and staff.
Seattle, 1970. 48p.
4014. WASSERMAN, Elga R. Coeducation comes to Yale College.
Educational record, v. 51 (Spring 1970), 143-7.
4015. WAYNE State University. College of Education. Counselor
bias and the female occupational role. By John J.
Pietrofesa and Nancy K. Schlossberg. Detroit, 1970.
13p. The theory that counselors are biased against

women seeking a "male" occupation.

4016. WELCH, W. H. Contribution of Bryn Mawr College to the
        higher education of women. Science, v. 56 (7 July
        1922), 1-8.

4017. WELLS, D. C. Higher education of women. American
        Sociological Society, proceedings and publications,
        v. 3 (1908), 115-23.

4018. WELLS, K. G. Education of women. National magazine,
        v. 10 (1899), 268.

4019. WHEELER, E. F. Colleges for the higher education of
        women. Critic, v. 15 (1889), 89.

4020. WHITE, Lynn T. The changing context of women's educa-
        tion. Marriage and family living, v. 17 (November
        1955), 291-5.

4021. _____. Educating our daughters; a challenge to the col-
        lege. New York, Harper, 1950. 166p.

4022. _____. Educating women in a man's world. Atlantic
        monthly, v. 185 (February 1950), 52-5. The need to
        develop a "distinctively feminine higher education" in
        order for women to see themselves as men's equals.

4023. _____. New yardsticks for women's education. American
        Association of University Women, journal, v. 41 (Octo-
        ber 1947), 1-7. The necessity for women to stop
        using men's values and points of view as a "yardstick"
        by which to measure themselves.

4024. WILCOX, Thomas. The lot of the woman: A report on the
        National Survey of Undergraduate English Programs.
        Association of Departments of English, bulletin, no.
        25 (May 1970), 53-9. Women as educators.

4025. WILSON, Pauline Park. College women who express futility;
        a study based on 50 selected life histories of women
        college graduates. New York, Columbia University
        Press, 1950. 166p.

4026. WINSTON, M. E. Education of women. Christian education,
        v. 28 (June 1945), 229-32.

4027. WOLFE, W. Beran. Why educate women? Forum, v. 81
        (March 1929), 165-8.

4028. WOMEN are losing out; the race for executive jobs. Michigan
        education journal, v. 42 (April 1965), 23.

4029. WOMEN as school directors in New York City. Science,
        v. 8 (1886), 470.

4030. WOMEN on campus: 1970; a symposium. Ann Arbor, Mich.,
        University of Michigan, Center for Continuing Educa-
        tion of Women, [1970?]. 65p. Partial contents:
        Barriers to women; the woman graduate student; the
        black women; the university and women; women at the
        University of Michigan.

4031. WOMEN profs fight back; discrimination against women.
        Newsweek, v. 77 (17 May 1971), 99-100+ .

4032. WOMEN'S studies; up and away from stereotypes? Nations
        schools, v. 86 (November 1970), 42+ .

4033. WOOD, J. M. Woman's right to a right education. Progres-
        sive education, v. 16 (January 1939), 44-50.

4034. WOODHOUSE, Chase Going.   Education of women as persons.
       National Association of Deans of Women, journal,
       v. 7 (June 1944), 157-9.
4035. WOODRING, Paul.   Sexism on the campus.   Saturday review,
       v. 53 (16 May 1970), 80+.   Women's rights in teach-
       ing and administrative positions.
4036. WOODWARD, Mary V.   Woman's education in the South.
       Educational review, v. 7 (May 1894), 466-78.   Prob-
       lems of the higher education of southern women due
       in part to the "ideal" objective of women: marriage.
4037. WOODY, Thomas.   A history of women's education in the
       United States.   New York, Science Press, 1929.   2v.
       Reprinted by Octagon Press, New York, 1966.
4038. WOOLLEY, M. E.   Educational problems in the colleges for
       women.   Education, v. 38 (May 1918), 650-4.
4039. _____. Values of college training for women.   Harper's
       bazaar, v. 38 (September 1904), 835-8.
4040. WOOLSON, A. G.   Work and wages of women in education.
       Granite monthly, v. 3 (1880), 11.
4041. WORTHINGTON, Daisy Lee.   Higher education of women.
       Educational review, v. 32 (November 1906), 405-14.
       Refutation of arguments that higher education for wom-
       en should be different from men's.
4042. WOTRING, Clayton Warren.   The legal status of married
       women teachers in the public schools of the United
       States as determined by judicial decisions and legal
       opinions.   PhD thesis, New York University, 1932.
       Covers from 1778 to 1932.
4043. WRIGHT, T. F.   Collegiate education of women.   New church
       review, v. 7 (1900), 112.
4044. YUDELSON, S.   Education and professional activities of
       women.   American Academy of Political and Social
       Science, annals, v. 25 (January 1905), 117-23.
4045. ZAPOLEON, Marguerite Wykoff.   Education and employment
       opportunities for women.   American Academy of Po-
       litical and Social Science, annals, v. 251 (May 1947),
       165-73.
4046. ZELLIOT, E. A.   Should collegiate schools of business give
       greater recognition to training for women's occupations?
       National business education quarterly, v. 5 (October
       1936), 19-20.
4047. ZWERDLING, D.   Womanpower problem: sex discrimination
       on campus.   New republic, v. 164 (20 March 1971),
       11-13.

RELIGION

4048. ACHTEMEIER, Elizabeth Rice. The feminine crisis in Christian faith. New York, Abingdon, 1965. 160p.

4049. ALTHOUSE, LaVonne. Ordain women? The woman's pulpit, v. 46 (July-September 1967), 4-5+.

4050. ANDERSON, Evelyn McCullough. It's a woman's privilege. Grand Rapids, Mich., Baker, 1970. 188p.

4051. ASHBROOK, J. B. The church as a matriarchy. Pastoral Psychology, v. 14 (Spring 1963), 38-49.

4052. BAROT, Madeleine. Cooperation between men and women in church, family, and society. New York, World Council of Churches, 1964.

4053. BEATON, Catherine. Does the church discriminate against women on the basis of their sex? Critic, v. 24 (June-July 1966), 20-7.

4054. BELL, B. I. Woman and religion. Atlantic monthly, v. 117 (March 1916), 378-82.

4055. BIBLE on women's public speaking. Louisville, Ky., Baptist Book Concern, 1895. 32p.

4056. BIG event at Wheeling; interim report from a special committee appointed to study the role of women in the ministry. Christian century, v. 83 (14 December 1966), 1529.

4057. BLISS, Kathleen. The service and status of women in the churches. Chicago, Allenson, 1952. 208p.

4058. BOCK, E. Wilbur. The female clergy: A case of professional marginality. American journal of Sociology, v. 72 (March 1967), 531-39. Shows little success on the part of female clergy.

4059. BOTTOME, Margaret. Women in the church. Homiletic and pastoral review, v. 21 (1891), 505-14.

4060. BOYER, C. Women and the altar. Unitas, v. 17 (Fall 1965), 227-30.

4061. BREAKTHROUGH for the woman minister. Christian century, v. 74 (23 January 1957), 100. Discussion: v. 74 (6 March 1957), 301.

4062. BREWER, Earl D. C. A study of employment of women in professional or executive positions in the churches at a national level. Information service (National Council of Churches, N.Y.), v. 48 (31 May 1969), 7-8.

4063. BRIN, R. F. Can a woman be a Jew? Reconstructionist, v. 34 (25 October 1968), 7-14.

4064. BROADUS, John Albert. Should women speak in mixed public assemblies? Louisville, Ky., Baptist Book Concern, 1890.

4065. BROWN, O. Place of women in the church. Monthly reli-
       gious magazine, v. 42 (1869), 26.
4066. BRUMMER, Peter. Regin Prenter on the ordination of wom-
       en. Springfielder, (March 1970), 23-6.
4067. BRYCE, James. The position of women in America. Luth-
       eran Church review, v. 18 (1899), 554-60.
4068. The BURIED talents. Sign, v. 46 (October 1966), 15-19.
4069. BURTON, K. Are women noticed? Sign, v. 40 (October
       1962), 11-39.
4070. _____. Return to the Gospels. St. Joan's alliance bul-
       letin, (June 1967), 4.
4071. _____. Why blame it on us women? Sign, v. 43 (March
       1954), 49.
4072. _____. Why not give us women a break. Sign, v. 42
       (April 1963), 62.
4073. _____. Women get inside the Council. Sign, v. 44 (No-
       vember 1964), 43. On Vatican II.
4074. BUTLER, Josephine. Woman's place in church work.
       Christian literature, v. 6 (1892), 30-7.
4075. BYRNS, K. Women's rights in the Catholic Church. Catho-
       lic mind, v. 39 (22 January 1941), 49-54.
4076. CAHN, J. Women and the ministry. View, v. 27 (January
       1963), 18-20.
4077. CALLAHAN, Sidney. The illusion of Eve. New York, Sheed
       and Ward, 1965.
4078. _____. No theological barriers to women priests, says
       woman author. U.S. Catholic and jubilee, v. 32 (No-
       vember 1966), 59.
4079. _____ and P. McGinley. Woman's place is...? Sign,
       v. 44 (July 1965), 22-6.
4080. CAMPION, D. Equal opportunity. America, v. 122 (24
       January 1970), 57. Women as ministers.
4081. CARTAYNE, A. The Council and women. Christus Rex,
       v. 20 (October 1966), 270-8. On Vatican II.
4082. CAVERT, Inez M. Women in American church life. New
       York, Friendship Press, 1949. 93p.
4083. CHAMPION, L. G. Ministerial service of women. Baptist
       quarterly, v. 20 (January 1964), 201-5.
4084. CHANEY, G. L. Ministry of women. Monthly religious
       magazine, v. 44 (1870), 231.
4085. CHARTERIS, A. H. Work of women in the church. Presby-
       terian review, v. 9 (1888), 285.
4086. CHRISTIANITY and the position of women. Homiletic and
       pastoral review, v. 35 (May 1935), 843-44.
4087. The CHURCH and women's liberation. Dialog, v. 10 (Spring
       1971), 93-139.
4088. CHURCH plan for women. Homiletic review, v. 107 (May
       1934), 374-75.
4089. CHURCHWOMEN and the church. Christian century, v. 54
       (5 May 1937), 576-78.
4090. CHURCHWOMEN ask where they stand. Christian century,
       v. 70 (8 April 1953), 405.
4091. CHURCHWOMEN get insights on womanpower. National

Council outlook, v. 8 (January 1958), 14. Concerning the United Church Women.

4092. COLE, M. An end to stag religion. Extension, v. 59 (November 1964), 18-21.

4093. COLLINS, S. D. Women and the church; poor psychology, worse theology. Christian century, v. 87 (30 December 1970), 1557-9.

4094. CONCERNING the ordination of women. Geneva, World Council of Churches, 1964.

4095. CONWAY, J. View of St. Thomas that male embryo acquires immortal soul after 40 days and female after 80 days. Catholic messenger, v. 82 (21 May 1964), 10.

4096. _____. What is taught or implied from the Scriptures and the oral tradition of Christianity about the position of women, single or married in society? Catholic messenger, v. 82 (1 October 1964), 14.

4097. _____. Why is it that young women are not ordained, or at least serving Mass? Catholic messenger, v. 82 (30 July 1964), 10.

4098. CORT, C. Women as preachers. Reformed quarterly review, v. 29 (1882), 123.

4099. COX, William M. The social and civil status of woman. Presbyterian quarterly, v. 9 (1895), 584-606.

4100. CRANE, C. B. Women ascend the pulpit. Woman's journal, n.s., v. 14 (December 1929), 16. Women as ministers.

4101. CREHAN, J. Ordination of women priests. Clergy review, v. 48 (January 1963), 48-51.

4102. CRIBARI, S. Theologians' recommendations: be open to women deacons. National Catholic reporter, v. 7 (15 March 1971), 1+.

4103. CROOK, Margaret. Women and religion. Boston, Beacon, 1965.

4104. CULVER, Elsie Thomas. Women in the world of religion. Garden City, N.Y., Doubleday, 1967. 340p. Concerns the role of women in the church, women in the Bible, and the early church.

4105. CUNNEEN, Sally M. Onward Christian sisters. Christian century, v. 88 (24 February 1971), 245-6.

4106. _____. Sex: female; religion: Catholic. New York, Holt, Rinehart, & Winston, 1968.

4107. CUNNINGHAM, A. The ministry of woman in the church. Catholic Theological Society of America, proceedings, v. 24 (June 1969), 124-41.

4108. _____. Why not women priests? U.S. Catholic and jubilee, v. 35 (June 1970), 10-12.

4109. CUNNINGHAM, A. C. F. Work of women in the church in America. Catholic Presbyterian, v. 9 (1883), 359.

4110. DALY, Mary. After the death of God the Father. Commonweal, v. 94 (12 March 1971), 7-11.

4111. _____. A built in bias. Commonweal, v. 81 (15 January 1965), 504-11.

4112. _____. The church and the second sex. New York,
        Harper & Row, 1968. 187p.
4113. _____. Mary Daly and the second sex. U.S. Catholic
        and jubilee, v. 34 (September 1968), 21-4.
4114. _____. The submission of women. St. Joan's Alliance
        bulletin, (August 1966), 10.
4115. _____. Three steps forward--one backward. Catholic
        citizen, v. 53 (September-October 1967), 125-6.
4116. _____. The woman intellectual and the church. Common-
        weal, v. 85 (27 January 1967), 446-56.
4117. DAMIAN, B. The priesthood for women? Friar, v. 25
        (February 1966), 14-17.
4118. DAVIS, J. J. It's a woman's church, too. Torch, v. 42
        (June-July 1958), 4-7.
4119. DEMAND social justice for women church workers. Christian
        century, v. 62 (26 December 1945), 1437.
4120. DEMUTH, J. Open up the Catholic Church for women. Na-
        tional Catholic reporter, v. 7 (22 January 1971), 1+.
4121. DEVER, M. Women; shall they preach? Lutheran quarterly,
        v. 34 (1904), 284.
4122. DIETRICK, Ellen Battelle. Women in the early Christian
        ministry. Philadelphia, n.p., 1897. 148p. An ap-
        peal for more women in the church.
4123. DOELY, Sarah Bentley. Women's liberation and the church;
        new demand for freedom in the life of the Christian
        Church. New York, Association Press, 1970. 158p.
4124. DOUGLAS, William. Women in the church; historical per-
        spectives and contemporary dilemmas. Pastoral psy-
        chology, v. 12 (June 1961), 13-20.
4125. DUREN, C. Place of women in the church, in religious
        meetings. Congregational review, v. 8 (1868), 22.
4126. EATON, Thomas Treadwell. Bible on women's public speak-
        ing. Louisville, Ky., Baptist Book Concern, [1912?].
        Women in the church.
4127. EBY, L. S. Can women make their way into the ministry?
        Christian education, v. 12 (June 1929), 534-9.
4128. EENIGENBURG, E. M. Ordination of women. Christianity
        today, v. 3 (27 April 1959), 15-16.
4129. ELDER H. Bussey, of Columbus, Georgia, presents his views,
        supported by Scriptures only, and not by the traditions
        of men; on some questions now being generally dis-
        cussed by primitive Baptists. n.p., n.d. 8p. Con-
        cerns, in part, women speaking in church.
4130. The ELIGIBILITY of women not a Scriptural question. Meth-
        odist review, v. 73 (1891), 287-91.
4131. ERMARTH, Margaret Sittler. Adam's fractured rib; obser-
        vations on women in the church. Philadelphia, For-
        tress, 1970. 159p. On the ordination of women.
4132. EYDEN, R. van. Women ministers in the Catholic Church?
        Sisters today, v. 40 (December 1968), 211-26.
4133. FAHERTY, William B. The destiny of modern woman in the
        light of papal teaching. Westminster, Md., Newman,
        1950. 206p.

4134.   FAITH of our feminists; question of ordination. Newsweek,
         v. 76 (2 November 1970), 81.
4135.   FARIANS, Elizabeth. Directive against women lectors not
         yet law. St. Joan's Alliance bulletin, (August 1966),
         9.
4136.   _____. The human dignity of women in the church.
         Washington, Ecumenical Task Force on Women and
         Religion, National Organization for Women, 1967. 2p.
4137.   _____. The status of women in the church. Washington,
         Ecumenical Task Force on Women and Religion, Na-
         tional Organization for Women, 1968. 5p.
4138.   _____. We will be silent no longer. Detroit, National
         Organization for Women, 1971. 2p. Accusations
         against the Roman Catholic Church and necessary ac-
         tion to be taken.
4139.   _____. Women in the church now. Washington, Ecumen-
         ical Task Force on Women and Religion, National Or-
         ganization for Women, 1968. 7p. On Discriminatory
         canons.
4140.   _____. Women, theologians and the priesthood. Wash-
         ington, Ecumenical Task Force on Women and Religion,
         National Organization for Women, 1971. 2p.
4141.   FEMALE clergy. Time, v. 72 (13 October 1958), 76.
4142.   FEMALES defeated: Laymen in the House of Deputies of the
         Protestant Episcopal Church have voted against allow-
         ing women to be members. Ave maria, v. 100 (14
         November 1964), 17.
4143.   FEMININE mystique. Christian century, v. 80 (5 June 1963),
         759.
4144.   FICHTER, Joseph H. Holy Father church; organized Chris-
         tianity is dominated by males. Commonweal, v. 92
         (15 May 1970), 216-18. Discussion: v. 92 (24 July
         1970), 355+ ; v. 93 (30 October 1970), 134-5; v. 93
         (4 December 1970), 237+ .
4145.   FINK, R. A. Women in the church. Lutheran quarterly,
         v. 4 (1874), 220.
4146.   FISHER, L. The angry ladies. Priest, v. 22 (January
         1966), 44-8. Women as ministers.
4147.   FITZWATER, Perry Braxton. Woman, her mission, posi-
         tion, and ministry. Grand Rapids, Mich., Eerdmans,
         1949. 86p.
4148.   FORD, Josephine M. The ordination of women? Continuum,
         v. 5 (Winter 1968), 738-43.
4149.   FOSTER, Hazel E. The church as a profession for women.
         Woman's press, v. 33 (July-August 1939), 312-13.
4150.   _____. The ecclesiastical status of women. Woman's
         pulpit, v. 44 (October-December 1967), 7-10. Women
         as ministers.
4151.   FOYE, Edward. Androgynous church. Front line, (Septem-
         ber 1967), entire issue.
4152.   FRAKES, M. Women's status in the churches; summary of
         the report to United Church Women. Christian cen-
         tury, v. 70 (14 October 1953), 1164-6.

4153. FRETZ, G. F. Shall we, too, preach? Homiletic review,
       v. 96 (July 1928), 45-6.
4154. GAGE, Matilda Joslyn. Woman, church, and state: histori-
       cal account of the status of woman through the Chris-
       tian ages. Chicago, Kerr, 1893. 554p. Concerns
       the relation of woman's inferior status to the church.
4155. GARDINER, B. A. Woman theologian is unique. Independ-
       ent woman, v. 34 (November 1955), 5-6.
4156. GIBSON, Elsie. Protestant women in religion. Review for
       religious, v. 26 (November 1967), 1011-25. Women
       as ministers.
4157. _____. When the minister is a woman. New York, Holt,
       Rinehart, and Winston, 1970. 174p.
4158. _____. Women as clergy? Ave maria, v. 102 (24 July
       1965), 5-8.
4159. GIERTZ, Bo. Twenty-three theses on the Holy Scriptures,
       the woman, and the office of the ministry. Spring-
       fielder, (March 1970), 10-22.
4160. GOD, male or female? Newsweek, v. 65 (12 July 1965),
       60-2. Women as ministers.
4161. GOODENOW, W. S. B. Voice of women in the church. New
       Englander, v. 36 (1877), 115.
4162. GORDON, A. J. The ministry of women. Missionary re-
       view of the world, n. s., v. 7 (1894), 910-21.
4163. GORRES, I. Women in holy orders. Month, v. 34 (August
       1965), 84-93.
4164. GOUDGE, Henry L. Place of women in the church. Mil-
       waukee, Morehouse, 1917.
4165. GRAEF, Hilda. As others see us: this masculine church.
       Priest, v. 25 (April 1969), 227-30.
4166. _____. Neither Eve nor Mary? Catholic world, v. 207
       (September 1968), 270+. Women and the church.
4167. _____. Women in the church of today. Catholic world,
       v. 207 (August 1968), 206-10. Ordination of women.
4168. GRAFF, M. W. Rebitzen--an old title with new meaning.
       Jewish digest, v. 12 (July 1967), 65-6.
4169. GRAHAM, B. Jesus and the liberated woman. Ladies home
       journal, v. 87 (December 1970), 40+.
4170. GREISCH, J. R. Distaff dissent. Christianity today, v. 14
       (5 June 1970), 37-8. Women as ministers and rabbis.
4171. The GROUND of woman's eligibility. Methodist review, v.
       73 (1891), 456-63.
4172. GRUMBACH, D. Father church and the motherhood of God;
       conference at Garrison, New York. Commonweal,
       v. 93 (11 December 1970), 268-9.
4173. HACKER, J. G. Does the church allow women to sing in
       our church choirs or does she not? Catholic choir-
       master, v. 20 (December 1934), 204-6.
4174. HALLINAN, P. Is she at home in the church? Sign, v. 45
       (January 1966), 16-17.
4175. HARGROVE, R. K. Woman's work in the church. Metho-
       dist review (South), v. 43 (1896), 3-14.
4176. HARPER, L. Woman's place is not where you think it is.

Catholic layman, v. 79 (June 1965), 40-4.
4177. HARPER, M. A. Woman's role in the church. America,
v. 115 (23 July 1966), 91-3. Discussion: v. 115
(27 August, 15 October 1966), 195-6, 436.
4178. HARRINGTON, M. P. Women ministers celebrate jubilee.
Christian century, v. 86 (8 October 1969), 1295-6.
4179. HARTLEY, L. R. Women as ministers: the pros and cons.
New York Times magazine, (13 April 1947), 19+.
4180. HARVEY, William Patrick. Shall women preach? Louisville,
Ky., Baptist Book Concern, 1905. 32p.
4181. HAUGHEY, J. C. Women's lib, Catholic style. America,
v. 123 (28 November 1970), 454.
4182. HAYS, George Pierce. May women speak? Evanston, Ill.,
National Woman's Christian Temperance Union, (1912?).
4183. HEATH, J. G. Careers for women preaching. Homiletic
review, v. 97 (March 1929), 203-6. Reply: v. 98
(July 1929), 41-2.
4184. HEFNER, P. J. Ministry of women. Lutheran quarterly,
v. 18 (May 1966), 101-3.
4185. HENDERSON, Eva. Revolution in woman's world. Woman's
pulpit, v. 44 (January-March 1965), 4-5. Ordination
of women.
4186. HENRICHSEN, Margaret. Woman minister. Religion in life,
v. 21, no. 2 (1952), 275-87.
4187. HODGSON, L. Theological objections to the ordination of
women. Expository times, v. 77 (April 1966), 210-13.
4188. HOLLAND, F. M. Our clergywomen. Open court, v. 6
(1892), 3121-3.
4189. HOMMES, N. J. Let women be silent in church; a message
concerning the worship service and the decorum to
be observed by women. Calvin theological journal,
v. 4 (April 1969), 5-22.
4190. HUMPHREYS, John F. Woman's work in the church.
Homiletic review, v. 25 (1893), 495-9.
4191. HUNGATE, Jesse Avery. The ordination of women to the
pastorate in Baptist churches. Hamilton, N.Y.,
J. B. Grant, 1899. 172p.
4192. HUNTER, Doris and Howard Hunter. Neither male nor female. Christian century, v. 82 (28 April 1965), 527-
8+; Discussion: v. 82 (23 June 1965), 814. Women
as ministers.
4193. HUNTER, Fannie McDowell. Women preachers. Dallas,
Texas, Berachah printing co., 1905. 100p.
4194. HUSBAND or wall. America, v. 109 (12 October 1963),
404. On women and the church.
4195. INTERNATIONAL assembly of women preachers: meeting,
1925, Detroit, Michigan. Christian century, v. 42
(17 December 1925), 1586.
4196. JORDAN, P. Women-priest stirs controversy. Catholic
messenger, v. 82 (16 April 1964), 8.
4197. JUNG, E. Women at the Council: spectators or collabora-
tors? Catholic world, v. 200 (February 1965), 277-
84. Vatican II.

4198. KELLY, Suzanne. Putting sisters in their place. America, v. 114 (1 January 1966), 10-11. Women and the church.
4199. KEPLER, Patricia B. Is Eve really Adam's helper? Trends, a journal of resources, v. 3 (October 1970), 18-20. Women's status in the church.
4200. KLAPERMAN, L. M. Heaven help the rebbetzin. Jewish digest, v. 15 (March 1969), 67-9.
4201. KRAMARSKY, L. President's column on the status of women. Hadassah magazine, v. 44 (November 1963), 2.
4202. KREBS, A. V. A church of silence. Commonweal, v. 81 (10 July 1964), 472.
4203. KUMLIEN, C. D. Suffragette nuns. Commonweal, v. 81 (16 October 1964), 95-7.
4204. LADIES of the cloth? Newsweek, v. 29 (24 March 1947), 80. Women as ministers.
4205. LADY goes round and round; the church and woman's coequal dignity with man. America, v. 108 (29 June 1963), 895.
4206. LADY in the pulpit. National Jewish monthly, v. 84 (January 1970), 31. Women as rabbis.
4207. LADY in waiting: Episcopal deaconess refused holy orders. Newsweek, v. 65 (26 April 1965), 62.
4208. LAMPE, G. W. Church tradition and the ordination of women. Expository times, v. 76 (January 1965), 123-5.
4209. _____. Women and holy orders. Modern churchman, v. 10 (April 1967), 226-30. Ordination of women.
4210. LARGER role for women. America, v. 106 (6 January 1962), 430.
4211. LAUER, Rosemary. Are women 'less equal' than men? Lamp, v. 63 (June 1965), 4-7.
4212. _____. Catholic woman professor commends NFTS' resolution on women as rabbis. American Judaism, v. 13 (September 1964), 32.
4213. _____. Women and the church. Commonweal, v. 79 (20 December 1963), 365-8. Discussion: v. 79 (14-28 February, 24 April 1964), 603-4, 634, 665-6; v. 80, 151.
4214. _____. Women lectors proper to American custom. St. Joan's Alliance bulletin, (August 1966), 5.
4215. LAWSON, W. How can the church pretend to admit woman's equality with man, yet keep the Nuptial Mass in its present form? Christian order, v. 5 (June 1964), 271-2.
4216. _____. Why couldn't the Redeemer have been a woman? Christian order, v. 4 (November 1963), 89-90.
4217. LEE, Rev. Luther. Woman's right to preach the Gospel; a sermon preached at the ordination of the Rev. Miss Antoinette L. Brown, at South Butler, Wayne County, New York, September 15, 1853. Syracuse, N.Y., The Author, 1853. 22p. Many references made to the Old and New Testaments.
4218. LINDBECK, Violette. Needed: a new status for the single

woman. Catholic world, v. 202 (December 1965), 151-7.

4219. _____. The ordination of women. Philadelphia, Lutheran Press, 1967.

4220. LOLLIS, Lorraine. The shape of Adam's rib; a lively history of women's work in the Christian Church. St. Louis, Bethany, 1970. 219p.

4221. LOOMIS, H. Women in the church. May they speak in meetings? Congregational quarterly, v. 16 (1874), 264.

4222. LOVE, W. Deloss. St. Paul and woman; or, Paul's requirement of woman's silence in churches reconciled with woman's modern practice of speaking in churches. Chicago, Revell, 1894.

4223. LOWERY, D. Should women be priests? Liguorian, v. 53 (May 1965), 20-5.

4224. LOY, Matthias. Rights of women in church. Columbus, Ohio, Lutheran Book Concern, (1912?).

4225. MACE, D. R. and G. Hagmaier. Equalitarianism and male dominance; a Catholic-Protestant dialogue on changing religious concepts. Pastoral psychology, v. 20 (November 1969), 49-62.

4226. MCKENNA, Mary Lawrence. Women of the church: Role and renewal. New York, P. J. Kenedy, 1967.

4227. MCMULLEN, F. D. Women in the pulpit. Woman citizen, n.s., v. 9 (21 February 1925), 12-13. Women as ministers.

4228. MADDEN, D. Women at the Council. Catholic digest, v. 29 (April 1965), 16-19. On Vatican Council II.

4229. MAGUIRE, D. No more second-class citizenship for women in the church. U.S. Catholic and jubilee, v. 32 (July 1966), 18-19.

4230. MAIER, Walter A. Some thoughts on the role of women in the church. Springfielder, (March 1970), 33-7. On the ordination of women.

4231. MAKING place for women: Vatican Council II. Christian century, v. 81 (24 June 1964), 821.

4232. MANGELS, Arthur C. The second declaration of independence. Philadelphia, Rolley & Reynolds, 1965. 249p. Women in Christianity.

4233. MATTISON, Robin. Student speaks out on women's liberation. Lutheran forum, (March 1970), 22. The ordination of women.

4234. MAYOR, S. H. Ministry of women; a report on the argument. Modern churchman, v. 12 (April 1969), 222-9.

4235. MAYSER, F. P. Shall women vote in the church? Lutheran Church review, v. 18 (1899), 479-86.

4236. MILLER, Elizabeth J. Retreat to tokenism; a study of the status of women on the executive staff of the American Baptist Convention. Valley Forge, Pa., American Baptist Convention, 1970. 21p.

4237. MONTGOMERY, Jane. Clerical celibacy demeans women. Christian herald, (January 1970), 51-4.

4238. MOORE, A. Women in the church. Congregational quarter-
      ly, v. 16 (1874), 279.
4239. MOW, A. B. Gee! Women in the ministry! Brethren life
      and thought, v. 12 (September 1967), 51-60.
4240. MULHERIN, K. and J. Gardner. Growing up a woman.
      Christianity and crisis, v. 30 (5 October 1970), 202-9.
4241. MURRAY, Pauli. Women's liberation--Pattern for the 70's?
      Church woman, (January 1970), 11-13.
4242. NAUMANN, Martin J. Natural orders. Springfielder,
      (March 1970), 4-9. Ordination of women.
4243. NEEDHAM, Elizabeth C. Woman's ministry: A spiritual
      exposition of woman's place in the church of God.
      new ed. Chicago, Revell, 1895.
4244. NICCOLLS, Samuel J. Woman's position in the church.
      Richmond, Va., Presbyterian Committee of Publica-
      tion, [1912?].
4245. _____. Work of women in the church. Presbyterian re-
      view, v. 10 (1889), 267.
4246. NO theological obstacle to ordination of women, states Msgr.
      Otto Mauer. Tablet, v. 220 (26 November 1966), 1341.
4247. NOVAK, M. Nuns in the world. Commonweal, v. 79 (29
      November 1963), 274-8.
4248. O'BRIEN, J. Women in the church: God's forgotten children.
      U.S. Catholic and jubilee, v. 36 (January 1971), 40-1.
4249. OPENING the pulpit to women. Literary digest, v. 100 (30
      March 1929), 27-8.
4250. ORDAIN women? Woman's pulpit, (July-September 1967), 4.
4251. PARVEY, C. F. Ordain her, ordain her not? Dialog, v. 8
      (Summer 1969), 203-8.
4252. PEABODY, Lucy McGill Waterbury. A wider world for wom-
      en. New York, F. H. Revell, 1936. 128p.
4253. PENNINGS, Burrell. Why we still say no to the ordination
      of women. Church herald, (23 January 1970), 10+.
4254. PETRIE, C. S. Women and the ministry; some guidance
      from St. Paul. Reformed theological review, v. 18
      (October 1959), 75-85.
4255. PFATTEICHER, Ernst P. H. Woman as a congregational
      voter. Lutheran Church review, v. 18 (1899), 460-78.
4256. PHELPS, E. S. Pulpit of woman. Atlantic monthly, v. 26
      (1870), 11.
4257. PLACE of women in the church. Catholic world, v. 21
      (1875), 324.
4258. PONSTEIN, Lambert J. Should we ordain women? Church
      herald, (16 January 1971), 11+.
4259. POPE recognizes women. Christian century, v. 81 (23
      September 1964), 1165.
4260. The PRIESTHOOD and women; a letter. Clergy review,
      v. 51 (February 1966), 154-7.
4261. PRIESTHOOD for women. Month, v. 155 (July 1930), 560-1.
4262. PROHL, Russell C. Woman in the church; a restudy of
      woman's place in building the kingdom. Grand Rapids,
      Mich., Eerdmans, 1957. 86p.
4263. PUBLIC still reluctant to accept women clergy. Christian

century, v. 64 (16 July 1947), 869.
4264. RAHNER, K. Equality for women in the church. U.S.
Catholic and jubilee, v. 30 (September 1964), 62.
4265. _____. True equality for women; excerpts. Catholic
messenger, v. 82 (2 July 1964), 1.
4266. RAMBUSCH, N. O blessed deviation. Commonweal, v. 86
(16 June 1967), 363-6.
4267. RAVEN, Charles Earle. Women and the ministry. Garden
City, N.Y., Doubleday, Doran, 1929. 139p.
4268. REED, G. E. Legal developments affecting the church.
Catholic action, v. 27 (August 1945), 9-10.
4269. The RIB uncaged. Time, v. 91 (19 April 1968), 70-1.
4270. RICE, John R. Bobbed hair, bossy wives and women
preachers; significant questions for honest Christian
women settled by the world of God. Wheaton, Ill.,
Sword of the Lord Publishers, 1941. 91p.
4271. RICHIE, Jeanne. Church, caste, and women. Christian
century, v. 87 (21 January 1970), 73-7. Discussion:
v. 87 (11 March 1970), 295-6+.
4272. RISHELL, Charles Wesley. Official recognition of woman
in the church. New York, Methodist Book Concern,
(1912?).
4273. ROHLER, Janet. Reverend ladies collars and curls.
Christianity today, v. 13 (22 August 1969), 34. Comments on the ministry for women during a meeting of
the American Association of Women Ministers.
4274. ROOT, G. M. Are church women exploited? Christian
century, v. 50 (8 November 1933), 1408-9.
4275. ROPER, J. B. Catholic Church and woman's freedom.
Truth, v. 36 (September 1932), 17-19.
4276. ROWE, M. A ministry for women. Sisters today, v. 40
(June-July 1969), 592-607.
4277. _____. Women in the church. Herder correspondence,
v. 6 (October 1969), 291-8.
4278. ROYDEN, Agnes Maude. The church and woman. New York,
Doran, (1925?). 255p.
4279. _____. What a woman preacher thinks of the church.
Ladies home journal, v. 39 (December 1922), 31.
4280. ROYS, Mrs. C. K. Status of women in church. Missionary
review of the world, v. 47 (May 1924), 382-4.
4281. RUETHER, Rosemary. The becoming of women in the church
and society. Cross currents, v. 17 (Fall 1967), 418-
26.
4282. _____. Women's liberation in historical and theological
perspective. Soundings, v. 53 (Winter 1970), 363-73.
4283. RYRIE, Charles Caldwell. The place of women in the
church. Chicago, Moody, 1968. 155p.
4284. SCHALK, A. The church and women. U.S. Catholic and
jubilee, v. 31 (September 1965), 21-6.
4285. SCHMAUK, Theodore E. The Epistle to Timothy and the
woman question. Lutheran Church review, v. 18
(1899), 525-36.
4286. _____. St. Paul and women. Lutheran Church review,

v. 18 (1899), 505-24.

4287. SCHMIDT, R. A. Second-class citizenship in the kingdom of God. Christianity today, v. 15 (1 January 1971), 13-14.

4288. SEEBACH, M. R. Women; shall they preach? Lutheran quarterly, v. 33 (1903), 579.

4289. SEX and the Sacraments. Christian century, v. 85 (13 November 1968), 1425. Women as ministers.

4290. SEX equality in church rule is blocked by male minorities. Newsweek, v. 16 (2 December 1940), 44.

4291. SHATTOCK, F. M. Theological exercise. Catholic citizen, v. 101 (September 1965), 61-2.

4292. SHAW, Anna Howard. Women in the ministry. Chautauquan, n.s., v. 8 (1898), 489-96.

4293. SHEED, W. Second sex, etc., etc. Commonweal, v. 80 (27 March 1964), 15-16. Reply: v. 80 (22 May 1964), 261.

4294. SHERWOOD, G. H. Church and the dignity of woman. Catholic action, v. 14 (July 1932), 11-12.

4295. SHOULD women be ordained? Episcopalians, no; Lutherans, yes. National Catholic reporter, v. 7 (6 November 1970), 9.

4296. SHOULD women be priests? symposium. Commonweal, v. 81 (15 January 1965), 504-11.

4297. SLAUGHTER, Philip. Man and woman; or, The law of honor applied to the solution of the problem, why are so many more women than men Christians? Philadelphia, J. B. Lippincott, 1860. 186p. Women and religion.

4298. SMITH, V. The woman and the Council: Will her voice be heard? Ave maria, v. 100 (3 October 1964), 26-30. On Vatican II.

4299. SPHERE and rights of woman in the church. Richmond, Va., Presbyterian Committee of Publication, (1912?).

4300. STAHL, Katherine. Early women preachers of Illinois. Illinois State Historical Society Journal, v. 9 (January 1917), 483-8.

4301. STAMM, R. T. Status of women workers in the church. Lutheran quarterly, v. 10 (May 1958), 139-60.

4302. The STATUS of women in church and society: A statement adopted by the Council for Christian Social Action and submitted as a proposed pronouncement to the General Synod of the United Church of Christ; Women's oppression: an overview, by Charlotte Bunch-Weeks; The problems of black women, by Pauli Murray; Women and the church: a dialogue, by Elizabeth Johns and Nelle Morton. Social action, v. 37 (April 1971), 5-35.

4303. STEHLE, W. Women and the clergy. Homiletic and pastoral review, v. 54 (January 1954), 326-30.

4304. STENDAHL, Krister. The Bible and the role of women. Philadelphia, Fortress, 1966.

4305. STEPHENSON, P. D. The woman question. Presbyterian quarterly, v. 13 (1899), 206-28, 685-724.

4306. STEVENSON, J. M.   Place of women in assemblies for
       public worship. Presbyterian quarterly, v. 2 (1873),
       42.
4307. STIER, J.   Women in the church.   College Theology Society,
       proceedings, (1967), 119-24.
4308. SUFFRAGETTES in the church. Ave maria, v. 12 (30 Octo-
       ber 1965), 16-17.
4309. SULLIVAN, D.   The arrogance of male power.   Jubilee,
       v. 15 (December 1967), 24-5.
4310. SURBURG, Raymond F.   Place of woman in the Old Testa-
       ment. Springfielder, (March 1970), 27-32. On the
       ordination of women.
4311. SUTHERS, H. B.   Religion and the feminine mystique.
       Christian century, v. 82 (21 July 1965), 911-14.
4312. SUZANNE, Sister.   Putting sisters in their place: Witness
       in the church and in the world. America, v. 114 (1
       January 1966), 10-11.
4313. SWIDLER, Arlene.   Ecumenical question: the status of wom-
       en. Journal of ecumenical studies, v. 4 (Winter 1967),
       113-15. Women as ministers.
4314. _____. The male church. Commonweal, v. 84 (24 June
       1966), 387-9. Women as ministers.
4315. SWIDLER, Leonard.   Can the churches avoid the next revolu-
       tion? Journal of ecumenical studies, v. 5 (Spring
       1968), 338-42.
4316. _____. Jesus was a feminist. Catholic world, v. 212
       (January 1971), 177-83.
4317. TANSEY, A.   Why must men run the show?   Catholic lay-
       man, v. 80 (June 1966), 51-8.
4318. TAVARD, George.   Women in the church: a theological
       problem? Ecumenist, v. 4 (November-December
       1965), 7-10.
4319. TERESA, M.   Women theologians in the church.   Sisters
       today, v. 37 (July 1966), 392-9.
4320. THOMAS, W. T.   Conference on role of church women.
       Christian century, v. 71 (1 September 1954), 1051-2.
4321. THOMPSON, B.   Sound and fury at assembly of Methodist
       women. Christian century, v. 87 (17 June 1970),
       773-4.
4322. TO study women's status. Christian century, v. 69 (4 June
       1952), 683. On the activities of the United Church
       Women.
4323. TO the hills, men! America, v. 118 (22 June 1968), 785.
       Women as ministers.
4324. TOBIN, T.   Women's new role in the church.   Liguorian,
       v. 56 (March 1968), 18-21.
4325. TORREY, C. W.   Sphere of women in the church.   Congre-
       gational quarterly, v. 9 (1867), 163.
4326. TOWNER, M.   Ladies in the pulpit.   Newsweek, v. 48 (5
       November 1956), 106. Women as ministers.
4327. TREINEN, S.   Underestimate a woman: The Council didn't.
       Priest, v. 22 (October 1966), 797-9. On Vatican
       Council II.

4328. TREVETT, Bernard. The place of women in the church.
         Catholic citizen, v. 53 (July-August 1968), 175-7.
4329. TREWICK, O. No place for women, or several? Catholic
         world, v. 210 (February 1970), 216-19. Women's
         status in the church.
4330. TROUT, E. J. Church: for men only? Spectrum, v. 47
         (March 1971), 17-19.
4331. TUCKER, R. L. Place of women in the church. Biblical
         world, v. 54 (November 1920), 578-87.
4332. TURNER, P. The contribution of women to theology. Col-
         lege Theology Society, proceedings, (1967), 109-18.
4333. TWING, M. A. E. Work of women in the church. Church
         review, v. 60 (1891), 182.
4334. TYRRELL, George. The old faith and the new woman.
         American Catholic quarterly, v. 22 (1897), 630-45.
4335. UNITED Presbyterian Church in the United States of America.
         Report of Standing Committee on Women to the 183d
         General Assembly, 1971. [Philadelphia, 1971?]. 32p.
         On the participation of women in the church.
4336. _____. Report of the Task Force on Women and The
         Standing Committee on Women, adopted by the 182d
         General Assembly, 1970. Reprinted from the minutes
         of the General Assembly, The Journal, part 1, 1970.
         [Philadelphia, 1970?]. 20p. Consists of recommenda-
         tions on women's status in the Presbyterian Church as
         well as a short account of the role of women in the
         Presbyterian Church.
4337. VAN SOEST, Bert. Rights of women to the offices of the
         church. Church herald, (9 January 1970), 11.
4338. The VATICAN Council; a new age for lay Catholics. Sign,
         v. 42 (October 1962), 11-39.
4339. VATICAN daily says no women priests. National Catholic
         reporter, v. 6 (4 February 1970), 3.
4340. VOGT, E. D. Role of women in the Protestant ministry.
         Unitas, v. 8 (Spring 1956), 41-5.
4341. WALLACE, Cecelia. How women were excluded. National
         Catholic reporter, v. 2 (5 January 1966), 6.
4342. _____. Women and the Council. Lamp, v. 68 (Septem-
         ber 1965), 12-13.
4343. WANGERMANN, E. Women in the church. Life of the
         spirit, v. 17 (May 1963), 475-82. Women as minis-
         ters.
4344. WARREN, W. F. Position of women in the church. Metho-
         dist review, v. 56 (1896), 81.
4345. WAY, Peggy. Church and (ordained) women. Christian
         ministry, (January 1970), 18-22.
4346. WEATHERS, P. A. News of the churches; Presbyterian
         Church in the United States. Reformed and Presby-
         terian world, v. 28 (March 1965), 224-5; (September
         1965), 317-18. Women as ministers.
4347. WEBSTER, Elaine. Woman's place. St. Joan's Alliance
         bulletin, (August 1966), 7-8.
4348. WEDEL, Cynthia. Church women and Christian unity. Catho-

lic world, v. 202 (February 1966), 278-82.
4349. _____. Employed women and the church. New York, National Council of Churches of Christ, 1959.
4350. _____. Woman power and the churches. Christian century, v. 74 (10 July 1957), 843-4. On the activities
of the United Church Women.
4351. WEIS, J. Status of women in the Missouri Synod in the
twentieth century. Springfielder, v. 33 (March 1970),
38-43.
4352. WHITE, Alma Bridwell. Woman's chains. Zarephath, N.J.,
Pillar of Fire, 1943. 184p. Women as ministers.
4353. WILKINSON, M. Women for pulpits. Woman citizen, n.s.,
v. 8 (9 February 1924), 17. Women as ministers.
4354. WILL women launch their own church? Christian century,
v. 65 (1 December 1948), 1291-2. On the activities
of the United Council of Church Women.
4355. WILLARD, Frances Elizabeth. Woman in the pulpit....
Chicago, Woman's Temperance Publication Association,
1889. 173p. An argument for more women preachers.
4356. _____. Women as preachers. Our day, v. 1 (1888), 21.
4357. _____. Women as preachers. Our day, v. 1 (1888), 286.
4358. WILLMARTH, J. W. Work of woman in the church. Baptist
review, v. 10 (1888), 466.
4359. WISE, W. G. and K. Taglauer, eds. Question of ordination
of women as reflected in Lutheran journals. Springfielder, v. 33 (March 1970), 44-54.
4360. WOMAN and the church. Bible world, v. 48 (December
1916), 366-7.
4361. WOMAN as pastor. Springfielder, v. 33 (March 1970), 1-2.
4362. WOMAN defying Paul's decree; ordaining of women to the
ministry. Literary digest, v. 68 (5 February 1921),
32-3.
4363. The WOMAN intellectual and the church; a Commonweal symposium. Commonweal, v. 85 (27 January 1967), 446-
56+ ; Discussion: v. 85 (3 March 1967), 611+.
4364. WOMAN seeks Episcopal ordination. Christian century,
v. 87 (21 January 1970), 72.
4365. WOMAN'S place in church work. Review of reviews, v. 5
(April 1892), 343. Women as ministers.
4366. WOMAN'S place in the church. America, v. 122 (28 February 1970), 204.
4367. WOMAN'S progress toward the pulpit. Literary digest,
v. 67 (23 October 1920), 34.
4368. WOMAN'S status in Protestant churches. Information service
(National Council of Churches, N.Y.), (16 November
1940), 1-12.
4369. WOMEN and the church. Renewal magazine, (October 1964),
entire issue.
4370. WOMEN and the pulpit. Newsweek, v. 45 (6 June 1955), 50.
4371. WOMEN as clergy. Literary digest, v. 121 (4 January
1936), 18.
4372. WOMEN at the altar. Time, v. 96 (2 November 1970), 71+.
4373. WOMEN in church. Time, v. 65 (6 June 1955), 65. On

women as ministers.
4374. WOMEN in the church. America, v. 107 (3 November 1962),
      972-3.
4375. WOMEN in the church. Christian century, v. 57 (11 Decem-
      ber 1940), 1542-3.
4376. WOMEN in the church. Congregational quarterly, v. 16
      (1874), 576.
4377. WOMEN in the church. Marriage, v. 56 (December 1964),
      17-18.
4378. WOMEN in the church. Time, v. 36 (2 December 1940), 40.
4379. WOMEN in the churches. Christian century, v. 69 (21 May
      1952), 606-7.
4380. WOMEN in the churches. National Council outlook, v. 3
      (June 1953), 8-9.
4381. WOMEN in the ministry. Literary digest, v. 96 (3 March
      1928), 30.
4382. WOMEN in the sanctuary? America, v. 103 (18 June 1960),
      367.
4383. WOMEN liberationists want bishops to act. National Catholic
      reporter, v. 7 (20 November 1970), 2.
4384. WOMEN preachers. Christian century, v. 40 (16 August
      1923), 1031-2.
4385. WOMEN seeking bigger role in churches. U. S. news and
      world report, v. 70 (18 January 1971), 24-5.
4386. WOMEN'S lib--Catholic style. America, v. 123 (28 Novem-
      ber 1970), 454.
4387. WOMEN'S lib hits seminary. National Catholic reporter,
      v. 6 (29 May 1970), 3.
4388. WOMEN'S lib stirs up churchly storms. National Catholic
      reporter, v. 6 (23 October 1970), 1+.
4389. WOMEN'S place in the church. New world outlook, v. 30
      (July 1970), 19-22.
4390. WOO, E. Theology confronts women's liberation. America,
      v. 124 (13 March 1971), 257-9.
4391. WORLD around us: liberation struggle generates tension on
      race, sex issues. Christian century, v. 87 (10 June
      1970), 736-42.
4392. WORLD Council of Churches. Concerning the ordination of
      women. New York, 1964. (World Council Studies,
      no. 1.)
4393. _____. The deaconess. New York, 1966. (World Council
      Studies, no. 4.)
4394. _____. Revised interim report of a study on the life and
      work of women in the church; including reports of an
      ecumenical conference of church women, Baarn, Hol-
      land, and of the Committee on "The life and work of
      women in the church" of the Assembly of the World
      Council of Churches, Amsterdam, 1948. Geneva, The
      Council, 1948. 76p.
4395. WYKER, Mossie. Church women in the scheme of things.
      St. Louis, Bethany, 1953.

BIOGRAPHY

ABBOTT, Edith, 1876-1957.
ABBOTT, Grace, 1878-1939.
(See also no. 3333)
4396. Abbott, Edith. Grace Abbott and Hull House, 1908-1921. Social service review, v. 24 (September-December 1950), 374-94, 493-518.
4397. Baker, H. C. The Abbotts of Nebraska. Survey graphic, v. 25 (June 1936), 370-372.
4398. Johnson, John Reuben. Representative Nebraskans. Lincoln, Neb., Johnsen Publishing Co., 1954. pp. 8-11.
4399. Lundberg, E. O. Pathfinders of the middle years. Social service review, v. 21 (March 1947), 22-5.
4400. Marks, R. Published writings of Edith Abbott. Social service review, v. 32 (March 1958), 51-6.
4401. Wisner, E. Edith Abbott's contributions to social work education. Social service review, v. 32 (March 1958), 1-10.
4402. Wright, N. R. Three against time: Edith and Grace Abbott and Sophonisba P. Breckinridge. Social service review, v. 28 (March 1954), 41-53.

ABZUG, Bella, 1920?-
4403. Bella. Newsweek, v. 76 (5 October 1970), 28-9.
4404. Newcomers in the House. Time, v. 96 (16 November 1970), 27.
4405. Who's new in Congress. Time, v. 97 (1 February 1971), 15.
4406. Women on the Hustings. Time, v. 96 (17 August 1970), 11.

ADAMS, Mary Newbury, 1837-1901.
4407. Noun, Louise R. Strong-minded women. Ames, Iowa State University Press, 1969. pp. 113-15, 263-4.

ADDAMS, Jane, 1860-1935.
4408. Abbott, E. Hull House of Jane Addams. Social service review, v. 26 (September 1952), 334-8.
4409. Addams, Jane. The second twenty years at Hull House, September 1909 to September 1929. New York, Macmillan, 1930. 413p.
4410. _____. The social thought of Jane Addams. Edited by Christopher Lasch. Indianapolis, Bobbs-Merrill, 1965. 266p.

ADDAMS, Jane. (cont.)

4411. _____. Twenty years at Hull House. New York, Macmillan, 1923. 467p. New York, NAL, 1971.

4412. Baldwin, R. Fighting pacifist. Saturday review, v. 44 (12 August 1961), 20-1.

4413. Conway, Jill. Jane Addams: An American heroine. Daedalus, v. 93 (Spring 1964), 761-80.

4414. Davis, Allen F. and Mary Lynn McCree, eds. Eighty years at Hull House. Chicago, Quandrangle, 1969. 256p.

4415. Elson, A. First principles of Jane Addams. Social service review, v. 28 (March 1954), 3-11.

4416. Farrell, John C. Beloved lady; a history of Jane Addams' ideas on reform and peace. Baltimore, Johns Hopkins Press, 1967. 272p.

4417. Harkness, G. Jane Addams in retrospect. Christian century, v. 77 (13 January 1960), 39-41.

4418. Kent, Muriel. Jane Addams: 1860-1935. Hibbert, journal, v. 35 (1937), 279-90.

4419. Levine, Daniel. Jane Addams and the liberal tradition. Madison, State Historical Society of Wisconsin, 1971. 277p.

4420. _____. Jane Addams: romantic radical, 1889-1912. Mid-America, v. 44, no. 4 (1962), 195-210.

4421. Linn, James Weber. Jane Addams; a biography. New York, Appleton-Century, 1935. 457p. Reprinted by Greenwood Press, Westport, Conn., 1970.

4422. Lynd, S. Jane Addams and the radical impulse. Commentary, v. 32 (July 1961), 54-9.

4423. Meigs, Cornelia. Jane Addams; pioneer for social justice; a biography. Boston, Little, Brown, 1970. 274p.

4424. Meiklejohn, D. Jane Addams and American democracy. Social service review, v. 34 (September 1960), 253-64.

4425. Oakley, Violet. Cathedral of compassion; dramatic outline of the life of Jane Addams, 1860-1935. Philadelphia, Jane Addams House, 1955. 104p.

4426. Perkins, M. Helen, comp. Preliminary checklist for a bibliography on Jane Addams; under the direction of the Rockford area Jane Addams centennial committee. [Rockford, Ill.?], Rockford College Library, 1960. 44p.

4427. Ratcliffe, S. K. Jane Addams of Chicago. Contemporary review, v. 148 (1935), 38-45.

4428. Scott, A. F. Jane Addams and the city. Virginia quarterly review, v. 43 (Winter 1967), 53-62.

4429. _____. Saint Jane and the ward boss. American heritage, v. 12 (December 1960), 12-17+.

4430. Tims, Margaret. Jane Addams of Hull House, 1860-1935; a centenary study. New York, Macmillan, 1961. 166p.

4431. Warm memories of Hull House. Life, v. 50 (17 March 1961), 141-2+.

ADDAMS, Jane. (cont.)
4432. Weybright, V. Memories. Saturday review, v. 44 (12
       August 1961), 21.
4433. Wise, Winifred E. Jane Addams of Hull House; a biog-
       raphy. New York, Harcourt, Brace, 1935. 255p.

ANDERSON, Mary, 1872-1964.
4434. Anderson, Mary. Woman at work: the autobiography of
       Mary Anderson as told to Mary Nelson Winslow.
       Minneapolis, University of Minnesota Press, 1951.
       266p. Autobiography of a former head of the U.S.
       Women's Bureau.

ANNEKE, Mathilda Fraziska, 1817-1884.
4435. Krueger, Lillian. Madam Mathilda Fraziska Anneke, an
       early Wisconsin journalist. Wisconsin magazine of
       history, v. 21 (December 1937), 160-7.

ANTHONY, Susan Brownell, 1820-1906.
       (See also no. 1045, 1427, 1966, 4549, 4890)
4436. Anthony, Katharine Susan. Susan B. Anthony; her person-
       al history and her era. New York, Doubleday,
       1954. 521p.
4437. Anthony, Susan B. An account of the proceedings of the
       trial of Susan B. Anthony, on the charge of illegal
       voting, at the presidential election in November
       1872, and on the trial of Beverly W. Jones, Edwin
       T. Marsh, and William B. Hall, the inspectors of
       election by whom her vote was received. Rochester,
       N.Y., Daily Democrat and Chronicle Book Print.,
       1874. 212p.
4438. Christensen, Thomas P. Susan B. Anthony in Iowa. Iowa
       journal of history and politics, v. 28 (July 1930),
       456-60.
4439. Dictionary of American Biography. New York, C. Scrib-
       ner, 1936. v. 1, pt. 1, pp. 318-20.
4440. Dorr, Rheta Childe. Susan B. Anthony, the woman who
       changed the mind of a nation. New York, Stokes,
       1928. 367p. Reprinted by AMS Press, New York,
       1970.
4441. Fishburn, E. Susan B. Anthony, apostle of freedom.
       National Education Association, journal, v. 31
       (February 1942), 49-50.
4442. Harper, Ida Husted. The life and work of Susan B.
       Anthony; including the triumphs of her last years,
       account of her death and funeral comments of the
       press. Indianapolis, Hollenback, 1898-1908. 3v.
       Reprinted by Arno Press, New York, 1972.
4443. _____. Susan B. Anthony. Independent, v. 60 (22
       March 1906), 676-82.
4444. _____. Susan B. Anthony. Review of reviews, v. 33
       (April 1906), 414-19.
4445. _____. Susan B. Anthony; the woman and her work.

ANTHONY, Susan Brownell. (cont.)
        North American review, v. 182 (April 1906), 604-
        16.
4446. Howe, M. A. Causes and their champions; woman suf-
        frage and its Napoleon, Susan B. Anthony. Ladies
        home journal, v. 43 (April 1926), 17.
4447. Just us girls. Newsweek, v. 44 (15 November 1954),
        118+.
4448. Ludwig, W. Her classroom was the nation. New York
        State Education, v. 43 (February 1956), 325-7.
4449. Lutz, Alma. Susan B. Anthony: rebel, crusader, hu-
        manitarian. Boston, Beacon, 1959. 340p.
4450. _____. Susan B. Anthony for the working woman.
        Boston Public Library quarterly, v. 11 (January
        1959), 33-43. On her activities to promote the or-
        ganization of employed women, admission into
        men's unions, and raising wages to those of men,
        1868-1904.
4451. Lyon, Peter. The herald angels of women's rights.
        American heritage, v. 10 (October 1959), 18-21,
        107-11.
4452. McKelvey, Blake. Susan B. Anthony. Rochester history
        [N.Y.], (April 1945), 1-24.
4453. Mason, Anna Dann. The most unforgettable character I've
        met. Genesee country scrapbook [Rochester, N.Y.
        Historical Society], v. 4 (1953), 22-4.
4454. Petition for remission of a fine. Praying for the remis-
        sion of a fine imposed upon her by the United States
        court for the northern district of New York, for
        illegal voting. Senate misc. docs. no. 39, 43d
        Cong., 1st Sess., v. 1. 22 January 1874. 4p.
4455. Picture on the cover. Independent woman, v. 33 (Febru-
        ary 1954), 44.
4456. Report on bill for relief of Susan B. Anthony. Recom-
        mends the passage of a bill for the relief of Susan
        B. Anthony. House Reports no. 608, 43d Cong.,
        1st Sess., v. 3. 25 May 1874. 4p.
4457. Report on case of Susan B. Anthony. Adverse to refund-
        ing or exempting by law Susan B. Anthony from
        paying a fine imposed upon her for illegal voting.
        House Reports no. 648, 43d Cong., 1st Sess., v. 4.
        16 June 1874. 8p.
4458. Report on case of Susan B. Anthony. Adverse to the
        petitioner's prayer for the remission of a fine im-
        posed upon her by the district court for the north-
        ern district of New York for having "knowingly
        voted without having a lawful right to vote." Views
        of Senator Carpenter. Senate reports, no. 472,
        43d Cong., 1st Sess., v. 2. 20 June 1874. 12p.
4459. Sisson, Adelaide Howe. Susan B. Anthony. Daughters
        of the American Revolution, magazine, v. 71 (1937),
        117-19.
4460. Susan B. Anthony; an appreciation and an appeal. West-

ANTHONY, Susan Brownell. (cont.)
          minster review, v. 165 (May 1906), 547-55.
4461. Susan B. Anthony elected to Hall of fame. Independent
          woman, v. 29 (December 1950), 379.
4462. Susan B. Anthony honored. National business woman,
          v. 38 (April 1959), 14.
4463. Susan B. Anthony placed in Hall of fame. Independent
          woman, v. 31 (June 1952), 165-6.
4464. U.S. vs. Susan B. Anthony for illegal voting, 1873. (In:
          Van Winkle, Marshall. Sixty famous cases:...29
          English cases...31 American cases, from 1778 to
          the present. Long Branch, N.Y., Ayres, 1956.
          10v.)
4465. Villard, Fanny G. Susan B. Anthony. Nation, v. 110
          (14 February 1920), 197-9.
4466. Wagner, R. F. She changed the mind of a nation: Susan
          B. Anthony. National Education Association, jour-
          nal, v. 27 (February 1938), 35-6.
4467. Weitz, A. C. Praise for a valiant soul. National Edu-
          cation Association, journal, v. 39 (February 1950),
          103.

ATKINSON, Ti-Grace, 1938?
4468. Four of a kind--yet different. Newsweek, v. 75 (23
          March 1970), 72-3.

AUSTIN, Mary Hunter, 1868-1934.
4469. Hunt, Rockwell Dennis. California's stately hall of fame.
          Stockton, Cal., College of the Pacific, 1950.
          pp. 565-9.
4470. Pearce, Thomas Matthews. Mary Hunter Austin. New
          York, Twayne, 1965. 158p.
4471. Powell, Lawrence C. A dedication to the memory of
          Mary Hunter Austin, 1868-1934. Arizona and the
          West, v. 10, no. 1 (1968), 1-4.

BEECHER, Catharine Esther, 1800-1878.
4472. Bacon, M. Miss Beecher in Hell. American heritage,
          v. 14 (December 1962), 28-31+.
4473. Biester, C. Catharine Beecher and education in the Mis-
          sissippi Valley. Practical Home Economics, v. 31
          (May 1953), 13+.
4474. _____. Catharine Beecher, pioneer. Journal of Home
          Economics, v. 41 (May 1949), 259-60.
4475. _____. Catharine Beecher: founder of home economics.
          American Dietetic Association, journal, v. 28
          (February 1952), 136-9.
4476. _____. Prelude--Catharine Beecher. Journal of Home
          Economics, v. 51 (September 1959), 549-51.
4477. Carson, Gerald. Catharine Beecher. New England galaxy,
          v. 5, no. 4 (1964), 3-10.
4478. Goodsell, Willystine, ed. Pioneers of women's education
          in the United States: Emma Willard, Catharine

BEECHER, Catharine Esther. (cont.)
        Beecher, Mary Lyon. New York, McGraw-Hill,
        1931. 311p. Reprinted by AMS Press, New York,
        1972.
4479. Harveson, Mae Elizabeth. Catharine Esther Beecher,
        pioneer educator. 295p. PhD thesis, University
        of Pennsylvania, 1931. Reprinted by Arno Press,
        New York, 1972.
4480. Soule, J. C. Catharine Esther Beecher; pioneer in the
        education of American women. National Education
        Association, journal, v. 35 (February 1946), 104-5.
4481. Thorp, Margaret F. Female persuasion. New Haven,
        Conn., Yale University Press, 1949. pp. 11-55.

BEECHER, Henry Ward, 1813-1887.
4482. Abbott, Lyman. Henry Ward Beecher. Boston, Houghton,
        Mifflin, 1903. 457p. Reprinted by Mnemosyne
        Press, Miami, Fla., 1969.
4483. _____. Henry Ward Beecher: a leader of men. Out-
        look, v. 105 (18 October 1913), 362-4.
4484. Dictionary of American Biography. New York, C. Scrib-
        ner, 1936. v. 1, pt. 2, pp. 129-35.
4485. Shaplen, Robert. Free love and heavenly sinners; the
        story of the great Henry Ward Beecher scandal.
        New York, Knopf, 1954. 273p.

BETHUNE, Mary McLeod, 1875-1955.
4486. Bethune, Mary McLeod. My last will and testament.
        Ebony, v. 18 (September 1963), 151-6.
4487. Bowie, Walter Russell. Women of light. New York,
        Harper and Row, 1963. pp. 112-27.
4488. Carter, E. A. A modern matriarch. Survey graphic,
        v. 25 (October 1936), 573-4.
4489. Finkelstein, Louis, ed. American spiritual autobiographies.
        New York, Harper, 1948. pp. 182-90, 267.
4490. Fleming, Alice. Great women teachers. Philadelphia,
        Lippincott, 1965. pp. 71-85.
4491. Holt, Margaret V. Mary McLeod Bethune; a biography.
        New York, Doubleday, 1964. 306p.
4492. Peare, Catherine Owens. Mary McLeod Bethune. New
        York, Vanguard, 1951. 219p.
4493. Richardson, Ben. Great American Negroes. New York,
        Crowell, 1956. pp. 178-96.
4494. Stoddard, Hope. Famous American women. New York,
        Crowell-Collier, 1970. pp. 71-80.

BLACKWELL, Alice Stone, 1857-1950.
4495. Kunitz, Stanley J., ed. Twentieth century authors. 1st
        supplement. New York, H. W. Wilson, 1955.
        p. 92.
4496. Time, v. 55 (27 March 1950), 98.
4497. Vartanes, Charles A. Alice Stone Blackwell--a sym-
        posium. Armenian affairs, v. 1 (Spring 1950),

BLACKWELL, Alice Stone. (cont.)
    135-50.
4498. Wilson library bulletin, v. 24 (May 1950), 634.

BLACKWELL, Antoinette Louisa Brown, 1825-1921.
    (See also no. 4217)
4499. Deen, Edith A. Great women of the Christian faith. New
       York, Harper, 1959. pp. 394-6.
4500. Dictionary of American Biography. New York, C. Scrib-
       ner, 1936. v. 1, pt. 2, pp. 319-20.
4501. Eliot, Samuel Atkins. Heralds of a liberal faith. Boston,
       Beacon, 1952. pp. 52-9.
4502. Kerr, Laura Nowak. Lady in the pulpit. New York,
       Woman's Press, 1951. 239p.
4503. Riegel, Robert Edward. American feminists. Lawrence,
       University of Kansas Press, 1963. pp. 116-19.

BLACKWELL, Elizabeth, 1821-1910.
    (See also no. 3253, 3254)
4504. Baker, Rachel M. First woman doctor; the story of
       Elizabeth Blackwell, M.D. London, Harrap, 1947.
       190p.
4505. Chambers, Peggy. Doctor alone; a biography of Elizabeth
       Blackwell, the first woman doctor, 1821-1910. New
       York, Abelard-Shuman, 1958. 191p.
4506. Dictionary of American Biography. New York, C. Scrib-
       ner, 1936. v. 1, pt. 2, pp. 320-1.
4507. Gillie, A. Elizabeth Blackwell and the medical register
       from 1858. British medical journal, no. 5107 (22
       November 1958), 1253-7.
4508. Hays, Elinor Rice. Those extraordinary Blackwells, the
       story of a journey to a better world. New York,
       Harcourt, Brace, 1967. 349p.
4509. Johnston, Malcolm Sanders. Elizabeth Blackwell and her
       alma mater; the story in the documents. Boston,
       Humphries, 1947. 29p.
4510. Lentz, J. America's first woman physician; Elizabeth
       Blackwell. Today's health, v. 42 (January 1964),
       36-7+.
4511. McFerran, Ann. Elizabeth Blackwell, first woman doctor.
       New York, Grosset and Dunlap, 1966. 175p.
4512. McNutt, Sarah J. Dr. Elizabeth Blackwell, her character
       and personality. Medical record, v. 100 (19 No-
       vember 1921), 922-6.
4513. Ross, Ishbel. Child of destiny: the life of Elizabeth
       Blackwell. New York, Harper, 1949. 309p.
4514. Roth, L. G. Elizabeth Blackwell, 1821-1910. Yale
       journal of biology and medicine, v. 20 (October
       1947), 1-18.
4515. Stack, N. Americans not everybody knows; Elizabeth
       Blackwell, the 1st American woman doctor. PTA
       magazine, v. 61 (February 1967), 26-7.
4516. Van Hoosen, Bertha. Elizabeth Blackwell: the woman

BLACKWELL, Elizabeth. (cont.)
            of the century. American Medical Women's As-
            sociation, journal, v. 4 (November 1949), 484-7.
4517.   Vaughan, E. The early days of Elizabeth Blackwell.
            Fortnightly review, n.s., v. 94 (November 1913),
            976-85.
4518.   Wilson, Dorothy Clarke. Lone woman; the story of
            Elizabeth Blackwell; the first woman doctor. Bos-
            ton, Little, Brown, 1970. 469p.

BLAKE, Lillie Devereux, 1835-1913.
4519.   Blake, Katherine Devereux and Margaret L. Wallace.
            Champion of women, the life of Lillie Devereux
            Blake. New York, Revell, 1943. 244p.
4520.   Dictionary of American Biography. New York, C. Scrib-
            ner, 1936. v. 1, pt. 2, pp. 343-4.

BLATCH, Harriot Eaton Stanton, 1856-1940.
4521.   Blatch, Harriot Stanton and Alma Lutz. Challenging
            years; the memoirs of Harriot Stanton Blatch.
            New York, Putnam, 1940. 347p.

BLOOMER, Amelia Jenks, 1818-1894.
            (See also no. 2114)
4522.   Bloomer, Dexter C. Life and writings of Amelia Bloomer.
            Boston, Arena, 1895. 387p. Reprinted by Garrett
            Press, New York, 1972.
4523.   Branch, E. Douglas. The Lily and the Bloomer. Colo-
            phon, pt. 12 (1932). 12p.
4524.   Dictionary of American Biography. New York, C. Scrib-
            ner, 1936. v. 1, pt. 2, pp. 385.
4525.   Fatout, Paul. Amelia Bloomer and Bloomerism. New
            York Historical Society, quarterly, v. 36 (October
            1952), 361-73.
4526.   Fox, L. H. Pioneer women's rights magazine. New
            York State Historical Society, quarterly, v. 42
            (January 1958), 71-4.
4527.   Gatley, Charles Neilson. The Bloomer girls. New York,
            Coward-McCann, 1967. 192p.
4528.   _____. Mrs. Bloomer. Saturday book, v. 23 (1963),
            175-89.
4529.   Goneiar, B. Amelia Jenks Bloomer, advocate of women's
            trousers. Hobbies, v. 53 (April 1948), 118-19.
4530.   Jordan, Philip D. The Bloomers in Iowa. Palimpsest,
            v. 20 (September 1939), 295-309.
4531.   Noun, Louise R. Strong-minded women. Ames, Iowa
            State University Press, 1969. pp. 12-20, 133-42,
            264-5.
4532.   Thorp, Margaret Farrand. Female persuasion. New
            Haven, Conn., Yale University Press, 1949.
            pp. 102-42.

BRECKINRIDGE, Sophonisba Preston, 1866-1948.
    (See also no. 4402)
4533. Abbott, E. Sophonisba Preston Breckinridge over the
          years. Social service review, v. 22 (December
          1948), 417-50.
4534. American sociological review, v. 13 (October 1948), 630.
4535. Lenroot, K. F. Sophonisba Preston Breckinridge, social
          pioneer. Social service review, v. 23 (March
          1949), 88-96; (September 1949), 377-8.
4536. Survey, v. 84 (August 1948), 251.
4537. Wilson library bulletin, v. 23 (September 1948), 10.

BROWN, Olympia, 1835-1926.
4538. Dictionary of American Biography. New York, C. Scrib-
          ner, 1936. v. 2, pt. 1, pp. 151.
4539. Neu, Charles E. Olympia Brown and the woman's suf-
          frage movement. Wisconsin magazine of history,
          v. 43 (Summer 1960), 277-87. The Reverend
          Brown's suffrage activities in Wisconsin and else-
          where around 1878 to 1920.
4540. Riegel, Robert Edgar. American feminists. Lawrence,
          University of Kansas Press, 1963. pp. 119-20.
4541. Willis, Gwendolen B. Olympia Brown. Universalist His-
          torical Society, journal, v. 4 (1963), 1-76. Covers
          the suffrage movement from 1867 until 1920.
4542. Willis, Olympia Brown. Acquaintances, old and new,
          among reformers. Milwaukee, S. E. Tate Printing
          Co., 1911. 115p. Autobiographical, with accounts
          of the suffrage campaigns in New York, Kansas,
          and Wisconsin.

BROWNSON, Orestes Augustus, 1803-1876.
4543. Lathrop, G. P. Orestes Brownson. Atlantic monthly,
          v. 77 (June 1896), 777-80.
4544. Swidler, Arlene. Brownson and the "woman question."
          American benedictine review, v. 19, no. 2 (1968),
          211-19.

CATT, Carrie Lane Chapman, 1859-1947.
    (See also no. 766, 854)
4545. Adams, M. Carrie Chapman Catt. Nation, v. 164 (22
          March 1947), 330-1.
4546. _____. Carrie Chapman Catt; leader of women, pioneer
          for peace. Pictorial review, v. 32 (January 1931),
          14-15.
4547. _____. The real Mrs. Catt. Woman citizen, n.s.,
          v. 9 (6 September 1924), 8-9.
4548. Brown, Margaret W. Medals awarded Mrs. Carrie Chap-
          man Catt, leader in the woman suffrage movement.
          Numismatist, v. 65 (February 1952), 114-24.
4549. Burnett, Constance Buel. Five for freedom: Lucretia
          Mott, Elizabeth Cady Stanton, Lucy Stone, Susan

CATT, Carrie Lane Chapman.   (cont.)
   B. Anthony, Carrie Chapman Catt. New York,
   Abelard, 1953. 317p. Reprinted by Greenwood
   Press, Westport, Conn., 1970.
4550. Changing the mind of a nation; story of Carrie Chapman
   Catt. World tomorrow, v. 13 (September 1930),
   358-61.
4551. Clevenger, Ima Fuchs. Invention and arrangement in the
   public address [1883-1947] of Carrie Chapman Catt.
   471p. PhD thesis, University of Oklahoma, 1955.
4552. Good housekeeping, v. 101 (November 1935), 35.
4553. Independent, v. 92 (17 November 1917), 324.
4554. Independent woman, v. 17 (November 1938), 343.
4555. Mrs. Carrie Chapman Catt--constructive decisionist.
   Everybody's magazine, v. 35 (November 1916),
   639-40.
4556. Miller, Helen Hill. Carrie Chapman Catt: the power of
   an idea. Washington, Carrie Chapman Catt Memorial Fund, Inc., 1958. 32p.
4557. Peck, Mary Gray. Carrie Chapman Catt, a biography.
   New York, H. W. Wilson, 1944. 495p.
4558. _____. Mrs. Catt at college: 1880-1930. Woman's
   journal, n.s., v. 15 (September 1930), 21+.
4559. Straus, D. Champion of women. Saturday review of
   literature, v. 27 (26 August 1944), 22.
4560. They stand out from the crowd. Literary digest, v. 117
   (20 January 1934), 9.

CHACE, Elizabeth Buffum, 1806-1899.
   (See also no. 1526)
4561. Dictionary of American Biography. New York, C. Scribner, 1936. v. 2, pt. 1, p. 584.

CHANNING, William Henry, 1810-1884.
4562. Dictionary of American Biography. New York, C. Scribner, 1936. v. 2, pt. 2, pp. 9-10.

CHAPIN, Nettie Sanford, 1830-1901.
4563. Noun, Louise. Strong-minded women. Ames, Iowa State
   University Press, 1969. pp. 95-6, 272.

CHAPMAN, Maria Weston, 1806-1885.
4564. Dictionary of American Biography. New York, C. Scribner, 1936. v. 2, pt. 2, p. 19.

CHENEY, Ednah Dow, 1824-1904.
4565. Dictionary of American Biography. New York, C. Scribner, 1936. v. 2, pt. 2, pp. 51-2.
4566. New England magazine, n.s., v. 28 (June 1903), 486.

CHILD, Lydia Maria Francis, 1802-1880.
4567. Baer, Helene Gilbert. Heart is like Heaven; the life of
   Lydia Maria Child. Philadelphia, University of

CHILD, Lydia Maria Francis. (cont.)
        Pennsylvania Press, 1964. 339p.
4568. _____. Mrs. Child and Miss Fuller. New England
        quarterly, v. 26 (June 1953), 249-55.
4569. Barnes, James A. Letters of a Massachusetts woman re-
        former to an Indiana radical. Indiana magazine of
        history, v. 26 (March 1930), 46-60. Letters be-
        tween 1862 and 1878 from Lydia Maria Child to
        George V. Julian concerning political and social
        matters.
4570. Curtis, G. T. Reminiscences of N. P. Willis and Lydia
        Maria Child. Harper's magazine, v. 81 (October
        1890), 717-20.
4571. Dictionary of American Biography. New York, C. Scrib-
        ner, 1936. v. 2, pt. 2, pp. 67-9.
4572. Hudson, A. S. Home of Lydia Maria Child. New England
        magazine, n.s., v. 2 (June 1890), 402-14.
4573. McDonald, Gerald P. A portrait from letters, Lydia
        Maria Child, 1802-1880. New York Public Library,
        bulletin, v. 36 (1932), 617-22. Her life between
        1862 and 1876.
4574. Meltzer, Milton. Tongue of flame: the life of Lydia
        Maria Child. New York, Crowell, 1965. 210p.
4575. Taylor, L. C. Lydia Maria Child: biographer. New
        England quarterly, v. 34 (July 1961), 211-27.
4576. _____. Reader I beseech you. Negro history bulletin,
        v. 20 (December 1956), 53-5.

CHISHOLM, Shirley St. Hill, 1924-
4577. Black lawmakers in Congress. Ebony, v. 26 (February
        1971), 118.
4578. Brine, R. Shirley in Wonderland. Time, v. 96 (2 No-
        vember 1970), 14+ .
4579. Chisholm, Shirley. Unbought and unbossed. New York,
        Avon, 1971. 191p.
4580. Drotning, Phillip. Up from the ghetto. New York,
        Cowles, 1970. pp. 132-42.
4581. Flynn, James J. Negroes of achievement in modern
        America. New York, Dodd, Mead, 1970. 200-9.
4582. New faces in Congress. Ebony, v. 24 (February 1969),
        58-9.
4583. These days black women are singing strong. Vogue,
        v. 153 (May 1969), 170.

CHURCHILL, Caroline Nichols, 1883-
4584. Churchill, Caroline Nichols. Active footsteps. Colorado
        Springs, The Author, 1909. 258p. Autobiography
        and Mrs. Nichols' activities for woman suffrage in
        Colorado.

CLAY, Laura, 1849-1941.
4585. Current biography, 1941. New York, H. W. Wilson,
        1941. pp. 155-6.

CLAY, Laura. (cont.)
4586. Goodman, Clavia. Bitter harvest: Laura Clay's suffrage
work. Lexington, Ky., Bur Press, 1946. 72p.

COGGESHALL, Mary Jane, 1836-1911.
4587. Noun, Louise R. Strong-minded women. Ames, Iowa
State University Press, 1969. pp. 153, 267-8.

COLBY, Clara Bewick.
4588. Brown, Olympia, ed. Democratic ideals: a memorial
sketch of Clara B. Colby. Racine, Wis., Carrie
Stebbins, 1917. 116p.

COOK, Tennessee Celeste Claflin, 1845-1923.
4589. Davenport, Walter. Ladies, gentlemen, and editors.
New York, Doubleday, 1960. pp. 109-24.
4590. Holbrook, Stewart Hall. Dreamers of the American
dream. New York, Doubleday, 1957. pp. 194-205.
4591. Riegel, Robert Edgar. American feminists. Lawrence,
University of Kansas Press, 1963. pp. 144-50.
4592. Ross, Ishbel. Charmers and cranks. New York, Harper
and Row, 1965. pp. 110-36.

CUNNINGHAM, Catherine Campbell, 1849-1908.
4593. Jones, Dorcey D. Catherine Campbell Cunningham, advocate of equal rights for women. Arkansas historical quarterly, v. 12 (Summer 1953), 85-90.

DALL, Caroline Wells Healey, 1822-1912.
4594. Riegel, Robert Edgar. American feminists. Lawrence,
University of Kansas Press, 1963. pp. 156-63.
4595. Welter, B. Merchant's daughter; a tale from life. New
England quarterly, v. 42 (March 1969), 3-32.

DARWIN, Mary Abigail Platt, 1821-1886.
4596. Noun, Louise R. Strong-minded women. Ames, Iowa
State University Press, 1969. pp. 146-7, 268-9.

DAVENPORT, Mattie Griffith, 1842-1928.
4597. Noun, Louise R. Strong-minded women. Ames, Iowa
State University Press, 1969. pp. 94-5, 269.

DAVIS, Paulina Kellogg Wright, 1813-1876.
4598. Dictionary of American Biography. New York, C. Scribner, 1936. v. 3, pt. 1, pp. 141-2.
4599. O'Connor, Lillian. Pioneer women orators. New York,
Columbia University Press, 1954. pp. 85-6.
4600. Riegel, Robert Edgar. American feminists. Lawrence,
University of Kansas Press, 1963. pp. 128-30.

DAY, Dorothy, 1899-
4601. Day, Dorothy. The long loneliness: the autobiography
of Dorothy Day. New York, Harper, 1952. 288p.

DENNETT, Mary Ware, 1872-1947.
4602.   Newsweek, v. 30 (4 August 1947), 56.
4603.   Publisher's weekly, v. 152 (9 August 1947), 550.

DEWSON, Mary, 1897-1962.
4604.   Patterson, James T.   Mary Dewson and the American
          minimum wage movement.   Labor history, v. 5,
          no. 2 (1964), 134-52.

DICKINSON, Anna Elizabeth, 1842-1932.
4605.   Anderson, Judith.   Anna Dickinson, antislavery radical.
          Pennsylvania history, v. 3 (1936), 147-63.
4606.   Chester, Giraud.   Embattled maiden; the life of Anna
          Dickinson.   New York, Putnam, 1951.   307p.
4607.   Noun, Louise R.   Strong-minded women.   Ames, Iowa
          State University Press, 1969.   pp. 58-64.
4608.   Riegel, Robert Edgar.   American feminists.   Lawrence,
          University of Kansas Press, 1963.   pp. 151-3.

DIGGS, Annie La Porte, 1853-1916.
4609.   Levinson, Harry.   Petticoat politician.   Kansas magazine,
          (1949), 20-3.   Concerning her work for suffrage in
          Kansas.

DIX, Dorothea Lynde, 1802-1887.
4610.   Bigelow, L. J.   Dorothea L. Dix.   Galaxy, v. 3 (1866),
          668.
4611.   Dictionary of American Biography.   New York, C. Scrib-
          ner, 1936.   v. 3, pt. 1, pp. 323-5.
4612.   Marshall, Helen E.   Dorothea Dix.   Forgotten samaritan.
          New York, Russell and Russell, 1967.   298p.
4613.   Olson, E. I.   We nominate for the Hall of fame.   Inde-
          pendent woman, v. 29 (October 1950), 301-2+.
4614.   Roe, Alfred S.   Dorothea Lynde Dix; a paper read before
          the Worcester Society of Antiquities, November 20,
          1888.   Worcester, Mass., Private Press of F. P.
          Rice, 1889.
4615.   Tiffany, Francis.   Life of Dorothea Lynde Dix.   Boston,
          Houghton Mifflin, 1918.   Rep., Plutarch Press, 1972.

DODGE, Grace Hoadley, 1856-1914.
4616.   Friend of workingwomen.   Outlook, v. 109 (6 January
          1915), 7-8.
4617.   Wildman, E.   What Grace Dodge has done for the working
          girl.   World to-day, v. 19 (December 1910), 1363-6.

DODGE, Mary Abigail, 1833-1896.
4618.   Pulsifer, Janice Goldsmith.   Gail Hamilton, 1833-1896.
          Essex Institute historical collections, v. 104, no. 3
          (1968), 165-216.   On Gail Hamilton, pen-name of
          Mary Abigail Dodge.
4619.   Thrasher, M. B.   Last years of Gail Hamilton's life,
          with extracts from letters written by her during

DODGE, Mary Abigail. (cont.)
    that time. Arena, v. 17 (December 1896), 112-19.

DORR, Rheta Childe, 1866-1948.
4620. Jakes, John. Great women reporters. New York, Put-
    nam, 1969. pp. 91-113.
4621. Review of reviews, v. 76 (December 1927), 650.
4622. Riegel, Robert Edgar. American feminists. Lawrence,
    University of Kansas Press, 1963. pp. 173-7.

DOUGLASS, Frederick, 1817-1895.
4623. Bennett, L. Up-to-date Frederick Douglass. Ebony,
    v. 19 (June 1964), 70-2+.
4624. Borome, J. A., ed. Frederick Douglass. Journal of
    Negro history, v. 33 (October 1948), 469-71.
4625. _____. Some additional light on Frederick Douglass.
    Journal of Negro history, v. 38 (April 1953), 216-
    24.
4626. Cooke, J. W. Freedom in the thoughts of Frederick
    Douglass, 1845-1860. Negro history bulletin, v.
    32 (February 1969), 6-10.
4627. Dictionary of American Biography. New York, C. Scrib-
    ner, 1936. v. 3, pt. 1, pp. 406-7.
4628. Douglass, Frederick. Life and writings of Frederick
    Douglass. Edited by Philip S. Foner. New York,
    International, 1950-55. 4v.
4629. Foner, Philip S. Frederick Douglass; a biography. New
    York, Citadel, 1964. 444p.
4630. Holland, Frederic May. Frederick Douglass: the colored
    orator. rev. ed. New York, Haskell House, 1969.
    431p.
4631. Quarles, Benjamin. Frederick Douglass. Washington,
    Associated Publishers, 1948. 378p.
4632. _____. Frederick Douglass. Englewood Cliffs, N.J.,
    Prentice-Hall, 1968. 184p.
4633. _____. Frederick Douglass and the woman's rights
    movement. Journal of Negro history, v. 25 (Janu-
    ary 1940), 35-44.
4634. Washington, Booker Taliaferro. Frederick Douglass.
    Philadelphia, Jacobs, 1907. 365p. Reprinted by
    Haskell House, New York, 1968.

DU BOIS, William Edward Burghardt, 1868-1963.
4635. Du Bois, Shirley Graham. His day is marching on.
    Philadelphia, Lippincott, 1971.

DUNBAR, Roxanne, 1938?-
4636. Four of a kind--yet different. Newsweek, v. 75 (23
    March 1970), 73.

DUNIWAY, Abigail Jane Scott, 1834-1915.
4637. Dictionary of American Biography. New York, C. Scrib-
    ner, 1936. v. 3, pt. 1, pp. 513-14.

DUNIWAY, Abigail Jane Scott. (cont.)
4638. Duniway, Abigail Scott. Path breaking; an autobiographical
history of the equal suffrage movement in the Pacific coast states. Portland, Ore., James, Kerns
and Abbott, 1914. 291p. Reprinted by Source Book
Press, New York, 1970.
4639. Groff, F. A. Woman pathfinder. Sunset, v. 27 (August
1911), 162-5.
4640. Holbrook, Stewart Hall. Dreamers of the American dream.
New York, Doubleday, 1957. pp. 205-12.
4641. Johnson, Jalmar. Builders of the Northwest. New York,
Dodd, Mead, 1963. pp. 151-69.
4642. Lockley, F. Mother of suffrage in the West. Overland
monthly, n.s., v. 67 (June 1916), 498-9.
4643. Walker, Sibyl. No doll was Abigail. American mercury,
v. 67 (August 1948), 164-8.
4644. West, Oswald. Reminiscences and anecdotes; political
history. Oregon historical quarterly, v. 50 (December 1949), 243-50.

EDSON, Katherine Philips, 1870-1933.
4645. Good housekeeping, v. 54 (February 1912), 154.
4646. Hundley, N. C. Katherine Philips Edson and the fight
for the California minimum wage, 1912-1923.
Pacific historical review, v. 29 (August 1960),
271-85.
4647. Loewy, Jean. Katherine Philips Edson and the California
suffragette movement, 1919-1920. California Historical Society, quarterly, v. 47, no. 4 (1968),
343-50.

ELMHIRST, Dorothy Payne, 1887-1968.
4648. New republic, v. 160 (4 January 1969), 13.

EMMET, Alida Chanler, 1873?-
4649. Grandes dames who grace America. Life, v. 64 (26
January 1968), 44.

FELTON, Rebecca Latimer, 1835-1930.
4650. Felton, Rebecca Latimer. Country life in Georgia in the
days of my youth; also addresses before the Georgia Legislature, women's clubs, women's organizations and other noted occasions. Atlanta, Index
Printing Co., 1919.
4651. Floyd, Josephine Bone. Rebecca Latimer Felton, champion of women's rights. Georgia historical quarterly, v. 30 (June 1946), 81-104.
4652. Talmadge, John Erwin. Rebecca Latimer Felton; nine
stormy decades. Athens, University of Georgia
Press, 1960. 187p.

FIELD, Sara Bard, 1882-
(See also no. 1642)

FIELD, Sara Bard. (cont.)
4653. Fry, A. Along the suffrage trail. American West, v. 6
       (January 1969), 16-25.

FLYNN, Elizabeth Gurley, 1890-
4654. Flynn, Elizabeth Gurley. I speak my own piece; auto-
       biography of "the rebel girl." New York, Masses
       and Mainstream, 1955. 326p.

FOSTER, Abigail Kelley, 1810-1887.
4655. Coombs, Zelotes W. Stephen Symonds and Abby Kelley
       Foster. Worcester Historical Society, publications,
       n.s., v. 1, no. 7 (1934), 376-90. Concerning Abby
       Kelley Foster and her husband, Stephen Symonds.
4656. Dictionary of American Biography. New York, C. Scrib-
       ner, 1936. v. 3, pt. 2, pp. 542-3.
4657. O'Connor, Lillian. Pioneer women orators. New York,
       Columbia University Press, 1954. pp. 59-65.
4658. Riegel, Robert Edgar. Abby Kelley. New England
       galaxy, v. 6, no. 4 (1965), 21-6.
4659. _____. American feminists. Lawrence, University of
       Kansas Press, 1963. pp. 34-40.
4660. Wyman, Lillie B. Reminiscences of two abolitionists.
       New England magazine, v. 33 (January 1903), 536-
       50. On Abby Kelley Foster and her husband.

FREEMAN, Jo, 1945?-
4661. Four of a kind--yet different. Newsweek, v. 75 (23
       March 1970), 73.

FRIEDAN, Betty.
       (See also no. 1000)
4662. Tornabene, L. Liberation of Betty Friedan. McCalls,
       v. 98 (May 1971), 84-5+ .

FULLER, Sarah Margaret, 1810-1850.
       (See also no. 175, 4567)
4663. Anthony, Katharine Susan. Margaret Fuller; a psycholog-
       ical biography. New York, Harcourt, 1921. 223p.
       Reprinted by Scholarly Press, St. Clair Shores,
       Mich., 1970.
4664. Barbour, Frances M. Margaret Fuller and the British
       reviewers. New England quarterly, v. 9 (1936),
       618-25.
4665. Bell, Margaret. Margaret Fuller, a biography. New
       York, Boni, 1930. 320p.
4666. Bradford, Gamaliel. Portrait of Margaret Fuller. North
       American review, v. 210 (July 1919), 109-21.
4667. Brown, Arthur W. Margaret Fuller. New York, Twayne,
       1964. 159p.
4668. Chipperfield, Faith. In quest of love; the life and death
       of Margaret Fuller. New York, Coward-McCann,
       1957. 320p.

FULLER, Sarah Margaret. (cont.)
4669.   Clarke, James Freeman.   Letters to Margaret Fuller.
        Indianapolis, Cram, 1957. 147p.
4670.   Colville, D.   Transcendental friends: Clarke and Margaret
        Fuller.   New England quarterly, v. 30 (September
        1957), 378-82.
4671.   Deiss, Joseph Jay.   Roman years of Margaret Fuller; a
        biography.   New York, Crowell-Collier, 1969.
        338p.
4672.   Dictionary of American Biography.   New York, C. Scrib-
        ner, 1936. v. 4, pt. 1, pp. 63-6.
4673.   Gale, Anna D.   Glimpses of Margaret Fuller: The Green
        Street School [Providence, R.I.] and Florence
        [Mass.].   New England quarterly, v. 29 (March
        1956), 87-98.   Excerpts from Miss Gale's diary
        while she was a student in Margaret Fuller's school.
4674.   Hess, M. Whitcomb.   Conversations in Boston, 1839.
        Catholic world, v. 149 (1939), 309-17.   Concerning
        the salons started by Margaret Fuller and their re-
        lation to the equal rights movement.
4675.   Higginson, Thomas Wentworth.   Margaret Fuller Ossoli.
        Boston, Houghton Mifflin, 1890. 323p.   Reprinted
        by Greenwood Press, Westport, Conn., 1972.
4676.   Howe, Julia Ward.   Margaret Fuller.   Boston, Roberts,
        1883. 298p.   Reprinted by Greenwood Press, West-
        port, Conn., 1972.
4677.   Kearns, F. E.   Margaret Fuller and the abolition move-
        ment.   Journal of the history of ideas, v. 25 (Janu-
        ary 1964), 120-7.
4678.   Miller, P.   I find no intellect comparable to my own.
        American heritage, v. 8 (February 1957), 22-5+.
4679.   Minot, John C.   Margaret Fuller Ossoli.   New England
        magazine, v. 42 (May 1910), 294-5.
4680.   Nicholas, Edward.   Hours and the ages.   Harper's maga-
        zine, v. 199 (July 1949), 66-76.
4681.   Ossoli, Sarah Margaret Fuller.   Love-letters of Margaret
        Fuller, 1845-1846.   New York, D. Appleton, 1903.
        228p.   Reprinted by Greenwood Press, Westport,
        Conn., 1969.
4682.   _____.   The writings of Margaret Fuller, selected and
        edited by Mason Wade.   New York, Viking, 1941.
        608p.
4683.   Stern, Madeleine Bettina.   The life of Margaret Fuller.
        New York, Haskell House, 1968. 549p.
4684.   _____.   Margaret Fuller's school days in Cambridge.
        New England quarterly, v. 12 (1940), 207-22.
4685.   _____.   Margaret Fuller's stay in Providence [R.I.],
        1837-1838.   Americana, v. 34 (1940), 353-69.
4686.   Wade, Mason.   Margaret Fuller, whetstone of genius.
        New York, Viking, 1940. 304p.

GAGE, Frances Dana Barker, 1808-1884.
4687.   Dictionary of American Biography.   New York, C. Scrib-

GAGE, Frances Dana Barker. (cont.)
      ner, 1936. v. 4, pt. 1, pp. 84-5.
  4688. O'Connor, Lillian. Pioneer women orators. New York,
      Columbia University Press, 1954. pp. 91-3.

GAGE, Matilda Joslyn, 1826-1898.
  4689. Dictionary of American Biography. New York, C. Scrib-
      ner, 1936. v. 4, pt. 1, pp. 86-7.
  4690. O'Connor, Lillian. Pioneer women orators. New York,
      Columbia University Press, 1954. p. 88.

GALE, Zona, 1874-1938.
  4691. Dictionary of American Biography. New York, C. Scrib-
      ner, 1958. Supplement 2, pp. 215-16.
  4692. Simonson, Harold Peter. Zona Gale. New York, Twayne,
      1962. 157p.
  4693. Wisconsin State Historical Society. Dictionary of Wiscon-
      sin biography. Madison, The Society, 1960. p. 140.

GARRISON, William Lloyd, 1805-1879.
  4694. American agitators. Time, v. 55 (30 January 1950), 94-6.
  4695. Chapman, John Jay. William Lloyd Garrison. New York,
      Moffat, Yard, 1913. 278p.
  4696. Dictionary of American Biography. New York, C. Scrib-
      ner, 1936. v. 4, pt. 1, pp. 168-72.
  4697. Fredrickson, George M., ed. William Lloyd Garrison.
      Englewood Cliffs, N.J., Prentice Hall, 1968. 182p.
  4698. Garrison, Wendell Phillips and Francis Jackson Garrison.
      William Lloyd Garrison, 1805-1879; the story of
      his life, told by his children. New York, Century,
      1885-1889. Reprinted by Negro Universities Press,
      Westport, Conn., 1969. 4v.
  4699. Grimke, Archibald Henry. William Lloyd Garrison, the
      abolitionist. New York, Funk and Wagnall's, 1891.
      405p. Reprinted by Negro Universities Press,
      Westport, Conn., 1969.
  4700. I will be heard. Newsweek, v. 61 (25 February 1963),
      97-8.
  4701. Johnson, Oliver. William Lloyd Garrison and his times.
      New York, C. Drew, 1880. 490p. Reprinted by
      Mnemosyne, Miami, Fla., 1969.
  4702. Merrill, Walter McIntosh. Against wind and tide; a biog-
      raphy of William Lloyd Garrison. Cambridge,
      Mass., Harvard University Press, 1963. 391p.
  4703. Nye, Russel Blaine. ' William Lloyd Garrison and the
      humanitarian reformers. Boston, Little, Brown,
      1955. 215p.
  4704. Swift, Lindsay. William Lloyd Garrison. Philadelphia,
      Jacobs, 1911. 412p.
  4705. Thomas, John L. Liberator: William Lloyd Garrison;
      a biography. Boston, Little, Brown, 1963. 502p.
  4706. Weakness for utopias. Time, v. 81 (1 March 1963), 80+.

GILMAN, Charlotte Perkins Stetson, 1860-1935.
     (See also no. 189, 283, 854)
4707. Bookman [N.Y.], v. 12 (November 1909), 204-6.
4708. Clarke, H. A. Charlotte Perkins Stetson as social
       philosopher and poet. Poetlore, v. 11 (January
       1899), 124-8.
4709. Current literature, v. 50 (May 1911), 550.
4710. Doyle, William T. Charlotte Perkins Gilman and the cycle
       of feminist reform. PhD thesis, University of Cali-
       fornia, 1960.
4711. Gilman, Charlotte Perkins Stetson. The living of Charlotte
       Perkins Gilman, an autobiography. New York, Ap-
       pleton-Century, 1935. 341p.
4712. Putnam's magazine, v. 7 (January 1910), 501.
4713. Riegel, Robert Edgar. American feminists. Lawrence,
       University of Kansas Press, 1963. pp. 163-73.

GOLDMAN, Emma, 1869-1940.
4714. Drinnon, Richard. Rebel in paradise; a biography of
       Emma Goldman. Chicago, University of Chicago
       Press, 1961. 349p.
4715. Goldman, Emma. Living my life. New York, Knopf,
       1931. 2v. Rep., DaCapo Press, New York, 1972.
4716. Ishill, Joseph. Emma Goldman, a challenging rebel.
       Translated by Herman Frank. Berkeley Heights,
       N.J., Oriole Press, 1957. 30p.
4717. Shulman, Alix. Emma Goldman, feminist and anarchist.
       Women, a journal of liberation, v. 1 (Spring 1970),
       21-4.

GRIFFING, Josephine Sophie White, 1814-1872.
4718. Dictionary of American Biography. New York, C. Scrib-
       ner, 1936. v. 4, pt. 1, pp. 622-3.

GRIFFITHS, Martha, 1912-
     (See no. 1320, 2416)

GRIMKE, Angelina Emily, 1805-1879.
GRIMKE, Sarah Moore, 1792-1873.
4719. Birney, Catherine H. The Grimke sisters. Sarah and
       Angelina Grimke, the first American women advo-
       cates of abolition and woman's rights. Boston,
       Lee and Shepard, 1885. 319p. Reprinted by
       Greenwood Press, Westport, Conn., 1970.
4720. [Birney on the Grimke sisters.] Literary world, v. 16
       (1885), 318.
4721. Dictionary of American Biography. New York, C. Scrib-
       ner, 1936. v. 4, pt. 1, pp. 634-5.
4722. Dubois, Ellen. Struggling into existence; the feminism
       of Sarah and Angelina Grimke. Women, a journal
       of liberation, v. 1 (Spring 1970), 4-11.
4723. Jones, F. Dudley. The Grimke sisters. South Carolina
       Historical Association, proceedings for 1933, 12-21.

GRIMKE, Angelina Emily.
GRIMKE, Sarah Moore. (cont.)
4724. Lerner, Gerda. The Grimke sisters and the struggle
            against race prejudice. Journal of Negro history,
            v. 48, no. 4 (1963), 277-91.
4725. _____. The Grimke sisters from South Carolina;
            rebels against slavery. Boston, Houghton Mifflin,
            1967. 479p.
4726. Lewis, Ruth Bartlett. Angelina Grimke Weld, reformer.
            134p. PhD thesis, Ohio State University, 1962.
4727. Melder, Keith E. Forerunners of freedom: the Grimke
            sisters in Massachusetts, 1837-1838. Essex In-
            stitute historical collections, v. 103, no. 3 (1967),
            223-49.
4728. Murphy, Carol. Two desegregated hearts. Quaker his-
            tory, v. 53, no. 2 (1964), 87-92.
4729. Weld, Theodore Dwight. Letters of Theodore Dwight
            Weld, Angelina Grimke Weld and Sarah Grimke,
            1822-1844. Edited by Gilbert H. Barnes and
            Dwight L. Dumond. New York, D. Appleton-
            Century, 1934. 2v.

HALE, Sarah Josepha Buell, 1788-1879.
4730. Hill, Ralph Nading. Mr. Godey's lady. American heri-
            tage, v. 9 (October 1958), 20-7, 97-101.

HAMER, Fannie Lou, 1917-
4731. Demuth, J. Tired of being sick and tired. Nation,
            v. 198 (1 June 1964), 548-51.
4732. Garland, P. Builders of a new South. Ebony, v. 21
            (August 1966), 27-30+.

HAMILTON, Alice, 1869-1970.
4733. Cook, W. A. Hall of fame of occupational disease in-
            vestigators. Industrial medicine, v. 31 (March
            1962), 130-1.
4734. Ellis, S. Alice Hamilton, M.D. Industrial medicine,
            v. 15 (November 1946), 664+.
4735. Hamilton, A. Edith and Alice Hamilton; students in
            Germany. Atlantic monthly, v. 215 (March 1965),
            129-32.
4736. Harvard honors Dr. Alice Hamilton. Social service re-
            view, v. 33 (June 1959), 170.
4737. Hygeia, v. 27 (August 1949), 535+.
4738. Johnstone, R. T. Climate for exploration. Archives of
            environmental health, v. 3 (November 1961), 559-
            62.
4739. Lasker awards for 1947. American journal of public
            health, v. 37 (December 1947), 1614.
4740. Time, v. 93 (7 March 1969), 40.
4741. Woman of the year. Time, v. 58 (19 November 1956),
            91.
4742. Woolf, S. J. Triumphs of a pioneer doctor. New York

HAMILTON, Alice. (cont.)
      Times magazine, (9 November 1947), 20+.

HARBERT, Elizabeth Morrisson Boynton, 1845-1925.
   4743. Noun, Louise R. Strong-minded women. Ames, Iowa
         State University Press, 1969. pp. 158, 270-1.

HARPER, Ida Husted, 1851-1931.
   4744. Banta, Richard E., comp. Indiana authors and their
         books, 1816-1916. Crawfordsville, Ind., Wabash
         College, 1949. pp. 134-5.
   4745. Dictionary of American Biography. New York, C. Scrib-
         ner, 1936. v. 4, pt. 2, pp. 281-2.
   4746. Woman's home companion, v. 31 (July 1904), 12.
   4747. Woman's journal, n.s., v. 16 (April 1931), 32.

HIGGINSON, Thomas Wentworth, 1823-1911.
   4748. Author and reformer. Chautauquan, v. 48 (November
         1907), 391-3.
   4749. Cooke, G. W. Thomas Wentworth Higginson at home.
         Critic, v. 6 (1884), 145.
   4750. Current literature, v. 29 (September 1900), 286.
   4751. Current literature, v. 38 (June 1905), 509-10.
   4752. Dial, v. 50 (16 May 1911), 375-6.
   4753. Eclectic magazine, v. 88 (1876), 631.
   4754. Higginson, Mary Thacher. Thomas Wentworth Higginson.
         Boston, Houghton, Mifflin, 1914.
   4755. Higginson, Thomas Wentworth. Cheerful yesterdays;
         autobiography. Atlantic monthly, v. 78 (1896),
         586, 758.
   4756. Jackson, A. W. Character sketch of Thomas Wentworth
         Higginson. New England magazine, n.s., v. 25
         (December 1901), 447-63.
   4757. Lamp, v. 26 (March 1903), 153-4.
   4758. [Life and work of Thomas Wentworth Higginson.] New
         England magazine, n.s., v. 21 (February 1900),
         760-71.
   4759. Man of letters as reformer. Living age, v. 233 (10 May
         1902), 373-6.
   4760. Mead, E. D. [Thomas Wentworth Higginson.] New
         England magazine, n.s., v. 44 (May 1911), 397-
         412.
   4761. Nation, v. 92 (18 May 1911), 497-8.
   4762. Reid, M. J. Thomas Wentworth Higginson. Review of
         reviews, v. 8 (August 1893), 213.

HILLES, Florence Bayard, 1865?-1954.
   4763. National Cyclopaedia of American Biography. New York,
         J. T. White, 1893- . v. 45, (1962), p. 408.

HOLTZMANN, Anne Fisher, 1923?-1967.
   4764. New York Times, (4 August 1967), 29.

HOOKER, Isabella Beecher, 1822-1907.
4765. Dictionary of American Biography. New York, C. Scrib-
       ner, 1936. v. 5, pt. 1, pp. 195-6.
4766. Who was who in America, 1897-1942. Chicago, Marquis,
       1942. p. 584.

HOOPER, Jessie Annette Jack, 1865-1935.
       (See also no. 766, 4794)
4767. Smith, James Howell. Mrs. Ben Hooper of Oshkosh:
       peace worker and politician. Wisconsin magazine
       of history, v. 46 (Winter 1962-63), 124-35.
4768. Wisconsin State Historical Society. Dictionary of Wiscon-
       sin biography. Madison, The Society, 1960.
       p. 176.

HOWE, Julia Ward, 1819-1910.
4769. Cooke, George Willis. Mrs. Howe as poet, lecturer,
       and clubwoman. New England magazine, v. 26
       (1902), 3-21.
4770. Dictionary of American Biography. New York, C. Scrib-
       ner, 1936. v. 5, pt. 1, pp. 291-3.
4771. Dole, Nathan Haskell. Julia Ward Howe and her talented
       family. Munsey's magazine, v. 42 (February 1910),
       613-20.
4772. Hall, Florence Marion Howe. Julia Ward Howe and
       Edwin Booth. New England magazine, n.s., v. 9
       (1893), 315.
4773. _____, ed. Julia Ward Howe and the woman suffrage
       movement; a selection from her speeches and es-
       says.... Boston, D. Estes, 1913. 241p. Re-
       printed by Arno Press, New York, 1969.
4774. Higginson, Thomas Wentworth. Julia Ward Howe. Out-
       look, v. 85 (26 January 1907), 167-78.
4775. Howe, Julia Ward. Reminiscences, 1819-1899. Boston,
       Houghton Mifflin, 1899. 465p. Reprinted by
       Greenwood Press, Westport, Conn., 1970.
4776. Mannering, Mitchell. Julia Ward Howe. National maga-
       zine, v. 30 (May 1909), 218-19.
4777. Maud, Constance Elisbeth. Mrs. Julia Ward Howe.
       Fortnightly review, n.s., v. 87 (February 1910),
       268-73.
4778. Painter, Florence. Julia Ward Howe. Putnam's maga-
       zine, v. 6 (May 1909), 148-55.
4779. Richards, Laura E. Julia Ward Howe, 1819-1910. Bos-
       ton, Houghton Mifflin, 1915. 2v. Reprinted by
       N. S. Berg, Dunwoody, Ga., 1970.
4780. _____. Two noble lives: Samuel Gridley Howe and
       Julia Ward Howe, by their daughter. Boston,
       Estes, 1911. 76p.
4781. Seventieth birthday of Julia Ward Howe. Critic, v. 14
       (1888), 276.
4782. Tharp, L. H. Song that wrote itself. American heritage,
       v. 8 (December 1956), 10-13+.

HOWE, Julia Ward. (cont.)
4783. _____. Three saints and a sinner; Julia Ward Howe,
          Louisa, Annie, and Sam Ward. Boston, Little,
          Brown, 1956. 406p.

HUNT, Harriot
4784. Hunt, Harriot K. Glances and glimpses; or, Fifty years
          social, including twenty years professional life.
          Boston, J. P. Jewett, 1856. 418p.
4785. Who was who in America, historical volume, 1607-1896.
          Rev. ed. Chicago, Marquis, 1967. p. 337.

HUTTON, May Arkwright.
4786. Howard, Joseph K. Humanitarian, mountain style.
          Pacific spectator, v. 3 (Spring 1949), 201-8.
4787. Kizer, Benjamin H. May Arkwright Hutton. Pacific
          Northwest quarterly, v. 57, no. 2 (1966), 49-56.

IRWIN, Inez Haynes, 1873-
4788. Kunitz, Stanley J., ed. Twentieth century authors. 1st
          supplement. New York, H. W. Wilson, 1955.
          pp. 478-9.

JACOBI, Mary Putnam, 1842-1906.
4789. Dictionary of American Biography. New York, C. Scrib-
          ner, 1936. v. 5, pt. 1, pp. 564-5.
4790. Gilder, R. W. Pioneer among women physicians. Put-
          nam's magazine, v. 2 (April 1907), 53-6.
4791. Putnam, Ruth, ed. Life and letters of Mary Putnam
          Jacobi. New York, Putnam, 1925.
4792. Riegel, Robert Edgar. American feminists. Lawrence,
          University of Kansas Press, 1963. pp. 124-7.
4793. Truax, Rhoda. Doctors Jacobi. Boston, Little, Brown,
          1952. 270p.

JAMES, Ada Lois, 1876-1952.
4794. Graves, Lawrence L. Two noteworthy Wisconsin women:
          Mrs. Ben Hooper and Ada James. Wisconsin
          magazine of history, v. 41 (Spring 1958), 174-80.

JOHNSTON, Mary, 1870-1936.
4795. Coleman, Elizabeth Dabney. Penwoman of Virginia's
          feminists. Virginia cavalcade, v. 6 (Winter 1956),
          8-11.
4796. Simonini, R. C., ed. Southern writers. Charlottesville,
          University Press of Virginia, 1964. pp. 71-102.

KELLEY, Florence, 1859-1932.
          (See also no. 4408)
4797. Blumberg, Dorothy Rose. Florence Kelley: The making
          of a social pioneer. New York, A. M. Kelley,
          1966. 194p.

KELLEY, Florence. (cont.)
  4798. Goldmark, Josephine. Fifty years--the National Con-
            sumers' League. Survey, v. 85 (December 1949),
            674-6.
  4799. _____. Impatient crusader: Florence Kelley's life
            story. Urbana, University of Illinois Press, 1953.
            217p.
  4800. _____. Twenty-five years of it. New republic, v. 40
            (12 November 1924), 271-2.
  4801. Kellogg, P. U. Secretary of the National Consumers'
            League. American mercury, v. 70 (July 1910),
            322-4.
  4802. Lathrop, J. C. Florence Kelley, 1859-1932. Survey,
            v. 67 (15 March 1932), 677.
  4803. Lundberg, E. O. Pathfinders of the middle years. Social
            service review, v. 21 (March 1947), 9-11.
  4804. Perkins, F. My recollections of Florence Kelley. Social
            service review, v. 28 (March 1954), 12-19.
  4805. World outlook, v. 2 (November 1916), 5.

KENT, Elizabeth Thacher.
  4806. Kent, Elizabeth Thacher. Biography of Elizabeth T. Kent.
            [Kentfield, Cal?], 1949. 16p.

KIMBALL, Martha, 1869-
  4807. Where are they now? Newsweek, v. 65 (29 March 1965),
            14.

LAFOLLETTE, Belle Case, 1859-1931.
  4808. Nation, v. 133 (2 September 1931), 217.
  4809. Woman citizen, n. s., v. 9 (9 August 1924), 4.
  4810. Woman citizen, n. s., v. 9 (1 November 1924), 22.

LAFOLLETTE, Fola, 1882?-1970.
  4811. Everybody's magazine, v. 26 (February 1912), 237.
  4812. Hampton's magazine, v. 26 (March 1911), 362.
  4813. McClure's magazine, v. 45 (September 1915), 19.
  4814. Middleton, George. These things are mine; the auto-
            biography of a journeyman playwright. New York,
            Macmillan, 1947. 448p.
  4815. New York Times, (18 February 1970), 47.

LAIDLAW, Harriet Burton, 1873-1949.
  4816. Good housekeeping, v. 54 (February 1912), 150.
  4817. Journal of social hygeine, v. 35 (April 1949), 183.
  4818. Literary digest, v. 75 (11 November 1922), 52.

LARCOM, Lucy, 1824-1893.
  4819. Addison, Daniel D. Lucy Larcom: life, letters, and
            diary. Boston, Houghton Mifflin, 1894. 295p.
  4820. American woman's life. Outlook, v. 51 (16 February
            1895), 270.
  4821. Book news, v. 5 (1887), 399.

LARCOM, Lucy. (cont.)
4822.   Critic, v. 22 (22 April 1893), 258.
4823.   Dial, v. 14 (1 May 1893), 267-8.
4824.   Dictionary of American Biography.   New York, C. Scrib-
            ner, 1936. v. 5, pt. 2, pp. 614-15.
4825.   Dow, Mary Larcom.   Old days at Beverly Farms.
            Beverly, Mass. , North Shore Print. Co. , n. d.
            81p.
4826.   Larcom, Lucy.   Lucy Larcom letters.   Extracts from
            the collection in the library of the Essex Institute.
            Essex Institute Historical Collections, v. 68 (1932),
            257-79.
4827.   _____. A New England girlhood.   Boston, Houghton
            Mifflin, 1924.   274p.   Reprinted by Corinth Books,
            New York, 1961.

LATHROP, Julia Clifford, 1858-1932.
4828.   Addams, Jane.   My friend, Julia Lathrop.   New York,
            Macmillan, 1935.   228p.
4829.   Chenery, W. L.   Great public servant.   Survey, v. 46
            (1 September 1921), 637-8.
4830.   Hackett, C. L   Julia Lathrop, friend at large.   Woman
            citizen, n. s. , v. 9 (12 July 1924), 12-13.
4831.   Holman, C. T.   [Julia Lathrop].   Christian century,
            v. 49 (27 April 1932), 550.
4832.   Honored at home.   Survey, v. 67 (15 November 1931),
            180.
4833.   Lundberg, E. O.   Pathfinders of the middle years.
            Social service review, v. 21 (March 1947), 11-14.
4834.   Nation, v. 134 (27 April 1932), 481.
4835.   Survey, v. 28 (27 April 1912), 176-8.
4836.   Wald, L. D.   Right woman in the right place.   American
            city, v. 6 (June 1912), 847.

LEOPOLD, Alice Koller, 1909-
4837.   New head of Women's Bureau takes office.   Independent
            woman, v. 33 (January 1954), 3.
4838.   Receives Jane Addams award.   National business woman,
            v. 39 (June 1960), 10.
4839.   Roosevelt, Eleanor.   Ladies of courage.   New York,
            Putnam, 1954.   pp. 119-30.

LIVERMORE, Mary Ashton Rice, 1820-1905.
4840.   Arena, v. 32 (August 1904), 159.
4841.   Arena, v. 34 (August 1905), 185-8.
4842.   Dictionary of American Biography.   New York, C. Scrib-
            ner, 1936. v. 5, pt. 1, pp. 306-7.
4843.   Livermore, Mary Ashton Rice.   The story of my life; or,
            The sunshine and shadow of seventy years....
            Hartford, Conn. , A. D. Worthington, 1897.   730p.
4844.   Outlook, v. 80 (3 June 1905), 260-1.
4845.   Review of reviews, v. 22 (December 1900), 698.
4846.   Review of reviews, v. 32 (July 1905), 34.

LOCKWOOD, Belva Ann, 1830-1917.
4847. Clark, Allen C. Belva Ann Lockwood. Columbia His-
          torical Society, records [Washington, D. C.], v. 35
          (1935), 205-21.
4848. [Efforts to become a lawyer]. Lippincott's magazine,
          v. 41 (1887), 215.
4849. Procter, John Claggett. Belva Ann Lockwood, only wom-
          an candidate for president of the United States.
          Columbia Historical Society, records [Washington,
          D. C.], v. 35 (1935), 192-204.

LOWELL, Josephine Shaw, 1843-1905.
4850. Charities and the commons, v. 15 (2 December 1905),
          309-35.
4851. Stewart, William Rhinelander. The philanthropic work
          of Josephine Shaw Lowell. New York, Macmillan
          1911. 584p. Reprinted by Patterson Smith, 1972.
4852. Who was who in America, 1897-1942. Chicago, Marquis,
          1942. p. 750.
4853. Work of Josephine Shaw Lowell. Chautauquan, v. 49
          (January 1908), 264-7.

MCCORMICK, Katherine Dexter, 1876-
4854. American women; the changes. Vogue, v. 149 (May
          1967), 184.
4855. Outlook, v. 102 (28 December 1912), 933.

MCDOWELL, Mary E. , 1854-1936.
4856. Who was who in America, 1897-1942. Chicago, Mar-
          quis, 1942. p. 809.

MAILER, Norman, 1923-
          (See no. 1264)

MANSFIELD, Arabella, 1846-1911.
4857. Noun, Louise R. Strong-minded women. Ames, Iowa
          State University Press, 1969. pp. 143-4, 271-2.

MARSDEN, Dora.
4858. Bjorkman, F. M. New prophetess of feminism: Dora
          Marsden. Forum, v. 48 (October 1912), 455-64.
4859. Feminism's new prophetess. Review of reviews, v. 46
          (December 1912), 739-41.

MARTIN, Anne Henrietta, 1875-1951.
4860. Cooley, W. H. How bold is Anne! The picturesque
          campaign of the first woman candidate for the
          U. S. Senate. Sunset, v. 41 (November 1918),
          39-40.
4861. Hutcheson, Austin E. , ed. The story of the Nevada
          equal suffrage campaign: memoirs of Anne
          Martin, 1912-1914. Reno, University of Nevada,
          1948. 19p. [Also in: University of Nevada bul-

MARTIN, Anne Henrietta.   (cont.)
        letin, v. 42, no. 7 (August 1948), 19p.]
4862. Independent, v. 89 (19 March 1917), 445.
4863. Independent, v. 93 (16 March 1918), 445.

MAY, Samuel Joseph, 1797-1871.
4864. Pease, William H. and Jane H. Pease. Samuel J. May:
        civil libertarian. Cornell Library journal, v. 3
        (1967), 7-25.

MEYER, Agnes Elizabeth Ernst, 1887-
4865. Meyer, Agnes Elizabeth Ernst. Out of these roots: the
        autobiography of an American woman. Boston,
        Little, Brown, 1953. 385p.

MILLER, Emma Guffy, 1874?-1970.
4866. Newsweek, v. 75 (9 March 1970), 61.
4867. Where are they now? Newsweek, v. 65 (29 March 1965),
        14.

MILLETT, Kate, 1934-
        (See also no. 1264)
4868. Edmiston, S. Day in the life of Kate Millett; interview.
        Mademoiselle, v. 72 (February 1971), 138-9+.
4869. Liberation of Kate Millett. Time, v. 96 (31 August
        1970), 18-19.
4870. Who's she? Women activists in U. S. history. Senior
        scholastic, v. 97 (9 November 1970), 14.
4871. Wrenn, M. C. Furious young philosopher who got it
        down on paper. Life, v. 69 (4 September 1970),
        22.

MINER, Myrtilla, 1815-1864.
4872. Who was who in America, historical volume, 1607-1896.
        Rev. ed. Chicago, Marquis, 1967. pp. 429-30.

MITCHELL, Maria, 1818-1889.
4873. Albertson, Alice Owen. Maria Mitchell. Nantucket
        Historical Association, proceedings, v. 29 (1923),
        47-52.
4874. Book news, v. 14 (1896), 536.
4875. Dictionary of American Biography. New York, C. Scrib-
        ner, 1936. v. 7, pt. 1, pp. 57-8.
4876. Hinchman, Lydia S. The Maria Mitchell house and
        memorial, Nantucket, Mass. Old-time New Eng-
        land, v. 16 (January 1926), 105-17.
4877. Howe, Mark Antony. Who lived here? Boston, Little,
        Brown, 1952. pp. 121-9.
4878. Matyas, C. J. Maria Mitchell, first woman astronomer
        in America. Science digest, v. 50 (September
        1961), 81-7.
4879. Mitchell, Maria. Maria Mitchell, life, letters, and
        journals. Compiled by Phebe Kendall. Boston,

MITCHELL, Maria.   (cont.)
                Lee and Shepard, 1896.   293p.
4880.   Popular science monthly, v. 50 (February 1897), 544-51.
4881.   Priestly, Alice E.   Maria Mitchell as an educator.   PhD
            thesis, New York University, 1947.
4882.   Spofford, H. P.   Maria Mitchell.   Chautauquan, v. 10
            (1889), 181.
4883.   Whitney, M. W.   Maria Mitchell.   Sidereal messenger,
            v. 9 (1890), 49.
4884.   Wright, Helen.   Sweeper in the sky: the life of Maria
            Mitchell, first woman astronomer in America.
            New York, Macmillan, 1949.   253p.

MORRIS, Esther Robart McQuigg, 1814-1902.
4885.   Dobler, Lavinia.   Esther Morris, mother of woman suf-
            frage.   Westerner's brandbook [New York], v. 4
            (1956?), 31-2, 47.
4886.   Friggens, P.   What Wyoming did for women.   Reader's
            digest, v. 77 (September 1960), 197-201+.

MOTT, Lucretia Coffin, 1793-1880.
            (See also no. 781, 4549)
4887.   Beard, Mary R.   Lucretia Mott.   American scholar,
            v. 2 (1933), 5-12.
4888.   Cromwell, Otelia.   Lucretia Mott.   Cambridge, Mass. ,
            Harvard University Press, 1958.   241p.
4889.   Dictionary of American Biography.   New York, C. Scrib-
            ner, 1936.   v. 7, pt. 1, pp. 288-90.
4890.   Field, Sara Bard.   The speech of Sara Bard Field pre-
            senting to Congress on behalf of the women of the
            nation the marble busts of three suffrage pioneers:
            Lucretia Mott, Elizabeth Stanton and Susan Brownell
            Anthony.   San Francisco, Nash, 1921.   9p.
4891.   Hallowell, Anna Davis.   James and Lucretia Mott: life
            and letters.   Boston, Houghton Mifflin, 1884.   566p.
4892.   _____. Lucretia Mott.   Medford historical register
            [Mass.], v. 14 (October 1911), 81-102.
4893.   Hare, Lloyd Custer Mayhew.   The greatest American
            woman, Lucretia Mott.   New York, American His-
            torical Society, 1937.   307p.   Reprinted by Green-
            wood Press, Westport, Conn. , 1970.
4894.   MacDonald, A. [Lucretia Mott].   Macmillan's magazine,
            v. 43 (1880), 452.
4895.   Rosenberger, Homer T.   Montgomery County's greatest
            lady: Lucretia Mott.   Montgomery County His-
            torical Society, bulletin [Pa.], v. 6 (April 1948),
            91-171.
4896.   Rush, N. Orwin.   Lucretia Mott and the antislavery
            fairs.   Friends Historical Association, bulletin
            [Pa.], v. 35 (1946), 69-75.
4897.   Smith, E. O. [Lucretia Mott].   Potter's American
            monthly, v. 16 (1880), 234.
4898.   Villard, Fanny Garrison.   Lucretia Mott.   Seneca Falls

MOTT, Lucretia Coffin. (cont.)
         Historical Society, papers, (1908), 47-51.
4899. Whitton, Mary Ormsbee. At home with Lucretia Mott.
        American scholar, v. 20 (Spring 1951), 175-84.

NATHAN, Maud Nathan, 1862-1946.
4900. Overland monthly, n. s., v. 61 (January 1913), 21.
4901. Survey, v. 35 (27 November 1915), 213.

NESTOR, Agnes, 1880?-1948.
4902. Nestor, Agnes. Experiences of a pioneer woman trade
        unionist. American federationist, v. 36 (August
        1929), 926-32.
4903. _____. Woman's labor leader, an autobiography.
        Rockford, Ill., Bellevue Books, 1954. 307p.
4904. Roberts, O. Lobbyist. American magazine, v. 73
        (February 1912), 422-5.

NICHOLS, Clarina Irene Howard, 1810-1885.
4905. Dictionary of American Biography. New York, C. Scrib-
        ner, 1936. v. 7, pt. 1, pp. 490-1.
4906. Who was who in America, historical volume, 1607-1896.
        Rev. ed. Chicago, Marquis, 1967. p. 450.

PACKARD, Elizabeth Parsons.
4907. Packard, Mrs. Elizabeth Parsons. Marital power ex-
        emplified in Mrs. Packard's trial, and self-
        defense from the charge of insanity; or three
        years' imprisonment for religious belief, by the
        arbitrary will of a husband, with an appeal to the
        government to so change the laws as to afford
        legal protection to married women. Chicago,
        Clarke, 1870. 137p.

PARK, Alice.
4908. Winter, Una Richardson. Alice Park of California,
        worker for woman suffrage and for children's
        rights. Upland, Cal., Susan B. Anthony Memorial
        Committee of California, 1948. 17p.

PARK, Maud Wood, 1871-1955.
4909. Good housekeeping, v. 70 (May 1920), 78.
4910. Good housekeeping, v. 73 (July 1921), 46.
4911. Hackett, C. I. Lady who made lobbying respectable.
        Woman citizen, n. s., v. 8 (19 April 1924), 12-13.
4912. Independent, v. 103 (17 July 1920), 84.
4913. Merk, Lois Bannister. The early career of Maud Wood
        Park. Radcliffe quarterly, v. 32 (May 1948),
        10-17. On her activities in promoting woman suf-
        frage between 1895 and 1917, especially in Mas-
        sachusetts.
4914. Review of reviews, v. 64 (September 1921), 277.
4915. Review of reviews, v. 65 (June 1922), 635.

PARK, Maud Wood. (cont.)
4916.   Woman's journal, n. s. , v. 15 (April 1930), 27.

PAUL, Alice, 1885-
        (See also no. 3333)
4917.   Current history magazine of the New York Times, v. 17
        (February 1923), 835.
4918.   Herendeen, A.   What the home town thinks of Alice Paul.
        Everybody's magazine, v. 41 (October 1919), 45.
4919.   Independent, v. 89 (19 March 1917), 489.
4920.   Kirchwey, F.   Alice Paul pulls the strings.   Nation,
        v. 112 (2 March 1921), 332-3.   Concerns her
        activities with the National Woman's Party.
4921.   New leader--Alice Paul--why she is.   Everybody's maga-
        zine, v. 35 (July 1916), 127-8.
4922.   Pan American magazine, v. 42 (October 1929), 108.
4923.   Riegel, Robert Edgar.   American feminists.   Lawrence,
        University of Kansas Press, 1963.   p. 181-2.
4924.   They stand out from the crowd.   Literary digest, v. 117
        (10 February 1934), 9.
4925.   Tittle, W.   Century, v. 106 (August 1923), 512.
4926.   Where are they now?   Newsweek, v. 75 (23 March 1970),
        18.
4927.   Zimmerman, Loretta Ellen.   Alice Paul and the National
        Woman's Party, 1912-1920.   353p.   PhD thesis,
        Tulane University, 1964.

PHILLIPS, Wendell, 1811-1884.
4928.   Dictionary of American Biography.   New York, C. Scrib-
        ner, 1936.   v. 7, pt. 2, pp. 546-7.
4929.   Phillips, Wendell.   Speeches, lectures and letters.   Bos-
        ton, Beacon, 1863-1891.   2v.   Reprinted by AMS
        Press, New York.   Volume two contains most of
        his writings on women's rights.

PORTER, Florence Collins, 1853-1930.
4930.   Who was who in America, 1897-1942.   Chicago, Marquis,
        1942.   p. 983.
4931.   Women in politics.   Outlook, v. 102 (28 September 1912),
        162-4.   Concerns the running of Mrs. Porter [of
        Los Angeles] for President of the United States
        with the Progressive Party.

PRATT, Iris Calderhead, 1888?-1966.
4932.   New York Times, (8 March 1966), 30.

RANKIN, Jeannette, 1880-
        (See also no. 1958)
4933.   Board, John C.   The lady from Montana.   Montana,
        v. 17, no. 3 (1967), 2-17.   An interview with
        Jeannette Rankin concerning her work as the first
        woman elected to Congress.
4934.   Congresswoman Rankin returns to the House.   Christian

RANKIN, Jeannette. (cont.)
        century, v. 57 (20 November 1940), 1437.
4935. Current history magazine of the New York Times, v. 17
        (February 1923), 835.
4936. First woman elected to Congress. Outlook, v. 114 (22
        November 1916), 623-4.
4937. Good housekeeping, v. 99 (July 1934), 51.
4938. Independent, v. 115 (26 December 1925), 727.
4939. Independent woman, v. 19 (December 1940), 379.
4940. Member from Montana. Literary digest, v. 53 (25 No-
        vember 1916), 1417.
4941. Political power in the hands of a woman. Survey, v. 38
        (21 July 1917), 357.
4942. Review of reviews, v. 54 (December 1916), 585.
4943. Schaffer, Ronald. Jeannette Rankin, progressive-isola-
        tionist. PhD thesis, Princeton University, 1959.
4944. Where are they now? Newsweek, v. 67 (14 February
        1966), 12.
4945. Wilhelm, D. Lady from Missoula. Independent, v. 90
        (2 April 1917), 25.

RIPLEY, Martha G. , 1843-1912.
4946. Solberg, Winton U. Martha G. Ripley: pioneer doctor
        and social reformer. Minnesota history, v. 39,
        no. 1 (1964), 1-17. Woman suffrage leader in
        the East and in Minnesota.

ROBINS, Margaret Dreier, 1868-1945.
4947. Current history magazine of the New York Times, v. 18
        (August 1923), 861.
4948. Dreier, Mary E. Margaret Dreier Robins: her life,
        letters, and work. New York, Island Press, 1950.
        278p. On her activities with the Chicago Federa-
        tion of Labor, the National Women's Trade Union
        League and other labor organizations, especially
        after 1907.
4949. Movement to organize women industrial workers into a
        labor union. American magazine, v. 70 (August
        1910), 464-5.
4950. Outlook, v. 123 (12 November 1919), 303.
4951. Survey, v. 23 (16 October 1909), 103.
4952. Survey, v. 48 (1 July 1922), 477.
4953. Wealthy worker for workers. Hampton's magazine, v. 26
        (March 1911), 367-8.

ROOSEVELT, Eleanor, 1884-1962.
        (See also no. 1235)
4954. Davidson, Margaret. Story of Eleanor Roosevelt. New
        York, Four Winds, 1968. 146p.
4955. Hareven, Tamara K. Eleanor Roosevelt; an American
        conscience. Chicago, Quadrangle, 1968. 332p.
4956. Lash, Joseph P. Eleanor and Franklin. New York,
        Norton, 1971.

ROOSEVELT, Eleanor. (cont.)
4957. _____. Eleanor Roosevelt; a friend's memoir. New
York, Doubleday, 1964. 374p.
4958. Peterson, Esther. Mrs. Roosevelt's legacy; report on
the status of women. McCall's, v. 91 (October
1963), 84+ .
4959. Reddy, J. Eleanor Roosevelt; first lady of the world.
American mercury, v. 68 (June 1949), 656-62.
4960. Roosevelt, Eleanor. Autobiography. New York, Harper,
1961. 454p.
4961. _____. If you ask me. New York, Appleton-Century,
1946. 156p.
4962. _____. On my own. New York, Harper, 1958. 214p.
4963. _____. This I remember. New York, Harper, 1949.
387p.
4964. United Nations pays tribute to the memory of Mrs. Roosevelt. U. S. Department of State bulletin, v. 48
(14 January 1963), 48-59.

ROOSEVELT, Theodore, 1858-1919.
(See no. 2052, 2060)

ROOT, Elihu, 1845-1937.
(See no. 2052)

ROSE, Ernestine Louise Potowski, 1810-1892.
4965. Dictionary of American Biography. New York, C. Scribner, 1936. v. 8, pt. 2, pp. 158-9.
4966. Friedman, Lee Max. Pilgrims in a new land. Philadelphia, Jewish Publishing Co. , 1948. pp. 248-60.
4967. Sillen, Samuel. Women against slavery. New York,
Masses and Mainstream, 1955. pp. 88-92.
4968. Suhl, Yuri. Eloquent crusader: Ernestine Rose. New
York, Messner, 1970. 191p.
4969. _____. Ernestine Rose and the battle for human rights.
New York, Reynal, 1959. 310p.

SANGER, Margaret Higgins, 1883-1966.
4970. Adams, M. Crusader. Delineator, v. 123 (September
1933), 15+ .
4971. Amidon, Beulah. Crusaders. New republic, v. 97 (7
December 1938), 152.
4972. Coigney, Virginia. Margaret Sanger; rebel with a cause.
Garden City, N. Y. , Doubleday, 1969. 185p.
4973. Douglas, Emily Taft. Margaret Sanger: Pioneer of the
future. New York, Holt, Rinehart and Winston,
1970. 274p.
4974. Kennedy, David M. Birth control in America; the career
of Margaret Sanger. New Haven, Conn. , Yale
University Press, 1970. 320p.
4975. Ketchum, R. M. Faces from the past. American heritage, v. 21 (June 1970), 53.
4976. Lader, Lawrence. The Margaret Sanger story and the

SANGER, Margaret Higgins. (cont.)
              fight for birth control.   Garden City, N. Y. , Double-
              day, 1955. 352p.
4977.   . Margaret Sanger; pioneer of birth control.
        New York, Crowell, 1969. 174p.
4978. Miller, L. M. Margaret Sanger; mother of planned
        parenthood. Reader's digest, v. 59 (July 1951),
        27-31. Discussion: v. 59 (December 1951), 139-
        42.
4979. Nichols, D. Sex and the law; raid on Mrs. Sanger's
        clinic. Nation, v. 128 (8 May 1929), 552-4.
4980. Rebel with a cause: Margaret Sanger. Newsweek, v. 68
        (19 September 1966), 34+ .
4981. Sabaroff, Nina. Margaret Sanger and voluntary mother-
        hood. Women; a journal of liberation, v. 1
        (Spring 1970), 28-32.
4982. Sanger, Margaret Higgins. Margaret Sanger; an autobi-
        ography. New York, W. W. Norton, 1938. 504p.
4983. Sanger at 66. Newsweek, v. 35 (6 February 1950), 48-9.
4984. Sanger milestone. Time, v. 28 (21 December 1936), 24.
4985. Story of Margaret Sanger. World tomorrow, v. 12 (July
        1929), 296-9.
4986. Wallace M. Personal history of a pioneer. Saturday
        review of literature, v. 19 (12 November 1938), 6.

SAVERY, Annie N. , 1831-1891.
4987. Noun, Louise R. Strong-minded women. Ames, Iowa
        State University Press, 1969. pp. 273-7.

SCHNEIDERMAN, Rose, 1884-
        (See also no. 2260)
4988. Good housekeeping, v. 102 (January 1936), 166.
4989. Independent, v. 58 (27 April 1905), 935.
4990. Literary digest, v. 116 (12 April 1933), 9.
4991. Schneiderman, Rose. All for one. New York, P. S.
        Eriksson, 1967. 264p. Concerning her work with
        the National Women's Trade Union League and the
        Women's Trade Union League of New York.

SCHOONMAKER, Nancy Musselman, 1873-1965.
4992. New York Times, (28 October 1965), 43.

SEARS, Julia.
4993. Crabb, A. L. Most remarkable woman. Peabody jour-
        nal of education, v. 46 (November 1968), 139-41.

SETON, Grace Gallatin, 1872-1959.
4994. Newsweek, v. 53 (30 March 1959), 72.
4995. Publishers weekly, v. 175 (13 April 1959), 28.
4996. Wilson library bulletin, v. 33 (May 1959), 614.

SEVERANCE, Caroline Maria Seymour, 1820-1914.
        (See also no. 540)

SEVERANCE, Caroline Maria Seymour. (cont.)
4997. Dictionary of American Biography. New York, C. Scrib-
             ner, 1936. v. 8, pt. 2, pp. 599-600.
4998. Groff, F. A. Mother of clubs. Sunset, v. 27 (August
             1911), 167-70.
4999. Hunt, Rockwell Dennis. California's stately hall of fame.
             Stockton, Cal. , College of the Pacific, 1950.
             pp. 535-40.
5000. Jensen, Joan M. After slavery; Caroline Severance in
             Los Angeles. Southern California quarterly, v. 48,
             no. 2 (1966), 175-86.
5001. New England magazine, n. s. , v. 38 (July 1908), 551.
5002. Ruddy, Ella Giles, ed. The mother of clubs: Caroline
             M. Seymour Severance: an estimate and an appre-
             ciation. Los Angeles, Baumgardt, 1906. 191p.

SHAW, Anna Howard, 1847-1919.
             (See also no. 854, 1799)
5003. American magazine, v. 68 (July 1909), 293.
5004. Bookman, v. 42 (October 1915), 120.
5005. Current literature, v. 47 (December 1909), 602.
5006. Dr. Shaw's revolt. Literary digest, v. 48 (10 January
             1914), 50-1.
5007. Dictionary of American Biography. New York, C. Scrib-
             ner, 1936. v. 9, pt. 1, pp. 35-7.
5008. Harper's bazaar, v. 39 (March 1905), 255.
5009. Independent, v. 56 (19 May 1904), 1138.
5010. Inveterate optimist of the woman suffrage movement.
             Current opinion, v. 59 (December 1915), 398-9.
5011. Nation, v. 109 (12 July 1919), 33.
5012. Shaw, Anna Howard. The story of a pioneer. New York,
             Harper, 1915. 337p. Reprinted by Kraus Reprint
             Co. , New York, 1971.
5013. _____. Why I went into suffrage work. Harper's
             bazaar, v. 46 (September 1912), 440.
5014. Simmons, E. B. Woman pioneer of the West. World
             outlook, v. 2 (April 1916), 10.
5015. World today, v. 13 (July 1907), 697.
5016. World today, v. 15 (October 1908), 1067.

SHERWIN, Belle, 1868-1955.
5017. National municipal review, v. 44 (September 1955), 448.

SMITH, Abby Hadassah, 1797-1878.
SMITH, Julia Evelina, 1792-1886.
5018. Speare, Elizabeth G. Abby, Julia and the cows. Ameri-
             can heritage, v. 8 (July 1957), 54-7, 96. On
             Abby and Julia Smith and their refusal to pay taxes
             without the right to vote in Connecticut.
5019. Who was who in America; historical volume, 1607-1896.
             Rev. ed. Chicago, Marquis, 1967. pp. 559, 563.

SMITH, Elizabeth Oakes, 1806-1893.
5020.   Critic, v. 23 (2 December 1893), 361.
5021.   Wyman, Mary Alice, ed.   Two American pioneers, Seba
        Smith and Elizabeth Oakes Smith.   New York,
        Columbia University Press, 1927.   251p.

SMITH, Gerrit, 1797-1874.
        (See also no. 5031)
5022.   Harlow, Ralph Volney.   Gerrit Smith, philanthropist and
        reformer.   New York, H. Holt, 1939.   501p.
5023.   Life of Gerrit Smith.   Potter's American monthly, v. 4
        (1875), 160.
5024.   Who was who in America, historical volume, 1607-1896.
        Rev. ed.   Chicago, Marquis, 1967.   p. 560.

SMITH, Jane Norman, 1874-1953.
5025.   Feminism and Jane Smith.   Harper's magazine, v. 155
        (June 1927), 1-10.
5026.   New York Times, (4 September 1953), 15.

STANTON, Elizabeth Cady, 1815-1902.
        (See also no. 1427, 4451, 4549)
5027.   Barth, R.   Feminist crusade.   Nation, v. 167 (17 July
        1948), 71-3.
5028.   Blatch, Harriot Stanton.   Elizabeth Cady Stanton.   Seneca
        Falls Historical Society, papers, (1908), 51-3.
5029.   Colby, Clara Bewick.   Elizabeth Cady Stanton.   Arena,
        v. 29 (February 1903), 152-60.
5030.   Cowing, Janet.   Mrs. Stanton our pioneer suffragist.
        State service [Albany, N. Y.], v. 3 (May 1919),
        12-18.
5031.   Galpin, W. Freeman.   Elizabeth Cady Stanton and Gerrit
        Smith.   New York history, v. 16 (1935), 321-8.
        Excerpts of their correspondence between 1856 and
        1875 pertaining to abolition and woman suffrage.
5032.   Harper, Ida Husted.   Suffrage and a woman's centenary.
        North American review, v. 211 (November 1915),
        730-5.
5033.   Lutz, Alma.   Created equal; a biography of Elizabeth
        Cady Stanton, 1815-1902.   New York, J. Day,
        1940.   368p.   Reprinted by University Microfilms,
        Ann Arbor, Mich.
5034.   Stanton, Elizabeth Cady.   Eighty years and more.   Remi-
        niscences of Elizabeth Cady Stanton.   New York,
        European Publishing Co. , 1898.   474p.   Reprinted
        by Source Book Press, New York, 1970.
5035.   Stanton, Theodore and Harriot Stanton Blatch, eds.
        Elizabeth Cady Stanton as revealed in her letters,
        diary, and reminiscences.   New York, Harper,
        1922.   2v.   Reprinted by Arno Press, New York,
        1969.
5036.   Wise, Winifred.   Rebel in petticoats; the life of Elizabeth
        Cady Stanton.   Philadelphia, Chilton, 1960.

STARBUCK, Kathryn H. , 1887-1965.
5037.   New York Times, (20 November 1965), 35.

STEINEM, Gloria, 1936-
5038.   Gloria Steinem; a liberated woman despite beauty, chic
        and success.   Newsweek, v. 78 (16 August 1971),
        51-5.
5039.   Smith, L.   Coming of age in America.   Vogue, v. 157
        (June 1971), 90-2+.

STEVENSON, Letitia Green, 1843-1914.
5040.   Stevenson, A. E.   Grandmother Stevenson, elder states-
        woman of the PTA.   PTA magazine, v. 60 (Sep-
        tember 1965), 20-1.

STONE, Lucy, 1818-1893.
        (See also no. 4549)
5041.   Blackwell, Alice Stone.   Lucy Stone, pioneer of woman's
        rights.   Boston, Little, Brown, 1930.   313p.
5042.   Dictionary of American Biography.   New York, C. Scrib-
        ner, 1936.   v. 9, pt. 2, pp. 80-1.
5043.   Garrison, W. P.   Mrs. Lucy Stone.   Nation, v. 57 (26
        October 1893), 302-3.
5044.   Hays, Elinor Rice.   Morning star: A biography of Lucy
        Stone, 1818-1893.   New York, Harcourt, Brace,
        and World, 1961.   339p.

STOW, Marietta.
5045.   Davis, Reda.   Woman's republic.   San Francisco, Cali-
        fornia Scene, 1969.

SUCHER, Nellie Dunn Mackenzie, 1883?-1966.
5046.   New York Times, (5 December 1966), 45.

SWING, Betty Gram, 1893?-1969.
5047.   New York Times, (4 September 1969), 47.
5048.   Time, v. 94 (12 September 1969), 85.

SWISSHELM, Jane Grey Cannon, 1815-1884.
5049.   Dictionary of American Biography.   New York, C. Scrib-
        ner, 1936.   v. 9, pt. 2, pp. 253-4.
5050.   Fisher, S. J.   Reminiscences of Jane Grey Swisshelm.
        Western Pennsylvania historical magazine, v. 4
        (July 1921), 165-74.
5051.   Klement, Frank.   Jane Grey Swisshelm and Lincoln: a
        feminist fusses and frets, 1860-1865.   Abraham
        Lincoln quarterly, v. 6 (December 1950), 227-38.
5052.   Shippee, Lester Burrell.   Jane Grey Swisshelm.   Mis-
        sissippi valley historical review, v. 7 (December
        1920), 206-27.
5053.   Swisshelm, Jane Grey Cannon.   Crusader and feminist;
        letters of Jane Grey Swisshelm, 1858-1865.   Edited
        by Arthur J. Larsen.   St. Paul, Minnesota His-

SWISSHELM, Jane Grey Cannon. (cont.)
          torical Society, 1934.   327p.
5054. _____ . Half a century.   Chicago, Jansen McClurg,
          1880.   363p.   Reprinted by Source Book Press,
          New York, 1970.

TARBELL, Ida Minerva, 1857-1944.
5055. American historical review, v. 49 (April 1944), 604-5.
5056. Independent, v. 90 (2 April 1917), 34.
5057. Keyes, H. J. [Thumbnail biography of Ida Tarbell].
          Woman's journal, n. s. , v. 16 (June 1931), 14-15+ .
5058. Literary digest, v. 98 (14 July 1928), 26.
5059. Memories of a muckraker.   Newsweek, v. 13 (24 April
          1939), 38.
5060. Newsweek, v. 23 (17 January 1944), 10.
5061. Outlook, v. 126 (13 October 1920), 283.
5062. Review of reviews, v. 78 (July 1928), 85.
5063. Tarbell, Ida Minerva.   All in a day's work; an auto-
          biography of Ida M. Tarbell.   New York, Mac-
          millan, 1939.   412p.
5064. They stand out from the crowd.   Literary digest, v. 117
          (13 January 1934), 11.
5065. Trambell, C. T.   Ida M. Tarbell and her farm.   Country
          life, v. 29 (November 1915), 19-22.

TERRELL, Mary Church, 1863-1954.
5066. Barton, Rebecca Chalmer.   Witnesses for freedom.   New
          York, Harper, 1948.   pp. 68-79.
5067. Negro history bulletin, v. 18 (October 1954), 2+ .
5068. New York Times, (29 July 1954), 23.
5069. No capital gains.   Time, v. 54 (4 July 1949), 39-40.
5070. Stokes, O. P.   Women of Africa and African descent.
          International journal of religious education, v. 44
          (October 1967), 7+ .

THERESA, Miriam.
5071. Freeman, O.   Sister Miriam Theresa and women's rights.
          Today's family digest, v. 26 (January 1971), 66-70.

THOMAS, Martha Carey, 1857-1935.
5072. Finch, Edith.   Carey Thomas of Bryn Mawr.   New York,
          Harper, 1947.   342p.
5073. Who was who in America, 1897-1942.   Chicago, Marquis,
          1967.   p. 1230.

THOMAS, Mary F.
5074. Heald, Pauline T.   Mary F. Thomas, M. D. , Richmond,
          Indiana.   Michigan history, v. 6 (1922), 369-74.
          Concerning Mrs. Thomas' activities for suffrage,
          especially in Indiana.

TRAIN, George Francis, 1829-1904.
5075. Bookman, v. 19 (March 1904), 6-8.

TRAIN, George Francis.   (cont.)
5076. Dictionary of American Biography. New York, C. Scrib-
       ner, 1936. v. 9, pt. 2, pp. 626-7.
5077. Outlook, v. 76 (January 1930), 252-3.
5078. Ross, C. Stuart. Two American types that left their
       stamp on Victorian history. Victorian historical
       magazine, v. 11 (July 1919), 126-34.

TRUTH, Sojourner, 1797?-1883.
5079. Bennett, Lerone. Sojourner Truth. Ebony, v. 19
       (October 1964), 63-4+.
5080. Bernard, Jaqueline. Journey toward freedom; the story
       of Sojourner Truth. New York, Norton, 1967.
       265p.
5081. Fauset, Arthur Huff. Sojourner Truth, God's faithful
       pilgrim. Chapel Hill, University of North Carolina
       Press, 1938. 187p.
5082. Gilbert, Olive. Narrative of Sojourner Truth, a bonds-
       woman of olden time... drawn from her Book of
       life. Battle Creek, Mich. , Review and Herald Of-
       fice, 1884. 240p. Reprinted by Johnson Publish-
       ing Co. , Chicago, 1970.
5083. Harlowe, M. Sojourner Truth, the first sit-in. Negro
       history bulletin, v. 29 (Fall 1966), 173-4.
5084. Pauli, H. E. Her name was Sojourner Truth. New
       York, Appleton, 1962. 250p.
5085. Ritter, E. J. Sojourner Truth. Negro history bulletin,
       v. 26 (May 1963), 254.
5086. White, W. Sojourner Truth: friend of freedom. New
       republic, v. 118 (24 May 1948), 15-18.

TUBMAN, Harriet Ross, 1815?-1913.
5087. Bennett, Lerone. Harriet Tubman. Ebony, v. 20
       (November 1964), 148+.
5088. Bradford, Sarah Elizabeth. Harriet Tubman, the Moses
       of her people. New York, Corinth, 1961. 149p.
5089. Conrad, Earl. Harriet Tubman. Washington, Associated
       Publishers, 1943. 248p. Reprinted by Eriksson
       Press, New York, 1969.
5090. Dennis, Charles. The work of Harriet Tubman. Ameri-
       cana, v. 6 (November 1911), 1067-72.
5091. Dictionary of American Biography. New York, C. Scrib-
       ner, 1936. v. 10, pt. 1, p. 27.
5092. Liberator, Harriet Tubman helped run the underground
       railroad. Life, v. 65 (22 November 1968), 101.
5093. Mary Eusebius, Sister. Modern Moses: Harriet Tub-
       man. Journal of Negro education, v. 19 (Winter
       1950), 16-27.
5094. Metcalf, George R. Black profiles. New York, McGraw
       Hill, 1968. pp. 169-94.
5095. Roy, J. H. Know your history. Negro history bulletin,
       v. 22 (November 1958), 38-40; v. 24 (January
       1961), 93-4.

TUBMAN, Harriet Ross.   (cont.)
5096.   Whiting, H. A.   Slave adventures.   Negro history bulletin,
          v. 19 (April 1956), 164.
5097.   Wyman, L. B.   Harriet Tubman.   New England magazine,
          n. s. , v. 14 (March 1896), 110-18.

UPTON, Harriet Taylor, d. 1945.
          (See also no. 3333)
5098.   Literary digest, v. 81 (24 May 1924), 6.
5099.   Outlook, v. 136 (23 January 1924), 149.
5100.   Savage, C.   Women as citizens.   Woman citizen, n. s. ,
          v. 8 (31 May 1924), 18-19.
5101.   Who was who in America.   Chicago, Marquis, 1950.
          v. 2, p. 543.

VALENTINE, Lila Meade, 1865-1921.
5102.   Coleman, Elizabeth Dabney.   Genteel crusader.   Virginia
          cavalcade, v. 4 (Autumn 1954), 29-32.   On Lila
          Meade Valentine's activities in the suffrage move-
          ment between 1909 and 1920.

VAN COTT, Maggie Newton.
5103.   Foster, John O.   Life and labors of Mrs. Maggie Newton
          Van Cott, the first lady licensed to preach in the
          Methodist Episcopal church in the United States.
          Cincinnati, Hitchcock and Walden, 1872.   339p.

VAN KLEECK, Mary, 1883-
5104.   Industrial citizenship for women; appointment of Miss
          Mary Van Kleeck as a member of the National
          War Labor Policies Board.   New republic, v. 15
          (13 July 1918), 304-5.
5105.   Who's who in America, with world notables, 1970-71.
          Chicago, Marquis, 1971.   p. 2335.

WAITE, Davis Hanson, 1825-1901.
          (See no. 1853)

WALD, Lillian D. , 1867-1940.
5106.   Alger, G. W.   Memories of an old friend.   Survey
          graphic, v. 29 (October 1940), 512-14.
5107.   Beatty, J.   She never gave up.   Forum, v. 96 (August
          1936), 70-3.
5108.   Duffus, Robert Luther.   Lillian Wald, neighbor and cru-
          sader.   New York, Macmillan, 1938.   871p.
5109.   Forty years on Henry Street.   Survey, v. 69 (May 1933),
          192.
5110.   House on Henry Street.   Atlantic monthly, v. 115 (March-
          August 1915), 289-300, 464-73, 649-62, 806-17.
5111.   Kellogg, P. U.   Settler and trail-blazer.   Survey, (15
          March 1927), 777-80.
5112.   _____ .   What about this Miss Wald?   Survey, v. 63
          (1 November 1929), 182-3.

WALD, Lillian D. (cont.)
5113.   Nation, v. 151 (14 September 1940), 203.
5114.   Stillman, C. G. Portrait of Lillian Wald.   Nation,
              v. 147 (26 November 1938), 569-70.
5115.   Wald, Lillian D. The house on Henry Street.   New
              York, H. Holt, 1915. 317p.
5116.   _____. Windows on Henry Street.   Boston, Little,
              Brown, 1934. 348p.
5117.   Williams, Beryl. Lillian Wald: angel of Henry Street.
              New York, Messner, 1948. 216p.

WALKER, Mary Edwards, 1832-1919.
5118.   Dr. Mary Walker and dress reform.   Independent, v. 97
              (15 March 1919), 357.
5119.   Dr. Mary E. Walker and her short dresses.   All the
              year round, v. 16 (1866), 514.
5120.   Dr. Mary Walker's eccentric dress drew attention away
              from her real achievements.   Literary digest,
              v. 60 (15 March 1919), 94.
5121.   Dictionary of American Biography. New York, C. Scrib-
              ner, 1936. v. 10, pt. 1, p. 352.
5122.   Snyder, Charles M. Dr. Mary Walker: the little lady
              in pants. New York, Vantage, 1962. 166p.
5123.   Woodward, Helen Beal. Bold women. New York,
              Farrar, Straus, 1953. pp. 281-98.

WEED, Helena Hill, 1874?-1958.
5124.   New York Times, (26 April 1958), 19.
5125.   Time, v. 71 (5 May 1958), 68.

WHITE, Sue Shelton.
5126.   Louis, James P.   Sue Shelton White and the woman suf-
              frage movement in Tennessee, 1913-1920.   Ten-
              nessee historical quarterly, v. 22, no. 2 (1963),
              170-90.   Concerning her activities with the Ameri-
              can Woman Suffrage Association and the National
              Woman's Party.

WILEY, Anna Campbell Kelton, 1877-1964.
5127.   Association of Official Agricultural Chemists, journal,
              v. 47 (April 1964), 408-9.

WILLARD, Emma Hart, 1787-1870.
        (See also no. 4478)
5128.   Brainerd, Ezra. Mrs. Emms Willard's life and work in
              Middlebury.   Middlebury, Vt. , Middlebury College,
              1918. 12p.
5129.   Dictionary of American Biography. New York, C. Scrib-
              ner, 1936. v. 10, pt. 2, pp. 231-3.
5130.   Fishburn, E. C. and M. S. Fenner. Emma Willard and
              her plan for improving female education.   National
              Education Association, journal, v. 30 (September
              1941), 177-8.

WILLARD, Emma Hart. (cont.)
5131. Holden, James A. Emma Willard; a sketch and a letter.
Educational review, v. 51 (April 1916), 387-96.
5132. Lutz, Alma. Emma Willard, daughter of democracy.
Boston, Houghton Mifflin, 1929. 291p.
5133. _____. Emma Willard, pioneer educator of American
women. Boston, Beacon, 1964. 143p.
5134. Meyer, M. R. Emma Willard and the New York state
teacher's institutes of 1845. Journal of educational
research, v. 44 (May 1951), 695-701.
5135. Stanton, Elizabeth Cady. Emma Willard, the pioneer in
the higher education of women. Westminster review, v. 140 (November 1893), 538-44.
5136. Tribute to Mrs. Emma Willard, the founder of Troy
Seminary. Magazine of American history, v. 26
(December 1891), 471-2.

WILLARD, Frances Elizabeth, 1839-1898.
(See also no. 4355)
5137. Dickinson, M. L. Frances E. Willard. Arena, v. 19
(May 1898), 658-69.
5138. Dictionary of American Biography. New York, C. Scribner, 1936. v. 10, pt. 2, pp. 233-4.
5139. Dillon, Mary Earhart. Frances Willard as an Illinois
teacher. Illinois State Historical Society, papers
for the year 1939. (1940), 27-38.
5140. _____. Frances Willard; from prayers to politics.
Chicago, University of Chicago Press, 1944. 417p.
5141. _____. The influence of Frances Willard on the woman's movement of the nineteenth century. PhD
thesis, Northwestern University, 1939.
5142. _____. A woman president; the story of Frances Willard and Northwestern University. National historical magazine, v. 73, no. 9 (1939), 54-8.
5143. Ferguson, C. W. Americans not everyone knows. PTA
magazine, v. 63 (November 1968), 10-12.
5144. Gates, Mildred L. Frances Elizabeth Willard, a great
woman; a brief story about her noble life, September 28, 1839-February 17, 1898. Memphis, Tenn.,
n. p., 1964. 24p.
5145. Gordon, Anna Adams. The life of Frances E. Willard.
Evanston, Ill., National Women's Christian Temperance Union, 1912. 337p.
5146. Morrill, M. A. Bow of white ribbon. Religion in life,
v. 19 (Winter 1949), 16-28.
5147. Somerset, I. C. Frances E. Willard. North American
review, v. 166 (April 1898), 429-36.
5148. _____. Frances E. Willard. Outlook, v. 53 (27 June
1896), 1184-90.
5149. Strachey, Rachel. Frances Willard, her life and work.
New York, Revell, 1913. 310p.
5150. Trowbridge, Lydia J. Frances Willard of Evanston.
Chicago, Willett, Clark, 1938. 209p.

WILLARD, Frances Elizabeth. (cont.)
5151.   Willard, Frances Elizabeth. Glimpses of fifty years.
        The autobiography of an American woman. Chi-
        cago, Woman's Temperance Publication Association,
        1889. 698p. Reprinted by Source Book Press,
        New York, 1970.
5152.   The Wisconsin home of Frances E. Willard. Wisconsin
        magazine of history, v. 2 (June 1919), 455-61.

WILSON, Woodrow, 1856-1924.
        (See no. 1925, 1926)

WOODHULL, Victoria Claflin, 1838-1927.
5153.   Cheshire, H. Woman for president. New York Times
        magazine, (27 May 1956), 60-1.
5154.   Dictionary of American Biography. New York, C. Scrib-
        ner, 1936. v. 10, pt. 2, pp. 493-4.
5155.   First teeny-bopper. Newsweek, v. 69 (10 April 1967),
        100-2+.
5156.   Johnson, G. W. Dynamic Victoria Woodhull. American
        heritage, v. 7 (June 1956), 44-7.
5157.   Johnston, Johanne. Mrs. Satan; the incredible saga of
        Victoria C. Woodhull. New York, Putnam, 1967.
        319p.
5158.   Marberry, M. Marion. Vicky; a biography of Victoria
        C. Woodhull. New York, Funk and Wagnalls, 1967.
        334p.
5159.   Noun, Louis R. Strong-minded women. Ames, Iowa
        State University Press, 1969. pp. 169-87.
5160.   Sachs, Emanie. The terrible siren, Victoria Woodhull.
        New York, Harper, 1928. 423p.
5161.   Trepte, E. H. No new thing under the sun. Independent
        woman, v. 35 (October 1956), 6+.

WRIGHT, Frances, 1795-1852.
5162.   Biography and notes of Frances Wright d'Arusmont.
        Boston, J. P. Mendum, printers, 1848. 48p.
5163.   Dictionary of American Biography. New York, C. Scrib-
        ner, 1936. v. 10, pt. 2, pp. 549-50.
5164.   Douglas, Emily Taft. Remember the ladies. New York,
        Putnam, 1966. pp. 66-84.
5165.   Perkins, Alice J. G. and Theresa Wolfson. Frances
        Wright, free enquirer. The study of a tempera-
        ment. New York, Harper, 1939. 393p.
5166.   Waterman, William Randall. Frances Wright. New
        York, Columbia University Press, 1924. 267p.
5167.   Woodward, Helen Beal. Bold women. New York,
        Farrar, Straus, 1953. pp. 24-52.

YOUNGER, Maud, 1870-1936.
5168.   Dictionary of American Biography. New York, C. Scrib-
        ner, 1958. Supplement 2, v. 11, pp. 743-4.
5169.   Edmondson, V. Feminist and laborite. Sunset, v. 34

YOUNGER, Maud. (cont.)
        (June 1915), 1179-80.
5170.   Woman's work for women workers.   Literary digest,
        v. 46 (18 January 1913), 137.

MANUSCRIPT SOURCES

ALABAMA

1. Heflin, James Thomas, 1869-1951.
   Papers: 1893-1951.
   In: University of Alabama Library, University.
   U. S. Representative and Senator from Alabama. Correspondence and other papers relate, in part, to his attitude toward woman suffrage.

ARIZONA

2. Women's Suffrage.
   Papers: 1879-1939.
   In: State of Arizona. Department of Library and Archives, Phoenix.
   Materials consist of anti-suffrage (1919); correspondence pro and con (1919); newspaper articles and some unsigned articles commenting on the subject.

CALIFORNIA

3. League of Women Voters of California.
   Records: 1911-1955.
   In: California Historical Society, San Francisco.
   Official archives including correspondence, minutes, committee reports, and printed material.
4. League of Women Voters of San Francisco.
   Records: 1911-1967.
   In: California Historical Society, San Francisco.
   Official archives including correspondence, minutes, committee reports, newspaper clippings, and other printed material.
5. Sorbier, Louise Agathe Josephine Bacon, 1847-1929.
   Papers: 1854-1956.
   In: California Historical Society, San Francisco.
   Correspondence, newspaper clippings, and other materials pertaining to the various organizations Mme. Sorbier was concerned with, such as the California State Woman Suffrage Educational Association, and the Women's Educational and Industrial Union.
6. Anthony Family.
   Papers: 1844-1945.
   In: Henry E. Huntington Library, San Marino.
   Includes correspondence relating to Susan B. Anthony.

CALIFORNIA (cont.)

7. Business Women's Legislative Council of California.
    Records: 1927-1943.
    In: Henry E. Huntington Library, San Marino.
    Correspondence and other records of the Council which
    was organized to bring about and maintain equal business
    opportunities for men and women.
8. Colby, Clara.
    Correspondence: 1882-1914.
    In: Henry E. Huntington Library, San Marino.
    Suffragist. Correspondence includes 117 letters from
    Susan B. Anthony to Mrs. Colby.
9. Collection. Woman Suffrage.
    Papers: 1886-1903.
    In: Henry E. Huntington Library, San Marino.
    Sixty pamphlets with the binder's title: Why women do
    not want the ballot.
10. Collection. Woman Suffrage.
    Scrapbooks: 1870-1950.
    In: Henry E. Huntington Library, San Marino.
    Scrapbooks containing ephemera relating to woman suf-
    frage and Elizabeth Harbert.
11. Field, Sara Bard.
    Papers: 1920-1953.
    In: Henry E. Huntington Library, San Marino.
    Collection of pamphlets on civil liberty, woman suffrage,
    Socialism, etc.
12. Harper, Ida Husted, 1851-1931.
    Correspondence: 1841-1910.
    In: Henry E. Huntington Library, San Marino.
    Letters on the woman suffrage movement in the United
    States.
13. Park, Alice.
    Correspondence: 1885-1946.
    In: Henry E. Huntington Library, San Marino.
    Her correspondence with other women suffragists in the
    United States and abroad.
14. Cator, Thomas Vincent.
    Papers
    In: Stanford University Library, Stanford.
    Correspondence during his involvement with the People's
    Party and the Populist movement in California, 1883-
    1915. His views are also stated on woman suffrage.
15. Irish, John Powell, 1843-1923.
    Papers: 1882-1923.
    In: Stanford University Library, Stanford.
    Journalist and member of the Iowa State Legislature.
    Articles and correspondence pertains, in part, to woman
    suffrage.
16. Jordan, David Starr.
    Papers
    In: Stanford University Library, University Archives,

CALIFORNIA (cont.)

            Stanford.
            General correspondence.
17.   Lissner, Meyer.
            Papers
            In: Stanford University Library, Stanford.
            General correspondence [1903-1925], articles, legal
            papers and speeches mostly of a political nature.
18.   Stanford, Jane L.
            Papers
            In: Stanford University Library, University Archives,
            Stanford.
            General correspondence.
19.   Field, Sara Bard.
            Oral history.
            In: University of California, Bancroft Library, Berkeley.
            Includes comments on the winning of suffrage in Nevada.
20.   Keith-Pond Family.
            Papers: ca. 1883-1947.
            In: University of California, Bancroft Library, Berkeley.
            Family letters and correspondence concerning woman suf-
            frage in California. Organizations represented include the
            California State Suffrage Association and the California
            Equal Suffrage Association. Correspondents include Susan
            B. Anthony, Lillian Harris Coffin, Ida Husted Harper,
            and Carrie Chapman Catt.
21.   Martin, Anne Henrietta, 1875-1951.
            Correspondence and papers: 1892-1951.
            In: University of California, Bancroft Library, Berkeley.
            Suffragist and pacifist, especially in Nevada. Some cor-
            respondents include Jane Addams, Charlotte Perkins Gil-
            man, Ida Husted Harper, Carrie Chapman Catt, Sara
            Bard Field, Belle La Follette, Harriet Stanton Blatch,
            Jeannette Rankin, Anna Howard Shaw, Mabel Vernon,
            Alice Paul, Mary Ritter Beard, and Katherine Devereux
            Blake. Materials consist of manuscripts, magazine and
            newspaper clippings, pamphlets, and scrapbooks.
22.   Suffrage in Nevada.
            Correspondence: 1914-1918.
            In: University of California, Bancroft Library, Berkeley.
            Correspondence relating to the suffrage campaign. Let-
            ters include those to and from Anna Howard Shaw, Maude
            McCreery, Edwin Ewing Roberts, Key Pittman, Anne
            Martin, Grace Bridges, Bessie Eichelberger, and Minnie
            Flannigan.
23.   Vernon, Mabel.
            Papers: 1914-1920.
            In: University of California, Bancroft Library, Berkeley.
            Suffragist. Correspondence, including campaign letters
            [1918-1921] and other papers of Miss Vernon who partici-
            pated in the Nevada suffrage campaign in 1914 and 1916.
            Includes papers and letters from Sara Bard Field, Alice

CALIFORNIA (cont.)

       Henkle, Alice Paul, Maud Younger, Doris Stevens, and
       Margaret Whittemore.
24. Catt, Carrie Chapman, 1859-1947.
       Correspondence: 1918-1920.
       In: University of California, Research Library, Los
         Angeles.
       Six letters pertaining to woman suffrage.
25. Cole Family.
       Papers: 1833-1943.
       In: University of California, Research Library, Los
         Angeles.
       Correspondence, clippings, and other materials relating,
       in part, to woman suffrage.
26. Edson, Katherine Philips, 1870-1933.
       Papers: 1909-1934.
       In: University of California, Research Library, Los
         Angeles.
       Correspondence, pamphlets and other materials pertaining
       to minimum wage laws, the National Woman's Party,
       woman suffrage in the United States and California, Car-
       rie Chapman Catt, the National Women's Trade Union
       League, and other political matters.
27. John Randolph Haynes and Dora Haynes Foundation Collection.
       John Randolph Haynes papers.
       In: University of California, Research Library, Public
         Affairs Service, Los Angeles.
       Pertains, in part, to employment of women and woman
       suffrage.

COLORADO

28. Meredith, Ellis, ca. 1860-1920.
       Papers
       In: State Historical Society of Colorado, Denver.
       Correspondence, notebooks, scrapbooks, and clippings
       about woman suffrage, child labor laws, and other mat-
       ters.
29. Colorado Federation of Women's Clubs.
       Papers: 1905-1952.
       In: University of Colorado Libraries, Western Historical
         Collections, Boulder.
       Materials include yearbooks for 1905-1935, 1958-1959,
       a program for 1910, and a history and chronology from
       1895 to 1952.

CONNECTICUT

30. Burr, F. E.
       Scrapbooks.
       In: Connecticut State Library, Hartford.
       Four scrapbooks consisting of newspaper clippings on

CONNECTICUT (cont.)

> woman suffrage and other subjects.
31. Connecticut Woman Suffrage Association.
>   Leaflets.
>   In: Connecticut State Library, Hartford.
>   Miscellaneous leaflets.

DISTRICT OF COLUMBIA

32. Grimké, Archibald Henry, 1849-1930.
>   Papers: ca. 1868-1930.
>   In: Howard University Library.
>   Lawyer, editor, author, lecturer, politician, and diplomat. Correspondence and official papers dealing with his duties. Correspondents include Sarah Moore Grimké, Angelina Emily Grimké, and others.
33. Terrell, Mary Church, 1863-1954.
>   Papers: 1895-1953.
>   In: Howard University Library.
>   Negro leader and author. Papers are mainly related to the National Association of Colored Women, of which Mrs. Terrell was the first president.
34. Banister, Marion Glass.
>   Papers: 1933-1951.
>   In: Library of Congress.
>   Leader in women's political affairs. Correspondence and publicity material relating to her life as assistant treasurer of the United States [1933-1951] and to the Democratic National Committee.
35. Catt, Carrie Lane Chapman, 1859-1947.
>   Papers: 1890-1947.
>   In: Library of Congress.
>   Leader in the woman suffrage movement. Correspondence and diaries relating to women's rights, etc. Correspondents include Alice Stone Blackwell, Ida Husted Harper, Maud Wood Park, Edna L. Stantial, Mary Gray Peck, and others.
36. Dickinson, Anna Elizabeth, 1842-1932.
>   Papers: 1860-1932.
>   In: Library of Congress.
>   Abolitionist, actress, author, and suffragist. Correspondence, speeches, and other documents relate, in part, to woman suffrage.
37. Hall, Olivia B.
>   Papers: 1869-1905.
>   In: Library of Congress.
>   Suffragist of Ann Arbor, Michigan. Correspondence and photos relating to the suffrage movement and Susan B. Anthony.
38. Howe, Julia Ward, 1819-1910.
>   Papers: 1861-1917.
>   In: Library of Congress.

DISTRICT OF COLUMBIA (cont.)

39. Johnson, Adelaide, 1859-1955.
    Papers: 1875-1947.
    In: Library of Congress.

Author and reformer. Consists of correspondence together with addresses, articles, lectures, and other
writings on suffrage, politics, and education.

Sculptress and suffragist. Correspondence, diaries,
and speeches concerning her life as a sculptress and
feminist. Correspondents include Susan B. Anthony,
Ida Husted Harper, Alice Paul, May Wright Sewall, and
others.

40. League of Women Voters of the United States.
    Papers: 1892-1956.
    In: Library of Congress.
    Consists of correspondence, papers, reports, and note-
    books. Correspondents include Carrie Chapman Catt,
    Jane Addams, Eleanor Roosevelt, Julia Lathrop, Grace
    and Edith Abbott, Sophonisba P. Breckinridge, Belle
    Sherwin, Cornelia Bryce Pinchot, Alice Hamilton,
    Florence Kelley, Ruth Hannah McCormick, and Ruth
    Bryan Rohde.

41. Leslie Woman Suffrage Commission.
    Records: 1911-1918.
    In: Library of Congress.
    Correspondence, press releases, articles and reports
    primarily written by Ida Husted Harper. Correspondence
    of the Commission, including materials relating to the
    suffrage movement.

42. National Women's Trade Union League of America.
    Records: 1903-1950.
    In: Library of Congress.
    Correspondence, records, reports, minutes of meetings,
    proceedings of national conventions, and International
    Congresses of Working Women, 1919-1921 and 1923.
    Includes much correspondence between the League and
    members of Congress concerning labor and social legis-
    lation and the later interests of the League in education,
    civil rights and price control. Correspondents include
    Jane Addams, Rose Schneiderman, Sophonisba P. Breck-
    inridge, Alice Henry, Eleanor Roosevelt, Margaret
    Dreier Robins, Mary Anderson, Elizabeth Christman.

43. Pittman, Key, 1872-1940.
    Papers: 1898-1951.
    In: Library of Congress.
    Lawyer and U. S. Senator from Nevada. Correspondence,
    speeches, clippings, etc. , pertain primarily to his ser-
    vice in the Senate, but with other materials dealing with
    woman suffrage.

44. Sanger, Margaret Higgins, 1883-1966.
    Papers: 1903-1957.
    In: Library of Congress.

DISTRICT OF COLUMBIA (cont.)

        Leader in the birth control movement. Diaries, (1914-
1936), articles, speeches, and other materials concern
her activities for the birth control movement in the
United States and abroad.
45. Susan B. Anthony Foundation, Washington, D. C.
     Records: 1896-1943.
     In: Library of Congress.
     Correspondence, bylaws and constitution, reports and
other records. Includes Susan B. Anthony biographical
papers and the records of the District of Columbia Woman Suffrage Association. Also includes materials relating to the General Federation of Women's Clubs.
46. Terrell, Mary Church, 1863-1954.
     Papers: 1886-1954.
     In: Library of Congress.
     Negro leader and author. Correspondence, diaries,
notebooks, etc. , part of which concerns the rights of
women. Relevant correspondents include Jane Addams,
Mary McLeod Bethune, Carrie Chapman Catt, and Ruth
Hanna McCormick.
47. Watterson, Henry, 1840-1921.
     Papers: 1863-1920.
     In: Library of Congress.
     Journalist, author, orator, and editor of the Louis-
ville Courier-Journal from 1868 to 1921. Papers relate,
in part, to woman suffrage.
48. Wiley, Anna Kelton, 1877-1964.
     Papers: 1798-1964.
     In: Library of Congress.
     Feminist and clubwoman of Washington, D. C. General
and family correspondence, speeches, etc. , mainly from
1925 to 1960, relating to Mrs. Wiley's activities for
women's rights and her work with clubs and associations.
49. Williams, John Sharp, 1854-1932.
     Papers: 1902-1924.
     In: Library of Congress.
     U. S. Senator from Mississippi. Voluminous correspond-
ence, including the woman suffrage amendment.

GEORGIA

50. Emma V. Paul.
     Scrapbook: 1913-1914.
     In: Atlanta Historical Society.
     Concerns woman suffrage in Atlanta and consists of
newspaper clippings, editorial cartoons, handbills issued
by the National American Woman Suffrage Association,
and a listing of 17 objectives of the Atlanta suffrage
movement.

GEORGIA (cont.)

51. Black, Nellie Peters.
        Papers: 1875-1920.
        In: University of Georgia Libraries, Athens.
        Letters, family papers, pictures, scrapbooks, etc. ,
        pertaining to club work in Georgia in the late 19th and
        early 20th century, including the Georgia Federation of
        Women's Clubs.
52. Felton, Rebecca Latimer, 1835-1930.
        Papers: 1851-1930.
        In: University of Georgia Libraries, Athens.
        U. S. Senator from Georgia, lecturer and educator. Cor-
        respondence, speeches, scrapbooks and other materials
        concerning Mrs. Felton's work in Georgia politics, wom-
        en's rights, and other subjects.

ILLINOIS

53. Anthony, Susan B.
        Letters
        In: Chicago Historical Society.
        Notes and letters pertaining to woman suffrage.
54. Cooper, Susan Fenimore, 1813-1894.
        Papers: 1874.
        In: Chicago Historical Society.
        Remarks in opposition to woman suffrage in New York
        State.
55. Herstein, Lillian, 1886-
        Papers: 1920-1958.
        In: Chicago Historical Society.
        Articles, speeches, newspaper clippings, etc. , pertain-
        ing to Miss Herstein's labor union activities, including
        her work with the Women's Trade Union League of
        Chicago.
56. Hess, Nina D.
        Letters: 1966
        In: Chicago Historical Society.
        Two letters with autobiographical information on Nina
        Hess, early Chicago suffragist.
57. Illinois League of Women Voters.
        Papers: 1921-1961.
        In: Chicago Historical Society.
        Letters, minutes, etc. , concerned with efforts to secure
        legal, political, and employment equalities for women.
        Also includes minutes of the National League in Wash-
        ington, D. C.
58. Nestor, Agnes, 1880-1948.
        Papers: 1896-1954.
        In: Chicago Historical Society.
        Labor union official.   The collection relates, in part,
        to the status of women in the field of labor, especially
        around 1900 to 1940.   Also includes material relevant

ILLINOIS (cont.)

      to hearings at Springfield, Ill. (April 1909) for woman
      suffrage in municipal elections.
59. Women. Suffrage.
      Petitions: ca. 1880.
      In: Chicago Historical Society.
      Miscellaneous woman suffrage petitions.
60. Willard, Frances Elizabeth, 1839-1898.
      Papers: 1855-1898.
      In: National Woman's Christian Temperance Union,
      Evanston.
      Educator and reformer. Correspondence, diaries, and
      other materials, much of it relating to her work with
      the WCTU.
61. Woodhull-Martin, Victoria Claflin, 1838-1927.
      Papers: 1870-1962.
      In: Southern Illinois University Archives, Carbondale.
      Social reformer. Correspondence and notes by Mrs.
      Woodhull-Martin (between 1870 and 1927) as well as cor-
      respondence of her sister, Tennessee Claflin Cook. Sev-
      eral prominent correspondents include Paulina Wright
      Davis, Isabella Beecher Hooker, Elizabeth Cady Stanton,
      and Susan B. Anthony.
62. Abbott, Edith, 1876-1957.
      Papers: 1903-1954.
      In: University of Chicago Library.
      Correspondence, notes, documents, pamphlets, and other
      papers (mostly since 1910) relating to the careers of
      Edith and Grace Abbott concerning equality of women in
      industry. Correspondents include Jane Addams, So-
      phonisba P. Breckinridge, Florence Kelley, Julia Lath-
      rop, and others.
63. Saperstein, Esther.
      Papers: 1949-1967.
      In: University of Illinois, Chicago Circle Campus Library.
      Member of the Illinois Legislature. Correspondence and
      other materials relate, in part, to discrimination against
      women in industry.

INDIANA

64. Woman's Suffrage Association of Indiana.
      Papers: 1851-1870.
      In: Indiana Historical Society, Indianapolis.
      Preamble and constitution of the Woman's Rights (changed
      to Suffrage in 1869) Association of Indiana with names of
      charter members; minutes of annual meetings from Octo-
      ber 1851 to January 1859 and from June 1869 to October
      1881; treasurer's report, 1870.
65. Clarke, Grace Giddings, 1865-1938.
      Papers: 1857-1936.
      In: Indiana State Library, Indianapolis.

INDIANA (cont.)

> Writer. Materials relate to the suffrage movement, the
> Indiana Federation of Women's Clubs (1910-1917), and
> the Woman's Franchise League.

66. Foulke, William Dudley, 1848-1935.
    Papers: 1849-1931.
    In: Indiana State Library, Indianapolis.
    Lawyer, author, and member of the Indiana Senate.
    Materials include Julia Ward Howe on woman suffrage
    and a history of the National American Woman Suf-
    frage Association.
67. Hays, Will H.
    Papers: 1896-1954.
    In: Indiana State Library, Indianapolis.
    Political letters, many concerning the national suffrage
    amendment.

IOWA

68. Bloomer, Amelia Jenks, 1818-1894.
    Correspondence: 1851-1869.
    In: Council Bluffs Free Public Library.
    Suffragist. Letters from Julia Ward Howe, Annie
    Savery, Lucy Stone, and others.
69. Iowa Suffrage Memorial Commission.
    Records: 1854-1949.
    In: Iowa State Department of History and Archives Collec-
    tions, Des Moines.
    Correspondence, biographies, speeches, records of the
    Iowa Equal Suffrage Association and other organizations.
    Also includes clippings and pictures related to Carrie
    Chapman Catt and women associated with her.
70. Adams, Mary Newbury, 1837-1901.
    Papers
    In: Iowa State University Library, Ames.
    Correspondence of Mrs. Adams, a suffrage advocate
    starting in 1868.

KANSAS

71. Johnston, Lucy Browne.
    Papers: 1886-1930.
    In: Kansas State Historical Society, Topeka.
    Correspondence (1886-1930); bulletins of the Kansas
    Equal Suffrage Association (April-October 1912); their
    minutes (1907-1911); and correspondence of the Men's
    League for Woman Suffrage (1912).
72. Woman suffrage collection.
    Papers: 1867-1909.
    In: Kansas State Historical Society, Topeka.
    Correspondence relating to the campaign of 1867; manu-
    scripts of Elizabeth Cady Stanton's first speech in

KANSAS (cont.)

> Kansas (1867); minutes of meetings of the Woman Suffrage Association of Topeka (1867-1875); and miscellaneous correspondence.

73. Stephens, Kate, 1853-1938.
> Papers: 1873-1937.
> In: University of Kansas Library, Lawrence.
> Author and professor at the University of Kansas. Correspondence, in part, pertains to woman suffrage leaders such as Ida Minerva Tarbell and Susan B. Anthony.

KENTUCKY

74. Clay, Cassius Marcellus, 1810-1903.
> Papers: 1844-1907.
> In: Filson Club Collections, Louisville.
> U.S. Minister to Russia, lawyer, and abolitionist of Kentucky. The collection includes letters to his daughter, Mary Bar Clay, from Susan B. Anthony, Alice Stone Blackwell, Lucy Stone, and other suffragists.

75. Clay, Laura, 1849-1941.
> Papers: 1882-1941.
> In: University of Kentucky Library, Lexington.
> Woman suffrage leader. Correspondence (most of which is from 1906 to 1920) includes woman suffrage and the Kentucky Equal Rights Association. Major correspondents include Susan B. Anthony, Anna Howard Shaw, Carrie Chapman Catt, and Harriett Taylor Upton.

76. Gibson Family.
> Gibson-Humphreys papers: 1840-1955.
> In: University of Kentucky Library, Lexington.
> Correspondence and papers of a Kentucky family. Materials include, in part, Sarah Humphreys' activities in the Kentucky Equal Rights Association.

77. Wilson, Mary Bullock Shelby, 1876-1959.
> Papers on Kentucky women in politics.
> In: University of Kentucky Library, Lexington.
> Political leader. Papers concerning state and local women's organizations in the first years of women's participation in politics as well as papers relating to the Kentucky Equal Rights Association and the Woman's State Democratic Club of Kentucky.

LOUISIANA

78. Douglas, Judith Hyams.
> Papers: 1897-1955.
> In: Louisiana State University Library, Baton Rouge.
> New Orleans lawyer. Correspondence, speeches, scrapbooks, pertaining, in part, to woman suffrage.

79. Era Club of New Orleans.
> Minutes: 1914-1919.

LOUISIANA (cont.)

> In: New Orleans Public Library.
> Minutes of the Era Club, a suffrage group of New Or-
> leans. Consists of 299 pages of minutes of general and
> board meetings including descriptions of the activities of
> the club, letters received and membership lists.

80. Hutson Family.
> Papers: 1807-1955.
> In: Tulane University Library, New Orleans.
> Consists, in part, of letters of Ethel Hutson discussing
> the woman suffrage movement, covering the period, 1912-
> 1919. Many pertain to the situation in New Orleans.

81. Saxon, Elizabeth Lyle.
> Scrapbook
> In: Tulane University Library, New Orleans.
> Scrapbook of newspaper clippings by and about Mrs.
> Saxon pertaining to women's rights and suffrage, pri-
> marily in Louisiana, Tennessee, and Alabama.

MARYLAND

82. Woman suffrage in Maryland.
> Papers: 1897-1906.
> In: Enoch Pratt Free Library, Baltimore.
> Minute book of the Maryland Woman Suffrage Associa-
> tion, 1904-1910; minute books of the Baltimore City Wom-
> an Suffrage Association, 1897-1902 and 1909-1910; scrap-
> book of clippings on woman suffrage and two letters from
> Susan B. Anthony to Mrs. Emma Maddox Funck.

83. Williamson Scrapbook: 1859-1921.
> In: Maryland Historical Society, Baltimore.
> Collection of clippings collected by Miss Mary Janet
> Williamson, part of which includes female suffrage move-
> ments.

MASSACHUSETTS

84. Litman, Ray Frank, 1864?-1948.
> Papers: 1871-1957.
> In: American Jewish Historical Society, Waltham.
> Lecturer and journalist. Sermons, essays, and scrap-
> book (1879-1901) reflecting Mrs. Litman's views on wom-
> an suffrage and other matters.

85. White, George Robert, 1847-1922.
> Papers: 1861-1927.
> In: Massachusetts Historical Society, Boston.
> Philanthropist. Correspondence includes, in part, the
> campaign objectives of the women suffragists. Corre-
> spondents include Alice Stone Blackwell.

86. Woman Suffrage.
> Correspondence: 1915-1920.
> In: Massachusetts Historical Society, Boston.

MASSACHUSETTS (cont.)

Correspondence concerning the Bay State Campaign Fund
of Woman Suffrage and the Boston Equal Suffrage Asso-
ciation.
87. American Association of University Women.
Records: 1881-
In: Radcliffe College, Schlesinger Library, Cambridge.
Materials consist of committee and division reports,
including several boxes of files on the Status of Women
Committee.
88. American Council on Education.   Commission on the Education
of Women.
Records: 1953-1961.
In: Radcliffe College, Schlesinger Library, Cambridge.
Correspondence, reports of meetings, and research.
89. Anderson, Mary, 1872-
Papers: 1921-1950.
In: Radcliffe College, Schlesinger Library, Cambridge.
Director of the U. S. Women's Bureau.   Personal letters
and other papers relating to equal rights for women and
the National Women's Trade Union League as well as the
International Federation of Working Women.   Important
persons represented include Alice Henry, Agnes Nestor,
Margaret Dreier, Mary Van Kleeck, Mary N. Winslow,
Eleanor Roosevelt, and Harriet Taylor Upton.
90. Anthony, Susan Brownell, 1820-1906.
Papers: 1815-1944.
In: Radcliffe College, Schlesinger Library, Cambridge.
Reformer and suffragist.   Diaries, letters, speeches,
family papers, and photographs.   Names and subjects
represented include Carrie Chapman Catt, Anna Howard
Shaw, and woman suffrage.
91. Armstrong, Florence Arzelia, 1884-1962.
Papers: 1901-1961.
In: Radcliffe College, Schlesinger Library, Cambridge.
Economist.   Correspondence concerns the status of wom-
en and the National Woman's Party.   Persons repre-
sented include Sue Shelton White, Eleanor Roosevelt,
and others.
92. Babcock, Caroline Lexow, 1882-
Papers of Caroline Lexow Babcock and Olive E. Hurlburt.
In: Radcliffe College, Schlesinger Library, Cambridge.
Material relating to Mrs. Babcock's activities in support
of woman suffrage in New York (1906-1915), and the Na-
tional Woman's Party.   Included is material related to
Elizabeth Cady Stanton, Olive E. Hurlburt, Harriet
Stanton Blatch, and Rosika Schwimmer.
93. Beecher Family.
Papers: 1798-1956.
In: Radcliffe College, Schlesinger Library, Cambridge.
Correspondence, clippings pertaining to members of the
Beecher family, including Lyman Beecher Stowe's cor-

MASSACHUSETTS (cont.)

respondence and research on Charlotte Perkins Gilman
and others.

94. Blackwell Family.
Papers: 1784-1944.
In: Radcliffe College, Schlesinger Library, Cambridge.
Correspondence, diaries and other papers relating, in
part, to Alice Stone Blackwell, Frances Willard, Susan
B. Anthony, Gerrit Smith, Lucy Stone, and woman suf-
frage. Also includes papers of Antoinette Brown Black-
well, the first ordained woman minister in the United
States. Also includes material on Isabella Beecher
Hooker and Frances Willard as well as materials on
women in medicine.

95. Coggeshall, Mary Jane Whitley.
Papers: 1882-1909.
In: Radcliffe College, Schlesinger Library, Cambridge.
Leader in the woman suffrage movement in Iowa.
Speeches and articles relating to the suffrage movement.

96. Consumers' League of Connecticut.
Records: 1907-1946.
In: Radcliffe College, Schlesinger Library, Cambridge.
Minutes of meetings and materials of its investigations
into minimum wage and other areas.

97. Consumers' League of Massachusetts.
Records: 1891-1955.
In: Radcliffe College, Schlesinger Library, Cambridge.
Correspondence with individuals and organizations, articles and reports, publications of the League and records of the National Consumers' League. Includes material, in part, relating to the working conditions of
women in industry, including wages and hours, sweat-
shops, and homework.

98. Dall, Caroline Wells Healey, 1822-1912.
Papers: 1841-1910.
In: Radcliffe College, Schlesinger Library, Cambridge.
Writer. Includes letters to Margaret Fuller and others
concerning her writings, journals and reminiscences.

99. Dewson, Mary Williams, 1874-
Papers: 1896-1958.
In: Radcliffe College, Schlesinger Library, Cambridge.
Leader in social causes. Materials reflect her interest
in matters such as the National Consumers' League on
wage problems and the Women's Division of the Democratic National Committee, woman suffrage, and other
matters.

100. Dillon, Mary Earhart.
Papers on suffrage and on the legal status of women.
In: Radcliffe College, Schlesinger Library, Cambridge.
Papers concerning the suffrage movement, especially in
Illinois and the changing legal status of women. Per-
sons whose papers appear in the collection include Carrie

MASSACHUSETTS (cont.)

    Chapman Catt, Elizabeth Boynton Harbert, Catharine
    Waugh McCulloch, Anna Howard Shaw, Edna Lamprey
    Stantial, and Lucy Anthony.
101. Dunham, Catherine Devenney.
    Papers: 1884?-1920.
    In: Radcliffe College, Schlesinger Library, Cambridge.
    Speaker for temperance and women's rights. Includes
    speeches and papers on women suffrage, rights of
    mothers as guardians of their children, and other wom-
    en's rights.
102. Elliman, Claiborne Catlin.
    Papers: 1914.
    In: Radcliffe College, Schlesinger Library, Cambridge.
    Suffragist. Account of a four-month tour through
    Massachusetts for the National American Woman Suf-
    frage Association in 1914.
103. Evans, Elizabeth Gardiner, 1856-1937.
    Papers: 1882-1937.
    In: Radcliffe College, Schlesinger Library, Cambridge.
    Writer and social worker. Correspondence includes
    her efforts to establish a minimum wage and woman
    suffrage. Some correspondents include Fola La Fol-
    lette and Elizabeth Cabot Putnam.
104. Gage, Matilda Joslyn, 1826-1898.
    Papers: 1850-1900.
    In: Radcliffe College, Schlesinger Library, Cambridge.
    Reformer. Correspondence, speeches, articles, and
    other papers concerning equal rights and the status
    of women. Correspondents include Susan B. Anthony,
    Lucretia Mott, Lucy Stone, and Matthew Vassar.
105. Gellhorn, Edna Fischel, 1878-
    Papers: 1919-1960.
    In: Radcliffe College, Schlessinger Library, Cambridge.
    Civic leader. Correspondence and biographical in-
    formation on her activities as director of the National
    American Woman Suffrage Association. Other ma-
    terials related to Carrie Chapman Catt, The Leslie
    Woman Suffrage Commission, and The Committee of
    Ten.
106. Hamilton, Alice, 1869-
    Papers: 1910-1952.
    In: Radcliffe College, Schlesinger Library, Cambridge.
    Physician, professor, and research worker. Papers
    and correspondence, part of which shows her interest
    in equal rights for women. Also includes material
    pertaining to Jane Addams.
107. Henrotin, Ellen M., 1847-1922.
    Papers: 1865-1921.
    In: Radcliffe College, Schlesinger Library, Cambridge.
    Correspondence, speeches, and other materials relating
    to Mrs. Henrotin's interests in suffrage, The General

MASSACHUSETTS (cont.)

        Federation of Women's Clubs, and other activities.
108. Howe, Julia Ward, 1819-1910.
        Papers: 1869-1910.
        In: Radcliffe College, Schlesinger Library, Cambridge.
        Author and reformer. Correspondence, scrapbooks
        and other papers relating to her work for woman suf-
        frage and other social problems. Materials also per-
        tain to The Woman's Journal, Association for the Ad-
        vancement of Women, and The New England Women's
        Club.
109. International Federation of Working Women.
        Records: 1919-1923.
        In: Radcliffe College, Schlesinger Library, Cambridge.
        Reports, speeches, articles, etc., pertaining to the
        National Women's Trade Union League and the employ-
        ment of women.
110. Irwin, Inez Haynes, 1873-
        Papers: 1872-
        In: Radcliffe College, Schlesinger Library, Cambridge.
        Author and reformer. Materials concerning woman
        suffrage work. Persons included are Maud Wood Park,
        Alice Paul, Maud Younger, Charlotte Perkins Gilman,
        and Alice Stone Blackwell.
111. Jacobi, Mary Putnam, 1842-1906.
        Papers: 1851-1906, 1923.
        In: Radcliffe College, Schlesinger Library, Cambridge.
        Correspondence, autobiographical notes, and other
        papers. Includes letters on religion, and medical edu-
        cation for women at the Harvard Medical School and
        other places.
112. Kitchelt, Florence Ledyard Cross, 1874-
        Papers: 1885-1956.
        In: Radcliffe College, Schlesinger Library, Cambridge.
        Social worker and feminist. Diary (1918) and other
        papers relating to Mrs. Kitchelt's work for suffrage
        in Rochester, New York, and Connecticut; and her
        work with the Connecticut Committee for the Equal
        Rights Amendment. Persons represented include Mary
        Ritter Beard, Carrie Chapman Catt, Charlotte Perkins
        Gilman, Mary T. L. Gannett, Alice Hamilton, Alma
        Lutz, Alice Paul, Anita Pollitzer, Mrs. Chase Going
        Woodhouse, Mary Emma Wooley, and others.
113. Kleinert, Margaret Noyes.
        Papers
        In: Radcliffe College, Schlesinger Library, Cambridge.
        Correspondence, biographical materials, and articles.
        Includes material on women in medicine.
114. Laidlaw, Harriet Burton, 1873-1949.
        Papers: 1886-1948.
        In: Radcliffe College, Schlesinger Library, Cambridge.
        Feminist. Articles and other papers relating to Mrs.

MASSACHUSETTS (cont.)

Laidlaw's life as a suffrage advocate. Includes letters from the New York State Woman Suffrage Association and the National American Woman Suffrage Association as well as the Men's League for Woman Suffrage. Persons represented include Jane Addams, Alice Stone Blackwell, Carrie Chapman Catt, Beatrice Forbes-Robertson, Julia Ward Howe, Jeannette Rankin, Eleanor Roosevelt, Anna Howard Shaw, and others.

115. Leopold, Alice Koller.
Papers: 1953-
In: Radcliffe College, Schlesinger Library, Cambridge.
Government official. Materials include her work as director of the U.S. Women's Bureau, 1953- . Also includes material on the Bureau's Conference on the Effective Use of Womanpower, 1955.

116. Lutz, Alma.
Papers: 1937-1953.
In: Radcliffe College, Schlesinger Library, Cambridge.
Author. Reports on the work of the National Woman's Party and its magazine, Equal Rights (1937-1940) and on the work of other organizations for the Equal Rights Amendment.

117. Lyman, Helen D.
Papers: 1882-1919.
In: Radcliffe College, Schlesinger Library, Cambridge.
Scrapbook of women in the ministry, an album (1893) of portraits of women ministers in the United States, kept by Julia Ward Howe.

118. May Family.
May-Goddard Family papers: 1766-1904.
In: Radcliffe College, Schlesinger Library, Cambridge.
Correspondence, diaries, and other documents of the May and Goddard families of New England, pertaining partly to woman suffrage. Part of the collection consists of letters from prominent women such as Lucy Stone and Julia Ward Howe.

119. Miller, Emma Guffey.
Papers: 1920-1960.
In: Radcliffe College, Schlesinger Library, Cambridge.
Democratic national committeewoman. Letter and speeches, part of which relate to equal rights for women and the National Woman's Party.

120. Miller, Frieda S., 1889-
Papers: 1939-1953.
In: Radcliffe College, Schlesinger Library, Cambridge.
Public official. Speeches and other papers relating to her as director of the U.S. Women's Bureau, concerning equal pay and jury service for women, and other matters.

121. Morgan, Laura Puffer, 1874-1962.
Morgan-Howes family papers: 1892-1962.

MASSACHUSETTS (cont.)

> In: Radcliffe College, Schlesinger Library, Cambridge.
> Correspondence, reports, articles, and other materials
> documenting her career for various social causes in-
> cluding woman suffrage. Persons represented include
> Carrie Chapman Catt, Julia Ward Howe, and others.

122. Nathan, Maud, 1862-1946.
> Scrapbooks: 1890-1938.
> In: Radcliffe College, Schlesinger Library, Cambridge.
> Author, speaker, and reformer. Mainly clippings and
> letters, pictures, etc. , relating to her work for woman
> suffrage, employment, and other social activities.
> Groups represented include the Consumers' League of
> New York and the National Consumers' League.

123. National Women's Trade Union League of America.
> Records: 1904-1949.
> In: Radcliffe College, Schlesinger Library, Cambridge.
> Correspondence, reports, and other materials of the
> League relating to its work concerning the legal status,
> employment, and suffrage of women and their status in
> trade unions.

124. Niles, Marion H.
> Papers: 1911-1946.
> In: Radcliffe College, Schlesinger Library, Cambridge.
> Reports and other papers showing Miss Niles' activities
> for working girls, especially in Massachusetts. Also
> represented is the National League of Women Workers
> and the Massachusetts League of Women Workers.

125. Norris, Katharine Augusta, d. 1949.
> Papers: 1943-1948.
> In: Radcliffe College, Schlesinger Library, Cambridge.
> Materials relating to the Women's Joint Legislative
> Committee for Equal Rights and the National Woman's
> Party.

126. O'Reilly, Leonora, 1870-1927.
> Papers: 1886-1928.
> In: Radcliffe College, Schlesinger Library, Cambridge.
> Labor organizer. Letters, diaries, and other material
> relate, in part, to woman suffrage and the National
> Women's Trade Union League.

127. Owens, Helen Brewster, 1881-
> Papers: 1899-1962.
> In: Radcliffe College, Schlesinger Library, Cambridge.
> New York suffragist and mathematician. Correspond-
> ence centering on New York and Kansas for woman suf-
> frage. Persons represented include Carrie Chapman
> Catt, Harriet B. Laidlaw, Catharine W. McCulloch,
> Anna Howard Shaw, Nettie K. Shuler, Margaret Topliff,
> and Harriet May Mills.

128. Powell, Rose Arnold, 1876-1961.
> Papers: 1922-1961.
> In: Radcliffe College, Schlesinger Library, Cambridge.

MASSACHUSETTS (cont.)

Correspondence, journals and articles, much of it concerning Susan B. Anthony, including correspondence
with Gutzon Borglum on the possibility of representing
Miss Anthony at Mount Rushmore. Other persons men-
tioned include Mary Ritter Beard, Carrie Chapman
Catt, Adelaide Johnson, Alma Lutz, Alice Paul, and
Charles Williams.

129. Radcliffe College. Women's Archives.
Miscellaneous manuscript collections, 1806-
In: Radcliffe College, Schlesinger Library, Cambridge.
Correspondence, diaries, journals concerning achievements of women in government service, medicine and
nursing, journalism, and other fields, and concerning
equal rights, suffrage, education, and other areas.

130. Ransom, Elizabeth Taylor, 1867-1955.
Papers: 1888-1955.
In: Radcliffe College, Schlesinger Library, Cambridge.
Physician. Correspondence, articles concerning her
education and practice of medicine in Boston.

131. Roberts, Margaret Stevenson, d. 1952.
Papers: 1900-1942.
In: Radcliffe College, Schlesinger Library, Cambridge.
Letters and telegrams from persons involved in the
woman suffrage movement including Carrie Chapman
Catt and Senator Borah. Much of the material dates
from between 1919 and 1921.

132. Robinson, Harriet Jane Hanson, 1825-1911.
Papers: 1833-1904.
In: Radcliffe College, Schlesinger Library, Cambridge.
Correspondence, diaries, and over fifty scrapbooks,
part of which concerns woman suffrage and the status
of women. Also includes material relating to the National American Woman Suffrage Association and correspondents including Susan B. Anthony, Matilda Joslyn
Gage, Lucy Stone, Elizabeth Cady Stanton, Lucy Larcom,
and Mary Ashton Rice Livermore.

133. Ryan, Agnes.
Papers: 1904-1955.
In: Radcliffe College, Schlesinger Library, Cambridge.
Writer and editor. Correspondents and diaries showing
her interest in suffrage. Some important correspond-
ents include Alice Stone Blackwell, Alice Park, Emily
Blackwell, and Henry Blackwell.

134. Seton, Grace Gallatin, 1872-1959.
Papers: 1911-1952.
In: Radcliffe College, Schlesinger Library, Cambridge.
Author and suffragist. Letters and other papers con-
cerning the Connecticut Woman Suffrage Association
between 1911 and 1912.

135. Sherwin, Belle, 1868-1955.
Papers: 1880-1950.

MASSACHUSETTS (cont.)

> In: Radcliffe College, Schlesinger Library, Cambridge.
> Civic leader. Correspondence and other papers per-
> taining to her as trustee of Wellesley College and
> president (1924-1934) of the League of Women Voters.
> Also includes material on women's work in World War
> I and the Consumers' League of Ohio.

136. Smith, Hattie Hyland.
> Papers: 1937-1959.
> In: Radcliffe College, Schlesinger Library, Cambridge.
> Government official. Articles, reports and other
> papers relating to her work in Massachusetts for
> minimum wages, equal pay, equal rights, and the
> National Committee on the Status of Women.

137. Smith, Hilda Worthington.
> Papers: 1835-1959.
> In: Radcliffe College, Schlesinger Library, Cambridge.
> Educator. Speeches, articles, reports and other ma-
> terial concerning her work in the education of working
> women.

138. Smith, Jane Norman, 1874-1953.
> Papers: 1913-1953.
> In: Radcliffe College, Schlesinger Library, Cambridge.
> Women's rights advocate. Papers concerning her
> activities with the National Woman's Party. The bulk
> of the collection is correspondence dealing with suffrage
> in New York and the Congressional Union for Woman
> Suffrage as well as the World Woman's Suffrage Al-
> liance. Persons represented include Mary Ritter Beard,
> Alva Belmont, Frances Bayard Hilles, Alma Lutz, Alice
> Paul, Anita Pollitzer, Mabel Vernon, Maud Younger,
> and others.

139. Somerville Family.
> Papers: 1852-1958.
> In: Radcliffe College, Schlesinger Library, Cambridge.
> Correspondence, speeches relating, in part, to the
> women suffrage movement and the Women's Division of
> the Democratic National Committee. Some important
> persons represented include Anna Howard Shaw and
> Frances E. Willard. Also includes materials pertain-
> ing to the legal profession activities of Nellie Nugent
> Somerville and her daughter, Lucy Somerville Howorth.

140. Tillinghast, Anna Churchill Moulton, 1874-1951.
> Papers: 1911-1945.
> In: Radcliffe College, Schlesinger Library, Cambridge.
> Minister and government official as well as an advocate
> of woman suffrage. Correspondence, scrapbook and
> other materials relating to her work as a minister and
> suffragist.

141. Wells, Agnes Ermina, 1876-1959.
> Papers: 1924-1956.
> In: Radcliffe College, Schlesinger Library, Cambridge.

MASSACHUSETTS (cont.)

Educator. Papers and clippings relating to her work
with the National Woman's Party, the American Association of University Women, and other organizations.
142. West, Helen Hunt, 1892-1963.
Papers: 1917-1964.
In: Radcliffe College, Schlesinger Library, Cambridge.
Lawyer and journalist of Florida. Correspondence,
speeches, photographs and other materials relating to
Mrs. West's activities in the suffrage movement and
the National Woman's Party as well as the campaign
for the passage of the Equal Rights Amendment. Per-
sons represented include Alice Paul and Jane Norman
Smith.
143. White, Sallie Elizabeth Joy, 1852?-1909.
Papers: 1828-1936.
In: Radcliffe College, Schlesinger Library, Cambridge.
Journalist of Boston. Includes clippings of Mrs.
White's newspaper articles, pertaining, in part, to
women's rights activities.
144. White, Sue Shelton, 1887-1943.
Papers: 1913-1943, 1959.
In: Radcliffe College, Schlesinger Library, Cambridge.
Lawyer and suffragist. Material concerning her work
for woman suffrage in Tennessee and the nation. Also
includes organizations such as the National American
Woman Suffrage Association, the National Woman's
Party, the Tennessee Equal Suffrage League, and the
Women's Division of the Democratic National Commit-
tee. Persons represented include Carrie Chapman
Catt, Alice Paul, and Eleanor Roosevelt.
145. Willis, Olympia Brown, 1835-1926.
Papers: 1849-1926, 1956.
In: Radcliffe College, Schlesinger Library, Cambridge.
Leader in the woman suffrage movement. Correspond-
ence pertains to the suffrage campaign in Kansas in
1867, the Wisconsin Woman Suffrage Association, and
the Federal Suffrage Association of the United States.
Persons included are Victoria C. Woodhull, Susan B.
Anthony, Alice Stone Blackwell, Antoinette Brown
Blackwell, William Lloyd Garrison, Phoebe Hanaford,
Ida Husted Harper, Isabella Beecher Hooker, Anna
Howard Shaw, Elizabeth Cady Stanton, Lucy Stone,
Henry B. Blackwell, Phoebe Couzins, and Mary A.
Livermore.
146. Winslow, Mary Nelson.
In: Radcliffe College, Schlesinger Library, Cambridge.
Social worker. Correspondence includes an autobiog-
raphy of Mary Anderson, and other materials concern-
ing the employment of married women. Includes ma-
terial related to the Inter-American Commission of
Women as well as the National Women's Trade Union

MASSACHUSETTS (cont.)

League.
147. Winsor, Mary.
      Papers: 1917-1940.
      In: Radcliffe College, Schlesinger Library, Cambridge.
      Personal papers and articles relating, in part, to suf-
      frage, equal rights, the Inter-American Commission of
      Women, and the National Woman's Party.
148. Woman's Rights Collection.
      Materials: 1633-1958.
      In: Radcliffe College, Schlesinger Library, Cambridge.
      Correspondence and other papers concerning 100 women
      and 4 men involved in furthering women's rights from
      colonial times to the present; the rights movement up
      to the 1920's, emphasizing Massachusetts; suffrage
      movement up to 1920; and gains for women in areas of
      protective legislation and employment opportunities.
149. Woodward, Ellen Sullivan.
      Papers: 1927-1954.
      In: Radcliffe College, Schlesinger Library, Cambridge.
      Public official. Correspondence, speeches, and other
      materials, part of which relate to Susan B. Anthony
      and Mary Ritter Beard.
150. Addams, Jane, 1860-1935.
      Papers: 1904-1935, ca. 1960.
      In: Smith College, Sophia Smith Collection, Northampton.
      Settlement worker, social reformer, and peace worker.
      Correspondence, speeches, relating in part to the
      status of women.
151. Allen, Florence Ellinwood, 1884-1966.
      Papers: 1920-1965.
      In: Smith College, Sophia Smith Collection, Northampton.
      Lawyer and judge of Cleveland, Ohio. Correspondence,
      in part, relates to her work for woman suffrage in
      Ohio. Also includes typescripts of subject's addresses
      to the International Federation of Women Lawyers, and
      other organizations.
152. American Association of University Women.
      Papers: 1923-1947.
      In: Smith College, Sophia Smith Collection, Northampton.
      Bulletins (1923-1926), convention material (1931, 1947),
      notices of meetings, and assorted pamphlets, clippings
      and reports.
153. Ames, Blanche Ames, 1878-1969.
      Papers: 1916-1967.
      In: Smith College, Sophia Smith Collection, Northampton.
      Suffragist, artist, women's rights advocate, especially
      of birth control. Birth control correspondence as
      well as a suffrage collection consisting of around 60
      letters (1914-1967), several hundred newspaper cartoons
      and drawings.

MASSACHUSETTS (cont.)

154. Anthony, Susan Brownell, 1820-1906.
         Papers: 1894-1955.
         In: Smith College, Sophia Smith Collection, Northampton.
         Reformer and suffragist. Includes 60 letters (1947-
         1955) from Una R. Winter, director of the Susan B.
         Anthony Memorial Committee of California, giving in-
         formation about Miss Anthony. Also consists of photo-
         graphs of Miss Anthony from her youth to old age.
155. Beard, Mary Ritter, 1876-1958.
         Papers: 1936-1958.
         In: Smith College, Sophia Smith Collection, Northampton.
         Historian. Correspondence, speeches, and records
         relate to women's rights and women in history.
156. Beggs, Vera.
         Papers: 1932-1946.
         In: Smith College, Sophia Smith Collection, Northampton.
         Suffragist, advocate of peace and equal citizenship.
         Around 40 letters (1932-1946) from Carrie Chapman
         Catt concerning suffrage activities. Other materials
         concern the International Alliance of Women for Suf-
         frage and Equal Citizenship as well as the Carrie Chap-
         man Catt Memorial Fund.
157. Blake, Lillie Devereaux, 1835-1913.
         Papers: 1871-1898.
         In: Smith College, Sophia Smith Collection, Northampton.
         Suffragist. Correspondence (1892-1898) to Isabel How-
         land and correspondence from Ethel E. V. Dreier,
         Florence G. Tuttle, and Carrie Chapman Catt pertain
         to suffrage activities and views. One scrapbook (1871-
         1875) contains clippings on Susan B. Anthony and the
         status of women.
158. Brush, Dorothy, 1896?-1968.
         Papers
         In: Smith College, Sophia Smith Collection, Northampton.
         Editor, writer, and advocate of women's rights, es-
         pecially birth control. Consists of articles and pam-
         phlets on birth control as well as a complete set of
         the International Planned Parenthood Federation News.
         Also includes photographs and script of an unpublished
         play.
159. Burr, Jane, pseud. (Winslow, Rosalind Guggenheim),
         1882-1958.
         Papers: 1914-1950.
         In: Smith College, Sophia Smith Collection, Northampton.
         Writer, advocate of women's rights and birth control.
         Approximately 150 letters (1914-1950) concerning mar-
         riage and divorce laws, status of women, and birth
         control.
160. Catt, Carrie Lane Chapman, 1859-1947.
         Papers: ca. 1902-1920.
         In: Smith College, Sophia Smith Collection, Northampton.

MASSACHUSETTS (cont.)

Suffragist and worker for peace. Correspondence,
books, and photographs relate to Mrs. Catt, the campaign for woman suffrage, and the International Woman
Suffrage Alliance. Also represented are the National
Woman Suffrage Association (1890-1900) and the League
of Women Voters (after 1920). Also consists of suffrage cartoons and photographs.

161. Committee of Correspondence.
Papers: 1952-1969.
In: Smith College, Sophia Smith Collection, Northampton.
New York organization whose purpose it was to prepare
women for leadership roles in their countries. Thousands of letters pertain to the status and activities of
women throughout the world. Also included are approximately 150 photographs.

162. Doty, Madeleine Zabriskie, 1879-1963.
Papers: 1907-1962.
In: Smith College, Sophia Smith Collection, Northampton.
Author, World War I correspondent, and reformer.
Correspondence and other papers relate to her work
in woman suffrage between 1907 and 1938 as well as
on other topics.

163. Dreier, Ethel Eyre Valentine, 1872-1958.
Papers: 1902-1957.
In: Smith College, Sophia Smith Collection, Northampton.
Civic leader, lecturer, and writer. Correspondence,
speeches and reports relate to the woman suffrage
movement, the New York State Woman Suffrage Association, and the National Woman Suffrage Association. Correspondents include Jane Addams, Carrie
Chapman Catt, Eleanor Roosevelt, and Theodore Roosevelt.

164. Education Collection.
Papers: 18th and 19th centuries.
In: Smith College, Sophia Smith Collection, Northampton.
Consists of 19 boxes pertaining to educational systems
in some states, higher education, Negro education and
continuing education. Materials relate to late 18th
century female education with writings of Emma Willard, Frances Wright and others. Also includes cata-
logs and reports of several female institutes of the
early 19th century as well as sources relating the
post-Civil War developments in higher education as
concerns Radcliffe College, Bryn Mawr, Mills College,
and Smith College.

165. Garrison Family Papers.
Papers: 1830 to date.
In: Smith College, Sophia Smith Collection, Northampton.
Thousands of letters pertaining to the family's involve-
ment in every major 19th and 20th century reform.
Family correspondence, diaries, clippings, articles,

MASSACHUSETTS (cont.)

photographs show William Lloyd Garrison's interests in
women's rights (1840's-1900), suffrage (1840's-1920),
and other reforms. Some of the correspondents include
Susan B. Anthony, Alice Stone Blackwell, Lucy Stone,
Lucretia Mott, Wendell Phillips, Theodore Dwight Weld,
and Elizabeth Cady Stanton.
166. Howland, Isabel.   d. 1942.
       Papers: 1888-1903.
       In: Smith College, Sophia Smith Collection, Northampton.
       Woman suffrage worker and reformer.   Correspondence
       and other papers concern her work with the New York
       State Woman Suffrage Association as well as the As-
       sociation for the Advancement of Women.   Correspond-
       ents include Susan B. Anthony, Carrie Chapman Catt,
       Alice Stone Blackwell, Lucy Stone, Anna Howard Shaw,
       and Frances E. Willard.
167. Hunt Family.
       Papers: ca. 1841-1903.
       In: Smith College, Sophia Smith Collection, Northampton.
       Papers and correspondence of Elizabeth B. Bisbee
       Hunt, n. d., suffragist; Mary Olive A., M. D., 1819-
       1908.   Family records and correspondence (ca. 1841-
       1903) pertain to 19th century women's medical educa-
       tion.   Several letters are from Susan B. Anthony (con-
       cerning New Hampshire suffrage activities) and several
       letters from Julia Ward Howe, also on suffrage.
168. International Woman Suffrage Alliance (International Alliance
       of Women).
       Papers: 1906-1961.
       In: Smith College, Sophia Smith Collection, Northampton.
       Consists of incomplete files of Congresses and reports.
169. Kitchelt, Florence L. Cross, 1876-1961.
       Papers
       In: Smith College, Sophia Smith Collection, Northampton.
       Settlement worker, writer, and social reformer.   Part
       of the collection consists of articles on Susan B.
       Anthony and on other subjects.
170. Law Collection
       Papers
       In: Smith College, Sophia Smith Collection, Northampton.
       Photographs and printed sources relating to Judge
       Dorothy Kenyon, Anna Dickinson, and Belva Lockwood.
171. McCullouch, Rhoda E., 1884-
       Papers
       In: Smith College, Sophia Smith Collection, Northampton.
       Editor, women's rights advocate, and peace worker.
       Consists of materials on education, marriage, and the
       attitudes of and on married working women.
172. National Council of Women.
       Papers: 1948-1967.
       In: Smith College, Sophia Smith Collection, Northampton.

MASSACHUSETTS (cont.)

Correspondence, files (1948-1961) pertain to cooperation
with organizations such as the New York Women's Trade
Union League. Also consists of lectures, reports, and
miscellaneous publications.
173. New England Hospital.
Papers: ca. 1820-1955.
In: Smith College, Sophia Smith Collection, Northampton.
Established in Boston in 1863 and staffed by women
doctors. Consists, in part, of notes on women's medical education. Correspondence from Alice Stone Black-
well, Elizabeth Blackwell, Lydia Maria Child, Horace
Greeley, Julia Ward Howe, Mary A. Livermore, Susan
B. Anthony, Angelina and Sarah Grimké, and others.
174. Parton, Sara Payson Willis, 1811-1872.
Papers: 1829-1966.
In: Smith College, Sophia Smith Collection, Northampton.
Writer, women's rights advocate. Family correspond-
ence (1829-1870) as well as that of descendants (1899-
1966) reveal her interests and activities.
175. Planned Parenthood Federation of America.
Papers: 1922-1953.
In: Smith College, Sophia Smith Collection, Northampton.
Materials pertain to meetings held between 1922 and
1947, committee reports between 1928 and 1949 as well
as legislative action and laws between 1929 and 1944.
Correspondence includes letters to and from Margaret
Sanger. Also includes materials relating to the Planned
Parenthood League of Massachusetts, general birth con-
trol materials and other subjects.
176. Planned Parenthood League of Massachusetts.
Papers: 1917-1956.
In: Smith College, Sophia Smith Collection, Northampton.
Reports and correspondence (including correspondence
of Margaret Sanger) relating, in part, to test cases in
order to change state birth control laws.
177. Sanger, Margaret Higgins, 1882-1966.
Papers: 1910-1966.
In: Smith College, Sophia Smith Collection, Northampton.
Nurse, author, lecturer and founder and leader of the
birth control movement and the Planned Parenthood
Federation of America. Consists of 191 boxes of
diaries (1914-1954), articles (1914-1960), address
(1915-1955) and other materials showing her work in
birth control. Also includes birth control periodicals
as well as materials relating to the International
Planned Parenthood Federation.
178. Schain, Josephine, 1886-
Papers: 1915-1954.
In: Smith College, Sophia Smith Collection, Northampton.
Suffragist, women's rights advocate. Correspondence
to and from Carrie Chapman Catt and others. Also

MASSACHUSETTS (cont.)

includes her work on the Democratic National Committee from 1940 to 1946. Suffrage pamphlets, notes and
organization reports indicate her role in groups such
as the New York Women Suffrage Association and other
groups.
179. Seton, Grace T. , 1872-1959.
       Papers: 1904-1940.
       In: Smith College, Sophia Smith Collection, Northampton.
       Author, explorer, and feminist. The collection con-
       sists, in part, of materials relating to the National
       Council of Women and the International Council of Wom-
       en and Suffrage.
180. Severance, Caroline M. S. , 1820-1914.
       Papers
       In: Smith College, Sophia Smith Collection, Northampton.
       Suffragist, birth control advocate. Part of the col-
       lection includes correspondence from Sarah Moore
       Grimké, Lucy Stone, Theodore Dwight Weld and others.
181. Sorosis, est. 1868.
       Papers: 1889-1965.
       In: Smith College, Sophia Smith Collection, Northampton.
       Materials include minutes (1925-1950, 1953-1965),
       yearbooks, programs, and bylaws. Several letters
       are included from Lucy Stone and Julia Ward Howe.
182. Suffrage and Anti-suffrage.
       Materials: 1840-1970.
       In: Smith College, Sophia Smith Collection, Northampton.
       Consists of the papers of Ohio suffragist, Frances M.
       Casement, 1840-1928, and a general 17-box suffrage
       collection. Includes records (1906-1970) of the Inter-
       national Woman Suffrage Alliance as well as many na-
       tional and state association publications. Also includes
       flyers and Woman Suffrage Calendar, published in 1910
       by the College Equal Suffrage League of New York
       City; the 1881 constitution of the American Woman Suf-
       frage Association and the sources relating to the Na-
       tional American Woman Suffrage Association. Ad-
       dresses are included from Jane Addams, Alice Stone
       Blackwell, Mary Dennett, Charlotte Perkins Gilman,
       Carrie Chapman Catt, and others. Also includes suf-
       frage materials for other countries, especially England.
       Anti-suffrage materials (for the United States and
       England) include many pamphlets and flyers.
183. Tarbell, Ida Minerva, 1857-1944.
       Papers: 1896-1939.
       In: Smith College, Sophia Smith Collection, Northampton.
       Author, critic, historian, editor, and advocate of
       political and social reform. Includes much correspond-
       ence on suffrage and other matters.
184. Tuttle, Florence Guertin, 1869-1951.
       Papers: 1917-1948.

MASSACHUSETTS (cont.)

In: Smith College, Sophia Smith Collection, Northampton. Writer, suffragist, birth control advocate. Correspondence between 1917 and 1936 gives views on suffrage, education, and other topics.

185. Van Kleeck, Mary, 1883-
Papers: 1919-1961.
In: Smith College, Sophia Smith Collection, Northampton. Pioneer, social research. Advocate of women's rights. Sources include books as well as articles written for professional and popular periodicals. Twenty scrapbooks containing material (1924-1961) pertaining to the economic status of women, trade unions, labor legislation, and other matters.

186. Ward, Emma France, 1886-1963.
Papers: 1922-1960.
In: Smith College, Sophia Smith Collection, Northampton. Expert, public health medicine. Correspondence between 1922 and 1960 indicates her career, views on women in industry, and other matters.

187. Women in Industry.
Papers: 1885-1965.
In: Smith College, Sophia Smith Collection, Northampton. Materials include biographical sketches of a number of labor leaders including Mary Van Kleeck and Margaret Dreier Robins. Also includes publications of the U. S. Women's Bureau on equal pay, equal employment opportunities, working mothers, trade unions, and other matters.

188. Women's Liberation.
Materials: 1950's to date.
In: Smith College, Sophia Smith Collection, Northampton. Includes 7 boxes of materials including special women's liberation issues of periodicals, flyers, posters, newsletters, lapel buttons, cartoons, and other materials. Also included are New England Free Press publications and a number of publications of the National Organization for Women as well as materials relating to women's liberation at Smith College.

189. Women's Rights.
Materials: 19th & 20th centuries.
In: Smith College, Sophia Smith Collection, Northampton. Consists (besides materials concerning foreign women's rights movements) of a microfilm of The Lily, (1849-1856), the earliest women's rights paper; many publications pertaining to women's rights leaders such as Amelia Bloomer, Lucretia Mott, Elizabeth Cady Stanton, and Lucy Stone, as well as the Seneca Falls convention of 1848.

190. Woodsmall, Ruth Frances, 1883-1963.
Papers: 1906-1963.
In: Smith College, Sophia Smith Collection, Northampton.

MASSACHUSETTS (cont.)

        International YWCA executive (1932-1948) and women's
        rights advocate. Consists of 72 boxes of personal
        papers (1906-1961), diaries (1920-1930, 1940-1950),
        business papers, and other materials. Includes ad-
        dresses and research papers and notes between 1930
        and 1960 on the status of women, education, and other
        topics. Also includes several hundred photographs.
191. Young Women's Christian Association.
      Papers: 1889-1959.
      In: Smith College, Sophia Smith Collection, Northampton.
      Many printed sources relating to business, women's
      movements, and other topics. Also included is a
      nearly complete file of Woman's Press (v. 1-46,
      1907-1952), the monthly magazine of the YWCA.

MICHIGAN

192. Dreier, Dorothea, 1870-1923.
      Papers: 1887-1916.
      In: Archives of American Art, Detroit.
      Artist. Correspondence, clippings, photos, etc.,
      pertaining, in part, to woman suffrage.
193. Emma Fox Collection.
      In: Detroit Public Library.
      Materials on the early woman's rights movement.
194. Stone, Lucinda Hinsdale, 1814-1900.
      Papers: 1879-1899.
      In: Kalamazoo Public Library.
      Educator. Letters dealing with the establishment of a
      woman's professorship at the University of Michigan
      and with the woman's suffrage movement. Includes
      letters from Susan B. Anthony.
195. Brotherton Collection [Mrs. Belle Brotherton].
      Papers: 1880-1920.
      In: State of Michigan, Department of Education, Bureau
        of Library Services, Lansing.
      Correspondence, files, clippings, pamphlets and broad-
      sides relating to the woman suffrage movement and the
      Michigan State Suffrage Association.
196. Gardner, Nannette Brown Ellingwood, 1828-1900.
      Papers: 1871-1889.
      In: University of Michigan, Michigan Historical Collec-
        tions, Ann Arbor.
      Woman suffrage leader. Scrapbooks containing bio-
      graphical sketches of Mrs. Gardner and members of
      her family and other papers relating to woman suffrage.
197. Grimes, Lucia Voorhees.
      Papers: 1912-1932.
      In: University of Michigan, Michigan Historical Collec-
        tions, Ann Arbor.
      Correspondence, scrapbooks, and other papers relating

MICHIGAN (cont.)

> to women's political activities in Michigan, woman suf-
> frage, and the Equal Rights Amendment.

198. McClure, Grace, 1884-1961.
> Reminiscences: 1958-1959.
> In: University of Michigan, Michigan Historical Collec-
> tions, Ann Arbor.
> State librarian and civic leader. The reminiscences
> of Mrs. Charles McClure of Saginaw including the
> woman suffrage movement.

199. Lampiden, Lily Gay.
> Student paper: 1960. 71p.
> In: University of Michigan, Michigan Historical Collec-
> tions, Ann Arbor.
> Teacher in Detroit. Student seminar paper, "Liquor,
> ladies, and the War of 1912, " concerns the women's
> rights movement in Michigan, 1912-1913.

200. Newkirk, Henry Wirt, 1854-1946.
> Papers: 1844-1936.
> In: University of Michigan, Michigan Historical Collec-
> tions, Ann Arbor.
> Lawyer and U. S. Representative from Michigan. Cor-
> respondence and miscellaneous material, largely con-
> cerning Michigan politics, including woman suffrage in
> that state in 1912.

201. Sawtell Family.
> Notebook: ca. 1850-1870.
> In: University of Michigan, Michigan Historical Collec-
> tions, Ann Arbor.
> Notebook of quotations and notes on the status of wom-
> en.

202. Selmon, Bertha Eugenia Loveland, 1877-
> Papers: 1932-1949.
> In: University of Michigan, Michigan Historical Collec-
> tions, Ann Arbor.
> Physician of Battle Creek. Correspondence with other
> women physicians on such topics as the Medical Wom-
> en's National Association, and women physicians, es-
> pecially in Michigan.

203. Taylor Family.
> Papers: 1827-1908.
> In: University of Michigan, Michigan Historical Collec-
> tions, Ann Arbor.
> Correspondence of Barton Stout Taylor (Methodist
> clergyman) and his wife Elizabeth. Includes sermons,
> articles, and addresses on various topics, among them
> woman suffrage.

204. Teed, Florence S. , 1901-1954.
> Papers: 1924-1954.
> In: University of Michigan, Michigan Historical Collec-
> tions, Ann Arbor.
> Minister and civic leader of Ann Arbor. Materials

MICHIGAN (cont.)

 relating to the rights and status of women and to other
 matters.
205. Thomas, Nathan Macy, 1803-1887.
      Papers: 1818-1889.
      In: University of Michigan, Michigan Historical Collec-
           tions, Ann Arbor.
      Physician in Mt. Pleasant, Ohio, and Schoolcraft,
      Michigan; Quaker abolitionist. Includes correspondence
      of his wife Pamela S. Brown, his children, and friends,
      pertaining, in part, to woman suffrage.
206. Weld Family.
      Papers: 1822-1898.
      In: University of Michigan, Michigan Historical Collec-
           tions, Ann Arbor.
      Correspondence, diaries, notebooks, and other papers
      of Angelina Grimké Weld and her sister Sarah Moore
      Grimké, relating to religious questions, anti-slavery,
      and social reform.
207. Crane, Carolina Bartlett, 1858-1935.
      Papers: 1843-1935.
      In: Western Michigan University, Regional History Collec-
           tions, Kalamazoo.
      Unitarian minister, civic leader, and reformer. Papers
      pertain to the woman suffrage movement and correspond-
      ence includes Anna Howard Shaw and Elizabeth Cady
      Stanton.

MINNESOTA

208. Brill, Hascal Russell and Family.
      Papers: 1805, 1849-1964.
      In: Minnesota Historical Society, St. Paul.
      Papers relating, in part, to the rights of women.
209. Brin, Fanny Fligelman, 1884-
      Papers: 1896-1958.
      In: Minnesota Historical Society, St. Paul.
      Teacher and resident of Minneapolis. Member of a
      number of organizations, among them the National
      American Woman Suffrage Association.
210. Christensen, Otto Augustus and Family.
      Papers: 1854-1964.
      In: Minnesota Historical Society, St. Paul.
      Papers pertaining, in part, to the rights of women.
211. Day, Frank Arah, 1855-1928.
      Papers: 1889-1928.
      In: Minnesota Historical Society, St. Paul.
      Journalist and public official of Minnesota. Materials
      include correspondence, newspapers, and clippings re-
      lating, in part, to woman suffrage.
212. Donnelly, Ignatius.
      Papers: 1850-1909.

MINNESOTA (cont.)

> In: Minnesota Historical Society, St. Paul.
> Papers pertaining, in part, to the rights of women.

213. Farmer, Eugenia B.
> Reminiscences: 1918.
> In: Minnesota Historical Society, St. Paul.
> In part, Mrs. Farmer's experiences of her activities
> for woman suffrage in Kentucky after 1888.

214. Hagen, Harold Christian.
> Papers: 1923-1957.
> In: Minnesota Historical Society, St. Paul.
> Papers relating, in part, to the rights of women.

215. Minnesota Equal Franchise League.
> Records: 1911-1917.
> In: Minnesota Historical Society, St. Paul.
> Correspondence includes the National American Woman
> Suffrage Association and the Congressional Union for
> Woman Suffrage. Also includes copies of bills con-
> sidered by the Minnesota Legislature to grant suffrage
> to women.

216. Minnesota Woman Suffrage Association.
> Records: 1894-1921.
> In: Minnesota Historical Society, St. Paul.
> Correspondence, newspaper clippings, and other records,
> part of which concerns a convention of the Mississippi
> Valley Suffrage Association in 1916. Also includes
> bills introduced in the Minnesota Legislature to allow
> women to vote in presidential elections.

217. Mitchell, William Bell and Family.
> Papers: 1806-1957.
> In: Minnesota Historical Society, St. Paul.
> Papers pertaining, in part, to the rights of women.

218. Nolan, William Ignatius, 1874-1943.
> Papers: 1900-1943.
> In: Minnesota Historical Society, St. Paul.
> Lecturer, state legislator, U. S. Representative from
> Minnesota. Correspondence, speeches and reports
> showing his opinions of woman suffrage and other mat-
> ters.

219. Paige, Mabeth Hurd.
> Papers: 1943-1958.
> In: Minnesota Historical Society, St. Paul.
> Member of the Minnesota Legislature. Part of the
> materials consist of Mrs. Paige's speeches on the
> history of the suffrage movement.

220. Pendergast, William Wirt and Family.
> Papers: 1816-1956.
> In: Minnesota Historical Society, St. Paul.
> Papers pertaining, in part, to the rights of women.

221. Peyton, Theresa Barbara, 1880-1929.
> Papers: 1898-1917.
> In: Minnesota Historical Society, St. Paul.

MINNESOTA (cont.)

Teacher. Papers related to suffrage and her activities
with the Minnesota Woman Suffrage Association, the
Minnesota Equal Franchise League, and the Political
Equality Club of St. Paul.
222.   Political Equality Club, Minneapolis.
Records: 1892-1920.
In: Minnesota Historical Society, St. Paul.
Besides correspondence, includes a list of woman suf-
frage clubs in Minnesota, reminiscences of Elizabeth
Cady Stanton, and a history of woman suffrage in Min-
nesota.
223.   Political Equality Club, St. Paul.
Records: 1910-1917.
In: Minnesota Historical Society, St. Paul.
Minutes of meetings showing efforts of the club in the
direction of suffrage for women in Minnesota.
224.   Sageng, Ole O., 1871-1963.
Papers: 1904-1953.
In: Minnesota Historical Society, St. Paul.
State Legislator of Minnesota. Correspondence con-
cerns, in part, woman suffrage.
225.   Simpson, David Ferguson and Family.
Papers: 1847-1956.
In: Minnesota Historical Society, St. Paul.
Papers pertaining, in part, to the rights of women.
226.   Wagner, Albert G.
Papers: 1908-1919.
In: Minnesota Historical Society, St. Paul.
Personal correspondence and articles received by him
due to his interest in the Industrial Workers of the
World. Includes information, in part, about the status
of women.
227.   Grevstad, Nicolay Andrew, 1851-1940.
Papers: 1889-1940.
In: Norwegian-American Historical Association, St. Olaf
College, Northfield.
Editor of Scandinavian-American newspapers in St.
Paul and Chicago. Correspondence and dispatches and
press releases relate, in part, to woman suffrage.
228.   Woman's Liberation/Woman's Rights Collection.
Papers
In: University of Minnesota Libraries, Social Welfare
History Archives Center, Minneapolis.
A continuing collection of all aspects of the women's
liberation movement, with the cooperation of a number
of women's organizations such as the National Organi-
zation for Women, Austin Women's Liberation, and
others.

MISSISSIPPI

229.   Mississippi Department of Archives and History.
         Records of Organizations: 1830-1938.
         In: Mississippi Department of Archives and History,
               Jackson.
               Correspondence, records and other papers of a number
               of groups, one of which is the Mississippi Woman Suf-
               frage Association from 1897 to 1920.
230.   Somerville, Nellie Nugent, 1863-1952.
         Papers: 1896-1951.
         In: Mississippi Department of Archives and History,
               Jackson.
               Leader in the woman's suffrage movement in Mississip-
               pi.   Consists of speeches, scrapbooks, and other papers
               relating to woman suffrage in Mississippi.
231.   Cavett, E. D., 1845-1919.
         Swann-Cavett papers: 1884-1929.
         In: Mississippi State University Library, State College.
               Soldier, State legislator, and Ku Klux Klan member.
               Collection includes pamphlets and reprints opposing
               woman suffrage.
232.   Thompson Collection - Mississippi Women's Suffrage Movement.
         In: University of Mississippi Library, University.
               Papers pertaining to the suffrage movement in Missis-
               sippi in the early 20th century.

MISSOURI

233.   Blake, Lillie Devereux, 1835-1913.
         Papers: 1847-1910.
         In: Missouri Historical Society, St. Louis.
               Author, lecturer, reformer, and suffragist.   Cor-
               respondence, autobiography (1873-1903), journals and
               other papers relating to the organization of the woman's
               rights movement, woman suffrage, and the National
               Woman Suffrage Association.   Includes letters of Susan
               B. Anthony, Carrie Chapman Catt, and Elizabeth Cady
               Stanton.
234.   Decker, Perl D., 1875-1934.
         Papers: 1897-1939.
         In: University of Missouri Library, Western Historical
               Manuscripts Collection, Columbia.
               Missouri lawyer and U. S. Congressman.   Correspond-
               ence includes woman suffrage and other political issues.
235.   McBeth, Kate.
         Women's suffrage speech: undated.   11 leaves.
         In: University of Missouri Library, Western Historical
               Manuscripts Collection, Columbia.
               A pro-suffrage speech indicating that many evils of
               woman would be remedied if she could vote.
236.   Shackelford, Thomas.
         Papers: 1820-1908.

MISSOURI (cont.)

In: University of Missouri Library, Western Historical
    Manuscripts Collection, Columbia.
    Lawyer and politician of Missouri. Correspondence
    consists, in part, of political letters relating to woman
    suffrage.
237. Gellhorn, Edna.
    Papers: 1917-1970.
    In: Washington University Libraries, St. Louis.
    First vice president of the National League of Women
    Voters. Correspondence, scrapbooks, etc. , pertaining,
    in part, to her activities in the woman's suffrage move-
    ment, 1919-1921.

MONTANA

238. Montana - Woman Suffrage.
    Papers: 1914.
    In: Montana Historical Society, Helena.
    Clippings and files of the Montana Suffrage Club.
239. Montana Women's Suffrage Association.
    Minutes: 1895.
    In: Montana Historical Society, Helena.
    Minutes of the first convention, September 2-3, 1895.
240. Woman Suffrage - Montana.
    Bills: 1895-1903.
    In: Montana Historical Society, Helena.
    Bills introduced in Montana Legislature in 1895, 1897,
    1899, and 1903 with roll call vote for 1895.

NEBRASKA

241. Carns, Margaret Jane Burke, 1859-1952.
    Papers: 1865-1952.
    In: Nebraska State Historical Society, Lincoln.
    Lawyer. Correspondence and other papers relate to
    the activities of the American Bar Association (of
    which she was its first woman member) and to the Na-
    tional Association of Women Lawyers.
242. Correll, Erasmus Michael.
    Papers: 1870-1913.
    In: Nebraska State Historical Society, Lincoln.
    Editor and state legislator of Nebraska. Correspond-
    ence, speeches, pamphlets and other papers relating
    to woman suffrage and to the Nebraska Woman Suffrage
    Convention of 6 July 1881 in Omaha.
243. Gerrard, Betty C.
    Papers: 1879-1913.
    In: Nebraska State Historical Society, Lincoln.
    Correspondence relating to Mrs. Gerrard's activities
    with the National Woman Suffrage Association.

NEBRASKA (cont.)

244. Miller, Annie Louise, 18??-1945.
        Papers: 1889-1941.
        In: Nebraska State Historical Society, Lincoln.
        Papers pertain, in part, to woman suffrage.
245. Nebraska Woman's Suffrage Association.
        Records: 1910-1940.
        In: Nebraska State Historical Society, Lincoln.
        Correspondence, minutes, legal records relating to
        their attempt to obtain the vote for women in that
        state. Correspondents include Mrs. William E.
        Barkley, Margretta Dietrich, Mrs. Draper Smith,
        Grace Wheeler, and Mary M. Williams.
246. Philbrick, Inez Celia.
        Papers: 1894-1953.
        In: Nebraska State Historical Society, Lincoln.
        Correspondence and printed matter relating to Dr.
        Philbrick's activities in support of woman suffrage and
        other matters. Correspondents include Susan B.
        Anthony and Elizabeth Cady Stanton.

NEW JERSEY

247. New Jersey Historical Society, Newark.
        Manuscript collection pertaining to the Women's
        Political Union and the struggle for the vote in 1915.
        Consists of photographs, pamphlets, banners, buttons,
        and newspaper clippings. Shows both the suffrage and
        anti-suffrage viewpoints.

NEW YORK

248. Blackwell, Elizabeth, 1821-1910.
        Letters: 1850-1884.
        In: Columbia University Libraries, New York.
        Physician. Letters from Dr. Blackwell to Barbara
        Smith Bodichon indicating the prejudice against women
        in medicine in the United States and England.
249. Gildersleeve, Virginia Crocheron, 1877-
        Papers: 1898-1962.
        In: Columbia University Libraries, New York.
        Dean of Barnard College. Materials relate, in part,
        to the American Association of University Women and
        the International Federation of University Women.
250. Griffing, Josephine Sophie White, 1814-1872.
        Papers: 1862-1872.
        In: Columbia University Libraries, New York.
        Social reformer. Letters written to Mrs. Griffing,
        part of which concern woman suffrage. Also repre-
        sented are Lucretia Mott, Henry Ward Beecher as
        well as a scrapbook of clippings about Mrs. Griffing's
        life.

NEW YORK (cont.)

251. League of Women Voters of New York City.
      New York woman suffrage collection: 1869-1919.
      In: Columbia University Libraries, New York.
          Minutes of the Woman Suffrage Association of New
          York State (1869-1917) and the Woman Suffrage Party
          of New York City (1910-1919), also including constitu-
          tions, membership lists, and other materials.
252. Cooper, Sarah Brown Ingersoll, 1836-1896.
      Papers: 1842-1910.
      In: Cornell University Library, Collection of Regional
          History and University Archives, Ithaca.
          Educator and social reformer. Correspondence relates,
          in part, to woman suffrage. Includes letters from
          Susan B. Anthony and Frances Willard.
253. Hazzard, Florence Woolsey, 1903-
      Papers: 1819-1965.
      In: Cornell University Libraries, Collection of Regional
          History and University Archives, Ithaca.
          Author and psychologist. Correspondence, manuscripts
          of writings, notes, etc., dealing mainly with Mrs. Haz-
          zard's studies of eminent American women. Includes
          personal and professional papers of the Hazzard Family,
          the World Center for Women's Archives, and the wom-
          en's rights movement in the United States. Women in-
          cluded are Abigail Adams, Susan B. Anthony, Elizabeth
          Blackwell, Lillie Devereux Blake, Lydia Maria Child,
          Margaret Fuller, Angelina and Sarah Grimké, Julia
          Ward Howe, Lucretia Mott, Elizabeth Cady Stanton,
          Lucy Stone, Harriet Tubman, and Emma Willard. The
          main correspondents are Mary Ritter Beard and Carrie
          Chapman Catt.
254. Howland, Emily, 1827-1929.
      Papers: 1797-1932.
      In: Cornell University Libraries, Collection of Regional
          History and University Archives, Ithaca.
          Educator, reformer, and philanthropist. Mainly letters
          (ca. 1850-1929) to Miss Howland, relating, in part, to
          the woman suffrage movement in New York state.
255. Kenney, Eudorus Catlin, 1857-1918.
      Papers: 1876-1916.
      In: Cornell University Libraries, Collection of Regional
          History and University Archives, Ithaca.
          Teacher, author, lecturer, and composer. Corres-
          pondence and other materials indicate his interest in
          the woman suffrage movement.
256. Smith, Goldwin, 1823-1910.
      Papers: 1820-1910.
      In: Cornell University Libraries, Collection of Regional
          History and University Archives, Ithaca.
          Historian, journalist, and university professor. Cor-

NEW YORK (cont.)

respondence and other papers relate, in part, to the
woman suffrage movement.

257. Democratic Party. National Committee. Women's Division.
Records: 1933-1944.
In: Franklin D. Roosevelt Library, Hyde Park.
Correspondence, memoranda, telegrams, and other
printed material concerning the role of women in
politics and other activities of the Women's Division
of the Democratic Party.

258. Dewson, Mary Williams, 1874-1962.
Papers: 1925-1951.
In: Franklin D. Roosevelt Library, Hyde Park.
Political leader and government official. Correspondence, photographs, notebooks and other materials
relating to the role of women in politics and other matters.

259. Bens, Glendolen T.
New York State Woman Suffrage Party papers: 1916-1918.
In: New York Public Library.
Correspondence and other papers dealing with the New
York State Woman Suffrage Party. Includes other
papers from the Party by Carrie Chapman Catt, Har-
riet B. Laidlaw, and Vivian Boarman Whitehouse.

260. Burge, Marie Louise.
Papers: 1849-1947.
In: New York Public Library.
Author. Correspondence, photographs, and clippings
relating to woman suffrage.

261. Catt, Carrie Lane Chapman, 1859-1947.
Papers: 1887-1947.
In: New York Public Library.
Lecturer, suffragist, and peace worker. Correspond-
ence, scrapbooks, relating to woman suffrage, the Na-
tional American Woman Suffrage Association, and the
International Alliance of Women for Suffrage and Equal
Citizenship.

262. Glasgow, Maude.
Letters: 1892-1935.
In: New York Public Library.
Letters relative to her internship and service in
Boston hospitals and her difficulties in establishing a
practice.

263. Harper, Ida Husted.
Scrapbook: 1898-1926.
In: New York Public Library.
Scrapbook containing newspaper and magazine articles
and leaflets on the suffrage movement.

264. Johnson, Helen Kendrick, 1844-1917. [Mrs. Rossiter
Johnson].
Papers: ca. 1871-1916.
In: New York Public Library.

NEW YORK (cont.)

> Correspondence with persons and organizations such as
> the National League for Opposing Woman Suffrage, New
> York State Association Opposed to Woman Suffrage, and
> others.

265. Johnson, Rossiter, 1840-1931.
> Papers: 1871-1931.
> In: New York Public Library.
> Author, editor, and lecturer; family correspondence as
> well as letters from the Man-Suffrage Association Op-
> posed to Political Suffrage for Women, the National
> Association Opposed to Woman Suffrage, and other
> papers.

266. Smith, Elizabeth Oakes Prince, 1806-1893.
> Papers: 1852-
> In: New York Public Library.
> Author and suffragist. Collection consists of scrap-
> books of her writings, among other materials.

267. Story, William Cumming.
> Diary: 1867-1870.
> In: New York Public Library.
> Diary kept by Mr. Story from October 1867 to May
> 1870 in Chicago, in part, pertaining to the woman's
> rights convention there on February 23, 1869.

268. Van Lew, Elizabeth L. , 1818-1900.
> Papers
> In: New York Public Library.
> Abolitionist, suffrage advocate and secret agent during
> the Civil War. Includes letters concerning her diffi-
> culties in being accepted in society.

269. Wheeler, Everett P. , 1840-1925.
> Papers: 1868-1925.
> In: New York Public Library.
> Lawyer, civil service reformer; correspondence, arti-
> cles and speeches, part of which relate to woman suf-
> frage between 1914 and 1920.

270. Consumers' League of New York.
> Records
> In: New York State School of Industrial and Labor Rela-
> tions, Collections, Cornell University, Ithaca.

271. New York State Association Opposed to Woman Suffrage.
> Scrapbooks and broadsides: 1915-1921.
> In: New York State University Library, Albany.

272. Chapman Family.
> Papers: ca. 1841-1954.
> In: Syracuse University Library, Syracuse.
> Correspondence, documents, and other personal papers.
> Part of the collection includes letters of Matilda
> Joslyn Gage, women's rights advocate.

273. Keifer, Joseph Warren, 1836-1932.
> Correspondence: 1858-1929.
> In: Syracuse University Library, Syracuse.

NEW YORK (cont.)

Lawyer, Union Army officer, State Legislator, and
U. S. Representative from Ohio. Letters to him, in
part, are from suffragists such as Susan B. Anthony
and Carrie Chapman Catt.

274. Walker, Mary Edwards, 1832-1919.
Papers: ca. 1863-ca. 1880.
In: Syracuse University Library, Syracuse.
Physician and suffragist. Letters and papers relating
to her medical career as a nurse and as an assistant
surgeon in the Union Army during the Civil War.

275. Anthony, Susan Brownell, 1820-1906.
Papers: 1855-1938.
In: University of Rochester Library, Rochester.
Reformer and suffragist. Documents, clippings, and
correspondence, much of which pertains to the Susan
B. Anthony Memorial Fund. Correspondents include
Harriet Taylor Upton, Ida Husted Harper, and Anna
Howard Shaw.

276. Sweet, Emma Biddlecom.
Papers: 1808-1951.
In: University of Rochester Library, Rochester.
Secretary to Susan B. Anthony. Correspondence and
other papers relating mainly to the woman suffrage
movement in Rochester, New York. Much correspond-
ence from Carrie Chapman Catt, Booker T. Washington,
Charlotte Perkins Gilman, and Susan B. Anthony.

277. Alma Lutz collection on the woman's rights movement.
Letters and manuscripts: ca. 1923-1942.
In: Vassar College Library, Poughkeepsie.
Consists of almost all of the publications of the Na-
tional Woman's Party, the Open Door International for
the Economic Emancipation of the Woman Worker, and
material on women in World War II. Also represented
are Amelia Bloomer, Lillie Devereux Blake, Alice
Carey, Phoebe Carey, George Combe, William Lloyd
Garrison, Horace Greeley, Gerrit Smith, James Mott,
Abigail Mott, Belva A. Lockwood, Mary Lyon, Maria
Mitchell, Ernestine Rose, Sarah Pugh, Parker Pillsbury,
Harriet Beecher Stowe, Theodore Tilton, George Francis
Train, Frances E. Willard, Victoria C. Woodhull,
Frances Wright, and Martha C. Wright.

278. Collection of woman suffrage materials.
In: Vassar College Library, Poughkeepsie.
Consists of both anti-suffrage and pro-suffrage publications, government documents and scrapbooks. Manuscripts of speeches by Howard A. Kelly, Amelia Mac-
Donald Putler, and Clara M. Hill, including correspondence of the National College Equal Suffrage League.

279. Davis, Paulina Wright, 1813-1876.
Papers: ca. 1840-1876.
In: Vassar College Library, Poughkeepsie.

NEW YORK (cont.)

> Editor, suffragist, and reformer. Correspondence con-
> sisting of writings, notebooks and books of autographs.
> Correspondents include Josephine S. Griffing, Lucretia
> Mott, Victoria Woodhull, Catharine Bullard Yale, Eliza-
> beth Cady Stanton, and others.

280. Furness, Caroline Ellen.
> Papers
> In: Vassar College Library, Poughkeepsie.
> Scientist and advocate of women's rights. Correspond-
> ence, notebooks, and notes, along with travel diaries.
> Member of the Vassar faculty from 1894 to 1936.

281. Hallowell, Anna Davis.
> Manuscripts
> In: Vassar College Library, Poughkeepsie.
> Included are the manuscript of "James and Lucretia
> Mott, life and letters," Boston, Houghton Mifflin, 1884,
> and a speech on Lydia Maria Child.

282. Mitchell, Maria, 1818-1889.
> Papers
> In: Vassar College Library, Poughkeepsie.
> Correspondence, notebooks, departmental reports of
> the astronomer and feminist, who taught at Vassar
> from 1865 to 1888.

283. Stanton, Elizabeth Cady, 1815-1902.
> Papers: 1792-1901.
> In: Vassar College Library, Poughkeepsie.
> Reformer and suffragist. Correspondents include Susan
> B. Anthony, Wendell Phillips, and Ernestine Rose.
> Also included are typescripts of a biographical sketch
> and articles about Mrs. Stanton by her daughter,
> Margaret Stanton Lawrence. Other correspondents in-
> clude Gerrit Smith, Antoinette B. Blackwell, Amelia
> Bloomer, Lydia Maria Child, Thomas Wentworth Hig-
> ginson, Angelina Grimké Weld, and Frances E. Willard.

284. Whitney, Marian I.
> Papers
> In: Vassar College Library, Poughkeepsie.
> Professor of German at Vassar from 1905 to 1929.
> Correspondence includes letters from Charlotte Perkins
> Gilman, Isabella Beecher Hooker; also includes scrap-
> books, diaries and notebooks relating to her career and
> activities in various women's organizations.

NORTH CAROLINA

285. Ambler-Brown Family.
> Papers: 1780-1865.
> In: Duke University Library, Durham.
> Papers pertaining to the education of women in Virginia.

286. Ball, William Watts.
> Papers: 1805-1952.

NORTH CAROLINA (cont.)

> In: Duke University Library, Durham.
> Materials pertain, in part, to woman suffrage and to
> the education of women.

287. Bartlett, Ellen.
> Correspondence: 1856-1888.
> In: Duke University Library, Durham.
> Personal letters to Miss Bartlett concerning teachers,
> salaries, and the education of women in Connecticut.

288. Barton, Gertrude Williamson.
> Letters: 1916.
> In: Duke University Library, Durham.
> Two letters (dated 22 and 26 November 1916) concern-
> ing woman suffrage.

289. Birckhead, Edward F.
> Letters: 1843-1895.
> In: Duke University Library, Durham.
> Letters pertaining to the education of women in Virginia.

290. Bryant, John Emory.
> Papers: 1882.
> In: Duke University Library, Durham.
> Consists of leaflet and letter (dated 6 June 1882) con-
> cerning woman suffrage in Missouri.

291. Campbell, James L. and James W. Campbell.
> Papers: 1805-1911.
> In: Duke University Library, Durham.
> Papers pertaining to the education of women.

292. Chamberlain, G. Hope Summerell.
> Papers
> In: Duke University Library, Durham.
> Letter (dated 4 February 1916) pertaining to the rights
> of women.

293. Clay, Clement Claiborne.
> Papers
> In: Duke University Library, Durham.
> Includes material pertaining to the Alabama Equal Suf-
> frage Association and the writings of Virginia C. Tun-
> stall Clay-Clopton.

294. Cook, Flavius Josephus.
> Papers: 1847-1916.
> In: Duke University Library, Durham.
> Papers pertaining to the education of women and to
> woman suffrage.

295. Cowper, Mary Octavine Thompson.
> Papers: 1903-1968.
> In: Duke University Library, Durham.
> Includes materials on the suffrage movement in Kansas
> and North Carolina, women in the textile industry in
> the South, and other areas.

296. Cronly Family.
> Papers
> In: Duke University Library, Durham.

NORTH CAROLINA (cont.)

              Letter (dated 30 May 1865) pertaining to the rights of
              women.
297.   Dandridge, Caroline Danske Bedinger.
              Papers: 1752-1954.
              In: Duke University Library, Durham.
              Papers pertaining to the education of women.
298.   Dearmont, Washington, 1829-1891.
              Papers: 1787-1944.
              In: Duke University Library, Durham.
              Farmer of Virginia. Correspondence, legal papers
              (primarily between 1851 and 1930) concerning, in part,
              woman suffrage in Colorado in 1912.
299.   Fasold, Emma J.
              Papers
              In: Duke University Library, Durham.
              Letter pertaining to woman suffrage, dated 19 Novem-
              ber 1915.
300.   Field-Musgrave Family.
              Papers: 1739-1938.
              In: Duke University Library, Durham.
              Papers pertaining to the legal status of women in the
              United States.
301.   Gardiner, Ann Henshaw.
              Papers
              In: Duke University Library, Durham.
              Letters dated between 19 July 1915 and 21 April 1916
              pertaining to woman suffrage.
302.   Gates, Addison W.
              Papers
              In: Duke University Library, Durham.
              Speech (undated) pertaining to woman suffrage.
303.   Hancock, Asenath Ellen Cox.
              Papers
              In: Duke University Library, Durham.
              Letter (dated 30 September 1926) pertaining to woman
              suffrage.
304.   Herdin, William D.
              Papers: 1838, 1870-1900, 1946.
              In: Duke University Library, Durham.
              Papers pertaining to the rights of women.
305.   Harrison, Henry Sydnor.
              Papers
              In: Duke University Library, Durham.
              Letter (dated 28 April 1915) pertaining to the rights
              of women.
306.   Hedrick, Benjamin Sherwood.
              Papers: 1848-1893.
              In: Duke University Library, Durham.
              Papers pertaining to the woman's rights convention
              in Worcester, Massachusetts, in 1851.

NORTH CAROLINA (cont.)

307. Hemphill Family.
        Papers: 1895.
        In: Duke University Library, Durham.
        Papers pertaining to woman suffrage.
308. Higginson, Thomas Wentworth.
        Papers: 1868-1906.
        In: Duke University Library, Durham.
        Papers pertaining to woman suffrage.
309. Holgate, William C.
        Papers: 1779-1911.
        In: Duke University Library, Durham.
        Papers and other materials pertaining to woman suf-
        frage.
310. Hundley-Owen Collection.
        Letters and papers: 1841-1921.
        In: Duke University Library, Durham.
        Materials pertaining to the education of women in
        Virginia.
311. King, Pendleton.
        Papers: 1876-1906.
        In: Duke University Library, Durham.
        Materials relating, in part, to woman suffrage.
312. Kirby, Ephraim.
        Papers: 1763, 1780-1804, 1878.
        In: Duke University Library, Durham.
        Papers pertaining to the education of women in Penn-
        sylvania.
313. Knight, John.
        Papers: 1788-1891.
        In: Duke University Library, Durham.
        Papers relating to the education of women.
314. McDowall, Susan.
        Diary and scrapbook: 1857-1880.
        In: Duke University Library, Durham.
        Materials pertaining to the education of women.
315. McIntosh, Thomas M.
        Papers: 1822-1895.
        In: Duke University Library, Durham.
        Papers pertaining to the medical education of women.
316. Magill, Sarah.
        Papers: 1836-1904.
        In: Duke University Library, Durham.
        Papers pertaining to the education of women.
317. Morriss, Beverly Preston.
        Papers: 1814-1947.
        In: Duke University Library, Durham.
        Papers pertain, in part, to woman suffrage.
318. Nesbitt, Charles Torrence.
        Papers
        In: Duke University Library, Durham.
        Papers and a clipping (including autobiography dated

NORTH CAROLINA (cont.)

1938) pertaining to woman suffrage.

319. Nutt, Haller.
       Papers: 1846-1911.
       In: Duke University Library, Durham.
       Papers relating to the education of women.
320. Nycum, John and John Q. Nycum.
       Papers: 1825-1900.
       In: Duke University Library, Durham.
       Papers relating to the education of women.
321. Patten, Mary Elizabeth.
       Papers
       In: Duke University Library, Durham.
       Consists of a diary pertaining to woman suffrage.
322. Plyler, Marion Timothy.
       Papers
       In: Duke University Library, Durham.
       Papers relating to the education of women and the
       Woman's College of Duke University.
323. Reid, Frank Lewis.
       Papers: 1893-1897.
       In: Duke University Library, Durham.
       Papers pertaining to woman suffrage.
324. Royston, William S.
       Letters and papers: 1823-1898.
       In: Duke University Library, Durham.
       Materials pertaining to the education of women in
       Virginia.
325. Shaeffer, Bartram A.
       Papers: 1850-1860.
       In: Duke University Library, Durham.
       Papers pertaining to the property rights of women.
326. Slade, William.
       Papers: 1816-1929.
       In: Duke University Library, Durham.
       Papers and other materials pertaining to woman suf-
       frage.
327. Small, John Humphrey.
       Papers: 1720-1946.
       In: Duke University Library, Durham.
       Papers and other materials pertaining to woman suf-
       frage.
328. Smith, William Patterson.
       Papers: 1791-1943.
       In: Duke University Library, Durham.
       Papers pertaining to the education of women in Virginia.
329. Socialist Party of America.
       Papers: 1900-1959.
       In: Duke University Library, Durham.
       Papers pertain, in part, to woman suffrage and to
       women in industry.

NORTH CAROLINA (cont.)

330. Southgate, James.
          Letters and papers: 1794, 1851-1935.
          In: Duke University Library, Durham.
          Materials pertaining to the education of women.
331. Sprunt, Alexander, & Son, Inc.
          Papers
          In: Duke University Library, Durham.
          Correspondence and other papers (between 1919 and
          1920) pertaining to woman suffrage.
332. Stephens, Alexander H.
          Papers: 1822-1911.
          In: Duke University Library, Durham.
          Materials relating to the education of women.
333. Thomas, Ella Gertrude Clanton.
          Journals: 1848-1889.
          In: Duke University Library, Durham.
          Materials pertaining to the education of women.
334. Thornton, William C.
          Papers: 1805-1854.
          In: Duke University Library, Durham.
          Papers pertaining to the rights of women.
335. Trent Collection - Manuscript Division.
          Sophia Jex-Blake Papers.
          In: Duke University Library, Durham.
          Papers pertaining to the medical education of women.
336. Tutt, James A.
          Papers: 1807-1908.
          In: Duke University Library, Durham.
          Papers pertaining to property rights of women.
337. Underwood, Ruth Elizabeth Newton.
          Papers: 1926-1931.
          In: Duke University Library, Durham.
          Papers pertaining to the employment of women.
338. Whittingham, William Rollinson.
          Papers: 1823, 1833-1867, 1879.
          In: Duke University Library, Durham.
          Papers pertaining to the education of women.
339. Young, Matilda.
          Papers: 1932-1933.
          In: Duke University Library, Durham.
          Letters of Miss Young, companion to Mrs. Alva
          Murray Vanderbilt Belmont, during 1932, commenting,
          in part, on Mrs. Belmont; together with Mrs. Belmont's
          memoirs, describing her personal life as child, wife,
          militant feminist, advocate of women's rights, and her
          marriage to Oliver Hazard Perry Belmont.
340. Lilly Family.
          Papers: 1924-1960.
          In: Historical Foundation of the Presbyterian and
          Reformed Churches, Montreat.
          Papers of David Clay Lilly (1870-1939), Presbyterian

NORTH CAROLINA (cont.)

        minister, part of which pertain to woman's status in
        the church.
341. Clark, Walter, 1846-1924.
        Papers: 1693, 1783-1920.
        In: North Carolina State Department of Archives and
             History, Raleigh.
        Judge and historian of North Carolina. Correspondence,
        in part, relates to woman suffrage.
342. Organizations: North Carolina League of Women Voters.
        Papers: 1920.
        In: North Carolina State Department of Archives and
             History, Raleigh.
        Letters and other materials from the 1920 woman's
        suffrage campaign in North Carolina. Materials con-
        sist of views of state senators on the suffrage question,
        pro and anti-suffrage materials.
343. Clark, Walter, 1846-1924.
        Papers: 1880-1919.
        In: University of North Carolina, Southern Historical
             Collection, Chapel Hill.
        Confederate soldier, historian and chief justice of
        North Carolina. In part, consists of papers pertaining
        to the legal rights of women.

NORTH DAKOTA

344. Slaughter, Linda Warfel, 1850-1920.
        Papers: 1870-1929.
        In: State Historical Society of North Dakota, Bismark.
        Pioneer and author. Letters to Mrs. Slaughter con-
        cerning, in part, woman suffrage.

OHIO

345. Woman suffrage in Cleveland and Cuyahoga County.
        Scrapbooks: 1911-1920.
        In: Cleveland Public Library.
        Clippings from local newspapers collected and mounted
        in scrapbooks by the Woman Suffrage Party of Cuyahoga
        County.
346. Women suffrage-League of Women Voters.
        Papers: 1869-1940.
        In: Dayton and Montgomery County Public Library,
             Dayton.
        Includes minutes (1869-1871) of the woman suffrage
        movement; scrapbooks, pamphlets, letters, etc., per-
        taining to the woman suffrage campaign for Montgomery
        County (1912-1919); 38 scrapbooks (1912-1940) covering
        news of local groups and some national; other materi-
        als consisting of periodicals, pamphlets, and photo-
        graphs (1912-1940).

OHIO (cont.)

347. Garford, Arthur Lovett, 1858-1933.
          Papers: 1877-1933.
          In: Ohio Historical Society, Columbus.
          Industrialist, politician, and philanthropist. Correspond-
          ence, speeches, articles and other papers concerning
          woman suffrage and other matters.
348. Henley, John Wesley, 1835-1903.
          Papers: 1848-1900.
          In: Ohio Historical Society, Columbus.
          Methodist and Universalist minister.   Includes sermons
          on woman suffrage.
349. Lawrence, William, 1819-1899.
          Letters: 1865, 1870.
          In: Ohio Historical Society, Columbus.
          Two letters, December 6, 1865, and February 5, 1870,
          of William Lawrence stating that universal suffrage
          must wait for an educated electorate, and the other re-
          ferring to a constitutional amendment.
350. Wheaton, Walter G.
          Papers: 1866-1945.
          In: Ohio Historical Society, Columbus.
          Papers of Walter G. Wheaton relating to his mother,
          Laura M. Wheaton Plantz, a doctor.   Includes her
          lecture, The True Woman, and other papers pertaining,
          in part, to woman suffrage.

OREGON

351. Dye, Eva Emery, 1855-1947.
          Papers: 1879-1936.
          In: Oregon Historical Society, Portland.
          Author and suffragist.   Correspondence, manuscripts
          of her books, notes, much of which include her work
          in the woman suffrage movement from 1904 to 1913.
352. Oregon State Woman's Suffrage Association.
          Records
          In: Oregon Historical Society, Portland.
          Consists of minutebook, account books, miscellaneous
          correspondence and papers.

PENNSYLVANIA

353. Mitchell, Maria, 1818-1889.
          Papers
          In: American Philosophical Society, Philadelphia.
354. Taylor Family.
          Papers of the Taylor and Shoemaker Families, ca. 1809-
              1953.
          In: Haverford College Library, Quaker Collection, Haver-
              ford.
          Primarily letters of the Taylor family and of the Shoe-

PENNSYLVANIA (cont.)

maker family concerning, in part, women's rights.

355. Katzenstein, Caroline.
    Papers: 1910-1963.
    In: Historical Society of Pennsylvania, Philadelphia.
        Suffragist of Philadelphia. Correspondence, clippings,
        photographs, etc. , relating to the suffrage movement,
        the Pennsylvania Woman Suffrage Association, and the
        National Woman's Party.

356. Preston Family.
    Sarah R. Meseroll Collection: 1733-1939.
    In: Pennsylvania Historical and Museum Commission Col-
        lections, Harrisburg.
        Correspondence and newspaper clippings relate, in
        part, to women's rights.

357. Suffrage in Pennsylvania.
    Papers: 1910-1917.
    In: Pennsylvania State University, University Park.
        Much of the material pertains to the acquiring of the
        vote for women in Pennsylvania in 1915. Materials
        included were issued by the Pennsylvania Woman Suf-
        frage Association, Congressional Union for Woman Suf-
        frage, Pennsylvania Men's League for Woman Suffrage,
        Pennsylvania Association Opposed to Woman's Suffrage,
        National Women's Trade Union League, The Equal
        Franchise Federation, The Woman Suffrage Society of
        The County of Philadelphia, and The Pittsburgh Men's
        League for Woman Suffrage. Included are 63 broad-
        sides, 13 pamphlets, and 4 periodicals.

358. Addams, Jane, 1860-1935.
    Papers: 1838-1959.
    In: Swarthmore College, Friends Historical Library,
        Swarthmore.
        Settlement worker, social reformer, and peace worker.
        Several persons represented in correspondence include
        Carrie Chapman Catt and Florence Kelley. The cor-
        respondence includes the rights of women.

359. Mott, Lucretia Coffin, 1793-1880.
    Papers: 1834-1896.
    In: Swarthmore College, Friends Historical Library,
        Swarthmore.
        Quaker minister active in social reform, anti-slavery,
        peace, women's rights, and education. Consists of a
        diary of her trip to the World Anti-slavery Convention
        in 1840 in England. Also includes correspondence with
        her husband, James Mott, as well as with William
        Lloyd Garrison, Elizabeth Cady Stanton, and Lucy
        Stone.

360. Spencer, Anna Garlin, 1851-1931.
    Papers: ca. 1830-1932.
    In: Swarthmore College, Friends Historical Library,
        Swarthmore.

PENNSYLVANIA (cont.)

> Pacifist and reformer. Correspondence, literary manu-
> scripts, published writings and other personal and family
> papers concern Mrs. Spencer's career. Correspondents
> include Edith Abbott, Susan B. Anthony, and David
> Starr Jordan.

361. National Organization for Women, Pittsburgh Chapter.
> Records: 1970-1971.
> In: University of Pittsburgh, Archives of Industrial
> Society, Hillman Library.
> Several hundred items consisting of minutes of general
> meetings, local chapter bulletins and newsletters, bro-
> chures, letters and news clippings as well as releases
> and publications of the national organization.

362. Roessing, Jennie Bradley.
> Papers: 1887-1961.
> In: University of Pittsburgh, Archives of Industrial
> Society, Hillman Library.
> Personal and business correspondence of a leading
> feminist and participant in the woman's suffrage move-
> ment. Correspondent includes Carrie Chapman Catt.
> Includes travel diaries (1850, 1853), scrapbook, photo-
> graphs, clippings, and pamphlets.

TENNESSEE

363. Benedict, Anne Scales, 1883-1958.
> Papers: 1911-1938.
> In: Joint University Libraries, Nashville.
> Social, civil, educational, and religious leader in
> Nashville. Correspondence and other items pertain to
> the education of women at Vanderbilt University.

364. Elliott, Collins D. , 1810-1899.
> Papers: 1816-1932.
> In: Tennessee State Library and Archives, Nashville.
> Minister, teacher, and chaplain. Includes papers re-
> lating to the woman suffrage movement, in particular
> the correspondence of Dr. Elliott's daughter, Elizabeth
> Porterfield Elliott.

365. Nashville Woman Suffrage Association.
> Papers: 1918-1919.
> In: Tennessee State Library and Archives, Nashville.
> Roll call and minutes of the Nashville Woman Suffrage
> Association, March 17, 1918, to January 23, 1919.
> Included in the minutes is a summary of the Associa-
> tion's convention held January 23, 1919.

366. Overall, Frances Holder, ca. 1877-ca. 1963.
> Papers: 1867-1919.
> In: Tennessee State Library and Archives, Nashville.
> Leader in the woman suffrage movement in Tennessee;
> consisting of clippings, speeches and a copy of the
> rules of the Nashville Woman Suffrage Association; a

TENNESSEE (cont.)

handbook, 1914-1915, of the Tennessee Equal Suffrage
Association as well as a scrapbook kept by Mrs. Overall.

367. Rankin, Anne Porterfield, 1869-1942.
Papers: 1887-1941.
In: Tennessee State Library and Archives, Nashville.
Newspaperwoman. Editor of the Southern Woman's
Magazine between 1908 and 1920. Letters pertain,
in part, to women's rights.

368. Sketches - General. "Woman's Suffrage" by Marie Sims
Jones.
1 item (9 page, typewritten copy), ca. 1967.
In: Tennessee State Library and Archives, Nashville.
Tells the part played by the Woman's Party and the
National American Woman Suffrage Association in the
struggle to obtain the vote for women.

369. Sketches - Places. McMinn County, Tennessee, 1819-1968.
1 item (51 pages).
In: Tennessee State Library and Archives, Nashville.
Includes a discussion of the tie-breaking vote cast by
Harry T. Burn in favor of Tennessee's ratification of
the Nineteenth Amendment.

370. Tennessee Federation of Business and Professional Women's
Clubs, Inc.
Records: 1920-1967.
In: Tennessee State Library and Archives, Nashville.
Includes questionnaires (1934) from Tennessee congressional candidates concerning (among other things) legislation about women. Also includes correspondence with
the Tennessee congressmen and others about equal
rights legislation for women in 1948 and 1953; and a
talk (1938) entitled "The Equal Rights Amendment to
the Federal Constitution. "

371. Woman Suffrage Movement in Tennessee.
Papers: 1 box.
In: Tennessee State Library and Archives, Nashville.

TEXAS

372. McCallum Family.
Papers: 1871-1957.
In: Austin Public Library, Austin-Travis County Collec-
tion.
Newspaper articles, manuscripts, periodicals, pam-
phlets, scrapbooks, etc. , relating to the woman's suf-
frage movement in Texas. Correspondence of Mrs.
Jane Yelvington McCallum and Mrs. Minnie Fisher
Cunningham as well as materials of the Texas Woman
Suffrage Association, and the Austin Woman Suffrage
Association.

TEXAS (cont.)

373. Bailey, Joseph Weldon, 1863-1929.
        Papers: 1880-1930.
        In: Dallas Historical Society.
        Lawyer and U. S. Representative and Senator from
        Texas. Correspondence and speeches, in part, per-
        tain to woman suffrage.
374. Texas Equal Suffrage Association.
        Papers
        In: University of Houston Libraries.
        Thirty-four boxes contain materials related to the suf-
        frage movement in Texas and the rest of the country.
        Also contains materials related to Mrs. Minnie Fisher
        Cunningham and her suffrage activities in Texas and
        with the National American Woman Suffrage Association.
375. Dancy, John Winfield, Scott, 1810-1856.
        Papers: 1832-1917.
        In: University of Texas Library, Austin.
        Lawyer, farmer, soldier, politician, editor, and rail-
        road developer of Nashville, Tennessee. Correspond-
        ence, diary, speech, and other papers relate, in part,
        to woman suffrage.
376. Glasgow Family.
        Papers: 1795-ca. 1889.
        In: University of Texas Library, Austin.
        The Alexander M. Glasgow family, planters of Virginia.
        Part of the materials consist of essays and speeches
        dealing with the status of women.
377. Henderson, Thomas Stalworth, 1859-1937.
        Papers: 1852-1937.
        In: University of Texas Library, Austin.
        Legislator, attorney, chairman of the University of
        Texas Board of Regents. Part of the papers pertain
        to the Texas Woman Suffrage Association.
378. Kleberg, Rudolph, 1847-1924.
        Papers: 1833-1932.
        In: University of Texas Library, Austin.
        Soldier, lawyer, politician, teacher, and reporter.
        Papers pertain, in part, to his advocacy of woman suf-
        frage. Some of the papers pertain to the Texas Wom-
        an Suffrage Association.
379. Lasseter, H. Elbert.
        Papers: 1913.
        In: University of Texas Library, Austin.
        Correspondence, journal, and clipping of the Texas
        Woman Suffrage Association.
380. Pennybacker, Anna J. Hardwicke, 1861-1938.
        Papers: 1878-1938.
        In: University of Texas Library, Austin.
        Teacher and author. Correspondence, telegrams,
        pamphlets, magazines, newspaper clippings, and photo-
        graphs, relating, in part, to the Texas and General

TEXAS (cont.)

> Federation of Women's Clubs and the National American
> Woman Suffrage Association.

VIRGINIA

381. Johnston, Mary, 1870-1936.
> Papers: 1898-1936.
> In: University of Virginia Library, Charlottesville.
> Author and suffragist. Correspondence, diaries (1907-
> 1915) and other papers concerning Miss Johnston's
> interest in woman suffrage, women's rights, and other
> matters. Some correspondents include Anna Howard
> Shaw, Zona Gale, Max Eastman, Ben Lindsey, and
> Fola La Follette.

382. Women's Organizations.
> Papers: 1918-1948.
> In: University of Virginia Library, Charlottesville.
> Materials concerning the Women's Suffrage and the
> Equal Suffrage League of Virginia and the Women's
> Trade Union League.

383. Virginia Woman Suffrage.
> Papers: 1910-1925.
> In: Virginia State Library, Archives Division, Richmond.
> Correspondence, press clippings, membership lists and
> other records of the Equal Suffrage League of Virginia.

WASHINGTON

384. Fick, Nellie Mitchell.
> Papers: 1917-1944.
> In: University of Washington Library, Seattle.
> Suffrage leader of Seattle. Correspondence and scrap-
> books relate to the woman suffrage movement in Wash-
> ington and the United States. Persons represented in-
> clude Adelaide Johnson, Bertha Knight Landes, and
> Reah M. Whitehead.

385. Semple, Eugene, 1840-1908.
> Papers: 1865-1908.
> In: University of Washington Library, Seattle.
> Lawyer, printer, and governor of Washington territory.
> Materials pertain, in part, to a woman suffrage bill
> passed in Washington in 1888.

386. Thompson, Walter J.
> Letters: 1878-1889.
> In: Washington State Historical Society, Tacoma.
> Letters to Mrs. Barbara J. Thompson, who worked for
> woman suffrage and the rights movement in Nebraska.
> Correspondents include Susan B. Anthony, Amelia
> Bloomer, Lucy Stone, and Elizabeth Cady Stanton.
> Also includes the movement in Washington State and
> materials from the National Woman Suffrage Association.

WASHINGTON (cont.)

387.   Devoe, Emma Smith.
         Scrapbooks: 1890-1920.
         In: Washington State Library, Olympia.
         Thirteen scrapbooks relating to the women's suffrage
         movement.   Consists of newspaper clippings, corre-
         spondence, published articles, pamphlets, etc. relating
         to the movement in Washington State.   Other materials
         relate to suffrage in South Dakota, Wisconsin, Iowa,
         Illinois, and other mid-western and western states.

WEST VIRGINIA

388.   Harmer, Harvey Walker, 1865-1961.
         Papers: 1842-1961.
         In: West Virginia University Library, Morgantown.
         Lawyer of Clarksburg, West Virginia and local historian.
         Part of the correspondence pertains to woman suffrage.
389.   Kump, Herman Guy, 1877-1962.
         Papers: 1907-1957.
         In: West Virginia University Library, Morgantown.
         Attorney, mayor, judge, and governor of West Virginia.
         Correspondence includes woman suffrage.

WISCONSIN

390.   Anneke, Fritz, 1818-1872, and his wife, Mathilde Fraziska,
         1817-1884.
         Papers: 1791-1884.
         In: State Historical Society of Wisconsin, Madison.
         Correspondence and papers deal, in part, with their
         involvement in woman's suffrage in Wisconsin.   Several
         correspondents include Susan B. Anthony and Elizabeth
         Cady Stanton.
391.   Catt, Carrie Chapman, 1859-1947.
         Diary: 1911-1912.
         In: State Historical Society of Wisconsin, Madison.
         Diary of her trip around the world.
392.   Esch, John Jacob, 1861-1941.
         Papers: 1891-1921.
         In: State Historical Society of Wisconsin, Madison.
         Republican congressman from Wisconsin.   Incoming
         correspondence between 1912 and 1919 reflect the views
         of suffrage proponents.
393.   Gale, Zona, 1874-1938.
         Papers: 1838-1941.
         In: State Historical Society of Wisconsin, Madison.
         Author.   Mainly literary manuscripts together with
         correspondence, notebooks, and reports concerning,
         in part, her promotion of woman suffrage.
394.   Hooper, Mrs. Jessie Annette Jack, 1864-1935.
         Papers: 1909-1934.

WISCONSIN (cont.)

> In: State Historical Society of Wisconsin, Madison.
> Suffrage speaker, Democratic Party leader, and worker
> for peace. The papers concern her work for the Wis-
> consin League of Women Voters as well as the General
> Federation of Women's Clubs, 1928-1932. Correspond-
> ents include Carrie Chapman Catt, Minnie Fisher Cun-
> ningham, and others.

395. James, Ada Lois, 1876-1952.
> Papers: 1816-1952.
> In: State Historical Society of Wisconsin, Madison.
> Suffragist, social worker, and reformer. Correspond-
> ence, diaries, articles showing her father's interests
> (David G. James) in employment for women, woman
> suffrage and other matters. Also included are her
> diaries (1865, 1882-1904) and proceedings of the meet-
> ings of the Wisconsin Woman Suffrage Association
> (1885-1903), correspondence with the National Woman's
> Party and the Political Equality League, 1911-1913.
> Includes letters from Jane Addams, Olympia Brown,
> Carrie Chapman Catt, Jessie J. Hooper, Catherine
> Waugh McCulloch, Theodora W. Youmans, Belle Case
> La Follette. Her additional diaries date 1892-1920
> and 1930-1947.

396. McGovern, Francis Edward, 1866-1946.
> Papers: 1909-1915.
> In: State Historical Society of Wisconsin, Madison.
> Governor of Wisconsin. Letters, in part, show his
> position on woman suffrage as well as correspondence
> from Theodore Roosevelt urging support for woman
> suffrage.

397. National Woman's Party.
> Records: 1946-1954.
> In: State Historical Society of Wisconsin, Madison.
> Correspondence, minutes, speeches, and press re-
> leases. Correspondents include Alice Paul from Mabel
> E. Griswold, a member of the National Woman's
> Party.

398. Richmond, Thomas C. , 1846-1920.
> Correspondence: 1882-1910.
> In: State Historical Society of Wisconsin, Madison.
> Attorney. Letters, in part, concern his attempts to
> get the Populist Party to accept woman suffrage.

399. Taggert, George W.
> Family papers: 1831-1939.
> In: State Historical Society of Wisconsin, Madison.
> Merchant and local official. Of the collection, letters
> and a scrapbook (1888-1928) record his daughter's
> interests (Hannah Taggert Patchin) in woman suffrage.

400. Wild, Robert, 1875-1928.
> Papers: 1828-1937.
> In: State Historical Society of Wisconsin, Madison.

WISCONSIN (cont.)

> Attorney and regent of the University of Wisconsin.
> Among his articles and speeches are those opposing
> woman suffrage.

401. Wisconsin Woman's Suffrage Association.
> Records: 1892-1925.
> In: State Historical Society of Wisconsin, Madison.
> Official correspondence, historical and biographical
> sketches along with correspondence related to Olympia
> Brown, Carrie Chapman Catt, Zona Gale, Ada L.
> James, Belle Case La Follette, and Theodora Youmans.
> Also includes correspondence of the Political Equality
> League of Wisconsin.

402. Young, Mrs. Frances Berkeley.
> Papers: 1912.
> In: State Historical Society of Wisconsin, Madison.
> Letters, notes, and clippings used by Mrs. Young for
> speeches and debates on women suffrage.

Associations (cont.)
  California, 3, 4, 5, 7, 14, 20, 154
  Colorado, 29
  Connecticut, 31, 96, 112, 134
  Georgia, 51
  Illinois, 55, 57
  Indiana, 64, 65
  Iowa, 69
  Kansas, 71, 72
  Kentucky, 75, 76, 77
  Louisiana, 79
  Maryland, 82
  Massachusetts, 86, 97, 124, 175, 176
  Michigan, 194, 195
  Minnesota, 215, 216, 221, 222, 223
  Mississippi, 229
  Montana, 238, 239
  Nebraska, 245
  New England, 108, 173
  New York (State), 114, 122, 163, 166, 172, 178, 251, 259, 261,
    264, 270, 271
  North Carolina, 342
  Ohio, 135, 345
  Oregon, 352
  Pennsylvania, 355, 357, 361
  Tennessee, 144, 365, 366, 370
  Texas, 372, 374, 377, 378, 379, 380
  Virginia, 382, 383
  Washington, D. C. , 45
  Wisconsin, 145, 394, 395, 401
Austin (Texas) Woman Suffrage Association, 372

Babcock, Caroline L. , 92
Bailey, Joseph W. , 373
Ball, William W. , 286
Baltimore (Maryland) City Woman Suffrage Association, 82
Banister, Marion G. , 34
Barkley, Mrs. William E. , 245
Barnard College, 249
Bartlett, Ellen, 287
Barton, Gertrude W. , 288
Bay State Campaign Fund of Woman Suffrage (Massachusetts), 86
Beard, Mary R. , 21, 112, 128, 138, 149, 155, 253
Beecher, Henry W. , 250
Beecher, Lyman, 93
Beecher Family, 93
Beggs, Vera, 156
Belmont, Alva, 138, 339
Belmont, Oliver H. , 339
Benedict, Anne S. , 363
Bens, Glendolen T. , 259
Bethune, Mary M. , 46
Birckhead, Edward F. , 289

Birth Control, 44, 153, 158, 159, 175, 177, 180, 184
  Massachusetts, 175, 176
Black, Nellie P., 51
Blackwell, Alice S., 35, 74, 85, 94, 110, 114, 133, 145, 165, 166,
  173, 182
Blackwell, Antoinette B., 94, 145, 283
Blackwell, Elizabeth, 173, 248, 253
Blackwell, Emily, 133
Blackwell, Henry B., 133, 145
Blackwell Family, 94
Blake, Katherine D., 21
Blake, Lillie D., 157, 233, 253, 277
Blatch, Harriot S., 21, 92
Bloomer, Amelia J., 68, 189, 277, 283, 386
Bodichon, Barbara S., 248
Borah, William E., 131
Borglum, Gutzon, 128
Boston (Massachusetts) Equal Suffrage Association, 86
Breckinridge, Sophonisba P., 40, 42, 62
Bridges, Grace, 22
Brill, Hascal R., 208
Brin, Fanny F., 209
Brotherton, Belle, 195
Brown, Olympia, 145, 395, 401
Brown, Pamela S., 205
Brush, Dorothy, 158
Bryant, John E., 290
Bryn Mawr College, 164
Bruge, Marie L., 260
Burr, F. E., 30
Business and the Professions
  California, 7
  Tennessee, 370
    See also names of individual professions beginning with the
    headings: "Women as..." and "Women in..."
Business Women's Legislative Council of California, 7

California
  Associations, 3, 4, 5, 7, 14, 20, 154
  Business and the Professions, 7
  Populist Party, 14
  Suffrage, 5, 20, 26
California Equal Suffrage Association, 20
California State Suffrage Association, 20
California State Woman Suffrage Educational Association, 5
Campbell, James L., 291
Carey, Alice, 277
Carey, Phoebe, 277
Carns, Margaret J., 241
Carrie Chapman Catt Memorial Fund, 156
Casement, Frances M., 182
Cator, Thomas V., 14
Catt, Carrie C., 20, 21, 24, 26, 35, 40, 46, 69, 75, 90, 100,

SELECTED REFERENCES

General Sources

American Historical Association. Guide to historical literature. New York, Macmillan, 1961. 962p.

Beers, Henry P. Bibliographies in American history. New York, Wilson, 1942. 487p.

Coulter, Edith M. Historical bibliographies; a systematic and annoted guide. Berkeley, University of California Press, 1935. 206p.

Gray, Wood. Historian's handbook; a key to the study and writing of history. 2d ed. Boston, Houghton Mifflin, 1964. 88p.

Handlin, Oscar, ed. Harvard guide to American history. Cambridge, Harvard University Press, 1954. 689p.

Larned, Joseph N. Literature of American history; a bibliographical guide. Boston, American Library Association Publication Board, 1902. Reprinted by Long's College Book Co., Columbus, Ohio, 1953. 596p.

U. S. Library of Congress. Guide to the study of the United States of America. Washington, 1960. 1193p.

Winchell, Constance. Guide to reference books. Chicago, American Library Association, 1967. 741p.

Special Libraries and Groups

Ash, Lee, ed. Subject collections. 3d ed. New York, Bowker, 1967. 1221p.

Kruzas, Anthony, ed. Directory of special libraries and information centers. Detroit, Gale Research, 1968. 2v.

Mushroom effect; a directory of women's liberation. Albany, Cal., Mushroon Effect, 1970. 14p. A listing of several hundred women's liberation organizations, films, plays, and periodicals.

Manuscript Sources

Carman, Harry H.   Guide to the principal sources for American
   civilization, 1800-1900, in the city of New York: Manuscripts.
   New York, Columbia University Press, 1962.

National union catalog of manuscript collections.   Hamden, Conn.,
   Shoe String, 1962- .

U. S. National Historical Publications Commission.   A guide to
   archives and manuscripts in the United States.   Edited by Philip
   M. Hamer.   New Haven, Conn., Yale University Press, 1961.
   775p.
   (See also Notable American Women in biography section.)

Biography

Biography index.   New York, H. W. Wilson, 1946- .

Dictionary of American biography.   New York, C. Scribner, 1946.
   11v.

Ireland, Norma O.   Index to women of the world.   Westwood, Mass.,
   Faxon, 1970.   573p.   An alphabetical listing of some 13,000
   women, with indications for biographical sources in books.

Notable American women, 1607-1950; a biographical dictionary.
   Edited by Edward T. James.   Cambridge, Harvard University
   Press, 1971.   3v.   Following each article is a brief indication
   of primary sources.

Outstanding young women of America.   Chicago, Outstanding Young
   Women of America, 1970.   896p.   Approximately 5000 biographical sketches, much like Who's Who of American Women.

Who's who of American women, a biographical dictionary of
   notable living American women.   Chicago, Marquis, 1971.
   1017p.

Willard, Frances E. and Mary A. Livermore, eds.   A woman of
   the century, 1470 biographical sketches accompanied by portraits
   of leading American women in all walks of life.   Buffalo, C. W.
   Moulton, 1893.   812p.   Reprinted by Gale Research, Detroit,
   1967.

Bibliographies and Indexes

Alternative press index.   Northfield, Minn., Carleton College,
   Radical Research Center, 1969- .

Barrow, John G. A bibliography of bibliographies in religion. Ann
    Arbor, Mich., Edwards, 1955. 489p.

Burr, Nelson. A critical bibliography of religion in America.
    Volume 4 of Religion in American life, edited by James W.
    Smith. Princeton, N.J., Princeton University Press, 1961.

California. Sacramento State College. Library. The changing role
    of women; a selected bibliography. Compiled by Leah Freeman.
    Sacramento, 1972. 50p. (Its Bibliographic series, no. 9.)

Catholic periodical and literature index. Haverford, Pa., Catholic
    Library Association, 1930- .

Cisler, Lucinda. Women: A bibliography. New York, The Author,
    1970. 36p.

Cumulated magazine subject index, 1907-1949. Boston, G. K. Hall,
    1964. 2v.

Current index to journals in education. New York, CCM Information
    Corp., 1969- .

Education index. New York, H. W. Wilson, 1929- .

Farians, Elizabeth. Selected bibliography on women and religion--
    1971. Cincinnati, National Organization for Women, 1971. 12p.

Franklin, Margaret Ladd. The case for woman suffrage; a bibliog-
    raphy. New York, National College Equal Suffrage League, 1913.
    315p.

Hughes, Marija Matich. The sexual barrier; legal and economic
    aspects of employment. San Francisco, Hastings College of the
    Law, Library, 1970. 35p. Supplement no. 1: 1971. 33p.

Index to religious periodical literature. Chicago, American Theo-
    logical Library Association, 1953- .

Kirby, Kathryn. The status of women in the church, Vatican II--
    1968, annotated bibliography: a research paper. Washington,
    Catholic University of America, Department of Library Science,
    1970.

Lee, Sylvia L. Implications of women's work patterns for vocational
    and technical education; an annotated bibliography. Columbus,
    Ohio State University, Center for Vocational Education, 1967.
    36p. A bibliography of annotated references pertaining to the
    status and changing roles, labor force participation, and legislation
    of women. Also includes several other bibliographies.

Mode, Peter G. Source book and bibliographical guide for American
    church history. Menasha, Wis., Banta, 1921. 735p.

Nineteenth century reader's guide. New York, H. W. Wilson, 1944.
2v.

Poole's index to periodical literature, 1802-1906. Boston, Houghton,
1891-1908. 7v. Reprinted by Peter Smith, New York, 1938.

Public affairs information service, bulletin. New York, Service,
1915- .

Reader's guide to periodical literature. New York, H. W. Wilson,
1905- .

Religious periodicals index. New York, Jarrow, 1970- .

Research in education. Washington, GPO, 1966- .

Shurter, Edwin Du Bois, ed. Woman suffrage: bibliography and
selected arguments. Bulletin of the University of Texas [Austin],
no. 31 (1 June 1915). 86p.

Spiegel, Jeanne. Sex role concepts; how women and men see themselves and each other; a selected annotated bibliography. Washington, Business and Professional Women's Foundation, 1969.
31p.

_____. Working mothers: a selected annotated bibliography.
Washington, Business and Professional Women's Foundation,
1968. 24p.

U. S. Department of Labor. Women--their social and economic
status. Selected references. By Julia A. Dupont. Washington,
GPO, 1970. 46p. A listing of 396 items along with a list of
special libraries.

_____. Library of Congress. Legislative Reference Service.
The new feminism: an annotated reading list. Washington, 1970.
4p.

Utah. University. Library. A selective bibliography on women's
liberation available in the Marriott Library. Salt Lake City,
1971. 62p.

Federal Government Documents

Ames, John G., comp. Comprehensive index to the publications of
the United States Government, 1881-1893. Washington, GPO,
1905. Reprinted by J. W. Edwards, Ann Arbor, Mich., 1953.

Poore, Benjamin P., comp. A discriptive catalogue of the government publications of the United States, September 5, 1774-March
4, 1881. Washington, GPO, 1885.

U. S. Superintendent of Documents. Catalogue of the public docu-
    ments of the _____ Congress and of all departments of the govern-
    ment of the United States. Washington, GPO, 1896-1945.   25v.

_____. _____. Monthly catalog of United States government
    publications. Washington, GPO, 1895- .

WOMEN'S LIBERATION SERIAL PUBLICATIONS

These serial titles are from 1968 and after. Titles limited to specific causes such as abortion, welfare rights, and peace are not included, nor are publications of women's clubs not directly involved in the movement. Also omitted are special issues of general publications.

The arrangement is by state and by city. Titles have been cited once only, unless the title has varied significantly, or it was not possible to establish a relationship for identical titles.

Not all titles are now being published or are available from the publishers. For aid in finding recalcitrants, contact the Women's History Research Center, 2325 Oak St., Berkeley, CA, enclosing a prestamped envelope. Their help has been invaluable in compiling this directory.

ARIZONA

Phoenix
NOW-Phoenix (Newsletter)
P.O. Box 7003
Phoenix, AZ   85011

CALIFORNIA

Albany
Mushroom Effect, a Directory
of Women's Liberation
P.O. Box 6024
Albany, CA   94704

Antioch
The Eagle's Eye
c/o Hill
Local #850 AWPPW
Rt. 1, Box 1155M
Antioch, CA   94509

Berkeley
Bay Area Women in Technical
Trades (Newsletter)
3021 Dana St. #1
Berkeley, CA   94705

Berkeley Women's Newsletter
Women's Refuge
2134 Allston Way
Berkeley, CA   95704

Common Woman
c/o Women's Center
1126 Addison
Berkeley, CA   94702

East Bay Feminists Newsletter
c/o Women's Center
1126 Addison St.
Berkeley, CA   94702

Employee Press
AFSCME Local #1695, AFL-CIO
2483-A Hearst
Berkeley, CA   94709

Female Liberation Newsletter
Box 300 Eshleman
U.C. Berkeley
Berkeley, CA   94720

It Ain't Me Babe
2325 Oak St.
Berkeley, CA   94708
(originally Spazm)

News NOW
Box 7024
Berkeley, CA   94707

Tooth and Nail
Bay Area Woman's Liberation
1800 Prince St.
Berkeley, CA   94703

Union W. A. G. E. Newsletter
Union Woman's Alliance to
   Gain Equality
c/o AFSCME #1695
2483A Hearst St.
Berkeley, CA   94709

Women's Newsletter
c/o Adam
2801 Ellsworth
Berkeley, CA   94705

Claremont
NOW-Pomona Valley (Newsletter)
P. O. Box 787
Claremont, CA   91711

Costa Mesa
Orange County Women's
   Coalition Newsletter
Women's Center
1926 Placentia #15
Costa Mesa, CA   92626

Davis
Women's Forum
Women's Liberation Center
UC Davis
Davis, CA   95616

Fairfax
Sappho 71
60 Steven Court
Fairfax, CA   94930

Fullerton
Action NOW
Orange County NOW
P. O. Box 4035
Fullerton, CA   93634

Goleta
Restless Eagle
The Isla Vista Women's Center
Goleta, CA   93017

Granada Hills
NOW-San Fernando Valley
   Now'sletter
c/o Henry
17716 Lajey St.
Granada Hills, CA   91344

La Jolla
Women: The Majority Report
Box 347
La Jolla, CA   92037

Livermore
Velvet Glove
Velvet Glove Press
P. O. Box 188
Livermore, CA   94550

Los Angeles
Every woman Magazine
2083 Westwood Blvd.
Los Angeles, CA   90025

Forever Amber
1822 West 4th St.
Los Angeles, CA   90057

The Lesbian Side
Tide Collective
1124 1/2 N. Ogden
Los Angeles, CA   90046

Matrix
Box 46067
Los Angeles, CA   90046

NOW Acts
1126 Hi Point St.
Los Angeles, CA   90035

NOW News
8864 West Pico Blvd.
Los Angeles, CA   90035

NOW West Regional News
8864 West Pico Blvd.
Los Angeles, CA   90035

Woman Worker
Box 26605
Los Angeles, CA   90026

Women's Liberation Newsletter
Los Angeles Women's Center
1027 South Crenshaw Blvd.
Los Angeles, CA   90019

Women's Caucus Newsletter-
    California Democratic
    Council
c/o Ehrlich
3332 Bennett Dr.
Los Angeles, CA   90028
(originally Women's RIGHTS
    Newsletter)

Millbrae
NOW-San Mateo (Newsletter)
c/o Miller
1354 Lasuon Dr.
Millbrae, CA   94030

Monterey
NOW Monterey Skylark
c/o Rose
735 Fillmore St.
Monterey, CA   93940

Oakland
The 4th World, an International
    Women's Paper
Box 8997
Oakland, CA   94608

Palo Alto
Off the Pedestal
376 Addison St.
Palo Alto, CA   94301

Riverside
NOW-Riverside; Women are
    Powerful
c/o Edwards
4951 Olivewood
Riverside, CA   92506

Sacramento
Capitol Alert
P.O. Box 13176
Sacramento, CA   95813

Muthah! A Magazine from
    Sacramento
c/o Saed
1420 22nd St.
Sacramento, CA   95816

NOW Sacramento (Newsletter)
4815 College Oak Dr.
Sacramento, CA   95841

Skirting the Capitol
c/o Ash
Box 4569
Sacramento, CA   95825

San Diego
Center for Women's Studies and
    Services (Newsletter)
c/o Nower
T 33 A Hardy St.
San Diego State Campus
San Diego, CA   92115

Goodbye to All That!
P.O. Box 3092
San Diego, CA   92103

Pandora's Box
Box 22094
San Diego, CA   92122

NOW-San Diego (Newsletter)
P.O. Box 22264
San Diego, CA   92122

WL Newsletter
c/o Pitkin
P.O. Box 22094
San Diego, CA   92122

San Francisco
Bay Area Women's Liberation
    Newsletter
2237 Pine St.
San Francisco, CA   94115

A Change is Gonna Come
1489 Sanchez
San Francisco, CA   94131

Connections
c/o C. Kornblith
7330 Ellis
San Francisco, CA   94110

Mother Lode Collective
P.O. Box 40213
San Francisco, CA 94140

NOW: News & Opinions of
   Women
330 Ellis
San Francisco, CA 94102

NOW-San Francisco Chapter
   (Newsletter)
P.O. Box 1267
San Francisco, CA 94101

San Francisco Women's Liberation Internal Newsletter
1380 Howard St.
San Francisco, CA 94103

Second Page
P.O. Box 14145
San Francisco, CA 94114
(originally Women's Page)

Sisters Magazine
1005 Market, Room 268
San Francisco, CA 94103

Sociologists for Women in
   Society Newsletter
4339 California St.
San Francisco, CA 94118
(originally Women's Caucus-
   ASA Newsletter)

San Lorenzo
Remember Our Fire
Shameless Hussy Press
Box 424
San Lorenzo, CA 94580

San Rafael
Marin NOW Newsletter
Box 2924
San Rafael, CA 94901

Santa Barbara
Beyond the Looking Glass
c/o Frankfurt
Associated Students
UC, Santa Barbara
Santa Barbara, CA 93106
(continued by Wild Flowers)

NOW Newsletter-Santa Barbara
2860 Kenmore Place
Santa Barbara, CA 93105

Wild Flowers
P.O. Box 14308 UCSB
Santa Barbara, CA 93107
(continues Beyond the Looking
   Glass)

Santa Clara
Maverick
P.O. Box 77
Agnew Station
Santa Clara, CA 93152

NOW Newsletter
NOW-South Bay Chapter
3498 Shafer Dr.
Santa Clara, CA 95051

South Pasadena
Women West
75 Monterey Rd.
South Pasadena, CA 91030

Stockton
NOW-San Joaquin Chapter
   (Newsletter)
P.O. Box 4073
Stockton, CA 95204

Ventura
NOW Ventura Newsletter
134 So. Palm St.
Ventura, CA 93001

COLORADO

Boulder
NOW Denver
1055 Roxwood Ln.
Boulder, CO 80303

Denver
SIS Newsletter
Sisters in Solidarity
1436 Lafayette
Denver, CO 80218
(originally Denver Women's
   Liberation Movement News-
   letter)

CONNECTICUT

Colchester
NOW-Connecticut
c/o Fedus
29 Prospect
Colchester, CT   06415

Middletown
Modern Language Association
   of America
Commission on Women
   (Newsletter)
c/o Ohmann
Wesleyan University West
   Station
Middletown, CT   06457
(also called Pre-Convention
   News)

New Haven
Yale Break
Durfee Hall
Yale Post Office
New Haven, CT   06513

Stamford
Women; By, For & Of
New Moon Publications
Dept. V-1A
Rox 3488 Ridgeway Station
Stamford, CT   06905

Stratford
Western Connecticut NOW
   Newsletter
c/o Sarkissian
340 Woodstock
Stratford, CT   06497
(originally Umbrella
   Newsletter)

FLORIDA

Atlantic Beach
Whitebook
P.O. Drawer 4
Atlantic Beach, FL   32233

Cocoanut Grove
NOW-Dade County (Newsletter)
P.O. Box 265
Cocoanut Grove, FL   33133

Tallahassee
Free and Proud
Tallahassee WL
Box U - 6800
Florida State University
Tallahassee, FL   32306

Ft. Lauderdale
New Woman
Box 24202
Ft. Lauderdale, FL   33307

New Port Richey
FEW's News and Views
Federally Employed Women
P.O. Box 1605
New Port Richey, FL   33552

GEORGIA

Atlanta
Just Like a Woman
Box 5432 Station E
Atlanta, GA   30307

NOW Notes (Newsletter)
Atlanta NOW
P.O. Box 54045
Atlanta, GA   30308

True to Life
69 Butler
Atlanta, GA   30303

HAWAII

Hawaii Women's Liberation
   Akami Sister
P.O. Box 11042
Honolulu, HI   96814

ILLINOIS

Charleston
Concerns
Women's Caucus for the
   Modern Languages
Department of English, Eastern
   Illinois University
Charleston, IL   61920

Chicago
Act NOW
7450 N. Sheridan Rd.
Chicago, IL 60600

Cassandra
P.O. Box 1797
Chicago, IL 60690

Chicago Woman's Liberation
    Union News
852 West Belmont
Chicago, IL 60657

Do it NOW
1957 E. 73d St.
Chicago, IL 60649

The Feminist Voice
227 E. Ontario
Chicago, IL 60611

Illinois Woman's Legislative
    Bulletin
5130 S. University
Chicago, IL 60615

NOW Newsletter
1952 E. 73d St.
Chicago, IL 60649

NUC Women's Caucus
    Newsletter
New University Conference
622 W. Diversey Parkway,
    Room 403a
Chicago, IL 60614

Rising up Angry
3746 Merchandise Mart
Chicago, IL 60654

The Spark
c/o Vasquez
6729 N. Ashland
Chicago, IL 60614

Spokeswoman
5464 S. Shore Drive
Chicago, IL 60615

Trans-Sister
NCCIS
1307 S. Wabash
Chicago, IL 60605

Trial
2150 N. Halsted
Chicago, IL 60614

University Women's Association
    News
6031 South Kimbark
Chicago, IL 20005

Voice of the Women's Liberation
    Movement
5336 So. Greenwood
Chicago, IL 60615

Downers Grove
Alliance Link
Equal Right Alliance
5256 Fairmont Ave.
Downers Grove, IL 60515

INDIANA

Bloomington
Bloomington Women's Liberation
    Movement
414 North Park
Bloomington, IN 41401
(originally Front Page)

Indianapolis
Indianapolis Women's Liberation
    Newsletter
P.O. Box 88365
Indianapolis, IN 46208

Middlebury
Progressive Woman
P.O. Box 510
Middlebury, IN 46540

Muncie
NOW-Muncie Indiana
c/o Newcomb
5 Cade Circle
Muncie, IN 47304

IOWA

Iowa City
Ain't I a Woman?
Women's Collective of Iowa
Box 1169
Iowa City, IA   52240

KANSAS

Lawrence
Feminine Focus
Intercollegiate Association
   of Women Students
c/o Rice
420 W. 11th St.
Lawrence, KA   66044
(also known as IAWS
   National Notes)

Wichita
WL-Wichita State University
   Newsletter
CAC
Wichita State University
Wichita, KA   67208

Wichita NOW Newsletter
3413 E. Murdock
Wichita, KA   67208

KENTUCKY

Louisville
Louisville WL Newsletter
WL Library
1131 S. Brook St. Apt. 1
Louisville, NY   40203

LOUISIANA

Baton Rouge
NOW Letter
NOW-Baton Rouge
c/o Madden
614 Park Blvd.
Baton Rouge, LA   70806

New Orleans
Her Own Right
1608 Milan St. Apt. 6
New Orleans, LA   70018

MARYLAND

Baltimore
Women; a Journal of Liberation
3028 Greenmount Ave.
Baltimore, MD   21218
(continuation of Female
   Liberation Journal)

Silver Springs
The Vocal Majority - NOW
   Washington, D.C.
10311 Folk St.
Silver Springs, MD   20902

MASSACHUSETTS

Allston
Boston Women United
   (Newsletter)
P.O. Box 278
Allston, MA   02134

Amherst
Connecticut Valley Newsletter
Women's Liberation
207 Hampshire House
Amherst, MA   01002

Boston
Female Liberation Newsletter
Box 303 Kenmore Square Station
Boston, MA   02215

Focus
1375 Commonwealth Ave.
Boston, MA   02134

New Broom
Box 341 Prudential Center
   Station
Boston, MA   02199

NOW-Eastern Mass. (Newsletter)
45 Newbury St.
Boston, MA   02171

Second Wave
c/o Female Liberation
Box 303 Kenmore Square Station
Boston, MA   02215

Unitarian Universalist
Women's Federation
25 Beacon St.
Boston, MA 02108

Cambridge
Bread and Roses Newsletter
Box 116
Cambridge, MA 02138

Cambridge Women's Liberation
(Newsletter)
Box 116
Cambridge, MA 02138

Hysteria
Box 116
Cambridge, MA 02138

Journal of Female Liberation;
No More Fun and Games
Cell 16
2 Brewer St.
Cambridge, MA 02138
(also called The Female State,
Dialectics of Sexism, The
First Revolution)

Lavender Vision
c/o Media Collective
2 Brookline
Cambridge, MA 02138

Newtonville
Voice of Women
811 Washington St.
Newtonville, MA 02160

Rockport
Essecondsex Newsletter
North Shore Feminists
58 High St.
Rockport, MA 01966

Springfield
Women's Newspaper
c/o Zaft
37 Warriner Ave.
Springfield, MA 01108

Worcester
Campus NOW News
c/o Volmer
Clark University
Box 1406
Worcester, MA 01610

MICHIGAN

Ann Arbor
Purple Star
c/o WL Office
Student Activities Building
University of Michigan
Ann Arbor, MI 48104

Spectre
Spectre Collective
P.O. Box 305
Ann Arbor, MI 48107

Dearborn
Beach Out
The New Detroit Daughters
of Bilitis
P.O. Box 244 Greenfield
Station
Dearborn, MI 48126

Detroit
Michigan Women's Liberation
Coalition Newsletter
5705 Woodward Ave.
Detroit, MI 48202

Moving Out
Wayne Women's Liberation
Publication Committee
Wayne State University
Detroit, MI 48201

NOW-Michigan
As We See It Now
P.O. Box 1455
Detroit, MI 48231

Notes on Women's Liberation;
· We Speak in Many Voices
1900 E. Jefferson
Detroit, MI 48207

East Lansing
Getting on Women Collective
  Newsletter
358 North Harrison
East Lansing, MI   48823

Lansing
Pissed Off Pink
1404 East Oakland
Lansing, MI   48906

MINNESOTA

Minneapolis
Twin Cities Female
  Liberation Newsletter
Box 8357, Lake St. Station
Minneapolis, MN   55468

A Feminist Journal
c/o Amazon Bookstore
705 7th St. S.E.
Minneapolis, MN   55414

OTTOTEM
c/o Chosa
1925 2nd Ave. South
Minneapolis, MN   55403

The Planner
Minnesota Women's Center
301 Walter Library
University of Minnesota
Minneapolis, MN   55455

St. Paul
Feminist Journal
c/o Women Unlimited
1132 Central Ave.
St. Paul, MN   55104

MISSOURI

Clayton
NOW News
Metropolitan St. Louis NOW
P.O. Box 11359
Clayton, MO   63130
(originally Alternatives NOW)

Independence
Here and NOW
2908 S. Hedges
Independence, MO   64052
(originally Greater Kansas
  City NOW Newsletter)

Kansas City
Women's Liberation Movement
Women's Liberation Union
3800 McGree
Kansas City, MO   64132

St. Louis
Real Women
The Women's Center
1411 Locust St.
St. Louis, MO   63103

Underground Woman
c/o Frederick
2505 St. Louis Ave.
St. Louis, MO   63106

NEVADA

Reno
The Ladder
P.O. Box 5025 G
Washington Station
Reno, NV   89503

NEW JERSEY

Princeton
NOW-Central New Jersey
  (Newsletter)
Box 2163
Princeton, NJ   08540

Washington
Times Change Press
Penwell Rd.
Washington, NJ   07882

Westwood
NOW-Northern New Jersey
  (Newsletter)
P.O. Box 435
Westwood, NJ   07675

NEW MEXICO

Albuquerque
Free Enquirer; vos de
  la Mujer
NOW-New Mexico
111 Laguna, N.W.
Albuquerque, NM   87104

New Mexico W. L. Newsletter
c/o Adair
804 Vassar, N.E.
Albuquerque, NM   87106

Sisters in Poverty
c/o NOW-New Mexico
Task Force on Women
  in Poverty
1712 Gold S.E.
Albuquerque, NM   87106

NEW YORK

Brooklyn
Feelings
c/o Coleman
243 Baltic St.
Brooklyn, NY   11201

Buffalo
Earth's Daughters
409 Richmond Ave.
Buffalo, NY   14222

NOW newsletter
NOW-Buffalo
610B Allenhurst
Buffalo, NY   14226

Great Neck
NOW-Long Island (Newsletter)
P.O. Box 158
Old Village Station
Great Neck, NY   11023

Jamaica
Majority Report
89-19 171 St., #5B
Jamaica, NY   11432

Lawrence
Sisterhood Week
379 Central Ave.
Lawrence, NY   11559

New York
Adam's Rib
Pussycat League, Inc.
255 W. 84th St.
New York, NY   10024

Aphra
Box 273 Village Station
New York, NY   10014

Association for Women in
  Psychology Newsletter
c/o Marlowe
180 West End Ave.
New York, NY   10023

Association of Women in
  Science Newsletter
Anne M. Brisco, editor
Harlem Hospital Center
New York, NY   10037

Battle Acts
YAWF Women
25 West 25th St.
New York, NY   10010

Broadside
41 Union Square West,
  Room 1328
New York, NY   10003

Catalyst
6 East 22nd St.
New York, NY   10028

Congress to Unite Women
  (Newsletter)
Box 114
New York, NY   10025

A Feminist Journal
c/o Betries
509 E. 5th St.
New York, NY   10009

Feminist Studies
c/o Calderwood
294 Riverside Drive
New York, NY   10025

Media Women's Monthly
G.P.O. Box 1692
New York, NY   10001

The Militant
14 Charles Lane
New York, NY   10014

Ms.
370 Lexington Ave.
New York, NY   10017

New Broadside
Box 390 Cooper Station,
   Dept. S
New York, NY   10003

The New Feminist
NOW-New York
28 East 56th St.
New York, NY   10022
(continues NOW in the News)

New York Feminist
2000 Broadway
New York, NY   10023

Notes from the 1st Year
Box AA Old Chelsea Station
New York, NY   10011

Persuasion
77 7th Avenue, Apt. 166
New York, NY   10011

Rat
241 East 14th St.
New York, NY   10003

Red Star; Organ of Red
   Women's Detachment
700 East 9th St.
New York, NY   10009

Sisterhood Songs
WL Front, WL Center
36 West 22nd St.
New York, NY   10010

Switchboard
Box 694 Peter Stuyvesant
   Station
New York, NY   10009

Title VII Report
Professional & Technical
   Programs Inc.
P.O. Box 848 Lenox Hill
   Station
New York, NY   10022

Up From Radicalism: A
   Feminist Journal
c/o Bantam Books
666 5th Ave.
New York, NY   10019

Up From Under
339 Lafayette St.
New York, NY   10009

WISE (Women for the Inclusion
   of Sexual Expression)
c/o Women's Strike Coalition
118 East 28th St.
New York, NY   10016

Women in City Government
   United
346 Broadway
New York, NY   10013

Women's Rights Law Reporter
119 F. Ave.
New York, NY   10003

Women's World
P.O. Box 949 Radio City
   Station
New York, NY   10019

The Working Mother; The Voice
   of Mother's & Children's
   Liberation
Maternal Information Services,
   Inc.
Suite 1E
46 West 96th St.
New York, NY   10025

Rochester
Statutes of Liberty
c/o Women's Liberation
8 Harvard St.
Rochester, NY   14620

Skaneateles
NOW-New York State
  (Newsletter)
West Lake Rd. RD #1
Skaneateles, NY 13152

Syracuse
NOW News & Notes
1404 State Tower Building
Syracuse, NY 13202

Whitestone
NOW York Woman
NOW-New York Chapter
c/o Loecher
162-11 Ninth Ave.
Whitestone, NY 11357

NORTH CAROLINA

Chapel Hill
Female Liberation Newsletter
Box 954
Chapel Hill, NC 27514

New Carolina Woman
Box 954
Chapel Hill, NC 27514

Newsletter American
  Library Association.
  Social Responsibilities
  Round Table. Task
  Force on Women.
c/o Robson
Undergraduate Library
University of North Carolina
Chapel Hill, NC 27514

Charlotte
To, For, By & About Women
Charlotte Women's Center
1615 Lyndhurst Ave.
Charlotte, NC 28203

NORTH DAKOTA

Minot
North Dakota Women's Health
  Resources Newsletter
Minot Women's Collective
P.O. Box 235
Minot, ND 58701

OHIO

Akron
Coordinating Committee on
  Women in History Profession
  Newsletter
Joanna Zangrando
History Dept.
University of Akron
Akron, OH 44304.

Cleveland
NOW-Cleveland (Newsletter)
"Channel C"
P.O. Box 7147
Cleveland, OH 44128

Cleveland Heights
Women Speak Out
1376 Hollister Rd.
Cleveland Heights, OH 44118

Columbus
Women's Action Collective
  Newsletter
326 Student Union
Ohio State University
Columbus, OH 43210

Under the Sign of Pisces
Publications Committee
Ohio State University Libraries
1858 Neil Ave.
Columbus, OH 43201

Dayton
Dayton Women's Liberation
1721 Burroughs Drive
Dayton, OH 45406

Shaker Heights
Women's Caucus for
  Political Science Newsletter
Women's Caucus of APSA
c/o Stevens
14609 S. Woodland Rd.
Shaker Heights, OH 44120

Yellow Springs
Antioch College Newsletter
Antioch College
c/o Auerbach
Yellow Springs, OH 45387

OREGON

Eugene
Women's Press
University of Oregon
Box 5306
Eugene, OR   97405

Portland
OCWE Newsletter
Oregon Council for
   Women's Equality
P.O. Box 8186
Portland, OR   97207

Salem
News and Views
Willamette Valley NOW
c/o Van Nale
P.O. Box 3422
Salem, OR   97302

PENNSYLVANIA

Philadelphia
Through the Looking Glass
Women's Center
4634 Chester Ave.
Philadelphia, PA   19143
(originally Awake and Move)

Women
Philadelphia Area Women's
   Liberation
c/o Turner
2015 Mount Vernon St.
Philadelphia, PA   19130

Pittsburgh
Know News Bulletin
P.O. Box 86031
Pittsburgh, PA   15221

NOW-Pittsburgh Chapter
   Newsletter
700 Penn Center Blvd.,
   Apt. 207
Pittsburgh, PA   15235

Slippery Rock
The Hand that Rocks the Rock
c/o Schmidt
Department of English
Slippery Rock State College
Slippery Rock, PA   16057
(originally Lysistrata)

State College
WEAL National Newsletter
Women's Equity Action League
325 Garner St., Apt. 101
State College, PA   16801

RHODE ISLAND

Providence
Women's Liberation Newsletter
P.O. Box 230 East Side Station
Providence, RI   02906

TEXAS

Austin
Second Coming
Box 8011 University of
   Texas Station
Austin, TX   78712

Bellaire
The Broadside
NOW-Houston
Box 384
Bellaire, TX   77401

Dallas
Turn of the Screwed
4213 Wycliff Ave.
Dallas, TX   75219

Ft. Worth
NOW-Ft. Worth (Newsletter)
2928 Owenwood Dr.
Ft. Worth, TX   76109

Houston
Sisters Unite
c/o Jarin
4334 Polk
Houston, TX   77023

VIRGINIA

Falls Church

National Ad Hoc Committee
for ERA Newsletter
2310 Barbour Rd.
Falls Church, VA 22043

The Woman Activist
2310 Barbour Rd.
Falls Church, VA 22043

WASHINGTON, D.C.

Citizen Advisory Council on
Status of Women Newsletter
U.S. Department of Labor
Washington, D.C. 20210

The Furies
Box 8843, S.E. Station
Washington, D.C. 20003

HRW Newsletter
Human Rights for Women
1128 National Press Building
Washington, D.C. 20044

National Committee on Household Employment News
1725 K St. N.W.
Washington, D.C. 20006

Off our Backs
#1013, 1346 Connecticut Ave.,
N.W.
Washington, D.C. 20036

Notes From the First Year
('68)
D.C. Women's Liberation
1520 N. Hampshire N.W.
Washington, D.C. 20036

Reflections
c/o Diana Press
2710 Woodley Place, N.W.
Washington, D.C. 20008

United Women's Contingent
Newsletter
1029 Vermont Ave. N.W.
Washington, D.C. 20005

Washington Newsletter for Women
c/o Barner & Associates, Inc.
1730 M St. N.W.
Washington, D.C. 20036

Women Today
1132 National Press Building
Washington, D.C. 20004

WASHINGTON

Edmonds

NOW-Snohomish County
(Newsletter)
c/o Underwood
19819 78th Place West
Edmonds, WA 98020

Mountlake Terrace

Action NOW
Snohomish Co. NOW
6301 234th S.W.
Mountlake Terrace, WA 98043

Seattle

And Ain't I a Woman
Seattle Women's Liberation
c/o Mayfried
3117 E. Thomas
Seattle, WA 98105

Lilith
c/o Women's Majority Union
Box 1895
Seattle, WA 98111

NOW-Seattle-King County
Newsletter
c/o Miller
3038 N.E. 85th St.
Seattle, WA 98115

Pandora
4224 University Way N.E.
Seattle, WA 98105

Traffic Jam
Women at AT & T
1601 41st Ave.
Seattle, WA 98102

WISCONSIN

Madison
Scarlet Letter Collective
923 W. Dayton
Madison, WI   53703

Wisconsin Women Newsletter
c/o University of Wisconsin
     Extension
Center for Women and
     Family Living Education
610 Langdon St.
Madison, WI   53706
(originally Women's Education
     Newsletter)

Milwaukee
St. Joan's Bulletin
U.S. Section
St. Joan's Alliance
2931 N. 37th St.
Milwaukee, WI   53208

What NOW
NOW-Milwaukee
P.O. Box 174
Milwaukee, WI   53201

Winneconne
Women in Struggle
Box 324
Winneconne, WI   54986

INDEX TO SERIALS

This index is limited to distinctive titles, and only those which do not include recognizable geographic locations as part of the title. For all others, including NOW and WL newsletters, use the geographical listing.

RETROSPECTIVE PERIODICALS;
A SELECTED TITLE CHECKLIST

These are some of the more important American periodicals documenting the social and intellectual history of U. S. women before 1968. They are available through the Sophia Smith Collection at Smith College and Greenwood Press microform reprints.

Aegis
Agitator
The Alpha
The Amulet & Ladies Literary
    Cabinet
Anti-Suffrage Review
Anti-Suffragist
Arena

Champion of Humanity
Chicago Magazine of Fashion,
    Music & Home Reading
Club Woman
Club Worker
Delta Newsletter

Equal Rights
Essence

Far & Near
The Fore Runner
The Forum Extra
Friend of Virtue

Genius of Liberty
Godey's Lady's Book

The Home Monthly
Hours at Home
Hull's Crucible

The Indian Ladies' Magazine
The Indian's Friend

Journal of Women's Work
Justitia

Keystone
Eleanor Kirk's Idea

The Ladies' Companion
The Lady's Friend
The Lady's Magazine
The Ladies Repository
The Ladies' World
The Laws of Life
The Liberal Thinker
Life & Labor
Life & Light for Women
Lily
Lotos
Lowell Offering
Lucy Stone League Bulletin

The Michigan Suffragist
Mother Earth Bulletin

National Citizen & Ballot Box
National Notes
National Suffrage Bulletin
National Woman's Party Bulletin
New England Offering
The New Era
The New Northwest
New York Suffrage Newsletter

The Open Door
Our Herald
Our New Humanity

Power & Woman's Advocate

Queen Bee
Queen Isabella Journal

Remonstrace
The Revolution

The Socialist Woman
Stiletto
Suffragist
Syndicalist

A True Republic

The Una

The Vote
Votes for Women

Western Woman Voter
Woman Citizen
Woman Patriot
Woman Rebel
Woman Voter
Woman's Advocate
Woman's Campaign
Woman's Chronicle
Woman's Column
Woman's Era
Woman's Exponent
Woman's Forum
Woman's Industrial News
Woman's Journal (Boston)
Woman's Journal (New York)
Woman's Press
Woman's Protest
Woman's Recorder
Woman's World & Jenness
    Miller Monthly
Women Speaking
Women's Freedom League
    Bulletin
Wonder Woman
Woodhull & Claflin's Weekly
Wood's Household Magazine
Working Women's Journal

Erskine, Lillian, 2399
Evans, Alvin E., 345
Evans, E. P., 346
Evans, Elizabeth G., 1251
Evans, Ernestine, 3333
Eyde, L. D., 3121
Eyden, R., 4132

Faherty, William B., 4133
Fairchild, J. E., 347
Fairchild, James H., 1621
Fairchild, S. C., 3122
Faivre, B. M., 2401
Famularo, Joseph J., 3123
Farber, Seymour M., 348,
349
Farians, Elizabeth, 4135-4140
Farley, G. M., 350
Farley, Jennie T., 351
Farmer, H. S., 2402
Farnham, Marynia B., 352
Farrell, John C., 4416
Fatout, Paul, 4525
Fauset, Arthur H., 5081
Faust, Jean, 353
Fava, Sylvia F., 3125
Fawcett, E., 2403
Fawcett, M. G., 3747
Fay, M., 3266, 3267
Felton, C. C., 354
Felton, Rebecca L., 4650
Fenberg, Matilda, 360
Fenner, Mildred S., 361
Ferber, Marianne, 3748
Ferguson, C. W., 5143
Ferguson, M. A., 2428
Ferrin, Mary U., 1623
Ferriss, Abbott L., 362
Fichter, Joseph H., 3126,
4144
Fidell, L. S., 3127
Field, A. E., 363
Field, Sara B., 1624, 4890
Fielding, W. J., 1625
Figueroa, Ana, 364
Filene, E. A., 2408
Finch, Edith, 5072
Finch, Jessica G., 1626
Finck, Henry T., 1627
Finigan, Frederick T., 3575
Fink, R. A., 4145
Finkelstein, Louis, 4489
Firestone, Shulamith, 365

Firkel, E., 366
Fisch, Edith L., 2409
Fishburn, Eleanor, 4441, 5130
Fisher, B. E., 367
Fisher, Dorothy C., 3128,
3749
Fisher, Katharine, 2410
Fisher, L., 4146
Fisher, Lettice, 2411
Fisher, M. J., 1629, 3750
Fisher, Marguerite J., 368,
369, 3334, 3577, 3578
Fisher, S. J., 5050
Fishman, Nathaniel, 370
Fitch, Charles H., 1630
Fitch, George L., 371
Fitzpatrick, E. A., 3751
Fitzwater, Perry B., 4147
Fleischman, Doris E., 373
Fleming, Alice, 4490
Fleming, E. D., 374
Flemming, A. S., 3579
Fletcher, Robert S., 3752
Flexner, Eleanor, 375
Flexner, Simon, 1631
Fley, J. A., 3753
Floerke, Jill, 2412
Flower, B. O., 378
Flynn, Elizabeth G., 379,
4654
Flynn, James J., 4581
Floyd, Josephine B., 4651
Foley, Paul, 380
Foner, Philip S., 4629
Ford, Josephine M., 4148
Forsyth, A., 1633
Forsyth, F. H., 381
Forsyth, Z. D., 381
Foster, G. B., 384
Foster, Hazel E., 4149, 4150
Foster, J. E., 385
Foster, John O., 5103
Foster, Lemuel H., 386
Fowler, Nathaniel C., 1634
Fowler, William W., 387
Fox, Karolena M., 1635
Fox, Louis H., 388
Foxcroft, F., 1636
Foye, Edward, 4151
Frakes, M., 4152
Francis, Barbara, 3754
Francis, Clarence, 3130
Francis, Philip, 389

Hicks, William W., 514
Higgins, Edwin, 515
Higginson, Mary T., 4754
Higginson, Thomas W., 1717,
    3784-3786, 4675, 4755,
    4774
Hill, C. M., 1718
Hill, Elsie, 1374
Hill, Helen, 2480
Hill, Joseph A., 2842
Hill, Ralph N., 4730
Hillyer, Curtis J., 1719
Hilton, M. E., 3142
Hilton, M. N., 2481
Hinchman, Lydia S., 4876
Hinckle, Warren, 521
Hinckle, Marianne, 521
Hines, F. T., 2482, 2483
Hinkle, Beatrice M., 522
Hinson, M. R., 523
Hoar, George F., 1721-1723
Hobbs, Lisa, 525
Hobbs, M. A., 2484
Hodge, P., 3448
Hodge, R. W., 3448
Hodgson, L., 4187
Hoffman, B. H., 3449
Hoffman, Lois N., 2485,
    2666
Holbrook, Stewart H., 4590
Holcombe, A. N., 3450
Holden, James A., 5131
Holden, Miriam Y., 3143
Holland, F. M., 4188
Holland, Frederic M., 4630
Hollingworth, Leta S., 526
Holmes, L. M., 527
Holsey, A. L., 3144
Holt, Margaret V., 4491
Holton, S. C., 3271
Holzapfel, Gottlieb, 1726
Hommes, N. J., 4189
Hooker, John, 528, 1727
Hooks, J. M., 2879
Horack, Frank E., 529, 1728
Hornaday, M., 1329
Horne, L., 530
Horner, Matina, 531
Hottel, Althea K., 3655,
    3791, 3792
Houghton, D. D., 3793
Howard, J., 535
Howard, Joseph K., 4786

Howe, F., 3145
Howe, Florence, 3795
Howe, Julia W., 1732-1734,
    2504, 3146, 4676, 4775
Howe, M. A., 4446
Howe, Mark A., 4877
Howells, W. D., 536
Howes, Ethel P., 537
Howes, Harvey, 1735
Howorth, L. S., 538
Hoyle, J., 3796
Hoyt, R., 539
Hubbard, Benjamin V., 1736
Hubbell, Thelma L., 540
Huber, Charlotte, 2505
Hubert, L. D., Jr., 541
Hudson, A. S., 4572
Hughes, J. L., 1737
Hughes, S. T., 542
Humphrey, Mattie L., 543
Humphreys, John F., 4190
Hundley, N. C., 4646
Hungate, Jesse A., 4191
Hunsucker, Suzanne, 545
Hunt, Harriot K., 3272
Hunt, Harry E., 546
Hunt, Morton, 547, 548
Hunt, R. L., 549
Hunt, Rockwell D., 4469
Hunter, Doris, 4192
Hunter, Fannie M., 4193
Hunter, Howard, 4192
Hunter, L. B., 3584
Huntington, F. D., 550
Hurd, Ethel E., 1738
Hurd-Mead, Kate C., 3273
Hurst, Fannie, 551
Hurst, Helen H., 552
Hurst, Sadie D., 819
Husbands, Clement M., 553
Hutcheson, Austin E., 4861
Hutchins, Grace, 2506
Hutchinson, Emilie J., 1739,
    2507, 3451, 3797
Hyer, M., 554, 555
Hymer, E. W., 556, 557,
    3585

Ingels, Margaret, 3379
Inman, Mary, 562, 563
Irvin, H. B., 2516
Irwin, Inez H., 1330, 1746-
    1748

Akron, Ohio
  Women's Rights Conventions, 1111
Alabama
  Economic Status, 2926, 3035
  Legal and Political Status, 1147, 1148
Amazons, The (Association), 302
American Association of University Women, 331, 922, 3978
American Equal Rights Association, 929, 1419
American Federation of Labor, 2410
American Woman Suffrage Association, 929, 1420, 5126
Anti-Suffrage, 1397, 1398, 1408, 1427, 1433, 1447, 1448, 1457,
    1464, 1468, 1469, 1472, 1475, 1489, 1497, 1500, 1538, 1556,
    1557, 1572, 1589, 1592, 1593, 1622, 1629, 1631, 1640, 1648,
    1652, 1660, 1672, 1687, 1736, 1737, 1762, 1764, 1804, 1824,
    1834, 1880, 1896, 1897, 1899, 1901, 1954, 1956, 1959, 1963,
    1964, 1982, 1986, 2005, 2011, 2081, 2095, 2101, 2133, 2150
  Illinois, 1742, 2133
  Massachusetts, 1431, 1460, 1792, 1898
  Michigan, 2133
  New York (State), 1488, 2075
  Oregon, 1468, 1528
  Virginia, 1409
  Washington, D. C. , 2000
  Wisconsin, 2133
Arizona
  Suffrage, 1812, 2120
Arkansas
  Economic Status, 2927, 3036
  Education, 34
  Legal and Political Status, 34
  Suffrage, 2041
Associations, 10, 40, 74, 145, 208, 254, 277, 302, 397, 439,
    504, 505, 540, 652, 749, 776, 792, 860, 929, 1026, 1121,
    1198, 1212, 1228, 1229, 1261, 1273, 1274, 1596, 4997-5002
  Chicago, Ill. , 2306
  Florida, 93
  Illinois, 271
  Iowa, 1103
  Michigan, 103, 582
  Mississippi, 2042
  New England, 1211
  New York (State), 2622
  North Dakota, 222
  Ohio, 1400

415

Associations (cont.)
   Oklahoma, 912
   Rhode Island, 1487
   Tennessee, 182
   Texas, 194
   Washington (State), 1435
      (See also names of individual associations)
Atlantic City, N. J.
   Women's Rights Conventions, 2122

Baltimore, Md.
   Economic Status, 2862
Baptist Church, 4191, 4236
Berkeley, Cal.
   Economic Status, 2759
Birth Control, 15, 423, 891, 961-978, 4970-4986
Boston, Mass.
   Millinery Employment, 2697
   Suffrage, 1839
   Trade-Unions, 2176, 3056
   Wages, 3417
   Women's Rights Conventions, 111
Brown University, 3821
Bryn Mawr College, 4016
Business and the Professions, 11, 20, 109, 1746, 2331, 2629,
      3078-3224, 3931
   California, 3152
   Kansas, 3203
   Southern States, 3198
      (See also: Married Women; Negro Women; and names of
      individual occupations as well as headings beginning "Women
      as _____ " and "Women in _____ ")

California
   Business and the Professions, 3152
   Economic Status, 2292, 2391, 2667, 2981
   Education, 162
   Higher Education, 3686, 3687, 3888
   Hours of Labor, 2626
   Labor Laws and Legislation, 2882
   Legal and Political Status, 162, 163, 777, 1149-1151
   Married Women, 112, 894
   Property Rights, 894
   Suffrage, 1424, 1542, 1543, 1576, 1577, 1580, 1698, 1714, 1831,
      1988, 2002, 2079, 4647, 4908
   Wages, 2293, 3465, 4646
   Women in Medicine, 3258
      (See also: Berkeley; San Francisco)
California. University. Berkeley, 3686
California. University. Santa Barbara, 3687
California State College at Fullerton, 3888
Catholic Church, 4075, 4132, 4133, 4138, 4181, 4225, 4259, 4339
Chicago. University, 3692, 3757, 3927

Chicago, Ill.
  Economic Status, 2180, 2526, 2642
  Higher Education, 3692, 3757, 3927
  Hours of Labor, 2441
  Stockyards, 2180
  Suffrage, 1392, 1607, 1718, 2017
  Trade-Unions, 2306
  Wages, 2182
  Women's Rights Conventions, 2017
Chicago Ladies' Garment Workers' Union, 2306
Cigar Manufacture, 2173, 2871
Cincinnati, Ohio
  Economic Status, 2335-2337
Civil Rights Act of 1964, 205, 340, 594, 712, 760, 785, 998, 1134,
    1187, 2594, 2624, 2755, 2773, 2774, 2806, 2843, 2890, 3022,
    3195
    (See also: Equal Employment Opportunity Commission)
Civil Service, 2647, 2738, 2846-2848, 2853, 2857, 2879, 2914,
    2944, 3041, 4837-4839, 5104, 5105
Clerical Occupations, 2212, 2392, 2876, 2946
  Philadelphia, Pa., 2945
Cleveland, Ohio
  Economic Status, 2321, 2737
  Suffrage, 1400
  Women's Rights Conventions, 801
Clothing Workers
  Wages, 2867, 3455
  Indiana, 2496
  New York (State), 2250, 3000
Clubs. See: Associations
College Equal Suffrage League, 1574
Colleges for Women, 3674, 3851, 3857, 3858, 4019
Colorado
  Equal Pay for Equal Work, 3547, 3548
  Higher Education, 3876
  Legal and Political Status, 1152
  Suffrage, 698, 1484, 1494, 1560, 1598, 1609, 1698, 1794, 1796,
    1798, 1814, 1838, 1853, 1935, 1951, 2033, 2047, 2135, 2136,
    2159, 2163
  Women as Educators, 3876
Colorado. University, 3876
Confectioners
  New York (City), 2341
  New York (State), 3440
Connecticut
  Economic Status, 2488, 2502
  Higher Education, 3728, 3777, 3832, 4014
  Laundry Industry, 2488, 2489
  Legal and Political Status, 7, 227
  Married Women, 513
  Night Work, 2660
  Suffrage, 1545, 1633
Consumers' League of New York, 2622
Consumers' Leagues, 2622

Georgia (cont.)
  Women in Politics, 4650-4652
Glass Manufacture, 2318
Greenwich Village, N. Y. , 1022
Grove Press, 2452-2454

Harvard University, 3738, 3780, 3794, 3920, 3924, 3966
Hawaii
  Economic Status, 2371, 2866
  Suffrage, 1710, 1711
  Women as Jurors, 494
High Schools, 520, 3685, 3731, 3764, 3932, 3954, 3976
Higher Education
  Nineteenth Century, 2014, 3684, 3695, 3711, 3717, 3718,
    3745, 3747, 3752, 3769, 3785, 3787, 3788, 3790, 3803,
    3806, 3811, 3822, 3824, 3846, 3877, 3891, 3900, 3917,
    3973, 3979, 3982, 3983, 3987, 3992, 3998, 4004, 5072,
    5073
  Twentieth Century, 3372, 3389, 3390, 3681, 3689, 3701, 3704,
    3707, 3715, 3716, 3719, 3722, 3723, 3729, 3753, 3763, 3765,
    3766, 3773, 3783, 3789, 3793, 3798, 3804, 3805, 3812-3815,
    3818, 3828, 3830, 3833-3836, 3840, 3842, 3843, 3847, 3848,
    3850, 3865, 3866, 3871, 3883, 3886, 3887, 3894, 3897-3899,
    3901-3905, 3907, 3914, 3916, 3918, 3922, 3937, 3940, 3944,
    3951-3953, 3960, 3963, 3967, 3969, 3981, 3984-3986, 3989,
    3990, 3995, 3999, 4007, 4008, 4017, 4021-4023, 4025, 4038,
    4039, 4041, 4043-4047
  California, 3686, 3687, 3888
  Chicago, Ill. , 3692, 3757, 3927
  Colorado, 3876
  Connecticut, 3728, 3777, 3832, 4014
  Eastern States, 3987
  Florida, 3654
  Georgia, 3746
  Illinois, 3692, 3748, 3757
  Indiana, 3649, 3673
  Kansas, 3650, 3808
  Maryland, 3943
  Massachusetts, 3678, 3698, 3738, 3776, 3780, 3794, 3824,
    3852, 3868, 3920, 3923, 3924, 3966
  Michigan, 3837, 3856, 3958, 4030
  Minnesota, 3726, 3949, 3997
  Missouri, 3986
  New York (City), 3873
  New York (State), 3754, 3878, 3947, 4010
  Pennsylvania, 3942, 4016
  Pittsburgh, Pa. , 3912, 3913
  Rhode Island, 3821
  Southern States, 3677, 3688, 3931, 3964, 4036
  Washington (State), 4013
  Wisconsin, 3755
    (See also: Colleges for Women; Nepotism; Women as
    Educators; names of specific colleges and universities)

Married Women, 133, 137, 299, 305, 399, 403, 452, 616, 629,
    642, 643, 646, 672, 733, 878, 1055, 1283, 1832, 1922
  Business and the Professions, 3085, 3097, 3103, 3113, 3115,
    3134, 3139, 3153, 3155, 3164, 3166, 3188, 3205, 3209, 3214,
    3216
  Contracts, 490, 1018
  Economic Status, 27, 2191, 2197, 2225, 2227, 2231, 2249, 2256,
    2272, 2278, 2291, 2294, 2302, 2305, 2322, 2324, 2325, 2332,
    2334, 2348, 2350, 2356, 2357, 2362, 2386, 2387, 2389, 2407,
    2411, 2414, 2420, 2431, 2451, 2461, 2468, 2472, 2501, 2505,
    2507, 2531, 2538, 2554, 2557, 2588, 2602, 2607, 2621, 2630,
    2631, 2644, 2666, 2679, 2681, 2683, 2687, 2688, 2721, 2727,
    2730, 2733, 2735, 2743, 2753, 2754, 2765, 2766, 2770, 2776,
    2780, 2792, 2812, 2820, 2827, 2872, 2873, 2886, 2904, 2947,
    2977, 2993, 2995, 2996, 2998, 3005, 3066, 3255, 3257, 3262
  Legal and Political Status, 21, 31, 46, 48, 96, 97, 114, 144,
    172, 178, 242, 275, 370, 373, 374, 386, 577, 591, 594, 606,
    620, 695, 765, 908, 994, 1004, 1031, 1105, 1120, 1127, 1129,
    1181, 1184, 3909, 4907
  Wills, 178
  Connecticut, 513
  Florida, 54, 788
  Georgia, 448
  Kentucky, 345
  Louisiana, 483, 541
  Massachusetts, 9, 177, 344, 2721
  Michigan, 1067
  New Hampshire, 314
  New Jersey, 623
  New York (State), 827, 1027
  North Carolina, 1018
  Pennsylvania, 335, 447, 553, 759
  Tennessee, 1084
  Texas, 655, 1029, 1086, 2644
    (See also: Divorce; Marriage; Property Rights)
Married Women's Property Acts, 717
Maryland
  Economic Status, 2495, 2667, 2902, 2933, 3031
  Higher Education, 3943
  Legal and Political Status, 515
  Property Rights, 87
    (See also: Baltimore)
Maryland. University, 3943
Massachusetts
  Anti-Suffrage, 1431, 1460, 1792, 1898
  Economic Status, 2182, 2721
  Higher Education, 3678, 3698, 3738, 3776, 3780, 3794, 3824,
    3852, 3868, 3920, 3923, 3924, 3966
  Hours of Labor, 2521, 2905
  Labor Laws and Legislation, 2882
  Legal and Political Status, 864, 938, 1035
  Married Women, 9, 177, 344, 2721
  Public Service, 2607

Virginia (cont.)
    Property Rights, 154
    Suffrage, 1451, 1615, 1761

Wages, 17, 122, 602, 1918, 2189, 2196, 2239, 2290, 2295, 2297,
    2304, 2307, 2757, 3116, 3117, 3186, 3405-3536
    Minimum Wage, 564, 2293, 2343, 2723, 3407, 3410, 3418, 3420,
        3430, 3438, 3445, 3450, 3455-3459, 3461, 3463-3466, 3468,
        3469, 3472, 3473, 3475, 3483, 3486, 3500, 3503, 3511, 3512,
        3528, 3529, 4604
    Boston, Mass. , 3417
    California, 2293, 3465, 4646
    Chicago, Ill. , 2182
    Illinois, 3434, 3435
    Indiana, 3423
    Kansas, 3515, 3531
    Maine, 3527
    Massachusetts, 3456, 3463, 3468, 3476
    New York (City), 2343, 3504, 3517
    New York (State), 3412, 3430, 3432, 3439, 3440, 3445, 3477-
        3479, 3485, 3526, 3532-3534
    Ohio, 3454, 3512
    Oregon, 3420, 3459, 3524
    Pennsylvania, 3411, 3481, 3520
    Rhode Island, 3438
    Tennessee, 3433
    Washington, D. C. , 3470, 3472, 3475
        (See also: Equal Pay Act of 1945; Equal Pay Act of 1963;
        Equal Pay for Equal Work; names of specific industries and
        occupations)
Walla Walla Woman's Club (Washington State), 1435
Want Ads, 2245, 2706
War Manpower Commission, 2708
Washington (State)
    Associations, 1435
    Higher Education, 4013
    Suffrage, 1434, 1435, 1438, 1684, 1698, 1902, 2155
    Women as Jurors, 350
        (See also: Seattle)
Washington. University, 4013
Washington, D. C.
    Anti-Suffrage, 2000
    Economic Status, 2497, 2952, 3018
    Legal and Political Status, 1153
    Suffrage, 1644, 1820, 1895
    Wages, 3470, 3472, 3475
Wellesley College, 3776
West Virginia
    Economic Status, 2951
Western States
    Suffrage, 1436, 1491, 1666, 1787, 1852, 1902, 1993, 2027,
        2078, 4637-4644
        (See also individual states)